MEDIA WRITING

Preparing Information for the Mass Media

Second Edition

From the Wadsworth Series in Mass Communication

Rebecca Hayden, Senior Editor

General

The New Communications by Frederick Williams

Media/Impact: An Introduction to Mass Media by Shirley Biagi

Mediamerica: Form, Content, and Consequence of Mass Communication, 3rd, by Edward Jay Whetmore

The Interplay of Influence: Mass Media & Their Publics in News, Advertising, Politics, 2nd, by Kathleen Hall Jamieson and Karlyn Kohrs Campbell

Mass Communication and Everyday Life: A Perspective on Theory and Effects by Dennis K. Davis and Stanley J. Baran

Technology and Communication Behavior by Frederick Williams

Mass Media Research: An Introduction, 2nd, by Roger D. Wimmer and Joseph R. Dominick

Communication Research: Strategies and Sources by Rebecca B. Rubin, Alan M. Rubin and Linda J. Piele

Journalism

Media Writing: Preparing Information for the Mass Media, 2nd, by Doug Newsom and James A. Wollert

Uncovering the News: A Journalist's Search for Information by Lauren Kessler and Duncan McDonald

When Words Collide: A Journalist's Guide to Grammar and Style, 2nd, by Lauren Kessler and Duncan McDonald

Interviews That Work: A Practical Guide for Journalists by Shirley Biagi

NewsTalk I: State-of-the-Art Conversations with Today's Print Journalists by Shirley Biagi

NewsTalk II: State-of-the-Art Conversations with Today's Broadcast Journalists by Shirley Biagi

Reporting Public Affairs: Problems and Solutions by Ronald P. Lovell

Newswriting for the Electronic Media: Principles, Examples, Applications by Daniel E. Garvey and William L. Rivers

Free-Lancer and Staff Writer: Newspaper Features and Magazine Articles, 4th, by William L. Rivers and Alison R. Work

This is PR: The Realities of Public Relations, 3rd, by Doug Newsom and Alan Scott

Public Relations Writing: Form and Style, 2nd, by Doug Newsom and Bob Carrell

Public Relations Cases by Jerry A. Hendrix

Creative Strategy in Advertising, 2nd, by A. Jerome Jewler

Fundamentals of Advertising Research, 3rd, by Alan D. Fletcher and Thomas A. Bowers

Broadcast, Cable and Film

Stay Tuned: A Concise History of American Broadcasting by Christopher H. Sterling and John M. Kittross

Writing for Television and Radio, 4th, by Robert L. Hilliard

Writing the Screenplay: TV and Film by Alan A. Armer

Announcing: Broadcast Communicating Today by Lewis B. O'Donnell, Carl Hausman and Philip Benoit

Modern Radio Production by Lewis B. O'Donnell, Philip Benoit and Carl Hausman

Audio in Media, 2nd, by Stanley R. Alten

Television Production Handbook, 4th, by Herbert Zettl

Directing Television and Film by Alan A. Armer

Sight-Sound-Motion: Applied Media Aesthetics by Herbert Zettl

Electronic Cinematography: Achieving Photographic Control over the Video Image by Harry Mathias and Richard Patterson

World Broadcasting Systems: A Comparative Analysis by Sydney W. Head

Broadcast/Cable Programming: Strategies and Practices, 2nd, by Susan Tyler Eastman, Sydney W. Head and Lewis Klein

Broadcast and Cable Selling by Charles Warner

Advertising in the Broadcast and Cable Media, 2nd, by Elizabeth J. Heighton and Don R. Cunningham

Copywriting for the Electronic Media: A Practical Guide by Milan D. Meeske and R. C. Norris

MEDIA WRITING
Preparing Information for the Mass Media

Second Edition

Doug Newsom
Texas Christian University

James A. Wollert
Memphis State University

Wadsworth Publishing Company
Belmont, California
A Division of Wadsworth, Inc.

Senior Editor: Rebecca Hayden
Editorial Assistant: Melissa Harris
Production Editor: Robin Lockwood, Bookman Productions
Designer: Hal Lockwood
Copy Editor: Anne Montague
Compositor: JGH Composition, Inc.
Cover: Stephen Osborn
Signing Representative: Dean Allsman
Cover photography: Erich Hartmann/Magnum Photos, Inc.

Printed in the United States of America
1 2 3 4 5 6 7 8 9 10—92 91 90 89 88

ISBN 0-534-08712-4

Library of Congress Cataloging-in-Publication Data

Newsom, Doug.
    Media writing: preparing information for the mass media / Doug
Newsom, James A. Wollert.
        p. cm. — (Wadsworth series in mass communication)
        Includes bibliographies and index.
        ISBN 0-534-08712-4
        1. Journalism—Authorship. 2. Reporters and reporting.
I. Wollert, James A. (James Alvin), 1940–1986. II. Title.
III. Series.
PN4781.N344 1988
808'.06607—dc 19   87-28958   CIP

Dr. James A. Wollert
(1940–1986)

This edition is dedicated to co-author Jim Wollert, who was head of the Memphis State University's broadcast journalism sequence and director of the graduate program in journalism.

He was a talented and versatile collaborator whose sturdy spirit lives in his students, many of whom were also his colleagues.

About the Authors

DOUG NEWSOM (Ph.D., University of Texas–Austin) is professor and former chair of the Journalism Department at Texas Christian University in Fort Worth. She is a past president of the Association for Education in Journalism and Mass Communication, and she has been chair of the Public Relations Division of the AEJMC. Long active as a practitioner and educator in the public relations field, she advises the Public Relations Student Society of America at Texas Christian University and has served as national faculty adviser to the PRSSA. She is an accredited member of the Public Relations Society of America and helped organize PRSA's Educator Section which she later headed. In 1982, PRSA named her Distinguished Educator of the Year. She is a trustee for the Foundation for Public Relations Research & Education. She is also a director of ONEOK, a diversified energy company, and is on the advisory committee of the Gas Research Institute. She frequently writes and prepares materials for all media and is also the senior coauthor of two other textbooks: *This Is PR: The Realities of Public Relations*, with Alan Scott; and *Public Relations Writing: Form & Style*, with Bob Carrell.

JAMES A. WOLLERT (Ph.D., Michigan State University) was professor and head of the broadcast journalism sequence at the Journalism Department at Memphis State University and had previously taught at the University of Texas–Austin and at Iowa State University. He was active in the Association for Education in Journalism and Mass Communication in which he served as head of the Radio-Television Journalism Division and was a cofounder of AEJMC's Committee on Communication Technology and Policy, serving as chair in 1984–85. He was also active in the Radio and Television News Directors Association and the Broadcast Education Association. Prior to teaching, he worked as a reporter and newswriter for WKOW Radio-TV in Madison, Wisconsin, and as executive producer of news for WAGA-TV, the CBS affiliate in Atlanta, Georgia; and he continued to write and produce programs and commercials as a freelancer. A tireless writer, he wrote and spoke widely on many subjects, including new communication technology, the media and the law, broadcast program practices, and journalism education.

Contents in Brief

Contents

Preface

This revised edition is a response to our audience. The first edition had been out only a few months when the phones began to ring: "Where's the advertising and public relations writing for the mass media?" We were besieged. The message was: "We'll use it, but you fix it." We hope it's "fixed."

Actually, we're a little smug about getting that kind of response. For years we worked under the assumption that writing is writing; all differences are created by audience, the medium and the nature of the message. It's rewarding to find others who look at all information as something to be crafted into the appropriate format for an audience and for delivery through a particular medium.

Thoughts like that were academic heresy not long ago. It took a student's demand to get a unified media-writing course taught at Texas Christian University in 1971. The student (who was getting degrees in both broadcast and print journalism) suggested an introductory writing course that would prepare students for either news route—print or broadcasting, or both.

After the class was formed, the search began for a text. There wasn't one. Over the years, teaching materials became an eclectic collection including print and broadcast newswriting, publicity and some commercial writing. Although the course was introduced at other universities over the years, instructors either accumulated materials as we had or tried to adapt basic print journalism texts. But broadcast, advertising and public relations majors soon began to outnumber news editorial majors, and those students couldn't identify with print news–oriented texts. Thus, some ten years after the course was established, frustration stimulated the development of this text.

SIGNIFICANCE OF THE COURSE

The *significance* of the course's concept was articulated by Christy Bulkeley, a thoughtful newspaperwoman who is now vice president of the Gannett Foundation after a career as a publisher for their newspapers; she is also a member of TCU's departmental advisory board. The following is from a letter she wrote in 1980:

I see the day when our photographers will be shooting videotape, serving both local cable news and our own paper from the same. The stills can be pulled from videotape frames and processed either in black and white or color for newspaper use, the tape then edited for the local news on the cable.

Our reporters will be serving multiple purposes as well—in addition to the local cable part (or low-frequency over-the-air broadcast) of local news as well as the newspaper itself. Similarly, our ad sales reps will be providing full service for their customers—all kinds of "traditional" newspaper print as well as cable verbal and visual and local community over-the-air broadcast verbal and visual.

Photographers and reporters alike will need to think visual almost as much as verbal. Charts, maps, other kinds of graphics and color should become a routine part of everyone's thinking.

Likewise, the editors and department managers and other executives will need to be much more versatile and knowledgable about all media than we have been.

Advertisers and advertising agencies, public relations firms and traditional broadcasters, all find themselves dealing with the same variety of ways of reaching the variety of publics they need to serve.

Which existing traditional news and advertising source becomes the information base in any community depends on who has the resources—particularly imagination and foresight—to take advantage of the myriad opportunities available. While the largest organizations in the metropolitan areas may still have plenty of room for professionals with only the traditional news and advertising skills, most of us are going to need people with far broader understanding and skills than we could have imagined a few years ago.

We agree that graduates in mass communication today may be preparing copy for more than one medium at the same time as print media expand into cable and other systems. For that reason, we have included coverage of teletext and videotex, electronic information delivery systems.

THE NEW EDITION

This edition is a genuine revision, not just an update. Most of the changes reflect suggestions from teachers using the book or considering using it. One key change is that the topics have been thoroughly reorganized. The new edition now has 14 chapters instead of 18, and these chapters are regrouped into four parts.

In Part I, Introduction to Media Writing, Chapters 1 and 2 now condense much of what was formerly covered in Chapters 1–4 (principles) and relevant portions of Chapter 9 (newsroom operations) and Chapter 18 (law); and the research chapter has shifted forward into Chapter 3.

Chapter 1, Media Writing Principles, introduces students to the principal considerations: the purpose for the copy, the medium, the audience and the message. We address critical questions every writer should ask. What is the intent of the message? Is it informative or persuasive? What are the characteristics of the medium that will carry the message? What is news and what factors affect a designation of information as "news"? How does the availability of information, media market size, nature of the medium and newsroom operations influence the message? What processes does information go through before it is presented to a mass media audience? Who are those audiences and what should a writer know about them? What is the impact of all of this on the message itself—its crafting and delivery?

Chapter 2, Media Writing Basics, acquaints students with the obstacles to be found in creating the message: obstacles from within the media, from within themselves as messengers and from without: laws. The emphasis of this chapter is on the writer as the messenger. The obligations of the writer as messenger are to be honest, fair and accurate. We discuss some of the ways to meet the obligations and some of the inherent difficulties. The writer also owes it to the audience to take care with the crafting of the message, to write using a style that promotes unity and clarity.

The final chapter in Part I, Chapter 3, considers information sources and research methods—where to find facts and how to use them. Since the focus in this book is on writing, we moved the fact-finding chapter forward to give teachers an opportunity to use a major research assignment as the base for a number of writing assignments.

Another major change in this edition is our simple-to-complex approach to story structure, with leads and basic skills for writing fundamental copy formats in Part II and the more complex structures in Part III.

In Part II, the first chapter (4) on leads and captions was written in direct response to colleagues who said it was needed.

Chapter 5 starts the student on some basic story formats for print and broadcast and takes them into writing three basic types of stories: the advance (the most generally used publicity format, too), the obituary and the rewrite.

Some of our colleagues who work for electronic news systems have convinced us that their jobs primarily involve rewriting and reformatting, not news gathering, so we've followed the chapter dealing with rewriting with the chapter on writing for electronic news (6).

The last chapter in this unit, Chapter 7, is on interviewing for print and broadcast. Interviews are a writer's basic tools, and perfecting interviewing techniques is critical to getting facts not available any other way.

Part III, Complex Story Structures, integrates the print and broadcast media in the discussions of the various types of stories. The development of a story for print is illustrated, and a shorter story with suggested sound bites for broadcasting follows. Chapter 8 covers speech stories, and Chapter 9 covers news conferences and meetings.

Chapter 10 is now devoted to public relations writing—both as a source and as a provider of information. Chapter 11 now combines both columns and features, since many columnists really present features in disguise. The features section includes some new material on magazine writing. The final chapter (12) in this part discusses the longer story—the depth piece. Although it may be some time before students need skill in these formats professionally, we've retained these chapters to aid students who start working in the student media in their sophomore or junior years. Students writing for their newspaper *will* be writing columns, reviews, editorials and depth pieces. The information here gives them a start.

Part IV has a new title: Persuasive Writing. It includes a new chapter (13) on writing for advertising, as well as Chapter 14 on opinion writing.

In addition to making changes in the text, I have revised the instructor's guide. As many of our colleagues suggested, I have moved some of the fundamental writing skills material from Part I in the first edition to the guide. The instructor's guide, together with the new exercise book, *Exercises for Media Writing,* should be used with the text for greatest effectiveness. The new exercise book—with 50 *writing* assignments suitable for use in labs or as homework—was written by Bruce Hinson of the University of Oklahoma.

PURPOSE   This book is designed to be as comprehensive as possible to introduce students to the different styles of writing demanded by the various media, the array of techniques and methods used to find information and present it accurately and appropriately for the medium, and the different forms information may take in the mass media. The expectation is that students in a beginning writing course may go into many different careers. The intent is to prepare all students in the course to gather information and communicate effectively to any mass audience. The hope is that students so prepared can better serve the media, the government, any corporate or non-profit institution they work for.

ACKNOWLEDGMENTS   Our students helped us write this book by showing us, often dramatically, what worked and what didn't in the classroom. To the first students in the course we are especially in debt. Our colleagues who used the first edition served us immeasurably in announcing firmly what we'd overlooked that they needed. Our reviewers of both editions offered solid criticism and helpful guidance, and we give the following our thanks: Claire Badaracco, Marquette University; Mary Benedict, Indiana University; Shirley Biagi, California State University, Sacramento; James Bow, Kent State University; Pat Flynn, University of Southern Mississippi; Bruce Garrison, University of Miami; Michael Kirkhorn, University of Kentucky; James F. Paschal, University of Oklahoma; Jon Roosenraad, University of Florida; Luther W. Sanders, University of Arkansas; Lynne Masel Walters, University of Houston; and Lee Wilkins, University of Colorado.

Jim Wollert and I also appreciated the colleagues at our own institutions who taught from the book and talked to us about what they wanted. Special credit is due Tom Siegfried, of the *Dallas Morning News,* who worked on initial drafts of the first edition and Ray Newton of Northern Arizona University, who was both a reviewer and contributor to the first edition.

Thanks are due the copy editor on both editions, Anne Montague. The patience of editor Rebecca Hayden in getting the final manuscript completed is greatly appreciated.

The dedication is a tribute to co-author Jim Wollert, who died—at 46—before we could complete this revision. Jim fought cancer for eight months while trying to work on this revision. He made significant contributions to both scholarly and professional journals; and he was a leader in professional and academic organizations. His energy and enthusiasm were matched only by his courage.

—DN

PART I

Introduction to Media Writing

"We are entering an era of extraordinary developments in communications, not just here but around the world. It is important that our perception of the relationship between the individual and the media develops and grows along with our new capacities. If it does, we shall understand better what is possible and what is not. If it does not, we shall go on finding phantom causes and proposing shadow cures for concerns that deserve, and need, harder and better thinking."

Gene F. Jankowski, president, CBS/Broadcast Group. Speech before the Radio and Television Commission of the Southern Baptist Convention, Fort Worth, Texas, Feb. 17, 1983.

"Communication is not just words, paint on canvas, math symbols or the equations and models of scientists; it is the interrelation of human beings trying to escape loneliness, trying to share experience, trying to implant ideas."

William A. Marsteller, founder of Marsteller Inc. advertising agency and co-founder, with Harold Burson, of Burson-Marsteller public relations agency, *Creative Management* (Chicago: Crain, 1981), p. 34.

Media Writing Principles

"The English professors don't understand me," the student complained. "I want to drop this course, and I need you to sign this." The adviser looked at her degree plan. "But you need an upper-level humanities class for your core," she said. "Well, it's not going to be English," the student responded. "And what's wrong with English?" asked the adviser. "As a mass communications major, I should think you'd be good in English." "No, I get Ds on my papers and the comment that my writing is too 'journalistic.'"

That scenario has played in hundreds of offices all over the country, unfortunately. Most English composition teachers know the difference between writing a scholarly paper or essay and writing a news or feature story. Mass media, particularly magazines, are an outlet for much of their own work. Certainly they would be sympathetic to the student's claim of being misunderstood, because they often are by their own departmental colleagues whose interest is in literature. The student should be urged to stay in the English class. She does need to learn how to change gears when she writes papers for that class.

She has chosen a writing profession, and writers are expected to be able to write, period. This expectation includes finding facts, arranging the facts in a logical, coherent and interesting way and writing in a style that is suitable to the message's purpose, to the audience and to the medium.

Regardless of title, writers begin each assignment with the same basic questions. You must have clear answers to these questions before you can begin your task: What exactly is the *message*? What *medium* is this message for? Who is the *audience*?

MESSAGES   The mass media present advertising, entertainment, opinion and news. A significant portion of information for news stories comes from professional public relations sources in the form of publicity or news releases.

All writers—reporters, public relations writers, ad copywriters—must think about what their messages are supposed to accomplish. Is it to inform, to educate, to entertain, or to persuade? Knowing the purpose determines the format of the piece.

Persuasive messages

Audiences are alerted to the persuasive nature of a message by both placement and format in the mass media. Print messages to persuade are in the form of advertisements, editorials or signed columns.

Print ads are generally set in a different typeface, usually in the lower portion of a page and along the two sides, forming a "well" or "table top" for the news and entertainment content. Editorials and op-ed (opposite editorial) pages are set aside specifically for opinion and clearly identified. The standing head, or regularly appearing title for a column, often accompanied by the writer's picture, clearly distinguishes the opinion piece from a news story, which merely carries an author's byline. Broadcast opinion pieces are often called "commentary" and generally are followed by a station's appeal for response from different points of view. Unless the commentaries are by the station's manager, they may also carry a disclaimer stating that the views of the writer are not necessarily those of the station or its advertisers.

What is news?

News, simply defined, is what people need to know and what is interesting to them—within the bounds of others' privacy and community standards of taste.

Characteristics of news.   Of course, many more elaborate definitions of news have been constructed. But it's probably more useful to describe news than to try to define it. Events and situations regarded as newsworthy have certain characteristics in common. Not all news stories will have all of the following qualities, but all news stories will have some of them.

1. *News is unusual.* News involves the out-of-the-ordinary. Disasters, accidents, epidemics are not the usual state of affairs. When something happens that's not expected to happen, it's usually news.

2. *News is change.* When the state passes a seat belt law, that's news. When the city hires a police chief, that's news. Whenever something important changes, the change is likely to be newsworthy.

3. *News has impact.* A new law, a drought, a downturn in the economy—all have an impact on people's lives. Anything that has a significant effect on people is news.

4. *News is interesting.* Sometimes an event doesn't have much effect on anybody, but it's interesting in itself. Human-interest stories, stories with drama, stories about things that are ironic or even bizarre, stories that are humorous or entertaining—all may qualify as news.

5. *News is timely.* Yesterday's news is old news, and old news isn't news unless it relates to current events. News is what's happening today, what wasn't known until today, or what takes on a different perspective with today's information.

6. *News is nearby.* The closer an event is, the more likely it will be news, other things being equal. A snowstorm in a neighboring city is news for local papers; a snowstorm in France is unlikely to be.

7. *News is information.* News is information useful to people in managing their lives, making decisions. What time is an event scheduled? Where is it going to be? What number can people call for help with their tax forms? Such information is news.

8. *News is conflict.* People disagree. When disagreements are widespread or when they're about matters of importance to people, they become news.

9. *News is about people.* When people accomplish something, do something wrong, or even when they die, a news story may result. The more prominent the person, the more likely it is that his or her activities will qualify as news.

10. *News is surprising.* Whenever something happens unexpectedly, or when something becomes known that no one had known before, it's likely to be news.

MEDIA

You'll hear the late media critic Marshall McLuhan quoted as having said the medium is the message.[1] He meant that in addition to the medium determining how a message is delivered, it also determines how an audience responds. The technology of the medium, McLuhan observed, affects how the audience accepts the message being sent through that medium. The capacities of a medium and the way audiences use a specific medium control how writers use it. The two major categories for media are print and electronic.

Print media

Print media are newspapers, magazines, posters, brochures, books—anything you read. Reading them requires a conscious effort. Print is concrete and permanent. Readers can reread anything they don't understand the first time, or return for reference. Points can be illustrated with photos and graphics.

Some magazines specialize in high-quality color photos. Some posters become art, carrying their message long beyond its timeliness. Magazines have long lives, as you know from looking through the copies in a doctor's office. But the elaborate production processes required for the glossy visuals preclude speed. You just can't put out a magazine as fast as you can a newspaper, or a poster as fast as you can a flyer. Good writers learn to exploit the different forms of print media to the best advantage.

Newspapers.   Although this familiar bearer of news is called a mass medium, it really isn't. Only a few of the nation's newspapers reach a national audience. Among these are the *New York Times* and the *Washington Post*. The Gannett Co. continues to support its effort at a national newspaper, *USA Today*, started in 1982. Although it is still not financially independent, the company's leadership has expressed a commitment to the publication. It may be the first truly intentionally national newspaper.

Two specialized papers come close to being mass media: the *Wall Street Journal*, with the largest circulation of any newspaper in the U.S., and *Women's Wear Daily*, a Capital Cities publication that also sends out features via its wire service.

One quality newspapers share that does put them nearer to mass media status is their dependency on wire services for much of their content. Some wire services are from individual publications, like the *New York Times* and the *Los Angeles Times*, and others from newspaper chains, like Gannett and Knight-Ridder. The giants are the Associated Press and United Press International.

Some other newspapers that might be assumed to be mass media are those sold in supermarkets, weekly tabloids like the *National Enquirer*. But a libel case against that publication (see Chapter 2) has resulted in the legal categorization of the tabloids as "magazines." Their sensationalized feature content and their non-daily publication would make such a category logical.

In addition to the 1,700 daily newspapers in the United States, some 6,800 weeklies offer exclusively local or regional coverage. And specialized newspapers, such as the educational tabloid the *Chronicle of Higher Education*, cover professions and industries. Many of these papers are the public relations vehicles of trade associations, unions or other such organizations.

Magazines.   Magazines also come under the category of mass media, but they are even less so than newspapers. With the possible exception of circulation leaders *TV Guide* and *Reader's Digest*, mass magazines no longer exist. Special-interest publications such as *Sports Illustrated, Sailing* and other such hobby or recreation-oriented publications have taken their place. Many non-profit public groups, like museums, universities and foundations, publish magazines. These publications are generally public relations vehicles, as are the magazines that are more functional than entertaining in their orientation, such as employee publications.

Newsletters.   Some membership organizations and some profit as well as non-profit institutions send newsletters. Newsletters are a message-oriented communications tool, to convey news and information at regular intervals to a certain constituency, whether they be contributors to the national Humane Society or the employees of a bank. Commercial newsletters are designed for particular audiences as diversified as personal investors or as specific as public relations practitioners. These commercial newsletters are expensive and a big publications business.

Posters and brochures.   These are primarily public relations publications, designed to call attention to something (product or service) or someone. Generally their graphics are as important as their words, because they must get readers involved in something they don't have to read or may not even have a particular interest in reading. You probably got a brochure about your college from the admissions office, and you walk past bulletin boards covered with posters trying to get you involved enough to read the content. The content is always persuasive, written to get you to think or to do something.

Books and pamphlets.   Pamphlets are really mini-books, different from brochures in that their graphics may not always be especially interesting— their producers count on you as an audience to get involved simply because of the subject matter. The same is true for books, although paperbacks count heavily on their packaging, the cover design, to "sell" the content.

Electronic media   Writers for electronic media include those preparing copy for radio and television (both over-the-air and cable) and for electronic message systems such as videotex and teletext. Included, too, are electronic message boards used as outdoor advertising and inside institutions for employee information.

Radio and television news.   Newswriters for both media strive for a conversational style. Generally their copy is briefer than print media stories.

Radio news, for example, offers a quick summary of what's happening that hour. The average commercial radio newscast runs about five minutes, so it must be made up of short synopses of as many top stories as will fit.

Radio information is also fleeting—in one ear and out the other. You can't go back and rehear a radio news story or catch the telephone number in a commercial the way you can reread information in a newspaper. Radio news copy must be immediately comprehensible and easy to recall.

Both radio and TV use tapes (audio and video) in their newscasts. This necessitates a form of "technical writing," or production-into-broadcast writing. The straight story read by the announcer becomes more difficult to write as tapes are introduced. We'll look at these writings formats in Chapter 5.

Radio and TV have the potential to provide live coverage from the scene of any breaking story. As a broadcast reporter, you may have to ad-lib these live reports from the scene. But this doesn't happen all that often; most radio and TV reports are scripted.

Another element of broadcast news is electronic news gathering (ENG). You've probably seen the TV vans about town with what looks like a satellite dish on top. They allow reporters to send back their reports from the field to the station for editing and scripting anytime during the day. Radio stations can do the same.

Commercials.   The same basic requirements of the medium that apply to news apply to radio and television advertising. Most broadcast and cablecast commercials are on tape, although at some radio stations commercials may be read live by an announcer. A major difference between the news messages and the commercial messages is the time limit. Commercial messages are usually 60 seconds, 30 seconds or 20 seconds.

Advertising messages that are not paid for also appear in commercial time slots. These may be promotional messages (promos) the station airs to alert audiences to special programs or public service announcements (PSA's) that are run without charge for non-profit organizations. These spots are written just like commercial messages and follow the same time restrictions.

Videotex and teletext.   This form of information delivery is generally called "electronic publishing." Some newspapers that have an electronic delivery system call it their electronic newspaper. It lets you get news and advertising copy from your TV set or home computer, either from the screen or from an attached printer. The technology will be explained more in Chapter 6. For now, it's enough to say that *videotex* is defined as electronic text that comes into the home via cable TV system or telephone line; *teletext* is delivered via the regular TV signal sent to the home.[2] Examples of this electronic text are shown in 1.1.

How the media shape the news

What actually appears in news stories is sometimes different from idealized, abstract news qualities, because factors having to do with the medium come into play.

Availability of information.   How easy is it to get the needed facts? A potentially newsworthy situation may not be reported simply because the news media are unable to get enough valid information.

Market size.   Location has a lot to do with determining what is considered newsworthy. A murder in Pittsburgh, Pa., is not the same as a murder in Pittsburg, Kan. In some big cities, crime is so common it's relegated to the back pages of the paper and not even reported at all on TV and radio. Farm news gets a lot of play in small rural towns and very little in most big cities, except when crops fail, sending food prices up 50 percent, or bank loans to farms cause city banks to go under.

Nature of the medium.   Radio news needs the voices of newsmakers and the sounds of news events, such as the roar of crowds or of rockets. Television news editors ask: "Is there action? Does it have visual appeal? Can it be photographed?" If not, TV may ignore the event, though it still warrants coverage in a newspaper.

At newspapers and some magazines, the size of the news hole—the amount of space available for news—is constantly changing. Both policy and advertising sales determine the news hole. More advertising means more pages, which increases the opportunity for more news to be included. However, an increase in advertising that isn't enough to pay for extra pages may actually reduce the size of the news hole. Most full-size newspapers must add pages in multiples of four (one double-page spread, printed both sides) to make it economical, but some presses allow added pages in multiples of two. Most newspapers and

1.1 Electronic Newspaper

These are the page formats for the Gainesville Cable Press, run by the University of Florida. The electronic newspaper is published every day except Christmas and New Year's. Formats are: National News, Daily Forecast, Weather Crawl, National World Headlines, Sports AP Scores, Movie Review and Events Calendar.

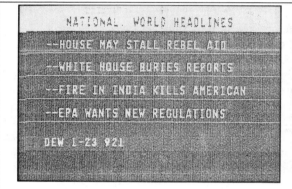

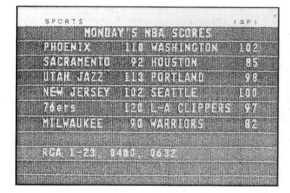

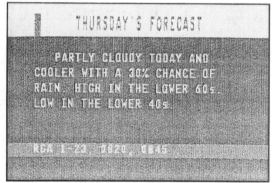

magazines have a flexible ratio of advertising to editorial content. Broadcast news holes are less flexible, but when a big story commands more time, other items, or even other programs, must be shortened, postponed or deleted. In neither medium are news holes in any way large enough to accommodate all available information. Choices must be made about what will be presented as "news."

News values.   The weighing of a story is a subjective decision by editors, who choose stories based on some traditional elements of news: *immediacy*, or timeliness; *proximity*, or how a non-local event affects the area; *prominence*, or what important people are involved; *conflict*; and *human interest*.

These qualities of news are interpreted by editors who have value systems of their own, and this controls the definitions of news.

For example, until recently almost all editors were white men, and their selection of news — their interpretation of news values — excluded, among others, prominent blacks and women whom the editors personally didn't know and therefore couldn't really consider "prominent." Women and minorities would be considered news only if they departed from stereotyped roles, such as a woman with a seat on the stock exchange.

Items that evoked emotion or curiosity were not considered front-page news; they were relegated to the less important human-interest category.

In 1983 a scholarly study of news values, *New Directions for News*, offered well-documented evidence for a need to recognize some broadened interpretations and recasting of traditional news values. Specific suggestions included more recognition of human news, or "soft news," and more coverage of the effects of change, such as new or proposed laws or court decisions, on the lives of readers.[3]

Newsroom organization   **Newspapers** have publishers at the top of the hierarchy, but although they may have some say about content, most of the daily decision making is left up to editors and those reporting to them. Levels of authority vary with the size of the paper. Larger papers assign corporate management tasks to the publisher and the executive editor (or editor-in-chief) and generally leave the management of the newsroom to a staff of subeditors. Titles vary; but most newspaper newsrooms are run by managing editors. The editorial-page editor generally reports directly to the publisher, since that page is the voice of the publisher, although on some papers that page's editor reports to the editor-in-chief (see 1.2).

Because so many people are involved in producing a newspaper, most papers have staff meetings daily to set the budget of news for the day and to discuss upcoming coverage. Working directly under the editor-in-chief or executive editor is the managing editor (ME), who has the most direct authority in the newsroom. Larger papers usually have one or more assistant MEs. The ME is responsible for seeing that the impossible does happen each day — that a newspaper is produced—and in addition must often deal with the public. The ME must coordinate the activities of the editorial division with advertising, handled by the advertising manager.

Assistant MEs report to the ME about the various departments: news from outside sources, such as national, state and regional bureaus, wire services, foreign correspondents and stringers (freelancers who send in stories from time to time); local news; photographers; section editors (such as sports, living, entertainment, business); and makeup. At smaller papers, several of these jobs are telescoped into one.

Each editor has an area of authority and usually a staff, but all have to work together so the paper has unity and presents stories in the most effective position. (A single story could conceivably appear on the front page, business page or local page, depending on the angle taken.)

Technology has made newspeople into technicians as well. Stories typed into the computer system on video display terminals (VDTs) can be printed

1.2 Newspaper Organization

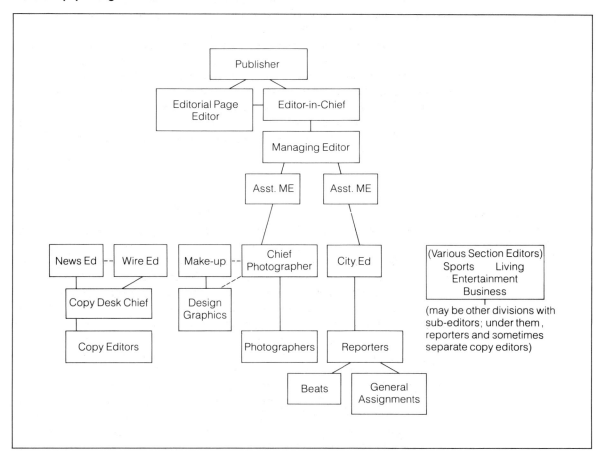

in type styles designated by the writer (italics, boldface, size and so on). Copy editors check the story and may change or add particular typesetting commands. Some systems have electronic pagination capabilities: Entire pages are laid out on the computer screen and are typeset as a unit.

Broadcast newsrooms are considerably smaller. According to the Radio and Television News Directors Association, most radio newsrooms employ about two people full time, except all-news stations. In many cases, the news director may be the only full-time newsperson at the station. A fourth of all radio stations (about 2,200) have no news department or full-time newspeople at all.

Television stations, on the other hand, usually have a news department, but only those in larger cities come close to the size of a typical newspaper newsroom. The usual complement of newspeople is about 20. The usual organizational structure of a TV news department is shown in 1.3. (All of the jobs outlined there are handled by the one or two staffers in most radio newsrooms.)

At the top of the organizational chart is the news director. At larger TV stations, news directors spend most of their time on budgets, personnel, equipment and other administrative matters. Content and quality of newscasts at those larger stations are the concern of producers.

The executive producer oversees all other producers but often also has primary responsibility for the quality of the evening newscast, the most important one of the day. Other news producers handle the early-morning, noon and late-night newscasts. Weekend newscasts also generally have their own producers. Special news programs, especially talk shows, may have their own staff and producers.

1.3 TV Newsroom Organization

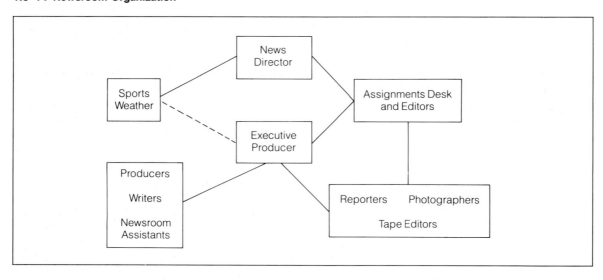

The content of news shows is determined by the assignment editor. It is at the assignment desk that decisions about what is news that day are often made. The assignment editor tells which reporters to cover which events. If the assignments given to reporters are poor, the newscast is usually poor, no matter how hard the producer may try to make it better.

This is why producers and assignment editors often work closely together. The executive producer in particular works with the assignment desk, attempting to ensure that all the important stories are covered, spot news is covered at all times and reporters and news crews are kept busy throughout the day. News directors also participate in this decision-making process, even in larger markets. In smaller and medium-size markets, the news director may be the producer and assignment editor all rolled into one.

When they return from the field, reporters usually begin editing their tapes immediately. Tape editors are assigned at larger stations. Producers set the length for each story. Reporters often spend all day on a story only to be told by a producer, "Your story gets one minute tonight."

Producers, assignment editors and the news director usually meet early in the afternoon each day to decide what the "lineup" or "rundown" will be for the early evening news. Every show must have a lead story. Other stories are then ranked in descending order of importance. Sports, weather and features are added, and a final lineup, with all in order, is typed.

The show's producer then assigns writers to each story. Producers sometimes write all "readers" themselves and assign the reporters who were in the field to write the lead-ins to the tape stories they covered that day. Producers also write these lead-ins themselves if reporters are busy editing tapes.

The TV news department employs a lot of people that the public never sees or hears. For every reporter on the street, there must be a photographer along to shoot the video. Larger stations have tape editors and writers. Desk assistants pull slides and line up other visuals that will appear on the screen during the newscast.

The news process   Information that might qualify as news must go through a series of steps before it gets into print or on the air. Some of that information survives, some doesn't (see 1.4).

Why is this so? The overall reason is that sufficient time and space aren't available to report everything. But there are specific reasons. A reporter may know about a story but may be too busy with another one to pursue it. An editor may decide to kill a story because it presents possible legal problems.

Gathering the news.   The first step in the news process is finding out something or getting an idea (see 1.4, step 1). Sometimes people call or write a newspaper or broadcast station with an idea for a story. On a more sophisticated level, public relations representatives for profit and non-profit institutions will suggest or even prepare stories in the form of news releases.

THE NEWS PROCESS
Story Ideas Generated
Phone calls, news releases, reporters, wire services, print, audio and video syndicates and satellite news services—all are sources for story ideas.
Ideas Evaluated
Importance, audience interest and other news values of the story idea are judged. Editor decides whether to assign story for further coverage or to just have it written up from information in the newsroom.
Stories Covered
Stories are assigned to reporters in the field. Reporters phone in stories or send them back electronically. Reporters also bring stories back to newsroom for processing.
Space/Time Assessed
Various editors or producers determine how much, if any, space (print) or time (broadcast) is available for each story.
Stories Assigned
Writers and reporters are assigned stories not yet written, new items for that day or later. Stories completed by reporters, but not used, may be assigned for updating and rewriting to meet space and time requirements.
Story Edited and Designated for Processing
In broadcast stories, tapes are edited to meet time requirements. In both print and broadcast, stories are edited for fit, accuracy, coherence, and style. Slides and graphics are prepared for broadcast stories. Headlines are written; type and sometimes photographs are produced for print stories.

1.4 The News Process

This chart highlights the usual path news stories follow from conception to communication.

For most news media, a more important source of information is the efforts of their own reporters. *Beats*, or areas of coverage, are often assigned in print newsrooms. One reporter might cover city hall, another the police station. Beats can be topics rather than places: education, business or local politics, for example.

Broadcast news reporters are general-assignment reporters in most cases. In a large city, a typical newspaper might field 100 reporters, while the average TV station might have 10 reporters and the average radio station one or two. Therefore, broadcast news reporters usually handle all areas of coverage rather than specific beats.

All reporters go to meetings, talk to people on their beats and all over town, examine documents and reports. Consequently, reporters are often the best source of information any news department can have.

Another large source of information is the wire services and syndicates. Wire services such as the Associated Press (AP) provide nationwide and worldwide news coverage to members or subscribers. Syndicates sell columns, features and specific kinds of news stories (such as science, education, medicine) to media outlets around the world. Many editorial-page columns, comic strips, advice columns and special features such as crossword puzzles are distributed by syndicates.

Satellite technology has spawned a wide variety of news services for broadcast media. Most TV stations and over half of all radio stations now have satellite dishes to receive these new services, which provide audio and video reports from all over the world that stations can use in their local newscasts. Additional services such as weather, sports, features and special-events coverage are also provided.

Public relations sources supply publicity to news media (mass and specialized) in a number of different ways. PR material for mass media has to meet all of the criteria for news and has to be prepared just the way the staffs for the various media would prepare it. Some publicity comes to news editors as typed releases on the organization's letterhead or the letterhead of the organization's public relations agency. Other publicity is sent on a public relations wire service furnished free to news media. Clients absorb the costs. Some public relations releases arrive over computer networks, like electronic mail, or are sent electronically directly from source to media.

News releases for broadcast media are often submitted on audio or videotape. Some television news directors don't like to use videotape their stations have not prepared, but even networks will use top-quality videotape if the message is genuinely news, and their staff hasn't been able to cover it. PR people provide this as backup even when major events are covered by news media.

PR people are significant sources of news and remain so as long as they are honest and straightforward with the news media contacts. Most PR practitioners know that all they really can offer to validate the information they present is their record for credibility. The ethical and responsible PR people work to preserve this in order to retain the effectiveness of their media relations.

To get coverage, PR people send news alerts—bulletins or memos to editors to let them now what's happening, when, where, its potential news value and who to contact to make arrangements for coverage. These alerts are often sent over the PR wire (see 1.5).

Evaluating the news.   Once information reaches a news medium or comes to the attention of a reporter, it is evaluated for its news value (see 1.4, step 2). A reporter attending a city council meeting, for example, rarely reports on everything that happens. Some matters are not of general interest. The reporter writes a story that covers only those points he or she deems important for the audience (see 1.4, step 3).

The editor will review the story about the meeting and may choose not to use it because he or she thinks it simply isn't newsworthy. Or it may be

1.5 PR Wire Service

Public relations news wires like this are offered free to
news media. News wire client fees cover the costs.

Tracor news

Tracor, Inc. 6500 Tracor Lane Austin, Texas 78725-2006 Telephone 512: 926 2800
Contact: Judith Asel Newby, Public Relations

Newly Formed Tracor Mermen, Inc., Uses Patented Tracor Technology To Provide First Brushless Underwater Cleaning System For Boats

AUSTIN, TEXAS, October 16, 1986 — Millions of small bubbles created from
Tracor-patented low-pressure water jets in a new-technology underwater cleaning
system, CaviSystem, destroy barnacles and algae on boat hulls and appendages. The
system is offered by Tracor Mermen, Inc., a recently formed and 50-percent-owned
subsidiary of Tracor, Inc.

William C. Moyer, Ph.D., a director of Tracor Mermen and a group vice
president and director of Tracor, Inc., and Roland J.N. Lever, president of Tracor
Mermen, today jointly announced that the new system will be available first to yacht
owners in the Fort Lauderdale area where the Tracor Mermen Hull-Maintenance
Service Program was established this month.

The CaviSystem Hull-Maintenance Service Program will be introduced to yacht
owners through video tape demonstrations at the Fort Lauderdale International
Boat Show, at the Bahia Mar, October 27-November 3, in Fort Lauderdale, Fla.

The brushless underwater cleaning system uses a patented CaviJet® concept
which was developed in an extensive research, development, and testing program
by the Jet Technology Systems Division of Tracor Hydronautics, Inc., a subsidiary of
Tracor headquartered in Laurel, Md. The CaviJet® nozzle design led to the invention
of a self-resonating, cavitating jet nozzle, the StratoJet®, and to the development of
the CaviSystem which uses the patented low-pressure water jets.

The water jets in the CaviSystem remove air that is trapped in water, pulsating
or streaming the air in the form of millions of small bubbles per second onto the
underwater surfaces to be cleaned. The bubbles burst on contact with the surface,
sending minute shock waves through the shells of barnacles or other crustaceans
and loosening adhesive pads of grass and algae growth. The pulsated water washes
away the debris to leave a clean surface.

Following development of the CaviSystem, field trials were conducted over a
10-month period in Stuart, Fla., in cooperation with Stuart Hatteras, Inc. During this
period, more than 75,000 square feet of hull surfaces were maintained, and both pre-
and post-cleaning sea trials were conducted. All field tests now completed, the
CaviSystem Hull-Maintenance Service Program is offered by service contract for a
minimum of one year.

Lever said, "Using a combination of low-pressure water enhanced by pulsation
and cavitation, the CaviSystem service brings a totally new dimension to underwater
hull, propulsion, and thorough hull cleaning.

"The specialized CaviSystem allows quick and environmentally responsible
underwater cleaning of boats. For example, the underside of a 60-foot yacht can be
cleaned totally in less than two hours using the water in which it sits.

"The maintenance contract offered by Tracor Mermen also is extremely
economical. The continued monitoring and quick removal of marine growth without
brushes or toxic chemicals saves time, prevents potential hazards, and increases the
useful life of the anti-fouling paint on boats. In addition, the thorough cleaning
assures drag-free vessel performance which saves fuel costs, reduces engine strain
and running-gear wear and tear, and maximizes power and speed availability."

-30-

Reprinted with permission of Tracor Inc. and Southwest Newswire, Inc.

considered newsworthy but there's no room for it—the editor decides other stories produced by other reporters are more important. Perhaps there's room for only part of the story, and some of the points judged significant by the reporter will have to be cut (see 1.4, step 4).

Some stories are held over because they are important enough to use, but not at that time. Others are assigned specifically for future use (see 1.4, step 5).

Production.   Once a story survives the first stages of the news process, it goes into production. Editors evaluate its importance and interest and decide how prominently it should be displayed (see 1.4, step 6). Should it be the lead story on the evening TV newscast, Page 1 of the morning paper? In some cases a story may be rewritten to "beef it up," that is, to add new or background material. The story must then be edited and prepared for print and broadcast.

For a newspaper story, a photograph may be taken to accompany it. A headline must be written. The story must be set in type. In broadcast news, the story may have a video or audiotape with it. Lead-ins to those tapes must be written after the tapes are edited to the time specifications set by the producers. Other visuals, such as slides, must also be written into the copy.

Cable TV news, videotex and teletext news and information—all news goes through this process, no matter how large or small the newsroom might be.

With an understanding of news and the news process, you can begin to learn the specific techniques of writing news for large and diverse audiences.

Advertising writers   Those who write advertising copy have a slightly different process. Their assignments come from their employers, whether they work for a company originating the advertising, an agency handling advertising for a client, or a news medium handling in house the advertising for its clients.

Print and broadcast commercial messages in the mass media run in purchased space or time. Most commercial messages come to the medium ready to print or air. Occasionally small advertisers will have their messages prepared by the medium and pay for that production in addition to the time and space.

Public service announcements are often prepared by the news media, although most national non-profit organizations, such as the American Heart Association, have sophisticated communication departments that prepare materials for immediate use. Another producer of public service messages for direct use is the Ad Council. This national association of advertising agencies selects a worthy non-profit organization or message and rotates among the agency members responsibility for production and placement. These public service announcements are used as time and space are available.

Ad writers' obligation is to capture attention and to persuade someone to think something (as in voting for a political candidate) or to buy something. Their responsibility to those who are information consumers is to practice the art of persuasion ethically so no one is misled. The media monitor their advertising content carefully and have standards for what they will present to their audiences. This includes national advertising that comes to news media from national space-buying operations as well as directly and through the networks.

The three major broadcast networks also have stringent regulations for the commercials they accept to be sure they don't run afoul of government regulations or the law.

These regulations often run counter to what some would call responsibility. There are debates over whether to advertise products either because someone considers them of questionable value (such as candy) or because people have different standards about them (such as birth control devices). Cigarette advertising can now appear only in print, and the American Medical Association has attempted to get cigarette print ads prohibited. But in February 1987, the American Bar Association declined support, saying such a prohibition would be an infringement of First Amendment freedom. The tastes and values of society are not homogeneous, and they are subject to change.

It is just such change that is at the root of another criticism of advertising: its contribution to (some say creation of) pop culture. The trends, the fads that often are introduced by advertising are seen by some as harmless entertainment. Others question the ethics of some, if not all, products and the persuasive way they are presented. A curious parallel to this criticism exists in cultures that don't have advertising. Advertising draws much of its innovation from the arts, and in cultures without advertising, it's the arts that are criticized for "corrupting" or at least "contaminating" the culture. In a commercially based culture, the quality of the advertising message is always an issue, even when the product (or service) isn't.

AUDIENCES

Audiences are the key to how messages are delivered, as electronic publishing so clearly illustrates. They are also the key to how messages are written for any medium. Audiences tend to treat news and commercial messages both as information, much to the dismay of the professionals producing these messages, who perceive the functions as clearly divided.

Expectations

Audience perceive media as fulfilling seven functions:

1. To provide information about the availability of products and services (advertising and publicity).
2. To entertain (special features).
3. To inform (basic news, advertising, publicity).
4. To provide a forum for ideas (editorials, interpretives, documentaries, commentaries).
5. To educate (in-depth pieces, self-help stories and columns and informative items presenting facts not otherwise readily available, as in science writing).
6. To serve as a watchdog of government (investigative reporting and coverage of trials and other public events).

7. To persuade through advertising, publicity, editorials and commentaries.

As a writer, you must remember these expectations in fullfilling the *purpose* of your writing, from your organization's perspective. You also must keep in mind how audiences will use the medium for which you are writing.

Use   When you listen to radio news, you probably want the immediate developments of a story. In the mornings you may turn on one of the network television shows to catch up with what happened when the other side of the world was working. You want to know what to expect during the day: a tropical storm off the coast that might bring rain or a strike that could mean loss of bus service.

You expect to get the kernel of the story, especially from television news. The broadcast media are more than a headline service, though. They offer a digest or summary of news that changes during the day as writers and editors anticipate what you need to know. Special bulletins during "drive time" help you avoid traffic snarls. Noon newscasts help you experience an event you missed, such as a president's message.

When you're the writer, putting yourself in the audience's place helps you meet its expectations. This is especially important for public relations people supplying information to the news media. You should know that medium's audience as well as any editor of that medium and be able to write as well or better than any of the professional staff you're competing with for space. Furthermore, you have to offer information valuable to that medium's audiences which the staff cannot provide or has not provided. Consulting statistics on media audiences can help you get a fix on who's using a medium and why.

Ad copywriters depend on such statistics to know how to slant their copy. Copy for a commercial that is going to be used on easy-listening stations isn't written the same way as a commercial to be used on rock or country-Western stations. Broadcast marketing and sales representatives as well as print ad salespeople can provide statistical pictures of their audiences.

Reprinted by permission of Jefferson Communications, Inc., Reston, Va.

Empathy   The empathic writer imagines being on the receiving end of the message, which helps in selecting facts and deciding which ones to emphasize, which to omit and how to arrange them for clarity.

Research data can help you visualize and understand your audiences. Who reads the morning newspaper? The research bureau of any newspaper prepares information for potential advertisers and can help writers understand the readership. The same is true of the research done on broadcast audiences. What age groups comprise your audiences? How much education do they have? How much money do they have, and how do they spend it? Under what conditions are these audiences reading or listening? What *audiences* do affects what *writers* must do to get attention and deliver a message.

Avoid stereotyping: Remember that a "homemaker" may be a man or a woman with a college degree and that a "blue-collar worker" may be an aircraft mechanic who owns a fixed-base operation that sells and services corporate jets. Developing a sense of empathy will help you bypass the trap of stereotyping.

General audience studies are available from academic institutions and from non-profit professional organizations such as the Television Information Office, which publishes an annual survey on the use of media (see 1.6). From it you learn that the most current information shows television ahead of newspapers as the news sources most relied upon. (The Television Information Office also reports that in 1984, television pulled 10 points ahead of newspapers as the source of news for college-educated people.) Television is also the most believed source for news by more than half of the public. In 1984, the most recent figures available from TIO, attitudes toward commercials were probed, and 64 percent of the people questioned said they got most of their information about products from television.

Education.   The background an audience brings to a news story or to a commercial message affects that presentation. This is a concern particularly in the broadcast media, since children can be exposed to information they don't have the maturity or educational background to put into perspective. It affects the way news of violence is presented on television, especially during the day and prime time, and the way products are advertised to children. Considering the educational level of the audience means deciding the kind of language to use, the amount of explanation needed and the impact the message is likely to have.

Taking education into consideration does not mean talking down to audiences at different levels; it only means talking differently to them. As a test, choose a prominent story in the news and compare the *Wall Street Journal*'s treatment of it with that of the daily newspaper in your area. Then compare these stories with the radio and TV versions. The writer's anticipation of what the audience will bring to the story affects the presentation.

The mass media have been accused of preparing material for the lowest level in order to reach the largest segment of the audience. The criticism of television news is especially harsh. TV news is, and must be, both information and entertainment, or audiences won't watch. But since so many depend on television for news, the burden of serious news coverage is there.

I'd like to ask you where you usually get most of your news about what's going on in the world today—from the newspapers, or radio, or television, or magazines, or talking to people or where? (DEC. 1986)

Newspapers	36%
Radio	14
Television	66
Magazines	4
People	4
Don't know	1

If you got conflicting or different reports of the same news story from radio, television, and magazines and the newspapers, which of the four versions would you be most inclined to believe—the one on radio, or television, or magazines, or newspapers? (DEC. 1986)

Radio	6%
Television	55
Magazines	7
Newspapers	21
Don't know	12

Different people have all sorts of things, both good and bad, to say about TV commercials—for example—that they are in poor taste, that they are informative, that they are amusing, that there are too many of them, etc. Now everything considered, do you agree or disagree that having commercials on TV is a fair price to pay for being able to watch it? (DEC. 1986)

Agree   75%   Disagree   20   Don't know   5

Turning to something else, where are you most likely to learn about products or brands of products you might like to try or buy—from radio commercials, or television commercials, or newspaper ads, or magazine ads? (OCT. 1986)

Radio commercials	5%
Television commercials	57
Newspaper ads	24
Magazine ads	16
Don't know	5

America''s Watching: Public Attitudes Toward Television. Television Information Office/Roper Report.

1.6 Sources of News

These excerpts from a 1987 Television Information Office study present statistics that illustrate how people generally use media.

THE COMMUNICATION PROCESS

This discussion of message, medium and audience is one way of looking at the communication process—what happens when you try to transfer an idea from one person to another. You've probably suffered enough misunderstandings to recognize that communication is a flawed process. When many people are involved, as in the mass media, the probability for error increases dramatically.

Steps in the process were described succinctly by political scientist Harold Lasswell in 1948, when he suggested that communication could best be analyzed by asking the following questions:[4]

> Who
> Says What
> In Which Channel
> To Whom
> With What Effect?

Mathematicians Claude Shannon and Warren Weaver devised a model of the communication process that included a "transmitter" and a "signal" for sending and carrying the message.[5] David Berlo adds an "encoder" for preparing a message to be sent and a "decoder" to be used by the receiver.[6]

Thus a convenient modern way of viewing communication as a process is something like this: A source encodes a message and sends it via some medium to a receiver who decodes the message and attaches meaning to it.

When you write something, you are the source. The encoding process is writing. How you write will be determined by the message you want to convey, the medium you will use to convey it, the audience you are conveying it to and the effect you wish that message to have on the audience to fulfill your purpose for writing it.

When a local government scandal erupts in Chicago, it may only merit a brief article on page 20 of your local paper in Oregon. Many libraries and bookstores, however, carry copies of the daily papers of major U.S. cities so you can keep up with the details of what's happening back home.

Jane Scherr/Jeroboam, Inc.

Whatever your role in this process, you will be expected to command the language, to master a variety of ever-changing equipment and to organize ideas, people and events successfully. Personal and mechanical skills must be second nature to you so you can accomplish the real work—the communication tasks.

MAIN POINTS

- Writers for mass media must consider the message, the medium and the audience.

- Messages in the mass media include ads, opinion and news; this book deals primarily with the news aspect.

- News is what people want and need to know. Criteria for news stories include: unusualness, newness, impact, interest, timeliness, proximity, information, conflict, humanity, surprise.

- The basic types of media are print and electronic, which includes radio and television as well as videotex and teletext.

- News presentation is affected by the availability of information, the market size in which the medium is located, the nature of the medium and newsroom operations.

- Reporters and editors act as "gatekeepers" who judge information based on the requirements of the medium.

- Newsroom operations affect the presentation of news because of the changing size of the news hole, news values that are applied to selection of stories to fit that hole, and who does that selecting.

- Newsroom organization is different for print and broadcast, with the primary difference being the size of staffs. Broadcast news staffs must be generalists, print reporters specialize more.

- The news process is basically the same, though, for all news media. That involves: (1) generating the story idea; (2) evaluating the idea; (3) covering the story; (4) assessing the availability of time or space; (5) assigning the story for writing or rewriting; (6) editing the story and preparing it for production; (7) producing it and delivering it to the audience.

- PR sources alert mass media editors and reporters to important stories in their organizations, often provide access for news media to cover a story and supply news coverage of events in the form of releases, photographs, audio and videotape.

- Advertising supplies information about products and services through the mass media. The mass media donate advertising time or space for special messages, their own promotional messages or those of non-profit organizations which they may also produce.

- Audiences use the different media differently and expect information to come from them in particular ways.

- Writers must have enough empathy with their audience to tailor messages appropriately.

- The whole process of communication is a hazardous one. Writers have to be concerned about the meanings of words and how words affect people. Communication has been described as a process with the following steps:

Who
Says What
In Which Channel
To Whom
With What Effect?

- Another way to look at the communication process is something like this: A source encodes a message and sends it via some medium to a receiver who decodes the message. You as a writer are the encoder of the message, sending it through a medium to be decoded by an audience on whom it will have some effect. You hope the effect achieves the purpose you had for writing the message.

EXERCISES

1. Read all the stories on the front page of a daily newspaper. For each story, list the applicable qualities of news given in this chapter. From your findings, how many of these qualities would you say are necessary to warrant a story's getting front-page display?

2. Which of the stories on the front page had you already gotten some information about from radio? Television? Did the broadcast story tell you everything you wanted to know, or did it make you curious to learn more about the event?

3. Compare the national news stories in today's newspaper with the stories broadcast on one of the national TV networks' evening news programs. Which stories were in the newspaper but not on TV? Which were on TV but not in the newspaper? What aspects of the news process can explain these differences?

4. How many of the front-page newspaper stories quoted some public relations source—a spokesperson or a government source (including the president of the United States, who has a press secretary). How many of these stories do you think were originated by the PR source? How many without acknowledged PR sources do you think came from PR sources? How many are responses to news media inquiries?

5. Find a story in the student newspaper or local newspaper on something you know about from firsthand experience—either you were at an event, such as a game, or you know about the subject, such as flying. Is the presentation an accurate one? If not, what's wrong? Why do you think that might happen?

NOTES

1. Herbert Marshall McLuhan and Quentin Fiore, *The Medium Is the Message: An Inventory of Effects* (New York: Random House, 1967).

2. "Teletex and Videotext in the Year 2000," Viewdata Corporation of America (Miami: Knight-Ridder, 1981). See also David Lachenbruck, "Revolutions on the Small Screen," *Encyclopaedia Britannica*, 1982 *Book of the Year*, pp. 659–60.

3. Virginia Allen, Catherine East and Dorothy Jurney, *New Directions for News* (Washington: Women's Studies Program and Policy Center of the George Washington University, 1983), p. 3.

4. Harold D. Lasswell, "The Structure and Function of Communication in Society," In *The Communication of Ideas*, ed. Lyman Bryson (New York: Institute for Religious and Social Studies, 1948), reprinted in Wilbur Schramm, *Mass Communications* (Urbana: University of Illinois Press, 1949), p. 1·17.

5. Claude Shannon and Warren Weaver, *The Mathematical Theory of Communication* (Urbana: University of Illinois Press, 1949). See the discussion of Shannon and Weaver's model in Werner Severin and James Tankard, Jr., *Communication Theories: Origins, Methods, Uses* (New York: Hastings House, 1979), pp. 31–32.

6. David Berlo, *The Process of Communication* (New York: Holt, Rinehart and Winston, 1960), pp. 30–32.

SUGGESTIONS FOR ADDITIONAL READING

For more detailed discussions of news and the news process, see:

Bogart, Leo. *Press and Public*. Hillsdale, N.J.: Lawrence Erlbaum Associates, 1981. Chapters 6 through 9 discuss the nature of newspaper and TV news content and readership study findings of what kinds of news people want to read or view.

Donohoe, George A., Phillip J. Tichenor and Clarice N. Olien. "Gatekeeping: Mass Media Systems and Information Control." In *Current Perspectives in Mass Communication Research*, edited by F. Kline and P. Tichenor, pp. 41–69. Beverly Hills: Sage, 1972.

Gans, Herbert J. *Deciding What's News*. New York: Vintage, 1979. An in-depth study of how news decisions are made at two news magazines (*Time* and *Newsweek*) and two TV networks (NBC and CBS) along with an analysis of the sociological factors influencing those decisions.

For public relations and advertising writing, see:

Newsom, Doug, and Bob Carrell. *Public Relations Writing, Form and Style*. 2nd ed. Belmont, Calif.: Wadsworth, 1986.

For a more detailed discussion of communication models and theories, see:

Berlo, David, *The Process of Communication*. New York: Holt, Rinehart and Winston, 1960. Though more than 20 years old, this book is still highly regarded and widely read. Chapters 1 through 3 outline Berlo's conception of the communication process.

DeFleur, Melvin L., and Sandra Ball-Rokeach. *Theories of Mass Communication*. 4th ed. New York: Longman, 1982. See Chapter 6 for theories on the nature and the effects of communication and Chapter 7 for the development of ideas about the effects of mass media.

Schramm, Wilbur. "The Nature of Communication between Humans." In *The Process and Effects of Mass Communication*, edited by W. Schramm and D. Roberts. Rev. ed. Urbana: University of Illinois Press, 1954. A sophisticated treatment of the communication process by one of the leading authorities.

Severin, Werner, and James Tankard, Jr. *Communication Theories: Origins, Methods, Uses*. New York: Hastings House, 1979. Chapter 3 gives a readable introduction to some of the popular communication models. Chapter 5 is an interesting discussion of semantics, and Chapter 6 is a thorough treatment of readability research.

Williams, Frederick. *Technologies and Communication Behavior*. Belmont, Calif.: Wadsworth, 1987.   Explains how people interact with communication technology from a social and behavioral standpoint.

For some criticism of the mass media, see:

Abel, Elie. *What's News*. San Francisco: Institute for Contemporary Studies, 1981.

Becker, Sam. *Discovering Mass Communication*. 2nd ed. Glenview, Ill.: Scott, Foresman, 1987.

Holloway, Harry, with John George. *Public Opinion*. 2nd ed. New York: St. Martin's, 1986.

Jamieson, Kathleen Hall, and Karlyn Kohrs Campbell. *The Interplay of Influence*, 2nd ed. Belmont, Calif.: Wadsworth, 1988.

Meyers, William. *The Image Makers*. New York: Times Books, 1984.

Media Writing Basics: Message Effectiveness

A popular bulletin-board sign is this short stanza commenting on the problem of misunderstanding messages:

> I know you believe you understand
> what you think I said,
> but I'm not sure you realize
> that what you heard
> is not what I meant.

The sign, though humorous, reflects a deep truth that everybody someday discovers: Communication isn't easy. There is unlimited opportunity for misunderstanding. For one thing, language isn't perfect. Reality is too complicated to be described by words. Or, as psychologist Daniel Katz expresses it, "The real world is more complex, more colorful, more fluid, more multidimensional than the pale words or oversimplified signs used to convey meaning."[1]

Additionally, there is the noise and confusion of information from multiple channels. The message you are trying to send in one medium to an audience is competing for attention with messages from many other media. To be successful in delivering a message, you must not only attract attention but keep it through the whole delivery of the message. Then you must count on that message being understood well enough to achieve your purpose.

CHALLENGES Everything you write has to work, or you've wasted your time and someone's money. To stay employed as a professional writer, you must master the language and the idiosyncrasies of all media. Challenges arise in these three areas: message, messenger, semantics.

Message

You have to remember what kind of message you are presenting and write accordingly. Keep your purpose in mind. A straight news report of a fire isn't written in quite the same way as an in-depth analysis of toxic-waste disposal. An editorial takes a different style and format than an obituary. An announcement news release is different from a feature about a person in the news, and both are quite different from a release explaining the impact of a crisis on an organization.

Commercial messages have more in common with editorials because they too are persuasive, but, like the different appeals of editorials, commercial messages make particular appeals based on purpose. It's important to remember what kind of message you are presenting and to write accordingly.

The problem occurs in understanding the times when purposes can successfully overlap and when they cannot. A news story written mainly to inform is more likely to be read through to the end if it's also entertaining. Features that entertain may also provide valuable information. Editorials that successfully persuade may also inform. Commercial messages that persuade may also entertain.

The difficulty of communicating through the mass media is the lack of immediate feedback from receivers as the message is delivered. In conversation, you can make a second effort to capture attention if you see it wandering, and you can respond to puzzled looks or questions. The mass media don't give you that opportunity.

Messenger

In writing for others, you must be acutely conscious of your own perspectives. You must be aware that some words you're accustomed to using may have different meanings to others.

Look at what you have written to see whether you have examined all the ways others might view it. This is a particular problem sometimes for public relations people who have to write a release that can be approved by top management yet will pass the careful scrutiny of news editors who routinely look out for missing or misleading information.

Mass media audiences are diverse. Your writing style must be accessible to all, and at the same time you must not forget that certain types of readers and listeners expect certain types of stories. On the sports page, for example, your style must be appropriate for sports enthusiasts yet clear enough to be understood by more casual readers.

Semantics

Most of the obstacles you'll have to overcome in writing are related to the encoding–decoding process—how words are used to express meaning. You have to be sure that the meaning you intended in encoding the message survives the decoding by someone else who may use the same words differently. The study of what words mean is called *semantics*.[2]

The word is not the thing. One of the first lessons of semantics is that words shouldn't be confused with the things they refer to. The word is a *symbol* that stands for the reality. No matter how close we come to describing reality with words, a gap between the word and the thing always remains. If you say "chair" to someone, how do you know that person's mental picture of a chair looks like yours? In giving directions, as in "Bring me a chair, please," you are not giving the person you are directing enough information if there is more than one chair from which to select and you want a particular chair.

Good communicators try to narrow the gap by making sure their words have obvious *referents*. The referent is the thing a word stands for. Beginning writers run into trouble using pronouns such as *it, this, them*. A beginner is likely to write: "The police chased the robbers for two hours. They lost them in a winding alleyway." Who lost whom?

If the audience has a clear notion of a word's referent, communication should succeed. Words with vague referents are said to be abstract. Abstraction is one of the chief concerns of semanticists.

Levels of abstraction. You have in mind one specific chair, the green upholstered office chair on rollers with the adjustable back. If the person who tries to follow your direction brings in a brown wooden classroom chair, you are likely to say, "No, I didn't mean that one." But you hadn't said what you meant. The brown wooden chair is also a chair.

Chair is an abstraction. Furthermore, it can be made more abstract by calling it furniture. You can carry that to an even higher level of abstraction by calling it building furnishings. It might appear on the university budget as assets. The further away you get from the specific, the less sure you can be that someone will know what you're talking about. Ordinarily, the less abstract—more specific—you can be, the better your audience will understand you.

Importance of context. The words surrounding a word help to explain it. The meaning never resides in the word alone. If you had asked for a chair "out of that office," you would have been less likely to get a classroom chair.

Context also helps explain a word that might be unfamiliar to your audience. Children acquire vocabularies by hearing words in context so that they learn what they mean.

But you also have to be sure the meanings are the same to your audience as they are to you. If you ask a friend who is helping you in the kitchen to hand you a "frying pan," you may or may not get the "skillet" you thought you were asking for. If you are in England and talk about having attended a public school, you'll find that what you have just said is that you attended a private school.

OBLIGATIONS You have some responsibilities to your audiences in the mass media. It is not a "buyer beware" marketplace of ideas. You are obliged to be honest, accurate

Reprinted by permission of Jefferson Communications, Inc., Reston, Va.

and fair. This applies across the board to news, public relations and advertising. In fact, professionals in all three fields are bound by codes of ethics that commit them to such standards. They are also constrained by a wide range of laws and regulations.

Honesty   Honesty means representing the reality of a situation as accurately as the language will allow.

Identifying statements: reports, inferences, judgments.   Perhaps the most useful contribution of semanticists to media writers is the division of statements into these three main groups.

Reports. A report is a statement of fact. It refers to something that can be observed and verified by checking reliable records. For example, "It snowed last night in Cleveland" is a report. Many people saw the snow, and official record keepers noted the event in a form that would permit anyone to verify the report at a later date.

Inferences. These are logical conclusions. Semanticist S.I. Hayakawa calls an inference "a statement about the unknown made on the basis of the known."[3] If we see that a puddle of water has frozen, we can infer that the temperature has dropped below 32 degrees Fahrenheit, even if we have no thermometer. A reporter covering a woman's murder might infer that her husband's checking in to a psychiatric hospital means that he killed his wife and is going to plead temporary insanity. But until adequate facts are found to document such a notion, writing a report based on this inference is risky. Audiences may infer guilt when news reports say a person had no comment to make in response to charges, even though the person is merely obeying legal counsel. As we gather additional information, we may find that some of our inferences were incorrect.

Judgments. A judgmental statement is an expression of approval or disapproval. "This rain is dreadful" is clearly an expression of disapproval; the statement is a judgment. Judgments, obviously, might not be shared by all observers. To the student who had planned to play tennis, the rain may be dreadful. To the farmer worried about his parched fields, the rain might be wonderful.

All three kinds of statements enter into most communication. The writer must know the difference between them to avoid misleading the audience. If a writer makes a report appear to be a judgment, for example, the audience may mistakenly disregard legitimate information as "just somebody's opinion." If an inference is disguised as a report, the audience may take important steps based on a belief that turns out to be false.

Fortunately, some simple tests can be applied. A report states a fact that any competent observer would agree with. If you report "It is raining outside," anyone who steps out and gets wet will agree with you. If you report "This doorway is three feet wide," anyone who bothers to check it with a tape measure will get the same result. Even if something isn't observed firsthand, such as a snowfall in Cleveland, weather bureau records would verify that the snow did indeed fall there that day.

Inferences are not as solidly based as reports. Yet some inferences are inescapable. If when you go to bed your lawn is clearly visible and when you awaken you find a foot of snow on the ground, you can infer that snow fell during the night.

Yet many inferences are made without such assurance. You might look around in certain parts of Kansas and infer from what you see that the earth is flat. Someone who drives up in a fancy Rolls-Royce may be rich—or a car thief.

Inferences, then, can be strong or weak, highly justified or risky. The strongest inferences are those based on broad knowledge and many observations. Inferences drawn on the basis of single observations by people who know little about the subject are less likely to prove accurate. Inferences are safest when no other inference can be drawn from what has been observed. In the case of the snow on the ground in the morning, very few other explanations could be offered besides the inferred snowfall during the night. But seldom is it true that *no* other explanation is possible. Someone could have hauled truckloads of snow into the area and dumped them on the ground. As a writer, you are obligated to point out the inference as something beyond what has been observed.

Judgments are opinions. One of the first rules for newswriters to learn is to leave their own opinions out, unless the copy is supposed to be an expression of opinion, as a column might be. While personal judgments should be omitted from news, quoting a responsible person's judgment of an issue he or she is involved with has its place.

When you are writing opinion copy for a broadcast commentary, a review, an editorial or a personal column, the judgment or opinion expressed is based on a knowledge of all aspects of the issue or situation. The opinion is usually more than just an expression of judgment; it is generally an effort to persuade others to share that opinion. Persuasion relies on inference as well as other techniques, some of which are propaganda devices. (See Part IV, Persuasive Writing.)

Lying.   In 1981 the *Washington Post* was publicly embarrassed by a reporter's misrepresentation. A *Post* story about an 8-year-old heroin addict won a Pulitzer Prize, the highest honor in journalism, but the story turned out to be a fabrication.[4] Shortly after Janet Cooke resigned from the *Washington Post, New York Daily News* columnist Michael Daly resigned for writing a column about events in Northern Ireland in which he quoted a British soldier, Christopher Spell, who didn't exist. Daly said Spell was a pseudonym for a real soldier, but that wasn't mentioned in the column, and other details of the events described were also questioned.

Most journalists believe such incidents occur infrequently. But no one denies that reporters sometimes add a few details they aren't sure of or make a direct quotation a little more dramatic and articulate than the speaker's actual words. No matter how widespread these practices are, though, they remain bad practices. Writers must be honest with readers. If you must use a fictional name to protect a person's identity, be sure to tell the readers that. Here's how one reporter handled a story about teen-age runaways:

> It was Friday afternoon in Austin and her mother was at work. Linda, 15, packed a small suitcase. Her parents were divorced. She had just had another fight with her mother.
>
> Linda brushed her short blond hair and, wearing jeans and sweatshirt, marched out the door, embarking on a journey that would lead through months of misery—drugs, prostitution, venereal disease. . . . Linda is not her real name, of course, but the story she tells is painfully real.

This kind of story could also be written by a public relations person seeking publicity for one of the city's social agencies. Whatever your role as a writer, set yourself these questions: Is the story completely true? Are the quotations exactly as people spoke? (You should have good notes and, perhaps, a tape recording of the interview as backup.) Have you avoided the temptation to make the story a little more interesting than it really is? If you have doubts about what you've written, don't submit the story.

Fiction in information is never justified. When a departure from reality is necessary in news material, such as changing a name to protect a person whose life may be in danger, for example, the audience should be told of the change.

Statements from interviewees can be incorrect or a matter of opinion and should therefore be clearly attributed to the source. When models are used in public relations photographs or advertising, that should be apparent or made clear.

Public relations people who are accredited are bound by a code of ethics not to provide false or misleading information or even to be deceptive by allowing someone to draw erroneous conclusions. The professional PR person who gets caught in a deception knows this is professional suicide, because credibility as a source of information is crucial. The PR writer supplying information for a publicly held company must under law be truthful and accurate, as must advertising copywriters. No one is eager to pay a fine or go to jail. That can happen to newswriters, too, if they libel with their fabrications.

Fairness   A writer can be truthful and still not fair. It's possible to communicate some facts while omitting others, thereby painting a misleading picture of the subject. Semanticists (and journalists) call such selective use of reports *slanting*. Consider the following facts about the performance of a baseball pitcher:

> He pitched one inning. He struck out three batters. He allowed one hit and no earned runs.

Sounds like what a sportswriter would call a "fine relief performance." But the reality of the situation might have been different. The following facts are consistent with those above:

> After striking out two batters, the pitcher walked the next three. The next batter hit an easy ground ball, but the pitcher threw it over the first baseman's head, allowing two runs to score. The pitcher hit the next batter with the pitch, then forced in a run by walking the next batter. The next batter swung and missed on the third strike, but the pitch was wild, the batter reached first safely and another run scored. The next batter hit a grand slam. The next batter flied out to end the inning. The pitcher had allowed eight runs, all unearned.

The first version of the pitcher's performance was completely true. Yet the version was slanted: Facts were chosen to create a certain impression. Other relevant facts were omitted. It's usually not possible, or even advisable, to say *everything* that could be said, but you must at least be sure not to select only those facts that might give a misleading impression.

Fairness is an elusive concept. There are, however, some guidelines that a writer can follow. Ben Bradlee, executive editor of the *Washington Post*, offers four:

1. No story is fair if it omits facts of major importance or significance.

2. No story is fair if it includes essentially irrelevant information at the expense of significant facts.

3. No story is fair if it consciously or unconsciously misleads or even deceives the reader.

4. No story is fair if reporters hide their biases or emotions behind such subtly pejorative words as *refused, despite, admit* and *massive*.[5]

In addition to these, three other notions of fairness are commonly practiced by the news media: giving all sides of the story, avoiding sexist and otherwise biased language and avoiding editorial comment.

Injecting editorial comment is a common flaw in most beginning writers' work, especially in public relations writing classes. Somehow the mind-set for writing a news release seems to be different for students than that for writing a news story. A news release *is* a news story, and it won't be accepted by the news media unless it avoids editorial comment, avoids biased language and gives all sides of the story. Where the public relations writer's skill comes in is determining which side to tell first, depending on the audience of the publication.

The PR writer ignores these rules of fairness at considerable risk. If a story is turned in that fails to meet these standards, there is a good chance it will be rewritten and become the kind of publicity an organization doesn't want.

A smart public relations writer uses research done for the organization that can be made public to develop a generic story, one that includes the organization but doesn't display it prominently. For example, a PR writer involved in real estate could do a major piece on available office space in the city, including quotes saying it's an important market contrasted with quotes saying it's already overbuilt. Although the PR person's institution may be mentioned only once in the story, that person has performed a service for the local newspaper and will be considered a reliable, fair and trustworthy source.

The PR writer's boss will be pleased, even though the institution is mentioned only once or twice, for two reasons: The story's appearing in a mass medium gives it what is called "third-person credibility." The idea is you can't brag about yourself and have many people believe you, but if someone else says it, it's likely to be believed. The other reason the PR person's boss will be pleased is once a PR person proves to be a reliable source for good stories that are not self-serving and are a well of information about a particular industry, profession or service, that PR person will be called on often by the news people and quoted, with title and organization in the attribution.

Giving all sides. A news medium can't afford to be seen as a vehicle for promoting one position. Anytime there's an issue, there will be several viewpoints. Newswriters must see to it that all responsible viewpoints are represented.

Thus if a government official says that inflation is caused by government spending, the reporter should seek out some other competent official for another view. The mayor might say a new housing project is desirable, but a local business leader or residents of the area might disagree, and the reporter should include such disagreement in the story.

Some reporters neglect to get all sides of the story for fear that what seems a good story will turn out to be not so newsworthy after all the facts are in. A few months after he left the presidency, Jimmy Carter complained that some reporters write what they know to be untrue, simply because it makes a good story.

Including all sides is especially important when a person or group is charged with wrongdoing. If A says something nasty about B, B's comments *must* be included in the story. Advice on this point from the *New York Times*:

It is of paramount importance that people or organizations accused, criticized or otherwise cast in a bad light have an opportunity to speak in their own defense. Thus it is imperative that the reporter make every effort to reach the accused, or criticized person or persons, or organization, and supply the opportunity to reply.[6]

Fairness as practiced by responsible public relations people means being available for the bad news as well as the good and keeping news media contacts aware of developing events as much as possible without breaching confidentiality.

UPI/Bettmann Archive

QUICK.
WHOSE SIDE ARE WE ON?

Central America is very complex. So are most news stories.

That's why you should watch The MacNeil/Lehrer NewsHour every weeknight. News stories get the time they deserve.

The time *you* deserve.

You get more facts about a story. You get different sides. And you get the analysis you need to understand completely.

Major funding for The MacNeil/Lehrer NewsHour is provided by AT&T, the national corporate underwriter.

The MacNeil/Lehrer
NEWSHOUR
Weeknights on PBS

Produced by WNET/13, N.Y., WETA, Wash., D.C., and
MacNeil-Lehrer-Gannett Prod. Funded by AT&T, Public Television Stations, and CPB. © AT&T 1984

AT&T

Time was when things seemed simple: Good cowboys wore white hats and the villains wore black; World War II was a clear battle between Us and Them. Those days of simple two-sided conflicts seem to have vanished. Today's audiences expect and demand to hear all sides of an issue. Photos: UPI/Bettmann Newsphotos.

Objectivity.   Giving all sides is sometimes described as a way of making news stories objective. But *objectivity* is a dangerous word to use, because it has different meanings for different people. For one thing, it can be used to mean "free from bias or prejudice." But no writer, no editor and no reader is completely free from bias. Objectivity is also used to describe a situation where the observer does not affect what is observed. Again, this is never completely achievable. In front of TV cameras or newspaper reporters, people will do and say things they wouldn't if reporters weren't present. No matter how much reporters attempt to stay in the background, their presence can affect events.

All writers have opinions, biases and prejudices that color their perceptions. Giving all sides and trying to be fair is what trained writers do to compensate for the fact that objectivity isn't possible.

Avoiding editorial comment.   The era of "yellow journalism," when not only opinion but vituperative comment in news stories was common, ended around the middle of this century. News stories should not contain editorial comment. This, of course, also applies to news releases that are submitted by public relations people for publication in the mass media. If the release smacks of opinion, it won't be used.

Sometimes editorial comments slip in almost unnoticed. If you write that a speech was "exciting" or even that it was "interesting," you have overstepped the proper limits. Not everyone will agree that a speech was interesting; not everyone will have been excited. Stick to the facts. If comment of some sort seems necessary, find some responsible person who is in a position to make such a comment and then quote him or her.

Here are some sentences written by students who had not yet learned to keep comment out of their news stories:

> Another company tradition has been innovative thinking and progressive practices that have proven it to be a true industry leader.

> The club's membership growth wasn't astonishing at first, but its accomplishments were.

Words like *progressive* and *astonishing* convey opinion. Note that favorable comment is just as bad as unfavorable comment in a news story. Being fair means being fair not only to the subjects of the story, but to those who might disagree with what you say. In each of these cases, the writer should have *attributed* the statement or rewritten the sentence. For example:

> The company's new ideas and progressive practices have made it an industry leader, said John Johnson, a local financial analyst.

> The club's membership growth was slow at first, its president said, but it did win three university service awards.

Public relations writers often overlook this simple means of getting otherwise taboo promotional-sounding sentences or phrases into their copy. PR writers, who also write most of the speeches given by top executives in their organization, can create quotes for attribution, the same way they put words in the mouths of speechmakers. They must clear the quotes with the "speaker," of course; otherwise a reporter or editor may ask the "speaker" about a quote that he or she knows nothing about. The best practice is to actually interview the people, not only for their speeches but for major announcements. Then you have legitimate quotes, and you don't have to worry about opinion creeping into a release.

Avoiding biased language.   Bias can be reflected by your use of nouns, pronouns and unnecessary descriptive adjectives (see 2.1). For example, if a newspaper's business page consistently refers to business*men*, the woman executive is excluded. If she hears only *he* used by broadcasters and sees the masculine pronoun used exclusively in print, she is likely to turn to more thoughtful sources.

Using the masculine pronoun generically to include men and women doesn't. It excludes. One solution to the pronoun problem is to use a plural noun; then the pronoun standing in its place can be plural (*they*, *them*).

> AVOID: The reporter assigned to a beat develops his own sources.

> USE: Reporters assigned to beats develop their own sources.

When a noun is exclusively one gender, choose another word.

> AVOID: Businessmen who fly often will find the new commuter airline routes useful.

> USE: Business passengers flying often will find the new commuter routes useful.

> AVOID: The petite, blue-eyed grandmother said that as mayor she would be meeting regularly with city planners.

You probably wouldn't have said "The small, blue-eyed grandfather said that as mayor . . .".

> AVOID: George Deukmejian, noted white California governor, met with articulate black presidential contender Jesse Jackson.

What does race have to do with the meeting? Also note the implication that Jackson, being black, would not be expected to be articulate.

Descriptive adjectives used when they do not contribute appropriately to the story are another way bias is often injected.

> AVOID: The blind professor said registration processes should be computerized for greater efficiency.

His sightlessness is not important; it is unfair to needlessly call attention to someone's handicap.

These and other sins of bias can be found—with ways to avoid them—in *Without Bias*, published by the International Association of Business Communicators (see list of readings at the end of the chapter).

Accuracy   Honesty and fairness have to do with character; accuracy has to do with competence. It's not enough to believe what you've written is true. It must *be* true.

Paula LaRocque, writing coach, *The Dallas Morning News.*

No one wants to write sexist and racist copy, yet sexism and racism in the press' reportorial approach continue to be major problems for many newspapers. This is so because of the very pervasiveness of discriminatory attitudes—which we all hold in varying degrees of strength and awareness. No one is exempt from assimilating cultural myth as truth; our only defense is constant vigilance. Those who say that the battle against racism and sexism is merely choking at gnats and swallowing camels should remember that "isms" are more pernicious for their subtlety. And camels slip down only with much practice on gnats.

The Mayor

Consider. The newly elected sheriff of Mayhem, Mass., is for the first time ever a man under 60. That is the story. Tradition has been broken: the new sheriff is 28. We write "How did he do it? How did a 28-year-old with curly red hair and male-model good looks win over his 60-year-old opponent.?" Is it OK? No. His curly red hair and good looks have nothing to do with the tradition that was broken and therefore have no business in that passage. They may have some business in the *story*, depending on what kind of story it is and the manner and reason for their inclusion. But they have no business here.

Or say that for the first time the mayor of Alabaster, Ala., is from New England instead of being Alabama-born. We write: "How did he do it? How did a 6-foot Yankee with thick black hair and all-American good looks win over the Alabama-born incumbent?" No, we won't write that—unless we're trying to suggest that the winner's lush locks and kitchy-koo face *are* relevant in this context.

If we would not print those two passages, why did we run this one:

> How did she do it? How did a 5-foot-tall woman with curly blonde hair and cheerleader good looks win over "good old boy" macho Houston—and defeat the burly 6-foot-4 sheriff of Harris County?

The woman as the girl with naturally curly hair: The story here is that Houston has a woman mayor for the first time ever. Her curly blonde hair and height have no business in *this particular passage*. If those attributes are of interest, they must be of interest in a different context. In other words, when we go beyond the significance of our story to include material that is extraneous—and material that would not be included if the subject were not a woman or a minority member—we may be writing discriminatory copy.

2.1 (continued)

The woman as a head of hair: An absent-minded blonde landed behind bars as a robbery suspect Saturday because she forgot to remove her pistol before visiting a Dallas County jail.

The 21-year-old East Dallas woman walked into the minimum security Woodlawn Jail at Maple and Oak Lawn avenues at 3:50 a.m. and asked to leave some money for a female inmate.

The woman as widow: After Marvella Bayh's 1979 death, was Birch Bayh identified automatically as "Senator Birch Bayh, an Indiana widower"? Of course not. Why? Because we accord men an individual identity that has to do with position and accomplishment rather than with marital status. Women and minority members are seeking the same treatment and many resent the implication that their merit is decided on the basis of their associates' or spouse's merit.

Houston mayor Kathy Whitmire was constantly referred to by the area news media as "Houston widow" or "widowed CPA from Houston."

The Prime Minister

The woman as mother: The British prime minister is named *Margaret Thatcher*. In this story, we identify by name Mark Thatcher, the son, and Denis Thatcher, the father—but we identify the prime minister as "his mother." And to compound this error, we fail to identify Margaret Thatcher by name through the *entirety* of the story.

Further, the writer here seems unsure how to address his subjects at all—he refers to Mark Thatcher variously as "Thatcher" and as "Mark."

Reprinted with permission, Paula LaRocque, *The Dallas Morning News*

In many college classes, professors grade on a 90–80–70–60 scale: 90 percent is an A, 80 percent is a B and so on. But in newswriting and publicity, the scale isn't so lenient: 90 percent right is an F. Stories for the mass media must be 100 percent accurate, 100 percent of the time.

Avoiding errors isn't easy, because there are so many different types of them. They range from simple spelling slips to mistakes in the names of people and places to out-and-out false statements about events, amounts or physical facts.

The reasons for such errors are many as well. Sometimes deadline pressure causes reporters to be careless. Sometimes reporters don't have adequate background information before writing a story. Sometimes they don't bother to check their facts with reliable sources. That source is often a public relations person. Accuracy is crucial to PR people. One error that costs a news medium a mistake creates distrust that seriously impairs effectiveness.

Research has revealed other causes of errors. These can include stress and the writer's personal involvement with the subject of a story—a built-in problem for PR writers. And one chief cause of inaccuracy is neglect of another important principle of writing: giving proper attribution.

Attribution.   An attribution is simply a phrase indicating the source of the information in a sentence. Unless a statement is common knowledge, on public record or describes something observed directly by the reporter, the source must be included.

Attribution isn't necessary for statements that can be easily checked in any standard reference book. "Columbus is the capital of Ohio," for example, doesn't need attribution. Most people know it, nobody disputes it and it can be easily checked. "The density of lead is 11.3 grams per cubic centimeter" is another statement that requires no attribution, even though most people don't know it. There's no dispute about that statement and it too can be easily checked in standard reference books (or, if necessary, in a laboratory).

But any fact that isn't generally known or easily looked up must be attributed to a source. And every statement of opinion, no matter how widely believed, must be attributed.

Here's a statement of fact that might appear in a hypothetical news story:

> ABC Electric Co.'s fuel contract with the XYZ Natural Gas Co. will expire in 1989.

Can that sentence stand without attribution? It depends. If the details of the contract are a matter of public record and the expiration date is widely known, attribution wouldn't be essential. But usually in such cases it's better to include the attribution, and the public relations writer preparing such an announcement for the news media should include the proper attribution in the release.

> ABC Electric Co.'s fuel contract with the XYZ Natural Gas Co. will expire in 1989, ABC spokesman George Smith said.

Now consider the following sentence:

> ABC Electric Co.'s main fuel contract will expire in 1989, raising the cost of electricity for customers in the area.

In this case, the sentence includes more than a simple factual statement about the expiration date of a contract. An inference is drawn: Electricity costs will increase. That may be a perfectly correct inference; nevertheless, it isn't a readily verifiable fact and must be attributed:

> ABC Electric Co.'s main fuel contract will expire in 1989, raising the cost of electricity for customers in the area, ABC spokesman George Smith said.

Reporters cannot observe everything they must report. Sometimes they have to get information from other people. Here's an example where a reporter had to rely on information provided by another person:

> There are no Tarrant County-based savings and loan associations on the Federal Home Loan Bank Board's "problem list" of those experiencing financial difficulties, Richard Greene, president of Arlington Savings, said Friday.

Why the attribution? Because the reporter had not seen the list, and therefore didn't know for certain that no Tarrant County firms were on it, only that one person—probably in a position to know—said so.

Had the reporter seen the list, the story could have been written differently:

> No Tarrant County-based savings and loan associations are on a list of those in financial trouble released by the Federal Home Loan Bank Board.

While attribution lets readers know where information comes from, it doesn't relieve the reporter of responsibility for accuracy. Just because an important person says something is so doesn't make it so. The reporter must verify statements whenever possible before using them. Once during congressional hearings on the safety of nuclear power plants, a scientist criticized a government study of nuclear plants because it didn't consider the possibility of human error contributing to a plant accident. Some reporters included that charge in their stories, carefully attributing the statement to the scientist. But later in the hearings, the author of the safety report in question testified that human error had indeed been considered and pointed out sections of the report where such calculations had been made. A thorough reporter would have checked the report or questioned the report's author before printing the original claim that human-error considerations were missing.

Verification.   Verifying something means being able to get the same information from another, independent, knowledgeable and reliable source. That source may be another person or some reference material. You should always check questionable information with at least one other source, and if a situation is sensitive, three. During the Watergate coverage in 1972–73, the two reporters doing most of the reporting and writing would not use any information for which they didn't have three-source verification. When potential litigation is involved, the truth has to be *provable*.

Being careful means checking everything. PR writers responsible for product publicity require the research and development office of their own company to provide notarized statements of product claims. They know that they as individuals, as well as the company, can be sued for errors in product publicity. Furthermore, the releases go to news media, who don't want a lawsuit either.

Reporters are responsible for verifying facts in their own stories, but at newspapers the copy desk is a backstop for them, holding up a story until facts that seem to be in question can be checked yet again. Cues to the copy desk that a story may need checking are words like *allegedly* and *reportedly*. Those words signal that a story may be missing some important facts. If facts are not available to complete a story, you either hold the story until they are or tell in the story what information is missing and what efforts were made to get it.

Verifying means not taking anything for granted, from the spelling of a name to the location of a city to a quotation from literature to a significant statistic.

MASS MEDIA WRITERS AND THE LAW: TWO MAJOR ISSUES

The First Amendment to the Constitution reads: "Congress shall make no law respecting an establishment of religion, or prohibiting the free exercise thereof; or abridging the freedom of speech, or of the press. . . ."

The framers of the Constitution didn't say exactly what they had in mind when they wrote those words, and for about 200 years the courts, and the media, have debated their exact interpretation and application.

The courts have rarely ever held that the phrase "no law" should be interpreted literally. The courts have agreed that Congress, and state and local governments, can make some laws that place some limits on press and speech. But what kind of laws can be made and how far government can go in its limitations are questions under continual discussion. (Cases applicable to each section in this chapter are listed at the end.)

One doctrine that applies to all areas of mass-communication law is "prior restraint." It states that no one can be punished for what he or she may be thinking or for what you might fear he or she might say, write or do. Even if that person has a long history of printing or saying the most scurrilous things imaginable, you can't prevent future printing or speaking.

However, even this doctrine of no prior restraints on speech and publishing is not absolute. Under some extreme conditions, often involving national or local security, some prior restraints may be acceptable. The news media are never absolutely protected by the First Amendment, and stand on even weaker constitutional ground if they libel people, invade their privacy, deny them a fair trial and so on.

Libel

Of all the areas of mass-communication law, libel is probably the best known. It is probably also the least understood, or most misunderstood, by many inside and outside the media. Here's a summary of where libel law stands today.

Defining libel. There are two types of defamation: libel and slander. A libel is written or printed; slander is spoken. Does that mean newspapers and magazines libel people, while broadcasters slander them? No. The courts have ruled that since broadcast news programs follow written scripts, they also belong to the category of libel.

We have always venerated the written word. In the eyes of many, including the courts, the written defamation is considered more injurious than the spoken one. That's especially true if the written defamation appears on the front page of the newspaper, or in the lead story on the 6 o'clock news, reaching several hundred thousand, or several million, people that day.

The dictionary defines *defame* as "to harm the reputation of . . .". Anyone can sue you for libel, claiming his or her reputation has been harmed somehow by your writing. However, this person (the "plaintiff") also has to have some proof of this for the courts to consider the case.

The elements of libel.   The plaintiff in a libel suit must show the following in court:

1. A publication or broadcast of the alleged libelous communication.
2. That he or she was identified in that publication or broadcast.
3. How the communication is defamatory.
4. In many instances, how the material was published or broadcast in disregard for the truth or through negligence and was not an honest error.

Defenses for libel.   If someone sues you for libel and presents these four elements against you, what are your defenses?

- *Truth*. Philosophers have been wrestling with the riddle of "what is truth" since time began. Truth in libel cases often seems just as elusive, for in most instances both sides believe they speak the truth.

  However, if the press can prove that what it published or broadcast is true, it wins the case. If you write a story about graft and corruption at city hall and can prove that everything you wrote is true, then you may see the mayor's libel suit against you thrown out of court. Note the word *may*. As you will see, there are a lot of qualifiers that must be used in libel cases.

  This also means some errors might be allowed to creep into your reporting on matters of legitimate and grave concern. However, these errors must be minor, not major errors of fact. Furthermore, errors must be honest, not malicious. Of course, it's best not to ever make an error of fact at all.

- *Privilege*. This defense is also called "qualified privilege." It means the news media can publish accurate reports of legislative, judicial or other public proceedings even if the words uttered by the officials are defamatory.

  Reporters, however, do have a responsibility to attempt to make sure that statements and public records being quoted in stories are fair and accurate. If a city councilman charges the mayor with "graft and corruption," you should research the charges or question the councilman further about the exact nature of the charges. You may have a qualified privilege to print and broadcast a lot of things said by others or appearing in public records, but the courts have also said: Be as fair as possible.

- *Fair comment*. Opinion and comment are also protected to some degree under libel laws. The courts have granted protection to a wide range of criticism and comment under the argument that such comment is in the public interest. If the press can show a legitimate public interest for the communication in question, then the press can be granted a greater degree of protection from any lawsuits that might result.

Categories. As far as libel law is concerned, there are three general types of people in the world: public officials, public figures and private persons. The seriousness attached to any possible falsehood you may write depends on its victim.

Public officials and public figures must demonstrate that for a libel to have occurred, the reporter was, at least, negligent. Under most circumstances, public officials and figures must also show some degree of malice. Malice means the reporter acted with a "reckless disregard for the truth" and published or broadcast the material knowing that it was false.

Private persons, on the other hand, need only show negligence on the part of the press. Generally negligence is carelessness, or sloppy journalism.

The *Washington Post* once ran a story about a lawyer named Harry Kennedy who was charged with forgery. The lawyer charged was actually named Harry P. Kennedy, and used his middle initial. Another lawyer named Harry F. Kennedy sued the paper and won a substantial judgment. Harry F. Kennedy never used his middle initial in his commonly known name and successfully convinced the court he was libeled because the *Post* printed a story about a Harry Kennedy.

Thus simply leaving out a middle initial can be construed as actionable under libel law. Negligence can extend to simple typos, misspelled names, placing the wrong caption under a picture, or any other of a number of so-called minor mistakes. Those small errors can result in large libel suits.

You may well ask, "How do you define public and private?" The courts have been trying to resolve that one for several decades now. Let's examine some of the results.

The general rule is that if a person is elected to office or receives pay or some other form of remuneration from the government, that person can be classified as a public official. So this definition includes not only elected officials but also appointed, or hired, public servants: the bureaucrats who work for the government (on all levels), the members of special boards and commissions (such as the state Board of Regents), consultants to the government who work on a daily or hourly fee basis. Public officials' actions while on the job are subject to the keenest scrutiny by the press; however, as will be seen, off the job is another matter.

Public *figures* receive no public money, but are also in the public eye. To be classified as a public figure, a person must usually (1) voluntarily thrust himself or herself into the limelight in some manner, and (2) achieve notoriety and become well known in some area for some time. Note the "voluntary" nature of being a public figure. The press cannot drag someone from obscurity onto the front page, then claim that person is a public figure for libel-defense purposes.

Public officials and public figures do enjoy some relief from the press; few of either type are "public" all the time. The president, your governor and a few other people may never enjoy a day off from the press, but most other public figures and officials do get to be treated as private persons.

"Limited" public figure is also a category defined by the courts. Circumstances often bring public attention to people for various reasons. A messy divorce proceeding, a lawyer in a famous murder trial, a doctor with a famous patient—all of these people and many others may be thrust into the limelight. These are people who may be famous for only that specific event and are quite private for the rest of their lives.

As was mentioned earlier, public officials and figures must often prove malice in some form if they are to win a libel judgment against the press, while private persons need only show negligence. Malice is very difficult to prove; negligence is much easier. If there is "absence of malice," the public personage's chance of winning the case is greatly reduced.

This doesn't mean you can feel safe libeling public people. The courts have looked unfavorably on reporters and writers who don't do all they can to get their facts straight, to make sure the people they write about are treated as fairly as possible and to see that everything they print and broadcast is in the spirit of ethical journalistic practice. If you don't act honestly and fairly at all times, you may be guilty of malice and can lose, and lose big.

Additional considerations.

1. Libel *per se* and libel *per quod*. Libel *per se* is libel "on the face of it." That is, any "reasonable" person would know that if you call someone a whore, thief, pervert or a host of other names in your writing, you mean to defame that person.

   In some instances you need not be so brazen in your defamations. In fact, your writing can appear to be quite innocent on the face of it and still be libelous. Libel *per quod* can be an instance where you imply someone is, say, a thief without using those exact words, and that person can prove identification and defamation. In one classic case, a newspaper reported that a woman gave birth to twins. That's quite an innocent story; however, many people knew she had been married only a month, and she sued for libel.

2. Third parties generally cannot sue for libel. Under this rule, no one can sue for libel on behalf of the dead.

3. In the United States a corporation is a person; thus corporations can sue for libel. So can organizations, associations and just plain groups and clubs.

4. If you repeat a libel, you may also be liable. If X libels Y and you repeat it, word for word, as a quote, can you be convicted? The courts have ruled "Not really," so long as the reporter reports and writes exactly what was said, without additional comment. If you go on to extend the libel somehow, you can lose the case.

Yesterday the Tattler-Tribune incorrectly identified Sen. Battson D. Belfry as a "low-down, slimy snake-in-the-grass."

In fact, the Senator is not slimy, nor is he, of course, a snake.

The Tattler-Tribune does not, however, regret the error.

Reprinted by permission of Jefferson Communications, Inc., Reston, Va.

In litigation pending as of this writing, the most critical cases for the press appear to be the ones in which public persons are attempting to find new means to show malice. It has been suggested that reporters take lie-detector tests, receive injections of truth serum or undergo hypnosis to discover their frame of mind when writing a story. Plaintiffs argue it's impossible to prove that reporters acted with malice without some resort to those techniques. So far there has been no definitive ruling on this matter.

Remember, damages can be large if you lose a libel case. *Penthouse* magazine, for example, was sued for $630 million in one libel action. In another, the magazine lost a $25 million libel suit. The Alton, Ill., *Telegraph* had to file for bankruptcy after losing a $9 million libel suit. Two San Francisco police officers successfully sued the *San Francisco Examiner* for $4.5 million for libel. In a celebrated case, Carol Burnett was awarded $800,000 in her successful lawsuit against the *National Enquirer*. Singer Wayne Newton was awarded $19.2 million in his successful lawsuit against NBC News. In other words, libel isn't something to take lightly, because those who claim you defamed them will certainly not take it lightly.

Privacy   In many ways, privacy law is a lot like libel law. Many people don't want their pictures taken and shown on the 6 o'clock news or in the newspaper the next day. Many also don't want even to be mentioned in the media. Privacy might be defined as the right to be left alone, especially by the news media.

Privacy law defines public officials, public figures and private persons in the same way as libel law. Just as with libel, anyone can sue you for invading his or her privacy. The defenses against an invasion-of-privacy suit do differ somewhat from those for libel.

- *Consent*. Photographers often carry consent forms with them and have their subjects sign them to ensure their defense just in case anyone sues.

- *Newsworthiness*. The courts have been rather lenient in the past in accepting the media's definition of what is news. In some cases the courts have accepted the defense of the "public's right to know."

- The media can also claim "no actual malice" was intended. This defense is similar to that in libel litigation.

There are four basic *torts* (wrongful acts) of privacy law: appropriation, false light, public disclosure of private facts and intrusion.

Appropriation.   The appropriation tort is defined as using someone's name, image or likeness for commercial or personal gain. Many people won't mind if you use their name or image and make money off of it, as long as you share the profits with them. Some people, of course, won't want to be associated with what you're associating them with, whether you try to pay them or not, such as if you use the picture of a Baptist preacher on a beer ad without that preacher's consent. These people can sue under the appropriation tort.

News presents a somewhat different case in appropriation, however. People have tried to sue the media for remuneration because their pictures appeared in the newspaper or on TV and newspapers and TV stations make money from publishing and airing these pictures. That argument has not stood up in court. However, the best advice still remains: When in doubt, get the person's consent.

False light.   This is one of the most difficult of the torts to understand. It would seem, at first, that the publication of any false information has no defense in the law. However, as was pointed out in the section on libel, the debate about "what is truth" has been going on for some time.

If you fabricate a story that harms some real person, that person can sue you for libel. That's why works of pure fiction can be held to be libelous. However, in false-light privacy cases the degree of falsity rather than total falsity is at issue.

As writers you must beware of leaving false impressions, especially of private persons. Photographs can also give the same false impressions, especially if the captions or accompanying stories create the mood of falsity. For example, the court once awarded damages to a taxicab driver whose picture had been used with a story about crooked cabbies in the *Saturday Evening Post*. The cab driver in question could show he wasn't crooked at all.

Public disclosure of private fact.   Publishing or broadcasting pictures of someone being arrested, someone hurt in an accident, someone out and about in public but in a situation the person didn't necessarily want displayed are all instances where people have sued the press for invasion of privacy under this tort.

Basically, we all want a lot of privacy at home and want to retain at least a little bit of privacy in public. The courts have ruled that, in general, anything the eye can see in public, the cameras can also see and record, and those pictures can be used as news pictures. However, the photojournalist should always keep in mind standards of good taste, ethics and fairness.

In your writing, the question is often one of using information obtained legitimately that nevertheless may reveal embarrassing private facts. Here again, the courts have ruled that if reporters dug for it, or just went and looked, the press can publish it.

What about digging up and publicizing past histories on people? Most of us have a skeleton in the closet. When the media drag these skeletons out, people sometimes sue. The question the courts have asked the news media when they reveal these embarrassing, or damaging, details of a subject's past, or even the personal side of the present, is "How pertinent is it to the issue at hand?" Even public officials and public figures have secrets the public doesn't have a right to know, and certainly private persons are even more protected in keeping their past and present private.

Intrusion.   You cannot break the law to gather the news. This means you can't trespass on private property in pursuit of a story; you can't tap the phone of someone you're investigating for a story; you can't rifle someone's desk or files to obtain information, no matter how worthy you think the story might be.

The news media usually don't engage in these types of activities, but the methods of some investigative reporters have been questioned under this privacy tort. Reporters have been known to dig through garbage cans, walk into restaurants with the cameras rolling to check on reported unhealthy conditions, or even walk into homes unannounced to get the story from unsuspecting people. The ethics of these reporters have been questioned, and zeal is no defense if you're hit with an invasion-of-privacy suit for illegally intruding on someone's property, or privacy, in some manner.

Additional comments.   Privacy is a relatively new concept in mass-communication law. It wasn't until the early 1900s that a so-called right to privacy was first mentioned in the courtroom. Since then it has been heard often.

Privacy law and libel law often go hand in hand. In some instances, plaintiffs appear to feel it's easier to win a judgment against the press through an invasion-of-privacy suit than through a libel suit, since the press often cannot use truth as a defense in privacy suits.

Privacy law also clashes with movements toward more freedom to gather and report information (see next section). It is a political issue today, as national computer networks are keeping some form of record on almost all Americans from birth. In the future, even more information will be available on almost everyone. What frightens many is the possibility that the "wrong" people will get their hands on this information, and many people fear those wrong people will be the members of the press.

The right to gather and report the news

The so-called right to gather, write and report the news is an umbrella category in mass media law covering three general areas: (1) the issues involving the debate over "free press—fair trial," (2) reporter privilege, and (3) access to information.

Free press—fair trial.   The right to a fair trial is a constitutional guarantee as strong as the First Amendment right of freedom of the press, in the mind of the courts and many citizens. So when these two critically important rights clash in some way, there's bound to be an uproar.

The news media have been charged with violating the fair-trial rights of citizens in several ways. First, there is pre-trial publicity—the media allegedly publish so much "sensationalized" information detrimental to the accused before a case begins that he or she cannot receive a fair trial. Second, there is publicity during a trial, which is often said to be just as damaging as pre-trial publicity.

The U.S. Supreme Court has reminded trial-court judges that they have a number of remedies to ensure that the defendant receives a fair trial. Among them:

1. *Change of venue*. The trial judge can move the trial to another town if the judge deems the local publicity harmful.

2. *Continuance*. A trial can be delayed until the publicity cools or dies out.

3. *Voir dire*. Here the attorneys for both sides, and the judge, can examine prospective jurors to determine whether they have formed prejudicial opinions one way or another about the outcome of the trial.

4. *Sequestering the jury*. This is a harsh remedy, for few people can afford to be totally away from their jobs, family and commitments for days, weeks or even months at a time.

    Instead of sequestering, the judge often admonishes the jury to not read newspapers or watch or listen to broadcast news accounts of the trial. The jury is also told not to discuss the trial with anyone.

Current law in this area is confusing, but generally reads that the judge must consider at least some of these remedies before ordering what is called a "gag" on the press. A gag order stops the press from printing or broadcasting anything more about the trial from the time of the order until the verdict is rendered. Gag orders are relatively rare these days, but some trial-court judges still try to stop all reporting of trials under way.

And there are other means beside outright gag orders to limit news coverage of a trial. Some trials can be held behind closed doors. Pre-trial hearings can be closed to the press, and often are. Juvenile trials are closed to the press in the majority of states. Jurors, attorneys, witnesses and everyone involved in the trial can be prohibited from speaking to the press about the trial.

Reporter privilege.   Their job often takes many reporters into areas where they uncover information from sources they would prefer to keep secret. Can the courts require reporters to appear and testify about anything they may have seen, heard or written about? To reveal their sources?

Most states have "shield laws" that allegedly protect the reporter from having to reveal sources. In general, these laws state that before the reporter can be asked to give up confidential information, the requesting party must demonstrate that:

1. The information sought cannot be obtained elsewhere.

2. The information is relevant to the case at hand.

3. The subject is one of "overriding and compelling state interest."

Journalists have been going to jail for contempt of court for refusing to reveal their sources. In two of the most publicized cases in recent years, William Farr of the *Los Angeles Times* went to jail for 46 days, and Myron Farber of the *New York Times* went to jail for 40 days. Reporters have also been hit with stiff fines. Up to today, the courts have ruled that reporters do not have an "absolute" right or privilege to refuse to reveal all sources. Sometimes, under some circumstances, reporters can be made to testify, and reveal sources and confidential information, just like everyone else.

Reporters argue that if they do reveal sources, other potential sources will dry up, and the courts have been willing to hear this argument to some degree. Circumstances will always dictate the outcome on a case-by-case basis, though.

Access.   Access to information by reporters is an area divided into three subcategories: open records, open meetings and access to people and places.

Open-records law.   These laws have been called "freedom of information" acts (FOIA). There is a federal FOIA, and all states have one as well. The spirit of an FOIA has been that of ensuring that all of the business of government is open to scrutiny by the press and the public. Therefore, in theory, all government records should be open. However, in practice it hasn't worked quite this way.

The federal FOIA contains nine exemptions, and states have exemptions ranging into the dozens each. In general, the concept of open records doesn't mean *all* records will be open. Some categories of exemptions found in the federal and state laws are personnel records, welfare, Social Security and tax records, trade secrets, police and law enforcement information, and matters pertaining to national security on the federal level.

Since all states have different laws in this area, as they do in libel, privacy and so many other areas, you should check your state's laws.

Open-meetings law.   All states and the federal government have open-meetings laws, but like open-records laws, this doesn't mean all meetings will be open to the press, or to the public. These open-meetings laws, sometimes called "sunshine laws," often have similar exemptions as FOIA's. Again, check the open-meetings law in the state where you'll be working for the exact guidelines.

Access to people and places.   Reporters cannot go everywhere and talk to everyone in their pursuit of the news. Some places, such as prisons, and people, such as prisoners, might be off-limits to reporters, except during normal visiting hours when the public is invited in. The courts have ruled that, in general, the press has about the same rights and privileges as the general public, whether it is access to courtrooms, records, meetings, people, places or things. The courts have refused to make reporters a privileged class.

Additional legal responsibilities for public relations and advertising copywriters

Besides sharing their news colleagues' legal responsibilities as individuals and as organizations, people in advertising and public relations have some additional concerns. Their legal responsibilities in the area of communications, particularly involving the news media, are open to interpretation by the Federal Trade Commission (see Chapter 13 on advertising and the FTC).

Public relations and advertising writers have to get a person's consent before using his or her name or picture. Most use a legal consent form for protection.

Both advertising and public relations writers are pulled in two directions by responsibilities to their organizations and to the consumers of information through the mass media. Difficulties often arise when the open-records and open-meetings laws are subject to interpretation. Organizations are likely to prefer a strict interpretation to the news media's more generally interpreted "public's right to know."

Yet another area of conflict of interpretation is the matter of who is a "public figure." Suppose a public relations person is handling publicity for the president of the board for the local symphony, for example. If the professional manager of the symphony runs the organization into debt, the news media will be writing a great deal about the board president's responsibility. There may be a good bit of prying into that individual's personal life, including finances. Where is the line drawn? Most court decisions have placed those who volunteer for positions of public trust in the same place as those elected or hired to fill them. So it's a problem sometimes for PR people.

Another privacy problem surrounds the families of people associated with the organization. Suppose the spouse of the bank president is kidnapped. The PR person is trying to work with the FBI, the family, the local police and the news media. Sometimes the problem is even more sensitive. Suppose the bank president checks into a drug rehabilitation center. Whose business is it? Does it matter whether that person is a president of a large bank or a small one? Whether that bank is publicly or privately held? There are few clear-cut rulings, and the public relations person will have to have copy approved by the institution's legal counsel.

PR practitioners often conflict with news media representatives on such need-to-know issues. The PR people usually try to protect their clients from unfair invasions. But who decides what is "unfair"? Hospital PR people and hospital administrators' associations have worked out an agreement with news representatives over what will and won't be released and under what conditions. Guidelines in other areas would reduce the tensions between PR and news people.

Copywriters for publicly held companies who are responsible to the Securities and Exchange Commission are required by law to make public any information likely to affect the price of the institution's stock. This means using mass media channels, and that information must not be deceptive, or the writer, as well as the organization, is subject to federal penalties.

Even non-profit organizations are under legal scrutiny, because they use money collected from the public. This is why many non-profit PR people publish annual reports for their organizations and refer to their contributors as *stakeholders*.

Suppose an institution is involved in a lawsuit and wants to make its position clear to the public by taking out an ad. The ad copywriter should be aware of the problems of potential contempt-of-court charges in such a case. Again, such advertising when a company is in major litigation must be cleared through the institution's lawyer. Institutional lawyers and news media lawyers may not agree on interpretation of the law. That's what lawsuits are about.

CONSIDERATIONS   Writers owe their audiences three major considerations: to compose with care, style and clarity.

Care   The *St. Petersburg Times*, often cited as one of the best daily newspapers in the United States, once began an account of the murder of a man whose body had been found by his parents thus:

> A 30-year-old St. Petersburg man was found murdered by his parents in his home late Saturday.

The writer unwittingly seemed to accuse the man's parents of the murder. The writer intended to say:

> Parents of a 30-year-old St. Petersburg man found him late Saturday, murdered in his own home.

Careless construction had created an enormous—and potentially libelous—error. While copy editors are supposed to catch such errors before they are printed, the writer has the responsibility not to create the problem. The writer who understands grammar and punctuation and who makes the effort to use words precisely stands a good chance of getting the intended message across to the reader.

Even an error so slight as a single out-of-place comma can cause confusion. The *New York Times*, generally a well-edited paper, once confused its readers in a story about albinos:

> But though they have poor eyesight, contrary to popular impressions, they are neither blind nor retarded.

As that sentence is punctuated, it could be inferred that most people believe albinos to have good eyesight. But from the rest of the story it's clear the writer meant the popular impressions are that albinos are blind and retarded. The comma after *impressions* should be eliminated.

Diligent readers might be able to untangle the meaning of such sentences, but they shouldn't have to. It's the writer's job to make the reader's job as easy as possible. The more effort you require of the reader, the fewer readers you'll have.

Even in broadcast writing, where the inflections of speech may make the meaning clear, grammar and punctuation must be taken into account. A punctuation error in a TV news script caused an announcer to utter these nonsensical sentences:

> Voyager is now about a billion miles from Earth, traveling at the speed of light. It will take the television signals more than an hour and a half to make the journey.

Voyager could not have been traveling at the speed of light. It will surely be several decades before warp drive is invented. The punctuation, not Einstein's theory of special relativity, is wrong. It should have been:

> Voyager is now about a billion miles from Earth. Traveling at the speed of light, it will take the television signals more than an hour and a half to make the journey.

Errors are easy to overlook because often we see what we expect to see. One of the authors, who gives an automatic grade of F for any piece of copy with an error in fact, grammar, spelling or punctuation, keeps on an office wall one advertising writer's $35,000 mistake: a poster with the word *remember* spelled "remmember" in elegant calligraphy. A few of the four-color posters had been distributed before the error was discovered. They had to be reprinted.

Style
Newswriters must know and observe the style rules of standard English. And they have the additional burden of obeying the rules of the medium they're working for. Most publications, broadcast stations and public relations operations have a stylebook that specifies certain company conventions on matters of abbreviation, capitalization, spelling and punctuation. PR staffs for organizations also develop manuals of usage for their logo, name and trademarks, including color specifications.

The style rules established by the Associated Press are widely followed by both newswriters and public relations writers.

For advertising copy, some agencies have a stylebook (1) to give consistency to spelling when there is a choice (for example, *advisor, adviser*); (2) to flag words *not* to use, because they are offensive; (3) to give direction for the use of partial sentences and other deviations from conventional usage.

You should own a wire service stylebook and use it as a guide when writing for a newspaper—unless the newspaper specifies other rules. The wire services also distribute style guides for broadcast copy.

Broadcast style characteristics.   Broadcast writers have two audiences: the announcer and the listening public. Copy must be very clearly edited: All words must be written as writers want them to be heard. For example, ".7%" might make an announcer hesitate. "Point seven percent" makes it much clearer.

Avoid alliteration. An announcer could stumble on a weather bulletin that reads "There should be some sunshine soon."

Some basic tenets for broadcast writing:

- *Keep it conversational.* It's been said before, but it must be said again: Broadcast news is written for the ear. You listen to radio and TV newscasts.

  We're used to certain styles when we listen to people talk. Our everyday speech usually consists of short, simple sentences, not complex and compound ones. That's the way to write broadcast news as well. For example, you probably wouldn't walk up to a friend and say:

  > "Wholesale prices, flattened by rapidly falling food and gasoline costs, dropped 0.2 percent last month, the government reported yesterday, all but ensuring the best inflation year in two decades."

  Chances are that conversation would start something like this:

  > "Hey . . . did you hear the price of gas is going down again?"

  Take the "hey" off that sentence and you almost have a broadcast news sentence. Here are several good broadcast news sentences:

  > The price of gas is still going down.

  > The price at the gas pump continues to fall.

  > You can continue to expect cheap prices the next time you fill up your gas tank.

  Use contractions—that's how people talk. People generally don't say "do not," won't say "will not," and there's a good chance "there is" is never uttered.

- *Keep it informal.* Don't use stuffy, stilted words. It's not conversational to say *physician, attorney, male, female, expired.* We generally say *doctor, lawyer, man, woman,* and *died* in conversation.

- *Make it personal.* Don't be afraid to use *you* in your broadcast copy. Broadcast writers write: "Your taxes will be going down next year"; "Our home heating bills will be going up next year"; "We can all expect a rise in food prices next month," and so on.

- *Don't overuse slang.* In trying to achieve a conversational style, you write the way the majority of people talk. Many slang words *have* crept into normal conversation and can be used when appropriate. *Kids, folks* and *bullish* are some new and old slang words that can be used with moderation. *Cop* is one that is never used, except in quoted material. In both print and broadcast writing, try to avoid the cute and flip. And street language doesn't fit at all.

- *Keep it simple*. Remember that listeners have only one chance to understand a story: they can't go back and rehear it.

    There are a lot of challenges involved in translating many of the day's stories into short and simple terms. The workings of government, business, industry and many newsworthy individuals are often complex. Statistics, data and numbers make stories confusing to listeners. That doesn't mean you must avoid them, just that you must make them understandable.

- *Keep it short*. In radio, of the 5 minutes slotted for news each hour or so, 1 minute is usually given over to commercials. Even the half-hour TV newscast must yield about 8 to 10 minutes to commercials, 4 minutes to sports, 3 minutes to weather; that leaves only about 15 minutes or so for news. And even a 24-hour-a-day all-news radio or TV operation has time constraints. Each hour is broken into segments, most of which are weather, sports, commentaries and special reports. The actual breaking-news portion of that hour may be as little as 10 or 15 minutes.

    A 30-second radio news story runs about seven or eight lines of typewritten copy. That's not many words to tell the top news stories of the hour, each hour—but a 30-second story is a long one by radio standards. If every story ran 30 seconds, only eight stories would fit into the 4-minute newscast. Often there are more than eight stories about international, national and local events that deserve mention each hour.

Clarity Good writing is not necessarily good media writing. Some of the world's great literature would certainly be out of place in a newspaper, not to mention on the air. But good newswriting must first be good writing. See 2.2 for some experts' advice on writing well.

The media writer must make the audience's task as easy as possible. Sentences should be instantly clear. Tangled syntax and confusing words cause readers to turn the page and listeners to turn the dial.

The key to clarity is writing simply and directly. Consider the lesson learned by the science writer Isaac Asimov, who is widely admired for his ability to explain complex subjects. Early in his career, Asimov had written, with much effort, a piece of fiction filled with flowery words and phrases and colorful sentences. An editor who reviewed the piece asked this question:

"Do you know how Hemingway says 'The sun rose the next morning'?"

"No," replied Asimov.

"Hemingway says 'The sun rose the next morning,'" said the editor.[7]

Asimov learned his lesson: Say what you have to say in plain English. And the lesson applies not only to fiction but to non-fiction as well. After all, Hemingway was a newspaperman before gaining fame as a novelist. He applied what he learned in journalism to his literary career: Write clearly, directly, to the point.

Among the principles of clear writing are being concise, keeping one idea to the sentence, using familiar words, being concrete and specific, writing in the active voice, phrasing sentences positively, using natural language and being well organized.

1. Think about what you want to say and organize your material. (Outline if it helps.)

2. Be brief, keep sentences short, avoid a succession of loose sentences, and when you are finished: stop.

3. Use specific but simple language; avoid jargon, redundancies and phrases that don't say anything or that tell your audience what they already know.

4. Use the active voice, inject variety into your choice of words and your sentence structure, cast statements in a positive form and use language familiar to your audience.

5. Think about what you are writing in terms of your audience and try to choose the words most meaningful to them that best express your thoughts.

6. Be sure you have used words correctly and that you have constructed your sentences so that they read well in addition to being grammatically correct.

7. Be logical in your development and presentation of ideas, keep construction parallel and in summaries stick to one tense.

8. Watch out for hidden bias, the "isms."

9. Trim from your material excess everything — words, phrases, anecdotes, information.

10. Get candid critiques of your writing from good writers and editors; don't count on being able to see your own mistakes.

2.2 Basic Writing Pointers

Various authorities have compiled basic writing pointers. Here are some distilled from the following: Strunk and White's *Elements of Style*, Robert Gunning's *Technique of Clear Writing*, Paula LaRocque's *FYI*, a newsletter distributed to writers at the *Dallas Morning News* where LaRocque is the writing coach, and *Reader's Digest* editor Edward T. Thompson's "How to Write Clearly."

Be concise.   Strive to get your message across in the fewest possible words. If a sentence has more words than it needs to be clear, cut them out.

Here is an example from a student newspaper. The article is about a group called Theological Reflections.

> Theological Reflections was first conceived and historically founded in the Wesley Foundation about two years ago.

First of all, *historically* is obviously not needed. It's clear that the group was founded at some time in the past, which is all *historically* means. Second, *first conceived* is redundant; it wasn't conceived twice. And in fact, *conceived* is not needed, either. Pointing out the time of conception would be useful only if conception had come at some time earlier than the founding. Thus a more concise version of the sentence would read:

> Theological Reflections was started in the Wesley Foundation about two years ago.

Sixteen words have become 12 with no loss in meaning.

Use familiar words.   A media writer is in the business of giving an audience information, not building their vocabulary. Use words that your audience will understand. If you use unfamiliar words, there's a good chance your audience will misunderstand the message. But even if they can figure out what an unfamiliar word means, it will require some effort. And many won't make the effort.

Much of the time the unfamiliar word can be replaced with a familiar one. There's no sense in using *remuneration* or *compensation* when *pay* works just as well. Why say *contusion* instead of *bruise?* Or *precipitation* instead of *rain?* The common word communicates much better.

Of course, sometimes the short word doesn't really mean the same thing as the long one. When the exactly right word is perhaps somewhat unfamiliar but no other word will do, you should use that word. But make sure that the context explains it. And don't take the approach of Humpty Dumpty in Lewis Carroll's *Through the Looking-Glass*, who says: "When *I* use a word, it means just what I choose it to mean." When a writer for the mass media uses a word, it must mean what the audience chooses it to mean.

Using familiar words is essential in stories about a specialized field. When writing on physics, or economics, or philosophy, or plumbing, you must avoid using the jargon of physicists, economists, philosophers, plumbers. Each profession has its own secret language that makes perfect sense to members of the profession but is meaningless to everybody else.

Consider this sentence from an engineer's report on solar energy:

> All solar thermal systems suffer from diurnal transients and rapid transients due to cloud passage during daily operation.

What does this mean? Only that solar power plants go on and off a lot because it gets dark at night and clouds sometimes block out the sun.

Sometimes jargon words are disguised as common, ordinary words. A printer may speak of a signature, but it has nothing to do with signing a name. A physicist's barn is not a farm building. Don't use such terms without explaining them.

Be concrete.   Many times the problem is not so much a word's unfamiliarity as its level of abstraction. The discussion of semantics earlier shows that all words, to some degree, are abstract. But the closer the word is to something visual, something real, the easier the word will be to understand. Good writers prefer words that give the reader something to see. A word like *sustenance* is fairly abstract—it could refer to too many different things. But *steak and beer* is concrete. Good writing is characterized by concrete nouns and action words.

Be specific.   Being concrete is closely related to the idea of being specific. General statements must be backed up by specific examples if communication is to be clear.

Consider this sentence: "People in the village eat a lot of fruit." The sentence is clear enough, but it is general. "Every villager eats two pounds of bananas, peaches and apples daily" is specific.

Specificity is the cure for vagueness. "He was a big hit with the audience" is vague. No reader or listener could be sure exactly what the writer meant. "The audience stood and applauded for five minutes" is a specific statement of fact. The meaning is clear.

Be positive. As Strunk and White point out in *The Elements of Style*, *not* is a weak word. "Consciously or unconsciously, the reader is dissatisfied with being told only what is not; he wishes to be told what is," they write.

Statements in positive form are easier to understand than evasive, negative constructions. And they make the message more forceful, more direct, more interesting. Compare:

Smithville did not escape the effects of the tornado.

The tornado devastated Smithville.

Or look at a sentence like "The governor did not sign the bill today as expected." What did the governor do? Positive statements reduce the chance for misunderstanding: "The governor vetoed the bill" or "The governor decided to wait until tomorrow to sign the bill."

Be organized. Good organization means the sentences and paragraphs come in the right order. One leads naturally to the next. Don't throw sentences at your audience haphazardly. Make a point clearly, support it and then make a smooth transition to the next point.

Good transitions are essential in guiding the audience from one sentence to the next, from one paragraph to the next. Changes in thought must be clearly signaled. The passage from a student's feature in 2.3 demonstrates how various thoughts can be tied together.

Be natural. Some people seem to think that writing calls for language that is more formal, more sophisticated than speech. It's true that some types of writing—things like royal proclamations and legal documents—traditionally are rather stilted. They're also hard to read. One of the golden rules of good writing is "Write the way you talk." This doesn't mean you should reproduce the repetitions, stutters and circumlocutions of everyday conversation. But you should use natural words and short, simple sentences.

Natural language is one of the media writer's most effective ways of making a story interesting. But natural language is also essential for clarity. Overly formal language often muddles the meaning. A favorite story told by critics of government jargon illustrates the point. A plumber wrote to a government agency about his discovery that hydrochloric acid was a good drain cleaner. A bureaucrat responded with a note saying: "The efficacy of hydrochloric acid

To her right stood a bookshelf jammed with books on nutrition, food, meal management. An apothecary jar filled with popcorn and another containing dried red peppines, small hot peppers, sat on a table behind her. "They're just for decoration," she said, adding, however, that she likes popcorn. "But without butter, and just a little bit of salt."

She said salt is one of the three culprits of the American diet that consumers should avoid. The other two are fat and sugar.

College students, in general, have poor diets because they don't have time to plan out their meals, she said. They often consume too many calories and fats and not enough essential vitamins and minerals.

"From some of the little dietary studies that we have done in some of our classes," Franklin said, "I would say they do not drink enough milk, they eat erratically, and I find also that they don't eat breakfast very much.

"Sometimes they indicate that they don't eat enough food. Some of them, especially the girls, are concerned about weight. They want to be very trim and look like Bo Derek."

She said, however, students can improve their eating habits by consuming more fresh foods--fruits and vegetables--throughout the day.

Looking at her petite, 5-foot-3 inch frame, one would imagine Franklin had no weight problems. She laughed at the thought.

"I've had a weight problem since I opened my mouth," she said. . . .

2.3 Transitions

Repetition can give unity to a story, as this student feature story shows.

is indisputable, but the ionic residues are incompatible with metallic permanence." The plumber wrote back, thanking the bureaucrat for the compliment and promising to tell his friends to use hydrochloric acid, too. The perplexed bureaucrat wrote the plumber again, in similar language, warning of hydrochloric acid's dangers. Again the plumber was pleased that the agency liked his idea so much, and he wrote promising to pass on any other good ideas he hit upon. Finally the bureaucrat tried English: "Don't use hydrochloric acid," he wrote. "It eats hell out of the pipes."[8]

Reprinted by permission of Jefferson Communications, Inc., Reston, Va.

Be readable.   There's nothing mysterious about making something readable. It's just a matter of applying the principles of readability developed by decades of research into the subject. The most important of these principles are:

- *Keep sentences short.* Information is easier to absorb when it's given in small chunks. Don't try to put more than one idea into a sentence. If you find a long sentence in your story, try inserting a period somewhere. Give the reader a chance to breathe.

- *Keep paragraphs short.* Because most newspaper stories are set in narrow columns, even a few sentences can make a long paragraph that looks hard to read. Announcers have good breath control, but they don't like to test it with long sentences. Don't worry if you have paragraphs of only one sentence, particularly near the beginning of a story. The first few paragraphs should have one or two sentences at the most. Later on in the story you may be able to get away with paragraphs that are a little longer. Even then, though, you shouldn't have more than one major idea in each paragraph.

- *Use short, common words.* The shorter the word the better. *Car* is better than *automobile*. And make sure the words you use are concrete and specific, not vague and abstract. Don't say *facilities* if you mean *building*.

Readability formulas   Mathematical formulas exist for testing the readability of a piece of writing. The most commonly used formulas test passages for average sentence length (in number of words) and use some measure of word length, usually in syllables. (It's easier to measure the length of a word than its familiarity. One readability testing method, though, known as the Dale-Chall formula, does attempt to measure word familiarity by comparing the words in a passage to a list of common words known by most fourth graders.)

At first glance, it might seem absurd that a mathematical formula could be of any use in measuring the readability of a piece of writing. But if you think about the principles of good writing, the formulas make sense. If you hold each sentence to one idea, your sentences will, on the average, be shorter than they would be otherwise. Sentences in the active voice are generally shorter than sentences in the passive voice. The same is true for sentences phrased positively instead of negatively. Familiar and concrete words tend to be short words. Thus measures of sentence length and word length are actually good indicators of a wide range of writing qualities.

Readability research has shown that the important consideration is the *average* sentence length in a piece of writing. An occasional long sentence (in the 30-to-40-word range) isn't necessarily a problem, if it's otherwise clear and well constructed. But an endless string of long sentences will drive readers away. A string of very short sentences, on the other hand, can be boring as well. The key is to vary the sentence length, with the average being in the readable range. One writing consultant suggests that 16 words per sentence is a good average to shoot for. Some consultants for newspaper wire services recommend 19 words.

The perceptive student will observe that a sentence with 16 short words isn't as long as a sentence with 16 long words. That's another reason readability researchers consider the average word length as well as the average sentence length.

Different experts compute word length in different ways. Rudolf Flesch gauged word length by counting all the syllables in a sample of writing. If a 100-word sample contains 150 syllables, the average word length is 1.5 syllables. Robert Gunning proposed a shortcut. Instead of counting all the syllables, Gunning merely counted the number of "long words": those of three syllables or more.

Many aspects of writing besides average sentence and word length affect readability. As early as the 1930s, researchers had identified more than 60 important factors. But most formulas stick to average sentence length for two reasons: Most of the other aspects are hard to measure, and many of them are closely related to sentence length or word length. An abundance of prepositional phrases increases the reading difficulty, for example. But the presence of many such phrases tends to make sentences longer, so sentence length is usually an adequate measure.

Readability tests are just mechanical tools to help you gauge the possible comprehension level of your writing. You are trying to communicate *ideas*, and you can write within levels of comprehension and still not accomplish that. As Gunning points out, "Nonsense written simply is still nonsense." A good readability score does not guarantee good writing. But it can be a useful check to see if your writing has a chance of being understood by your audience.

Research in readability has shown that readable writing has two main benefits: People will be more likely to read what you write, and they will be more likely to understand it. It doesn't matter how informative your story is if nobody reads it.

You need to make writing interesting, and Flesch's formula offers a key to

Perhaps the most famous of readability measures is the Flesch formula. His approach combines average sentence length with average number of syllables per word to produce a "reading ease" score, usually between 0 and 100. A score of 100 is extremely readable; a score of 0 is next to impossible. (Some government documents get scores in the negative numbers.) Gunning's formula is a little simpler. The average sentence length is added to the number of long words per 100 words. The sum is multiplied by 0.4, giving a score equal to the grade level of the writing. A Gunning score of 12, for example, indicates that the material could be understood by the average high school senior.

The preceding paragraph, for instance, contains eight sentences and 117 words, for an average of 14.6 words per sentence. There are 16 long words. (Gunning does not count words made into three syllables by the addition of -*ed* or -*es*, and does not count compound words made up of simple, short words—*butterfly*, for example.)

Thus:

$$\frac{16 \; long \; words}{117 \; words} \times 100 = 13.7 \; long \; words$$

Then: $13.7 + 14.6 = 28.3$

And: $28.3 \times .04 = 11.3$

So the previous paragraph is a little more advanced than the high school junior level.

You might like to know that you don't have to do the math to get your writing scores. Computer programs you can buy will do the counting for you.[9]

2.4 The Gunning Formula

that. In his system, a "personal word" is any pronoun that refers to people, all nouns that suggest masculine or feminine gender (like *father* or *sister*), and words like *people* or *folks*. "Personal sentences" are questions, commands, other sentences where the reader is addressed directly and sentence fragments where the "full meaning has to be inferred from the context—like 'Well, he wasn't.'"[10] While writing for the mass media doesn't permit much personal writing, you should take advantage of opportunities.

Instead of writing this:

> Residents who have not filed city income tax forms by midnight may face fines up to $500.

Write this:

> If you don't file a city income tax form by midnight, you may be hit with a $500 fine.

MAIN POINTS

- The major obstacles in good message delivery: the different types of messages a writer must learn to master and the encoding process the writer must accomplish to ensure fidelity of the decoding.

- Some principles of semantics that writers should keep in mind are:

  1. The word is not the thing. Words are symbols; thus they can never completely correspond to reality.

  2. Words are abstractions. Words at high levels of abstraction say very little about the things to which they refer.

  3. Words do not have "true" meanings apart from context. Words mean different things in different situations.

- A writer is obligated to be honest, fair and accurate.

- Statements can be classified as reports, inferences and judgments. Reports are statements of fact based on observations of easily verified information. Inferences are statements about the unknown made on the basis of the known. Judgments are expressions of the writer's approval or disapproval.

- A writer can be dishonest by not being specific in presenting a statement correctly as a report, inference or judgment, or by lying.

- Quotations in news stories must be verbatim. If a public relations writer develops quotes for a news release, these must be cleared with the person they're attributed to.

- If a name is changed, your audience must be informed.

- Slanting can mislead. If the writer selects only those facts that support a certain viewpoint and has omitted others, the story can be deceptive.

- Fairness involves presenting all valid points of view, but this should not be confused with objectivity. Total objectivity cannot be achieved.

- A person accused of wrongdoing must always be given an opportunity to respond in the same story in which he or she is accused.

- Editorial comment has no place in any writing except that clearly labeled as opinion or commercial copy.

- Biased language, including sexist terms and pronouns, is not being fair.

- Readers have a right to expect absolute accuracy in what you write.

- All statements of opinion or facts not commonly known must be attributed to the source.

- Two principal concerns for mass media writers are libel and invasion of privacy.

- Libel applies to both print and broadcast media, and slander laws cover ad-libbed (non-scripted) comments as well.

- In libel suits, the plaintiff must show publication, identification, defamation and some negligence or disregard for the truth. Defenses against libel are truth, privilege and fair comment.

- People are categorized as public officials, public figures and private persons in libel cases. Public officials and figures must often prove malice, while private persons need only show negligence.

- In privacy cases, consent, newsworthiness and absence of malice are defenses.

- The four torts of privacy are appropriation, false light, public disclosure of private fact and intrusion.

- Gag orders are last resorts to keep reporters from covering trials, but other methods are used to accomplish much the same thing.

- Reporters have been going to jail and are being fined for refusing to reveal their sources.

- The press has access to information under freedom-of-information acts and sunshine laws; however, exemptions and loopholes often render these laws less than effective.

- The courts have ruled that in the areas of free press—fair trial, privilege and access— the news media have no greater, and no lesser, rights than the general public.

- The right of privacy affects the use in publicity or advertising of a person's picture, letter or name. Consent is the best defense.

- The Freedom of Information Act protects trade secrets and confidential information of a commercial or financial nature obtained from outside government sources.

- Legal responsibilities for PR and advertising writers who are placing information in the mass media include fulfilling requirements of the Federal Trade Commission and the Securities and Exchange Commission.

- Conflicts between public relations people and news media representatives are likely to occur over interpretations of open records, open meetings and who can be identified as a "public figure."

- All writers and their employers are responsible for violations of the law and can be subject to fine or imprisonment.

- Using the language carefully is important for clear communication.

- Correct grammar and proper punctuation are needed to convey meaning successfully.

- Writers of news must be aware of specific style requirements for the media. Most newspapers observe the rules set forth by the major wire service, AP.

- Broadcast writers must write copy for the announcer to read and the audience to understand.

- Some of the fundamentals of clear writing: Be concise; use familiar words; be concrete and specific; use the active voice; phrase sentences positively; use natural language; be organized.

EXERCISES

1. Select a news story at random from a local newspaper. Attempt to categorize each statement in the story as a report, inference or judgment. Compute the percentage of each kind of statement and draw a conclusion about the journalistic quality of the story.

2. In the same story, look at descriptive words to see how many influence the way the action being reported is perceived.

3. Look at several stories from any daily newspaper to find statements without attribution. Make a list of those statements and decide for each one whether you think (a) attribution should have been included or (b) attribution was properly omitted. Write the reasons attribution was or was not needed in each case.

4. Record some television and/or radio newscasts. Compare the way broadcast writers and newspaper writers handle attributions. Are broadcast writers more likely to leave out attributions? If so, is this a proper practice?

5. Ben Bradlee says that newswriters shouldn't hide their biases behind words like *refused, despite, admit* and *massive*. Read through several newspaper articles to find instances where reporters did use such words. In your opinion, did the use of these words indicate a subtle bias on the writer's part? In the course of your reading, viewing and listening, watch for other words that might suggest bias. Compile a list of at least 20.

6. Find a news story in which you feel an organization (company, non-profit, any type) has not been treated fairly. Assume that you are the public relations director of that organization and write the reporter (if a byline is given) or managing editor to explain why you think the story is biased, attaching a version of the piece that you think would be fair.

7. Part of fair journalism is providing the name of the source of information used in a story. But sometimes sources don't want to be named, and writers must promise not to use the name before the source will talk. Under what circumstances should a reporter promise not to use a source's name?

8. Watch a local television newscast and read that same day's newspaper to see whether you discover anything that seems to you to be an invasion of privacy. Why would you think so?

9. Tape a radio newscast from an all-news station, if possible. See how many stories were included and the approximate length of each.

10. Tape the audio of a TV network newscast. How many minutes of news, excluding sports and weather, were in the newscast? How much of that was actually scripted (the non-scripted would be tapes and "patter"—conversation of the anchors)?

11. Select two articles from a daily newspaper: one that you consider easy to read and one that you consider difficult. Using one of the formulas discussed in 2.4, test the readability of each article. (Choose two samples of about 100 words each from each article.) How do the articles score? Do the scores confirm your subjective impression of reading difficulty?

NOTES

1. Daniel Katz, "Psychological Barriers to Communication," in *Mass Communications*, ed. Wilbur Schramm, 2nd ed. (Urbana: University of Illinois Press, 1960), pp. 316–17.

2. Perhaps the most famous semanticist is S.I. Hayakawa, well known as a professor before gaining wider fame as president of San Francisco State University and then as a United States senator. His studies of language and meaning are important for a writer. See the suggested readings for some of his works. S.I. Hayakawa, *Language in Thought and Action*, 4th ed. (New York: Harcourt Brace Jovanovich, 1978), p. 25.

3. Ibid., p. 155.

4. *Washington Post*, Sept. 28, 1980, p. 1A.

5. Robert A. Webb, ed., *The Washington Post Deskbook on Style* (New York: McGraw-Hill, 1978), p. 4. Reprinted with permission of the *Washington Post.*

6. Lewis Jordan, ed., *The New York Times Manual of Style and Usage* (New York: Times Books, 1976), p. 75.

7. C.C. Waldrip, "'I'm Paid Enormous Amounts of Money to Be Great,' and Other Good-Natured Self-Appraisals from Isaac Asimov," *Writer's Yearbook 1980* (Cincinnati: Writer's Digest), p. 79.

8. Terry Dunkle, "Obfuscatory Scrivenry (Foggy Writing)," *Science '82* 3:82–3.

9. Wayne Danielson, *Four Readability Formulas*, software package.

10. Rudolf Flesch, *The Art of Readable Writing, 25th Anniversary Edition* (New York: Harper & Row, 1974), p. 249.

SUGGESTIONS FOR ADDITIONAL READING

For more detailed discussions of semantics, see:

Hayakawa, S.I. *Language in Thought and Action.* 4th ed. New York: Harcourt Brace Jovanovich, 1978. An accessible yet thorough account of language, focusing on the ways it can facilitate or impair interactions among people.

Hayakawa, S.I., ed. *The Use and Misuse of Language.* Greenwich, Conn.: Fawcett, 1962. A collection of articles addressing various applications of semantics to life.

Johnson, Wendell. "The Communication Process and General Semantic Principles." In *Mass Communications,* edited by W. Schramm, pp. 301–15. 2nd ed. Urbana: University of Illinois Press, 1960. A sophisticated discussion of semantics by one of the early leaders in the field. This selection is part of a paper first published in 1948 and so doesn't reflect recent literature on the issues of semantics.

For more information on libel and privacy, see:

Bensman, Marvin R. *Broadcast Regulation: Selected Cases and Decisions.* 2nd ed. Lanham, Md.: University Press of America, 1985.

Braverman, Burt A., and Frances J. Chetwynd. *Information Law: Freedom of Information, Privacy, Open Meetings, Other Access Laws.* New York: Practicing Law Institute, 1985.

Carter, T. Barton, Marc A. Franklin and Jay B. Wright. *The First Amendment and the Fourth Estate: The Law of Mass Media.* 3rd ed. Mineola, N.Y.: Foundation Press, 1985.

Christensen, Gary L. *The New Era in CATV: The Cable Franchise Policy and Communications Act of 1984.* New York: Practicing Law Institute, 1985.

Dill, Barbara. *The Journalist's Handbook on Libel and Privacy.* New York: Free Press, 1986.

Gillmor, Donald M., and Jerome Barron. *Mass Communication Law.* 4th ed. St. Paul: West, 1984.

Holsinger, Ralph. *Media Law.* New York: Random House, 1985.

Kane, Peter E. *Murder, Courts, and the Press: Issues in Free Press/Fair Trial.* Carbondale: Southern Illinois University Press, 1986.

Nelson, Harold L., and Dwight L. Teeter Jr. *Law of Mass Communications: Freedom and Control of Print and Broadcast Media*. 5th ed. Mineola, N.Y.: Foundation Press, 1986.

Pember, Don R. *Mass Media Law*. Dubuque, Iowa: Wm. C. Brown, 1984.

Robertson, Geoffrey, and Andrew Nicol. *Media Law*. London: Sage, 1986.

Smolla, Rodney A. *Suing the Press*. New York: Oxford University Press, 1986. Includes famous libel cases like Westmoreland vs. CBS, Carol Burnett vs. *National Enquirer*, Lillian Hellman vs. Mary McCarthy, Miss America Pageant vs. *Penthouse*, Jerry Falwell vs. *Hustler*.

For more information on style, see:

Brooks, Brian S., and others (The Missouri Group). *News Reporting and Writing*. 2nd ed. New York: St. Martin's, 1985. Has an excellent overview of the problems of quotation and attribution.

Chapman, Robert L., ed. *New Dictionary of American Slang*. New York: Harper & Row, 1986.

French, Christopher, Eileen Alt Powell and Howard Angione, eds. *The Associated Press Stylebook and Libel Manual*. New York: Associated Press, 1980.

Holley, Frederick S., ed. *Los Angeles Times Stylebook*. New York: New American Library, 1981. Besides being a thorough stylebook, this volume contains some good general advice for newswriters, especially under the headings of dialect; obscenity, profanity and vulgarity; quotations; *said, says*; and sequence of tenses in direct quotations.

Hood, James R., and Brad Kalfbeld, eds. *The Associated Press Broadcast News Handbook*. New York: Associated Press, 1982.

Jewler, A. Jerome. *Creative Strategies in Advertising*. 2nd ed. Belmont, Calif: Wadsworth, 1985.

Jordan, Lewis, ed. *The New York Times Manual of Style and Usage*. New York: Times Books, 1976. See the entries on dialect; fairness and impartiality; jargon; obscenity, vulgarity, profanity; parenthetical attribution; quotations; and sources of news.

Miller, Bobby Rae. *The UPI Stylebook*. New York: United Press International, 1977.

Moriarity, Sandra. *Advertising Copywriting and Design: Creative Advertising: Theory and Practice*. Englewood Cliffs, N.J.: Prentice-Hall, 1986.

Newsom, Doug, and Bob Carrell. *Public Relations Writing: Form and Style*. Belmont, Calif.: Wadsworth, 1986. Includes all types of PR writing from backgrounders to news releases.

Pickens, Judy, Patricia Walsh Rao and Linda Cook Roberts. *Without Bias: A Guidebook for Nondiscriminatory Communication*. 2nd ed. New York: John Wiley, 1982. International Association of Business Communicators, 1977. Should be in every writer's library.

Prejean, Blanche G., and Wayne A. Danielson. *Programmed Newspaper Style*. Fort Worth, Texas: American Continental, 1971.

Webb, Robert A., ed. *The Washington Post Deskbook on Style*. New York: McGraw-Hill, 1978. This stylebook offers an excellent commentary on standards and ethics by executive editor Ben Bradlee.

For more information on grammar, see:

Berner, R. Thomas. *Language Skills for Journalists*. 2nd ed. Boston: Houghton Mifflin, 1984.

Bernstein, Theodore. *The Careful Writer*. New York: Atheneum, 1965.

Copperud, Roy H. *American Usage and Style: The Consensus*. New York: Van Nostrand Reinhold, 1980.

Ebbitt, Wilma R., and David R. Ebbitt. *Perrin's Index to English*. 7th ed. Glenview, Ill.: Scott, Foresman, 1982.

Johnson, Eleanor, and Pat Gerkin, eds. *Directory of Editorial Resources 1985–86*. Alexandria, Va.: Editorial Experts.   Includes grammar hotlines.

Kessler, Lauren, and Duncan McDonald. *When Words Collide: A Journalist's Guide to Grammar and Style*. Belmont, Calif.: Wadsworth, 1984.

Montgomery, Michael, and John Stratton. *The Writer's Hotline Handbook*. New York: New American Library, 1981.

Rosen, Leonard. *The Everyday English Handbook*. Garden City, N.Y.: Doubleday, 1985.

For more information on the principles of good writing and readability, see:

Flesch, Rudolf. *The Art of Readable Writing, 25th Anniversary Edition*. New York: Harper & Row, 1974.

Gunning, Robert. *The Technique of Clear Writing*. Rev. ed. New York: McGraw-Hill, 1968.

Strunk, William, and E.B. White. *The Elements of Style*. 3rd ed. New York: Macmillan, 1979.

Zinsser, William. *On Writing Well*. 2nd ed. rev. New York: Harper & Row, 1985.

For current information on journalism-related software, you can request a newsletter from the Oates Clearinghouse for Computer-based Education in Journalism and Mass Communication, P.O. Box 248127, University of Miami, Coral Gables, Fla. 33124.

Information Sources
and Research Methods

Strong writing is based on information gathered through objective observation and thorough research. Gathering this information is the first part of your job.

Newswriters often report what they observe directly. Reporters attending a speech or meeting, battlefield correspondents, sportswriters covering a football game all report what they see and hear. Their colleagues with cameras do the same.

But rarely is the news limited to firsthand observations. Reporters ask other people what they have seen and heard. Reporters interview the participants in news events to learn their thoughts and feelings and to gain new information from a different perspective. They check records and documents to glean background information and to verify the assertions of participants and observers.

The information reporters get, whether from their own observations or from the reports of others, is sometimes not trustworthy (see 3.1). Reporters may see only part of what has happened. Observers may tell only part of the story or distort the part they tell. Printed sources may contain mistakes. "There's nothing more deceptive than an obvious fact," Sherlock Holmes told Dr. Watson in "The Bascombe Valley Mystery." An "obvious fact," the detective knew, often turns out not to be a fact at all. For the writer whose work will appear in the mass media, there is great danger in reporting an obvious fact without first making sure the statement is indeed accurate. You can't take anything for granted, no matter how obvious it may seem. Reporters have to be careful to distinguish between reports and inferences from those reports, and they must be on the lookout for judgments disguised as reports or inferences.

The word *reporter* is used deliberately; public relations writers need to adjust to the idea that they are internal (sometimes external) reporters for their organization. They can't sit waiting for someone to tell them what to write. The president of the organization either may not know what makes a good story or may simply be wrong. Just like the news media reporter, the public relations writer has to sense a story, get to the sources, sort out conflicting information and write a comprehensible story. The PR writer may also do

3.1
Even Supreme Court justices aren't always right, as this
story shows.

For a quotable high court view, never let facts stand in the way

By Stephen Wermiel
Staff Reporter of The Wall Street Journal

WASHINGTON—If Perry Mason practiced in the Supreme Court, this might be called "The Case of the Curious Quote."

It all began last June 26 when Chief Justice Warren Burger used a Supreme Court libel decision as a vehicle to remind the news media to act responsibly.

"Consideration of these issues," the chief justice wrote in a separate opinion, "inevitably recalls the aphorism of journalism attributed to the late Roy Howard that 'too much checking on the facts has ruined many a good news story.'"

Although Chief Justice Burger's comment raised the hackles of a few journalists, it was extraneous to the court's ruling and no one paid much attention to it.

A Pair of Skeptics

No one, that is, but Bruce Sanford, a lawyer here for E.W. Scripps Co.'s Scripps-Howard newspaper chain, and William Burleigh, vice president of the chain.

The two men had never seen such a statement attributed to Mr. Howard, who for many years was editor-in-chief of Scripps-Howard. Since there was no footnote to the chief justice's opinion, they wondered where and when the statement might have been made.

So Mr. Burleigh put a sleuth on the case: James Roche, a researcher at the Roy Howard Memorial Center at Indiana University's School of Journalism. Mr. Roche says he has read all the collected papers and memorabilia of Mr. Howard. "I'm confident," he says of the missing quote, "that it was never said by Mr. Howard in a professional, recorded way."

No Record Found

That was good enough for Mr. Bur-

leigh and for Mr. Sanford. They told Henry Lind, the Supreme Court reporter of decisions, that there was no record of Mr. Howard's having made the statement.

No explanation was ever offered, but in December Mr. Lind's office changed the language of the chief justice's opinion for the version that will appear in the permanent, bound record of Supreme Court decisions. When lawyers in the future look up the case of **Dun & Bradstreet Inc. v. Greenmoss Builders, Inc.**, the last paragraph of the chief justice's concurring opinion will say:

"Consideration of these issues inevitably recalls an aphorism of journalism that 'too much checking on the facts has ruined many a good news story.'"

research for internal documents from which decisions are made. The information must be comprehensive, timely and accurate, so the **PR** person uses internal electronic data banks and external sources.

Ad copywriters don't have it all handed to them, either. A new account means extensive research into the product or service and the market—particularly the competition and the industry the product or service is part of, including the regulatory agencies that govern the industry and control to some degree what an advertiser can say. If you think that's an easy job, try doing some research on a product, such as bathroom fixtures, assuming your new client is one of the smaller companies in the marketplace. Or consider a service industry that's regulated, such as insurance. You have to become as good a fact finder as Sherlock Holmes.

In short, writers for the mass media must be skilled researchers. Reporters call research *backgrounding*, and PR writers prepare formal documents for management called *backgrounders*. As information becomes more complex, the need for people skilled at fact-finding becomes even greater. Such skill comes from experience, but even the beginner must know the basic sources of information available.

There are two kinds of information sources: primary and secondary. For the most part, primary sources are people directly involved in an issue. (Strictly speaking, primary sources also include the reports and documents prepared and written by these people.) Writers try to talk to primary sources whenever possible: the candidate running for office, the scientist who conducted a research project, the designer of the new museum exhibit.

Secondary sources are the reports of people who have gathered the findings of others. Newswriters generally go to them to gather background before approaching a primary source or to verify information from other sources. Such secondary information can be found in books, periodicals and other documents. Most serious writers maintain their own considerable reference libraries of atlases, dictionaries, encyclopedias, indexes and professional periodicals. Public libraries offer extensive reference rooms staffed by reference specialists to help you locate elusive facts or sources.

Some of the most helpful librarians are those in charge of electronic information-retrieval systems. The search capabilities of these systems make them excellent time-savers. The microfilm and electronic files of some major publications, such as the *New York Times*, are made available to libraries. Libraries with electronic retrieval systems also can access journal and magazine articles. The latest such source is the *data base*, a computerized information-retrieval system accessed via telephone lines.

In addition, organizations with large staffs and budgets often undertake original research projects such as public opinion polls.

Thus the writer uses three classes of information sources: primary, mainly people; secondary, mainly paper and printouts; and original research methods. Any one story may involve two or more methods of fact-finding.

PAPER AND PRINTOUTS

Some paper sources, such as books and magazines, are familiar to everybody. Newspapers themselves are a valuable source of information. The *New York Times, Wall Street Journal* and *Washington Post* are widely read by writers.

Other paper sources commonly used for research are reference books: dictionaries, encyclopedias, almanacs, yearbooks and a variety of specialized publications such as compilations of biographical sketches and bibliographies for a specific subject area.

Less publicized but possibly more useful sources are research journals, government documents and records, and various data bases available through electronic retrieval systems.

Reference books Reference books usually don't provide all the background information a writer needs on a given subject, but they're often the best source of answers to specific questions or for statistical information: the capital of a country, the population of a city, the number of pounds of potatoes grown on U.S. farms each year.

Most writers and organizations where a great deal of writing is done keep almanacs—compact volumes of statistics and numbers and miscellaneous data about everything from weights and measures to celebrities' birthdays. Among the most frequently used almanacs are *The World Almanac and Book of Facts*, the *Information Please Almanac*, the *Reader's Digest Almanac* and the *Associated Press Almanac*.

An especially useful reference source similar to an almanac is the *Statistical Abstract of the United States*, published annually by the U.S. Department of Commerce. It contains a wealth of information on all aspects of American society: population, education, health and nutrition, crime, employment, banking, finance and the economy, food and agriculture, health and medicine, energy, the environment, transportation, business and industry.

For any given industry or subject of interest, more specific information is often available from a trade association. Gale Research Co.'s *Encyclopedia of Associations* lists names, addresses and phone numbers of these organizations.

You shouldn't overlook the more traditional reference sources such as dictionaries and encyclopedias. Many elementary questions are often answered in the definitions of standard dictionaries, especially the large unabridged versions (such as *Webster's Third New International Dictionary* and the *Random House Dictionary of the English Language*). How high are the walls of the moon's crater Copernicus? You can find the answer (12,000 feet) in the *Random House Dictionary*, in the second definition under *Copernicus*. If your research has to do with the history of words or certain terminology, the *Oxford English Dictionary* is an essential source.

Encyclopedias, of course, go into much greater depth. For a writer setting out to do a story on an unfamiliar subject, an encyclopedia is one of the best places to go first (along with an introductory textbook), because it will give a general introduction to a subject, its basic issues and terminology.

Not all encyclopedias are equally reliable. For serious research, the best choices are the *Encyclopaedia Britannica* and the *Encyclopedia Americana*. The authors of the articles in these encyclopedias are usually well-qualified authorities.

Most library reference rooms also have numerous specialized encyclopedias and dictionaries, covering such diverse fields as physics, art, sociology, music and political science. A writer seeking to understand the specialized terminology of a given field may have to go to such sources for help.

Books Often the first stop in a research project is the card catalog (see 3.2 and 3.3). But writers should keep in mind that most books are somewhat out of date the day they hit the bookstores. It can take anywhere from several months to two or three years for a book, once written, to be published. The writer researching subjects where events move rapidly will find that most books aren't much help.

3.2 Cards from a Library Card Catalog

Books are listed under title, author's name, and topic. The three cards shown here all represent the same book, but they're found in different sections of the catalog. The books can be located in the library through their *call* *numbers*. The Library of Congress call-number system, used by many libraries, is shown in 3.3. (Libraries now are converting to electronic display of card catalog information.)

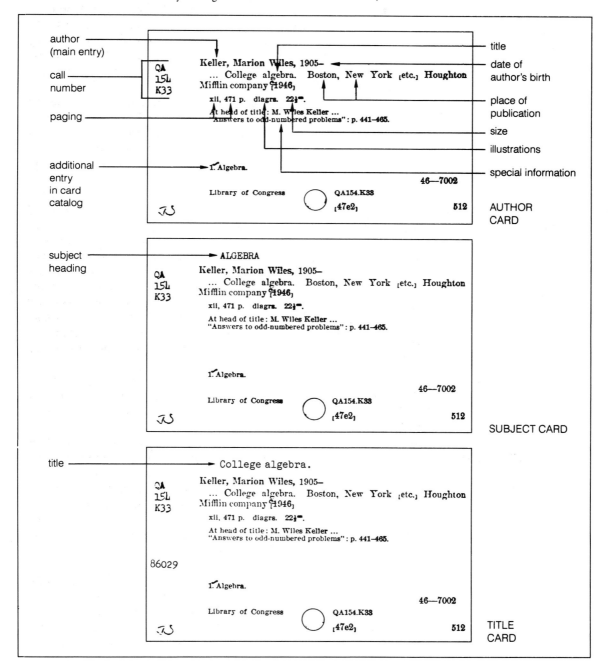

A	General Work–Polygraphy
B	Philosophy–Religion
C	History–Auxiliary Sciences
D	History and Topography (except America)
E–F	America
G	Geography–Anthropology
H	Social Sciences
J	Political Science
K	Law
L	Education
M	Music
N	Fine Arts
P	Language and Literature
Q	Science
R	Medicine
S	Agriculture–Plant and Animal Husbandry
T	Technology
U	Military Science
V	Naval Science
Z	Bibliography and Library Science

3.3 Library of Congress System

The Library of Congress classification was introduced in 1897. The system appears here in its severest brevity. Its flexibility has made it appealing to librarians. For a thorough discussion of both this system and the Dewey decimal system, see *Finding Facts* by William L. Rivers, pp. 77–81.

Introductory textbooks in various fields may prove useful, though, for some basic background and terminology. Perusing a text on astronomy, say, can give you some preparation in doing a story on black holes. But you must then go to primary sources to get the latest developments.

When evaluating the information contained in books, you must keep an important distinction in mind. Some books present primary research findings— they are written by the researchers themselves. Other books are secondary works—surveys and discussions of the research of others. The latter are sometimes valuable syntheses of important but scattered information, but often they are merely collections of a given author's opinions and prejudices. It's up to you to sort the valuable and valid from the worthless and invalid.

Magazines   As sources of information, magazines have some advantages over books, but also some of the same disadvantages. Datedness is less a problem, but—depending on the subject—it can still exist. Some magazines, such as the major news weeklies, appear on the newsstands within days of being written. For other magazines, the time lag ranges from a week or so to a few months.

Like some books, most magazines are written not by the primary researchers but by writers who have surveyed what others have done. Some magazines are produced by skilled journalists and have a reputation for accuracy. Others aren't and don't. Studies of accuracy reveal a wide range of difference among various publications. A panel of experts who rated the accuracy of various science articles found an average of only 0.3 errors in an article in *Scientific American* (whose contributors are practicing scientists) and an average of 9.9 errors in an article in *Ms.* magazine.[1] The writer using a magazine as a research tool must first investigate its reliability and reputation.

Journals Journals are periodicals that publish research studies. These are valuable because it is primary information—the original reports of findings by the people who did the research. The reliability of information in most journals is increased by the process of peer review: Before publication, experts in the field review each study to make sure that the research was conducted properly and that the conclusions of the researchers are sound. (Journals that use such a review process are called "refereed" journals.)

Every important field of study has a journal for publication of research—and most fields have more than one. In medicine, research findings are reported in the *New England Journal of Medicine* and the *Journal of the American Medical Association*, among others. Historical research is published in the *Journal of American History* and the *American Historical Review*. Studies of literature and language appear in *College English* and *Philological Quarterly*. Chemists publish in the *Journal of the American Chemical Society* and in any of dozens of more specialized journals. Other scientists report research findings in *Science* and in the British journal *Nature*.

Many journals are published only four times a year; others come out more frequently. Not even journals printed weekly are always timely. The research studies reported in a journal may have been conducted several months or even more than a year before publication.

Newspapers Newspapers are used as sources of information by all sorts of writers, from historians and creative writers to other media writers. Most newspapers maintain a library (in old newspaper jargon, the morgue), a collection of back issues and clippings from those issues usually filed by subject; at larger papers the files are on an electronic system, so searches go somewhat faster. Public libraries have had microfilm for decades. The advantage of that system is the preservation of the graphics. However, content is now on various forms of electronic storage, floppy or hard discs.

In all communities, the newspaper is the medium "of record." It's what you consult to find out the most information about everything that happened on a certain date in that community and surrounding area. Broadcast tapes of newscasts cannot begin to provide the same amount of detail. That's the reason many broadcast stations also clip and file local newspapers.

Newspapers are valuable information sources. They provide clues that a reporter can investigate to find a story that was missed. And newspapers of record, such as the *New York Times*, often provide useful background information—the complete text of presidential speeches or important pieces of legislation, for instance.

Most of all, newspaper research is valuable because it is timely. If you know your information is up to date as of a month ago, you can review newspaper reports since then to learn of any new developments. One problem with news reports, though, is that because of immediacy, they may be less accurate or complete, missing details that put the facts into perspective. A book can do that better.

Government documents

Government agencies churn out vast numbers of publications, ranging from single sheet flyers to multivolume reports, on almost any subject imaginable. New ones appear almost daily. This important source is often overlooked because it is often not recorded in card catalogs or standard indexes.

To help researchers keep up with what's available, the U.S. Government Printing Office issues a monthly catalog of new documents. Annual indexes are issued to help find listings in these catalogs, which were first published in 1895. There are indexes to government statistical publications and to publications of Congress as well.

Certain libraries designated as official "depository" libraries receive many of these documents directly from the printing office. Other documents are available from the printing office or from the National Technical Information Service in Springfield, Va.

Government publications are valuable because they're prepared by people with access to the latest information. They generally offer a level of detail — particularly of statistical information — beyond that presented in books or magazines.

Yet there are drawbacks. Government documents are especially susceptible to the influences of politics. The ways facts are presented can change from one president's administration to the next. During Jimmy Carter's term in office, some government booklets on nuclear energy were taken out of print and revised to reflect Carter's new policy toward breeder reactors. The facts hadn't changed — just the politics. Writers of government documents are sometimes instructed to quote, or not to quote, certain individuals because of their party affiliations or positions on congressional committees. Government documents must not, therefore, be blindly accepted as politically neutral and factual.

There is an important distinction to be made between government documents and government records. Documents are usually prepared by government agencies to make information public and accessible. Agencies at all levels of government also maintain many records that are open for public inspection — records of proceedings in open court, financial reports filed by corporations.

Such records can provide a wealth of information to a writer, but they aren't always easily obtained. The federal Freedom of Information Act, and similar acts in many states, can be used to force a reluctant agency to turn over certain records. Writers should know the law regarding public records in their state and be familiar with the necessary procedures for obtaining records under Freedom of Information provisions.

Data bases Data bases have come to prominence since the introduction of the personal computer in 1975 and its subsequent proliferation in homes, libraries and offices. Data bases were developed to fill the growing demand for instant information. The concept is essentially that of videotex. Both are large repositories of information, but whereas videotex is localized, data bases are national.

A check of computer magazines indicates about 700 such data bases are available to home-computer owners, businesses and journalists. *Personal Computing* magazine notes there are data bases for

law, medicine, corporate profiles, agribusiness, technical and professional journals in 40 languages, consumer buying habits, solar energy, financial management and planning, coal, oil and forestry resources, commodities, pharmacology, aquatic sciences, alcoholism, Latin America, the Middle East, money markets, supermarkets, and even the fertilizer market.[2]

The more familiar data bases are CompuServe, The Source, Dow Jones, News/Retrieval Service and NEXIS/LEXIS. One that serves primarily the advertising, public relations and marketing area is MARS. All generally provide abstracts from newspapers and magazines, as well as information on hundreds of topics. LEXIS is designed for lawyers and law schools; NEXIS is a news service especially attractive to journalists.

These services enable people from all over the country to connect their microcomputers to the large mainframe computers where the data is stored. To gain access, you connect your home or business computer to a modem, a device sold at all computer stores that allows your computer to use the telephone lines to contact the mainframe, which may be thousands of miles away.

Once on-line with the mainframe, you can select information from a number of "menus." Most data banks work by searching for key words in the computer's memory. For example, a reporter planning a series about how college lifestyles have led to great stress for students might submit the words *college students lifestyle, college students stress*, and, perhaps, *college students mental health* to the computer. The computer would then search its data base for articles with those words in the titles (or in specially prepared descriptions of articles that include key words). Part of the printout resulting from such a search is shown in 3.4.

With some data bases you can then ask to see the entire text of any article that interests you. Others will only tell you where to go to get the information, providing the title of an article and the journal in which to find it, sometimes along with a brief summary, or abstract, of the article's contents. You can also call for bibliographies on subjects and let the computer do in seconds what it would take hours to do in the library.

But while using a data base is certainly faster, it also costs money. You can wander into a library and search through books for free, but most data bases charge for an initial subscription, then charge about a dollar a minute for use. You also pay for the long-distance phone calls to the central computer.

3.4 Electronic Searching

A search asking for descriptions of marketing functions
resulted in printouts like this. Data bases charge by the
contact minute.

```
                                                                        26
      Print 6/7/2-70
      DIALOG File16: PROMT - 72-83/A (Item    1 of   69) User 8356  5jul83


        *1USA *United States *9914110 *Organization of the Marketing Function *221
          *planning
          Cable TV may cause package goods companies to restructure their marketing
        staffs, according to G Karalekas, sr VP, exec director media, D'Arcy-MacManus
        & Masius. Marketers have traditionally set up their sales staffs by
        predefined divisions, regions, sales territories, etc. As the media became
        more impactful, client marketing teams redefined their territories to better
        match media coverage. With the growth of cable and the increasingly bigger
        role played by interconnects, new evolutionary sales and marketing
        distribution patterns may emerge as the medium matures and is better able to
        refine geographic and demographic prospects. In order to become more
        productively efficient, the marketer, faced with continually rising costs of
        doing business, will be pressured into further refining where he does his
        business and which prospects are most viable. The planner will need to have
        the understanding, the sensitivity and the resources that can pinpoint the
        media overlay required. Interconnects can make this job much easier,
        especially for the planner, in that they can reduce the number of geographic
        and demographic pieces to the search for the right media overlay mix.
        Currently, only some 20 markets are thought to be interconnected, according
        to the Cable Ad Bureau.
          816900 Market Com 82/09      P18


        *1USA *United States *9914110 *Organization of the Marketing Function *221
          *planning
          A media vehicle plan (MVP) can aid industrial marketing communications
        execs in meshing their selling and advertising efforts. An MVP combines the
        advertising and sales functions early in the planning cycle and spells out
        the complementary roles both functions play in achieving marketing
        objectives. The objectives set by an MVP improve advertising and selling
        accountability and cost effectiveness. In addition, the MVP can serve as a
        sales forecasting tool. The MVP's objective is to deliver the most messages
        to key buying influences in a target market for the lowest possible cost. In
        order for the benefits of the plan to be realized it is necessary to review
        the role of personal selling in the marketing mix. Information about a
        company's products or services can be communicated either by telling a
        prospect through face-to-face personal selling or letting the prospect read
        it in non-personal marketing tools such as direct mailers, advertisements and
        publicity. The 'cost per message delivered'--the company's cost to deliver a
        benefit message to a buying influence--is a useful concept for analyzing cost
        effectiveness of alternatives for the MVP. Further explanation of the MVP
        process is presented. Tables showing the planning process, and a completed
        MVP are included.
          814976 #Ind Mktng 82/09      P68,72+


        *1USA *United States *9914110 *Organization of the Marketing Function *243
          *market research
          The best market for goods and services during the 1980s will be Americans
        over 60, according to Heublein chrmn SD Watson. 'Unlike the younger
        generation, their income will not be consumed by housing costs. They will
        travel more, eat out more and buy more of all kinds of consumer goods,'
        Watson says. (article contains little further information)
          756221 Ad Age 82/04/19 P75
```

Database Search by *DIALOG*/Predicast, Inc.

News releases News releases flood most newsrooms daily. PR people keep the news media informed about the company, industry or institution they represent in the hope that reporters will cover certain events, people or issues. While most of the releases are sent by mail, some are personally delivered, some arrive via the public relations wire service and others are delivered from the PR source's computer directly to the news media's computer.

PR releases are written from the organization's perspective, even when they tell bad news—a painting discovered missing from a museum, an unusually low quarterly earnings report, an official involved in some unethical or illegal act. Effective, efficient PR people want to get to the news media first with their version of the story. Thus reporters generally regard all news releases with some degree of skepticism.

But PR sources are important to the news media because they can help with research. They can supply information from their resources that it would take a reporter a considerable amount of digging to find. In addition to prepared materials, PR representatives often can get reporters interviews with people in their organization who are well insulated from the press.

Suppose a reporter is preparing a series on the local economy. There's no better place to start than the Chamber of Commerce. Because it is the PR arm of local business, its view is likely to be optimistic, unless there's a political reason to be otherwise, such as exaggerating storm damage to influence government assistance. For an opposing view, check with the PR people at labor unions, in social agencies and government sources. They'll furnish information from their perspective, perhaps on how bad the economy is and how working people are not getting a fair shake. The reporter knows the truth probably lies somewhere in between but will use the information provided to develop a story.

PEOPLE Once background has been gleaned from paper sources, a writer is ready to approach the primary sources: people.

Sources and strategies Before you start phoning people and asking questions, see what's in your organization's files, not only what's there but who the contacts were. Talk to colleagues who know something about the individuals or the subject you're writing about. Colleagues will generally offer some suggestions when you ask, like "You need to talk to Elaine Brown at XYZ organization. She can help." If that offer is made, ask if you can use their name. It sometimes makes a difference in getting through to the person they told you to talk to. If you do your initial research where you work, you'll get some leads to sources and avoid the embarrassment of having someone outside direct you to your own organization or someone in it.

Even when the major source for a story is published research, it's essential to talk to the people involved. There may have been new developments in the interval between completion of the study and its publication. And no matter how thorough your spadework, there is never time to read everything. Talking to experts can be a way of getting the information you missed. Experts can clarify points raised by your research and help you avoid drawing unwarranted conclusions.

Different kinds of stories call for different kinds of sources. The important thing to remember is that it is rarely advisable to interview only one person for a story. Every individual has a personal point of view, experiences and prejudices. You must talk to people who have differing perspectives and prejudices. For a story on crime, interview criminals as well as victims. It might be appropriate to interview legislators or sociologists who specialize in the study of crime.

If your first searches don't help, don't hesitate to seek out the person who gave you the assignment, tell him or her where you have looked, what you have found and what you think you still need to know to do the best job. Ask for help and you'll usually get it.

There are some points to remember about this fact-finding. Take careful notes to be sure the information you recorded is accurate. Spell back names of people and places. Repeat figures, and say them a different way to be sure. If the source said "fifty thousand," ask, "You said five-oh-zero-zero-zero, fifty thousand, right?" *Fifty* can sound like *fifteen*.

Be sure to keep the information sources straight. Keep a card file on your contacts. If you use an electronic system for such records, keep updated hard copies handy for days when the system is down or the power fails.

Some writers organize their sources by subject of expertise. Some record just the names and numbers of sources, not their credentials or their possible relationship to stories, so others will not benefit from this proprietary information. Use your indexes of sources to record home telephone numbers, unlisted numbers and switchboard bypass numbers for people who work in their offices during off-hours.

A natural question for the beginning writer building a list of sources is "Who should I interview?" For many articles you'll be able to find a government agency or non-profit organization that deals with the subject. For a story on depression and suicide, for example, you could start by calling the local chapter of the Mental Health Association.

In addition, various organizations publish directories of people who are experts in given fields. The *Directory of American Scholars*, published by R.R. Bowker, lists college professors and their fields of expertise. Individual colleges and universities often provide such lists as well through their public relations department. Directories of public relations representatives with various companies and trade groups are also available. PR people can answer some questions and also tell a writer who the experts are for more in-depth interviews.

Most interviewers take a tape recorder to be sure they get the information correctly and capture the nuances of the person's voice. Of course, the interviewee must give permission, but most are not reluctant. Generally they forget the machine is operating, and the interviewer should too, except to change the tapes. The interviewer needs to be taking notes just as if the machine were not there.

When interviewing people for a story, you should ask appropriate questions—questions that the interviewee is qualified to answer. You would not, for instance, ask the victim of a crime to interpret the meaning of the statutes that the criminal violated. That's a question for lawyers or judges. But you might well ask for the victim's opinion on whether the laws are fair.

The best way to retain sources is to be direct and honest with them. This applies to all information sources, not just news. The internal politics of a public relations piece or sometimes even an ad can be unsettling to the naive. You need to be aware of the egos and reputations involved and who stands to benefit.

Quote sources accurately and you'll earn their trust. If you make a mistake, apologize. Try to correct it if you can.

Always thank sources for their help, and be considerate of their time. Organize your questions so you don't have to call back (but it's better to call back than to make a mistake). You may prepare a source for a second call by saying, "I think I have it all straight, but if I hit a snag, I may want to get back to you. Where will you be this afternoon?" or "Will it be all right to call you tomorrow?"

Don't be in too big a hurry. You may have to listen to more than you called for, but listening shows you care about the source as a person, not just as a handy resource. There's a utilitarian aspect, too: Sometimes you pick up ideas from them you wouldn't have gotten otherwise, or you get some additional insight. You have to be alert also for non-verbal cues—signs of enthusiasm, of impatience, of anger, of anxiety. The interviewee's silent language often will tell you how far you can go with a line of questioning.

Sometimes sources want to see your finished piece before it's published or broadcast. Ordinarily that's not a problem in advertising and publicity, since there is an approval chain, but it could be. Tell them you'll check and get back to them. That's the standard line for newswriters, too. You would say something like, "I can check with my editor (or news director), but usually the only time we ask someone to check a story before it's used is when we want to verify the accuracy of what was said." A newswriter is under no obligation to show a source a story before it's used—but you are obligated to be certain that what you write is accurate, balanced and fair. That's where a newswriter is in a very different position from a public relations writer, who may clear the release not only with the source but also with top officials in the organization.

More actual interviewing techniques are discussed in Chapter 7. The best writers work hard at developing interviewing skills, because the interview is one of the most important of all information-gathering tools.

Knowing that research sources and methods exist is not enough. You must know how to use them, where to start, what to do. You need a strategy.

For some situations, your research needs will be small and your strategy simple. Suppose you must cover a speech by a famous author. You already know quite a bit about her, you've read some of her books, and you think you're well prepared. But you need to know a few things not mentioned in the publicity material sent out to announce the speech. What year was she born, maybe, and when was her Pulitzer Prize–winning book published?

Such questions as these are easily answered if you have the appropriate reference books on hand. If not, a call to the reference desk of the local library should do the job. Most libraries have reference workers who will be happy to answer questions over the phone. The Brooklyn Public Library, for example, reports that its reference-desk staff receives more than 1,000 calls a day.[3]

But suppose you've never heard of the author whose speech you must cover. In that case, you can call a library's reference desk for some guidance; you can also consult *Current Biography* or *Who's Who in America* for basic biographical information. You should find some of the author's writings as well. And if the author is speaking on a topic unfamiliar to you, you must do background research on that, too.

In this case, the reference library might offer helpful suggestions on where to look, but you won't get all the answers you need over the phone. Many libraries restrict the amount of time they'll devote to any one question. The New York City Public Library's reference service will give answers that can be found in less than five minutes.

Consider the case of writing a story on an unfamiliar subject: the possibility of climate changes as carbon dioxide builds up in the atmosphere from the burning of fossil fuels. This is the sort of assignment a public relations writer as well as a reporter might receive if employed, for example, by an agency whose new client is a coal company or an industry that uses fossil fuels. Where do you begin? Certainly not with the latest research report published in a technical journal—you won't understand it. You must begin with background research in sources you will understand and proceed from there to more specialized and technical sources.

Step 1: *Consult a general encyclopedia.* Let's say all you can get your hands on is a somewhat out-of-date *Encyclopaedia Britannica.* It certainly won't have the latest developments, but it's good enough to tell you what carbon dioxide is: "a colourless gas, possessing a faint pungent smell and a slightly acid taste." Its chemical symbol is CO_2. It was discovered by J.B. van Helmont (1577–1644), who noted that it was produced both by fermentation and combustion. You learn that it is found in the atmosphere in small amounts (3 parts per 10,000 by volume), that it is formed in the process of respiration and that it is a basic ingredient in the process of photosynthesis. There is some more chemical information, but nothing about carbon dioxide–induced climatic changes.

Step 2: *Consult a specialized encyclopedia.* There are several possibilities, but you choose *Van Nostrand's Scientific Encyclopedia*, because you don't know very much about your subject yet and *Van Nostrand's* is less specialized than other scientific reference books—and you happen to have a copy. Reading the entry on carbon dioxide gives you more information and also introduces you to the first pitfall of research: conflicting information. *Britannica* says carbon dioxide has "a faint pungent smell"; *Van Nostrand's* says the gas is "odorless . . . at standard conditions." When you get to the interviewing stage, you might want to ask a chemist about that discrepancy.

Van Nostrand's confirms that carbon dioxide is found in the air, but it puts the amount at 0.05 percent by weight, compared to the *Britannica's* 3 parts per 10,000, or 0.03 percent, by volume. You now know to be careful when expressing proportions of gases—you must specify whether volumes or weights are being measured.

You learn that carbon dioxide is used in fire extinguishers and in carbonated beverages, and then find a key clue: ". . . the presence of CO_2 in the atmosphere disturbs the environmental energy balance." The encyclopedia directs you to the article on air pollution for further discussion.

In the article "Pollution (Air)," you find nothing useful. So much for *Van Nostrand's*.

Since the carbon dioxide issue is related to energy production, you head for the library and check the *McGraw-Hill Encyclopedia for Energy* and find a paragraph that sets forth the issue:

Some scientists speculate that the increasing carbon dioxide content of the atmosphere will increase its capacity to absorb solar energy, leading to a gradual warming of the troposphere (the greenhouse effect). If the concentration of carbon dioxide were to become high enough, some scientists warn, the temperature increase could melt the polar icecaps, with catastrophic flooding of coastal areas throughout the world.

Step 3: *Seek magazine articles.* You search through the last few years of the *Readers' Guide to Periodical Literature* and find a reference to an article by George M. Woodwell in the January 1978 issue of *Scientific American*. It is a thorough discussion of the carbon dioxide issue. You now have a solid basis of understanding to continue your research.

You find other articles relating carbon dioxide to climate: "Scientists Grapple with CO_2 Problem" in the Jan. 26, 1981, *Chemical Engineering News*; a report in the April 1982 edition of *Discover*, and several others. Each offers new statistics, insights and references to experts in the field. You make a list of people and publications to consult later.

Step 4: *Consult the card catalog.* You find several books on the weather, but one titled *Climatic Change* seems to be most directly related to the topic. It's a collection of analyses of different climate issues, and two of the chapters relate to the carbon dioxide problem. Extensive bibliographies direct you to other sources.

Step 5: *Examine government documents.* By now your reading has identified for you several important government documents on the subject, including a major report by the National Academy of Sciences, "Energy and Climate," published in 1977, and "Global Energy Futures and the Carbon Dioxide Problem," published by the Council on Environmental Quality in 1981.

Step 6: *Consult journal articles or major published studies.* The bibliographies of the government documents and books you consult will lead you to numerous articles in scientific journals. Some of these articles will treat the carbon dioxide issue broadly; some will deal with only one narrow aspect of the problem. Studies will be found in such journals as *Science, American Scientist* and the *Journal of Atmospheric Chemistry.* Checking recent issues of these publications will help you avoid missing important new studies.

Step 7: *Consult newspapers and news magazines.* In addition to checking recent copies of important journals, it is wise to check the *New York Times Index* and the latest news magazines, *Time* and *Newsweek,* and in this case scientific news magazines such as *Science News* and *Chemical & Engineering News* for recent developments. New legislation may have been proposed to deal with the carbon dioxide problem. This is also a good time to check electronic data bases for information if you haven't used that approach earlier in the process (as when searching for magazine articles).

Step 8: *Interview the appropriate people.* Now that you know who the experts are, call them for analysis and interpretation. They should be able to tell you about current research and point out any important sources you have missed.

Researching this way appears to be a long, exhausting process. You won't always have time to go through all of it on deadline. But with a systematic, organized approach, you can acquire a lot of information in a short time.

SURVEYS AND POLLS

Even beginning reporters do surveys of sorts.

- Who robbed you?
- What did the robber look like?
- How did the robber get away?
- When did the robbery occur?
- Why didn't the guard dog attack?
- How much money was stolen?

A reporter asking those questions of people at the scene of the robbery is doing a crude survey—asking individuals in a select group the same questions.

If you were to go about it haphazardly, asking different questions of a few people you find on the street near the scene of the crime, that would not be a survey or a poll at all. Why not?

Samples and populations

A true survey or poll uses a rather large sample drawn at random from an identifiable population. To conduct a survey, you first must have a research idea or question; then you must identify the population you want to sample.

Let's say you're interested in finding out what the people of Boston think about crime in their city. You ask a sample of, say, 1,000 Boston residents. Can such a sample really tell us what all of the half-million people of Boston think? Yes, it can. The doctor doesn't need to drain all of your blood and look at it ounce by ounce to give you an adequate physical. He or she takes a blood sample, from which the exact state of all of your blood can be determined.

However, that sample of your blood cannot tell the doctor the condition of someone else's blood, and the same is true in survey research. You must always know the exact population from which the sample is drawn so as not to make erroneous inferences. For example, a survey of University of California students might turn up the amazing results that 90 percent of them read their campus newspaper daily. Now, you cannot assume that 90 percent of all University of Virginia students also read their campus newspaper daily, or that 90 percent of all college students read their campus newspaper daily. Too often reports state or imply that the results of a survey done on one population hold true for another population.

Surveys can be conducted of entire populations, or of select populations from the whole. If the research questions require only select groups, then only those groups should be sampled. For example, you may want to extend the crime survey from Boston to other cities, including Atlanta. And now you also want to find out more about what blacks think of crime. So in Atlanta you conduct a *stratified* sample, polling only blacks. You can stratify by race, sex, age, income, education and just about any demographic or geographic variable you can think of.

Drawing the sample

The critical part of survey research is the *sampling frame*, the list from which the sample is drawn. A telephone book is a sampling frame for telephone surveys.

Many sampling frames are difficult to get. Suppose you want to do a study of all recovering alcoholics in the city. How do you go about getting a list of their names? If you can come up with that complete list for your community, you certainly pass this part of the course in research.

An entire industry has grown up around buying and selling lists of addresses and phone numbers of people, businesses and institutions to use in survey research, direct mail and marketing. Marketing researchers use surveys and polls daily, and the lives of many companies depend on this research.

When you get the list, you must decide whether it's complete, accurate and up to date. If it isn't, you'll have some error in the sample you pull from this list. That's the trouble with using telephone books: People move quite often and change their telephone numbers; many people have unlisted numbers. It's possible to generate some additional numbers using the prefixes (first three digits) of the area and random mixes of numbers.

Once you have a list you feel is as complete as possible, you pull the sample. This must be done at random; otherwise, error will result. Random sampling means everyone in the population from which the sample is drawn has an equal chance of being included.

Questionnaires

The next step is to decide how you want to administer a questionnaire to the people in your sample. The most common way to conduct surveys is by phone, because it's the cheapest and most effective. Personal interviews are expensive, and mail questionnaires traditionally have a low rate of response. It's important to design your questionnaire carefully so that it's free from bias and asks the right questions. Many surveys fail because the questionnaire was faulty.

Many questionnaires try to determine the degree of feeling people have about a subject. This is accomplished through *scaling* techniques. Thus you don't ask, "Do you like the *New York Times?* Yes or no?" You ask subjects to respond to the statement "I like the *New York Times*" by indicating "strongly agree; agree somewhat, don't know; disagree somewhat; strongly disagree."

These are called *closed-ended* questions and are used most often in survey research. *Open-ended* questions are of the type "Tell us what you like, or dislike, about the *New York Times*." Responses to these questions are much more difficult to code, that is, assign numerical values so that they can be entered into the computer for analysis.

Questionnaires that force a yes-or-no response not only don't offer degree of agreement/disagreement but also sometimes suffer from a biased structuring of the question. This is occasionally deliberate so that the results will support a particular position. Politicians often send out this type of questionnaire. Questions are worded so that the only "responsible" sort of responses are supportive of a certain position. Political PR people risk their credibility when they write news releases based on such "questionnaires," and newswriters should ask for the whole questionnaire, the number sent, to whom they were sent, how many were received and how many were considered "valid," as well as the statistical margin of error.

Statistical analyses

Statistics can be used for any purpose, to anyone's advantage or disadvantage. In other words, you can lie with statistics. No matter what results surveys and polls yield, anyone can use any one of them to his or her advantage.

Suppose a poll of voters last week showed 99 percent saying they would vote for Jones and 1 percent favoring Smith. This week the poll shows Jones 98 percent, Smith 2 percent. Smith now takes a full-page ad:

SUPPORT FOR SMITH DOUBLES IN JUST ONE WEEK!

Independent poll shows twice as many voters now prefer Smith over his opponent!

Is Smith lying? Well, not really. He just isn't telling the whole truth.

Hence you must exercise caution in writing about the results of surveys and polls. In addition, there is the factor called *statistical error*, which comes through sample size. In general, the larger the sample, the smaller the error. The idea behind surveys is that the resulting data should indicate what the entire population from which the sample was drawn thinks and how it will act. The more people you question, the better your ability to tell something about the entire population, in theory.

A sample size of 384 will give an error rate of about 5 percent, at the 95 percent confidence level, whereas a sample size of 1,500 gives an error rate of just over 2.5 percent. What this means to you as reporters is to beware of close calls.

Let's take the Jones–Smith political race again as an example and this time say our poll shows Jones 50 percent, Smith 49 percent, Other 1 percent.

Now, if the sample in the poll were 384, there is a possible statistical error of plus or minus 5 percent. What that means is the actual percentage of voters who will vote for Jones can range from 55 percent to 45 percent, and for Smith it's 54 percent to 44 percent. The election outcome could read Smith 54 percent, Jones 45 percent, Other 1 percent and the poll would still be correct because of the error factor. If, though, the poll shows Jones 98 percent and Smith 2 percent, no amount of error can overcome these differences, and you can safely report Jones will win the election, unless, of course, you did not pull a random sample, or you made gross errors someplace else.

UPI/Bettmann Newsphotos

The point is that when statistics come out very close, you shouldn't try to predict from them. Even with a sample size of 1,500 and an error rate of just over 2.5 percent, the final outcome could still be Smith 50 percent, Jones 49 percent, because that falls within our 1 percent error rate.

However, there's nothing wrong with *reporting* close statistics. You can certainly report the results of a poll that shows Jones 50 percent, Smith 49 percent and write a story about the closeness of the race, the fact that it's too close to call, Jones appears to be leading at this time and so on. If you're handling a story like this for a newspaper's copy desk, just don't headline your story "Jones will win by 1%," or you may find yourself in the history books along with those newspaper writers who predicted Thomas Dewey would beat Harry Truman in the 1948 presidential race.

Although we generally think of politics when we think of polls, polls are also administered on topical questions. Television and radio stations and some newspapers use these as mail-backs or call-ins. Some of these polls are serious, such as opinions on increasing the salaries of lawmakers. Others are just for fun, such as choosing the person you'd like to be stranded on a deserted island with. Which product doctors would choose to have with them on that deserted island is a survey an aspirin company based an advertising campaign on. Some newspapers run person-in-the-street columns featuring the responses of six or seven "ordinary people" to a current-events question (see 3.5).

Media market Markets are defined by audience measurement firms hired by both local and national media to gauge audience characteristics. Information gathered from readership and broadcast audience surveys can be taken to potential advertisers. But these surveys can be used in determining which features are most important to the audience and which ones they'd like to see added.

A newspaper survey might ask readers about the type of news and information that affects them most. Say the results were, in rank order: (1) the economy; (2) jobs and employment; (3) consumer buying information; (4) leisure activities; and (5) the computer. The news department might then plan special feature articles on the local economy, jobs and employment. Another new section could be added on consumer buying tips, and several more reporters could be added to the section titled "Where to Go and What to Do." A special column on computers could be introduced.

Research covers even those audiences not served by the media. Many newspapers are expanding into suburbs and surrounding smaller towns. Research is conducted to find out what kind of news these areas want, and special editions are printed to serve the new subscribers. The same is true for new content areas. For example, when a newspaper decides to start a special business section once a week, a survey discovers what local business people want to read.

Broadcasters depend on periodic surveys called *ratings*. A rating is, simply, the number of sets (radio or TV) tuned to a program divided by the total number of sets in the market. In a market with 100,000 TV sets, if 30,000 are tuned in to a station's 5 p.m. news, its rating will be 30.

3.5 Person-in-the-Street Feature

VOICES FROM ACROSS THE USA

Do you think there should be mandatory seat-belt laws?

NANCY SLOCUM, 22
Student
Chapel Hill, N.C.

Although seat-belt laws can be helpful, wearing seat belts should not be mandatory. If someone does not want to wear a seat belt, that should be their right as long as they're aware of the consequences. We should also be aware that in the event of an accident, wearing a seat belt in the back seat could be detrimental to health.

ROY TASSI, 73
Retired
Lodi, Calif.

I do not like to be told what to do, but I tell myself that it is good wisdom to wear a seat belt. We should use seat belts for the purpose they were intended — to save lives — and not because someone told us to wear them. Wearing seat belts should be as universal and as mandatory as brakes on automobiles.

ELMA VAN BUREN, 31
Homemaker
Fremont, Neb.

It should be left up to individuals whether or not they want to wear seat belts. My parents were once in a pickup truck accident and they would have been killed outright if they *had* been wearing their seat belts. I buckle up every once in a while, but my parents' accident always makes me stop and think.

KELUNNI MENON, 33
Accountant
New York, N.Y.

Statistics have shown that seat belts have saved quite a lot of lives. The safety of one's life carries a higher priority than one's individual rights. It is good to have rights, but a person has to give in to common sense. It is just a matter of time before people will realize that wearing seat belts is for their own good.

MELISSA SALENGO, 21
Student
West Rutland, Vt.

Wearing seat belts should not be mandatory. It is more of a personal choice. The seat belt issue is confusing because seat belts can trap passengers and aid in their deaths, or they can save lives. If you're trapped in a car, it would probably be more dangerous to wear a seat belt because you would be too disoriented to unbuckle it.

LEONARD BROWN, 48
Factory supervisor
Chicago, Ill.

Seat-belt laws should be mandatory in every state. I feel safer when I wear my seat belt. Although it is mandatory to wear seat belts in Illinois, the law is not strongly enforced. If there is going to be a law requiring seat-belt use, then law enforcement officers should not be as lenient as they are with drivers.

JOY GRIFFIN, 31
Department chairman
Silver City, N.M.

The U.S. Department of Transportation tells us that traffic crashes kill more than 30,000 people a year, and nearly half of those killed are under 25 years old. Seat belts can reduce the number of fatalities and injuries by 50 to 60 percent. For these reasons, mandatory seat-belt laws are a good idea.

News departments, especially those of TV stations, must be constantly aware of their programs' ratings, for if the ratings drop—or don't rise—drastic changes in content and personnel often result.

Advertising and public relations people define their audiences by their demographics and psychographics. Demographic information is statistical, such as age, sex, education. Psychographic information is what people have in common despite their demographic characteristics, such as lifestyle. Because advertising and public relations both use the mass media to reach these audiences, they are very interested in the research the media generate. Usually, they also either do independent research or commission it from a research agency.

MAIN POINTS

- Gathering and checking information is essential to writing. Thus all professional writers must be experts in methods of research. Common information sources include books, magazines, newspapers, encyclopedias and dictionaries, almanacs and yearbooks, journals, government documents, electronic data bases, news releases and people.

- Check the medium's files to see what information is on hand before you start making calls.

- Be careful in notetaking.

- Be direct and honest with your sources.

- Writers gathering information in a hurry should follow an organized, systematic strategy. One possible approach to a research problem:

    1. Consult a general encyclopedia.
    2. Consult a specialized encyclopedia.
    3. Seek major magazine articles.
    4. Consult the card catalog.
    5. Examine government documents.
    6. Consult journal articles or major published studies.
    7. Consult newspapers and news magazines.
    8. Interview the appropriate people.

- Surveys are used for many purposes by many organizations today. You will be expected to write about the results of surveys, so you must know something about how surveys are conducted. In some news organizations, reporters are expected to initiate and direct surveys, generally based on some significant issue.

- News organizations also use surveys and polls for information about themselves. Broadcast ratings often directly affect those news departments.

EXERCISES

1. List the reference books you have and make a list of those you think you need to keep right at hand.

2. Find three reports in newspapers or news magazines of the results of a public opinion poll. For each report, make a list of (a) the possible sources of error in the results; (b) the deficiencies or omissions in the publication's presentation of the poll results.

3. Outline a research strategy for a writer about to do an in-depth series on one of these topics:

   - use of cocaine by athletes
   - escalating costs of a college education
   - genetic engineering
   - problems of overpopulation in developing nations

   In constructing the outline, be sure to list the following:

   general reference books

   specialized reference books

   magazines likely to contain relevant articles

   journals likely to contain reports of relevant studies

   electronic data bases that might be useful

   organizations or companies whose executives or PR people might be appropriate to interview

NOTES

1. Susan Gray Borman, "Communication Accuracy in Science News Reporting," *Journalism Quarterly* 55 (Summer 1978):345.

2. Marvin Grosswirth, "Getting the Best from Data Banks," *Personal Computing*, May 1983.

3. Claudia M. Caruana, "Get the Most out of Your Research Time," *Writer's Digest*, May 1982, p. 26.

SUGGESTIONS FOR ADDITIONAL READING

Babbie, Earl. *The Practice of Social Research.* 4th ed. Belmont, Calif.: Wadsworth, 1986. The basic research book for social scientists.

Barzun, Jacques, and Henry F. Graff. *The Modern Researcher.* 4th ed. New York: Harcourt Brace Jovanovich, 1985. A thorough examination of the process of research from the point of view of historians. Though not oriented to journalistic research, many of the same principles apply, especially those discussed in chapters on verification, handling ideas and truth and causation.

Druck, Kalman B., ed. *New Technology and Public Relations.* New York: Foundation for Public Relations Research and Education, 1986.

Horowitz, Lois. *Knowing Where to Look.* New York: Macmillan, 1986.

Kessler, Lauren, and Duncan McDonald. *Uncovering the News.* Belmont, Calif.: Wadsworth, 1987.

Larimi Communications. *Media Directories Set.* 5 West 37th St., New York, N.Y. 10018.

McCormick, Mona. *The New York Times Guide to Reference Materials.* New York: Popular Library, 1985. A convenient paperback that describes general reference sources as well as specialized sources in various fields.

Osgood, Charles, George J. Suci and Percy Tannenbaum. *The Measurement of Meaning.* Urbana: University of Illinois Press, 1967. A classic in research methods.

Rivers, William L. *Finding Facts.* Englewood Cliffs, N.J.: Prentice-Hall, 1975. A guide to information-seeking with excellent advice for the journalist on interviewing, observing and library use as research methods. The section on central sources is an invaluable guide to reference books and journals in various specialized fields.

Webb, Eugene J., Donald T. Campbell, Richard D. Schwartz and Lee Sechrest. *Unobstrusive Measures: Nonreactive Research in the Social Sciences.* 2nd ed. Chicago: Rand McNally, 1981. A good guide to using techniques of observation and some built-in controls.

Weinberg, Steve. *Trade Secrets of Washington Journalists.* Washington: Acropolis, 1981. Excellent suggestions on doing—and finding jobs in—research.

Wimmer, Roger D., and Joseph R. Dominick. *Mass Media Research.* 2nd ed. Belmont, Calif.: Wadsworth, 1987. A good guide to all types of mass communication research.

Writing Basics and Copy Formats

". . . You can find out just about anything you need to know, legitimately. I'm not talking about a dossier on someone who deliberately cultivates an aura of mystery, but about the average citizen."

Louis J. Rose, *St. Louis Post-Dispatch* investigative reporter, in interview with Claire Eyrich, "How to play detective," *Fort Worth Star-Telegram*, May 23, 1982, p. 5C.

"I see the day when our photographers will be shooting videotape, serving both local cable news and our own paper . . . Our reporters will be serving multiple purposes as well. . . . Similarly, our ad reps will be providing full service for their customers — all kinds of 'traditional' newspaper print [ads] as well as cable verbal and visual [ads] and local community over-the-air broadcast verbal and visual. . . .

Advertisers and advertising agencies, public relations firms and traditional broadcasts, all find themselves dealing with the same variety of ways of reaching the variety of publics they need to serve."

Christy C. Bulkeley, vice president, Gannett Foundation.

Leads and Captions

If you want to concentrate on what gets the most attention from mass media audiences, here's your chance: leads and captions. There's substantial research that suggests they provide the information from which audiences draw their conclusions about the story itself.

The lead (pronounced *leed* and sometimes spelled *lede* in the business) is the first sentence or paragraph of the news story—in print and broadcast.

Don't confuse broadcast story leads with *lead-ins*, the sentence or phrase that provides a transition from one news item to the next. *Lead* can also refer to the first story in a newscast or the main story in a newspaper section or in a magazine. And reporters sometimes will say they have a lead on an important story. They don't mean that they have written the first paragraph—they have a tip about a potential story.

Captions, the copy that goes with an illustration (photograph, graphics or other artwork), are also called *cutlines*. In olden days, photographs went through an acid-etching engraving process and were called *cuts*. The lines that went with them were therefore called cutlines.

But something that hasn't changed is that audiences pay more attention to these brief sentences than anything else you write. They won't get to anything else in your story if you don't capture their attention with the lead. Captions for pictures that go with stories give you another chance to draw readers into the story. Captions are also written for "wild art"—a photo or graphic that has no accompanying story. These are used not only to liven up the look of a printed page but to pull the reader into the page so that other items have a better chance of being read.

LEADS Many students and professional writers consider leads the most difficult part of a story to write. Actually, that is mostly apprehension resulting from an acute awareness of the significance of the lead to the story.

People talk in leads all the time: "Did you hear Jack Smith totaled his car last night? Yes, on the North/South Freeway, about 10 o'clock. Slid on the ice and hit the Sixth Street overpass. He wasn't hurt, but that Mustang's not going anywhere again." All that's missing is who Jack Smith is, but in personal conversation, the individual generally is known. If not, the conversational lead would start like this: "Remember Jack Smith, that business major from Phoenix who used to study with us? Well, he totaled his car last night." The conversation may continue about who was or wasn't with him, how he got home and so on. But someone overhearing the conversation would already know the basic information. Only the details are left.

Of course, had Jack Smith been killed or injured, the telling would be different: "Have you heard that Jack Smith was killed last night? His car slid on the ice on the North/South Freeway and hit the Sixth Street overpass." What would be described in a conversation to follow would be whether he died on impact or later—at the scene, on the way to the hospital or at the hospital. You'd also tell whether anyone was with him and whether there were any other circumstances surrounding the accident—other cars involved, and so on.

If the event had occurred some time ago, but the news was just now being conveyed, the conversation might go like this: "Did you know about Jack Smith's getting killed in a car accident? He hit some ice on the North/South Freeway and slid into the Sixth Street overpass. It happened last Friday night. He died immediately." Again, details would follow.

Look at those leads. What orders the priorities? It's the most important fact among the *who, what, when, where* and *how*. You, as the writer, have to make that determination, based on the audience—what they already know about the information; the importance of the information to them; the timeliness of the information in terms of delivery to them; the outcome or the significance of the information to them. You know this instinctively, but as a writer you have to practice it consciously.

Using the previous example, you can't imagine someone saying: "Last Friday night there was a bad accident on the North/South Freeway. It was at the Sixth Street overpass. There was some ice on the freeway, because of the overpass, I guess. A car hit the ice and slid into the overpass. It was a Ford Mustang. As a matter of fact, it was Jack Smith's car. Remember him? He was that business major from Phoenix who used to study with us. Dreadful accident. He was killed." Someone hearing such a rendition is likely to say, "Why didn't you tell me that *first*?"

Leads as story patterns   The lead is more than a hook to capture the attention of your audience, though, and it's more than their news digest; it is your story theme and format.

The lead is supposed to answer the major questions of a story: who, what, when, where, why and how. The order in which you introduce those elements indicates their significance. That ordering of significance provides you with a pattern for the development of the story: the inverted pyramid style.

While the structure is not followed slavishly, and shouldn't be, it exists because it is useful. It summarizes for the audience the most important elements in the story. It also makes it easy for copy editors cutting stories hurriedly to fit a layout. They expect to be able to cut from the bottom up and still preserve the meat of the story.

Some texts and some professionals still say the lead of a news story should give *all* the important elements (who, what, when, where, why and how) in the first sentence—a tight one of 16 to 25 words. This approach to newswriting originated during the Civil War, when battlefield correspondents sent their dispatches back to their newspapers by telegraph. The telegraph lines were frequently cut during transmission, so reporters developed the technique of getting *all* of the crucial facts across in the first sentence. Details came later, if the line was still open.

Severed telegraph lines rarely present a problem today. But conveying the news to readers in a readable package does. Trying to include *all* of the significant facts in the lead usually results in a long, hard-to-read sentence. It's better to write a shorter sentence that identifies the *single most important point of the story*, leaving the less critical details for later.

The lead, then, can refer to the first paragraph (or *graph*, in newspaper lingo), which might contain only one sentence but could have two or three. In feature stories the lead may be several paragraphs long. For straight news stories, though, it's convenient to think of the lead as just the first sentence. And it's usually best to start a new paragraph after that sentence. Experienced writers will sometimes break this rule when dealing with a complicated story. The second paragraph may answer the remaining who, what, when, where, why and how elements, as well as serve as a tie-in to the body of the story.

The lead of the news story (not always the feature) gives the conclusion right away. It tells the main point of the story, its significance, immediately. You wouldn't write:

> The polls opened at 7 a.m. Tuesday as area voters turned out to elect a new mayor.

A good lead would give the results of the election:

> Jane Smith won a landslide victory in the mayor's race Tuesday.

Determining which of the six critical elements to use in the lead is a challenge. Choose the three or four that alone tell the story best. Follow with the other two or three in a transitional sentence, one that will best connect the lead to the body of the story.

Usually the *who* is essential and should be in the lead. *What* is also frequently one of the most important points to include. *Where, when, how* and *why* will be part of some leads but not others.

When Neil Armstrong and Edwin Aldrin walked on the moon, the lead of the *New York Times* story was "Men have landed and walked on the moon." The *where* was obviously the key point of the story.

LEAD: Who What When Where Why How   16 to 25 words

TIE-IN: One sentence connecting *one* element of the lead to the body.

BODY: Development of most important of the WWWWWH elements
         of lead
         Second most important element of WWWWWH
         Further development of most important element
         Other elements
         The least important facts of the story—nothing new introduced

LEAD 5W&H

Tie-In

Most Important

2nd Important

Other

Least

4.1 Traditional Inverted Pyramid

Time is sometimes the focus of a lead, as in anniversary stories. A story about a missing child began: "More than a year has passed since 9-year-old Laura Savillas disappeared, but her parents' hopes are kept alive by occasional reports of sightings."

How leads are sometimes a challenge to write, since that aspect of a story is generally more complex. A story about plant pests in a suburban city began: "Small killers are stalking city plants, so Arlington has hired equally small hunters —thousands upon thousands of ladybugs."

A story's *why* is also complex and seldom the most important element, but it can be. "Citing rapidly dwindling foreign reserves, Brazil President José Sarney announced Friday that his country would suspend interest payments." The tie-in sentence from the lead to the body of the story was this: "Brazil's $108.8 billion is the world's largest foreign debt."

Fortunately, the most important element of a story is often the most interesting one. The writer must just make sure that the most important element is presented in an interesting way.

The following lead gives the most important point of the story, but it doesn't sound very interesting:

LEAD: Major theme, could be significance of event, rather than fact

                May be two sentences

                May not include all 5Ws&H

TIE-IN: The leftovers of the 5Ws&H not mentioned in lead

1st Graph: Explication of lead—incident, quote, meaning or background of event—how something came to be

2nd Graph: Additional information about most important fact of lead

                Something to give credibility or significance to lead information

3rd Graph: Secondary theme or supporting documentation for lead

4th Graph: Any other details, in order of significance to lead

<u>LEAD</u>

Documentation or Explication=Background or History

Elaboration of Lead

Secondary Theme
or
Supporting Facts, Quotes

Least Significant
details

4.2 Modified Pyramid

Campus organizations will compete in the annual blood drive next week.

With a little imagination, the writer could have said the same thing in an attention-grabbing way:

Campus organizations will compete next week in a contest sure to draw blood.

For a story about a nutritionist, a student could have written a lead like this:

Ruth Ann Franklin, a professor of home economics, has been concerned with nutrition for most of her life.

That would have been accurate, but dull. Instead, the writer opened with something livelier:

> Nutrition is more than just food for thought for Ruth Ann Franklin. It's what her life has centered on since childhood.

Hard-news stories especially need to provoke attention, and all it takes is imagination.

> Budget deficits may put an 11 p.m. curfew on most campus buildings, says Provost Jane Taylor.
> Common use areas like the student union, library and fitness center may eventually be included to save on utility costs, she added.

Readers want to know what's special about a story, what makes it worth reading. The writer should ask, How is this event different from other events like it? What sets it apart? Is it the first time something like this has happened? Was more money spent on this than on any other such project? Is it the only time this century that it snowed in May? Whatever is unique, out of the ordinary, even bizarre should be in the lead. Public relations writers particularly strive for this in their copy because they know the lead must sell the story to the editor.

One warning: The lead must not mislead. In their zeal to attract attention, some writers go overboard. You should emphasize what's interesting, but not at the expense of accuracy. Stories with "the only," "the first" or other exclusive claims bear careful checking.

It would be inappropriate to use a lead like this with the story that follows it:

> It's confirmed—everything causes cancer.
> A new study has concluded that it is impossible for anyone to completely avoid cancer-causing substances in the environment.

The lead is certainly attention-getting, but it's not borne out by the story, which says only that people cannot avoid substances that cause cancer, not that every substance causes cancer.

Types of print news leads

The following types of leads are some of the most common found in the print media.

- *Summary*—generally used for straight news stories.

  > Five TCU geology students and two faculty members were injured Sunday night when their van slid out of control on icy roads in the Texas Panhandle.

- *Contrast*—provides insight and sets the tone for the story.

  > A prospective faculty member responding to an ad for a position paying $21,000 will find that salary will not make it possible to qualify for a mortgage in most U.S. cities.

- *Question* — a way to get readers involved.

  Will the student vote affect state elections? Not if students are not registered to cast their ballots.

  Representatives from the Wisconsin Attorney General's office will be in the Student Center on Thursday and Friday to register all students who claim Wisconsin as a legal residence.

- *Direct address* — uses personal pronoun, *you*, to involve reader immediately.

  You wouldn't expect to be held up by a snake-toting robber, would you?

  That's exactly what happened to a convenience store clerk who was confronted by two teen-agers carrying a three-foot-long snake.

  Their "take" was one six-pack of beer. They left the snake.

- *Background* — sets the scene for the action to be told.

  Cafeteria lines are short this week as fasting students contribute their meal money to the International Hunger Week Fund.

- *Picture or description* — a way to stimulate reader interest in the storyline.

  Sitting in the dorm window, the tiny calico cat looked almost like a stuffed toy. But she wasn't. She was an illegal resident of Shirley Dorm.

- *Punch* — quickly hits the reader with something of interest; can be an exclamation.

  In the restaurant business, it's called the Vat of Death.

  Every day restaurants churn out bucketfuls of old grease that, because of health standards, cannot be thrown out with the garbage or poured into the sewer system. Instead, the grease is stored in 55-gallon drums and is usually kept somewhere out back. (The story goes on to explain that some people buy the grease and refine it into something called yellow grease used in cattle feed and cosmetics.)

- *Quotation* — a common feature lead, and often a speech story lead.

  "My plane is taking off without me," shouted a student pilot to his instructor as he dashed down the runway after the runaway Cessna 140.

- *Freak* — whimsical feature leads that might begin with the lyrics of a song, a poem or something unusual.

  Mash the Ash
  Can the Trash
  City park superintendent Marilyn Abbott penned this couplet and proposed that it be stenciled on park garbage cans.

Guidelines for print news leads

Certain principles can help guide writers in framing their leads properly.

Be brief. The lead should be direct and to the point. You can give the details in subsequent paragraphs.

How long should a lead be? That's a controversial question. But it's probably safe to say this: the shorter the better. Leads on Associated Press stories average about 25 words (some are surely much longer than the average). Wire services write longer leads because some papers may want to use only the lead or first two paragraphs of a story.

The best length for a lead is probably 20 words or less. You won't be able to write a good lead that short for every story, though. Use as many words as you need to convey the main point and get the reader's attention. Just make sure each of those words is really needed.

The following 52-word lead, which appeared in a major daily, is too long because of unnecessary information and excessive detail:

> The United States has stockpiled 215 million barrels of crude oil in underground salt caverns in Texas and Louisiana, yet has no plan on how to use the reserves in the event of an import interruption such as the 1973 Arab oil embargo or the 1979 Iranian crisis, a federal study shows.

Here is the 29-word rewrite suggested by that paper's writing critic:

> The United States has an emergency stash of 215 million barrels of crude oil in Texas and Louisiana salt caverns, but no plan for its use in an emergency.

Another example from the same paper:

> Owners of the Comanche Peak nuclear power plant, as a result of a ruling Tuesday by a three-member panel of the U.S. Atomic Safety and Licensing Board in Fort Worth, must prove they are financially capable of operating the twin 1,150-megawatt reactors in a safe manner.

A rewrite:

> Owners of the Comanche Peak nuclear power plant must prove to the U.S. Atomic Safety and Licensing Board that they are financially capable of operating the plant safely.[1]

Be specific.   The biggest fault in most beginning newswriters' leads is vagueness. The lead must tell the reader exactly what the main point is, not just hint at it.

A reporter covering a psychologist's speech about depression would not want to write a lead like this, for example:

> Lyn Abramson, psychologist and author, spoke here Thursday.

The next version isn't much better:

> Lyn Abramson, psychologist and author, spoke about depression here Thursday.

That gives some idea of what the talk was about, but it's still not specific enough. What did the psychologist *say* about depression? What was the most important point?

A student writer actually covering such a speech came up with this lead:

> Depressed people may have a more accurate view of reality than people who are not depressed, says psychologist and author Lyn Abramson.

Now, at last, the reader knows what the point is.

It may sometimes take several rewrites to get a lead that focuses sharply enough on the point of the story. Consider this lead, written by a student from a fact sheet on a speech:

> Dr. Rodney Mayhew, state director of public health, spoke to 89 members of the American College of Angiology, meeting at the Alamo Hotel last night.

Another student did a little better.

> The state director of public health, Dr. Rodney Mayhew, released his analysis of the patterns of coronary patients at a meeting last night.

Now we know the topic. But we still don't know what he said. The lead should give the *result* of his analysis, not just the fact that he did one.

One student tried:

> Dr. Rodney Mayhew, state director of public health, said that coronary patients' trouble is self-induced.

This is better, but the statement is still vague. Self-induced in what way?

Two students did a reasonably good job of summarizing the point in their leads:

> The conscientious working man is a good candidate for a heart attack, says Dr. Rodney Mayhew.

> Young men holding high-pressure jobs may be prime candidates for heart attacks, says Dr. Rodney Mayhew.

Both of these leads tell the reader right off what the point is: Working under pressure can lead to heart attacks. The second lead is a little better than the first: it's more explicit about the type of work ("high-pressure") and specifies that the doctor is talking about young men.

Identify the news.   The lead must give the most newsworthy of the specific points; it must answer the reader's question, What's the news in this story? Here's a lead that clearly does not answer the question of identification:

Hindus make up 83 percent of India's population, Muslims 11 percent and Christians 2.6 percent.

Certainly that's specific, but it's a "so what" lead. The information could be found in reference books. What is the news?

Watch question and quotation leads.   While these can attract attention, they can also be pointless. The lead should give answers, so don't pose a question unless it is the major problem or quandary of the story. And the lead should give answers to the question clearly, concisely and directly as well as explain why it is at the core of the story. Rarely does anyone speak well enough to provide a suitable quotation that is precisely the key element of a story. Unless the quote captures the gist of the story, don't use it just to be different.
It would be a mistake to begin a story like this:

What is the most likely site for the 1988 Republican Convention?
From all indications, it will be Denver.

The first sentence is a waste of space. Come right out with a positive statement.

All signs point to Denver as the likely site for the 1988 Republican Convention.

Direct quotations present a similar problem. Here's how a student began a story about a talk by a military-science professor.

"With the gross imbalance in defense spending between the United States and the Soviet Union, there is indeed potential for war in Europe."

The writer made one obvious mistake: not attributing the quotation. But she made another one as well: She assumed that she couldn't write as well as the professor talked. The professor's point could have been condensed, clarified and presented much more directly:

War in Europe is possible because the Soviet Union is spending more for defense than the United States is, a military-science professor says.

Give proper attribution.   The desire for brevity sometimes causes writers to drop an attribution from a lead. Thus a story occasionally begins something like this:

The United States must immediately stop sending foreign aid to nations in Africa, South America, Europe and the Far East.
That's the opinion of Joe Jones, candidate for mayor.

Without attribution, the sentence reads as though the information is factual. Whenever the lead is a matter of opinion, attribution is essential.

Naming the information source is often necessary so that readers can judge how much credence to give it. For example, if a speaker declares that coffee drinking does not present a danger to pregnant women, attribution in the lead is essential — it makes a big difference whether the speaker is a coffee-industry executive or the state director of public health. For the sake of brevity, it isn't always necessary to give both name and title. You might write:

> Drinking coffee is not as hazardous for pregnant women as some reports have indicated, the state public health director said today.

Be timely. Deciding what the news is in a story is a matter of judgment, involving a consideration of all the characteristics of news discussed in Chapter 1. One of the most important of those characteristics is the time element, and it is more significant for broadcast news than for print, as you'll see in the discussion that follows about the differences between print and broadcast leads. This also is the element that news editors say is most ignored by public relations writers trying to get their news releases placed. *News is new.* Because the time element is so crucial, it is frequently included in the lead — especially if the time is *today.*

Leads with *today* usually appear only in afternoon papers, though. A morning paper's final deadline is generally about midnight the night before, so a story with a *today* time element is rarely possible, unless it is an advance. For example: "A decision about Arlington's new police chief will be made today."

The *Associated Press Stylebook* says to use "today, this morning, this afternoon, tonight, etc. as appropriate" in stories for afternoon papers. In other cases, use the day of the week. *Yesterday* is considered taboo by many editors, especially in the lead: It calls attention to the staleness of the news. According to the *Associated Press Stylebook*, it should be used only in direct quotations or in phrases where it refers to the general past: "Yesterday when we were young."

If a story breaks in the morning paper, the lead in the afternoon paper on the same day will have a new angle. Consider this lead appearing in a Thursday morning paper:

> Pennsylvania Electric Service Co. will file a request for an $88 million systemwide rate increase Thursday with the city of Scranton and the Public Utilities Commission in Harrisburg.

The news was the filing of the rate-increase request. But the wire story written for Thursday's afternoon papers included fresh information in the lead — the estimated monthly increase for the company's customers:

> Customers of Pennsylvania Electric Service Co. would pay an estimated $5 more monthly under an $88 million rate hike request filed Thursday by the utility.

When an event happened the previous day but hasn't yet been reported, the lead should contain a *today* time element, if possible. For example, the day after an amusement park accident, an afternoon paper would not use a lead announcing the accident as though it had just occurred. Some new information would be emphasized in the lead; the background would be given in the following paragraphs. Instead of saying "One person died after a sky bucket accident Sunday," the lead might be:

> Investigators said today that they could not determine the cause of a sky bucket accident that killed one man at the state fair Sunday.

Sometimes you will have to write about an event that occurred several days ago (a particular problem on weekly or semiweekly papers). In these cases the lead must rely on some interesting angle. A story about a mayor's plan to renovate part of the city began this way:

> The boy who grew up to be mayor of Fort Worth went back to his old neighborhood last week and announced a program to save it from further deterioration.

Another approach to the second-day lead is to emphasize some detail not reported in earlier accounts. When reports of the atomic bomb explosion at Hiroshima appeared in a Los Angeles newspaper two days after the event, the lead was built on a detail not available in the first accounts:

> The single bomb dropped on Hiroshima completely destroyed 4.1 square miles of the city in a cataclysmic blast.

Another timeliness problem in lead writing is the temptation to begin a story at the beginning, in the distant past. Consider this lead:

> Two years ago a professor complained about discrimination by campus fraternities, leading to an investigation by the Student Organization Committee.

The story is about the results of the investigation. The results are the news. This sentence belonged further down in the story, as background.

That doesn't mean you should never use an old time element in the lead. Sometimes the contrast between the past and now is the significance of the story. Here's an example of a two-sentence lead with two time elements:

> Erratic heartbeats that led to cardiac arrests almost killed Magellon Walker twice in February. In May, doctors deliberately started the spasms again— to save his life.

Getting started. Beginning writers who have difficulty ordering the items for a lead might benefit from making a physical list of the who, what, when, where, why and how and assigning priorities to them. Then start to structure a lead from the principal elements:

> WHO: The president of the university
> WHAT: New alcohol policy
> WHEN: Goes into effect immediately
> WHERE: On all university property
> WHY: New host liability law
> HOW: Meetings with residence hall officers, student government officers, student organization officers and sponsors

Priorities are:

1. What: no alcohol

2. When: immediately

3. Where: all university property

4. Why: new host liability law

5. Who: university president

6. How: meetings

Now you can start:

> No alcohol/immediate/all university property.
>
> Host liability law/university president/meetings.

First draft:

> "No alcohol" starting today anywhere on university property because of the new host liability law, said President William S. Moore, who will take the word to the university community through meetings with resident hall, student government and student organization officers and their sponsors.

Second draft to clear up major problems:

1. Too long,

2. Not clear,

3. Awkward, uninteresting and doesn't involve reader.

Next effort:

> You can't drink or serve alcohol any more on this campus.
> The new host liability law is the reason, says President William S. Moore, who will be discussing the new ruling with student organization officers and their sponsors.

Problem: Still too long.

> Alcohol is no longer allowed on university property. That's the message President William S. Moore will be giving student organization officers and their sponsors.
> Moore cites the new host liability law as the reason.

Close, but dull. Likely to be missed by readers.

Another try:

> Prohibition is back, at least on university property, as a result of the new host liability law.
> President William S. Moore will meet with student officers and organization sponsors to explain the new policy.

And yet one more:

> You can't drink or serve alcoholic drinks on university property any more. (12 words)
> A host liability law is the reason, said President William S. Moore, who will be meeting with student organization officers to explain. (20 words—name is 1 word; total of 32 words)

Can you improve?

Broadcast leads   After working for years on the newspaper wire of UPI, Charles Collingwood was hired by CBS's most famous correspondent, Edward R. Murrow, to write for CBS radio. In later years, Collingwood (who himself went on to become a correspondent) was fond of relating this anecdote about his initial exposure to his new environment:

I was fascinated by the difference between writing for this new, bumptious medium of radio and conforming to the canons of wire service journalism. So even before I went on the CBS payroll, I went around to Murrow's office and pored over his script files, looking for clues. "It seems to me," I said, "that your formula is to write short, vivid declarative sentences, using dependent clauses only to vary the pace or for ornamentation." Ed looked at me in some surprise and said, "Oh, is *that* what I do. I never thought about it."[2]

The lead sentence is as important in a broadcast news story as it is in a print story. Its primary purpose is to catch the listener's attention.

A good broadcast lead, like a good print lead, doesn't contain all of the facts of who, what, when, where, why and how; it may contain only one or two at most. Still, that doesn't mean the broadcast lead doesn't convey information. Many broadcast leads are as informative as they are catchy. Catchy doesn't mean that broadcast style is headline style, except in the headline segments of newscasts.

Some writers insist on never using the past tense in a broadcast news lead. The philosophy behind this rule is that broadcast news is immediate, or can be. Almost all broadcast news can be delivered to an audience at about the same time the event is happening. And these writers maintain that *any* story can be updated to the present in the lead. If Congress passed a bill yesterday raising taxes, the broadcast lead might be "Your taxes will soon be going up."

The present perfect tense is a good one for broadcast newswriters to use in leads, for it implies some immediacy, even though the action occurred in the past. Thus you would write *has been* instead of *was, have been* instead of *were* and so on. If someone asks you "Where have you been?" you could answer "Oh, I was in the Caribbean last month." But if you reply "Oh, I've been to the Caribbean," it sounds like you just got back this morning.

The best rule for writing broadcast leads that convey a sense of immediacy is *Get a current angle*. If a fire destroyed an apartment complex last night, call the fire department and find out what's happening today—right now. Is the cause of the fire known? Are the firefighters still at the scene? Is arson suspected? Will the owners rebuild? If you do that, you have the basis for an updated story and a new lead.

Broadcasters update leads constantly during the day—at least on the hour, so the story sounds fresh. The trouble with that practice is that the genuine emphasis of the story can become distorted unintentionally. You have to rewrite while remaining faithful to the original story if you have no new information to add.

Types of broadcast leads

Here are a few general categories of leads used at all TV and radio stations. A particular type of story might dictate which type is to be used, but often it's at the writer's discretion.

- *Traditional leads.* Traditional leads are also called "hard-news leads" or "main-point leads." An example:

    Mayor Preston Kindrick announced this morning he will not seek a second term of office.

    A lead like that is certainly hard news, and it is certainly the main point of the story to follow, which will probably tell a little about why the mayor made this decision, what he plans to do next, when he will begin to do it and so on.

- *Angle leads*. Often broadcast newswriters look for an unusual angle to catch the listener's attention. There are several ways to do this.
  Try leading with a question:

  > Do you own a 1981 General Motors car? If you do, then it may be recalled.

  There's a good chance many in the audience own such a car and will listen up. But don't get cute or overdo it. Don't write a lead like:

  > Do you have AIDS? If you do, here's some medical news for you.

  That's going too far; be sure to stay within the bounds of taste.
- *Umbrella leads*. Umbrella, or comprehensive, leads occur in some complex stories. They're also used to tie together two or more stories of the same type. Here's one example.

  > There was some good news and some bad news on the economic front today.

  The story went on to say that while the jobless rate dropped slightly in the past month, the inflation rate was up. Other examples: "Bad weather hit the entire nation today," for a roundup story about the various forms the bad weather took in different parts of the country; "City council has a full agenda for tonight's meeting," with all the items on the agenda given in the story.
- *Throwaway leads*. This type seems to be a favorite of many broadcast newswriters. It often doesn't give much information at all, but it's effective in getting attention. "Welfare recipients got some good news today" is a throwaway lead.

Guidelines for writing broadcast leads

The best way to begin is to imagine that you're trying to tell the story to a friend who's hurrying to catch a bus that's ready to pull away. Say the words aloud to see whether they sound right. Write them. Be sure you've used personal pronouns and contractions. See whether you can say the same thing in half the words. Start getting rid of all clauses. If it's still too long, start looking at phrases you can delete. Now read it aloud. Try to imagine you're hearing it for the first time. Would you know what it meant, or is something essential missing? To practice, tape your copy and listen to it an hour or so after you've written it. How does it sound coming to you on the tape recorder? If your copy passes these tests, let someone else read it. If you get a puzzled look, start over. You don't have a lead yet.

Getting started.   Take the story on university alcohol policy to work on.

First draft:

> The university's new alcoholic beverage policy is now in effect. The rule is simple: you can't drink or serve alcohol on university property. A new host liability law is the reason, the president says. (35 words, nearly 20 seconds; too long.)

Try this:

> There's a new rule about drinking or serving alcohol on university property. It's forbidden. A new host liability law is responsible for the change, the president says. (27 words: better, but too long, and "host liability law" is going to be difficult for the ear.)

Again:

> A new university rule says you can't drink or serve alcohol on the campus. A liability law prompted the change, the president says. (23 words, about 16–18 seconds, depending on the announcer.)

Can you do better?

CAPTIONS   Some photojournalists are under the misconception that they don't have to deal with the written word. But the photographer must take down the basic who, what, where and when about the photos, because he or she may be the only representative of the news organization on the scene. For a story, a photographer *may* work with the reporter, but he or she cannot depend on the reporter's getting the caption information even then. The photojournalist, still camera or TV, has to think in two dimensions—words and pictures.

Wild art   For wild art, art without a story, the caption writer has a special responsibility to tell the reader enough. If it's a seasonal picture, such as children enjoying a sprinkler on the first official day of summer, explaining the photo sometimes seems to detract from it. But the children and the location should be identified, and the readers may need to be reminded that it's the first official day of summer, which is why the picture is there. See 4.3–4.5 for other examples of wild art.

4.3 Seasonal Wild Art

Robert Lebow of Fort Worth is sprayed by friends at the Wet 'N' Wild water park in Arlington on Tuesday. The 5-year-old and his friends were playing with the park's water cannons.

Gary Dunkin, *The Dallas Morning News*

Art with a story   Sometimes a picture will be on a page alone but isn't really wild art. The story it accompanies is somewhere else in the newspaper. This is quite common with special events. The royal wedding picture (4.6a carries a deep cation ending with "refers" (pronounced REEFers) that tell where to find related stories (4.6b).

The questions to ask about writing any caption are: How much space is there? (This is the ad copywriter's constant query.) How much explanation does the art need? What are all the facts — who, what, when, where, why and how?

Getting good facts and photos means you can pull facts from a story, write them into a caption and let the picture and caption tell that portion; thus the story can be shorter. Or you can use the caption and picture to emphasize some element in the story, which will also carry the same information, written in a different way. Still another option is to use the photo and its caption as a sidebar, something that relates to the story but functions better as its own unit, rather than integrated into the story.

Paula Nelson, *The Dallas Morning News*

4.4 Event Wild Art

Mr. Bear greets Jesus Jimenez, 7, at the United Way Affiliates Fair in Bell Plaza downtown Tuesday. This fair coincided with Southwestern Bell's United Way fund drive.

4.5

Stand-alone graphics call for clear, informative captions. (Reprinted by permission of *The Wall Street Journal,* © Dow Jones & Company, Inc. 1986. All rights reserved.)

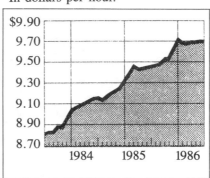

Hourly Earnings

In dollars per hour.

AVERAGE HOURLY PAY of factory workers in June fell to $9.70 from a revised $9.71 the preceding month, the Labor Department reports.

The important point to remember in writing captions is to be sure the tone of the copy is appropriate for the picture. As with leads, resist being gimmicky or cute. Look at the caption for the royal wedding (4.6a). The tone is neither familiar nor reverent. It is informative. People in the United States might not remember which one of the sons this is, and perhaps they didn't know that Fergie is really Sarah.

Public relations people often are the suppliers of information for captions, as they probably were for the United Way photo (4.4). They often furnish photographs suitable for wild art as well. The photos must be of especially high quality, because the photo editor will be asked to approve them. Also, identify the photo well and give office and home phone numbers where an editor can find someone to talk to if necessary. Be sure the suggested caption is attached with rubber cement, not tape or clips, that the photo itself has identification on the back (rubber stamp or felt-tip pen) in the border of the print, not on the print. Write the caption in AP style.

4.6a Stand-Alone Photo with "Refers"

Royal newlyweds
Prince Andrew, Queen Elizabeth's second son, and his bride, Sarah, leave Westminster Abbey on Wednesday after a wedding ceremony seen by 300 million people worldwide. (Related stories on 8A, 33A, 37A and 38A). *The Dallas Morning News.*

Wide World Photos

4.6b Stories Related to 4.6a

Couples' nuptials get royal results

By Mercedes Olivares
Staff Writer of The News

It was about 4,800 miles and worlds apart from Westminster Abbey, but couples getting married Wednesday at the Dallas County Courthouse within hours of England's regal ceremony came out feeling like Andrew and Sarah.

"You don't have to be in charge of a country to feel like royalty," said Dale Murray, 27, a Tulsa County deputy sheriff who was married before Justice of the Peace Robert Cole.

"She's my queen," he said, pointing to his bride, Monica Angieri, 28.

Instead of a cruise on the Britannica, the Oklahoma couple will honeymoon on the log flume at Six Flags Over Texas before returning home.

And although the couples tying the knot in Dallas did without British pomp, "we're having a jolly good

ROYAL WEDDING	
■ Sarah, Andrew wed.	**8A**
■ Commoners' fanfare.	**8A**
■ Weddings for $25.	**37A**
■ Plaza gala.	**38A**

time," said Robert Burnam, 43, a general contractor who selected Wednesday as a wedding date because it was "very convenient."

"Actually, they (Andrew and Sarah) chose to do it the same day as we did," he added. "We planned to get married about six months ago."

Burnam and his bride, Eve Harris-Troost, 47, were dressed in Dallas chic: She wore a bright blue pantsuit, gold Porsche sunglasses, sandals and gold chains. He sported a white polo shirt, a Rolex watch and cowboy boots.

Both have been married before and have seven children between them.

Asked about their honeymoon plans, Burnam said, "It depends on how the afternoon goes."

The Dallas and British ceremonies differed in other ways.

Instead of several hundred television crews recording the event, one couple brought an instant camera—that didn't work. In place of a floral bouquet, one young bride carried a manila envelope with the marriage license inside.

None of the grooms wore a suit, but several of the brides wore lace, although it was usually blue, and sometimes red. Instead of a postwedding breakfast, one couple ran through the cafeteria line in the courthouse.

But like the royal couple, all of their Dallas counterparts cooed, giggled or smiled.

"He treats me like a queen," echoed 25-year-old Sandra L. Landrum, after marrying Donald Ray Furr, 45, in a two-minute ceremony in Cole's chamber.

The new Mrs. Furr said she was reminded by her mother of the royal wedding taking place on the same day as their marriage.

"We should remember this, because we're getting married the same day as important people today," she said.

Christopher Meregini, 27, said he felt the same way.

"I thought if my marriage certificate could read the same as the prince's, what's wrong with that?" said Meregini, a native of Nigeria. "But I always feel like royalty."

Donald Ray Furr gets a big hug from his new bride, Sandra L. Landrum. Photo: Juan Garcia, *The Dallas Morning News.*

4.6b (continued)

Bride and groom can marry royally for $25 in Dallas

Just what did Prince Andrew and Sarah Ferguson get Wednesday for sticking to tradition? Carriage rides, blaring horns, pealing bells and a fruitcake cooked by the Royal Navy.

What if they had eloped to the Colonies, particularly a Western outpost?

Cindy and Steve—"no last names, please," she asks—scheduled their ceremony Wednesday night at Angelic Weddings in Northeast Dallas. Cindy says that "in all honesty, no, we didn't think about getting married on the same day as the royal wedding."

In Grand Prairie at the Chapel of Love, a gray frame house with red trim, H. Eddy Heldt, who acquired his doctor of divinity degree four years ago from Kings College in Des Moines, Iowa, was prepared to do any wedding up royally.

For $25 any couple—royal, common or otherwise—can get *The Wed-*ding *March* as performed by cassette recorder, wedding arches and a ceremony viewed by up to about 50 people.

And, Heldt says, for the same $25 a couple gets one free renewal of their vows and "free counseling service for people as long as they want it after they're married."

And, unlike the British press, nobody measures the bride's hips.

Reprinted by permission of *The Dallas Morning News*

4.6b (continued)

They're there—in spirit
Transplanted Britons toast royal nuptials

By Joe Drape
Staff Writer of the *News*

John F. Rhodes, *The Dallas Morning News*

So what if it was a rerun?

Everyone loves a wedding. Especially transplanted Britons who after years of living in Texas would gladly turn in their spurs for a royal coach ride 'round Buckingham Palace.

"I just do cry whenever I hear the pipes play," said British emigre Mary Taylor, who has called Dallas her home now for 18 years. "It's so . . . so British. This whole wedding makes me homesick."

Such were the sentiments among scores of loyal—in heart at least—British subjects who attended a gala centering around a videotaped replay of the royal wedding of Prince Andrew and Sarah Ferguson Wednesday night at the Plaza of the Americas Hotel.

The hotel, which is owned by

4.6b (continued)

Britain's Trusthouse Forte Hotels, responded with a decidedly authentic rendition of a royal wedding reception for the more than 600 guests.

Beefeaters served as parking valets, impeccably uniformed London bobbies patrolled the ballroom and a lavish spread of English fare was served up, topped off with a 500-pound fruitcake.

"We've tried to create, in spirit at least, a royal palace atmosphere," said hotel General Manager Wolfgang Von Baumbach, who said a portion of the proceeds from the $25-per-person affair would be donated to the Variety Club Children's Charities at the request of the royal couple.

Von Baumbach and British Consul David Hallett offered toasts to Queen Elizabeth II, President Reagan and "to the royal couple, the Duke and Duchess of York."

All were answered with muffled "Hear, hears" from the nattily attired crowd—double-breasted pin-striped suits for the men, stylish hats for the women.

When the ballroom wasn't booming with the sounds of blue-faced bagpipers, it was abuzz with curses for that "bloody awful" British press.

"They'll write anything," said Daphne Wolfson, now of Plano, referring to Fleet Street's pre-wedding debate over Ms. Ferguson's hip size —a mere 39 inches, or a larger 41. "I know some Texas women who are equally large and impressive."

Ms. Wolfson added that she might be a spot cranky because she had been up since 4 a.m. watching the live broadcast of the royal wedding "with my tea set and tissues."

There was at least one confused Texan at Wednesday's royal wedding reception.

Hotel security guard Tim Moore, outfitted in a London bobby's gear, was asked what a bobby did at a party.

"Stand around and look good," said Moore, eyes staring straight ahead. "It adds to the flavor, don't you think?"

Reprinted by permission of *The Dallas Morning News*

An Associated Press model laserphoto machine called AP Dataphoto used exclusively by foreign members for photo transmissions.

Wide World Photos

MAIN POINTS

- When writing print leads:

  1. Include the most important and most interesting aspects of the story.
  2. Tell the main point.
  3. Be brief.
  4. Be specific.
  5. Identify the news.
  6. Be sure to use attribution.
  7. Watch question and quote leads to be sure you get the gist of the story.
  8. Be timely.

- When writing broadcast leads, keep it catchy and current. Broadcast leads are not headlines. Write in headline style only for the headline segment of the newscast.

- When writing captions, tell the reader why the art is there and what it means. Keep the tone of the caption appropriate to the art. When art appears with a story, use the caption to add information or to emphasize, not merely to repeat.

EXERCISES

1. Find examples of the different types of leads from a local newspaper. Identify good and bad leads. What makes the good ones work? Can you make the bad ones better?

2. See if you can improve the question and direct-quote leads by changing them to a summary lead. Decide in each case why the type of lead was or wasn't most effective for that story.

3. Find captions for both wild art and art that goes with a story. How are they different? How would you have rewritten the wild art caption to improve it? What about the art that goes with the story? Does it add to the story or detract from it? Did the information in the caption come directly from the story, or is it additional to what is in the story?

NOTES

1. Paula LaRocque, *FYI* (Dallas, Texas: The Belo Corporation, *Dallas Morning News*).

2. Edward Bliss Jr. and John M. Patterson, *Writing News for Broadcast*, 2nd ed. (New York: Columbia University Press, 1978).

SUGGESTIONS FOR ADDITIONAL READING

Bliss, Edward, Jr., and John M. Patterson. *Writing News for Broadcast*. 2nd ed. New York: Columbia University Press, 1978.

Brooks, Brian S., and others (The Missouri Group). *News Reporting and Writing*. 2nd ed. New York: St. Martin's, 1985.

Fang, Irving E. *Television News, Radio News*. 4th ed. rev. St. Paul: RADA Press, 1985.

French, Christopher W., Eileen Alt Powell and Howard Angione, eds. *The Associated Press Stylebook and Libel Manual*. New York: Associated Press, 1980. See, especially, material on captions.

Hood, James R., and Brad Kalbfeld, eds. *The Associated Press Broadcast News Handbook*. New York: Associated Press, 1982.

Mencher, Melvin. *News Reporting and Writing*. 3rd ed. Dubuque, Iowa: Wm. C. Brown, 1983.

Shook, Frederick. *The Process of Electronic News Gathering*. Englewood, Colo.: Morton, 1982.

Shook, Frederick, and Dan Lattimore. *The Broadcast News Process*. 2nd ed. Denver: Morton, 1983.

Smeyak, G. Paul. *Broadcast News Writing*. 2nd ed. Columbus, Ohio: Grid, 1983.

Stephens, Mitchell. *Broadcast News*. New York: Holt, Rinehart and Winston, 1980.

Simple Story Structure, Rewrites, Advances and Obits

One characteristic of writing for the mass media that makes the process easier is the existence of patterns—story structures you can follow. The simplest story structures for print and broadcast have many elements in common, the most significant being the placement of emphasis on a single item in the story. However, there are some differences, so we'll deal first with the structure for print, then radio and then television.

PRINT STORY STRUCTURE

Manuscript mechanics

Most newswriters now work on computer systems, which have their own individual formats and styles. However, when copy is typed on paper, as in news releases, a few conventions remain. No paragraphs are divided at the end of a page. If there's not enough room, the copy is taken to the top of the second page. The word *more* is typed in the bottom center of the first page, as well as any pages that follow until the end of the story.

The second page is generally labeled *Add 1*, the third page is *Add 2* and so on. At the end, a tradition from the Civil War wireless days remains: -30- or ### is placed at the end. War correspondents in the field used ### to indicate the end of their "send," so if the transmission was interrupted editors would know that they didn't have all of the story yet.

Organization

Most news stories have the following elements (see 4.1 for story diagram):

1. The lead (the main point)
2. Secondary points in a tie-in transition
3. Elaboration on the main point
4. Support for the lead
5. Background
6. Development of the main idea
7. Details

The role of the lead and secondary points. The lead captures the essence of the main point but doesn't give a complete, thorough account of it. If there are major secondary points, you should introduce them right behind the lead. A major secondary point that turns up suddenly three-fourths of the way into the story will surprise the reader. Surprises make stories hard to follow. So

5.1 Print Story Format

```
Your Name
Story I.D.  (Slug Line)
Date
(When a story is typed on a terminal, these may follow
each other in a single line.)


     (A dateline here, if not local.)  Your lead is

here.  Generally a 60-space line is used.  Remember

that if printed in a single column, about five words

will comprise a single line.

     Your transition from lead to body of story goes

here, usually one sentence.

     The body of your story starts here.  You always

double space.  Don't divide paragraphs between pages

or on the screen between page division indicators.

     You may be incorporating indicators in your

copy that are peculiar to the electronic system you

are using--signs that indicate italics or boldface.

     If you have to go to a second page, complete

your paragraph on the first page and put (more) at

the bottom.        (more)
```

5.1 (continued)

```
             On the second page, put your name, your news-

paper's indicator for the second page of the copy,

which may be "Take 1" or "Add 1" and the slug line

or story identification.  At the end of the story,

use ### or -30- to signify that's the conclusion

of that piece.  If you are using a terminal and are

putting in a second story, scroll to the next page

designation to begin.

                        -30-
```

you begin something like this: Here is the main point (lead). By the way, some other important things—namely this and that—will be discussed later in the story, after we talk about the main point.

Consider the lead written by the student who covered the psychologist's talk:

> Depressed people may have a more accurate view of reality than people who are not depressed, says psychologist and author Lyn Abramson.

That lead gives the *who* and *what*. In elaborating on the lead, the writer worked in the remaining elements of the story:

Reprinted by permission of Jefferson Communications, Inc., Reston, Va.

> Abramson, who spoke here Thursday on "Depression, Non-depression and Cognitive Bias," discussed research on theories of depression. Her book *Feeling Low?* was published last year. The program was sponsored by the psychology department.

Now the reader knows where (here), when (Thursday) and why (the psychology department invited her).

Elaboration on the main point.   There is further elaboration to be made on the lead, however. The next paragraph did so:

> Abramson said she has discovered through her research that depressed people judge reality well, but non-depressed people tend to have illusions of control that protect them from depression.

Support for the lead.   The lead makes a claim; the story should prove it. Thus it's necessary to give specific supporting evidence for the point made in the lead. Sometimes the support can be simple and brief—one direct quote, for example, might provide all the support a lead needs. In other cases you might need several paragraphs of statistics, examples or expert testimony.

Consider a lead like "John Smith says he will not vote for the president's new tax proposal." One direct quote from John Smith might be enough support to prove that point:

> "If they tied me to the rails and put a gun to my head, I wouldn't vote for that stupid bill," Smith said.

Here's a real example from a student newswriter. The lead:

> World hunger is caused not by overpopulation but by politics, the keynote speaker for Hunger Week said Monday.

Shortly thereafter came the direct quote supporting the lead:

> "The reason people remain hungry in this world is that they are powerless," said Joe Short, executive director of Oxfam-America, an organization that advocates self-help in underdeveloped nations.

Background.   All beginning newswriters soon learn this cardinal rule of journalism: Never assume anything. And the most important thing not to assume is knowledge on the part of your readers.

That's not to say readers are stupid—just don't assume they will know or understand what happened yesterday, or last week, or last month. You may have given the background in a story you wrote for yesterday's paper, but some readers will have missed that issue. So you must repeat essential background information in every story. Ask yourself this: What must readers know to be able to understand the facts you are reporting? You don't need to devote seven paragraphs to a detailed history of the matter. But you must briefly summarize essential background.

For example, when a school board was about to vote on an outline for teaching evolutionary and non-evolutionary theory, a reporter interviewed four scientists who criticized inaccurate statements in the non-evolutionary theory outline. The reporter wrote a story based on the scientists' criticism. But it was necessary to include background information explaining what the flap was all about.

> The dispute over how to teach the origin of life surfaced in the district March 3 when the board refused to adopt two earth science textbooks that presented only the evolutionary account. The board subsequently adopted the two textbooks but instructed the staff to write a plan that presents both sides of the question.

This paragraph allowed readers not already aware of the controversy to understand the story.

Stories that continue over a period of time, such as a kidnapping, or stories that reappear after being out of the news for a while, such as trials, need backgrounding. A few lines may be adequate in some instances to give readers enough information to be able to understand the current story. Sometimes it may take several paragraphs.

Some of the background a story must contain isn't a matter of repeating information from earlier stories. Some stories just aren't comprehensible without simple explanatory information. A student writing about a work-study program had to provide background information about the source of funds for the program.

> The work-study program is federally funded. The government pays 80 percent of a work-study student's salary and 20 percent is paid by the institution employing the student. Some of the non-profit institutions that have an agreement with the university to hire work-study students are YWCA, YMCA, the General Services Administration and the U.S. Attorney's Office.

Development of the main idea.   The lead, its elaboration and support, and background information are the basics of the news story. But the complete news story doesn't stop there. What are the consequences of this news? How will it affect the upcoming elections, or the economy, or the environment? How will it affect residents of the area? What will happen next? The newswriter must explain the significance of an event, not just present the facts of it.

Details.   In a news story details are the subsidiary points that relate to the main one. They should be worked into the story in the course of elaborating on the lead. But others might not be so easily assimilated. Exactly where to put them depends on their importance. Very important details will be introduced right after the lead, and returned to later on—perhaps before the lead is developed, perhaps after. Less important ones may be introduced near the beginning or may be held back until after the development of the main point is exhausted.

Throwaway paragraphs are the way writers have traditionally ended their stories. These contain information that they expect may be deleted if the story is too long to fit the allotted space.

Electronic editing has made it easier to cut stories from within, not just from the bottom. However, most stories still have the least important information at the end because if a story has to be moved in the redesign of a page, it's convenient to be able to discard that last paragraph without worry.

Examples 5.2 and 5.3 show two ways the elements of a story can be put together. Despite the AZT story's length, its construction is simple, not complex. Other structures are possible; there is no one right way—the same story could be structured in several different ways by different writers. But whatever way you choose, it must read smoothly, so that the parts of the story give the appearance of being in the "right" order. One way to accomplish this is to use words or ideas in the last part of a sentence closing a paragraph to begin the following paragraph. Such transitions provide a smooth passage from one idea to another.

Holding reader interest

Some stylistic methods to keep a reader interested were presented in Chapter 2. There are also some structural ways: use direct quotes; show, don't tell; answer readers' questions.

Use direct quotes.   Using direct quotes makes writing sound more natural and helps credibility too. Both reasons are why broadcast writers use so many actualities, or tapes. Choosing quotes carefully is essential, though, because most people don't speak all that clearly and concisely. That also means you shouldn't use too many quotes. Often you can effectively paraphrase what was said.

Quotes also break up the monotony of a straightforward presentation of the facts and vary the pace of the story. They add human interest to the piece as well as providing illustrations or examples and substantiation. And they let readers know the speaker's exact words. Sometimes that's very important, as when the president makes a major policy statement. Many people will be commenting on what he meant and what the significance is, so your readers should have the specific words.

Consider this sentence:

Smith said the plan was ridiculous, outrageous and stupid.

Did Smith actually use those words, or did the reporter summarize and paraphrase? Direct quotation would clarify:

"This parking plan is ridiculous, it's outrageous and it's stupid to boot," Smith said.

5.2a Wire Story

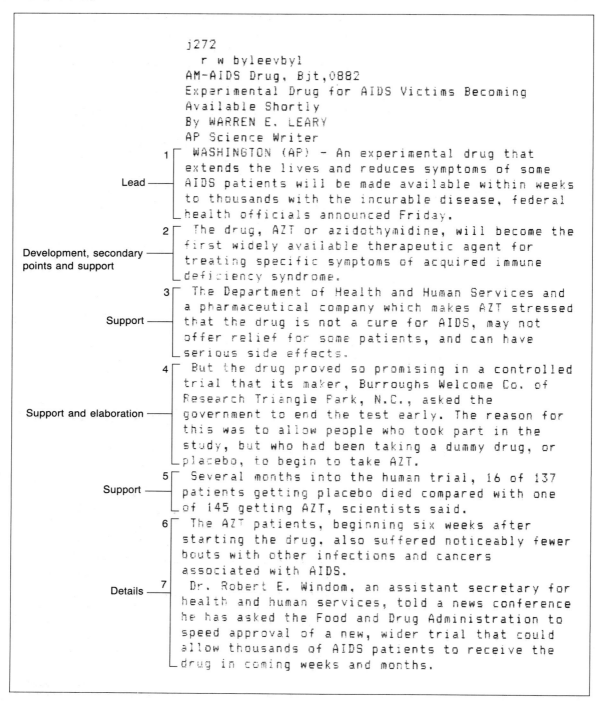

j272
  r w byleevbyl
AM-AIDS Drug, Bjt,0882
Experimental Drug for AIDS Victims Becoming
Available Shortly
By WARREN E. LEARY
AP Science Writer

Lead

1 WASHINGTON (AP) - An experimental drug that
extends the lives and reduces symptoms of some
AIDS patients will be made available within weeks
to thousands with the incurable disease, federal
health officials announced Friday.

Development, secondary points and support

2 The drug, AZT or azidothymidine, will become the
first widely available therapeutic agent for
treating specific symptoms of acquired immune
deficiency syndrome.

Support

3 The Department of Health and Human Services and
a pharmaceutical company which makes AZT stressed
that the drug is not a cure for AIDS, may not
offer relief for some patients, and can have
serious side effects.

Support and elaboration

4 But the drug proved so promising in a controlled
trial that its maker, Burroughs Welcome Co. of
Research Triangle Park, N.C., asked the
government to end the test early. The reason for
this was to allow people who took part in the
study, but who had been taking a dummy drug, or
placebo, to begin to take AZT.

Support

5 Several months into the human trial, 16 of 137
patients getting placebo died compared with one
of 145 getting AZT, scientists said.

6 The AZT patients, beginning six weeks after
starting the drug, also suffered noticeably fewer
bouts with other infections and cancers
associated with AIDS.

Details

7 Dr. Robert E. Windom, an assistant secretary for
health and human services, told a news conference
he has asked the Food and Drug Administration to
speed approval of a new, wider trial that could
allow thousands of AIDS patients to receive the
drug in coming weeks and months.

Details (continued) ——

8 "Today's announcement represents an important step forward in the search for an effective therapy for treating persons infected with the AIDS virus, but it is only one step," Windom said.

9 AIDS, an incurable condition that results in destruction of the body's infection-fighting immune system, has been diagnosed in 24,859 Americans to date, 13,689 of whom have died. There is no effective treatment for the disease and no one is known to have survived it.

Background ——
10 The virus that causes it, known as HTLV-3, or LAV, is spread through intimate contact with victims' bodily fluids, such as blood and semen, and more than 70 percent of cases have involved male homosexuals. Other high-risk groups include intravenous drug abusers and those receiving infected blood or blood products.

11 The Treatment Investigational New Drug Trial would be open to AIDS patients around the country who meet criteria established in earlier tests for those who might benefit from taking AZT.

Details ——
12 The drug will become available to those AIDS sufferers who also have suffered bouts with Pneumocystis carnii pneumonia, a form of pneumonia that frequently springs up in patients and against which the recently suspended trial was targeted.

Background ——
13 Dr. Anthony Fauci of the National Institutes of Health estimated that between 50 percent and 60 percent of the 12,000 living AIDS patients in the United States have this accompanying pneumonia.

Development ——
14 Fauci said additional criteria will be developed by health officials in the next couple of weeks, and said he felt "several thousand" patients could prove elegible for the new AZT test.

15 Dr. David W. Barry, vice president for research at Burroughs Wellcome, said the company would make the drug available free of charge for those in the expanded test. But he also said it would take several months for the company to get production to the point where it can make enough

(continued)

5.2a (continued)

16 of the drug for the anticipated number who will
enroll in the study.
    The federal department and the company have set
up a special toll-free telephone number
(1-800-843-9388) for those wishing information
about AZT or about getting into the new trial.

17 To be considered for the expanded studies, AIDS
patients will have to get their doctors to
certify that they meet the criteria. The doctor's
would have to agree to both supervise
administration of the drug and to file test
reports to researchers. The prescription drug
will be made available at specially authorized
pharmacies in all parts of the country, officials
said.

18 Researchers said the major side effects of the
drug, taken orally several times a day, are bone
marrow suppression and the resulting severe
anemia that may require blood transfusions.
People who are too weak or whose bone marrow
counts are very low may not be eligible to take
the drug, he added.

19 Because of many remaining questions about AZT,
the drug will remain in other tests to determine
whether it continues to have beneficial effects,
scientists said.

20 Dr. Samuel Broder of the National Cancer
Institute, who is coordinating new AIDS drug
testing, said a few AZT patients who have taken
the drug for more than a year seem to be
tolerating it and living better lives.

21 "I'd say there was a noticeable benefit in
quality of life," Broder said. The drug appears
to halt disease progression in many patients and
even allows some rebuilding of the immune system
in others, he said.

22 AZT is one of a battery of potential drugs
against AIDS being tested at 14 university
research centers around the country. The drug
interferes with the reproduction of the AIDS
virus within cells by inhibiting an enzyme
essential to the process.

Details ——

5.2b Newspaper Version of Wire Story

Note that the details in the 16th paragraph in the AP wire version have been broken out and put in a box in the newspaper story. The graph has been slightly rewritten for this display. Also notice that the last line of the 18th graph to the end of the original story have been cut for space.

Experimental drug OK'd for AIDS use

Associated Press

Lead 1   WASHINGTON — An experimental drug that extends the lives and reduces symptoms of some AIDS patients will be made available within weeks to thousands with the deadly, incurable disease, federal health officials announced Friday. — What, when (2), who (2), why, where.

Tie-in 2   The drug, AZT or azidothymidine, will become the first widely available therapeutic agent for treating specific symptoms of acquired immune deficiency syndrome. — Transition, significance of what.

Details 3   The Department of Health and Human Services and a pharmaceutical company that makes AZT stressed that the drug is not a cure for AIDS, may not offer relief for some patients — and can have serious side effects. — Who (2) and a new who introduced.

4   But the drug proved so promising in a controlled trial that its maker, Burroughs-Wellcome Co. of Research Triangle Park, N.C., asked the government to end the test early. The reason for this was to allow people who took part in the study, but who had been taking a dummy drug, or placebo, to begin to take AZT. — What, why.

5   Several months into the human trial, 16 of 137 patients getting placebo died compared with one of 145 getting AZT, scientists said. — Background of what and who.

6   The AZT patients, beginning six weeks after starting the drug, also suffered noticeably fewer bouts with other infections and cancers associated with AIDS. — Results — why.

7   Dr. Robert E. Windom, an assistant secretary for health and human services, told a news conference he has asked the Food and Drug Administration to speed approval of a new, wider trial that could allow thousands of AIDS patients to receive the drug in coming weeks and months. — Authority cited, where, another who.

(continued)

5.2b (continued)

8   "Today's announcement represents an important step forward in the search for an effective therapy for treating persons infected with the AIDS virus, but it is only one step," Windom said.

— Quote from an authority.

9   AIDS, an incurable condition that results in destruction of the body's infection-fighting immune system, has been diagnosed in 24,859 Americans to date, 13,689 of whom have died. There is no effective treatment for the disease, and no one is known to have survived it.

— Background of the disease stressing impact.

10   The virus that causes it, known as HTLV-3 or LAV, is spread through intimate contact with victims' bodily fluids, such as blood and semen, and more than 70 percent of cases have involved male homosexuals. Other high-risk groups include intravenous drug abusers and those receiving infected blood or blood products.

— Background of the disease stressing cause.

11   The Treatment Investigational New Drug Trial would be open to AIDS patients around the country who meet criteria established in earlier tests for those who might benefit from taking AZT.

— First graph that was.

12   The drug will become available to those AIDS sufferers who also have suffered bouts with *Pneumocystis carinii* pneumonia, a form of pneumonia that frequently springs up in patients and against which the recently supended trial was targeted.

— Discussion of why.

13   Dr. Anthony Fauci of the National Institutes of Health estimated that between 50 and 60 percent of the 12,000 living AIDS patients in the United States have this accompanying pneumonia.

— Another authority introduced for amplification of who.[2]

14   Fauci said additional criteria will be developed by health officials in the next few weeks and that he believed "several thousand" patients would prove eligible for the new AZT test.

— Paraphrase of quote amplifies why.

5.2b (continued)

15   Dr. David W. Barry, vice president for research at Burroughs-Wellcome, said the company would make the drug available free for those in the expanded test. But he also said it would take several months for the company to get production to the point where it can make enough of the drug for the anticipated number of patients who will enroll in the study.

— Third authority gives maker's position on availability of drug, a <u>how</u>.

For more information

The Health and Human Services Department and Burroughs Wellcome Co. have set up a special toll-free telephone number, 1-800-843-9388, for those wishing information about azidothymidine or about getting into the new trial.

— Block with phone number used for emphasis.

16   To be considered for the expanded studies, AIDS patients will have to get their doctors to certify that they meet the criteria.

— who[2] that receives more elaboration in Example 5.12, which comes from several wire stories.

17   Researchers said the major side effects of the drug, taken orally several times a day, are bone marrow suppression and the resulting severe anemia that may require blood transfusions.

— A <u>what</u> that is also amplified in Example 5.12.

Fort Worth Star-Telegram

One other rule to remember about direct quotations: Quote only those sentences that are worth quoting. Use quotations when a speaker says something that is extraordinarily dramatic or expressive or significant. Do not quote bland, straightforward information:

"The meeting will begin at 4 p.m.," Johnson said.

Instead, paraphrase:

Johnson said the meeting will begin at 4 p.m.

It's usually best to place the attribution for a direct quotation at the end. One of the main reasons for quoting is to make the story more interesting and conversational, and you destroy the conversational nature of the quote if you begin it with "He said."

5.3 Structure in a Student Exercise

Lead
> Working too hard and worrying too much can cause heart attacks in people under 40, Dr. Rodney Mayhew says.

Development and secondary points and support
> On-the-job stress, frustrations and an inability to relax all increase the risk of heart attacks, the state director of public health said here Monday.

Support
> "The perfect candidate for a heart attack is the serious-minded young man who feels guilty if he relaxes for 10 minutes, who works at a job filled with deadlines, frustrations, worry or discontent," Mayhew told 89 members of the American College of Angiology.

Support and elaboration
> "This sort of person burns himself out trying to meet life's challenges with extremely conscientious work," the doctor added.
>
> Mayhew's remarks were based on his recent study of 220 heart patients, all under 40. He found that 198 of the victims had jobs where they encountered stress, frustration or undue fear.

Support
> Nearly half—92 of the 198—held down two jobs or worked more than 60 hours a week on one job, Mayhew said.

Elaboration
> He pointed out that nearly all the patients were "victims of their own personalities, almost literally slaves to situations they created." The typical victim, Mayhew said, finds little satisfaction in his accomplishments and sets higher goals as soon as old goals are achieved. Such a person is "almost doomed"

Details
> to a heart attack if he is overweight, eats a high-fat diet, and has a history of heart attacks in his family, Mayhew said.

Throwaway
> Mayhew, 54, is a native of Austin. He was director of public health in New Mexico before assuming similar duties in Texas in 1968.
>
> His talk was presented at the Alamo Hotel, where the American College of Angiology is meeting. Angiology is the study of blood vessels and lymph vessels.

In the following example, which method of attribution would be more effective?

> One man said, "I think the whole project is a waste of money."

> "I think the whole project is a waste of money," one man charged.

Clearly the second sentence is more interesting.

There are exceptions to this general rule, however. Whenever more than one speaker is being quoted in a story, you must make sure the reader knows who's speaking.

> "As long as the case is in court, I'm not going to comment on it," said attorney Susan Smith.
> "We're still working with the city to see if we can reach a compromise," said city manager Roger Jones.

The reader is surprised at the end of the second quote to find that Smith is no longer talking. The second quotation should have the attribution first. Or a sentence could have been inserted to indicate the change in the speaker.

> "As long as the case is in court, I'm not going to comment on it," said attorney Susan Smith.
> But city manager Roger Jones said a solution to the problem is still possible. "We're still working . . ."

Inexperienced writers feel compelled to alternate explanatory paragraphs and quotes. You can avoid a style trap and enliven your story by using partial quotes.

> Attorney Susan Smith would not comment on the case "as long as [it] is in court." City manager Roger Jones said they were still working with the city "to see if we can reach a compromise."

Show, don't tell. Stimulate your readers' imaginations by creating pictures in their minds. A statement like "The speaker was well received by the audience" doesn't create much of a picture. But "The 5,000 people in the audience stood and cheered when the speaker had finished" describes a scene that readers can imagine. Use specific nouns and action verbs to paint the scene.

Answer readers' questions. People are curious. The reporter's job is to anticipate what readers will want to know and to provide that information in the story.

Every story is different, so readers will want to know different things about different stories. But there are several guidelines that reporters follow in determining what to include—information that most readers demand from most stories. Here are some general guidelines.

- *Explain effects on people.* If the utility company raises electric rates, don't just say how much more money the utility will get—tell how much more individuals will have to pay. If a fire destroys an apartment complex, don't stop with giving the amount of damages and the cause of the fire. What will the tenants do? Where will they stay? People like to read about people.

- *Include all relevant times, places, dates and names.* What time of day did the event take place? What time is the speech Wednesday? Where did the accident occur? How far from the city is the new construction project? Who is the owner? Who is the builder? When will construction be finished?

   Such questions must be answered in almost every news story. They might not all be answered at once, but the information must be included in the story somewhere. People will be looking for it. They will abandon a story that lacks the basic information they need.

- *Identify people and organizations.* Don't just say "Joe Smith said." Who is Joe Smith? Why should anyone care what he said? Vice president of Gizmo Corp.? Research scientist at the local university? Identify him, but use identification pertinent to the story. The university scientist probably is a teacher too, but identifying him as a chemistry professor will not suggest his research field. For instance:

   > Dr. Jack Barchas, a Stanford University research psychiatrist, says it is becoming clear that the amount and combination of certain chemicals in a person's brain regulate aggression and grief.

   In the same way, it's necessary to identify organizations. Just what is Gizmo Corp., anyway? A multinational computer company or a local car parts firm? Identify the organization:

   > The complaint was brought by a former meat wrapper for Pak-n-Pay, a Cleveland-based supermarket chain.

- *Present relevant numbers.* Don't just say that the state senate passed a bill— what was the vote? If a motion fails to carry, how many votes would have been needed? What was the score of the game? How many people attended? How long did it last? Be especially careful to include any figures having to do with money. Always tell how much something cost, or how much was saved. Talk about numbers in ways that they can be understood. When possible, relate them to something familiar: "The disputed property is the size of two football fields placed end to end." Always reduce millions. Use 2.84 million, rather than 2,840,000.

- *Support generalities with specifics.* "The candidate has vast experience in government" is a vague, general statement. What kind of experience? What branch of government? Such a sentence must be followed by specific examples. "She served four terms in the state legislature and three terms in the U.S. House of Representatives before serving four years as state attorney general."

- *Give background* beyond what is needed to make a story understandable. What past legislation has contributed to the current situation? Have public school teachers ever had to take a state test before? What was the test like?

  In a story about the resignation of U.S. Sen. Harrison Williams, one writer provided this background paragraph:

  > Williams, 62, who was convicted of bribery and conspiracy in the FBI Abscam investigation, ended his 23-year Senate career when he signed his letter of resignation.

  This paragraph works in Williams' age, the length of his tenure in the Senate and the key event leading to his resignation. The writer went on to give additional background information of historical interest.

  > During the 193-year history of the Senate, only 15 of its members have been expelled, all for treason or disloyalty.

  This sentence is certainly not essential to making the story understandable, but it gives perspective.

- *Describe the circumstances* when covering an event. Don't just report what was said or done—describe the environment surrounding the action. What sorts of people were in the audience? How big was the crowd? What were the weather conditions at the time of the accident?

- *Note any unusual aspects* that distinguish the story. While newswriters are often criticized for their preoccupation with the first, biggest, most and other such records, the citations, if accurate, are of legitimate interest to readers. If the city adopts the largest budget in its history, you should say so.

- *Discuss expected future developments*. It's not enough just to tell what happened. Readers want to know what's going to happen next. Sometimes no one knows, of course, and you should never speculate without a basis. But you can interview knowledgeable people who have some idea. Certain events are scheduled for coming weeks and months, certain people have the power to make things happen, and they may indicate what they're going to do. You owe it to the readers to find out as much as you can about possible future developments and to pass that information on.

WRITING RADIO NEWS

About 8,755 commercial and 1,247 non-commercial radio stations are operating in the United States. There are also 22 radio networks offering news to local radio stations. Only 400 radio stations are all-news. Cable systems are also beginning audio services. About 250 systems, or 5 percent of the 5,000 cable systems in the country, now originate audio programming, including newscasts. That figure is expected to grow to 2,090 by 1990, according to surveys.

Formats and style Radio news copy is typed full-page, using regular left- and right-hand margins. Each story is typed on a separate page so that stories can be shuffled around as the newscast is being put together. Each page is slugged with the writer's name, the date, the time of the newscast and some brief identifier as to what the story is about. A typical slug, typed in the upper left-hand corner of each page, might look like this:

GRETCHEN KIA

11/10/88

10 AM NEWSCAST

DIPHTHERIA OUTBREAK

Slugs containing this information can also be typed across the top of each page on a single line. If a story is continued to the next page, which is rare, the word *more* is used, and the slug line appears on the second page, ADD 1. At the end of each story, instead of -30-, the indication is -0-; -30- is reserved for the end of the newscast itself.

Some radio writers type their stories in all caps; others use upper- and lower-case. Broadcast news copy is written for someone to read over the air, so the copy should be typed according to the announcer's preference.

Broadcast news is written to fill time, not space, so all broadcast copy must be timed out. In radio news, one typewritten 60-space line equals about 4 seconds of reading time. Thus a 20-second story would equal five lines of copy, a 30-second story seven to eight lines, and so on.

Writing the reader *Readers* are stories without audiotape inserts in radio, or videotape in TV. When beginning a radio (or TV) reader, the writer often has some idea of how long the story should be. Copy can always be edited down or increased in length if necessary.

The writer sets about answering the most important questions, as discussed in Chapter 4. However, all the questions generally can't be answered in the usual 5 to 10 lines of copy. Broadcast newswriters must choose only the most crucial facts. Comparing the 1:30 story in 5.4 with the 20- and the 15-second versions in 5.5 shows how much can be eliminated. Some newscasts run stories as short as 10 seconds. For an idea of how that would look:

THE U-S HEALTH DEPARTMENT SAYS AN
EXPERIMENTAL DRUG TO BE RELEASED
SOON MAY EXTEND THE LIVES OF AIDS
VICTIMS.

You must ask, Of all those facts in 5.2 (the print version) and even 5.4, which are *really* essential for the audience to know? And because broadcast writers must leave out so much information, the information included must be well organized, make sense and support the lead.

5.4a Broadcast Wire Stories

This preview story moved on the Associated Press broadcast wire at 7:11 a.m. CDT, as the numbers in the last line indicate.

```
AP-"AIDS DRUG"

     (WASHINGTON) -- SOURCES SAY AN EXPERIMENTAL
DRUG THAT SEEMS TO OFFER RELIEF FROM SOME OF THE
SYMPTOMS OF "AIDS" MAY BE MADE MORE WIDELY
AVAILABLE TO VICTIMS OF THE INCURABLE DISEASE.
THE DEPARTMENT OF HEALTH AND HUMAN SERVICES AND A
PHARMACEUTICAL COMPANY HAVE SCHEDULED A NEWS
CONFERENCE FOR TODAY TO DISCUSS THE DRUG A-Z-T.
     RESEARCHERS WHO HAVE WORKED WITH THE DRUG
STRESS THAT IT IS NOT A CURE FOR ACQUIRED IMMUNE
DEFICIENCY SYNDROME AND MAY NOT BE EFFECTIVE IN
RELIEVING SOME SYMPTOMS OF THE DISEASE. BUT THEY
SAY IT IS ONE OF THE MORE PROMISING OF SEVERAL
DRUGS BEING TESTED AND COULD BE THE FIRST TO
OFFER DISEASE VICTIMS EVEN A FEW EXTRA MONTHS OF
LIFE.
     ONE OF THE DISCOVERERS OF THE VIRUS THAT
CAUSES THE DEADLY DISEASE SAID IN A RECENT
INTERVIEW THAT A-Z-T PROBABLY IS NOT EVEN A
TREMENDOUS ADVANCE IN TREATMENT. BUT DR. ROBERT
GALLO OF THE NATIONAL CANCER INSTITUTE SAYS HE
DOES THINK "IT'S LIKELY TO BE AMONG THE BEST
THINGS WE HAVE NOW -- PERHAPS THE BEST."
     A-Z-T IS ONE OF A BATTERY OF POTENTIAL DRUGS
AGAINST AIDS BEING TESTED AT 14 UNIVERSITY
RESEARCH CENTERS AROUND THE COUNTRY. THE DRUG
INTERFERES WITH THE REPRODUCTION OF THE AIDS
VIRUS WITHIN CELLS BY INHIBITING AN ENZYME
ESSENTIAL TO THE PROCESS.
     SCIENTISTS REPORT THAT IN EARLY TESTS THIS
YEAR, A-Z-T IMPROVED THE CONDITION OF 15 OF 19
ADVANCED AIDS PATIENTS. THEY SAY LEVELS OF A
WHITE BLOOD CELL KILLED BY THE VIRUS BEGAN
INCREASING.
     -
AP-DN-09-19-86 0711CDT
```

5.4b

This AP broadcast story reporting the AZT news conference moved at 12:13 p.m. CDT, six hours earlier than the print version (5.2a).

```
AP-AIDS DRUG (TOPS)

    (WASHINGTON) -- DOCTORS SAID TODAY THAT THE

EXPERIMENTAL DRUG A-Z-T APPEARS TO EXTEND THE

LIVES OF SOME "AIDS" PATIENTS -- AND WILL BECOME

THE FIRST THERAPEUTIC AGENT MADE AVAILABLE TO A

WIDER NUMBER OF THOSE WITH THE INCURABLE DISEASE.

    GOVERNMENT HEALTH OFFICIALS AND THE COMPANY
THAT MAKES A-Z-T (AZIDOTHYMIDINE) HELD A
WASHINGTON NEWS CONFERENCE TODAY. THERE, THEY
TOLD REPORTERS THE DRUG HAS PROVED SO BENEFICIAL
IN LIMITED CONTROLLED TESTS, THEY SUSPENDED THE
TRIAL SO PARTICIPANTS GETTING A DUMMY DRUG COULD
GET A-Z-T.
    THEY STRESSED HOWEVER, THAT A-Z-T IS NOT A
CURE FOR ACQUIRED IMMUNE DEFICIENCY SYNDROME.
    THEY DO SAY, THOUGH THAT THE DRUG ALSO COULD
BE AVAILABLE WITHIN A FEW WEEKS FOR THOUSANDS OF
AIDS SUFFERERS WHO MEET CERTAIN CRITERIA, MAINLY
THAT THEY SUFFER FROM PNEUMOCYSTIS CARINII
PNEUMONIA.
    THIS FORM OF PNEUMONIA IS A MAJOR SIDE
INFECTION OF AIDS AND EXPERTS ESTIMATE THAT UP TO
60 PERCENT OF AIDS PATIENTS HAVE BEEN AFFLICTED
WITH IT FROM TIME TO TIME.
    BURROUGHS-WELLCOME OF RESEARCH TRIANGLE PARK,
NORTH CAROLINA HAS BEEN MEETING WITH GOVERNMENT
HEALTH OFFICIALS FOR A WEEK TO DISCUSS ENDING A
TRIAL THAT SHOWED A-Z-T SIGNIFICANTLY REDUCED THE
NUMBER OF DEATHS AMONG THOSE WHO TOOK THE DRUG.
    DR. ROBERT WINDOM, ASSISTANT SECRETARY FOR
HEALTH AT THE DEPARTMENT OF HEALTH AND HUMAN
SERVICES, TOLD THE NEWS BRIEFING HE'S ASKED THE
FOOD AND DRUG ADMINISTRATION TO SPEED PAPERWORK
ON A NEW, WIDER TRIAL THAT COULD ALLOW THOUSANDS
OF AIDS PATIENTS TO RECEIVE THE DRUG WITHIN
WEEKS.

AP-DN-09-19-86 1213CDT
```

5.5 A 20-Second Radio Story

```
AP-8TH NEWSMINUTE

    HERE IS THE LATEST NEWS FROM THE ASSOCIATED
PRESS:

    SOURCES SAY AN EXPERIMENTAL DRUG CALLED A-Z-T
THAT APPEARS TO HELP PEOPLE SUFFERING FROM "AIDS"
MAY BE MADE MORE WIDELY AVAILABLE TO VICTIMS OF
THE DEADLY DISEASE. REPORTS HAVE SAID THE DRUG IS
SO PROMISING THAT ITS MAKER WANTS TO ABANDON
FURTHER TESTS AND GIVE IT TO MORE AIDS SUFFERERS
INVOLVED IN THE STUDIES. DOCTORS STRESS IT'S NOT
A CURE, THOUGH.

    NEW STUDIES INDICATE THERE'S A LINK BETWEEN
AIDS AND TUBERCULOSIS. FEDERAL HEALTH OFFICIALS
IN ATLANTA SAY AIDS VICTIMS CAN CONTRACT THE
DISEASE BECAUSE OF THEIR WEAKENED IMMUNE SYSTEMS.
THEY SAY ABOUT TEN

AFTER REPORTED THREATS THAT AN AMERICAN WOULD BE
KIDNAPPED FROM THE DISCO THIS WEEKEND.

AP-DN-09-19-86 0705CDT
```

AP Thru   Date & Time
    Dallas   Cleared Wire
    Computer

```
GOT A CALL THAT AN AMERICAN MAY BE KIDNAPPED
THERE -- AND ASKS SOLDIERS AND THEIR FAMILIES TO
STAY AWAY.

    THERE MAY BE SOME RELIEF ON THE WAY FOR
"AIDS" VICTIMS. RESEARCHERS REPORT THERE'S A NEW
DRUG THAT SEEMS TO RELIEVE SOME OF THE SYMPTOMS
OF THE DEADLY DISEASE. OFFICIALS SAY THE DRUG --
CALLED "A-Z-T" MAY SOON BE MADE MORE WIDELY
AVAILABLE.

    PHILIPPINE PRESIDENT CORAZON AQUINO
(KOR-AH-ZOHN  AH-KEE'-NOH) IS DUE IN NEW YORK
TODAY AS PART OF HER NINE-DAY TOUR OF THE U.S.
SHE ADDRESSED A JOINT MEETING OF CONGRESS
YESTERDAY - AFTER WHICH THE HOUSE APPROVED 200
(M) MILLION DOLLARS IN NEW AID.

AP-DN-09-19-86 0814CDT
```

In many stories, the final sentence makes reference to the future, somehow:

The Board of Education will meet tonight to discuss this matter.

Congress will begin deliberations on the bill next week.

Writing to tape   Let's say the radio reporter covering the AZT news conference taped the following statement there:

"Today's announcement represents an important step forward in the search for an effective therapy for treating persons infected with the AIDS virus, but it is only one step." (Dr. Robert E. Windom, an assistant secretary for health and human services.)

Some days, only one good quote, such as this, is uttered. You'll see that it was used, in summary, to close the 5.4a broadcast story.

The radio reporter now wants to write a story. To do that, he or she starts by writing a *lead-in* to the taped quote.

Lead-ins.   Two types of taped segments are used in radio newscasts: An *actuality* is the actual voice of the newsmaker or news source speaking; a *voicer* is the voice of the station's reporter. The first step in writing the story is writing the *lead-in* to the tape. Examples of lead-ins to actualities and to voicers are shown in 5.6 and 5.7.

Lead-ins to both actualities and voicers should identify the person speaking on the tape that follows. The audience wants to know who's talking when a different voice comes on. And the lead-in should never repeat what's on the tape.

Cues are typed into all tape stories to give the broadcast personnel directions. All tape stories must contain these cues: *take tape* (or just *tape*); *time*; and *end cue* (or *outcue*). The cue *take tape* simply indicates to all involved that a tape is to be inserted at this spot in the newscast. The total times of all stories must be known so that the copy time equals the time allocated for news. *End cue* tells the announcer how the tape ends, so he or she can prepare to read copy once again.

Tape IDs are the notations within parentheses that follow the take-tape cues. Most radio stations record all *tape cuts* (taped segments) to be used on the air on cartridge ("cart") or cassette tape, one cut per cart or cassette. Each cart or cassette is then labeled with the name of the person speaking on that cut or with a number. This system is designed to eliminate such mix-ups as the announcer reading "And the mayor says . . ." followed by a tape cut of the president.

5.6 Lead-ins to Radio Actualities

Example 1

THE DEPARTMENT OF HEALTH AND HUMAN SERVICES AND A
PHARMACEUTICAL COMPANY HAVE ANNOUNCED THE EXPERIMENTAL DRUG
A-Z-T WILL BE USED FOR SOME AIDS PATIENTS. THE NEW DRUG APPEARS TO
EXTEND THE LIFE OF AIDS PATIENTS.

TAKE TAPE (WINDOM)   TIME: 10   END CUE "ONLY ONE STEP."

> "Today's announcement represents an important step forward in the search for an effective therapy for treating persons infected with the AIDS virus; but it is only one step."

THAT WAS DR. ROBERT WINDOM, ASSISTANT SECRETARY FOR HEALTH AT THE
DEPARTMENT OF HEALTH AND HUMAN SERVICES. THE 800 NUMBER TO CALL
FOR MORE INFORMATION IS . . .

Example 2

THERE MAY BE SOME RELIEF ON THE WAY FOR "AIDS" PATIENTS.
RESEARCHERS REPORT THERE'S A NEW DRUG THAT SEEMS TO RELIEVE SOME
OF THE SYMPTOMS OF THE DEADLY DISEASE. OFFICIALS SAY THE DRUG—
"A-Z-T" MAY SOON BE MADE MORE WIDELY AVAILABLE. HEALTH AND HUMAN
SERVICES ASSISTANT SECRETARY ROBERT WINDOM TOLD KXAX NEWS . . .

TAPE (#23)   TIME: 10   OUTCUE: "ONLY ONE STEP."

> "Today's announcement . . . only one step."

THE DRUG WILL BECOME AVAILABLE TO AIDS SUFFERERS WHO HAVE HAD
THE FORM OF PNEUMONIA THAT FREQUENTLY SPRINGS UP IN AIDS PATIENTS.
FOR MORE INFORMATION ABOUT THE NEW DRUG, A-Z-T, YOU CAN CALL THIS
800 NUMBER 843-9388. TO FIND OUT ABOUT THE AVAILABILITY OF THE NEW
DRUG FOR AIDS SUFFERERS, CALL 1-800-843-9388.)

Taglines are copy read by the announcer after the tape is played. Some stations amend the rule that all lead-ins must contain the name of the person speaking on tape by identifying the speaker in the tagline, as in Example 1 of 5.6.

A voicer is a reporter's summary of events (see 5.7). It implies the reporter was at the scene. Voicers are often written out beforehand, then recorded for air use. Learning to write voicers is an integral part of the broadcast newswriter's

5.7 Lead-ins to Radio Voicers

Example 1

THE DEPARTMENT OF HEALTH AND HUMAN SERVICES AND A
PHARMACEUTICAL COMPANY TODAY ANNOUNCED THE RELEASE OF AN
EXPERIMENTAL DRUG THAT EXTENDS THE LIVES OF AIDS PATIENTS. KXAX'S
EVAN KENDRICK WAS AT THE NEWS CONFERENCE AND HAS THIS REPORT . . .

TAKE TAPE (#33)   TIME: 20   END CUE ''EVAN KENDRICK.''

> Doctors said today that the experimental drug A-Z-T appears to extend the lives of some AIDS patients—and will become the first therapeutic agent made available to a wider number of those suffering from the incurable disease. Doctors stressed that the new drug is not a cure. For KXAX news, this is Evan Kendrick.

Example 2

THERE MAY BE SOME RELIEF ON THE WAY FOR AIDS PATIENTS. RESEARCHERS
REPORT THERE'S A NEW DRUG THAT SEEMS TO RELIEVE SOME OF THE
SYMPTOMS OF THE DEADLY DISEASE. OFFICIALS SAY THAT THE DRUG—
CALLED ''A-Z-T''—MAY SOON BE MADE MORE WIDELY AVAILABLE, AS KXAX'S
EVAN KENDRICK REPORTS . . .

TAPE (KENDRICK)   TIME: 20   END CUE: ''EVAN KENDRICK.''

> Doctors said today that the experimental drug A-Z-T appears to extend the lives of some "AIDS" patients—and will become the first therapeutic agent made available to a wider number of those with the incurable disease. Doctors stressed that the new drug is not a cure. For KXAX news, I'm Evan Kendrick.

---

job. Some voicers, however, are ad-libbed these days, as both radio and TV newscasts are doing more and more live coverage. A live voicer tests a reporter's ability to organize facts in a meaningful way.

Technological techniques.   Tape-editing techniques and equipment allow actualities to be incorporated into voicers and can be used for much more complex tasks as well. Live coverage from the scene, telephone reporting ("phoners"), intricate tape pieces—all are produced by broadcast newswriters and incorporated into the newscast. Radio newswriting, then, involves much more than simply rewriting the wire.

But when it comes to technology and incorporating it into newscasts, radio isn't half so complex as TV.

WRITING TV NEWS YOU NOW MIGHT BE WONDERING
WHETHER THE PUBLISHER GOOFED
HERE. WHY IS THIS WRITTEN ON
ONLY HALF OF THE PAGE, AND IN
ALL CAPS? YOU MIGHT ASK. WELCOME
TO A NEW MEDIUM—THE WORLD OF
TV NEWS, AND TV NEWSWRITING.

Formats and style Writing for television is technically more complicated than writing for radio. That's why the copy setup of TV news differs from that of radio. The copy the announcer will read is typed on the right-hand side of the page; the left-hand side is reserved for the cues to the director, audio control people and other technicians. These cues almost always indicate what pictures the TV newswriter wants shown as the copy is being read.

As in radio, all TV copy is slugged. In radio it's rare for a story to run more than one page, but in TV this often happens because of the half-page format. When more than one page is needed, PAGE 2 should be noted somewhere in the slug, and at the bottom of the preceding page should appear

-MORE-

Because TV copy is typed on a half page, you count 2 seconds per line, as compared to 4 seconds per line in radio. In TV, then, a 30-second story would run 15 lines, a 20-second story 10 lines, and so on.

Typing in all caps is pretty much a habit with TV newswriters. However, as in radio, there's no hard and fast rule, and it's usually left to the preference of the announcer. In TV, most announcers and writers seem to prefer all caps.

Writing copy for TV This means learning how to write for the technology. TV newswriters can't just put words down on paper for announcers to read. They have to think and write for the mechanics of the newscast.

There are about 1,000 broadcast TV stations and more than 5,000 cable TV systems in the country, many of them doing local news. The principles of TV newswriting outlined in this section apply to both broadcast and cable TV.

In surveying more than 100 TV newsrooms in the past several years and obtaining sample scripts from each one, we've found that there are four basic types of TV news stories the beginner should know how to write: (1) the reader, (2) the slide or chromakey story, (3) the lead-in to videotape, (4) the voice-over tape story.

The reader is very similar to a radio reader. If you compare 5.8 with 5.4, you'll notice that apart from the different copy setup, this could be a radio news reader.

The way reporters and writers write cues varies from station to station. For example, to call up the shot seen in 5.8, any one of the following could be used:

ANNCR.

ANNOUNCER

ANCR.

ANCHOR

ON-CAMERA SHOT

TATE

(The announcer in the picture is named Jerry Tate.)

The slide, or chromakey, shot and story involves one picture superimposed over another. Compare 5.8 to 5.9. The written copy is exactly the same, but the pictures are different. That picture framed over the announcer's shoulder in 5.9 is a slide electronically produced on the screen. This type of shot and story is also called a picture *chromakey*, or just *key*, shot (and story). The technology used to achieve this effect changes from station to station (thus the variation in terminology), but the result is the same.

All TV stations are capable of making several pictures appear in one shot. TV newswriters must know how to incorporate this capability into their writing. Thus in 5.9 the writer calls for a slide shot with the cue SL. The identifier (FIRE) after the cue is a precaution. You don't want the announcer reading a story about a fire and having a picture of the first lady appear on the screen.

The lead-in to tapes differs little from radio lead-ins; the same rules apply. The TV lead-in does not repeat what is said on the videotape and identifies who's speaking on tape. An example of a lead-in to a videotape story is shown in 5.10. About the only difference between this TV version and the radio lead-in to the AZT actuality (5.6, Example 1) is the visual cues.

5.8 TV News Story Without Visuals (Reader)

ANNCR

FIRE OFFICIALS ARE STILL ON THE SCENE OF AN OVERNIGHT FIRE AT THE POPLAR STREET APARTMENTS. FIRE CHIEF JACK HANSON TOLD CHANNEL THREE NEWS ARSON IS SUSPECTED. THE APARTMENTS ARE LOCATED AT THE CORNER OF POPLAR AND MICHIGAN STREETS.

LAST NIGHT'S FIRE CAUSED MINOR DAMAGE TO AT LEAST FIVE UNITS IN THE COMPLEX. THERE WERE NO INJURIES, AND THE AMOUNT OF DAMAGE IS STILL UNKNOWN.

5.9 TV News Story With Slide

ANNCR.
SL (FIRE)

FIRE OFFICIALS ARE STILL ON THE SCENE OF AN OVERNIGHT FIRE AT THE POPLAR STREET APARTMENTS. FIRE CHIEF JACK HANSON TOLD CHANNEL THREE NEWS ARSON IS SUSPECTED. THE APARTMENTS ARE LOCATED ON THE CORNER OF POPLAR AND MICHIGAN STREETS.

LAST NIGHT'S FIRE CAUSED MAJOR DAMAGE TO AT LEAST FIVE UNITS IN THE COMPLEX. THERE WERE NO INJURIES, AND THE AMOUNT OF DAMAGE IS STILL UNKNOWN.

The cue SOT that appears in 5.10 means "sound on tape." (If this interview with Chief Hanson had been shot on film instead of tape, the cue would have been SOF, "sound on film"; film is rarely used now in TV news, though.) The SOT cue, used as a signal to the audio control people, indicates there is sound on a particular cut of tape. Not all tape cuts have sound on them, as you will see in the next section on voice-overs.

Another cue that appears in 5.10 is SUPER, short for *superimposed*. Words, letters and numbers can all be *supered*. They're typed into an electronic *character generator*, which is a microcomputer. An example of what a super looks like on the screen is shown in 5.11. The super allows the TV newswriter a freedom radio writers don't have: It identifies the person speaking on videotape, so this information doesn't need to be included in the lead-in.

Note that in 5.10 the tagline following the tape is accompanied by a cue. The director has to know what picture to put on the screen at all times; for everything written on the right-hand side of the page, some sort of shot must be indicated on the left-hand side.

Voice-overs involve an announcer reading copy "over" a videotape. You've seen these many times. Sportscasters use them as much as anyone in TV news, describing the videotaped highlights of a game that appear on the screen. Many stories demand voice-overs. It doesn't make much sense to interview someone about a parade that took place downtown this afternoon. Instead, you'd shoot some tape of the parade and write copy for the announcer to read as the tape is shown.

The cue V/O in 5.11 means voice-over. SIL means the tape appearing on the screen is silent. Note there is a short lead-in before the tape begins. This is standard procedure in many TV newsrooms. After the tape is over, the writer can tag the story with more copy and a studio shot of the announcer. That's also standard procedure in some newsrooms.

5.10 Lead-in to Videotape Story

ANNCR
SL (CHANNEL 3 LOGO)

TAKE TAP (SOT)
SUPER (CHIEF HANSON)
TAPE RUNS :15
END CUE "LOOKING FOR THE
ARSONISTS"
ANNCR

FIRE OFFICIALS ARE STILL ON THE SCENE
OF AN OVERNIGHT FIRE AT THE POPLAR
STREET APARTMENTS LOCATED ON THE
CORNER OF POPLAR AND MICHIGAN
STREETS. FIRE CHIEF JACK HANSON SAYS
ARSON IS SUSPECTED AS THE CAUSE . . .

THERE WERE NO INJURIES IN LAST
NIGHT'S FIRE, AND THE AMOUNT OF
DAMAGE IS STILL UNKNOWN.

5.11 Example of a Voice-Over Tape Story

ANCHOR
SL (CHANNEL 3 LOGO)

TAKE TAPE (SIL) V/O
SUPER (DOWNTOWN)

SUPER (3 NEWSTAPE)

ARSON IS SUSPECTED AS THE CAUSE OF A
FIRE LAST NIGHT AT THE POPLAR STREET
APARTMENTS LOCATED AT THE CORNER
OF POPLAR AND MICHIGAN STREETS.

FIRE CHIEF JACK HANSON TOLD TV-3
NEWS THERE HAVE BEEN FIVE
APARTMENT HOUSE FIRES IN THIS PART
OF TOWN IN THE PAST TWO MONTHS . . .
AND FOUR OF THEM WERE SET BY
ARSONISTS.

THAT'S WHY THE ARSON SQUAD WAS
CALLED IN TODAY TO INVESTIGATE THIS
FIRE.

AT LEAST FIVE APARTMENT UNITS
WERE DAMAGED IN LAST NIGHT'S FIRE
. . . BUT NO ONE WAS INJURED.

Another type of tape used in voice-overs is called *natural sound* or *background sound*. Natural sound on the tape cut in 5.11 might be the sound of the fire-fighters cleaning up at the scene, the pumps pumping water, traffic on Poplar and Michigan streets, sirens as another fire truck pulls up to help.

Because cameras and field equipment have become so light and portable, it's no problem to shoot sound along with the pictures for most stories, so most videotapes shot for TV news today contain natural sound.

When you want the natural sound in the background on your voice-overs, you write it like this:

ANNCR	ARSON IS SUSPECTED AS THE CAUSE OF A
	FIRE LAST NIGHT AT THE POPLAR STREET
TAKE TAPE	APARTMENTS, LOCATED AT THE CORNER
(NAT SOT) V/O	OF POPLAR AND MICHIGAN STREETS. . . .

Writing copy for the announcer to read is still the most important part of all broadcast newswriting. Unintelligible copy results in an unintelligible story, no matter how good the pictures are. If the lead-in to the tape (radio or TV) doesn't make sense, chances are good the words the speaker utters on tape won't make sense either.

The technical devices shouldn't dominate or detract, but they often do, according to two TV news critics. They also say that TV news often fails to explain the significance of the news, the *why*. Authors of *The Main Learning Source: Learning from TV News* Mark R. Levy and John F. Robinson analyzed news on the three networks to develop their critique. Much of the difficulty centers on the brevity of the stories, which suggests that perhaps fewer stories better told might be the answer.

Electronic news gathering

Electronic news gathering, or ENG, is so much a part of everyday news operations in TV, and to some extent in radio, that the beginning broadcast newswriter and reporter must have some knowledge of this area.

Starting around 1975, various advances in broadcast and communications technology enabled TV reporting crews in the field to send back live reports from the scene. ENG vans are common sights in most larger communities these days. The vans are mobile newsrooms. TV reporters can write their copy in the field, shoot and edit the tape in the field, and then send it all back to the station via microwave in the form of a finished report. Many live reports from the field are ad-libbed by reporters; the ability to ad-lib on the spot is a skill that's difficult to teach and learn and probably impossible to teach or learn from a book. Becoming a good ad-libber just takes practice.

These field reports can also be taped back at the station for editing and replay within the newscasts. However, the primary contribution of ENG is that ability to go live when called for.

In visions of the future, there is the notion that ENG transmissions will be captured in the newsroom by computerized voice transmission units that will convert the spoken words to print. Then the story will exist on paper for reworking either for print or broadcast. Rewriting, drafting different versions of a story, is already a basic newsroom task.

REWRITES   Whether you start in news, public relations or advertising, you will spend a great deal of time rewriting—reworking someone else's efforts or your own. You'll be updating stories, rewriting release material or putting a slightly different twist on some copy for a different audience. All three of those tasks can fit all three types of occupations.

Rewriting anything will challenge your creativity. How can you take a story and make it not only fresh but better? If you write advertising or publicity copy, you'll work with the same body of facts until you could easily recite them in your sleep. How can you write each new draft with enthusiasm? Broadcast copywriters have the same volume of rewriting, but they do have different material to work with. Broadcast wire news stories are rewritten every hour to give a new sound to the news. How can you dig into a story and come up with fresh leads without distorting the emphasis? Television news, because of production considerations, is likely to use some of the same stories in the late evening news that appeared on the earlier afternoon broadcasts. But if they are breaking stories, like a fire or flood, these repeats will have fresh leads.

This discussion will deal only with rewriting news stories for print and broadcast, since that affects both newswriters and public relations people handling publicity. Additional information about rewriting for public relations is in Chapter 10, and all of the discussion about reworking material for ad copy is in Chapter 13.

Four story types require reworking: combined stories, holdover copy, followups and futures. You assess the information you have, discover what's missing, find it and put it in place.

Reprinted by permission of Jefferson Communications, Inc., Reston, Va.

Combined stories When there's a crisis, such as a tornado, or a holiday that involves many types of celebrations and observations, there are likely to be a number of stories from different sources that are written as separate pieces. Your job may be to weave them into one cohesive article, sometimes referred to as a *combine* (pronounced COM-bine). Or you may be given the police blotter reports to rewrite into a single crime-over-the-weekend piece, or all of the traffic accidents and fires over July 4 to write as one story. Wire service stories are frequently combined, as in 5.12, another newspaper's version of the piece in 5.2b. Note the differences between the two.

Holdover copy Stories about honors, awards and meetings are often held to make room for ones about robberies, fires and accidents. A rewrite for a story that has been put on hold is fairly simple. A new lead giving new information is added. Times and dates need to be checked. Words like *today*, if used, may need replacing. If new material changes the emphasis of the story, restructuring may be needed.

At the first-day story about a weeklong festival, for example, didn't get used, obviously the secondary events become the lead. The opening can be covered as a past event in a subsequent paragraph. The next paragraph can include a summary of the rest of the week's events with some quotes from the organizers about the festival's history or significance.

Follow-ups New developments are the important aspect of these second-day stories and dominate the lead. Has the kidnapped child been found? Was the fire caused by arson? A summary of the events from previous reports should follow the lead. Checking for completeness and accuracy in the original report is especially critical, because the initial coverage may have been rushed. Verify all names, identification and figures.

In writing the follow-up story, you have to be especially conscious of other news reports the audience may have received. Also, be aware of conflicting early reports. Preliminary broadcast reports of the attempted assassination of President Ronald Reagan in 1981 said Reagan was not injured and press secretary James Brady was dead.

You want your story to sound new; at the same time, you have to consider the person who has had no previous exposure to the story—someone returning from a trip, a visitor in town, a new resident. Enough information has to be included so the story can stand on its own, not dependent on the audience's memory of previous reports. Look at three follow-ups on the AZT story in 5.2. One was published three days after the news conference (5.13) and the other nine days after that (5.14). A local version of the story was published more than three weeks after the conference (5.15). See how the writers have brought the public up to date on what has happened since the story broke.

When you are the public relations person supplying information on a follow-up story, your real job is to anticipate the needs and questions of the various news media—actuality for broadcast, some additional activity for television—for

5.12 Wire Combine

Anti-AIDS drug OK'd for victims
AZT is believed to prolong lives

From Wire Reports

Simple advance stories like this one can appear to be complex because of backgrounding and attributions. Look at how the writer handled these elements.

Lead—a simple announcement. ——

Note *two* time elements, always present in an advance: 1) when the event will occur; 2) when the announcement was made.

Often there are also two *who* elements in announcements: 1) who made the announcement —the attribution here is not specific; the Department of Health and Human Services is mentioned later; 2) who the announcement is about. This story really has three *Whos*—the third is the developer, Burroughs-Wellcome.

WASHINGTON—An experimental drug that extends the lives and reduces symptoms of some AIDS patients will be made available within weeks to thousands with the deadly disease, federal health officials announced Friday.

What: an experimental drug that extends life and reduces symptoms of AIDS patients.

When: 1) available in a few weeks; 2) announced Friday.

Who: 1) federal health authorities; 2) thousands of AIDS patients.

Why: (relief from) the disease.

Where: Dateline says Washington, but not important.

The significance of the *what* provides the tie-in. ——

Note the use of terms: "first *widely available therapeutic agent* for treating *specific symptoms*." Scientists are very careful about qualifying occurrences, especially discoveries or breakthroughs.

Also notice this is the first time the full name of AIDS is used. That deviates from the usual practice of using abbreviations only on second reference. This deviation is preferred, though, with well-known abbreviations such as AIDS.

The drug—known as azidothymidine, or AZT—will become the first widely available therapeutic agent for treating specific symptoms of acquired immune deficiency syndrome.

Transition/Tie-in: The drug AZT first widely available.

Elaboration on elements in the lead. Federal health authorities are more fully identified; the third *who* implied in the lead is introduced here but not yet named.

New information on *what*.

New information, elaboration of *why*.

These four graphs are the basic elements of the story. The reader could stop there and still have substantive information.

Background dealing with the *what* and *who*—the two essential elements in the story.

About now the reader would begin to ask, "Who said so?" So this graph focuses on the details of who[2]—the Department of Health and Human Services, but now we have a name: Dr. Robert Windom.

A *where* is introduced, and yet another *who*—the Food and Drug Administration, which must approve all new drugs. The writer supposes most U.S. readers would understand this, but puts it in a context so that someone from another country would draw the correct conclusion.

Quote breaks the monotony of the story structure and gives credibility and significance to the story.

The Department of Health and Human Services and a pharmaceutical company that makes AZT stressed that the drug is not a cure for AIDS, may not offer relief for some patients and can have serious side effects.

But the drug proved so promising in a controlled trial that its maker, Burroughs-Wellcome Co. of Research Triangle Park, N.C., asked the government to end the test early. Doctors involved in the tests wanted to make the drug available to those patients receiving a dummy drug, or placebo, saying it was unethical to withhold AZT from them since it is thought to be an effective treatment.

Several months into the human trial, 16 of 137 patients getting the placebo had died, compared with one of 145 getting AZT, scientists said.

The AZT patients, beginning six weeks after starting the drug, also suffered noticeably fewer bouts with other infections and cancers associated with AIDS.

Dr. Robert E. Windom, an assistant secretary for the Department of Health and Human Services, said at a news conference that he has asked the Food and Drug Administration to speed approval of a new, wider trial that could allow thousands of AIDS patients to receive the drug in coming weeks and months.

"Today's announcement represents an important step forward in the search for an effective therapy for treating persons infected with the AIDS virus, but it is only one step," Windom said. He called the test results "exciting and potentially important."

Details: who[2] Dept. of Health; who[3] maker of AZT; who[1] patients what drug not cure.

Where: News conference
What: Asked for early release of drug
Who[4]: (asked) the FDA
Why: to allow AIDS victims to get drug.

(continued)

5.12 (continued)

AIDS, an incurable condition that results in destruction of the body's infection-fighting immune system, has been diagnosed in 24,859 Americans to date, 13,689 of whom have died. There is no effective treatment for the disease and no one is known to have survived it.

Explanation of the disease and
its severity. ——

The virus that causes it, known as HTLV-3 or LAV, is spread through intimate contact with victims' body fluids, such as blood and semen, and more than 70 percent of cases have involved male homosexuals. Other high-risk groups include intravenous drug abusers and those receiving infected blood or blood products.

The expanded trial program, the Treatment Investigational New Drug Trial, would be open to AIDS patients around the country who meet criteria established in earlier tests for those who might benefit from taking AZT.

Discussion of the new drug and
its usefulness. ——

The drug will become available to those AIDS sufferers who also have suffered bouts with pneumocystis carinii pneumonia, a form of pneumonia that frequently springs up in patients and against which the recently suspended trial was targeted.

Introduces two more authorities
and what they have to say. ——

Dr. Anthony Fauci of the National Institutes of Health estimated that between 50 percent and 60 percent of the 12,000 living AIDS patients in the United States have this accompanying pneumonia.

Fauci said additional criteria will be developed by health officials in the next couple of weeks, and said he felt that "several thousand" patients would prove eligible for the new AZT test.

Dr. David W. Barry, vice president for research at Burroughs-Wellcome, said the company would make the drug available free of charge for those in the expanded test. But he also said it would take several months for the company to boost production to make enough of the drug for the anticipated number of patients who will enroll in the study.

Information about the toll-free number for inquiries. One editor chose to break out this information and box it.

The federal department and the company have set up a special toll-free telephone number (1-800-843-9388) for those seeking information about AZT or about getting into the new trial.

To be considered for the expanded studies, AIDS patients will have to get their doctors to certify that they meet the criteria. The doctors would have to agree to both supervise administration of the drug and to file test reports to researchers. The prescription drug will be made available at authorized pharmacies in all parts of the country.

Discussion of the drug and studies involving it.

Researchers said the major side effects of the drug, taken orally several times a day, are bone-marrow suppression and the resulting severe anemia that may require blood transfusions. People who are too weak or whose bone-marrow counts are very low may not be eligible to take the drug, they added.

Yet another authority is introduced. His quote follows.

Dr. Samuel Broder of the National Cancer Institute, who is coordinating new AIDS-drug testing, said a few AZT patients who have taken the drug for more than a year seem to be tolerating it and living better lives.

"I'd say there was a noticeable benefit in quality of life," Broder said. The drug appears to halt disease progression in many patients and even allows some rebuilding of the immune system in others.

Summary with some additional details begins here.

The drug interferes with the reproduction of the AIDS virus within cells by inhibiting an enzyme essential to the process.

The drug was designed more than 20 years ago by Detroit chemist Jerome Horwitz, who experimented with it in preventing tumor cells from dividing.

(continued)

5.12 (continued)

Summary, which could be cut without losing any vital information. ___

But Burroughs-Wellcome researchers discovered in 1984 that AZT appeared promising as an anti-viral agent. Hiroaki Mitsuya, a Japanese researcher at the Bethesda, Md.-based National Institutes of Health, then found that AZT worked to protect healthy cells against the AIDS virus.

Preliminary tests on humans began in July 1985 to determine doses and side effects.

In early tests this year at the cancer institute and Duke University, AZT improved the condition of 15 of 19 advanced AIDS patients, and levels of a white blood cell killed by the virus began increasing, scientists reported.

The current phase of testing began in June at several centers, with more than 100 patients with AIDS and a less-severe form of the disease called AIDS-related complex, receiving the drug and a like number getting a placebo.

Dallas Morning News, Sept. 20, 1986, p. 1A
Reprinted with permission.

5.13 Second-day Follow-up Story

AIDS victims flood hotline with calls after study shows drug prolongs life

By Marilyn Chase
Staff Reporter of The Wall Street Journal

WASHINGTON—A National Institutes of Health telephone hotline has lit up with more than 3,000 telephone calls since Friday's disclosure that the drug azidothymidine, or AZT, prolongs life in certain patients with acquired immune deficiency syndrome.

Calls from patients, their physicians and families have flooded the special switchboard at a rate of 1,000 a day asking for information about eligibility to receive the Burroughs-Wellcome Co. drug free on a "compassionate-plea basis."

On Friday, U.S. health officials ended weeks of speculation and suspense by announcing the results of a six-month controlled study of the drug.

Burroughs-Wellcome said at that time it plans to file a new drug application with the Food and Drug Administration within the next four to six weeks. Robert E. Windom, assistant secretary of health, said he has asked the FDA to put the drug on a fast track, and he forecast that market approval could come as early as Jan. 1.

Burroughs also said that in the meantime it will make AZT available free of charge to patients who meet the strict criteria of the test participants—principally AIDS with early AIDS-linked pneumonia. This could include 60% of the roughly 10,000 AIDS patients in the U.S. today. In all, about 25,000 cases of the fatal syndrome have been diagnosed in the U.S., with an additional one million to two million persons believed infected. The known death toll as of Sept. 15 is about 14,000.

The study evaluated 282 patients with AIDS or AIDS-related complex, which is a set of symptoms including fevers, infections and weight loss that falls outside the technical definition of AIDS. Only one patient died out of a group of 145 patients receiving the drug. But in the control group of 137, which was given a placebo, 16 patients died. Statistically, that is a very significant difference, doctors said, and its chance of occurring randomly is only five in 10,000.

Patients receiving AZT also suffered fewer "serious events," such as infections, during the six-month course of therapy. Their immune systems also improved, as measured by an increase in T-cells, which help fight infection. The drug's most serious side effect so far has been anemia, which may limit AZT treatments or require transfusions.

"Today's announcement represents an important step forward . . . but it is only one step," said Dr. Windom, the assistant secretary for health. "AZT isn't a cure for AIDS," he added. Rather, it is a palliative, which eases symptoms and extends patients' lives. Other researchers were also careful to note the limits of the test.

"It's not a single magic bullet," said David Barry, Burroughs-Wellcome's vice president of research. And Dannie King, head of the company's department of infectious diseases, noted the study "doesn't show how long patients may tolerate the drug, or how long the patients' responses may be maintained." Nor did the test address whether AZT works for any other group of AIDS patients, such as children or patients with Kaposi's Sarcoma, an AIDS-linked malignancy. Further, some clinicians suggested that over long periods the immune-system improvement in AIDS patients may plateau, since some patients' T-cells initially rebound, then level or even drop again. T-cells in patients with AIDS-related complex, or ARC, show a more sustained rise, perhaps because their disease is less severe.

Because the AIDS virus seeks refuge in the brain, doctors are excited by the possibility that AZT may help AIDS patients with brain infections and related neurological ills. These range from pain and muscle weakness to paralysis and psychosis. One researcher, Margaret Fischl of the University of Miami Medical Center, said Friday she has "subjective evidence of (neurological) improvement. But the full meaning of that isn't known," and the question begs further study.

The doctor who initiated the AZT trial, Samuel Broder, clinical oncology chief at the National Cancer Institute, explained that the drug probably works by inhibiting replication of the virus, by allowing the immune system to regenerate and by fostering "a meaningful, not just a statistical improvement" in the quality of life of AIDS patients.

The end of this AZT trial doesn't signify the end of drug tests. Many other possible therapies are currently being studied. It does mean, however, that AZT becomes the "index drug," or current standard against which future drugs will be measured, for AIDS patients with pneumonia.

It also means that for AIDS patients with pneumonia, controversial placebo controls will be ended. Already, patients in the test's control group have begun receiving AZT. Nevertheless, Anthony Fauci, director of the National Institute for Allergy and Infectious Diseases, cautioned that "there's still a place for placebo-controlled trials in other components of AIDS," such as for people with an early-stage infection who haven't yet developed symptoms.

While Burroughs-Wellcome will be supplying free AZT to AIDS patients, it can't do the same for ARC victims, Dr. King said, because the company had to limit its offer to "those people most at risk, that is AIDS patients." However, since estimates of the number of people with ARC run 10 times higher than those with AIDS, others suggested cost might be a factor. "They can't afford to give it out to everyone with ARC," speculated Samuel Isaly, a pharmaceutical industry analyst for S.G. Warburg & Co., New York, the company's investment bankers.

The product of an intense collaboration between the public and private sectors, AZT was discovered nearly two decades ago by Jerome Horwitz of the Michigan Cancer Foundation. When it failed as a cancer chemotherapy, it was shelved until Burroughs-Wellcome developed it as a possible anti-viral drug. When the AIDS epidemic struck, the company sent the compound to the National Cancer Institute, where it was screened with hundreds of other drugs and shown effective against the virus in the test tube. The first patient received AZT at the institute's clinical center in Bethesda, Md., in July 1985.

Wall Street Journal, Sept. 22, 1986, p. 8.

5.14 Follow-up Based on New Development

More AIDS patients eligible for new drug

New York Times News Service

NEW YORK—Most of the 7,000 AIDS patients who have suffered a specific form of pneumonia are now eligible to receive azidothymidine, or AZT, the first drug to show promise against AIDS.

Less than two weeks ago, officials of Burroughs-Wellcome Co., which makes AZT, said that until the drug is licensed for commercial marketing, they would provide it free only to pa-tients who have had a single attack of the form of pneumonia, Pneumo-cystis carinii, within 120 days.

But under the new policy, patients eligible for treatment with AZT include any who have recovered from one or more cases of the pneumonia, who are not receiving other experimental drugs and who have sufficient blood cell counts and adequate liver and kidney function.

How to apply

Physicians can obtain eligibility requirements and patient application forms by calling (800) 843-9388.

From the New York Times News Service, printed in the *Fort Worth Star-Telegram*, Oct. 1, 1986, p. 2A

5.15 Local Follow-up to National Story

Tarrant to get new AIDS drug
By Carolyn Poirot
Star-Telegram Writer

The first experimental drug to show real promise against AIDS should be available in Tarrant County within two weeks, doctors say.

Azidothymidine, or AZT, reduced the symptoms and extended the lives of most AIDS patients who used it in initial human trials, according to reports released by the National Institutes of Health in late September.

It showed such promise that the controlled study was expanded so more AIDS patients would have access to the drug.

"That is fairly common when you are talking about people who are dying of a particular disease and a drug that shows a statistically significant effect against it," said Dr. Alan Kelly, one of several Fort Worth specialists treating patients suffering from the acquired immune deficiency syndrome.

AIDS destroys the immune system, leaving its victims open to deadly infections. It is spread through intimate sexual contact and contaminated drug needles, and no cure is known.

While protocol, or treatment plan, sheets must be submitted for each doctor, patient and pharmacy involved, the drug should be available within two weeks for AIDS patients who have had pneumocystis carinii pneumonia.

"People have been calling. They see a ray of hope and want to make sure they benefit from that ray," said Dr. Okey Nwanyanwu, epidemiologist for the Fort Worth-Tarrant County Health Department.

"We tell them this is not a cure. Not all the answers are in. Not all the questions have even been asked, but anything that will improve the level of care for AIDS patients is most welcome," Nwanyanwu said.

Another doctor agreed but advised caution.

"Preliminary data indicates this drug may be worthwhile, but by no means is anything proven," said Dr. Steve Sotman, an infectious disease specialist. "I think it's great that we have the opportunity to try this, but we should be a little skeptical. It may backfire when we give a safe dose."

Through September, 56 Tarrant County residents had been diagnosed as having AIDS. Twenty-eight have died, Nwanyanwu said. Another half-dozen cases are being processed.

Of those diagnosed, 35 had pneumocystis.

Physicians and patients last week began processing the paperwork necessary to obtain AZT.

The drug affects the bone marrow and can cause anemia. Some patients become so anemic that they need blood transfusions during treatment. Headaches, mild confusion and anxiety, skin rashes and itching also have been reported, but side effects are mild considering the disease, Kelly said.

"This is an inevitably fatal disease. When death is inevitable, the risks of toxicity are not as significant," he said.

"Once they develop pneumocystis, AIDS patients are about 90 percent sure of dying within two years, usually less," Kelly said. "It's an important drug, a dramatic change in the way we can treat this disease."

He said the new study is being confined to patients who have had pneumocystis only because it is the most common marker of AIDS and is very easy to diagnose under the microscope. AZT actually is effective against the AIDS virus, not the pneumonia, which is caused by a common parasite that causes disease only in people whose immune systems are significantly weakened.

"Sixty to 70 percent of all AIDS patients are diagnosed on the basis of pneumocystis pneumonia or will get this infection," said Kelly, who is treating five AIDS patients, including two who have completed the paperwork necessary to get the new drug.

Sotman, who had four through Friday who were completing the application process, said he is advising "all people sitting out there with no hope to try it."

The drug is being supplied free by the manufacturer, Burroughs-Wellcome Co.

Dr. David Beyer said he has a number of patients who have requested information on AZT, and he plans to apply for the drug through Fort Worth Osteopathic Medical Center.

"It looked promising in preliminary trials, but that was a small sample," Beyer said. "But since (AIDS) is uniformly fatal, people are willing to say, 'Let's try something.' They seem to have simplified the protocols to make it more readily available. I'm delighted that it's going to be available."

By Friday, more than 12,000 phone calls had reached the new AIDS hot line, set up by the National Institutes of Health to answer questions concerning the drug, said Walt Martin, a hot line operator.

"We've had applications from all over the country. They have not yet been separated by state or county," Martin said when asked the number of doctors and pharmacies from this area who are applying for the drug.

"It is being forwarded to hospital pharmacies only, because it is felt they are more secure than drugstores," he said. "We will begin sending it out just as soon as the paperwork is processed, probably within the next two weeks."

Harris Hospital in Fort Worth is applying for the drug. Both John Peter Smith and St. Joseph hospitals are considering making it available, and Arlington Memorial likely will apply if doctors treating AIDS patients request it, hospital spokesmen said.

Hot line

A toll-free hot line, (800) 843-9388, has been set up at the National Institutes of Health for questions on AZT, an experimental treatment for AIDS. The hot line operates daily between 7 a.m. and 11 p.m.

Fort Worth Star-Telegram, Oct. 13, 1986.

---

all the latest information covering all specifics, as well as some quotes from persons of authority.

Many news editors fault PR people for failure to carry out this function. "We hear a lot from them in advance when they want the space to call attention to something," they say, "but once it's over and we need a wrap-up, they're nowhere to be found." If something is news, it's news afterward, too.

Futures   Stories from the futures file are often of a public service nature, announcing the routine, such as school board meetings, and the special, such as the opening of an art exhibit. The only information you might have is a time, place and contact logged into a futures book. Some people use a calendar book (such as a Daytimer). You can log in all expected events (such as holiday observances), firm events (for example, the lighting of the city's Christmas tree) and casual ones (such as the expected time for a new building to be completed). If you cover a news beat, you'll be able to jot down meeting times and recurring events such as election of an organization's officers (school board, chamber of commerce and so on).

When you get some information about a future event, it may be skimpy—a note with some clips of the initial stories that says to check on an architect's plans for a new school, for example, or a news release describing the scheduled arrival of a circus. You'll integrate information from the files and the release with what you discover by calling sources. Use a checklist to be sure all of the who–what–when–where–why–and–how information is there.

ADVANCES

The advance describes something that is to happen, anything from a meeting of the city council to the first opera of the season. Advances flood into newsrooms because people involved in an event want recognition. Some information comes from public relations sources, but a great deal of it comes from organizations with publicity committees. Reporters also generate information about upcoming events on their beats. On top of that, an endless variety of calendars listing all the events in the state, or city, or county, or meeting place come to the news desk. Beginning reporters are often assigned to deal with this deluge to free more experienced staff for more complex assignments.

Sometimes advances are carried in an "around town" column with each event being an item. Radio is likely to use the calendar-of-events approach; television will use an advance only if there is something interesting to show, such as the circus unloading animals or an antique show going into a big exhibit hall.

When you're asked to write an advance, ordinarily you'll be given the name and phone number of a contact. When you call, you need to start with this checklist:

- Official name of the group (any national connections to a larger group).
- Time and place for the event.
- Major items on the agenda.
- Names of officers, speakers, any visiting dignitaries.
- Why the event is important.
- Whether the public is invited, and if so the cost of admission, meals, registration and so on.

These are the basics that give you the clues about where to go from there to fill out the story.

The structure is the inverted pyramid for print and a slightly modified version for broadcasting.

Print structure

WHO: The University's Symphony Orchestra

WHAT: opens its 20th season on campus

WHEN: this Sunday at 3 p.m.

WHERE: in the Music Hall Auditorium

Concertmaster Dr. Johnanna First will be the soloist in Brahms' Violin Concerto.

Dr. I.R. Arms, music director, will conduct the orchestra in the first of its five-week subscription series.

HOW: Tickets to the series are available to students and faculty for $1.00 at the Music Hall Box Office. Some individual tickets will be sold at the door for $2.50.

The series is underwritten by the Citywide Foundation for the Performing Arts.

What's missing? You could provide more complete information by adding the other pieces to be presented on the program. You could do the readers a service by advising students and faculty to bring ID cards when purchasing tickets. You could tell how much tickets cost for people outside the university. Can the community buy series tickets? What if someone from the campus wants to bring someone from outside? Can two come at campus rates and sit together? A good editor may send you back for those details. A sharp editor will ask you whether the symphony is doing anything special for this 20th-anniversary year. If so, what is it? Has some music been commissioned? Who is the composer? Who paid for the commissioned work? Why is the series sponsored by a local group from the community? There may be more to the story than the bare bones.

Broadcast structure   Probably not even all of the bare bones will be used in the broadcast story. A likely version for the student radio station:

WHO: The University's symphony orchestra begins

WHAT: its 20th season on campus this fall. The

WHEN: first concert of the fall series is Sunday

WHERE: afternoon at 3 o'clock in the Music Hall Auditorium.

HOW: Series tickets are still available to faculty and students at the box office.

Although the broadcast story is much briefer, the station's news director should have on hand as much information about the event as the newspaper's editor. The radio station may rewrite the story often during the week. The same words will be threadbare by Saturday and Sunday, an important time for the story to be used, unless tickets are sold out. A sample rewrite:

> Series tickets to the University Symphony Orchestra's fall performances are available now. The symphony's first concert is Sunday afternoon. Faculty and students can get their tickets at the Music Hall Auditorium box office.

A rewrite for Saturday:

> Tomorrow afternoon the University's symphony orchestra begins its 20th year on the campus. The first concert of the fall season is at 3 o'clock in the Music Hall Auditorium. Single tickets and series tickets are available at the Auditorium box office.

Notice in both the print and broadcast versions, the last sentence can be deleted without harm to the story. The print version can be cut up to its first paragraph.

OBITUARIES   Obits, too, are among the most common stories handled by beginning reporters, especially on smaller papers, which are more likely to use a large number of obits. Editors often give these stories to beginners to test both their accuracy and their creativity—their ability to make the routine interesting. In major markets some papers will carry staff-written obituaries, but others will carry only obituaries of famous people, for many of whom the wire services have "standing obits" waiting for use (see 5.16). Broadcast obits are presented only for well-known people. All newspapers publish in the classifieds notices from the funeral homes of burial services.

Both stories and notices get a great deal of attention, especially from people associated with the story. Yet it seems the obituaries written by the newspaper's staff often contain many errors. Perhaps the simplicity of the stories makes them subject to careless handling.

The *Orlando Sentinel* is one newspaper that daily publishes obituaries of ordinary people, some 13,000 to 14,000 a year. To ensure against errors or misidentifications when people have the same or similar names, the paper requires the age and address of the person who died. The names of organizations the person belonged to and the names and cities of relatives usually cause the most accuracy problems.[1]

Credit is given to E. Clifton Daniel Jr. for developing at the *New York Times* the system of standing obits for famous people.[2] The first writer of these standing obits was Alden Whitman, who always tried to interview the subjects. Although some of the famous he interviewed teased him about being the *Times'* "ghoul," he said:

> . . . no necrophilious thought passes through my brain as I talk with men and women about themselves in preparation for writing the profiles that will accompany the news of their deaths . . . The practice makes an enormous amount of good sense. Newspapers interview people all the time about everything under the sun. Why not interview them about themselves?[3]

Whitman's skill at his craft is cited in a manual for newsroom supervisors:

Some wire service obits on the late Sen. William Benton reported he graduated from Yale. It remained for Alden Whitman of the *New York Times* to tell us he worked his way through Yale playing high-stakes auction bridge, although he had denied he made $25,000 in one year. Whitman interviews famous persons while they are still alive, and also talks to associates and friends for leads. . . . The Benton obit . . . fascinated readers because it told that he . . . invented the singing commercial . . . first used live audiences on radio and first cued audiences with "applaud" cards . . . "discovered" and got a sponsor for "Amos n' Andy" on radio . . . sold Muzak music to thousands of buildings and dentists' offices.[4]

A successor as the *Times'* standing obit writer, Marilyn Berger, said: "Some biographies might take a week to write. Others might take two or three weeks . . . There's an emphasis on writing them well, and there are sometimes huge amounts of material to go through."[5]

Information about people who have died generally results from interviews with official sources at the scene of the death (hospital, police, fire or company officials) or at funeral homes after arrangements are made. The funeral home relies on family members to supply information. Information from any source is likely to be just the basic facts: name, address, year and place of birth, family, education, civic or military service, employment, memberships, cause of death (sometimes) and survivors. Most people's lives are more interesting than these facts would imply. Discovering who the person was and what he or she did can make the obituary a profile, not a death notice.

The good reporter uses the interview to collect such details. Contact friends and neighbors of the deceased to get a better idea of how that person lived. What hobbies did the person have? Some people's hobbies become almost a vocation. A prominent lawyer may have been better known to neighbors and close friends as a highly skilled lapidarist who polished and mounted special stones for friends on important occasions. A graphic artist is especially missed by the handicapped children in a home where she had spent every Saturday teaching art. If you interview the friends and associates of the deceased, it will make discussions with family members easier because you'll have something to talk about.

You may find it easier to talk with relatives outside the immediate family, especially if the death was unexpected, and it is often these relatives who answer the telephone.

What do you do if there's no one to talk to? There's always someone. One illustration may provide suggestions. A neighborhood character died in a large city. She frequented one restaurant and was a "housemother" of the streets to many younger transients, lending them money, caring for them when they were sick. She was known as Princess; no one was sure where she lived. A reporter was tenacious enough to find out the facts of her life, verify them and describe her as she was known in the neighborhood and how the people she had befriended felt about her death.

Public relations people sometimes have difficulty writing the "standing obits" for the people in their organization. It's easy to imagine the reluctance of a top officer in the organization to be interviewed for such a purpose. One PR person overcame this by saying to the director, who didn't hold reporters in high regard, "Would you rather they write the story or me?" Actually, the news media *do* have final control over what appears, but they'll generally use material supplied to them by the organization. In fact, they expect it. The organization where someone worked is on the obit writer's list to call just after the funeral home.

Some PR writers approach the standing obits for their top people more subtly; they simply call them background features. That's not just a euphemism; much of the information is used from time to time in feature profiles they will write as well as introductions for the person when he or she is speaking somewhere.

Broadcast obituaries   Most obituaries on radio and television are for prominent people. Obituaries of the well known are transmitted by wire services both to print and broadcast media. For a national or international celebrity, the television networks will pull from their libraries a videotape prepared in advance of scenes from the life of the person. Ordinarily these are prepared only for very prominent people, such as heads of state. However, when any distinguished person dies, television news staffs at the station or network level can put together material, voice and pictures, from the files for an obituary.

For most broadcast obituaries, the introduction is generally descriptive, identifying the person. Next comes a simple statement of where or how the death occurred. Circumstances or cause of death and burial sometimes are used. An example:

> The state's poet laureate, Robert Willis, died today in an Auburn hospital. He was 71. Willis was hospitalized early last month after collapsing at a reading of his poetry. Burial is tomorrow afternoon at the state capitol.

In reducing even that small amount of copy, an editor may cut the third sentence, making the entire obit less than 10 seconds long.

If there is a story in the lives of ordinary people, there certainly is more than enough to write about the lives of the famous. How do you find it? Most beginning writers won't have the opportunity to write the story about an internationally known person, but they may about a community celebrity.

Obituaries can—and should—be interesting, because people are. If as a beginning writer you ever complain that you're only doing rewrites and obits while other people get to do the features, you might need to see whether you're passing up the feature elements in the stories you're writing.

5.16 Obituary for National Figure

The Associated Press obituary for Bess Truman was very much the same for both print and broadcast on announcement. Later broadcasts, both television and radio, carried quotes from such prominent figures as another first lady, Lady Bird (Mrs. Lyndon B.) Johnson. The AP Broadcast Service's assistant broadcast editor, Sue Cuneff, noted that they had enough material already prepared to move on the wire two long pieces, about 90 minutes' airtime, immediately after the initial bulletin around 4:45 a.m. "We were able to provide these strong capsules while the nation's radio stations were still in their morning drive news period." The additional items illustrate how easily a story can be made to sound different over several hours if the material is available.

```
AP-U R G E N T

BESS TRUMAN (DETAILS)

     (KANSAS CITY)--FORMER FIRST LADY BESS TRUMAN,
THE WOMAN FORMER PRESIDENT HARRY TRUMAN REFERRED
TO AS "THE BOSS," IS DEAD AT AGE 97.
     A SPOKESMAN FOR THE RESEARCH MEDICAL CENTER
IN KANSAS CITY SAYS TRUMAN WAS PRONOUNCED DEAD ON
ARRIVAL AT THE HOSPITAL AT ABOUT 4:30 THIS
MORNING. THE TRUMAN FAMILY PHYSICIAN, DR. WALLACE
GRAHAM, SAID SHE DIED OF CONGESTIVE HEART
FAILURE.
     TRUMAN HAD BEEN PLAGUED IN RECENT YEARS BY A
VARIETY OF AILMENTS, INCLUDING ARTHRITIS,
ABDOMINAL STRESS AND HIGH BLOOD PRESSURE.
     ON SEPTEMBER SECOND, SHE WAS RUSHED TO THE
HOSPITAL FROM HER HOME IN NEARBY INDEPENDENCE,
MISSOURI WITH INTERNAL BLEEDING. DOCTORS SAID THE
BLEEDING, WHICH RESULTED FROM AN ULCER, STOPPED
THE NEXT DAY, BUT THE FORMER FIRST LADY WAS NOT
RELEASED FROM THE HOSPITAL FOR THREE WEEKS.
     MRS. TRUMAN OUTLIVED HER HUSBAND BY NEARLY
TEN YEARS. SHE ALSO LIVED LONGER THAN ANY OTHER
FORMER FIRST LADY. EDITH WILSON, WIFE OF
PRESIDENT WOODROW WILSON, DIED AT AGE 89 IN
1961.  THE OLDEST LIVING FIRST LADY IS
70-YEAR-OLD PAT NIXON.
     IN 53 YEARS OF MARRIAGE, BESS TRUMAN ENJOYED
THE TRADITIONAL WOMAN'S ROLE OF THE QUIET AND
UNASSUMING BUT THOROUGHLY DEVOTED WIFE AND
MOTHER. BUT HER HUSBAND SAID SHE WAS HIS CLOSEST
CONFIDANTE AND ADVISER ON EVERY IMPORTAMT THING
HE EVER DID--INCLUDING DECISIONS LEADING TO HIS
UPSET VICTORY OVER THOMAS DEWEY IN 1948.
     SHE SAID ONCE THAT BEING FIRST LADY REQUIRED
```

(continued)

5.16 (continued)

"GOOD HEALTH AND A SENSE OF HUMOR."
     BY THE TIME HER HUSBAND DIED AT AGE 88 TEN
YEARS AGO, ARTHRITIS IN HER RIGHT LEG HAD
ADVANCED TO THE POINT WHERE MRS TRUMAN HAD
CURTAILED HER ACTIVITIES.
     HER HUSBAND'S WILL SPECIFIES THAT SHE BE
BURIED BESIDE HIM IN THE GARDEN OF THE TRUMAN
LIBRARY, A FEW BLOCKS FROM THE FAMILY MANSION.

AP-NY-10-18-82 072 EDT

AP-BESS TRUMAN OBIT

(INDEPENDENCE, MISSOURI)--ELIZABETH WALLACE
TRUMAN WAS A QUIET AND UNASSUMING WOMAN. WHEREVER
SHE WENT DURING HER HUSBAND'S PRESIDENCY, SHE WAS
HERSELF...BESS TRUMAN, A HOUSEWIFE AND HOMEMAKER
FROM INDEPENDENCE, MISSOURI. BEING FIRST LADY
DURING THE ADMINISTRATION OF HARRY S. TRUMAN WAS
ENTIRELY SECONDARY.
     IN THE 53 YEARS OF THEIR MARRIAGE, BESS
TRUMAN SAW HER HUSBAND RISE FROM COUNTY OFFICIAL
TO SENATOR, VICE PRESIDENT, AND--FINALLY--EIGHT
YEARS IN THE OVAL OFFICE BEGINNING IN 1945. BUT
SHE ALWAYS REFUSED TO BE SWAYED BY THE GLITTER OF
THEIR LIFE AND PREFERRED HER HOMETOWN CIRCLE OF
FRIENDS. SO THE FIRST LADY LEFT THE SPOTLIGHT TO
PRESIDENT TRUMAN.
     YET, IN SPITE OF HER PREFERENCE FOR PRIVACY,
BESS TRUMAN DEVOTEDLY SUPPORTED HER HUSBAND'S
PUBLIC CAREER. SHE WORKED FOR A TIME IN HER
HUSBAND'S SENATE OFFICE, WHILE ALSO SUPERVISING
THEIR HOUSEHOLD DUTIES AND THE UPBRINGING OF
THEIR DAUGHTER MARGARET. HE FREQUENTLY CREDITED
HER WITH GREAT HELP AND ADVICE, REFERRING TO HER
LOVINGLY AS "THE BOSS."
     IT WAS A HAPPY DAY FOR BESS TRUMAN IN JANUARY
1953 WHEN SHE, HARRY AND MARGARET RETURNED TO
INDEPENDENCE TO STAY AFTER HARRY LEFT OFFICE. SHE
WAS BACK AT THE HOUSE WHERE SHE WAS BORN ON

FEBRUARY 13TH, 1885...A RAMBLING, THREE-STORY
VICTORIAN STRUCTURE BUILT BY HER GRANDFATHER.

AFTER PRESIDENT TRUMAN'S DEATH ON THE DAY
AFTER CHRISTMAS IN 1972, BESS QUIETLY LIVED ALONE
IN THAT HOUSE--EXCEPT FOR A DOMESTIC STAFF AND
SECRET SERVICE AGENTS.

IN THE EARLY MORNING HOURS OF AUGUST FIRST,
MRS. TRUMAN WAS ADMITTED TO RESEARCH MEDICAL
CENTER IN KANSAS CITY. SHE WAS HOSPITALIZED AFTER
HER RESPIRATION AND PULSE BECAME IRREGULAR.
BECAUSE OF BESS TRUMAN'S AGE--97--SHE WAS
INITIALLY LISTED IN SERIOUS CONDITION. SHE
RETURNED TO THE HOSPITAL IN EARLY SEPTEMBER WITH
INTERNAL BLEEDING, WHICH DOCTORS ATTRIBUTED TO AN
ULCER.

TODAY, BESS TRUMAN WAS RUSHED BACK TO THE
HOSPITAL--WHERE SHE WAS PRONOUNCED DEAD ON
ARRIVAL. DOCTORS SAID SHE DIED OF CONGESTIVE
HEART FAILURE.

FORMER FIRST LADY BESS TRUMAN...DEAD AT THE
AGE OF 97.

BESS TRUMAN, WHO SHARED HER HUSBAND'S RISE
FROM COUNTY OFFICIAL TO U-S PRESIDENT, HAS DIED
AT THE AGE OF 97. HER DOCTOR SAYS THE FORMER
FIRST LADY SUFFERED CONGESTIVE HEART FAILURE
EARLY TODAY AND WAS DEAD ON ARRIVAL AT RESEARCH
MEDICAL CENTER IN KANSAS CITY. MRS. TRUMAN
OUTLIVED HER HUSBAND, HARRY, BY NEARLY TEN YEARS.
FRIENDS SAY THEIR CHILDHOOD ROMANCE HAD NEVER
FLAGGED, THAT TRUMAN WAS THE ONLY MAN SHE EVER
REALLY LOVED--AND SHE, THE ONLY SWEETHEART HE
EVER HAD.

BESS TRUMAN NEVER HAD AN OFFICIAL JOB IN
GOVERNMENT OTHER THAN AS A CLERK AND A SECRETARY.
BUT HER HUSBAND OF 53 YEARS ONCE DESCRIBED HER AS
HIS CLOSEST CONFIDANTE AND ADVISER. MRS. TRUMAN,
WHO'D BEEN IN POOR HEALTH FOR SOME TIME, DIED
THIS MORNING OF CONGESTIVE HEART FAILURE. THE
FORMER FIRST LADY WAS 97, AND SHE'D OUTLIVED HER
HUSBAND BY NEARLY TEN YEARS. PRESIDENT HARRY
TRUMAN DIED DECEMBER 26TH, 1972.

(continued)

THE NATION IS NOW LEFT WITH ONLY FIVE LIVING FORMER FIRST LADIES--JACQUELINE KENNEDY ONASSIS, LADY BIRD JOHNSON, PAT NIXON, BETTY FORD AND ROSALYNN (ROH'-ZUH-LIN) CARTER.

PRESIDENT HARRY TRUMAN ONCE WROTE TO A FRIEND THAT THE MOST JOYOUS MOMENT OF HIS LIFE WAS WHEN HIS CHILDHOOD SWEETHEART AGREED TO MARRY HIM. TRUMAN'S CHILDHOOD SWEETHEART AND THE NATION'S FORMER FIRST LADY DIED EARLY TODAY OF CONGESTIVE HEART FAILURE. BESS TRUMAN WAS 97.

THE GARDEN OF THE TRUMAN LIBRARY IN INDEPENDENCE, MISSOURI IS EXPECTED TO BE THE FINAL RESTING PLACE FOR FORMER FIRST LADY BESS TRUMAN. SHE DIED THIS MORNING IN KANSAS CITY AT AGE 97. PRESIDENT HARRY TRUMAN'S WILL SPECIFIED THAT HIS WIFE OF 53 YEARS BE BURIED NEXT TO HIM.
MRS. TRUMAN IS SURVIVED BY HER DAUGHTER, MARGARET TRUMAN DANIEL. THE DANIELS ARE SAID TO BE IN LONDON AND ARE EXPECTED TO FLY TO INDEPENDENCE, MISSOURI THIS EVENING.

AMERICANS ARE MOURNING THE DEATH TODAY OF BESS TRUMAN, WHO AT 97 HAD LIVED LONGER THAN ANY OTHER FORMER FIRST LADY. SHE'S BEING REMEMBERED AS PRESIDENT HARRY TRUMAN'S CLOSEST ADVISER, AND A WOMAN OF DIGNITY AND QUALITY. PRESIDENT REAGAN CALLED HER A "GRACIOUS, UNASSUMING FIRST LADY."
BESS TRUMAN'S DOCTOR SAYS HE KNEW "THE END WAS NEAR" WHEN SHE LEFT A KANSAS CITY HOSPITAL ON SEPTEMBER 24TH AFTER TREATMENT FOR AN ULCER. MRS. TRUMAN DIED THIS MORNING OF CONGESTIVE HEART FAILURE. DR. WALLACE GRAHAM SAYS NONE OF THE DRUGS GIVEN THE FORMER FIRST LADY OVER THE WEEKEND SEEMED TO WORK. AND, IN HIS WORDS, "THERE WAS NOTHING MORE THAT WE COULD HAVE DONE." MRS. TRUMAN, WHO WAS MARRIED TO AMERICA'S 33RD PRESIDENT FOR 53 YEARS, IS TO BE BURIED BESIDE HIM AT THEIR HOME IN INDEPENDENCE, MISSOURI.

(continued)

```
     FUNERAL SERVICES FOR FORMER FIRST LADY BESS
TRUMAN ARE TENTATIVELY SET FOR THURSDAY. A FAMILY
SPOKESMAN SAYS IT'LL BE A PRIVATE AFFAIR. MRS.
TRUMAN DIED OF CONGESTIVE HEART FAILURE AT THE
FAMILY HOME IN INDEPENDENCE, MISSOURI TODAY AT
THE AGE OF 97. ACCORDING TO FAMILY PHYSICIAN DR.
WALLACE GRAHAM "THE OLD ENGINE JUST RAN OUT."
MRS. TRUMAN HAD BEEN BATTLING A SERIES OF
AILMENTS FOR THE LAST SEVERAL YEARS. SHE WAS
REMEMBERED BY KANSAS CITY MAYOR RICHARD BERKLEY
AS "A WOMAN OF SPIRIT AND COURAGE."
```

```
AP-WITH 'ESS TRUMAN-REAGAN

     (WASHINGTON)--PRESIDENT REAGAN IS LEADING THE
NATION IN MOURNING THE DEATH TODAY OF FORMER
FIRST LADY BESS TRUMAN.
     THE PRESIDENT ISSUED A STATEMENT SAYING THE
97-YEAR-OLD MRS. TRUMAN HAD "LIVED A LONG, FULL
LIFE SERVING HER HUSBAND, HER FAMILY AND HER
COUNTRY WITH DIGNITY."
     REAGAN CALLED MRS. TRUMAN "A DEVOTED WIFE, A
LOVING MOTHER AND A GRACIOUS, UNASSUMING FIRST
LADY." AND HE SAID SHE "EMBODIED THE BASIC
DECENCY OF AMERICA."
     THE PRESIDENT CONCLUDED BY SAYING, "NANCY AND
I CONVEY OUR DEEPEST SYMPATHY TO HER FAMILY AND
TO ALL WHO WILL MISS THIS FINE LADY'S GOODNESS."

AP-NY-10-18-82 1203EST
```

From Associated Press Broadcast Services. Reprinted with permission.

(continued)

5.16 (continued)

Bess Truman dies at age 97

KANSAS CITY, Mo. (AP)—Bess Truman, the nation's oldest former first lady and the lifelong sweetheart President Harry S. Truman called "The Boss," died early today. She was 97.

The Truman family physician, Dr. Wallace Graham, said Mrs. Truman died of congestive heart failure. Research Medical Center said she was pronounced dead on arrival at the hospital at 4:38 a.m.

Mrs. Truman outlived her husband by nearly 10 years. Friends say their childhood romance never flagged—that he was the only man she ever really loved and she the only sweetheart he ever had.

In 53 years of marriage, Mrs. Truman much enjoyed the traditional woman's role of the quiet and unassuming but thoroughly devoted wife and mother. But Truman said she was his closest confidante and adviser on every important thing he ever did—including decisions leading to his upset victory over Thomas E. Dewey in 1948.

"I never wrote a speech without going over it with her," he said of the woman who shared his rise from county official to U.S. senator to president.

Mrs. Truman had been plagued in recent years by a variety of ailments—arthritis, abdominal stress and high blood pressure. On Sept. 2, she was rushed to the hospital from her home in nearby Independence, Mo., with internal bleeding. Graham said the hemorrhaging, which he attributed to an ulcer in her duodenum, stopped the next day, but Mrs. Truman was not released from the hospital until Sept. 24.

She was hospitalized for six days in August for treatment of hyperkalemia, a potassium build-up caused by diminished kidney function.

To some, Mrs. Truman's dignity and reserve left the impression that she was austere, withdrawn and colorless, but those intimates entitled to call her Bessie knew her as warm and gracious, witty and wise.

She said in 1948 that being first lady required "good health and a sense of humor." Of criticism of her husband, she said once, "after 25 years in politics, I've learned to accept it—almost."

And despite her eagerness to avoid publicity for herself, Mrs. Truman became known as a gracious White House hostess and a woman with an amazing ability to remember names.

Observers regarded it as characteristic that she reduced the White House staff by almost half after her husband became president. Guests described her as a housekeeping genius, both in the White House and at the family mansion in Independence.

Mrs. Truman lived longer than any other former first lady.

Edith Wilson, wife of Woodrow Wilson, was the oldest at age 89 in 1961. Mary Scott Harrison, the second wife of Benjamin Harrison, died in 1948 at age 90, but was never first lady. The oldest living first lady is 70-year-old Pat Nixon.

Known as independent and athletic during her girlhood in Independence—where one magazine writer reported she was the only girl able to whistle through her teeth—Bess Truman was the only daughter in a socially prominent family. She was born in the three-story Victorian mansion in Independence that her grandfather built in 1865, and it was her home for nearly all her life.

Although primarily a homemaker and helpmate, she was active in social organizations, and did draw a salary for a time—she spent two years on Truman's Senate staff as a clerk and secretary, at $4,500 a year.

After leaving the White House, Mrs. Truman said she missed some things about life there—notably its able gardeners and household staff—but not the "big receptions where hundreds and hundreds of strange hands had to be shaken," the mountains of mail and many appointments.

The Trumans retired to Independence from Washington, and in 1955 she told of her unsuccessful efforts to get her husband to put their power mower to use—a tale that strikes a familiar chord for followers of the scrappy former president.

"Finally he did. 11 o'clock on a Sunday morning, with all the Methodists and Baptists going by our house on the way to church," Mrs. Truman recalled. "There's not a doubt in my mind he planned the whole thing deliberately to save himself from ever touching that mower again. And he hasn't."

Born Elizabeth Virginia Wallace on Feb. 13, 1885, a birthday Truman said he could always remember because it fell before Valentine's Day, Mrs. Truman was known as Bess to the world and Bessie to intimates.

Her husband's will specified that she be buried beside him in the garden of the Truman Library, a few blocks from the family mansion. With her name and other pertinent information, Truman directed that the inscription on his wife's slab read: "First Lady, The United States of America, April 12, 1945-January 20, 1953."

First lady was not a role Bess Truman sought. When Truman was nominated as Franklin Roosevelt's running mate in 1944, Mrs. Truman said she didn't want her husband to be vice president but was "reconciled" to the idea. The Democrats won, and within a few months, Roosevelt was dead and Truman was the nation's 33rd chief executive.

"I've had several moments of great joy . . . but the greatest joy of them all was when my sweetheart from 6 years old consented to become Mrs. Truman," Truman wrote in a 1958 letter to Arkansas Superior Court Justice Edward McFaddin published in *Off the Record, the Private Papers of Harry S. Truman.*

By the time Truman died at age 88 on Dec. 26, 1972, arthritis in her right leg had advanced to the point where Mrs. Truman had curtailed her activities.

Nevertheless, she built a new life with the help of a few close friends. It was perhaps a mark of fastidiousness rather than vanity that she continued to make regular trips to the beauty parlor.

A routine checkup in March 1978 turned into a four-week hospital stay and Mrs. Truman was hospitalized twice more that year for a variety of ailments.

Mrs. Truman continued into her mid-90s to receive some dignitaries.

Her last visit by a president was in September 1980 when President Jimmy Carter spent about 10 minutes with her during a campaign swing.

President Gerald Ford visited her for a few minutes in May 1976 when he dedicated a statue of Truman in the Old Courthouse Square in Independence. She did not take part in the ceremonies.

©1982 *Fort Worth Star-Telegram*, Oct. 18, 1982. Used with permission.

MAIN POINTS

- Structuring stories properly requires the right arrangement of these elements:

  1. The lead (the main point)
  2. Secondary points
  3. Elaboration on the main point
  4. Support for the lead
  5. Background
  6. Development of the main idea
  7. Details

- To make a story interesting:

  1. Use direct quotations.
  2. Show, don't tell.
  3. Answer people's questions about a story.
     a. Explain effects on people.
     b. Include all relevant times, places, dates, names.
     c. Identify people and organizations.
     d. Present relevant numbers.
     e. Support generalities with specifics.
     f. Give background.
     g. Describe the circumstances.
     h. Note any unusual aspects.
     i. Discuss expected future developments.

- Radio news copy is typed full-page and is timed at four seconds per line.
- Radio news stories can be readers or lead-ins and tags to audiotape: actualities and voicers.
- TV copy is typed in a half-page format with the right-hand side used for copy and the left-hand side for technical cues.
- A TV news reader, a slide or chromakey shot, a lead-in to videotape, a voice-over, and incorporating supers into the scripts are the basics of TV newswriting.
- Beginning writers are often given rewrites—combined stories, holdover copy, news stories that need a follow-up and futures assignments from the file. A rewrite means taking a fresh approach to make the copy lively, interesting and "new."
- The advance describes something that is to happen. The story needs to be as complete as possible, because it will be read carefully by people who might want to participate.
- The obit is an important story to family and friends, and although only famous people's obits make the front page or broadcast news, some obits of ordinary people can be poignant features.

EXERCISES

1. Select four news stories from a current paper. Try to label each paragraph with its function in the story: lead, development of the lead, background, secondary points, details and so on. Then make lists of which elements of a news story are sometimes omitted and which seldom or never are.

2. If your university received a bomb threat and you were assigned the story, list all of the sources you would need to call. Include names, complete titles, addresses and phone numbers.

3. Find an advance story in the newspaper. See whether it gives all of the information that you would need to attend that event. What is missing, if anything? Why? Compare print and broadcast versions of the story. How do they differ? Why?

NOTES

1. "The Last Word," *Sentinel Communications Quarterly* 4, no. 2 (Summer 1986): 12.

2. Ibid., pp. 12–13.

3. Alden Whitman, "So You Want to Be an Obit Writer," *Saturday Review*, Dec. 11, 1971, p. 70.

4. John L. Dougherty, *Learning in the Newsroom: A Manual for Supervisors* (Reston, Va.: American Newspaper Publishers Association Foundation, 1975), pp. 117, 119.

5. "Postscript," *Sentinel Communications Quarterly*, p. 13.

SUGGESTIONS FOR ADDITIONAL READING

Capon, René. *The Word: An Associated Press Guide to Good News Writing*. New York: Associated Press, 1982.

French, Christopher W., Eileen Alt Powell and Howard Angione, eds. *The Associated Press Stylebook and Libel Manual*. New York: Associated Press, 1980.

Garcia, Mario R. *Contemporary Newspaper Design: A Structural Approach*. 2nd ed. Englewood Cliffs, N.J.: Prentice-Hall, 1987.

Holley, Frederick S., ed. *The Los Angeles Times Stylebook*. New York: New American Library, 1981.

Hood, James R., and Brad Kalbfeld, eds. *The Associated Press Broadcast News Handbook*. New York: Associated Press, 1982.

Jewler, A. Jerome. *Creative Strategies in Advertising*. 2nd ed. Belmont, Calif.: Wadsworth, 1985.

Jordan, Lewis, ed. *The New York Times Manual of Style and Usage*. New York: Times Books, 1976.

Meeske, Milan D., and R.C. Norris. *Copywriting for the Electronic Media: A Practical Guide*. Belmont, Calif.: Wadsworth, 1987.

Miller, Bobby Ray. *The UPI Stylebook*. New York: United Press International, 1977.

O'Donnell, Lewis B., Carl Hausman and Philip Benoit. *Announcing: Broadcast Communicating Today*. Belmont, Calif.: Wadsworth, 1987.   See Chapter 8, "The Craft of Interviewing."

Shook, Frederick. *The Process of Electronic News Gathering*. Englewood, Colo.: Morton, 1982.

Smeyak, G. Paul. *Broadcast News Writing*. 2nd ed. Columbus, Ohio: Grid, 1983.

Utz, Peter. *Today's Video: Equipment, Setup and Production 1987*. Englewood Cliffs, N.J.: Prentice-Hall, 1987.

Webb, Robert A., ed. *The Washington Post Deskbook on Style*. New York: McGraw-Hill, 1978.

Westin, Av. *Newswatch: How TV Decides the News*. New York: Simon & Schuster, 1982.   Written by a powerful veteran TV newsman, this book explains the technical and production aspects of news in the network and local newsrooms.

Yoakum, Richard, and Charles F. Cremer. *ENG: TV News and the New Technology*. New York: Random House, 1985.

CHAPTER 6

Writing for the New Electronic Media: Teletext and Videotex

We live in an era of rapidly changing communications technology. Satellites are sending signals directly to homes equipped with satellite dishes; home and office computers are affecting how we communicate; such things as "electronic mail" may replace the postal service. Videotape recorders, compact discs, large-screen TVs and miniature TVs are found in increasing numbers of homes. Anyone who doesn't have these devices today probably will in the future.

These technologies offer new opportunities to communicators. In addition to the proliferation of cable TV systems, thousands of new low-power television (LPTV) and radio stations will be signing on the air over the next few years. New transmission technology makes it possible for more of these low-power stations to be approved. That means more potential jobs and additional, creative ways to use these new media.

An emerging communications innovation is teletext and videotex, which combine many aspects of broadcasting and print. They've been dubbed "electronic publishing," and they function as an electronic newspaper. Several hundred of these systems are in operation in communities around the country.

Both are electronically generated letters, numbers, symbols and graphics that are read from the TV screen or the home computer monitor (see 6.1). Both systems are computer-based: Copy is entered into a computer at a central location for transmission to the home.

TELETEXT Teletext is one-way. The teletext subscriber can't request specific information to be sent to one specific home. Teletext is more like the local TV newscast and newspaper. In general, it is delivered to the home via a regular TV broadcast signal. The subscriber has a decoder similar to a cable TV converter, which allows the subscriber to read the text on the TV screen at any time.

The British introduced teletext in 1974. The French and Japanese now have systems in various stages of development. The BBC's CEEFX (seefacts) system can transmit a 100-page newspaper or magazine to the home in 24 seconds.

This digital transmission of information appears on home screens in "video pages," which can be selected for reading in order or at random, much like a newspaper. The television network's captioning service for the hearing-impaired is a form of teletext. Captions are sent over one of the unused, and unnoticed, electronic lines that form the TV picture. Retail stores sell the decoding devices necessary to make the captions appear.

VIDEOTEX Videotex (also spelled *videotext* by some, but *videotex* is more common) is two-way communication. It's delivered to the home via a cable TV system or the telephone lines, which allows more items to be transmitted than a TV signal does. In Europe, where the technology originated, delivery of the electronic messages is called *viewdata*.

Videotex messages are also delivered to the home through a decoder on the TV set, or they can be sent directly to home computers. In 1984, about 8 million homes had computers of one type or another. These computer households already have access to national videotex services, such as The Source and CompuServe. As noted in Chapter 3, these are national data bases from which subscribers can request information. The idea behind local videotex systems is to provide data bases filled with local information.

The modem makes videotex a two-way communication system, allowing it to interact with a contact, as in ordering information from a data base. The *Fort Worth Star-Telegram*'s Startext is such a system (see 6.1). The interaction makes videotex ideal for home banking or shopping. The "Viewtron" electronic newspaper of Knight-Ridder in South Florida at one time had 2,500 users. Lipton offered an 80-screen catalog of high-tech products. A display of product photos was kept on line so users could order from their computer terminals. Stories from Startext about the demise of the videotex operations of Times-Mirror and Knight-Ridder appear in 6.7.

But commercial potential for the electronic systems is there, as some other types of commercial ventures indicate. Public relations firm Burson-Marsteller in a 1985 newsletter said that Metropolitan Life had created "a new set of advertiser/consumer relationships" with videotex.[1] The insurance company offered an insurance planning service using CompuServe's national Electronic Mall test with 130,000 users. Although forbidden by law to sell insurance electronically, Metropolitan nevertheless developed a 150-screen interactive data base for its insurance planning. The company said that although sales couldn't be actually made by the medium, the sales leads were of higher quality because users had access to this technology.

As this example suggests, the success of this medium will be market-driven. If it is demanded, and used, it will continue. Critical to success are the costs, the hardware, the services, the ease of use and the security of information, such as banking transactions.

6.1 A Look at Videotex

Subscribers to Startext, from Capital Cities' *Fort Worth Star-Telegram*, can call up not only news but also weather, sports scores, entertainment and other services on their home computer.

Used with permission of Startext, a registered trademark of the *Fort Worth Star-Telegram*.

NEWS SERVICES   Many studies have been conducted of the potential audience for teletext and videotex. In a number of communities, experiments have been going on for several years now with teletext and videotex systems offered to select homes. In other communities, full-scale teletext and videotex systems are in opera-

6.2 Startext Output

A close up look

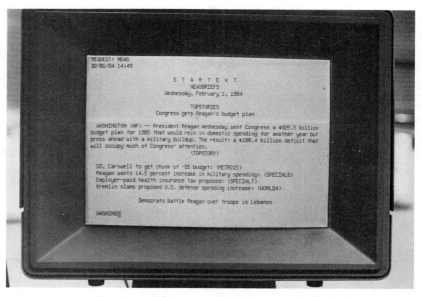

Used with permission of Startext, a registered trademark of the *Fort Worth Star-Telegram*.

tion. In all of these communities, users and potential users of this technology have been quite specific about the types of services they want.

Topping almost all surveys and studies about the services most desired is local news. What people seem to want is a newspaper that's constantly updated throughout the day. Think of everything that's in every section of your local newspaper. The front sections often contain international, national, state and regional news. The sports section is a mainstay of all daily newspapers. Also included are a classified ad section, plus sections on fashion, trends, lifestyle and so on. Subscribers want all of this on their teletext/videotex services as well, and they want it to be kept current.

Suppose sometime in the future you're living in a city far away from where you are today. And suppose you're dying to know how your alma mater did in the big football game on Friday night or Saturday. You just can't wait for the Sunday newspapers and their comprehensive listing of scores. What can you do?

You could watch the network sports news in the hope that they will scroll all of the scores across the nation. Or you could call the local newspaper or broadcast station and ask someone in the sports department to check the wire for you—but you may not get cooperation. Finding that one score among the many hundreds coming in each Saturday is a time-consuming task. With videotex, or so the idea goes, you simply use a keypad or computer terminal connected to the phone line or cable system to request such information from a central computer.

This central computer will also allow you to request weather reports for Paducah, Dubuque, Peoria and all points in between; the location of the garden club's meeting in town today; the up-to-the-minute news on war in the Middle East; facts about gorillas for a school research report; reviews of all the movies in town and a listing of where they're showing; and so much more it would take 10 pages to list them all here.

COMMERCIAL USE

Some companies such as Disney, General Electric, Sears and Merrill Lynch, are using cable TV or computer information systems. The potential for immediate response from the consumer is especially attractive to advertisers. If you want to buy a new VCR, you need to know what's available at what price. You might be able to dial up "VCR" and get all of the possibilities, with descriptions of their features. Or, in another system, perhaps you could order only if you knew the outlets and could call into each of these to see what was being offered and then order. The latter probably is preferable to sellers, while buyers would probably like to see all sorts of VCRs shown in comparison with each other. While commercial interests have controlled to a large extent what is advertised and when in traditional media, with the new technologies the power seems to be in the hands of the consumers. This is partially because the new technologies have further splintered the "mass media" into a collection of specialized channels, much as the magazine market has dissolved from large-circulation national publications into specialized ones.

The Burson-Marsteller newsletter makes an insightful observation:

> With their growing emphasis on choice, options and control, consumers have told us what they want from media. Business, therefore, must not be tied to the success of any one of these message outlets, but must track how consumers use, and are affected by, all of them. If it was not the case in the beginning (when some media were referred to as "solutions without a problem"), their growth will almost certainly be market-driven.[2]

The newsletter also noted that public relations professionals were scrambling to develop expertise to help sort out all of the new message systems and to figure out how to use them.[3]

You'll notice we've been talking here about what computer people call "outputs." Of course, someone must do the input: gathering the information, writing, editing and producing for the new technologies.

WRITING FOR TELETEXT/ VIDEOTEX

Through a series of grants, the Electronic Text Center (ETC) at the University of Florida has become the largest center in the United States for teletext/videotex journalism education. It was also one of the first to provide a student-originated local videotex news and information service.

The introduction to the Center's stylebook notes that no one is quite sure how to write for teletext or videotex. However, videotex and teletext pioneers have centuries of newspaper and decades of broadcast writing history to draw on. That's not like starting from scratch.

Formats and style   Writing for teletext is more like headline writing, since the stories scroll and to be read easily must fit the screen. If the type is large enough to be read comfortably, the limitation is about eight lines, about five words to the line. These brief bulletins are bare-bones news. Writing these bulletins, as anyone who has tried to write headlines or radio news knows, is not easy. Capturing the gist of the story (the basic facts) and the tone in a few lines is a challenge.

A videotex news item may require two separate stories: a summary or news brief for the casual reader and a longer version for those especially interested in the topic.

The interactive nature of the system makes the longer stories possible. If the reader doesn't like a story or finds it boring, the daily menu offers plenty to choose from. But even the long news stories aren't comparable in length to an 8-to-10-inch news story. They're more like broadcast news stories. Much longer pieces, generally analyses and features, are in the system, though, for audiences to call up.

Part of the appeal of the electronic delivery system is the brevity, the staccato delivery, the "short takes." One style that doesn't work too well is the feature that uses suspended interest. Since the electronic systems are basically *editing* operations, as a writer you run the risk of having the main point of the story cut off by a hasty editor.

The system demands skill with tight summary leads—either creating them or paring a lead down to its basics. Stories from the wire are often cut to a mere 50 or 75 words. As an example, see what the AZT story in Chapter 5 might look like:

```
AIDS VICTIMS TO GET SOME HELP

        AIDS VICTIMS WILL HAVE A LIFE-EXTENDING DRUG
AVAILABLE TO THEM WITHIN A FEW WEEKS, FEDERAL
HEALTH OFFICIALS SAID FRIDAY.
        THE EXPERIMENTAL DRUG, AZT, OR
AZIDOTHYMIDINE, ALSO REDUCES SYMPTOMS OF ACQUIRED
IMMUNE DEFICIENCY SYNDROME BUT CAN CAUSE SERIOUS
SIDE EFFECTS.
        THE DEPARTMENT OF HEALTH AND HUMAN SERVICES
AND THE DRUG'S MAKER, BURROUGHS-WELLCOME, ASKED
THE GOVERNMENT TO END A CONTROLLED TEST EARLY TO
ALLOW THE DRUG'S USE.
        FOR INFORMATIONM ABOUT AZT CALL
1-800-843-9388.
```

Another version might be:

```
AIDS VICTIMS TO GET SOME HELP
        AN EXPERIMENTAL DRUG, AZT (AZIDOTHYMIDINE),
THAT HELPS, BUT DOESN'T CURE, PATIENTS WITH AIDS
```

```
(ACQUIRED IMMUNE DEFICIENCY), WILL BE RELEASED IN
A FEW WEEKS, FEDERAL HEALTH OFFICIALS ANNOUNCED
FRIDAY.
     DRUG-MAKER BURROUGHS-WELLCOME SAID AZT
PROVED SO PROMISING IN A CONTROLLED TRIAL THAT
THE GOVERNMENT WAS GOING TO SPEED THE APPROVAL
PROCESS SO OTHERS COULD BENEFIT.
     THE GOVERNMENT AND THE DRUG COMPANY HAVE SET
UP A TOLL-FREE NUMBER TO CALL FOR INFORMATION:
1-800- 843-9388
```

Examples of progress of copy through a videotex system can be examined for clues to what the style of writing for teletext and videotex is now. Material displayed in 6.3 and 6.4 shows a story from its origin as a newspaper story to its viewing by the videotex subscriber. The subscriber looks at a list of news headlines to determine which story to read (6.5). The word in parentheses following each headline is the *keyword* the subscriber uses to call up the whole story. Feature files are available as well as news stories. Startext calls this listing the *keyword index*.

The stories can be ordered up from the videotex central computer, or the reader can order up the menu again and scan another category, repeating this information-on-demand process as often as desired. To aid consumers, Startext publishes a monthly tabloid, *Startext Ink*, that is distributed to current subscribers and area computer stores (see 6.8).

Teletext is more of a magazine digest format. The home subscriber can't order up personalized information. Instead, a table of contents (or menu) presents the subscriber with a list of the stories that can be called up from the 100 or so pages sent to the home.

Writing and production

The information prepared for teletext and videotex systems must come from somewhere. If audiences are demanding local news and information from these systems, local reporting must take place. Because of these demands, we may soon have videotex and teletext newsrooms nationwide, probably as a part of some already existing publication's operation.

Although teletext and videotex are not broadcast news formats, they do share with TV newscasts a reliance on graphics. TV newsrooms are becoming production centers for elaborate and sophisticated computer art and graphics. Studies have shown that the potential audience for teletext demands no less in the way of high-quality art and graphics on their systems. Writers will have to determine how they can best depict the news story or graphically deliver the commercial message as well as writing the electronic text. A chart on, say, unemployment figures may convey the message much more efficiently than any written story could. That need to consider the visual element at all times may give the teletext/videotex writer a lot in common with the TV writer.

6.3 Newspaper Story Submitted to Videotex System

This is what a story looks like when it arrives in the Startext system from a *Star-Telegram* copy editor. Copy editors designate stories from the newspaper's bank of stories for Startext transmission. Editing for the Startext system is handled by writers assigned to Startext. Sometimes a story needs only to be reformatted for transmission (see 6.4).

```
added a bit. friouf>

fb]3fc 9a 22 NEW HED with 38.9-45-2 jump to 10a--red in 1 stor[fr]/]
 ']
 ']
 ']
 ']
 ']
*45M*
 [P43V47][]
[ransportation system/]            <           -- 1.1 CHARS, 2.1 PICAS>
[es96]
in Dallas getting off track@       <           -- 0.2 CHARS, 0.5 PICAS>
/1
*22*[FB]Continued from Page 9<>[FR]c
/]
/]
/]
/]
*2129*@
*22*
*9by2*jackie Koszczuk@
bruce millar@
*9stws*
/mDallas' $8.7 billion public transit plan is running behind schedule,
and its leaders are working to head off a derailment by restoring
public confidence. In August 1983 Dallas County voters approved the
plan whose centerpiece was a 147-mile rail system, heralded as second
in size only to New York's.
Despite its breath and ambition, the Dal<D-
>las Area Rapid Transit plan was viewed as yet
another attainable star in a city whose think-big
leaders were accustomed to erecting constella<L-
>tions.</P>
But now the number of proposed rail miles has
been scaled back by a third. Construction, which
was to have started this year, won't be under way
until at least the end of next year, according to
the most optimistic timetable. The first rail
```

(continued)

6.3 (continued)

```
line, which was to be in operation by the end of
the decade, will be in service in 1994 at the
earliest.<P> Meanwhile, 90,000 additional cars a
year take to the roads in Dallas and Tarrant
counties, a num<D-ber that one former DART
official observed is sufficient for a bumper-
to-bumper line from Dallas to Little Rock,
Ark.</P>
```

Used with permission of Startext, a registered trademark of the *Fort Worth Star-Telegram.*

Writing, reporting, editing and production are the skills that will be required of the teletext/videotex journalist, just as they are for the newspaper and broadcast reporter. If you look at the basics of writing for all of these areas, you find these steps to a good story: Boil to the basics, cutting out all non-essential information; pare to fit a specific news hole.

Special problems   Some major decisions have yet to be made regarding teletext: To start, what is it? What shall it be called for regulatory purposes? Although newspapers are not absolutely free from government regulation, they enjoy more freedom than broadcast properties. Newspapers, like all other businesses, must pay taxes, take out business licenses, abide by local zoning ordinances, refrain from polluting the air and discriminating against workers, and reporters must be law-abiding in their pursuit of the news just as their counterparts in the advertising department must be law-abiding about truth in advertising. But little direct government interference is aimed at the content of the newspaper. That is censorship.

The courts, it is true, must delve into content in libel cases to determine guilt or innocence. Still, the government cannot order the newspaper to print something, and only under the most extreme conditions can it order the newspaper not to print something. Publishing instructions on how to make an H-bomb is a recent example.

Broadcasting is different.

The Communications Act of 1934 forbids the FCC from engaging in censorship. Direct and overt censorship by the commission is rare, but indirect and covert censorship certainly does exist, and censorship is censorship in the minds of many.

Direct censorship with court approval has affected broadcasters. In the case of "seven dirty words," an album cut by comedian George Carlin used the seven words you could not say over the nation's airwaves. The routine was humorous, perhaps educational in that it traced the origins of these words. A non-commercial radio station in New York City played the cut over the

6.4 Newspaper Story Reformatted for Videotex

The story has two types of identification used by a subscriber: a headline, or summary, which gives the subscriber a general notion of what the story or feature is about, and a keyword, which the subscriber uses to call up the story. The keyword is also used by videotex editors to log in stories on the system each day (see 6.6). Here the keyword is METRO8.

```
<<R:METRO8
DART's rail plans off track/L
/L
By Jackie Koszczuk/L
& Bruce Millar/L
Star-Telegram Writers/L
/L
   Dallas' $8.7 billion public transit plan is
running behind schedule, and its leaders are
working to head off a derailment by restoring
public confidence./L
   In August 1983 Dallas County voters approved
the plan whose centerpiece was a 147-mile rail
system, heralded as second in size only to New
York's./L
   Despite its breadth and ambition, the Dallas
Area Rapid Transit plan was viewed as yet another
attainable star in a city whose think-big leaders
were accustomed to erecting constellations./L
   But now the number of proposed rail miles has
been scaled back by a third. Construction, which
was to have started this year, won't be under way
until at least the end of next year, according to
the most optimistic timetable. The first rail
line, which was to be in operation by the end of
the decade, will be in service in 1994 at the
earliest./L
   Meanwhile, 90,000 additional cars a year take
to the roads in Dallas and Tarrant counties, a
number that one former DART official observed is
sufficient for a bumper-to-bumper line from
Dallas to Little Rock, Ark./L
```

Used with permission of Startext, a registered trademark of the *Fort Worth Star-Telegram*.

air, and the FCC, finding little humor in this broadcast, took action against the station. The U.S. Supreme Court upheld the FCC's action.

The court's decision shocked many. In effect, it banned seven specific words from the nation's airwaves for reasons of taste. That decision poses this fundamental question: If the government can ban specific words on a "moral" judgment, can it then proceed to whole sentences, or even to thoughts and ideas?

6.5 Keyword Index

A summary of the day's headlines gives the subscriber an
idea of what news is available. The features, with their
headlines, follow.

```
<<R:METRO
=== METROPLEX HEADLINES ===/L
/L
/L
DART's rail plans off track: (METRO8)/L
/L
TCOM library may go unoccupied if Legislature's
budget cuts are approved: (METRO4)/L
/L
Pilot, 10, begins 7,000-mile trek: (METRO6)/L
/L
Employees fight stigma of age bias: (METRO5)/L
/L
Quadriplegic seeks respect, autonomy: (METRO7)/L
/L
Texans put state pride on the record: (METRO9)/L
/L
IN DALLAS: Memorbilia, drawings of Dallas
veterans memorial monument sought: (INDALLAS)/L
/L
Johnson closes fashion boutique, plans to reopen
in North Dallas: (METRO30/L
/L
Dallas newspaper survey links drugs, crime binge:
(METRO34)/L
/L
Three in family killed in I-35 collision:
(METRO39)/L
/L
Man killed in shooting at party: (METRO37)/L
/L
Joshua athletic director fighting cutback:
(METRO36)/L
/L
City to block streets from Cooper cruisers:
(METRO1)/L
Attack motivates Arlington homemaker to take up
law career: (METRO40)/L
```

(continued)

```
/L
Social solutions developing 3 years after study:
(METRO2)/L
/L
Metroplex rehab services found inadequate:
(METRO38)/L
/L
/L
-----------------------/L
STAR-TELEGRAM COLUMNISTS/L
-----------------------/L
/L
  MIKE NICHOLS: Compared to this, communism is a
Red herring: (NICHOLS)/L
/L
  GEORGE DOLAN: If he lifts another half-inch he
really will need relief: (DOLAN)/L
/L
  KATIE SHERROD: War against drugs should also be
for life: (SHERROD)/L
/L
  BILL YOUNGBLOOD: Nyaa, nyaa; I'm on mailing
lists and you're not: (YOUNGBLOOD)/L
/L
  CISSY STEWART: Ruto Lee stars as Pied Piper:
(CISSY)/L
/L
/L
 * List of volunteer work needed in Tarrant
County: (VOL)/L
 * Star-Telegram's DWI series: (DWI)/L
 * Best selling books in the Metroplex:
(METROBOOKS)/L
 * Area news shorts: (METBRIEFS)/L
 * Local obituaries now available: (0994) and
(0995)/L
------------/L
/L
END -- METRO/L
<<E:
```

6.6 Features Log

Each day's completed log lists the keywords designating
each story in the system. Stories are logged as they are
put on line.

WORLD (20)	NATION (20)	BUSINESS (40)	TOPSTORY
(8) S.A.	(16) R-Maid	(14) Baby Bell	Cowboys
(9) Pakistan	(17) Arms talks	(15) Oil Prices	SURPRISE
(10) Castaways	(18) Gramm/Rudman	(16) Bank	XGR Prayer
( )	(19) Airline	(17) Howe	NY AMX OTC MF TV
( )	(20) Rehnquist	(18) Bentzen	STOCKS NEWS
( )	(1) US-Nic	( )	DOLLAR TODAY
( )	(2) Tax overhaul	( )	GOLD ~~DOW~~
( )	(3) NW fires	( )	SILVER ~~TBONDS~~
( )	( )	( )	FOREXCH ~~BONDS~~
		( )	CHIBOARD ~~MONEYRATE~~

STATE (20)

			GOLDSIL BIZMIRROR
(1) Budget	( )	( )	BRITMETAL REALESTATE
(2) Richards	( )	( )	PLAT DRILL
(3) Lottery	( )	( )	SCRAP

METRO (40)

CHIMERC
COTTON
OIL
DEFENSE _Spending_
NASA _SHT-Cong._
POLITICS

(1) Coopes	(8) DART	( )	~~BROOKS~~ ~~EDDRICE~~
(2) Social	(9) Pride	( )	CISSY NICHOLS
(3) Johnson	(34) Crime	( )	CHAPMAN SHERROD
(4) Library	(37) Shooting	( )	DOLAN YOUNGBLOOD
(5) Age bias	(38) Rehab	( )	
(6) Pilot	(39) Fatal	( )	USWEA FOODREPORT
(7) Quadriplegic	(40) Attack	( )	FORECASTS METBRIEFS

SPORTS (20)   SCIENCE (20)   MED (20)

POLLEN   SCOTUS
USTEMPS   BRITES
TEXTEMPS   DEATHS
GLOBE   PEOPLE

(18) Walker strategy	(19) Oldest birds	(10) Pill/breast cancer	LEBRETON SWC
(19) NFL Meet	(20) Sea change	(11) Runner/hormone	WILKINS ARKANSAS
(20) Bass	( )	(12) Nutrisweet	BLACKIE BAYLOR
(1) Spud Game	( )	(13) M attack	RANGERS HOUSTON
(2) Cow react	( )	(14) UA Surgery	ALSTANDINGS NTSU
(3) Gwiz	( )	(15) Rehab (MED)	NLSTANDINGS RICE
(4) Dorsett	COMP (20)	( )	ALGAMES SOONERS
( )	(11) AI	( )	NLGAMES SMU
( )	(12) Lotus	WEATHER (5)	RBOX TCU
( )	( )	(4) Drought	SCORES TECH

COWBOYS   TEXAS
POKESTATS TEXASAM
NFLRDP   TWC
WRESTLING UTA
RELIGION (10)
-- OBITS --

AMUSE (10)

LIFESTYLE (10)

SPECIAL (20)

(19) R-S.A.	(1) Fires	( )	( )
( )	( )	( )	( )

(3)
(2)

6.7a Startext Stories about Other Videotex Systems

Two stories on the demise of other videotex systems were carried on Startext. Example 6.7a describes the shutting down of the Times-Mirror operation and 6.7b tells of Knight-Ridder's Viewtron.

```
                                              PAGE: 1


          Times Mirror to close Gateway videotex service
          27feb86


          By James Granelli
          Copr. 1986, Los Angeles Times


             SANTA ANA, Calif. -- After more than four years
          of research, including 15 months of commercial
          trials, Times Mirror Co. said Thursday that it
          will close down its Gateway videotex service next
          Friday and lay off most of the 120 employees.
             The termination also will affect about 3,000
          subscribers, mostly personal computer users in
          Los Angeles and Orange counties, and about 45
          advertisers. Gateway's demise also means the end
          of in-home banking services for subscribers with
          accounts at Security Pacific National Bank.
             Times Mirror, which publishes the Los Angeles
          Times, said low consumer use of the once
          trend-setting idea left doubt about the future
          marketability and profitability of videotex.
             "The reaction among consumers, while
          gratifying, was not sufficient to warrant
          full-scale development of Gateway as an ongoing
          business," said James H. Holly, president of
          Times Mirror Videotex Services.
             The termination did not surprise industry
          analysts. They believe that videotex, a computer
          service providing in-home news, advertising,
          banking and shopping services, is an idea whose
          time has not arrived -- and may never arrive.
             Times Mirror executives would not disclose the
          company's investment in the videotex subsidiary,
          but securities analysts said the company
          committed more than $15 million to the
          experiment. Times Mirror, the analysts said, will


                                              (continued)
```

6.7a (continued)

not show much in the way of losses because the company has been writing off the costs all along.

"Basically, it (Gateway) was always considered to be a market test, and the results didn't seem to indicate that it would be a profitable business," Holly said.

Gateway started with "dedicated" terminals, like pay-television decoder boxes, which consumers could connect to their television sets and telephones to gain access to the service. But Gateway soon marketed its services only to customers with personal computers, who did not need the special terminals. Those customers, Holly said, are mainly hobbyists, and they presented several problems. While it is easy to sign them up for little or no fees, it was much more difficult to get them to use the videotex services, which Gateway sold at $3 an hour. Other similar services cost up to $12 an hour.

Also, he said, the market was limited. While there are some 12 million personal computers in homes nationwide, only about 1 million owners have the modems needed for telephone hookups and only 6 percent of them, at best, were located in the Times Mirror market.

The fate of the division remains uncertain, Holly said. "I can't say what will happen. There are other things we have an interest in that are related."

Folding Gateway removes one of the last home computer systems for general information and interactive service, like home banking.

A few, including one joint venture by CBS, Inc., Sears, Roebuck and IBM, are still in their infancy. Other videotex ventures, like Keycomp Publishers in Chicago, quit some time ago, as did experiments by Time, Inc.

Another general-interest videotex, Viewtron, owned by Knight-Ridder Newspapers, has narrowed its focus and "repositioned" itself to serve personal computer users, said Frank Hawkins, a Knight-Ridder vice president.

6.7b

```
<KW:BC-VIDEO>
<KO205/Mknigo
r f BC-VIDEO -- Attn. 03-17-86 0571>
<ON-LINE WIRE WI3:K0205;FRBX;03>
[WB]BC-VIDEO -- Attn. business editors
```

By Ronald Rosenberg
Boston Globe
BOSTON -- Knight-Ridder Newspapers Inc., whose videotex service called Viewtron promised to bring a broad array of electronic information and financial services to consumers, said Monday it will fold the nearly five-year-old venture.

The termination comes less than three weeks after Times-Mirror Corp. of Los Angeles announced the shutdown of its videotex services, at a reported loss of $20 million to $30 million. Some analysts estimate Knight-Ridder has lost $50 million although the company has stated the costs of the project have been met annually and there would be no significant writeoffs.

"Despite steady growth in the number of subscribers (to about 20,000), usage numbers have not kept pace," said James K. Botten, Knight-Ridder president. "Over time we might have been able to turn Viewtron into a viable business. But in weighing the continuing cost of investment against other competing uses for corporate funds, we decided it was in the best interests of our shareholders not to continue."

Videotex, a rather amorphous term, is essentially an easy-to-use two-way information transmission service of text and graphics to and from a video screen such as a television or home computer terminal in home or office.

Viewtron's videotex service enabled computer users with a modem -- a telephone device for sending and receiving data -- or a Viewtron hand-held terminal to receive the latest news, weather and current sports scores, stock and commodity quotes, flight schedules and fares. Users could also perform home banking, participate in electronic auctions, do catalog shopping and participate in electronic mail.

(continued)

6.7b (continued)

Several industry watchers said they were not surprised that Knight-Ridder pulled the plug. They cited Viewtron's overpriced services, failure to move quickly to personal computers and competition from more established on-line computer service firms, notably CompuServe, Dow Jones and The Source.

"Knight-Ridder was not running Viewtron as a business, but rather a giant test market," said Myron Kassaraba, executive vice president of Applied Videotex Services, a local vidotex service provider that is relocating to Boston's World Trade Center from Belmont, Mass.

Some of the first hints that Viewtron was on shaky ground came early last year when Affiliated Publications Inc., parent company of the Boston Globe, decided against signing a Viewtron contract after spending more than $1 million as part of a pilot program on providing videotex services in the Boston area.

Another major problem was Viewtron's inability to hold onto subscribers, some of whom spent as much as $600, or nearly $25 a month, for a hand-held terminal that provided two-way communications. In addition, Viewtron users were expected to pay about $20 a month for services.

"Knight-Ridder came out with a technology-driven system which from day one made them losers," said Elizabeth Ferrarini, author of two books on on-line computer services. "Knight-Ridder ignored the market forces of CompuServe and the others. They just went off and did their own thing. It took them five years before they put their service onto personal computers."

Despite the failures of two major newspaper publishing firms, some of America's largest corporations are planning to enter the market. Last month, Citicorp, NYNEX Corp. and RCA said they will form a joint venture to study home banking, home shopping and similar services. Another group, called Trintex, is a joint venture of CBS Inc., IBM Corp. and Sears Roebuck and Co. It is developing a videotex service for households with personal computers.

Page: 2

AP-NY-03-17-86 2122EST

6.8 Startext Tabloid

This guide to the system is sent to subscribers and is available to customers in computer stores.

StarTexan

Volume 2, Number 10   STARTEXT is the online service of The Fort Worth Star-Telegram   **August, 1986**

Photo by SUSAN SHIELDS

ENGROSSED -- What are these kids so interested in? To find out, see page 7.

Improved stocks coming soon

In mid-August, STARTEXT will introduce several changes that will improve access to the closing stock prices.

There are two key changes.

The first change involves how the stock data is displayed. Under the new format, the data will be tabular, making it more convenient to access and use.

The other major change involves the symbols used to access the individual stock quotes.

For the past four years, STARTEXT has used the AP symbol for the stocks on the New York, American and Over the Counter exchanges. Beginning later this month, we will switch to the official New York exchange symbols.

To make the transition easier, there are six new directories for matching new and old symbols.

If you want to match the **old** AP symbol with the **new** New York symbols, use **NYDIR, AMXDIR** or **OTCDIR**.

If you want to type a New York symbol and match with the old STARTEXT symbol, use: **NYSYM, AMXSYM** or **OTCSYM**.

These directories also include the full name of the company represented.

Closing prices are generally available by late afternoon on each business day. For more information on using the stock data bases, request **HELP.STOCKS** on STARTEXT.

New temps, airport index added

STARTEXT offers subscribers all sorts of news and information. Sometimes however, that information is not always available in the best possible format.

Take for example the long list of cities and their associated weather conditions provided by the Associated Press. This has traditionally been split into three long keywords: **USTEMPS, TEXTEMPS** and **GLOBAL.** If you wanted to find out how hot it was in Yucca Flats, you could request **USTEMPS** and wait for all the cities from A thru X to scroll by.

Now that same information is presented in a manner similar to the **MAILDIR** and the stock exchanges. Type the new keyword **TEMPS** and ALL weather data across the world is available to you. Inside the TEMPS database simply enter all or part of the city name you are interested in, and all cities you are interested in will be displayed.

A similar problem existed with the airline flight schedules. You could look at **DELTACITIES** or **AACITIES** to find out the airport code of the city you were flying to, but if that happened to be Zurich, Switzerland you would be a long time waiting for the Z's to show up.

The airline cities now have been converted into a file called **AIRIN-DEX.** Request that keyword and then type as much or as little of the city name as you think you need to find a match. Three letters is the minimum length you should use. You'll get a list of cities which match what you typed in.

COPYRIGHT 1986 FORT WORTH STAR-TELEGRAM

STARTEXT
PO Box 1870
Fort Worth, Tx. 76101

BULK RATE
U.S. Postage
PAID
Fort Worth, Tx.
Permit No. 1259

6.9 Excerpts from the Electronic Text Center Stylebook

Writing for electronically delivered print systems demands conciseness and clarity since users are obviously using such media for instant information. The stylebook from which excerpts appear here was designed for student editors at the Electronic Text Center in the University of Florida's College of Journalism and Communications. To get an idea of how students operate the system, look at the instructions for opening, closing and preparing a four-minute update.

PART 1—STYLE

Acronyms

1. All listed are OK on 1st reference.
2. Those noted with "SPORTS" may be used only in sports stories. (Elsewhere spell out).
3. If an acronym spells a word, use hyphens.
4. To create the plural form of acronyms, use a lower case "s".

AA DEGREE	AAA	ABC-TV	ACC	ACLU
AFL-CIO	AIDS	AL	Amtrak	AMA
AP (news wire)	ASPCA	AT&T	AWOL	B1 BOMBER
BA DEGREE	BBC	BIG-10	BS DEGREE	CB
CBS-TV	Comsat	Conrail	CIA	DC10
DDT	DJ	D-O-T	DMZ	DUI
EDB	EdD DEGREE	EKG	EPA	E-R-A
ESPN-TV	F1 JET	F14 JET	FAA	FBI
FCC	FDA	FDIC	FHA	FPL
FSU	FTC	FM	GE	GI
GM (cars)	GNP	GOP	HBO	HRS
IBM	IFAS	IOU	IQ	IRA
IRS	IUD	KGB	LSD	LPGA
MA DEGREE	MGM	MIA	MiG	MS DEGREE
NAACP	NASA	NASCAR	NATO	NBA
NBC-TV	NCAA	NEA	NFL	NHL
NL	N-O-W	OK	OPEC	PAC-10
PBS-TV	PGA	PhD	PLO	P-O-W
PTA	QB	RBI (not RBIs)	RCA	ROTC
RSVP	S-A-L-T	SEC (SPORTS)	SOS	TASS
TNT	TV	TWA	UAW	UCF
UF	UFO	U-M	U-N	UNESCO
UNF	UNICEF	UPI	U-S	USF
USFL	USSR	V-A	VD	VFW
VIP	YMCA	YWCA	WBA	WBC
WWI	WWII	3-D	49ers	76ers

Cities (Int'l)

1. These can stand without a country.
2. Others require the nation in commas: "SEOUL, S KOREA, IS A DUMP"

AMSTERDAM	ATHENS	BANGKOK	BEIRUT
BERLIN	BOMBAY	BRUSSELS	BUENOS AIRES

6.9 (continued)

CAIRO	CALCUTTA	DUBLIN	E BERLIN
GENEVA	GIBRALTAR	GUATEMALA	HANOI
HAVANA	JERUSALEM	JOHANNESBURG	KUWAIT
LENINGRAD	LONDON	LUXEMBOURG	MADRID
MANILA	MEXICO CITY	MONACO	MONTREAL
MOSCOW	NEW DELHI	OTTAWA	PARIS
PEKING	QUEBEC	RIO DE JANEIRO	ROME
SAIGON	SAN SALVADOR	SHANGHAI	SINGAPORE
TEHERAN	TOKYO	TORONTO	VATICAN CITY
VIENNA	WARSAW	W BERLIN	

Opening

1. Open curtains, turn all monitors on.
2. Update crawl pg 64 and change
   from ". . . GAINESVILLE CABLE PRESS . . . TOP HEADLINES"
   to ". . . GOOD MORNING, GAINESVILLE . . . TOP HEADLINES"
   Try to make this the 1st thing you do.
3. Check wire for today's news. Pull ALL "takes" of the most recent NEWSWATCH, FLORIDA NEWSWATCH, AND SPORTSWATCH.
4. Watch for "FLORIDA ZONE FORECASTS" for use on page 8 & 12. (Gainesville is in zone 9.)
5. Review and update pp 90-101, the 4-minute update. These pages run continuously between 6:30-8:30am. Be concerned with the 4-minute update during this time.
6. Sometime before 8:30am, move new stories out of pp 90-101 and into the regular pp. 8-47. Make sure you review all of pp 8-47 for updates and redundant stories. You should complete this by 8:30am—that's when the program switches to GCP and the 4-minute-update will be over.
7. When you have time, visit the radio station newsrooms and get the local news from our baskets. Check off the "RADIO NEWS" box on the run sheet once this is done.
8. Manage the paper as usual. Tend to headlines, weather, etc.

Closing

1. At approximately 9pm start preparing pp 8-47 for the next day:
   a. change occurrences of "TODAY" so that the days are named ("THURSDAY").
   b. review the whole paper and check for errors, redundant stories, or stories that are outdated.
   c. rewrite the weather pages 8 & 12 as if it is 6am the next day.
2. Get the other clipboard with the morning log sheets on it. Copy the slugs of the current stories into each box under the PREP column. Record tomorrow's date.
3. Prepare the 4-MINUTE UPDATE. See procedure, next page.
4. Review the events calendar (p. 130+) and Weimer Communi-Cable (p. 145+) for deletions. Once this is done check off the boxes on the new run sheet marked WEIMER and EVENTS.

(continued)

5. Go to the auxiliary keyboard. Transfer (FETCH) pp 8-47 to the auxiliary keyboard so that we have 2 copies of the "paper."
6. Update the p. 64 crawl to refer to only stories which appear in the 4-MINUTE UPDATE and check for accuracy. Then change
   from ". . . GOOD EVENING, GAINESVILLE . . . TOP HEADLINES"
   to ". . . GAINESVILLE CABLE PRESS . . . TOP HEADLINES"
7. Place a roll of paper at least 3" in diameter on the printer. Otherwise, the printer will run out during the night. Make sure the core is seated on spindles properly or it will not "feed" properly.
8. Throw all AP paper in the LIVE COPY basket away. Throw out soda cans and stray wrappers. Turn off all TV monitors. Leave all computers ON and running. Make sure AP printer is printing OK. If it is 10pm you may leave. Turn off room lights, close curtains and lock door.

Preparing the 4-Minute Update

1. Once you have the stories updated in pp 8-47, choose the TOP ones and move them to pp 90-101:

page	subject
90	Nat'l News
91	"
92	"
93	World News
94	"
95	World or Business News
96	State News
97	"
98	"
99	"
100	Sports
101	"

2. To move the pages
   RECALL　　the page number you want to transfer.
   STORE　　the page number you want to move onto.
3. Review pp 90-101 to make sure the stories are where you want them. Enter them on the morning log sheet under 4-MIN UPDATE.
4. Write the headline crawl to mention only the 12 stories you moved so people don't wait for a story that isn't coming.

　　　Suppose the *New York Times* chose to cover this court decision and printed those seven words letter for letter in the paper. Could the government then order the nation's newspapers never to publish those words again in their columns? The answer has been a clear *no*.

　　　This fact of life was brought home during the Watergate days. Despite the harassment tactics that were employed, the Nixon White House knew it could not stop the *Washington Post* from publishing its articles, and punitive action against the *Post* would be most difficult. But Post-Newsweek is a major broadcaster in the United States, and the White House did go after its broadcast licenses, an action the House Judiciary Committee considered investigating as grounds for impeaching President Nixon. The attempt to challenge failed. The licenses of the *Post*'s Florida stations, WJXT in Jacksonville and WPLG in Miami, were renewed.[4] The frightening lesson, though, was there for the learning.

But suppose the *Post* had been delivered to our home via teletext at that time, using the *Post*-owned WTOP-TV. Could the White House then have put both WTOP-TV and the teletext-delivered *Post* itself out of business by ordering the FCC to yank its license? When he was chairman of the Federal Communications Commission (FCC), Charles D. Ferris posed the question in a speech to broadcasters. He mused aloud whether such "newspapers" (his quote) were broadcasts, thus subject to governmental regulation by the federal agency, "or should they be governed by the absence of regulation, like print?" Print journalists throughout the country fear the classification of teletext as broadcasts, should the day come when all newspapers are delivered to the home electronically.

As Bernard Kilgore, president of the *Wall Street Journal* in 1961, said in a speech: "The argument that freedom of the press protects a licensed medium from the authority of the government that issues the license is double-talk."[5] What the government giveth, the government can taketh away, and this is what disturbs many print journalists today about any rulings on the new information delivery systems, teletext and videotex.

MAIN POINTS

- New communication technologies and services include satellites, home computers, video recorders, low-power TV and radio stations, teletext and videotex.

- Teletext and videotex are computer-based electronic text services to the home or office. Teletext is one-way; videotex is two-way, or interactive.

- Studies have shown that local news and information are among the things people want most from these new services.

- Advertising and public relations professionals are studying the impact of these systems on the audiences they are trying to reach.

- Teletext and videotex writing styles are in their developmental stage, just like the technology itself. Writing for both teletext and videotex demands a style between print and broadcast, with elements of both.

- Because videotex is two-way, and people can request more information, news items on videotex take two forms: a brief broadcast-style summary and a full-length newspaper-style article.

- Because teletext is one-way, stories will tend to be longer than videotex summary items.

- Graphics will play a large role in both services; thus you as writers will have to learn how to use graphics and artwork, as in writing for TV news.

EXERCISES
1. (a) Find a long newspaper article (probably in a science, lifestyle or business section). Write the very terse summary that would be used for the casual reader. (b) Edit the longer piece for inclusion in the "call-up" section of the menu. (c) What graphics does the piece call for?

2. Look at the Startext features log (6.6). What would you consider adding to it? Why? Deleting? Why?

3. What do you think the new electronic systems, videotex and teletext, are most like: print or broadcasting? How should the government regard them for regulation? Defend your answer.

NOTES
1. "New Communication Technologies: Chasing Elusive Audiences," *Burson-Marsteller Report* no. 72, (Summer 1985), p. 2.

2. Ibid., p. 3.

3. Ibid., p. 1.

4. Barry Sussman, *The Great Cover-Up: Nixon and the Scandal of Watergate* (New York: Signet, Times-Mirror, 1974), pp. 136–37. (For more details, read all of Part IV.)

5. This section and parts of others where the legal differences between print and broadcasting have been discussed in light of the new technologies is adapted from the following: James A. Wollert, "The Communications Era," *National Forum* special edition of *The Phi Kappa Phi Journal* 60, no. 3 (Summer 1980).

SUGGESTIONS FOR ADDITIONAL READING

Ahlhauser, John W., ed. *Electronic Home News Delivery: Journalism and Public Policy Implications*. Bloomington, Ind.: School of Journalism and Center for New Communications, 1981.   A comprehensive look at the impact of the new technology.

Compaine, Benjamin M. *The Newspaper Industry in the 1980s: An Assessment of Economics and Technology*. White Plains, N.Y.: Knowledge Industry Publications, 1980.   A look at the economic feasibility of new information systems.

Cross, Lynne C. *The New Technologies*. Dubuque, Iowa: W. C. Brown, 1986.

Neustadt, Richard M. *The Birth of Electronic Publishing*. White Plains, N.Y.: Knowledge Industry Publications, 1982.   A book that covers many of the possibilities of the new technology.

Weaver, David H. *Videotex Journalism: Teletext, Journalism and the News*. Hillsdale, N.J.: Lawrence Erlbaum Associates, 1983.   Covers the impact on print journalism and the industry's involvement.

Interviewing

Interview stories are media staples. The Q&A story appears in magazines and newspapers, and its broadcast version is the talk show. The person who generally gets credit for popularizing this story form is Horace Greeley, probably more famous for popularizing the command "Go west, young man."

Greeley probably didn't write the first interview story, but as editor of the *New York Tribune*, he was one of the most influential journalists of the 19th century and was the first to write interview stories well.

He wrote the most famous of his early interview stories in 1859, when he himself went west and interviewed the Mormon leader Brigham Young in Salt Lake City.[1] Greeley published the two-hour interview in question-and-answer format, substantially verbatim. Most interview stories aren't written that way today. But the idea of talking to important people and reporting what they say has remained.

PRE-INTERVIEW BASICS

In preparing an interview story, some basic decisions must be made, most of them based on the type of interview and the medium. Other considerations are the topic and who is available to talk about it.

Types of interviews

Before Greeley popularized the format, other reporters had conducted interviews to get information for stories, but the stories weren't constructed as a report of the interviews themselves. In the years since Greeley, the interview story has developed into several types. The *routine* (or news) interview involves gathering information about news events or issues from someone in a position to know something about them. The *personality* interview records a conversation with celebrities—movie stars, sports figures, politicians (see 7.1). The *symposium* interview entails talking to several people on the same topic to get a variety of viewpoints.

7.1 **The Personality Interview**

Spoonful of success and loads of talent

By Bob Thomas
Associated Press Writer

Wide World Photos

LOS ANGELES — Most movie star careers follow the pattern of an arc, rising to the highest point and then curving downward. But not Julie Andrews'.

She started at the top in 1964, winning an Academy Award for her first movie, *Mary Poppins*, and followed that with *The Sound of Music*, which became the top money-making film.

Then there were more box-office winners, *Torn Curtain, Hawaii, Thoroughly Modern Millie.*

After three failures, *Start, Darling Lili* and *The Tamarind Seed*, she abandoned films for a series of TV specials and a quiet life in Gstadt, Switzerland.

Since 1979, her films have been comedy hits made by her husband, Blake Edwards: *10, S.O.B., Victor/ Victoria.*

Julie Andrews will appear this fall in two disparate movies: *Duet for One*, based on the Tom Kempinski play, directed by Andrei Konchalovsky and co-starring Alan Bates and

The lead tells the gist of the story so you'll know what to expect.

Establishes her identity, because she may not be all that familiar to younger people.

Following a brief chronology of hits and failures, the news of her next two films is given here. This information is not in the lead because the films already have

Max von Sydow; and *That's Life*, directed by Blake Edwards and co-starring Jack Lemmon, Sally Kellerman and Robert Loggia.

This graph sets the time and location of the interview. The next three paragraphs are quotes that fit together, whether or not they actually were said in exactly that order without any other words in between.

Andrews recently talked about the two movies and other matters at her 16th-floor office in a Century City high-rise, part of the Blake Edwards Enterprises complex.

"*Duet for One* happened very fast," she said. "I heard about it last November, and I started shooting in London in February. At first I thought, should I go or not? Should I uproot the children and take them along? The answer was yes. It was too good an opportunity to miss.

"It was also the hardest work I've ever done—six-day weeks, and extended days at that. It was an eight-week schedule because Konchalovsky had an opera he had to direct.

"I played a concert violinist who at the prime of her career becomes a victim of multiple sclerosis. The story concerns how her family and others around her handle it. I did a lot of research on the subject and discovered that some families rally around the victim, but some husbands simply quit, unable to cope with the situation."

Andrews also discovered something about the violin: "It is the most killingly difficult instrument to learn. I would have required 10 years to play as well as I should have."

— Summary

The movie project *That's Life* was something else.

— Transition leading into the following quote graph.

"Blake was sitting in the Jacuzzi one day and he said, 'You know what I'd like to do next? An intimate piece about a family. And I'd like to do it for ourselves.' That surprised me, and I thought he might forget about it. But six weeks later he was ready to go," she said.

The cast of *That's Life* includes Lemmon's wife, Felicia Farr, and son, Chris; Edwards' daughter, Jen-

— Factual information.

been announced; yet this is the real "news peg" for the feature, the reason to write about the star.

(continued)

7.1 (continued)

nifer; and Andrews' daughter, Emma. However, the Edwardses' adopted Vietnamese childen, Amy, 12, and Joanna, 11, are not in the movie, which was primarily shot at the Edwardses' Malibu compound.

Andrews' devotion to her family ——— has been partly responsible for the lapses in her film career. "We try to spend Christmas and summer together at Gstadt," she said. "This summer we couldn't, because Blake was filming *Blind Date*. So afterward we did my second-favorite thing: We all went to British Columbia, chartered a boat for 2½ weeks and went fishing."

——— Explanation for her career interruptions as well as giving some insight into Andrews.

Associated Press, published in *Fort Worth Star-Telegram*, Sept. 22, 1986, p. 48. Reprinted with permission.

Choosing a subject

In selecting a topic, you need to consider who other than yourself would be interested in learning about the topic? Who is your audience? What would that audience be likely to know about the topic already? How much are you going to have to fill them in through the content of the interview? How much material is available to you, and how accessible is it? How much time do you have to prepare? For an interview like Greeley's, you'd have to know about the history and doctrines of the Mormon Church as well as about Brigham Young. Sometimes the person you've chosen to interview *is* the topic, as is usually the case with a celebrity. You still have to have an angle for the interview—that person's most recent performance, work, award. You can't just begin the interview, "This story is about you. Tell me about yourself."

Selecting the interviewee

Determining whom to interview depends on the type of story you're writing. For a news interview, you must talk to people who have special knowledge about the subject or hold a position of power or influence related to the subject.

For a story on nuclear fusion, then, you might interview an engineer who has worked on projects to design fusion reactors. But you might also interview a member of Congress who knows little or nothing about fusion but who sits on a committee that will decide whether the fusion project gets federal research funds. You also should talk with some physicists—in industry and academia.

Some critical considerations in choosing your interview subjects are their *accessibility*, especially within the time frame needed to meet your deadline; their *willingness to talk* on the topic you've chosen; their *veracity*, not only their personal reliability to tell the truth but also their knowledge about the topic that would make what they say likely to be accurate; their *quotability*, or their tendency to speak with directness, color and wit.

Preparing for the interview

In preparing for the interview, you should do as much preliminary work on the story as possible. As we said before, you must research the *subject* and the *person* to be interviewed. In researching the subject, read authoritative publications until you are able to talk with ease about it to others, and then do just that: Talk informally with others about the subject. You might get an angle you hadn't thought of. Check public records that might relate to the subject. As you're reading, keep a list of questions you have about the subject: conflicting information you discover (as noted in Chapter 3) and anything you don't understand about what you've read.

Organize your list of questions so that they follow in a logical sequence. You should know what answers to expect before you ask the questions. If the interviewee gives wrong answers, you can sometimes conclude that he or she doesn't know much about the subject or is lying. But the person may know more than the sources you consulted and the sources are wrong. Give the person the opportunity to explain why he or she is right and other sources are wrong, then judge the validity of the explanation. You might need to do further research to confirm which position is right.

GETTING THE INFORMATION

Good writers work as hard to develop interviewing skills as they do to develop writing skills. When a subject is awkward, the interviewee difficult or the situation a crisis, strong interviewing skills are essential. Your interviews may be on the telephone, by closed-circuit television or in person. In all cases, some fundamentals always apply.

- *Introduce yourself clearly and accurately.* If you are representing a news medium (including "in-house" or institutional media), be sure to make your role clear. To assume a role other than reporter is unethical.

- *Get the person's name and title.* Although you should have gotten this in advance, you need to confirm it. Your source could have been wrong, or a title could have changed. Have the person confirm the spelling of his or her name. Asking the question is not as embarrassing as making a mistake in print. Then get other routine information before you launch the tough questions. Those routine questions will help to build rapport with your interviewee and to develop a sense of trust.

- *Let the interviewee talk freely.* Generally don't interrupt, but make mental notes of points you need clarification or more detail about (exact dates, locations and so on). If the interviewee tends to ramble, though, you may need to put him or her back on course to get your story. Always save the toughest questions for the end of the interview. Remember, the purpose of the interview is to get information. Asking a question the interviewee may be reluctant to answer early may end the discussion.

- *Be courteous and sensitive* to the reactions of the interviewee. If he or she keeps looking at the clock or seems to be tiring, you should recognize the obvious cue that time is limited.

- *Observe the interviewee's behavior*, such as mannerisms of speech or body, and if you are on that person's turf, note the surroundings. These not only will tell you something about the person but may give you a topic of conversation if the interview gets awkward. Pictures and replicas of cars, planes, turtles or horses, for example, suggest a special interest that can give a personal dimension to the story. An orderly or cluttered desk might also give you another insight into the person. One TV personality has a desk piled with a foot or so of debris, but colleagues say any item can be retrieved instantly. Details like this add to a story.

- *Don't be afraid to depart from your list* of prepared questions if responses to them could open a new, interesting line of discussion. And once you've asked all of the questions you'd prepared, be sure to ask whether there's anything you should have asked or anything else the interviewee would like to say. Some of your best information can come out of questions like that.

- *Phrase your questions carefully.* Unless you're looking specifically for a yes-or-no answer, ask open-ended questions. For example, ask "What is your opinion on the new research funding proposal?" rather than "Do you favor the new research funding proposal?" If you get stuck with a yes or no without elaboration, asking "Why?" can be helpful. With a hostile person, though, asking why can sometimes cause a defensive reaction. Return to open-ended questions.

- *Rephrase questions* if the response is not clear or the source is reluctant to talk. Make sure you understand what the person interviewed has said. Don't stop probing until complicated points are explained to your satisfaction. If you hit an especially rough area that threatens to disrupt the interview, go on to other things, returning to that point later on. But recognize that the source is not under an obligation to talk to you.

- *Get facts straight* by asking for a chronological development. You might accomplish that with a series of questions along these lines: "When did you start this hobby? . . . Then you picked it up again after you retired? . . . But didn't you show some paintings while you were the company president? . . . Let's just start from the very beginning with your art lessons so I can get it all in order."

- *Make your subject a good storyteller* by asking for problems encountered along the way to a goal or best-times and worst-times stories. You'll need to edge into this with something like, "What was the moment you felt most successful?" You might try to balance an overly positive story with something like, "Was it a straight shot for you from the first (recording, book) to the (Grammy award, best-seller list)?" Skillful celebrity TV interviewer Barbara Walters asked musician Lionel Richie: "If your life were a country music song or a Lionel Richie song, what would its title be?" Richie's response: "I'm Just Out Here Living a Dream.[2]"

- *Be persistent.* TV talk show hostess Bobbie Wygant's personality picklock question is what book the respondent has read recently. Or if that gets a dead-end response ("None."), she asks what his or her favorite book is. Sometimes the next question, "Why?", really gives the insight. If that doesn't work, she has some "imagine" kinds of questions to ask: "If you were King/Queen for a Day, won the New York Lottery" and so on.

- *Use a tape recorder.* Your foremost concern should be accuracy, and to quote completely accurately without a tape is impossible. Many print journalists have reservations about using tape recorders. In some cases, their reasons are simply excuses for not doing the extra work of listening to the tape. When working on deadline for a newspaper, you may indeed not have time to listen to the entire tape. But you can spot-check it to verify specific direct quotations.

  Have the courtesy to ask whether the interviewee minds a tape recorder being used. Most people today are familiar with tape recorders; certainly someone who's interviewed with any frequency will not object. If you detect any uneasiness, just say, "I want to be sure to get everything right."

  But even when using a tape recorder, you should also take notes. Machines don't always work as they're supposed to. And even if you have no mechanical problems, you'll find reviewing the tape is easier and faster with notes to go by. Without notes, finding a certain passage on the tape is difficult. Always record in your notes critical information like names, dates, locations and spellings of any unfamiliar terms. The tape won't help you there, and you may commit an embarrassing error like the student reporter who gave the Vice Chancellor for Fiscal Affairs the title of Vice Chancellor for Physical Affairs.

- *Tell the interviewee how to get in touch with you.* Something might come to mind later that he or she wants to add. And it makes an interviewee more secure to know exactly who you are and where you can be located.

- *Remain neutral.* Never let your attitude toward the subject or the person you are interviewing come to the surface or enter into the discussion. You should neither offer your opinion nor respond to the interviewee's expressions of opinion or inquiries about yours. You can be supportive of the interviewee and encourage responsiveness without agreeing. Most important, don't argue with the interviewee. Arguing is a sure way to restrict the information you'll be able to get out of the interview.

- *Use additional sources* for personality interviews where the interviewee is the subject as well as the source. Talk to everyday contacts that person has—family, friends, associates at work. If the person is well known in her or his field, talk to other authorities to see what they consider that person's major contributions.

Interviewing reluctant sources

Most experienced interviewers develop their own style: conversational, dynamic, impersonal and so on. However, they also respond to their subjects. The response should be an intellectual one, but emotional elements are difficult to put aside. The interviewer has to maintain control of the interview. Sometimes that's easy. Some people are easy to talk to because they like people and like to talk. Some sources, such as PR people, public officials and celebrities, are used to being interviewed, and their skill may make the interview go smoothly. But sometimes you must interview people who rarely speak in public, people who are by nature reserved, people who distrust anyone who is going to record or write about what they say. Special interviewing tactics can get these people to talk.

- *The "play it dumb" routine.* People may be reluctant to talk because they have something to hide, but ordinarily reluctance is just shyness. Frequently you can get such people to talk by acting dumb and helpless. Ask for an explanation of what the source knows so much about and you know so little of. This pose enhances the source's self-esteem, making him or her more likely to talk. People usually like to explain things they know a lot about. This technique can backfire, though. Knowledgeable people are often exasperated by ignorance. Don't ask stupid questions—just ask for explanations.

- *The "play it smart" routine.* Often sources think the person asking the questions is too ignorant of something like technical material to get it right. Public relations writers can run into this problem when interviewing the technical people (scientists, engineers, doctors) in their institution. Out of fear that what they say will be garbled, these people may refuse to say anything. In this situation, you must show that you've done some research by asking a sophisticated question. If the source discovers that you can converse intelligently on the subject, he or she is likely to open up and answer your questions.

- *The "it's in your best interest" routine.* There are several ways to play this game. "It's going to look bad if I have to say you refused to comment on what your company is doing with that federal money" will get a public official talking in a hurry. So will something like, "I have reports from all of the other departments for the company magazine, and the boss is going to wonder why there's nothing about yours." Lines like those are threats, though. It's better to try a positive approach. "Your department doesn't get much visibility. This story should help people understand all that you do." But if youre working for the news media and trying to get an important story on a subject the public needs to know about, don't hesitate to use pressure. PR interviewers who work in an institutional setting try to get some pressure exerted through the system instead of exerting it personally when the gentle approach doesn't work.

- *The thin edge of the wedge.* Especially when the story is controversial, sources might not want to talk. But if you can just get them started, they might not stop. If they begin by saying, "I just don't want to discuss the commissioners controversy," you might say something like, "Well, I know you aren't going to talk about it, but could you at least tell me this . . .". Then ask some trivial question that the source probably won't mind answering. That might lead naturally to another easy question, and if you're lucky, the person will lose the initial reluctance and keep on talking, giving you the whole story.

Probing for elusive facts from a reluctant source is not as common as being overwhelmed with unimportant, uninteresting information. Experienced sources know how to say a great deal without revealing much. Picking at small threads until a story begins to unravel is a skill developed by practice.

Some sources may have their public relations person sitting in on the interview. It's highly likely that the PR person will want to record the session—only on audiotape if it's a print story, but maybe even on videotape if it's for television. In several lawsuits, the original videotape has been shown to prove that misrepresentation occurred in the editing. Public relations people do even more to protect the people they are responsible for, training them for the news media interview experience and rehearsing them on likely questions.

The public relations person has a right to be in the interview to observe, but monitoring is a bad practice. News media expect the source, not the PR person, to answer the questions. If the encounter is likely to be fractious, the public relations person will probably set some guidelines before the interview begins, perhaps even when the interview is first granted. For every bad experience a newsperson can relate about PR-controlled interviews, the PR person can recite an equal number about misquotes, "no-win" questions ("When did you stop beating your wife?") and rearrangement of information that gives an unflattering slant.

PRESENTING THE INFORMATION IN PRINT

Two problems face the reporter: what to do with all of that quoted material and how to explain the nature of the question that provoked the response. Horace Greeley didn't have either problem when he interviewed Brigham Young. The published story was like a transcript of a tape—questions followed by answers. Greeley began simply by saying he had stopped to visit Young in Salt Lake City and that

[a]fter some unimportant conversation on general topics I stated that I had come to quest of fuller knowledge respecting the doctrines and polity of the Mormon church and would like to ask some questions bearing directly on these, if there were no objection.

Greeley then went on to report the substance of the interview, giving Young's views on the Mormon Church, slavery and polygamy. For example:

H.G.: What is the position of your church with respect to slavery?

B.Y.: We consider it of divine institution and not to be abolished until the curse pronounced on Ham shall have been removed from his descendants.[2]

Today most interview stories are not written in this format, except in some magazines. Most interview stories are either structured like news stories or like feature stories (see Chapter 11).

Personality interviews are almost always feature stories or columns; symposium interviews are often news features. The difference is a personality feature focuses on the individual and the news feature's emphasis is on information the person gives. The most common type of symposium interview is the "person-in-the-street" approach, where various people are asked their views on something in the news (see 3.5). Sometimes the people questioned are chosen simply because they are available; sometimes they're from a specific group. During the Watergate scandal, one reporter called plumbers around town to get their reaction or reports of the White House "plumbers" group formed to plug news leaks.

Even when an interview story is written like other news sories, with a lead that tells the most important point, development and elaboration of the main point, and so on, some special rules apply:

- *Make sure the lead isolates a specific point.* Your interview probably covered a wide range of topics, and you have collections of quotes around these topics. Mentioning all of these topics in the lead is usually a mistake. Choose one that is the most interesting or important and introduce the other matters further down. Try to relate them to the main topic so the story doesn't appear to be segmented. You may have to leave out whole areas of discussion.

- *Structure the story in order of importance.* Rarely is it a good idea to present the points in the order they came up in the interview. The most important things may have been mentioned near the end of the interview— but they belong at the beginning of the story.

  Furthermore, a person may refer to something early in the interview, then return to it later. In writing the interview story, you will group related subject matter together.

Reprinted by permission of Jefferson Communication, Inc., Reston, Va.

In moving parts of the interview around, though, you must be careful not to strip a remark of its context or to juxtapose elements in ways that distort the discussion.

- *Indicate the occasion of the interview.* Generally an interview story is written for a reason. It might be that an important person had come to town for a meeting or speaking engagement. Or the person may be an authority on an issue that has just emerged as significant. In any event, the story should indicate why the person was interviewed or the circumstances of the interview. For example:

> Video games are replacing drugs as an addiction for teen-agers, says sociologist John Smith.
> Smith, a professor of sociology at XYZ College, was in the city Tuesday for the annual video game convention.

- *Include the qualifications of the speaker.* Part of showing why someone was interviewed is giving that person's qualifications to speak on the subject. In the hypothetical example above, the next paragraph might say something like this:

> Smith has conducted several studies of teen-agers' recreational habits, including a study of video games published last month in the *Journal of Leisurely Sociology.*

In news interviews the emphasis is on the person's qualifications: education, experience or position. In a feature story on the person, the emphasis is on all aspects of the individual, including physical description. In a symposium interview, the emphasis is on the variety or, maybe, commonality of responses. Direct quotations are important in the symposium story, mixed with background to put the quotes in perspective, because the stories are generally on issues. Events or news features often call for multiple-source interviews (see 7.2 and 7.4).

Quotation   A central part of structuring the interview story is incorporating direct quotations. Some beginning writers just string them together—the Q&A format minus the Q. But ordinarily that's not a very good idea.

The writer's job is to distill the information collected in the interview and present it to the reader clearly and concisely. Rarely are the interviewee's exact words the clearest and most concise way to present the information. As noted in Chapter 5, paraphrasing and summarizing help get the major points across and give the story unity.

The role of quotes is to lend authority to points, to provide support for them and to capture the flavor of the person who was the source for the information. Quotes have a mechanical use, too—to break up the monotony of an otherwise dry, straightforward account.

Choose quotes for their drama or expressiveness, but be careful about attribution. Consider this sentence:

7.2 Multiple-Source Interview

This is fairly typical of the multiple interview for a news event (Person-in-the-street collective interviews are generally on issues: "What do you think of giving military aid to Latin American governments?")

Few rules to cut fire risk are in effect

By Mark Nelson
and Stephen Engelberg
Washington Bureau of *The News*

WASHINGTON—Air-safety officials have proposed, with little success, dozens of regulations during the past 20 years to eliminate the danger of fires in airline cabins.

The lead is a summary of conclusions based on the interviews.

Although fires aboard commercial jetliners are rare, National Transportation and Safety Board officials have issued repeated warnings about materials that give off toxic fumes and dense smoke.

The first person cited is an FAA spokesman, since the FAA regulates the airline industry.

But the Federal Aviation Administration has implemented few of the proposals, which might have prevented some of the 23 deaths in the Air Canada flight from Dallas/Fort Worth Airport that made an emergency landing at Greater Cincinnati Airport Thursday.

"The present standards are totally inadequate, and the federal regulations are far behind the state of the art," said Rep. Elliott Levitas, D-Ga. He directs a subcommittee that has called for improved fire-prevention measures in airline cabins.

FAA spokesman Fred Farrar said Friday that research into fire safety "has been given top priority" by the agency. He said that fires in the passenger compartment are extinguished easily and that jet fuel poses a greater hazard.

Since the mid-1960s, the NTSB— the government agency that investigates air accidents—has issued more than three dozen recommendations dealing with cabin fires. A 1973 NTSB proposal called for fire detectors in aircraft lavatories, and in 1974

Information from the NTSB, the government agency that investigates aircraft accidents, is probably from a report, although an official also is quoted.

(continued)

The FAA was asked to re- ——
spond to the report, an
attempt to be fair in the
reporting.

the board recommended that automatic fire extinguishers be installed in
airplane restrooms. Neither regulation has been issued.

Investigators believe the Air Canada fire started in a rear lavatory of
the DC-9.

The proposed standards were not
issued because the FAA argued that
airplane manufacturers could not
reasonably be expected to meet the
new requirements.

Other NTSB proposals urged the
government to require that manufacturers develop materials for seats and
interior walls that slow the spread of
flames and limit the danger from toxic smoke and fumes.

But the FAA said action already
had been taken to preclude hazardous
fire conditions and that such fires
were not "a continuing safety problem."

Airplane manufacturers insist that —— A manufacturer also was
fire-prevention technology has im-   interviewed, since the way
proved during the past two decades.   planes are built is a factor
But a McDonnell-Douglas spokes-   in accidents.
man said Friday that the federal government has not required airlines to
incorporate these advances into older
aircraft like the 1968 Air Canada
DC-9.

The opposite side is the —— "The 'after-the-crash' mentality
opinion of the Aviation Con-   often plays a role in this," said Mat-
sumer Action Project.   thew Finucane, director of the Aviation Consumer Action Project, an or-
ganization associated with consumer
activist Ralph Nader. "Ultimately,
deaths have to be closely tied to the
problem before you finally get action."

Finucane said Congess is well
aware of the problem of fires in aircraft cabins.

"You may see some final solutions
coming out of this crash," he said.

Former NTSB chairman James
King told a House subcommittee in
1980 that the effects of smoke and

(continued)

7.2 (continued)

flames are fatal to 20 percent of the people who die in fiery airplane crashes.

"Unless the FAA acts forcefully and decisively, there will be no appreciable difference in these statistics in the foreseeable future," King said.

Virtually all materials in airline cabins are flammable. Wool carpets give off deadly cyanide gas when they burn. The cabin walls of most airliners are coated with a substance that can give off hydrogen cyanide. In addition to the toxic fumes that these materials produce, they also give off dense smoke.

"Everything that isn't metal poses a problem," one NTSB official said.

"It's difficult to find something in this world that won't burn," said Tom Cole, a spokesman for Boeing Commercial Airplane Co. Flame-retardant chemicals used on aircraft materials sometimes can add problems. "The more flame retardant you make something, apparently the more toxic it is when it does finally burn or melt," he said.

Passengers have no more than a few minutes to escape the cramped environs of an aircraft cabin before they are overcome by smoke, researchers have estimated.

"Our concern is that the FAA set standards for the amount of smoke and toxic gas that can be emitted from burning cabin materials," Finucane said. "Right now, there are no standards."

The FAA requires that seat cushions and carpets in airplane cabins pass flammability tests. But the agency's safety experts say it is difficult to determine the potential of those materials for emitting toxic fumes and smoke.

Materials treated for flame resistance are especially difficult to rate because the chemicals used in the process sometimes produce more

—— Another plane manufacturer was asked to comment, since fabrics used in most planes are treated with flame-retardant chemical products.

(continued)

dangerous gases than the materials they protect.

John O'Brien, a safety specialist with the Air Line Pilots Association, said the pilots' union has been pushing for stronger government regulations for years.

Because pilots are in the planes all the time, a representative of the pilots' association was interviewed.

"There is material available" that will restrict the spread of flames and reduce the dangers of toxic fumes," O'Brien said. "The biggest problem is cost."

After reading this story, do you have any questions? What is missing? Was the reporter fair, objective? What is your conclusion after reading the story?

Industry officials estimate the cost at hundreds of millions of dollars to equip the nation's commercial airline fleet of more than 2,000 planes with flame-retardant cabin materials.

Dallas Morning News, June 6, 1983.
Reprinted with permission.

Smith said the program was an outrageous, unconscionable use of public funds.

The reader wonders if *outrageous* and *unconscionable* are the words of the writer or of Smith. A direct quote would have been better because the speaker was using colorful words.

"This program is the most outrageous, unconscionable waste of public funds I've ever encountered," Smith said.

Sometimes the speaker's point can be made most clearly by a paraphrase, but a direct quote is nevertheless helpful to support and elaborate on the point. Consider this lead:

Homicides and rapes tend to increase as the temperature climbs, according to a study by a Rice University researcher.

That's a concise statement of the point. The support, in the form of a direct quotation, came several paragraphs later:

"The data isn't clean enough to allow a specific prediction," Anderson said in an interview, "But if you plot it on a graph, the shape is fairly consistent. Highly aggressive crimes tend to increase as temperatures increase."

In all cases, you need to look for that strong opening or supporting quote to give focus to the story. It should capture the essence of the story—either facts or emotion. Then you need a transitional quote that will carry the story from one of the interview topics to another to show how the information is related. And you always should look for the concluding quote that will tie the topics of the story together. These are difficult to get, and not every story will have three strong examples, but you should go into an interview looking for ways to make the story hang together. Most experienced interviewers will recognize these quotes as they are uttered. You'll need to practice listening for the points the interviewee makes that will help you tell the story best in his or her own words.

Showing the responses to questions

Beginning writers seem to have difficulty obeying the edict to keep yourself out of the story while showing how quotes, or even topics, came to be. You can state in the story that a quote came from an interview or from some other source. The news peg or the reason for the reporter's interview is usually clear—the publication of a book or some research, the release of a film or recording.

Sometimes it's not that simple. An interviewer may introduce a topic that doesn't seem to come from any of the quotes, or the circumstances. In a case like that it's easy enough to say, "In response to a question about her recent trip to India, Dr. Turner said she presented a paper drawn from her research at an international conference." It's not necessary to say who asked the question.

A problem does occur when an interviewee has responded to a question with something like, "I'll tell you, but it's off the record." Off- and on-the-record material in an interview may put the writer in some risk of betraying a confidence.

On and off the record

Some writers have a policy of never permitting an interviewee to go off the record. That reduces the risk of confusing what is on and off the record in a story. However, sometimes permitting an interviewee to tell you something off the record can help to put the story in better perspective. Occasionally, you can talk the person into going on the record with it if you can negotiate how it will be presented. (See the discussion of government terminology in Chapter 10.)

If you get permission to use the material without attribution, you should check claims of fact with at least one other source.

Off-the-record interviews are common with government officials who don't always want the public to know what they think. Writers can get used that way. Nevertheless, reporters often accept off-the-record information when the story is important to the public and they can't get it any other way. Some top bureaucrats will grant interviews only if identification is vague, as in "'War in the Middle East is likely,' said a high-ranking government official, who asked not to be identified." The public may be mystified by the attribution, but often insiders know who it is.

Attribution As with other news stories, you must make sure that statements of opinion or facts not commonly known are attributed. (Some of the conventions of attribution are reviewed in 7.3.) But your source in most instances is the per-

7.3 Quotation and Attribution

Give the source of any statement not commonly known to be true.

WRONG: Tacoma will have an adequate supply of electricity in the future.
RIGHT: Tacoma will have an adequate supply of electricity in the future, George Henderson says.
WRONG: The company's largest natural gas contract will expire in 1991, making the cost of natural gas much higher than in the past.
RIGHT: The company's largest natural gas contract will expire in 1991, making the cost of natural gas much higher than in the past, Henderson said.

Always give attribution for direct quotations:

WRONG: "It is quite possible that the president would order that part of our electricity be sent to other parts of the nation."
RIGHT: "It is quite possible that the president would order that part of our electricity be sent to other parts of the nation," Henderson said.

Begin the sentence with the quotation; put attribution at the middle or end.

WRONG: Henderson said, "The fact is still that the overall supply of natural gas discovered and available has declined each year."
RIGHT: "The fact is still that the overall supply of natural gas discovered and available has declined each year," Henderson said.

Always separate attribution following a quote or statement with a comma.

WRONG: "We learned that safety systems will work and the public can be protected from harm" said Henderson.
RIGHT: "We learned that safety systems will work and the public can be protected from harm," said Henderson.
WRONG: If electricity use stopped growing Henderson said the company would continue to build plants for two purposes.
RIGHT: If electricity use stopped growing, Henderson said, the company would continue to build plants for two purposes.

Don't use "according to" when "says" or "said" can be used.

WRONG: Tacoma Electric is optimistic that its nuclear plant will receive a license, according to Henderson.
RIGHT: Tacoma Electric is optimistic that its nuclear plant will receive a license, Henderson says.

---

son interviewed, and a continual string of identical attributions can get monotonous. That doesn't mean attribution can be omitted. But certain techniques can reduce the monotony. You can alternate the use of the person's last name and a pronoun, as "Anderson said" with "he said." And you can avoid giving double attribution to a single quotation. If an attribution appears between two quoted sentences, there is no need to repeat the attribution after the second sentence. As an example:

> "The data isn't clean enough to allow a specific prediction," Anderson said in an interview. "But if you plot it on a graph, the shape is fairly consistent."

The attribution pattern can also be varied by giving the attribution before the quote. But avoid burying the quote behind an attribution, as in

> He said, "I agree with the president's economic plan."

Instead, introduce the quote with a sentence containing the attribution:

> Smith expressed support for the president. "I agree with the president's economic plan."

When the story is quoting only one person, this technique poses no problems, but when other speakers are quoted, it might lead to some confusion. Make sure the context makes your attribution clear.

Verification

Finally, be aware that accurately reporting what a person says in an interview does not fulfill all of your responsibilities. You have an obligation to your readers to verify questionable statements. During the 1980 presidential election campaign, Ronald Reagan accused Jimmy Carter of starting his campaign at the birthplace of the Klu Klux Klan. Reporters who merely repeated Reagan's comment didn't do their job. Conscientious reporters checked the history books to find the Klan's actual birthplace—which wasn't even in the same state that Reagan cited.

Writing an interview story from only one interview always poses some risk. If matters of controversy are discussed, you have an obligation to see that other viewpoints are represented in your story. And you have the further obligation of investigating the claims made by either side so you can inform your readers of the facts. Such an effort ensures balance and gives your story credibility.

You'll lose credibility with your source if you take quotations out of context so that you misrepresent what the interviewee intended to say. Broadcast stories are particularly vulnerable to this error, because you'll be choosing actualities from the bulk of the interview.

INTERVIEWS IN THE BROADCAST MEDIA

In addition to facing all of the challenges of an interviewer who's preparing an interview for print presentation, broadcasters have some particular concerns.

Equipment

Radio reporters go everywhere with their audiocassette tape recorders; TV reporters with their cameras, lights and videotape recorders, often in large vans to carry it all.

As Chapter 5 pointed out, the primary goal in radio and TV news is to capture the story on tape. So it's critical that you keep your equipment in perfect operating order at all times. News directors and producers will never accept the excuse that you couldn't get the interview because your batteries were dead. No reporter who wants to work very long in broadcast news ever goes out without first checking the condition of the batteries and of the other crucial parts. Batteries must be fully charged, lights must be in working order, enough audiotapes and videotapes must be carried along to record on, all recorders and cameras must be in top shape, and the van or news car must have plenty of gas.

Broadcast reporters often carry spare batteries and even spare parts, just in case. Radio reporters might even carry a spare tape recorder.

Preparation

Because broadcast newsrooms have fewer reporters than newspapers do, the broadcast reporter often has far less time than a newspaper reporter to research and prepare for each interview. It's imperative for the broadcast journalist to read widely to keep on top of events as well as trends.

Assignment editors are often used as resources for broadcast reporters in the field. Reporters just finishing one story will call in to the station and ask the assignment editor for help in researching the next story. Assignment editors make phone calls for background information and then relay it.

The interviewer still has to think through the questions to be asked and try to anticipate the responses. You have to remember the focus of the interview and not let the person responding get too far afield. As in the print interview, though, you have to be sensitive to tangents introduced by a response that might give you a better story than the one you went to get. Listen carefully to the responses; the audience (and the interviewee) will notice if you're preoccupied with the next question you're going to ask. If you establish a conversation between the two of you, the person forgets the equipment and the audience and talks (see 7.4).

Reluctant and overeager interviewees

The audiotape recorder and the TV cameras scare some people off. And some people seek out the broadcast reporter just to hear themselves talk on radio or see themselves on TV. Both types require careful handling.

The reluctant ones are often the off-the-record type. Off the record in broadcast means no cameras or tape recorders. Many news directors declare that

7.4 TV Interview Feature

A segment on the TV news magazine *20/20* on Dec. 12, 1985, dealt with insomnia. Three self-described insomniacs were interviewed, and one (Fran) presented a film of one of her sleepless nights made by her nephew, who makes medical films. Doctors in a sleep clinic were also interviewed to show what they had done for each one of these people. Only a portion of the segment is represented here, and some of that has deletions, as indicated.

[Host Hugh] DOWNS: There's probably not one of us who hasn't had some trouble at some time or another getting to sleep. Some 20 million Americans suffer from insomnia, and it's really a miserable condition. We have found three real insomniacs who were willing to show us how bad this can be. They let 20/20 stay with them through the night, when they hardly sleep anyway, and through the day, when their lack of sleep really shows. They did this to let people know what insomnia is like and to help John Stossel show other insomniacs that there are new treatments that work. . . .

JOHN STOSSEL *[voice-over]*: First, let me introduce you to three people who cannot sleep and don't know why.

Paul Garrison is one of them. Here he's taking a walk with his wife. He's a successful businessman who's had insomnia for 20 years.

Mrs. GARRISON: Oh, every time we go to someone's house he falls asleep. It's a big joke already, because everybody knows that when they invite Paul he's not going to be there for dessert.

STOSSEL *[voice-over]*: It's not funny to Paul. Recently he hired someone to drive him to work, because several times when he was driving his car, he started dozing off.

PAUL GARRISON, **insomniac:** And I got scared. There were many times when I would really feel, hey, pull over before it's too late.

STOSSEL *[voice-over]*: He falls asleep in the car, at parties and at work—
[interviewing] But at night in your own bed you can't sleep?

Mr. GARRISON: I'm supposed to sleep. I don't sleep.

STOSSEL: How much sleep do you get?

Mr. GARRISON: Two hours, maybe three hours at best.

STOSSEL *[voice-over]*: Lately he's tried drinking himself to sleep. We filmed him making his usual before-bed drink. But the real problem starts when he wakes up, around 2:00 or 3:00 in the morning.

Mr. GARRISON: It started with one martini, then it went to two martinis, then it went to three martinis. And at that point I said it's enough. I got to do something about it.

STOSSEL *[voice-over]*: Dana Saltsman is a 30-year-old pipefitter at a power plant. For the last eight years he hasn't slept more than four hours a night.

DANA SALTSMAN, **insomniac:** I try to go to bed, like, at 11:00, usually don't fall asleep til, like, 1:00 or so, normally. Maybe get up two or three times during the night.

STOSSEL *[voice-over]*: He often wakes up thinking about the sports cars he races as a hobby, and usually works on late into the evening. Dana might not mind his sleeplessness, except that it makes him so irritable during the day.

Mr. SALTSMAN: If something irritates you, you know, you're more apt to, you know, jump the gun a little bit because you are tired than you would be—

STOSSEL: You broke your ex-wife's nose.

(continued)

Mr. SALTSMAN: Yeah.

STOSSEL: Do you think your lack of sleep contributed to two divorces?

Mr. SALTSMAN: Yeah. Quite a bit, actually.

STOSSEL [voice-over]: Fran Canfield has not slept straight through the night for as long as she can remember.

FRAN CANFIELD, **insomniac:** Hi, my name is Fran, and I'm going to admit you.

STOSSEL [voice-over]: By day she works as a nurse in the local hospital. Then she goes home to give dinner to her husband and two children.

Ms. CANFIELD: Okay, let's—we're going to have some supper, you guys.

STOSSEL [voice-over]: It's hard enough to hold down a full-time job and raise a family. Imagine what it's like if you're sleepy all the time.

Ms. CANFIELD: I work hard and I have two children. I have a lot of things going on, and I don't have energy. I don't have the energy to keep up.

STOSSEL [voice-over]: Fran's also upset because she's overweight. She blames the insomnia for that. She says when she gets up at night, the only way she can get back to sleep is by eating peanut butter sandwiches. To get a sense of what she goes through, we spent a night with the Canfields.

Ms. CANFIELD: Time to go to bed.

STOSSEL [voice-over]: Fran went to bed at 11:00. Our camera crew stayed in the living room. Fran's husband wanted his privacy, so he slept in another room. We arranged for a special black and white camera to be in Fran's room.

On this night Fran tosses and turns for awhile. She later said she was sleeping fitfully. And at a little after 1:00 she's up. She goes to the living room and reads the paper.

Ms. CANFIELD: I'm tired and yet I'm not tired. I don't know how to describe it. But I, you know, I feel like I know I have to go back to bed but I really don't feel like it. I can't—I don't know any other way to say it.

STOSSEL [voice-over]: A half-hour later she tries to sleep again, and for the next three hours she tosses and turns. This time she's not asleep. You can see her looking at the clock. Just before 5:00, she gets up for the second time.

Ms. CANFIELD: I'm hungry now.

STOSSEL [voice-over]: This time she makes the peanut butter sandwich.

Ms. CANFIELD: I was hungry. I was not getting away from it. I knew. I'd probably have indigestion by the time I have to get up.

STOSSEL [voice-over]: The neighborhood's quiet except for Fran's house. She's wide awake.

Ms. CANFIELD: I don't know. I guess I'm aggravated now. I was trying to go back to sleep in there and I couldn't.

(continued)

7.4 (continued)

> **STOSSEL** *[voice-over]*: At 5:35 Fran goes back to bed. After tossing and turning awhile, she finally does get some sleep, but only until 8:00, when she's wakened by a friend's phone call.
>
> **Ms. CANFIELD:** Some nights when I get up, I feel worse than when I went to bed, figure I might as well not have bothered, you know, that I didn't sleep at all.
>
> **STOSSEL** *[voice-over]*: Fran, Paul and Dana—none of them has had a good night's sleep for years. *[on camera]* What can they do about it? Well, if insomnia persists, your doctor may recommend that you go to a sleep laboratory. We visited one here at the University of Pittsburgh.
>
>   *[voice-over]* Both Fran and Dana were referred here for help. Paul went to a sleep clinic at Montefiore Medical Center in New York. Their sleep will be analyzed by a staff of experts, who want to know the patients' medical histories and details about their sleeping habits. . . .
>

Potential interview subjects sometimes appear as you're en route to the actual event. Broadcast reporters must be prepared to do an interview on the spur of the moment.

they'll just leave if any source says "No cameras or tape recorders." Sometimes a compromise can be worked out. Stations sometimes muffle the voice of a source who doesn't want to be identified, or they obscure the person's face on TV. But few sources will agree to this because they can usually be recognized anyway.

A newspaper reporter can write:

> A high city official today said, "The mayor has been stealing from the city treasury for the last 10 years."

But that high city official would hesitate to say the same thing on radio or TV for fear of being recognized. Broadcast reporters in those cases must resort to the voicer (radio) or standup (TV)—that is, reading their report:

> A high city official told KXAX news today . . . and I quote . . . "The mayor has been stealing from the city treasury for the last 10 years." We tried to talk with the mayor about these charges, but his office said he was in the Bahamas on business. For KXAX news, I'm Gretchen Kia.

Unlike the print interviewer, the broadcast reporter *never* goes into an interview and asks whether the interview can be taped. As a broadcast reporter, you just set up your equipment as if nothing is happening, and the person will tell you if you can't use it. People who agree to be interviewed by reporters or institutional PR people should *expect* the interviewer to arrive with equipment.

When a subject says no to recording, the public relations person needs to do some persuasive talking and negotiating. The broadcast news reporter can try to reason with the person, playing on the importance of getting his or her ideas and points of view to the thousands out there in the audience. For some people, an ego appeal works, and for others, playing on their sense of responsibility helps.

Even when someone agrees to be recorded, he or she may be ill at ease with the equipment. Starting with small talk helps. Talk about the weather, sports, their hometown, ask some of the routine information questions you'll need answered anyway. During this time, simply say something like, "I'm going to turn on the tape recorder (camera) to get a level on our voices here. This won't take long . . ." and most people will have overcome their shyness by that point.

Then there are the hams and publicity seekers who gravitate to tape recorders and cameras. Some politicians and public figures are among them, and you have to beware. Their lack of reticence makes them tempting interview subjects, but they often present only one side of any issue. If you rely on them too often for interviews, your coverage won't be fair and balanced.

Telephone interviewing

The recorded telephone interview is the backbone of radio news reporting, although it sometimes is also used in television news. Print media reporters have to rely on the phone, too, since travel budgets are limited. Most of the time they let the readers know that the information came from a telephone interview.

The telephone interviewer is handicapped by the impersonality of the instrument. You can't see the other person and he or she can't see you. In fact, you don't really know if the person on the line is the real source or not. Sometimes a request to record a conversation, even if you are writing for print, gives you some protection. A statement about the recording procedure is usually followed by asking the person to give his or her name and title. Some reporters note the telephone number if the source called in; that information is evidence of an attempt to verify. Another disadvantage is the loss of non-verbal cues. And it's more difficult to establish rapport. Radio reporters especially try to make a lot of personal contacts so when they do call someone, they're known. Radio reporters learn to make friends of the gatekeepers of the people they want to talk with—the public relations representatives who can provide the access, the receptionists and secretaries and staff who work with them.

The major problem with broadcast telephone interviewing, besides the impersonality of the device, is, generally, the brevity of the call. You have little time to establish your credentials, get permission to tape the call (required by the Federal Communications Commission) and get focused responses to clear questions.

If you're going to use the tape on the air or if you're on the air live, there are some major points to remember:

1. Always identify yourself and who you represent at the outset.

2. Identify the person you're talking with so listeners will know who it is and what position that person holds (also to be sure you do have that person on the line).

3. Give the purpose of your call even before the question is asked, and make it sound critical that you get the person to respond on tape right at that moment.

4. Tell the person that he or she is being taped, not just for legal reasons; sometimes it helps the person to frame responses more carefully.

5. Use open-ended questions; when you hit a dead response (yes or no), employ the "Why?" approach.

6. Keep quiet while the other person is talking. Don't acknowledge responses as you do in ordinary conversation, with "I see" or "uh-huh"; it complicates editing the tape.

7. Interrupt with questions, if necessary, to keep the subject on track.

8. Act friendly and interested. Never act pushy.

9. Don't "frame" your respondent by putting words in his or her mouth or asking leading questions. A quick respondent is likely to call your hand on the air and also terminate the interview.

10. Don't ask questions that take so long to pose that the respondent has forgotten where you started, or two-part questions. Even if the person being interviewed can follow them, the audience can't.

11. Beware of respondents who ignore your question and reply by telling you what they wanted to say, usually an opinion. Often they'll begin with, "That's a good question, but . . .". Don't let them escape without answering.

12. Don't ask permission to use a comment—the person agreed to being taped.

Editing a story for broadcast

Editing tape for radio and TV requires many of the same skills as writing the interview story for print.

You still need good opening, transitional and concluding quotes. You still have to weave these into the fabric of a story, but you'll write less copy than the print writer; you'll depend more on quotes (actualities).

Suppose an interview with a news source runs five minutes. As noted in Chapter 5, perhaps only 30 seconds of that five minutes will be used on radio, about a minute or so on TV.

Writers and tape editors must decide which cut, or cuts, to pull from that five-minute interview to use in the newscast. This is not always an easy process. Broadcast writers, reporters, producers and editors face this process with speeches, meetings and news conferences as well, as you will see in the following chapters.

MAIN POINTS

- Interviews can be categorized as news gathering, personality or symposium, where several people are interviewed on a topic.

- You need to choose an interview subject that people need to know about or are interested in and to select as an interviewee the person most knowledgeable about that subject.

- Doing interview stories for all media requires mastery of certain interviewing skills: researching the subject and the person, compiling a list of questions carefully phrased to get the best responses, presented in the right order (toughest questions last), and taking good notes with a tape recorder for backup.

- When interviewing people who are reluctant to talk to reporters, you must attempt to get information by the most appropriate strategy. Some of these are: playing dumb — appearing to be a non-challenging interviewer merely seeking explanations; playing smart — asking sophisticated questions that show the interviewee you are knowledgeable and will understand what he or she says; saying "It's in your own best interest" — showing the interviewee the advantages of talking, or the disadvantages of being quoted as unwilling to comment; applying the thin edge of the wedge — beginning by asking harmless questions that get the person talking, eventually leading to matters of importance.

- In writing the interview story, make sure the lead isolates a specific point; structure the story in order of importance; indicate the occasion of the interview; and include the qualifications of the speaker.

- Problems in presenting the information in the print media include finding effective ways to pull together all of the topics of the interview and to use quotes. You should have a good opening, transitional and closing quotes.

- When information can be obtained in no other way, a reporter may allow some of an interview to be off the record, but ordinarily, off-the-record interviews should be avoided.

- In handling quotes, especially if some material is given off the record, you need to be careful about the attribution and you should always verify facts given in the story. The audience should know if someone says something that doesn't happen to be true or if controversy surrounds the fact.

- Because equipment is a fundamental part of the broadcast interview, you have to be sure that everything is in good working order and that you have spares.

- The equipment used for broadcast interviews intimidates some interviewees; it encourages others. Either extreme can be a problem.

- Whether the interview is in person or on the phone, the broadcast reporter seeks substantive answers on tape that can be used on the air.

EXERCISES

1. Find a Q&A format interview in *U.S. News & World Report* or some other magazine. Rewrite the interview as a newspaper story, crafting an appropriate lead, including other items of importance and leaving out unimportant details.

2. Choose one of the following people as the subject for a hypothetical interview on the subject listed. Do the preparation you would if you were actually going to interview the person. Be sure to gather information about the person and the subject, then prepare a list of at least 10 questions.

   Philippe de Montebello on museum's holding of antiquities from other nations.

   Jacques Cousteau on mining the sea.

   John Strohm on the international environment, especially endangered species.

   Carl Sagan on the possibility of space colonies for some of Earth's inhabitants.

   Marshall Loeb on the U.S. economy.

   Jeffrey Z. Rubin on international terrorism.

   Stanley Marcus on men's and women's fashions.

   Barbara Walters or William Buckley on interviewing.

   William Raspberry on editorial writing.

3. Choose a current news topic and ask 10 other students for their opinions. Record their responses and write a symposium interview story. Then list the weaknesses and strengths of this type of story.

NOTES

1. Louis L. Snyder and Richard B. Morris, *A Treasury of Great Reporting*, 2nd ed. (New York: Simon & Schuster, 1962), p. 106.

2. Ibid. p. 107.

SUGGESTIONS FOR ADDITIONAL READING

Biagi, Shirley. *Interviews That Work*. Belmont, Calif.: Wadsworth, 1986.   An excellent book especially for help with broadcast interviews; includes some case studies by expert interviewers.

Biagi, Shirley, ed. *NewsTalk I and NewsTalk II*. Belmont, Calif.: Wadsworth, 1987. The expert interviewer has talked to people in print (book I) and broadcasting (book II) and displays her craft as well as their information in this set of paperbacks.

Blumberg, Skip. "Interviews with Interviewers, about Interviewing" (videotape). New York: Electronic Arts Intermix, 1986.

Brady, John. *The Craft of Interviewing*. Cincinnati: Writer's Digest, 1976.   Covers interviewing for news and features. Easy to read and has especially good information on asking questions.

Metzler, Ken. *Creative Interviewing*. Englewood Cliffs, N.J.: Prentice-Hall, 1977.   A standard supplement in print news courses.

O'Donnell, Lewis B., Carl Hausman and Philip Benoit. *Announcing*. Belmont, Calif.: Wadsworth, 1987. See Chapter 8 on interviewing.

Zinsser, William. *On Writing Well*, Rev. ed. New York: Harper & Row, 1985. Chapter 2 gives some beneficial insights on writing interview stories.

Complex Story Structures

"Too much of what you write on many of these beats is written for the approval of your fellow participants in the game, for your editors to some degree, and hardly at all for the comprehension and approval of a wider public, most of which you tend to think of with the same contempt as government officials. This public doesn't have the background to understand the stuff anyway, and you can't really write what you know because it would go over their heads."

Hodding Carter, "Making Sense of News," speech at the Modern Media Institute, St. Petersburg, Fla., 1983.

"The commission and many serious students of the urban riot (Watts) could only conclude that the press played a major role as a causative factor, that our failure to report on the conditions of the inner city left those inside its walls with no way to make the rest of us out there in illusion land understand how deep was their anguish. . . . Our neighbors had to set a fire to gain our attention. . . . But I am persuaded today that we learned almost nothing."

Robert C. Maynard, "Ralph McGill's America and Mind," the fifth Ralph McGill Lecture, Oct. 20, 1982, at the Henry W. Grady School of Journalism and Mass Communication, University of Georgia, Athens.

Speech Stories

"Put in a bulk order for 60 hearing aids," said a seasoned newspaper reporter teaching a college class as a visiting professor. His reason: speech stories. "First, I told them all week to start speech stories with what the person said, not to write the coverage lead like an advance. Next, I told them they would have to listen and take careful notes so their quotes would be accurate," he said.

So why order hearing aids? Only 10 students used any quotes at all from a speech he had read as a class exercise. Of these 10, only 3 had captured accurate quotes. More than half the class began the story with the standard summary lead and put what the speaker said in the *second* graph. These students made the two most common errors of any beginner writing a speech story. Finding just the right quote that sums up the speech is difficult, but you can paraphrase and begin with the most important information from the speech.

Covering speeches makes up a significant percentage of day-to-day reporting. Print and broadcast journalists sometimes seem to follow each other around all day long from speech to speech. Speech stories are seldom coveted assignments; they can be boring or frustrating. But they are such a staple that you have to develop skill in handling them. In most small communities, at least one speaker a day is on the calendar of activities. In big cities, the calendar is so crowded that only the really newsworthy speakers are covered—and then only if they're discussing something of significance to the media audience.

Most of these speeches are written by public relations staff people after interviews with the person who is to give the speech. The PR writers also prepare an introduction to the speaker, which is often used if provided. And the speaker has copies of the speech, introduction and a news release. If the speaker is important, a PR person may be there to see that the news people get the information and pictures they need.

Often the PR person issues the speech and the introduction in a brochure to selected audiences. If the speaker makes changes in addressing the audience, or if the person introducing the speaker changes the prepared introduction, the brochure should reflect these changes. The brochure with the introduction, speech, pictures of speaker and principal hosts, as well as something about the occasion extend the audience for the speech and often result in quotes used by writers long after the event.

Speeches generally have some focus or purpose, and the public relations writer's news release stresses the elements in the speech that the speaker and his or her institution want emphasized. But reporters covering the speech may pick up on something the speaker says that they feel is particularly important to their audiences. Good reporters will always find something in a speech that will give the story a special focus for their audiences. Examining three common formats for writing speech stories may help you tackle this job.

TYPES OF SPEECH STORIES

Speech stories always focus on (1) what is said; (2) the speaker (personality); or (3) the event (action). One of the three becomes the news peg.

1. Attention is given to what was said when the speaker isn't well known. The announcement of medical breakthroughs, for example, usually come from researchers or doctors who were previously not newsmakers.

2. The speaker sometimes is the news focus, and the occasion for the talk is only a subsidiary element. Brooke Shields speaking at a youth conference on the dangers of smoking is an example. So is a U.S. national security adviser making a major policy statement in a commencement address. Of course, to the graduating class, the event was probably more important, but to news media audiences, the policy statement is the news.

3. On some occasions, a speaker is a mere formality, as at July 4 or Cinco de Mayo celebrations. These are really event-centered speaker stories. However, a prominent speaker's message at a routine occasion can become headline news, as 8.1 shows. How such a story is written depends on a careful weighing of the news values.

Personality stories

The significance of the visit from a head of state is often lost in the flurry of news out of Washington. Many come, and often they address Congress, but seldom do they get the attention that Corazon Aquino received in 1986. This news story (8.2) is more about the person who is the leader of the Republic of the Philippines than it is about her words to the U.S. Congress. Note how direct quotes from the speaker and details about her background are woven into the story.

Event stories

The job of the reporter is to explain the significance of the event, a portion of which is a speech. The keynote speaker at an international meeting of wildlife conservationists may set the agenda for the meeting by outlining the most threatened elements to the environment. A speaker at a dedication of a building or a memorial ceremony may be less newsworthy than the occasion but needs to be reported nonetheless. Sometimes the speaker's remarks underscore the event (see 8.3).

8.1 Prominent Speaker, Routine Event

Reagan marks Flag Day with scorn for Nicaragua

Associated Press

Note how the lead captures the president's symbolic gesture. ____

BALTIMORE—President Reagan wrapped an attack on "communist bullying" in Central America into a red-white-and-blue Flag Day ceremony Friday at Fort McHenry, where Francis Scott Key was inspired to write the *Star Spangled Banner*.

Completes the essentials and explains the symbolism suggested in the *where* of the lead. ____

In a speech at the Baltimore harbor fort where Key saw the tattered flag that inspired the national anthem, Reagan derided leftist Nicaragua. He compared El Salvador to the flag that inspired Key to write his famous poem while viewing a battle in the War of 1812.

Quote. ____

"El Salvador, beset by terrorists supported by the communist regime in Nicaragua, has come securely through its own perilous night, and its democratic flag still proudly waves over a free land," the president said.

Summary, then a quote. ____

Reagan railed against Nicaragua, charging it with inspiring "years of armed communist subversion" and "outright military attacks" against democratic Honduras and Costa Rica.

"But the communists' bullying tactics have only bolstered the determination of the democratic Central American nations to defend their freedom," Reagan said.

Summary of the president's prepared text versus what he actually said. The writer explains that the president reworked his text and gives a spokesman's reason for the rewrite. ____

Reagan's prepared text also contained a pitch for his tax overhaul program, but the president did not include that section in his actual address. In that portion, he contended his plan is one that will make the system more equitable and that Americans believe "everyone deserves a fair break."

Reagan reworked his text at the last minute "because he wanted the event to have a patriotic focus," spokesman Pete Roussel said.

Wide World Photos

(continued)

(8.1 continued)

The president spoke inside the star-shaped red brick fort, which was built from 1794–1805 and stands guard over the mouth of the Baltimore Harbor.

His audience was composed of students and sponsors of the National Flag Day Foundation, who gathered at the fort for a ceremony reciting the pledge of allegiance to the flag.

"I always get a chill up and down my spine when I say the pledge," Reagan said.

Above the platform, a stiff breeze caused a replica of the 42-by-32-foot, 15-star flag sighted by Key to flap smartly in the wind.

Bursts of fireworks exploded and parachutists circled above in the air as the crowd belted out Key's song before the president spoke.

Key, a young Washington attorney, was apprehended by British soldiers while attempting to negotiate the release of an American doctor held by the British during the Sept. 13–14 attack on the fort in 1814.

Key watched the fierce bombardment of the tiny fort throughout the night and was inspired to pen his poem—later put to music and adopted as the anthem—when he spotted the torn and tattered flag that marked the fact that the Americans had held off the British assault.

Reagan recalled the patriotism that inspired Key during the 25-hour bombardment.

"You can imagine his joy when the next morning—in the dawn's early light—he looked out and saw the banner still flying—a little tattered and torn and worse for wear—but still flying proudly above the ramparts," Reagan said. "The United States, this great experiment in human freedom, as George Washington described it, would endure.

"Thinking back to those times, one realizes that our democracy is so strong because it was forged in the fires of adversity," Reagan said.

The nation's patriots kept faith in

The rest of the piece, describing the audience and the historical character involved (Francis Scott Key) and concluding with quotes, is not essential as information. They are important to the story, though, because of the occasion and the setting.

the flag and what it stood for, despite perils of war, Reagan said, and this spirit has been carried on by American men and women for two centuries.

"Our flag flies free today because of their sacrifice," he said.

Reprinted with permission of Associated Press.

8.2 Personality Speech Story

Aquino asks Congress to nourish democracy
Lawmakers applaud leader's pledge to try to keep power by peace

By Richard Whittle
Washington Bureau of The News

Lead gives the focus of her speech—a request for aid—but also gives the mood in which her address was received, "an emotional welcome."

WASHINGTON—Philippine President Corazon Aquino received an emotional welcome Thursday as she asked a joint session of Congress to help her nation keep the democracy it won in February's bloodless revolution.

Quote ties the lead to next graph, which gives an idea of the strong emotions that the lead suggests.

"You have spent many lives and much treasure to bring freedom to many lands that were reluctant to receive it," Mrs. Aquino said. "Here you have a people who won it by themselves and need only the help to preserve it."

Details to explain and describe the symbolic support—the wearing of yellow by the members of Congress.

Mrs. Aquino, whose speech was interrupted 12 times by applause, wore a suit in her trademark color, yellow. Many people in the House chamber wore yellow clothing or bright yellow rosebuds.

The 240 rosebuds were bought and distributed by House Majority Leader Jim Wright, D-Fort Worth, who wore a yellow sweater and yellow bow tie for the occasion. Secretary of State George Schulz wore a yellow shirt and a yellow handkerchief in his suit breast pocket.

Quotes plus background.

"As I came to power peacefully, so shall I keep it," Mrs. Aquino said,

(continued)

Associated Press

Philippine President Corazon Aquino flashes her campaign sign, which means to fight, Thursday while addressing a joint session of Congress where she received a rousing welcome. Behind Mrs. Aquino are House Speaker Tip O'Neill (left) and Senate President Pro Tem Strom Thurmond. (Story on Page 11A.)

alluding to the non-violent popular uprising that drove former president Ferdinand Marcos from office. "That is my contract with my people and my commitment to God."

But she said that if she fails to negotiate peace with the communist and Moslem rebels who are continuing to resist her government as they did Marcos', "I will not stand by and allow an insurgent leadership to spurn our offer of peace and kill our young soldiers and threaten our new freedom."

(continued)

President Reagan told Mrs. Aquino in their first meeting Wednesday he supports her strategy, according to aides to both leaders, but unidentified U.S. officials were quoted last month as criticizing as too weak Mrs. Aquino's approach to the insurgents.

"I must explore the path of peace to the utmost, for at its end, whatever disappointment I meet there, is the moral basis for laying down the olive branch of peace and taking up the sword of war," Mrs. Aquino told Congress.

Summary. ____ Mrs. Aquino refrained from asking directly for more than the $505 million in economic and military aid the United States has given the Philippines since she took power, but she made it clear she wanted more.

Skillful use of the partial quote. ____ Noting her country's "other slavery —our $26 billion foreign debt," she complained that "no assistance or liberality commensurate with the calamity that was visited on us has been extended. Yet ours must have been the cheapest revolution ever."

Reaction to the speech, represented by a quote. ____ House Speaker Thomas "Tip" O'Neill, D-Mass, said afterward, "That's the finest speech I've heard in my 34 years in Congress."

Within hours of her speech, the House passed 203-197 a bill giving the Philippines a $200 million cash infusion to help deal with economic distress. The measure was sent to the Senate, where prospects for approval were uncertain.

Rep. David Obey, D-Wis., chairman of the House Appropriations foreign aid subcommittee, said the measure was brought to the floor spontaneously in the immediate aftermath of the Aquino speech.

Concluding graph emphasizes speech's impact. Note that much of this story is drawn from the writer's observation of the audience during the speech. ____ Many in the audience, including Sen. Phil Gramm, R-Texas, could be seen wiping tears from their eyes during the first half of Mrs. Aquino's address when she recalled her late husband, Benigno, who was jailed and then forced into exile by Marcos.

8.3 Event Speech Story

The significance of this speech is the event—a convention of the Society of Professional Journalists, Sigma Delta Chi, to which many members of the working news media belong. The speaker is telling them that newspaper profits are the result of the editorial product (content written by the reporters), not the result of the business side, hence the headline, "Andy Rooney Declares War." The speech was an event that stimulated discussions at the meeting.

```
CMD=ID:AMUSEMENTS2
TIME: 11/11 20:00
ANDY ROONEY DECLARES WAR
-
    MILWAUKEE--JOURNALISTS SHOULD REALIZE THAT THEY
ARE AT WAR WITH THEIR BUSINESS DEPARTMENTS,
COLUMNIST ANDY ROONEY SAID THURSDAY.
    "LET'S FACE IT, THEY'RE THE ENEMY," ROONEY TOLD
THE CONVENTION OF THE SOCIETY OF PROFESSIONAL
JOURNALISTS, SIGMA DELTA CHI. "THEY PRETEND TO BE
ON OUR SIDE BY TELLING US IF IT WASN'T FOR THEM
WE'D BE NOWHERE, BUT I REJECT THAT. IF IT WASN'T
FOR US, THEY'D BE NOWHERE."
    HE SAID NEWS HAS BECOME BIG BUSINESS AND THE
DANGER IS THAT PROFITS WILL BECOME MORE IMPORTANT
TO JOURNALISTS THAN THE PRODUCT--NEWS.
    WHEN EDITORS AND REPORTERS BOW TO PRESSURE FROM
THEIR BUSINESS OFFICES, THE PROFESSION IS IN
TROUBLE, HE SAID.
    THE NEWS MEDIA ARE REFLECTING THE TREND IN
BUSINESS OF SPENDING TIME AND MONEY ON PACKAGING
RATHER THAN ON IMPROVING THE PRODUCT, HE SAID.
    ROONEY ATTACKED THE HIGH SALARIES HE SAYS
ADVERTISING SALESMEN GET AT NEWSPAPERS AND
TELEVISION STATIONS.
    "THE PEOPLE PRODUCING THE PRODUCT IN ANY
ENDEAVOR SHOULD BE PRIMARY TO THAT OPERATION," HE
SAID. "I KNOW A LOT OF ADVERTISING SALESMEN ARE
NICE GUYS. WHY SHOULDN'T THEY BE? THAT'S WHAT
THEY'RE PAID FOR.
    "REPORTERS AREN'T NICE GUYS, ON THE OTHER HAND,
'CAUSE THEY'RE NOT PAID FOR THAT. THEY'RE PAID TO

BE ACCURATE AND HONEST, AND THERE JUST DOESN'T
SEEM TO BE MUCH MONEY IN THAT ANYMORE."
    ROONEY IS KNOWN FOR HIS HUMOROUS COMMENTARIES
ON THE TELEVISION SHOW "60 MINUTES." HE IS ALSO A
```

```
SYNDICATED COLUMNIST, AUTHOR OF FIVE BOOKS AND
RECIPIENT OF TWO EMMYS, SIX WRITERS GUILD AWARDS
AND A PEABODY AWARD.
    HE SAID THE TELEVISION NETWORKS, WITH THEIR
LARGE FINANCIAL BASE, HAVE BEEN ABLE TO REMAIN
MORE INDEPENDENT THAN SOME AREAS OF THE MEDIA,
AND HAVE PRODUCED JOURNALISM OF SURPRISINGLY GOOD
QUALITY.
    IN SPITE OF WHAT HE PERCEIVED AS A TREND TOWARD
COMMERCIALIZATION, ROONEY SAID HE WAS NOT
DISCOURAGED ABOUT JOURNALISM'S FUTURE.
    IN OTHER CONVENTION NEWS, THE SOCIETY'S BOARD
OF DIRECTORS DECIDED TO PRESENT THE SOCIETY'S
FIRST AMENDMENT AWARD TO THE MISSOULIAN, A
NEWSPAPER IN MISSOULA, MONT., FOR ASSISTING A
NEWSPAPER IN LIBBY, MONT., IN ITS FIGHT TO KEEP A
TRIAL FROM BEING CLOSED TO THE PRESS AND THE
PUBLIC.
-

FROM ASSOCIATED PRESS
CMD=CLOSE
```

Reprinted with permission of AP Newsfeatures.

COVERING SPEECHES FOR PRINT MEDIA

When a reporter is assigned a speech, the direction is often brief and general: "Someone with the UN is talking to Rotary today. Go and see what you can get." Sometimes the reporter gets a copy of the advance story. If not, the reporter has to find out who the Rotary program chair is, then call to check time and location and get some information about the speaker and the topic. If the program chair can't be located, the reporter is stuck with arriving at the meeting early enough to find out some of the basics before the speech. Occasionally a photocopying machine can be located to make a copy of the speech before it's presented, if the speaker will let it out of his or her hands. Some speakers come prepared for such a request with an extra copy. Other speakers may talk only from notes or without any aids; that's when having a tape recorder is helpful. Always take notes, though. Good notes also help in organizing a story.

Sometimes a reporter may get an advance copy of the speech, the speaker's biographical data, a photograph and an invitation to meet with the speaker before or after the talk. Such arrangements give a reporter a base to work from, but relying on the accuracy of any of the material is a potential error. Reporters should check even the biographical data with the speaker.

The reporter must observe and listen attentively during a speech. The speaker's inflections, the gestures, the audience reaction—all are potentially a part of the story.

Among possibilities the reporter should be prepared for are these:

- The speech may be extemporaneous or disjointed. The speaker may tend to wander or digress. Finding a central theme may be difficult. The reporter must take careful notes and review them thoroughly before writing the story.

- The speech may differ from the prepared text. Many speakers try to tailor a speech to the event and the audience, so a reporter shouldn't use just the written text and ignore the spoken comments. Experienced reporters tell horror stories of deciding not to attend the event and writing a speech story in advance, based on a distributed text, only to find out the speaker had tossed the prepared speech aside and addressed a new topic.

   If you have a copy, follow it as the speaker delivers the speech, noting any major changes so they can be reflected in the final story.

   If you are the public relations person "covering" the speaking event and find the speaker departing from the prepared text, you also need to note the changes in your copy. You should always arrange to have the speech taped. If you don't and the speaker is misquoted, you won't be able to offer evidence.

- The speech may be dull. The fact that a speaker is a national figure doesn't guarantee he or she will be interesting. Some speeches are just plain dull—but you still have the responsibility to your editor and your public to report what was said. And the written word might turn out to be more revealing, more emphatic than the spoken one. Dullness may be the result of poor delivery rather than weak content.

Speech story structure

Three main tasks are involved in organizing and writing a speech story, none of which are different from those involved in writing any general news story: (1) choosing what information to use in the story; (2) deciding how to use that information to tell the story—what the focus is; (3) selecting the quotes, determining how to use them—directly, indirectly or paraphrased. Once you have chosen the quotes, you can work on summarizing the rest of the content.

Don't make the mistake so many beginners do of writing the speech in chronological order. Many times a speaker will save the best till last. You need to listen continually and carefully to what's being said. Pay particular attention if you hear a phrase such as "and in summary" or "to conclude." Often these are clues that the major points are going to be re-emphasized.

If you don't have an advance copy of the speech, take careful notes. As you take notes, jot down or highlight what seem to be the key points. In most speeches, only two or three main points are stressed.

You use the principal point the speaker makes for the lead and the other who–what–when–where–why information that didn't fit comfortably in the lead as the tie-in. These are followed by the other points the speaker made, presented in a combination of summaries and quotes, much like the interview story.

The well-written speech story includes good quotes. Not all of them must be direct. In fact, a balance of direct and indirect quotes is preferable. Choose succinct direct quotes that capture the speaker's main points. You can use paraphrases and summaries for the least significant statements. For example, in reporting a scientist's speech on a highly specialized topic, you wouldn't want to quote the technical jargon verbatim. Readers won't understand it. You need to translate the scientist's remarks into everyday language. This means you need to have some background in the topic, or else you need to talk to the speaker afterward to clarify the exact meaning.

The structure of the speech story parallels that of most straight news stories. The lead should summarize the major point made by the speaker. It should also indicate the qualifications or background of the speaker. This can be done briefly: "nationally known physicist," "U.S. ambassador to Spain." Often the lead will note the occasion of the speech: dedication of a building, tribute to a person or event, announcement of a new invention. In the transition between the lead and the body, try to include information about the audience who was there: the size, their responses and some identification for them (the sponsoring organization, if the audience is a public one).

The graphs following the lead usually expand on the major points. They also provide a transition into the body of the story, which ordinarily will focus on the key comments of the speaker. If some information was gathered in a news conference before or after the speech or in a special interview, be sure to make clear what was said where.

The body of the story enlarges on the speaker's central theme, using a mixture of direct and indirect quotes. It may also contain phrases about audience reaction, as in 8.2. The speaker's subsidiary points are then introduced in descending order of significance.

To see how this format works, look at this portion of a speech story:

School districts need to face the dropout problem, said José Cardenas of the Intercultural Developmental Research Association, which compiled a state study on dropout rates.

Cardenas addressed his comment to officials from 35 school districts gathered at the convention center here Friday to consider common problems.

Expressing his support for pending state legislation, Cardenas said that would provide for at least one person at each school to be responsible for dropouts.

"So few districts have a plan to deal with dropouts," he said. "I think it's a step in the right direction."

The focus, Cardenas said, should be on dropout prevention.

Drawing from his study, Cardenas said the dropout problem is costing the state $17.1 billion per year in lost income and tax revenues as well as increased costs in welfare, crime, incarceration, unemployment insurance and education.

He praised a dropout plan developed by . . .

The rest of the story summarized the plan submitted by one school district and closed with a quote from another district official there saying it was about time they went to work on the problem.

When a speaker's background deserves more extensive treatment, it can be woven into the story, or the last paragraphs can summarize the biographical data.[1]

As we noted in Chapter 5, you want to avoid monotony in using "he said" or "she said" as attribution after each statement or quote. Instead, you can use qualifying phrases such as "The former congressman said," or "The U.S. Olympic hopeful said." By using such qualifiers carefully, you can weave part of the speaker's background into the story.[2]

In using quotes and summaries, avoid redundancy. Don't summarize a point and then follow that with the quote that makes the same point. That's a common flaw in beginner's speech stories (see 8.4).

Should you edit a speaker's quote to make the quote grammatically correct? Because spoken language is more informal than written, you may have some ungrammatical constructions to deal with in a quote, particularly when the speech is extemporaneous. Certainly it's all right to correct a quote to make the subject and verb agree, for example. You don't want to change construction, though, if it is contrary to the way the person ordinarily speaks. If you have serious doubts about cleaning up a speaker's grammar, don't use the quote. Summarize what was said or paraphrase the quote.

8.4 The Future of Newspapers

This speech (delivered to newspaper controllers and finance officers) is especially well-written and therefore easy to follow. Note the clues signaling the main points, the support for those points, and some lively, provocative quotes. To outline:

THEME:	Newspapers will be around beyond the next 20 years, but the speaker is only going to deal with changes in that period.
REASONS (support for theme):	Future of newspapers *promising*, as newspapers *change* from mass to class publications.

PROMISE:	Power and efficiency of printed word and its precision. News is a valuable commodity. Newspapers have character that appeals and wins loyalty.
CHANGES:	Smaller circulations and higher prices. Smaller papers. Fewer newspapers but better ones; some national. No bulk advertising, but class, not mass to suit audience.

(The italics in the speech are ours, indicating significant words or phrases.)

Today's Newspaper — 2002

by Clayton Kirkpatrick

A couple of nights ago I listened in amazement to a television anchorman as he summarized the history of communication and prophesied the demise of newspapers in about 10 sentences. First, he said, in the dim early days of mankind, there was speech. (Starting with "ugh," I suppose.) Then there

(continued)

was writing. (Maybe starting with "I"?) Then there was imagery complemented by audio. (Mickey Mouse?) The progress of communication had made the written word obsolete, he concluded solemnly, and that is why newspapers would disappear.

It just happens that I know that broadcaster and I know that he has the capacity to think more rationally if only he had taken a few minutes to consider what he was saying. In fact, if he had had to put his thoughts in writing, he never would have been trapped into such a ridiculous historical analysis and conclusion. That is one of the great virtues of the written word. It makes it difficult to propound nonsense masquerading as significant communication.

CLUE ▶   *This afternoon I want to go one step beyond your theme.* I suggest that
THEME ▶ newspapers will survive long past the term of your examination, and long past the scope of my topic, the next 20 years. However, 20 years is a term that appeals to me. It is about the limit that I can expect to experience, and I
▶ think it is a period that promises *interesting changes* and tantalizing rewards.

QUOTE ▶   Let me concede that I begin with a bias, a rational bias, I think. *The*
FOR *sun is not setting on newspapers.* The news, printed on paper, permanently
THEME recorded, portable, accessible, reasonably inexpensive, will be distributed as long as men and women are concerned with serious subjects and abstract thought.

Maybe the time will come when cognition will pass on to individuals and to masses by the millions through some kind of instantaneous telepathy. Maybe each will have a memory bank like a computer served by instant
CLUE: retrieval. Then we will not need newspapers. Until then we do.
SUPPORT ▶   Now let me expound some of the *reasons* why I think the future of news-
FOR THEME paper publishing is promising, some of the changes I think I see coming,
COMING and finally, how they may affect you in your profession as managers and financial strategists.

WATCH FOR ▶   *First*, I would assert that the best thing newspapers have going for them
LISTS is the *power* and the *efficiency* of the printed word. News in print has a
SUPPORT special efficacy and appeal. It is the most comprehensible medium for
FOR THE abstract thought. It communicates the language of scholars. It focuses upon
FIRST the intellect as its target. It has its greatest effect upon the rational faculties
STATEMENT of man rather than upon his emotional faculties. The spoken words of broad-
IN THE LIST casting, the vivid and immediate images of TV have powerful effects, but they are colored by the senses. They have the strongest impact upon the emotions, and they are commonly transitory, better suited for entertainment than the sterner responsibility of imparting an understanding of complex issues.

Reflect upon your own experience. If you are really serious about wanting accurate and comprehensible information, what do you say? You say: Put it in writing. Give me a memo. I want a copy of that. The connotation I take from this is that while talk may be cheap, there is something precious and valuable about the printed word. Much of the worth we attribute to it arises from the process of its creation. Writing is work—frequently lonely and agonizing work. As in all human endeavor, it is labor that creates value.

Written discourse rarely takes the form of idle chatter, even among practitioners with a very light and amusing style. When you sit down to write,

(continued)

8.4 (continued)

you are forced to think, you are forced to select, you are forced to organize, you are forced to provide a fund of information from which the writing flows. Somehow when the words are filtered through the fingers, nonsense and bombast and error and ignorance tend to be strained out. Almost without exception the noblest, clearest, most perceptive and most persuasive expressions of human intelligence are written. Conversely, shoddy, shallow, and dishonest content reduced to writing becomes transparently revealed in all its defects. Demagogues like Hitler, Mussolini, or Huey Long could sway hundreds of thousands with speech. Their words in print were insignificant.

Permanence is one of the great assets of news in print. Newspapers constitute the lasting record of contemporary history. They are always available for review and analysis. No mysterious formulae, no intrusive mechanisms are required to recall and reproduce the records they keep. It is all there each day, and, what is really quite important for the understanding of historical events, the record is in context with the other contemporary significant events which tend to impinge upon and affect each the other. Newspapers are a researcher's delight.

CLUE:
MORE
SUPPORT
FOR ITEM 1
IN THE LIST

►   *Another* important virtue of the printed news is precision. The progress of oral communication from auditing to memory to recall and finally to reproduction again in speech is notoriously strewn with error. The conflicts and contradictions among witnesses in court testifying about the same evidence is well known. In appeals when final decisions are reached, the weight always comes down on the side of the written record rather than oral presentations.

The lack of precision in oral communications is particularly common in the utterances of politicians. Presidents whose words are carefully scrutinized and analyzed frequently delegate to their staffs the embarrassing duty of eating their words for them when they misstate facts. A recent example would be President Reagan's assertion that fetuses delivered at four months have lived. The list of such errors is long. I do not believe these misstatements resulted from sloppy carelessness or that they stemmed from a malevolent desire to deceive.

I think these errors are inherent in a system where men and women in positions of leadership are stuffed with information by their staffs in oral cram sessions. After all, they are supposed to know everything about everything aren't they? When they try to bring it back under pressure, garbling is almost inevitable.

The Reagan White House staff finally appealed to correspondents to report the thrust of what the President said rather than specific details. And they limited the occasions when such slips might be made. I hasten to add that Reagan is not unique in this regard. All others in high office have been similarly embarrassed.

Back in the days when Richard J. Daley was mayor of Chicago, his staff suggested to reporters that they not report what he said, but rather report what he meant to say. The present mayor seems simply to ignore the contradiction and misstatements that crop up in her oral discourse.

The written record has its share of error, to be sure, but it is light years ahead of the spoken word in precision. That is one of the reasons why most audible news originates from a script. The broadcaster relies upon this invaluable tool. The auditor has no such assistance; he comes away with vague, transitory and frequently erroneous impressions. He has the same trouble with oral briefings as politicians do. The process is quick and effortless but defective.

ITEM 2 IN THE LIST ► The *second* great asset of newspapers is the value of news *as a commodity*. There is a huge market for news, both the news of events and ideas and the commercial news that we describe as advertising. Newspapers once held a monopoly in this market. Now it is shared by an impressive number of competitors. They include magazines, radio, television, cable, newsletters, weekly newspapers as contrasted to daily newspapers and advertising shoppers.

The broadcast industry first and now the cable industry have been particularly aggressive in claiming a share of this market. Some of us remember when radio was almost purely an entertainment medium. News was broadcast in five-minute segments. Now we have some radio stations broadcasting news 24 hours a day. The movement of television into news has been massive. Television news once came in 15-minute segments once or twice a day. Now it comes in two-hour segments in the morning, a brief midday period, up to two hours in an early evening segment, and 30 minutes to an hour in the late evening segment. Cable has gone much further, with Ted Turner's Cable Network News leading the way. It provides virtually round-the-clock news, and his second cable network supplements the first with a headline service also available throughout the day.

This competition has forced the broadcast networks to start news programming earlier and to extend it later. CBS is offering network news now through the early morning hours from 2 to 7. NBC is offering news from 1:30 a.m. to 2:30 a.m. ABC has added another hour of news from 6 to 7 a.m.

SUPPORT FOR ITEM 2 ► This headlong rush by the electronic news media is another demonstration of the value of the newspapers' historic franchise on a most *marketable commodity*.

Part of the reason for the extension of news time on cable and television is a perceived need to make news accessible. Anybody who has listened for an extended period to all-news radio knows how repetitive it is. Two-hour television news has the same problem, but the objective is to have a complete budget of news for those who tune in at different times. To satisfy the need for accessibility, broadcasting must repeat itself.

Here the written record of the news has big advantages. It is constantly accessible at any time of the reader's choosing. Also, it is portable, traveling easily and conveniently for the benefit of its audience. There should be important economic advantages to a medium that can prepare its news report once a day and achieve constant accessibility over a medium that must constantly repeat its service hour after hour in order to be accessible.

To be sure, broadcasters can update the news frequently as newspapers once did, but this changes the character of the news, making it a headline service, committed to reporting events in a superficial way. This leaves

(continued)

8.4 (continued)

a better field open to the newspapers, comprising interpretation, analysis, commentary, historical perspective and educational services. There is time, human resources and space to give depth and richness to the reporting of the news that far outweighs whatever advantages broadcast news can claim in timeliness.

CLUE
ITEM 3
IN LIST

► There is *one other area* of vitality in the printed news that is difficult
► to define and assess. It lies in the *intangibles of character and personality* which newspapers have assumed through centuries of development. Newspapers do have character and they do have personality and readers recognize these qualities and cherish them sometimes and sometimes they resent them. They seldom are indifferent to them.

The other media, being newer, lack these qualities totally or in large degree. Newspapers themselves have these qualities in varying degrees, but my observation has been that those which have the strongest personalities, the most incisive characters are the most successful.

SUPPORT
FOR ITEM 3

► What are some of these *traits*? One is an almost obsessive interest in the political process. This grows out of a perception in the earliest days of the formation of our republic that a free press was necessary if popular government was to succeed. The obligation placed upon newspapers in the First Amendment was twofold: They were to be instruments of education to inform citizens so that they could govern themselves wisely, and they were to be watchdogs to prevent government from deteriorating into tyranny as it had too often in Europe.

QUOTE

► *So newspapers took on the character of monitors teaching the art of self-government and watchmen correcting through exposure the tendency to corruption.* Other characteristics followed, some good and some less good. Some newspapers took on the character of super-patriot and that character sold well at one period of history. Some took on the character of defender of the common man and his interests, a populist position. That too prospered from time to time. Some took their political responsibilities too

QUOTE

► seriously and became flag bearers for partisan factions. *Newspaper character has been de-emphasized in recent years, but the ability of a newspaper to identify with its audience and to assume the position of leadership in causes generally recognized as altruistic and in the public interest is a great intangible asset unique in its power.*

CLUE TO
SUMMARY

► I have *mentioned* the *changes* in the character of the news—more thoughtful, less timely, more analytical, less oriented to events—which we already see in progress. They add dimensions of value to the printed news that broadcast news cannot match.

I believe that there are other major changes in progress or in perspective that can be traced to this competition. One of these is the growing interest in demographic marketing. Newspaper managers historically have regarded them as mass media. They were thought to appeal to everyone and that their market stretched across the complete human spectrum.

In my opinion, it is becoming quite clear that a large faction of their former audience now is committed to competing electronic media for news and information. They are non-readers and nothing will change them.

There remains a numerically smaller potential audience, but qualitatively a superior audience. These are thoughtful men and women, concerned with public affairs, involved enough to give the time and effort necessary to be informed in depth and with the precision that the written word provides.

ITEM 1
IN CHANGES

► For the most part this is an *able, affluent audience willing and able to pay the higher prices that scaled-down circulations require.* In other words, the future of newspapers lies in becoming the *class information medium,*

2ND QUOTE
FOR THEME

► *not the mass information medium.*

I predict that this transition will go hard in traditional circles because numbers, big numbers, have been cherished by newspaper managers and editors. To accept smaller circulation figures will be difficult. To persuade advertisers to accept them will be even more difficult, but the demographics will support the strategy. And, of course, the economic health of the enterprise must remain strong. That means higher prices for what seems to be less—a difficult sale in any context. Nevertheless, newspapers have been underpriced for years. It is time for creative managers to solve this problem.

Actually, the relative share of market both in readership and advertising revenue has been declining for years. It has failed to keep up with population increase, and it has failed to match gains made by competing media, notably television and weekly newspapers. It is time to recognize the reality of these changes and adjust strategy accordingly.

ITEM 2
IN
CHANGES

► While these changes are going on, *I am sure that newspapers in broadsheet format will continue to shrink in size.* You are familiar with some of the economic reasons for this, although production experts are likely to argue that the economy would be on the side of the larger sheets if only production costs were considered.

However, from the reader's viewpoint the smaller sizes will be a big plus. In my opinion, the ideal broadsheet for the reader would be about three-fourths the size of the present sheet, still sectionalized for convenience and internal emphasis on major interest area, and much less bulky.

To meet these problems, there will be a continued progress in *consoli-*

ITEM 3
IN
CHANGES

► *dation.* There will be *fewer newspapers, but better ones; some national papers*—after all, communication improvements are making the country smaller and homogenizing its population. I think Al Neuharth's *USA Today* has a good chance to find a viable market.

SUMMARY
QUOTE
FOR
CHANGES

Competition will force most newspaper organizations left after the period of consolidation to become organized as horizontal communications conglomerates offering a variety of services for increasingly complex markets fragmented by the special needs and special interests of consumers.

On the publishing side, they probably will be putting out special-interest newspapers and magazines, shoppers and weekly local newspapers, as well

ITEM 4
IN
CHANGES

► as the publications we now regard as general-circulation dailies. *One consequence* of this variety of products is that the general-circulation newspaper will no longer be forced to carry the bulk advertising that now makes it cumbersome and expensive to produce, difficult to deliver, and exasperating to try to read. The bulk will still be there, but in other associated publications, where it will be welcomed by an audience that wants it. The newspaper will become a *news*paper, with very high rates for the very classy and smaller ads that appear in it.   **(continued)**

8.4 (continued)

These changes will have some important consequences for you who are controllers and finance officers. The transitions are already in progress. The consolidation of ownership in publicly held corporations, the conglomerate character of the enterprise, the emphasis on marketing, the proliferation of products and activities—all of these have begun.

Newspapers which once were simple, straight-line operations, usually managed by editors who lacked interest in administration but had to learn how to operate a business, have become complex financial institutions. The old progression from editor to publisher to chairman is becoming rare. Most editors find it difficult to master the science of financial management, marketing and corporate organization. Not too many want to.

The new candidates for top executive responsibilities are general managers and financial managers. Some of you, I am sure, are such candidates. The new progression will require that you learn more about the concerns outside your special fields. You will have to sensitize yourselves to those intangibles I have mentioned—the elements of character and personality and responsibility that bring a publication to life and make it prosper. You will have to think more in terms of what a reader needs and wants. And you must be ready to invest some of those dollars you cherish to provide for those needs and wants. Finally, you must guard against the blind worship of numbers. It is difficult to accept, but consider whether in circulation and linage, less may be more.

Clayton Kirkpatrick, "Today's Newspaper—2002," speech to Institute of Newspaper Controllers and Finance Officers, Dearborn, Mich., Oct. 20, 1982. Reprinted with permission of the author.

Speech story sidebars

Once in a while, a story related to the speech may emerge. The good reporter will recognize the relationship and write a sidebar: a story associated with but not directly part of the main article. The well-written sidebar can enhance the main story, perhaps revealing a few interesting facts that didn't fit into it.

Speech sidebars can develop from several sources. Audience reaction may be one. Was there criticism? Was there praise? Did direct action result from the speech? Are there likely to be long-range effects?

For instance, when the mayor of Scottsdale, Ariz., proposes to limit industrial growth in an address to the Scottsdale Chamber of Commerce, it's likely that some of the business community will react vehemently. The writer covering that speech should identify two or three opponents and seek responses. A good sidebar can give additional depth to a story.

Accompanying the Aquino story reprinted in 8.2 was a related Associated Press report noting that while Aquino was addressing the U.S. Congress, a panel in the Philippines drafting a new constitution approved a provision that would make new leases for U.S. military bases in that country subject to legislative approval or even public referendums. Reporters who had read the AP story before arriving at the Capitol interviewed legislators assembled for her speech to get reactions to the events in the Philippines. Those reactions went into a sidebar. Read the AP story in 8.5 and decide whom you would have chosen for a reaction.

8.5 Related Story

Philippines panel proposes vote on bases

Associated Press

MANILA, Philippines—The panel drafting a new constitution approved a provision Thursday that could make new leases for U.S. military bases in the Philippines subject to legislative approval or even a public referendum.

The panel voted 26-15 to approve the provision, a compromise between those who want the bases closed when the current lease expires in 1991 and those who think the issue does not belong in the constitution.

The compromise provision would require that the lease be a formal treaty between the two countries and that both the Philippine legislature and the U.S. Senate approve it. Under the provision, the Philippine legislature could vote to submit the treaty to a public referendum.

Currently the lease for Clark Air Base and Subic Naval Base—the largest U.S. bases overseas—as well as three smaller facilities, can be extended by presidential endorsement.

"The Philippine government cannot enter in a mere executive agreement," said the Rev. Joaquin Bernas, a critic of the bases and co-author of the compromise agreement. "Certainly the provision allows for renewal of the U.S. military bases under certain con-

ditions. . . . But it will be more difficult now."

The commission is scheduled to finish the draft constitution and submit it to the voters later this year.

The continued American military presence is one of the thorniest issues facing President Corazon Aquino.

The U.S. military has maintained installations in the Philippines since taking the country from Spain in the 1898 Spanish-American War.

COVERING SPEECHES FOR BROADCAST   A broadcast reporter's approach to speeches differs from a print reporter's. Because of limited time and personnel, the speech usually has to be an important one before radio and TV will cover it, and broadcast reporters usually don't stay from start to finish of the entire proceedings. Speeches are a long process, often entailing a meal, preliminary speakers, awards, jokes and much, much more before the main event. Broadcast reporters with four or five or more stories to cover that day or night just don't have that kind of time. Even if the main speaker gets up to speak first, broadcast reporters may still not

be able to stay for the whole speech. Therefore, they've developed several shortcuts.

Interviewing speakers

Instead of attending the speech, broadcast reporters will try to have a public relations person set up an interview for them with the speaker before or after the speech. Radio reporters may ask for a telephone interview.

A risk of interviewing the speaker before the speech is that the speech may turn out to be different from what the speaker had promised. If a speaker strays from the prepared text and makes startling announcements, the broadcast reporter may miss the story.

In March 1967, President Lyndon Johnson scheduled another (read, boring) speech on the Vietnam War. The networks covered it, and it got a little long (and boring). Then, at the very end, Johnson dropped the bombshell that he would not run for another term. That caught everyone by surprise, including the networks.

It's unlikely the president would have told reporters that news if he had been interviewed beforehand. However, the practice of interviewing speakers beforehand and afterward will continue of necessity.

Covering the main points

When advance copies of the speech are available, some broadcast reporters may stick around for only a few major points. While that may be impolite, the assignment schedule requires it if the speech is to be covered at all.

Many seasoned speakers, aware of broadcast reporters' tight schedules, don't mind this practice. Many have even been known to write their speeches to this practice, making major points at the beginning, then keeping right on going as the radio and TV crews pack up and leave.

Advance copies of the speech may allow broadcast crews to come in late for speeches as well, if major points are to be made at the end. This requires close timing, but it is done. If major points are missed, the interview afterward will get the speaker on tape.

Covering entire speeches

The advance copy of the speech may show that the speaker will be making major points throughout, and so full coverage, from beginning to end, is demanded. Full coverage may also be demanded when no advance copies are available.

Full coverage presents no technical problem. Equipped with plenty of blank tapes, radio and TV reporters could record a speech for hours. And some speeches do last that long. The question most reporters and assignment editors ask is: Is all that time worth it? Usually it isn't. Besides, covering entire speeches presents an editing problem. Searching through an hour or more of tape for some cuts to air in the newscast can be very time-consuming.

Editing tape The key to effective broadcast coverage of speeches, meetings and news conferences is in the final editing process.

Audio and videotape editing is not a very difficult technical skill to acquire. It's a matter of learning which buttons to push when. The difficult part is making decisions about content. The broadcaster must go through all the tape gathered at the speech and decide what to use and how to use it. These content decisions are no different from those made by the print writer about which quotes to use and where to place them in the story.

Look at the speech story excerpt on dropouts presented earlier in the chapter. If you were writing it for broadcast, you would write something like this:

OFFICIALS FROM THIRTY-FIVE STATE SCHOOL DISTRICTS MEETING TODAY HEARD HOW BIG A PROBLEM DROPOUTS ARE.

TAKE TAPE (Cardenas) TIME: 12 END CUE "STEP IN THE RIGHT DIRECTION."

"PENDING STATE LEGISLATION WOULD REQUIRE SCHOOL DISTRICTS TO DESIGNATE AT LEAST ONE PERSON AT EACH SCHOOL TO DEAL WITH DROPOUTS. SO FEW DISTRICTS HAVE A PLAN TO DEAL WITH DROPOUTS, I THINK IT'S A STEP IN THE RIGHT DIRECTION."

THE AUTHORITY ON DROPOUTS IS JOSE CARDENAS FROM THE INTERCULTURAL DEVELOPMENTAL RESEARCH ASSOCIATION. THE ASSOCIATION COMPILED A STATE STUDY ON DROPOUT RATES. ACCORDING TO THE STUDY, DROPOUTS ARE COSTING THE STATE MORE THAN 17 BILLION DOLLARS A YEAR IN LOST WAGES AND TAXES AND SOCIAL PROGRAMS.

Public relations people preparing news release tapes or videotape presentations from their own coverage of a speech must also keep in mind how the videotape will be used, who the audiences are. A special emphasis may be needed for certain audiences who are not immediate ones like those who watch newscasts.

There may be an hour or more of tape from which to pull as little as 30 seconds. The tape cut has to accurately represent the speech, not be out of context and not display any bias. Generally in a speech, interview or news conference, only one side is given; the presentation format may allow for questions and answers, though. Any Q&A would be covered as part of the event. If someone is attacked in the speech or news conference, the reporter will want to identify the person making the charge and should contact the person attacked for a response.

The public relations person may or may not want to include the attack in a release. Sometimes doing so makes a point. Politicians' PR people may do it to show what sort of undesirable conduct a candidate is having to take from the opposition and how well he or she is handling it. If the attack commands significant attention, not just a few boos or one shouted remark, the public relations person should include it. News media covering the event will have it anyway and not to include it looks like a cover-up.

MAIN POINTS

- The beginner needs to be aware that covering speeches will be a common assignment. The obligation is to present the substance of the speech, the circumstances of the speech and the speaker's qualifications.

- Get as much information in advance as possible and try to determine which will be more important, the personality of the speaker or the event. That will help to focus the story.

- If an advance copy of the speech is available, refer to it as the speaker is talking and note any significant deviations from it. If advance copies aren't available, take good notes.

- Observe carefully the setting, audience reaction and other circumstances that may affect the impact of the speech.

- Isolate the key points made in the speech. Don't attempt to report every subordinate detail.

- Use both direct and indirect quotes. Use clear paraphrases and summaries, particularly for supporting statements. Use summaries as transitions.

- Be certain that attribution is clear, but vary the attribution pattern so that facts or qualifiers about the speaker are included.

- Be aware of sidebar possibilities.

- Edit the speaker if necessary, but keep the meaning, emphasis and focus faithful to the speaker's presentation.

- PR people often release print and videotape versions of presentations of key people from their organizations.

- Proper tape editing techniques are essential to convey the main points of the speech to the audience.

- Broadcast reporters, pressed for time, often must resort to abbreviated coverage: interviewing the speaker or covering just part of a speech.

- In either a print or broadcast story, make clear to your audience where the speaker made the remarks—in a speech, interview or news conference before or after the speech. Don't mislead.

EXERCISES

1. Arrange to cover two speeches on your campus. These should be formal speeches, not classroom lectures. Prepare a 60-second radio story for each. Also write a story for the campus newspaper on each. Briefly describe how the versions are different and why.

2. Arrange to attend a local civic, service or professional organization's meeting: Chamber of Commerce, Rotary, Kiwanis, Business and Professional Women's Club, Public Relations Society of America, Society of Professional Journalists, Sigma Delta Chi, Women in Communications Inc., Ad Club. Write a 300- to 400-word story about the speech, being certain to include the major point(s) in the lead sentence. Then rewrite the story as a 30-second radio story. Briefly compare the approaches you used in writing the story for two different media.

3. Cover a major speaker either on campus or in the community, and assume you are doing it for television with videotape. Write the intro and the script for a 45-second television story. Be sure to include specific directions about the shots, voice-overs and cuts you want. Write a print story for the local (not campus) newspaper on the same speech. Explain your choices of quotes for each story.

4. Cover a major speech on campus and plan your coverage far enough in advance to arrange an interview with the speaker. Write your story using information from both the speech and the interview.

5. Write a newspaper speech story from the speech in 8.4.

NOTES

1. Construction of a speech story is diagramed in Melvin Mencher, *Basic News Writing* (Dubuque, Iowa: Wm. C. Brown, 1983), pp. 327–33.

2. Some good suggestions for handling quotes appear in W. L. Rivers, *Writing: Craft and Art* (Englewood Cliffs, N.J.: Prentice-Hall, 1975), pp. 93–9.

SUGGESTIONS FOR ADDITIONAL READING

Dennis, Everette E., and Arnold H. Ismach. *Reporting Processes and Practices: Newswriting for Today's Readers*. Belmont, Calif.: Wadsworth, 1981.

Fedler, Fred. *Writing for the Print Media*. 3rd ed. New York: Harcourt Brace Jovanovich, 1984.

Hough, George III. *Newswriting*. 3rd ed. Boston: Houghton Mifflin, 1984.

Smeyak, Paul. *Broadcast News Writing*. 2nd ed. Columbus, Ohio: Grid, 1983.

Stephens, Mitchell. *Broadcast News*. New York: Holt, Rinehart and Winston, 1980.

Covering Meetings and News Conferences

The station's videotape editor was working under deadline pressure for an afternoon newscast when the news director appeared and said, "I'm having Susan take over for you. You're going to a press conference for a prizefighter." The young man, a recent graduate in journalism and music, had never even seen a prizefight, nor did he want to. As he began to protest, the news director interrupted, "But you speak French fluently, right?" He said he did. "Then," said the news director, "you're going. This guy is big stuff for the boxing fans and we don't have anyone else who can talk to him. He's French and speaks no English."

That's not the best way to set out for a news conference or a meeting. You should have time to do some research on the individual (or the group), the occasion (or the meeting agenda) and what the person (or group) is going to say or do that is of interest to your audience.

Two key points to remember are: (1) You represent the public that can't be there to get information, so you have to think of what people want to know. (2) Information that is not discussed or action not taken may be as significant as what did occur. You won't be able to recognize these significant omissions without a thorough background—not always possible to get at the last minute.

MEETINGS Scarcely a day passes in a major city that a meeting or news conference doesn't take place. Smaller communities may have fewer large-scale formal meetings, but various organizations will convene and will believe that what they do warrants coverage in the local media.

Of all the assignments a beginning reporter gets, covering a meeting may be the most difficult. Some meetings don't have a central focus or clear-cut purpose. Sometimes organizations will meet just to meet. And sometimes so many different people are involved that finding a dominant purpose—the news peg you need to write the story—is almost impossible. If a speaker is on the agenda, that may be your story. But some meetings, particularly dinner meetings, feature speakers who are just entertainers. Even with a speech, the beginner always wonders what to do about all the rest that goes on: committee reports, recognition and awards, announcements. The point is you are there to write about the event so that it has meaning and significance to the audience.

Types of meetings   Meetings can be categorized into two general types: the civic/social/professional, as the speeches in 8.3 and 8.4 illustrate, and the political/governmental, as 9.1 shows. Certainly these categories aren't rigid, for sometimes civic and social meetings take on political overtones. The opposite is also true. Some political meetings are really social events—opportunities to be seen publicly.

A purely social meeting might be something like an autograph party for a local author or a Chamber of Commerce cocktail party at a newly established business. A purely civic meeting might be something like a gathering of the coordinating council for the United Way to plan strategy for future fund-raising activities. These social/civic meetings usually don't result in as much hard news as the political/governmental ones do.

Political/governmental stories vary considerably in newsworthiness. Obviously the local precinct committee meeting doesn't merit the same kind of coverage in a daily paper as the state convention to select party delegates. The greater the organization's impact, the more coverage it's going to get.

Covering a meeting   For background, a reporter covering a meeting can generally consult an advance story—one written by a public relations person or a media staff writer. If not, a reporter will look for a fact sheet that tells what the organization is, who the officers are, the purpose of the meeting and who the speaker or speakers will be. (This agenda can help you structure your notetaking at the meeting.) The news medium's own files may have clips of past coverage of the organization. These stories can help fill you in on the "actors" and the "plot." The program chair or meeting coordinator can also provide background. If the organization is a large one, the public relations person will see to the reporter's needs. In some cases, an organization's publicity chair, though not a public relations professional, may understand the function well enough to be helpful. You may get caught, though, with no help and no prior information. That's when you need good interviewing and persuasion skills. Plan to arrive ahead of time so you can interview some of the main participants.

Know in advance the time, precise location (room number, not just building or street address) and details such as where to find a telephone or electrical outlets.

If you want to use a tape recorder, get permission, then place the microphone so that it picks up every speaker's voice. You may have some difficulty, though, identifying speakers. Take careful notes, and be sure you can distinguish when one speaker stops and another begins. Few errors are more embarrassing than to attribute a quote to the wrong source, particularly when covering a meeting

9.1 Political Meeting Story

The story was not the forum or meeting, as this reporter recognized. The story was the reaction of a candidate's mother to the attacks on her son.

Mother stands up for Oliver
Candidate's mom criticizes his rival

By Kevin Merida
Staff Writer of The News

An increasingly combative Democratic state Senate race took an emotional turn Tuesday when the mother of state Rep. Jesse Oliver passionately defended her son at a political forum and struck back at one of his opponents.

During a question-and-answer period, Mary Small accused Bishop College chemistry professor Jesse Jones of pursuing the race out of "personal selfishness" and of "suppressing everything" that her son had accomplished.

As a result, Mrs. Small said, "the public is not informed" of Oliver's legislative achievements.

Jones said later that he was taken aback by the "personal attacks" of Mrs. Small.

The forum was part of the weekly Community Leadership Luncheon at St. Luke Community United Methodist Church. Jones, Oliver and former state Rep. Eddie Bernice Johnson —all of whom attended—are locked in a Democratic primary battle for the southern Dallas County seat being vacated by State Sen. Oscar Mauzy.

As in recent forums, Ms. Johnson was not brought into the fray. She again talked about her many years of work in community affairs. Later, an official of her campaign touted the latest results from an ongoing telephone survey conducted by the Johnson camp of likely Democratic primary voters. In that survey to date, 2,410 respondents have favored Ms. Johnson, 71 have opposed her and 658 have been undecided, the official said, adding that more than 1,300 re-

At some meetings like this convention, the technology often overwhelms the action·and may influence it. Photo: *The Dallas Morning News.*

spondents agreed to take yard signs for the Johnson campaign.

Meanwhile, a source close to the Oliver campaign said a poll taken by his campaign 3½ weeks ago showed Ms. Johnson was ahead in the race, followed by Oliver and Jones. A subsequent tracking poll, the source said, showed Oliver was in a virtual dead heat with Ms. Johnson, with Jones far behind.

The forum, broadcast live over KKDA-AM radio, was one of several being sponsored this month by the Progressive Voters League—a political organization tied to candidate

Jones and Dallas County Commissioner John Wiley Price.

As Mrs. Small spoke Tuesday during the question-and-answer period, Price—who served as moderator—motioned in vain for her to limit her remarks and to ask her question.

Finally, Mrs. Small said she wanted to know of Jones: "Will he be as selfish as he is now? He doesn't care how he gets this office and who he steps on."

Jones responded: "I have given all, even sacrificing my family for this community." He said that during Bishop College's financial crises, he had once worked four months "without getting a dime."

The tone of the forum mirrored that of other recent forums in the 23rd District race.

On Tuesday, Jones stepped up his criticism of Oliver's large contributions from Austin-based lobbying interests, saying the money would particularly influence "a person who is young and inexperienced in politics."

Oliver said the 23rd District needed "not a voice that will stand around and talk about personalities, but a voice that will get results." In defending his independence, Oliver noted that he had battled the Texas Hospital Association—an Austin-based contributor to his campaigns—over indigent healthcare legislation.

"The real problem I have with Dr. Jones is he has to attack me directly," Oliver said after the forum. "One day he talks about needing role models for black kids, and the next day he cuts one up in public."

Jones said he was "just reading the record" and denied that he had made derogatory statements about Oliver.

In recent weeks, however, Jones has zeroed in on Oliver as if the two were in a two-man race.

Jones said many of the criticisms he directed at Oliver also applied to Ms. Johnson, but added: "I'm not going to talk about any ladies. I'm just not. It's inappropriate as far as politics go."

Ms. Johnson could not be reached for comment later in the day.

Shirley Miller, a campaign consultant for Ms. Johnson, said, "Her stand on that is she is running against two friends. And she expects they will be friends after the election. She is not fighting against either one of them. She is running on her record. She didn't sign up to fight. She signed up for an office."

Reprinted with permission of *The Dallas Morning News.*

where sensitive issues are being explored or controversial opinions are being exposed.

It's worth noting that some reporters don't want to be recognized as reporters, not because of any ulterior motive but because they believe they can report more accurately if they're less visible, a fly on the wall, as columnist–editor Walter Lippmann put it. Lippmann suggested a reporter could be more effective in reporting the details of a story by being unobtrusive yet all-seeing. (Granted, it's a bit difficult to remain inconspicuous if you're lugging a TV camera, lights and a sound pack.)

Sometimes when you are in a meeting covering it, the chairperson may declare the meeting closed. Or a scheduled meeting may be declared closed in advance. You need to know when this can be done and when it cannot. Private organizations are under no obligation to open meetings. Public organizations must abide by state and federal laws. The statutes are different for different states, so you'll need to check on which government bodies are covered by the open meetings laws; under what conditions a meeting can be closed; what notice is required to hold a public meeting. Generally, closed meetings are allowed when people's futures are involved (personnel matters, paroles, and such) and when special discussions of money must be held (real estate transactions, investments, salary negotiations, including negotiations with unions).

Publicly held companies are required to have annual meetings for stockholders, and these are generally open to the public. Some publicly held companies that are regulated, such as utilities, are, in most cases, subject to open-meetings laws. Non-profit organizations that collect money from the public also generally open their meetings out of a sense of responsibility to the community. Whether you are working for the news media or another organization, even as a private citizen, you should make it a point to know what the open meeting laws are in your community.

Writing the meeting story   Meeting stories are often difficult to write cohesively, because a number of unrelated items are likely to be on the agenda. You can rely on the summary lead for help.

> Increasing fees for garbage pickup stimulated more discussion than the five other items on Lake Highlands City Council's agenda Tuesday.
>
> No action was taken on the garbage fees or on the other agenda items: a progress report on the town lake study; one-way street designations downtown; zoning changes for property across from Lake Highlands High School, city employees' retirement insurance and the purchase of new Christmas decorations for downtown.

Introduce discussion of each of the lesser items in the same order as given in the second paragraph. Implied in your ranking of them is the degree of emphasis on them in the council meeting *or* their significance to the community.

The easiest meeting to cover is the one where only a single speaker is involved. These are common at civic and service clubs. Writing the story generally becomes a matter of isolating the major point or points made. Depending on the complexity of the topic, you can use a single-feature lead, a summary lead, a direct-address lead—whatever you believe will best capture the gist of the story as well as reader interest.

The rest of the story should follow the typical inverted-pyramid pattern: support for major points, with subordinate details near the end. Avoid chronological order.

Circumstances.   As noted in Chapter 5, in writing the story you need to make clear where the information came from. Did direct quotations come from a speech or meeting? An interview? Did the person speak off the cuff or did he or she read a prepared statement? Were comments quoted from a news conference made during opening remarks or in response to a question?

All of the circumstances surrounding the event influence what is said. For the reader to understand the event, the reporter must paint a complete picture. Who's in the audience who may influence what a speaker will or will not say? How big was the audience? How did it react? Did the meeting adjourn early for some reason? Later than usual? Answers to these questions create a complete story. You may want to include a paragraph or two about a discussion period or question-and-answer session, especially if these relate to the main points in the story.

Attribution.   In meeting stories you have to be especially careful to make attributions clear. If you're balancing the statements of two speakers, use the technique illustrated below:

> "I do not understand how the public can possibly accept a major tax increase such as the governor is proposing, especially when unemployment is so high," said Howard James, chair for the Conservative Citizens' Group.

Martha Swartz, leader of the Citizens for Civic Improvement organization, countered James' comment: "We simply must accept a tax increase if city and county services, especially those associated with health and environmental problems, are to be solved."

Note that in the second paragraph, attribution occurs at the beginning to signal a change of speaker.

Judicious placement of attribution is possible no matter how many people speak during a meeting. Always remember to give attribution for both direct and indirect quotes to avoid misleading the reader.

Yet another problem with the quotes may be in explaining them. The jargon of politics, science, academics is unintelligible to the outsider. You may have to paraphrase most of what was said.

The unusual. Many meeting stories are boringly routine, but sometimes something happens that brings a meeting to life. An outburst in the audience, for example, may reveal more about the topic than any statement from a speaker.

The unassigned story. As with speeches, an angle totally different from the one assigned may emerge. Be aware of such possibilities. Listen for a hint of a departure from the scheduled topic, a new development.

For example: At a public licensing hearing for a nuclear power plant, the chief executive of a utility company had just finished answering some questions from the licensing panel. The chairman of the panel called a 15-minute recess. Most reporters went across the street for coffee. One reporter remained behind. The utility executive had said something puzzling. When asked how much time the company's top nuclear experts would spend at the plant, the executive had responded, "With this one in operation and one more under consideration, I'd say about 40 percent of the time."

The reporter knew that plans for only one nuclear plant had been announced. While the other reporters were drinking coffee, he cornered the executive and asked about future plans. Sure enough, the company was considering another plant, even though its first one had not yet been licensed. A scoop.

Scoops are not all that common, but sidebar story opportunities are. During breaks, conversation is informal. People begin to talk about what's on their minds. They also like to share news. What is frequently referred to as "gossiping" is actually the sharing of news and information. Develop a sense for when there's a story in the chatter so you can get some facts, names and phone numbers while you're there. Some sidebar stories result from unexpected events at the meeting—a demonstration by protesters, the awarding of special recognition to someone.

Meeting stories usually result in notes to a futures book for follow-up or coverage of the next meeting. If this is not your beat, give such tips to the editor when you turn in the story. Although most such tips are for news, a feature or depth story idea can come from a meeting, too.

**Broadcast coverage
of meetings**

For the broadcast reporter, meetings are much more difficult to cover than speeches. Consequently, few meetings get full coverage by the broadcast media. Broadcast reporters just don't have the time to spend at lengthy meetings. In addition, meetings and at times news conferences present a technical problem: Getting the newsmakers' voices on tape is often next to impossible. Meetings are usually held around tables. At some meetings, such as those of a city council, people address a dais. In either situation, proper microphone placement is hard to achieve.

Some media-alert meeting planners try to set up for meetings like they do for a speech to encourage broadcast coverage. When a speaker's podium is used, radio and TV reporters can place a mike at the podium, and they can all use the same mike if the room has a multiple-plug box ("mult" box) that allows all audio recorders to tap into a single source. This eliminates the need for a number of "coverage" mikes. If the meeting is an occasion where only a few speakers walk to and from the speaker's podium, such an arrangement works.

However, most meetings involve participation from a number of different people. Rooms are often set up with a microphone at a podium for the person in charge of the meeting and microphones in front of each participant or every two or three participants. Even if the sound can be captured technically (most meetings like this are taped by the membership for transcription and minutes), the sound is not of broadcast quality.

The dynamics of people interacting makes meetings unpredictable, so planning in advance for certain shots is difficult. Agendas are very little help, because they are often ignored. Certainly you can't interview someone before a meeting to find out what will be said. Thus most broadcast reporters attend meetings to take notes and look for sources to interview when the meeting breaks up. Reporters may ask key figures and speakers to summarize their comments and their position, to elaborate on positions taken and to summarize the results of the entire meeting. At a meeting held by an organization that keeps minutes, ask the secretary for such a summary. His or her notetaking is probably more reliable than someone else's recollection, and the secretary also knows the participants. Some organizations have professional public relations staff who can supply the information.

In this way, the newsmakers provide the comments on and summaries of what happened at the meeting. If for some reason they cannot, or will not, comment, the broadcast reporter does the summarizing in the form of a voicer or stand-up.

TV photographers are often sent to meetings to shoot general footage of people sitting around talking. The TV writer then writes a voice-over that summarizes what happened at the meeting.

**NEWS
CONFERENCES**

The news conference is intended to present the media, hence the public, with information. Note that the AZT story in 5.2 is from a news conference.

Library of Congress

Racks of news releases are common at government meetings, conferences and in times of crises.

News conferences are generally called by public relations officials, in cases where access to someone, like the vice president of the United States who is getting an honorary degree at a university, is limited, or when a crisis or controversy erupts in which interaction between the reporters and the news source is needed.

Reporters cover news conferences in much the same manner as they do meetings. But they have to work more quickly, filing the story minutes after the conference ends. The PR people have a story to write, too. They must issue a release immediately after the news conference and provide cuts to the broadcast people who didn't get there. Ordinarily the audio is chosen quickly from the tape (the entire news conference is almost always taped by the PR people), a script written for the lead-in and the lead-out and a feed given to one of the regional radio networks.

The approach you take to writing the news conference story will vary, depending on the news being released.

The news of news conferences

News conference stories generally fall into two categories: information and personality. A research scientist's news conference about a drug she just developed is likely to result in an information story. A celebrity animal news conference will result in a personality story (see 9.2).

Unlike the meeting, where several issues may be discussed, the news conference usually has a single motive. An exception to this are presidential press conferences, where the president is expected to field questions on any government issue — foreign or domestic.

The key to the news conference is the give-and-take, as different reporters open up avenues of discussion that others might not have thought of alone.

9.2 Personality–Event News Conference

You might get an assignment to attend the press conference of a celebrity animal, and it's difficult to do that without an interpreter. The interpreter in this story, and also the source, is the famous feline's owner, accompanying him on a promotional tour for National Cat Health Month.

Fame hasn't turned Morris into a party animal
America's favorite cat prefers his quiet life at home to his celebrity status on the road

By Leslie Pound
Staff Writer of The News

Like a true celebrity, Morris travels with his doctor, Laura Pasten. Photo: Randy Eli Grothe.

Sometimes, celebrities let us down. Sean Penn punching photographers, Julie Andrews (Mary Poppins!) appearing topless in a movie. John Riggins calling Justice Sandra Day O'Connor "Sandy baby" at a banquet, then passing out.

But one celebrity, thankfully, is the same in real life as he is on the screen. Truly cool. Macho. Laid-back.

He may travel first-class and shoot commercials about two months out of the year. But the remaining 10 months, Morris is the epitome of the word "cat."

"He's a typical cat," says his owner, animal trainer Bob Martwick, who wears a tie with miniature Morrises embroidered on it. "He doesn't do any tricks. He's quite nocturnal when we're home. Sometimes I can hear him prowling around at night."

Martwick and Morris were in Dallas last week, their second visit in six years. Last trip, they were promoting Morris' book. This time, they were promoting September as National Cat Health Month.

Morris hasn't changed much since 1980. He remains a cat of few mews. If he has any wrinkles, they are hidden beneath his well-groomed coiffure. His legs are still like pogo sticks, catapulting him onto windowsills and tables.

Although Morris seemed to be enjoying his Dallas visit, Martwick says that the cat was ready to end his seven-city tour. He was ready to go home and do what he always does when Martwick lets him out of his cage after a road trip: rub against Martwick's legs and jump on the counter to see what there is to eat.

Some nights, Morris sleeps with Martwick. Other nights, he prefers to lie at the base of a lamp on Martwick's desk. When Morris sleeps during the day, he changes his napping position as the sun goes down, following a spot of sunlight as it moves across the floor.

Such cat-next-door qualities account for Morris' phenomenal following, Martwick says.

"Everybody who sees the commercials sees something of their cat in him," he says. "I've had people tell me that their cat is just like Morris— except theirs is a black-and-white female that weighs seven pounds."

Morris, who is 8 years old, is a whopping 14-pounder. He eats two cans of cat food a day, plus any tidbits he can nab from Martwick.

Martwick keeps a careful eye on Morris—not just because he's a celebrity but also because the man obviously is crazy about the cat, whom he calls "Morts."

He owned Morris' predecessor, too, and his eyes still get a little misty when he talks about the original. The cat died of a stroke eight years ago, when he was 19 years old.

"I made him a little coffin and buried him under a beautiful tree—a cherry tree," Martwick says. "I missed him quite a bit. I'd lock the door at night and he wasn't there and I missed him."

He didn't want another cat right

Morris eats two cans of cat food a day, plus snacks from owner-trainer Bob Martwick, and weighs in at 14 pounds. Photo: Randy Eli Grothe.

away, he says. But when a new Morris was found at a humane society in Massachusetts, Martwick befriended the cat.

"The new Morris is pretty good," he says. "I like the way he's laid-back. When he wants to be with me, he will. When he doesn't—goodbye."

The biggest problem he has with Morris is getting him to respond during the filming of the commercials.

"He's getting so blase," Martwick says. "Only food excites him."

Cat lovers interested in getting a free copy of The Morris Prescription, *a pamphlet on cat health, can write to 211 E. Ontario, Suite 1300, Chicago, Ill. 60611.*

Reprinted with permission of *The Dallas Morning News.*

Reporters may compete fiercely at these events if their organizations are rivals and the pressure to be first and be best is on. Sometimes in a more relaxed setting, they may work together, helping each other with missed responses. The disadvantage of this set-up is that it results in what some refer to as herd journalism. Everyone at the conference writes basically the same story.

To avoid this trap, look for the unusual angle. One lifestyle editor remembers a news conference with the first lady attended by about 50 other editors. As they were leaving, they got to shake hands and thank her. The editor commented on the meat loaf they had been served at the luncheon in the White House and learned the recipe was the first lady's own. She recited the simple recipe, and the editor had at least a lead different from everyone else's. Along more serious lines, a reporter attending a State Department briefing noted the name of a study the official quoted from, stopped at the library on the way back to the newsroom and added substantial depth to the story by quoting from the original material that had been merely mentioned in passing.

A danger lurks in taking a different tack, and that is that the reporter may seize on an unimportant aspect of the story. If the reason for the news conference is serious, the story can be critically distorted for the readers or viewers by a reporter's being different just for the sake of being different. The unusual slant should be one that has news value.

The person in charge of a news conference often will give reporters a written statement summarizing the major announcement being made. Don't make the mistake of accepting the written statement at face value. Remember the organization is concerned with putting its best foot forward. Some organizations believe

9.3 Event-Related News Conference

The two officials had simultaneous news conferences, both of which had to be covered and then combined for the story.

Stage is set for decision on summit

Associated Press

WASHINGTON—Preparations for a second meeting between President Reagan and Soviet leader Mikhail Gorbachev moved forward during talks that ended Saturday.

Progress was made despite high-level disagreement over the Daniloff case and the U.S. expulsion of 25 persons from the Soviet mission to the United Nations.

Secretary of State George Shultz said it was "difficult to think of a fruitful summit" without the case of *U.S. News & World Report* correspondent Nicholas Daniloff being resolved in advance.

In simultaneous early evening news conferences, Shultz and Soviet Foreign Minister Eduard Shevardnadze said they had made progress on some of the main issues that would be discussed at a summit.

Shevardnadze, speaking at the Soviet embassy, said the superpowers were "moving forward" on arms and other issues and that he and Shultz had set "a foundation for holding a productive summit meeting."

In fact, on having Reagan and Gorbachev decide on holding a summit, he said, "The recommendations have been made, it's up to them to decide."

At the State Department, Shultz said, "There were quite a few items that seemed insoluble a year ago that are working themselves out."

He said there had been some progress made on intermediate-range nuclear forces and said he thought Shevardnadze would agree that had been "one of the promising areas."

Nevertheless, they ended their 14 hours of talks over two days—the highest-level U.S.-Soviet discussions in 10 months—with complaints about the treatment of their citizens in each other's country.

Shultz said the detention of Daniloff on spy charges in Moscow is "a cloud that hangs over this." Before Daniloff was arrested on spy charges Aug. 30, it was thought the weekend meetings would result in a date being set for the summit.

At the State Department, Shultz said there were long discussions about Daniloff and said, "It is hard to think that progress is made (toward a U.S.-Soviet summit) as long as he is there and unable to leave.

"I think it is difficult to think of a fruitful summit without these cases being resolved because they're going to wind up consuming great blocks of time," Shultz said.

Officials said the men would continue their discussions—with Daniloff on the agenda—this coming week in New York, site of the U.N. controversy.

Shevardnadze blasted the U.S. expulsion of 25 Soviet officials from the United Nations as "unlawful, irresponsible and provocative," and said, "If the American side believes that it can act arbitrarily, with impunity, it is mistaken.

"I must say this is most unfortunate; someone's malicious hand has tried to block" progress toward a summit, he said. He threatened retaliation for the expulsion of the Soviet officials from New York.

Yet, Shevardnadze said of the Friday-Saturday talks, "This work, in a way, creates a foundation for holding a productive summit meeting, and in this area, we are indeed moving forward.

"It is good that common sense has prevailed as well as the understanding of the fact that . . . ultimatums are unfit for our relations."

Of Daniloff, he said: "Please give us a chance through diplomatic channels in a calm and coolheaded way to discuss those issues and find the most wise . . . decision on that."

At another point, he said: "So far as I am concerned, Daniloff was engaged in impermissible activities directed against the interests of the Soviet Union. If there is no resolution of that case before trial, then he will be answerable to all Soviet laws and will be tried . . . We would prefer a normal resolution to this issue, and the administration is aware of that." Shultz said Daniloff was not a spy.

Shevardnadze's remarks on the U.N. matter were harsh and uncompromising.

Shevardnadze welcomed reporters to the Soviet Embassy and promptly blasted the U.S. expulsion of 25 Soviet officials from the United Nations.

Asked about Shevardnadze's veiled warning of Soviet retaliation, Shultz said the action in which the United States moved to limit the size of the Soviet delegation because of past espionage was unrelated to the Daniloff matter.

Shultz said he explained that to Shevardnadze and, "He argued with it."

In the midst of the Daniloff-U.N. controversies, the officials seemed optimistic about summit preparations overall.

Schultz was asked if there could be preparations for the summit in light of the Daniloff arrest. "Certainly, there can be preparations and we spent a great deal of time discussing the substance of issues that need to be worked out to make a summit meeting a successful meeting."

He indicated there had been some progress on arms control issues, saying that on the thorny areas of the Strategic Defense Initiative—dubbed "Star Wars"—he felt the discourse was "better" than before. Still, he conceded, "I can't say that we had anything to say to each other that genuinely narrowed the issues."

Shevardnadze began his remarks by referring to the 1985 Geneva summit in which Reagan and Gorbachev agreed to meet again in 1986.

He then said one of the stumbling blocks to a summit is the U.S. demand to reduce the Soviet U.N. staff. And so, in this way, he used the expulsions as a Soviet card to counter the U.S. anger over Daniloff.

Before their separate news conferences, the two diplomats shook hands at the State Department, where they held their discussions. Shultz ate lunch at the Soviet Embassy.

Later, the Soviet foreign minister was to fly to New York to attend a U.N. General Assembly meeting that

Shultz also planned to attend. The two men may resume talks on some issues there.

The two began their Saturday session with an hourlong private meeting in one of Shultz's offices while the rest of both delegations waited in a conference room.

After the private meeting, Shultz and Shevardnadze joined their delegations and posed for photographs. The Soviet and U.S. officials, seated on opposite sides of the table, smiled and burst into laughter when Shultz made a whispered comment.

The president's national security adviser, Vice Adm. John Poindexter, who did not participate on Friday, took part in the talks Saturday.

The issue of Daniloff was first raised by Shultz on Friday. Daniloff was freed from jail on Sept. 12 but has not been permitted to leave Moscow.

Shevardnadze came to the meeting with a letter from Gorbachev, which the White House said was a reply to a lengthy message on arms control from Reagan in July.

It was the latest correspondence in a series that began in June with a proposal by Gorbachev for major re-

ductions in long-range, offensive weapons if the United States would continue abiding by the 1972 Anti-Ballistic Missile Treaty.

Adherence to the treaty would bar deployment of a "Star Wars" strategic missile defense. Reagan has committed vast amounts of money to the project.

In July, Reagan offered to adhere to the treaty for five years and then begin negotiations to adjust the pact to permit both sides to deploy defensive systems. If those talks failed, the United States would give six months notice and proceed with "Star Wars."

Since early 1985, administration officials have said an understanding on defensive weapons is the key to an overall settlement that would include interim cuts in medium- and long-range offensive weapons.

The United States has also continued to press Moscow with such human rights demands as renewal of higher levels of Jewish emigration from the Soviet Union and withdrawal of Soviet troops from Afghanistan.

9.3b News Conference Sidebar

Sidebars are always to be found at special events, and this was certainly that—an international summit. This story gives a human perspective to the meeting by focusing on those working before the leaders meet, throughout that period and afterward.

Landmark security accord near

Conferees optimistic about agreement to reduce risk of war

Associated Press

STOCKHOLM, Sweden—Soviet and U.S. delegations to the Stockholm security conference expressed weary optimism Saturday as the meeting adjourned for the night on the threshold of a landmark East-West accord.

Negotiations were to continue Sunday with delegates to the 35-nation conference working on borrowed time after freezing the clock at one hour before midnight on Friday, when the conference had been scheduled to close.

"Everything is going well. I am pretty sure the outstanding questions will be solved, and I see clear prospects for success," Oleg Grinevsky, the chief Soviet delegate said.

Robert Barry, the chief U.S. delegate, told reporters, "We are moving

(continued)

9.3b (continued)

ahead, getting closer on both issues, although slowly. I hope we will be finished tomorrow, but I am not sure. We are working day and night in an atmosphere of good will" by all 35 nations.

In addition to the United States and the Soviet Union, Canada and all European nations except Albania are represented at the talks.

The conference began Jan. 17, 1984. Formally called the Stockholm Conference on Security- and Confidence-Building Measures and Disarmament in Europe, its mandate is to forge a package of binding military measures designed to lessen the risk of an accidental war in Europe. It is an offshoot of the 1975 Helsinki accords.

If delegates reach agreement, it will be the first East-West accord on European security in seven years.

Both East and West have agreed to exchange information and to invite observers for military activities. The two blocs remained deadlocked on issues that included the size of military maneuvers that would have to be announced to the other side and on-site inspection techniques by the opposite camp.

The smallest details of inspections, such as the placement of windows in airplanes for observers or the type of radio links they would be allowed, are all subject to discussion.

Both NATO and Warsaw Pact delegates said good progress was still being made in hectic negotiations Saturday, with conference clocks stopped.

Stopping the clock, used at several previous similar conferences, allows delegates to work on while time "stands still" and to forge a final document that can be dated Friday, Sept. 19.

If the two sides agree on a final document, which would be the first East-West security accord since the SALT II pact in 1979, it could not be presented in final shape until Sunday.

That is the real deadline for the conference, since the opening in Vienna of a preparatory meeting for a review conference to follow up Stockholm is scheduled for Tuesday. Many delegates had booked flights out of Stockholm for late Sunday and Monday.

in candor, and others, while they probably aren't so dumb as to lie, may not tell all sides. Read any hand-out statement carefully, listen to what is said about it—and ask questions. Be alert to hidden messages, ulterior motives. You may pick up on an angle that wasn't apparent at the outset.

In deference to some print reporters who complain that news conferences serve television best, some public relations people schedule two conferences, back to back—one for print and one for broadcast.

Broadcast coverage of news conferences

For broadcast reporters, news conferences are much like speeches. At a news conference the speaker is usually standing at a podium, speaking or answering questions; thus the podium can be miked or a mult box can be used. Whether a reporter will be on camera while asking a question is generally decided in advance. Often, though, the camera coverage is of all speakers and all questions.

Unfortunately, the questions from other reporters and anyone else in the audience often cannot be miked. So broadcast reporters take notes of questions asked, then write in those questions for the announcer or anchor to read, with the answers supplied on tape. For example, the radio story might be written:

MAYOR SAMUELS HELD A NEWS CONFERENCE THIS MORNING TO ANSWER CHARGES HE HAS BEEN INVOLVED IN A THEFT OF CITY FUNDS. EARLIER, WE REPORTED AN UNIDENTIFIED CITY OFFICIAL HAS CHARGED THE MAYOR WITH . . . AND I QUOTE . . . "STEALING FROM THE CITY TREASURY." THE MAYOR ANSWERED THAT CHARGE DIRECTLY IN HIS OPENING COMMENTS . . .

TAKE TAPE TIME :32 END CUE "I'M INNOCENT"

A REPORTER THEN ASKED THE MAYOR WHY HE HAS REFUSED TO AUTHORIZE AN AUDIT OF THE CITY TREASURY BY AN OUTSIDE AUDIT FIRM. THE MAYOR RESPONDED . . .

TAKE TAPE TIME :16 END CUE "WHEN I'M READY"

TV writers write their stories the same way.

MAIN POINTS

- Background research is necessary before covering meetings and news conferences.
- Finding the central focus of a meeting is usually more difficult than getting one for a news conference, which usually is called for a specific purpose.
- The advance for a meeting sometimes helps with the focus, but if the meeting is non-structured, the reporter must be continually listening and observing to find the news peg. Having a copy of the formal program or agenda can assist in planning for the story.
- When covering a meeting or news conference, know in advance the time, precise location (room number, not just building or street address) and other details (such as telephone or electrical outlets) of the facility where the meeting or news conference is to be.
- Be on time, or early if possible, to locate the central participants so you can get advance information or exclusive comments.
- Be particularly careful about citing the source for statements and quotes.
- Take good notes, even if you have electronic equipment as aids. You may be under deadline pressure and may have to file a story rapidly.
- Voicers and stand-ups can be used to summarize meetings.
- Be continually alert to possibilities for stories other than the obvious one.
- Be attuned to clues that may reveal more than what is forthrightly said.

EXERCISES

1. Arrange to cover two meetings on your campus. One should be a student government meeting and the other an organization's regularly scheduled meeting involving business and a speaker. Prepare a 60-second radio story for each. Also write a story for the campus newspaper on each. Briefly describe how the versions are different and why.

2. Attend a business meeting of a group or a club (a local service club, for instance) where more than one person speaks. Write a 300- to 500-word story, using direct quotes and solid attribution.

3. Attend a news conference at your school. (The campus news bureau director or sports information director will have a schedule of such conferences.) Write a 250- to 300-word print story. Write a 30-second radio story. Which of the two was harder to write? Why?

4. Attend a meeting of city council or the school board. Write a 750- to 1,000-word story. Compare what you wrote with the coverage given the same event by the local newspaper. How do the stories differ? How are they similar?

5. Attend a political meeting or conference. Write a 300- to 500-word summary story for print. Write a 45-second radio story in which you use an actuality.

SUGGESTIONS FOR ADDITIONAL READING

Bacharach, Samuel B., and Edward J. Lawler. *Power and Politics in Organizations*. San Francisco: Jossey-Bass, 1980.

Bard, Rachel. *Newswriting Guide: A Handbook for Student Reporters*. Tacoma, Wash.: Writer's Helpers, 1985.

Conrad, Charles. *Strategic Organizational Communications: Cultures, Situations and Adaptations*. New York: Holt, Rinehart and Winston, 1985.

Jamieson, Kathleen Hall, and Karlyn Kohrs Campbell. *The Interplay of Influence*. Belmont, Calif.: Wadsworth, 1983.

Kessler, Lauren, and Duncan McDonald. *Uncovering the News*. Belmont, Calif.: Wadsworth, 1987.

Lau, James, and Marianne Kelinele. *Behavior and Organizations*. Homewood, Ill.: Irwin, 1983.

Mehrabian, Albert. *Silent Messages*. 2nd ed. Belmont, Calif.: Wadsworth, 1981.

Rivers, William L. *Finding Facts*. Englewood Cliffs, N.J.: Prentice-Hall, 1975.

Smeyak, Paul. *Broadcast News Writing*. 2nd ed. Columbus, Ohio: Grid, 1983.

Stephens, Mitchell. *Broadcast News*. New York: Holt, Rinehart and Winston, 1980.

Public Relations Writing

When a book titled *PR: How the Public Relations Industry Writes the News* by Marie Hodge Blyskal and Jeff Blyskal appeared with its thesis that the majority of stories in the public media have PR origins, the disclosure might have been news to a few, but the media and PR people greeted it with a yawn. In fact, public relations texts have been making this statement for at least 10 years. The point of the book was to suggest that public relations sources control and manipulate the news. The fact is that PR is the principal source of all news, and much of that is indeed "controlled," in the sense that the PR people know when something is going to occur before anyone else and they decide when to release it. Ordinarily this is when all of the facts are firm. This doesn't mean that the news media are not going to investigate facts they think are suspect or tell the other side in a biased or slanted story before using it.

The authors called particular attention to the *Wall Street Journal* as publishing mostly PR-based stories. The financial news daily shares with *USA Today* the claim of having the largest circulation in the country. All publicly held companies are required by the Securities and Exchange Commission to release information about anything likely to affect the price of its stock. A constant flow of disclosure releases moves from publicly held companies to the Dow Jones wire. Rest assured that these releases are accurate. No PR writer, much less the company, wants jail sentences or SEC fines. On the other hand, the *Journal* regularly runs on the front page tough stories that give background for the economic news, and it didn't flinch from front-paging a story about one of its own writers who was accused of insider trading—making a profit on the knowledge he gained from his reporting activities.

Public relations writing does appear in the mass media, but most of it is done for specialized media, such as trade, association, employee and audio-visual productions. Whether mass or specialized media, though, public relations writing involves all the story structures and styles outlined in this book, and more.

Since so much mass media content has public relations origins,[1] looking at the public relations person both as a writer and a source may be useful.

263

THE PUBLIC RELATIONS WRITER

The PR person goes through the same research process as any writer, gathering information from primary and secondary sources. The difference is the PR writer must play the role of reporter within an organization in order to furnish material both inside and outside the organization.

Besides being a skillful fact finder, the public relations writer becomes a masterful rewriter. One collection of facts often serves the PR writer for preparing a backgrounder (a summary of all research findings), a briefing (for breaking news) or a position paper (presenting the organization's stand on a controversial matter, such as divestiture of investments in South Africa, and supporting it with documentation). From this accumulation of material, to which the good researcher is always adding, the PR person draws a wide variety of writing: material for a media kit, including a fact sheet; news releases; features; biographical or historical information or both; and copy for brochures, slide–tape presentations, speeches, ads and commercials. In addition to this great variety, a public relations writer is responsible for all the other writing chores of the organization, from letters and memos to the annual report. And in a controversial situation, or when an executive of the organization needs to be there to respond to questions, or when a celebrity is in town, the PR person organizes a news conference.

PR writers must know the technicalities of all these different tasks and prepare suitable materials. And they must know the appropriate writing styles for all media and follow them in preparing copy.

In writing a news release for the mass media, the public relations person is going to present the information in a way that serves the organization. This can mean being up front, even first, with a story of a problem or a crisis. It can even mean including more than one side of a controversial issue. However, it generally doesn't mean the evenhanded representation of all sides of an issue that is expected from a newswriter.

Another difference is that public relations writers often have more control over their materials than writers in the mass media, because their organization generally is originating the information.

Public relations writers must also be editors. They often control not only the substance but also the form of information from their organization. This is especially true of PR writers in the broadcast area. They are busy preparing external films and videotapes as well as training films for employees.

These are not, as you might think, dull teaching tools. For example, Public Service Electric and Gas produced a film, "The Sixth Sense," as a part of their customer relations improvement training program. The film is designed to sensitize employees to the problems of older customers, and it's available to others through the National Council on the Aging. Other companies have made historical films about aspects of their industry. Many of these are available through film distribution companies.

Public relations writing tasks are heavy for entry-level people, some of whom may start as publicists for an organization. Publicists write what is given to them to prepare in whatever form necessary; they have no control over policy. *Staff writer* is another beginning job. In an agency, the writers are a part of the creative department and work with the senior-level public relations person in the agency.

Senior public relations people may occasionally take on a publicity or promotion enterprise, especially in an agency, but usually they are involved at the management level. They may head a corporate communications section to which public relations reports, or they may be the PR person for the company. In either case, they report directly to top management and have a voice in what the organization does, what it says it does and how it relates to all of its constituencies.

THE PUBLIC RELATIONS SOURCE
If you work in the mass media, you'll be relying on PR people as sources. Consider the following situation.

The assignment: In advance of a celebrity's arrival in town, to obtain the agenda for a visiting celebrity, set up an interview and secure a photo along with a copy of a speech to be given at a benefit.

The assignment was given to a summer intern working for a metropolitan newspaper. The celebrity was to be in town for two weeks to star in a musical at a theater owned by the city; the benefit, for a local non-profit group, was to be hosted by a department store.

The effort: The intern called City Hall and was told by the receptionist to call the theater directly. The theater's receptionist referred the call to the public relations department. The intern, who had been indoctrinated never to trust a PR person, asked only for the dates the celebrity was to appear at the theater, the name of the musical, and the role the star was playing. Then she called the department store, where the receptionist referred her to the publicity chairwoman for the benefit. That person wasn't home. Recalling that all professional actors have agents, she called the library to find out who the actor's agent was.

The solution: Several hours later, when the information was needed by the entertainment section, the intern reported on her efforts. The editor immediately called the theater, asked for the PR person, set up the interview and determined the time of arrival and departure, where the celebrity would be staying, a list of all personal appearances booked so far and information on the benefit. Before saying goodbye, the editor requested a copy of the forthcoming speech and a photograph.

Within an hour, a messenger arrived with black-and-white photos, a color slide, a fact sheet about the benefit, a biography of the celebrity and a confirmation of the interview time and place, including arrangements for the photographer who'd accompany the reporter doing the interview.

The intern was dismayed. She'd wasted a good deal of her (and other people's) time by not taking the direct route. The editor told her that the PR person is most often the best source to contact, even when the situation is less than auspicious—for example, if the musical were a flop and the city decided to close the theater, or if the celebrity had experienced an accident en route, or if the benefit were to lose money.

With a large percentage of news being supplied or stimulated by public relations sources, the job of a reporter requires using such sources effectively. On any given day, a reporter is deluged with mailed releases, business wire (PR wire) copy,[2] telephone calls and messages from public relations contacts. In addition, already marked on the calendar for coverage is a news conference or special event managed by a PR person.

When reporters are on assignment, their contacts are often PR people. The news sources of most government, business and cultural offices are public information or public affairs people, whose jobs are in the PR category. Public officials and corporate officers generally rely on their PR professionals to provide information to print and broadcast reporters. Reporters and editors expect to receive everyday news through PR channels, and they also expect PR professionals to set up interviews and appointments for them with the top people when the extraordinary occurs, or when a writer has an idea for a special story.

Well-trained PR representatives know the news values of the different media and understand how to prepare information to meet their technical requirements. They also learn which reporters are reliable. Reporters, too, learn which PR sources can be trusted to perform professionally. Not all of them are accurate, responsive and responsible, any more than all reporters are fair and accurate in their coverage. Reporters need to know how to extract and demand the best from PR sources and are obligated to be accurate and responsible in turn in order to get the best cooperation from them. If the two don't cooperate, the real losers are audiences, who are deprived of information.

News releases   Reporters look to news releases when writing an advance, covering an event, speeches and meetings included, and doing a follow-up after an event. They rely most on PR advances. PR people are the first to know about plans the institution or organization they represent is making. When the plans are complete enough for a story, they write one and distribute it to the news media. If an event is significant enough, the media may choose to cover it. When that occurs, the PR person is in a position to assist reporters in getting what's needed for the story: information, pictures, access to newsmakers. Some PR people also write coverage stories that resemble news stories for reporters to draw from, especially for complex events, such as a space launch, for which daily releases are prepared in addition to the daily news briefings. Most PR people generally prepare a follow-up story; reporters may use that to flesh out their own coverage or as primary information about the event if they couldn't cover it (see 10.1).

Both the coverage and follow-up stories are less likely than an advance to be used verbatim (see 10.2). Although most reporters will insist that they always rewrite an advance, and they should, the fact is that a straightforward, well-written advance by a PR person usually doesn't need major rewriting. If it passes the newsworthiness test, it generally gets used as is, with minor editing for style.

10.1 GRI Technology Profile

Gas Research Institute

TECHNOLOGY PROFILE

August 1986

Guided Horizontal Piercing Tool

The guided horizontal piercing tool potentially can reduce a utility's cost of installation and restoration for underground gas distribution piping by underground gas distribution piping by at least 25%, and up to 50% in urban areas.

Problem

For repairs and new service installations, utilities try to avoid the high cost of pavement removal and restoration by boring under paved surfaces. Available tools (ground-piercing impactors, pipe-pushers, and augers) are typically adequate for boring distances up to 60 feet but cannot be controlled with accuracy over longer distances. If a tool deviates from a straight course there is no mechanism to correct it. Local soil conditions or rocks may cause a boring tool to deviate from its intended path and cannot be detected from above the ground. As a result, the tool may miss its target, bury itself, or in the worst case, damage adjacent utility lines.

GRI Solution

Funded by GRI, a "guided" horizontal piercing tool is being developed by Maurer Engineering, Inc., with technical support from IIT Research Institute and CyberSense Corporation. The tool incorporates electronic tracking/navigation and mechanical steering systems that will allow operators to control accurately the direction of the device. The tool has been designed so that it can be adapted easily to commercially available piercing tools. It is capable of boring holes of four inches in diameter for up to 120 feet within a 2-foot-diameter target range.

Benefits

The guided horizontal piercing tool potentially can reduce the utility's cost of installation and restoration for underground gas distribution piping by at least 25%—up to 50% in urban areas—when compared to trenching,

backfilling, and reinstatement costs. Pipe can be installed more rapidly over longer distances, thereby increasing the productivity of the work crew. Additionally, the tool requires a minimal amount of excavation for

launching and retrieval. Because of this, trees, landscaped yards, or other environmentally sensitive areas are less likely to be disturbed; traffic disruptions and public inconvenience will be kept to a minimum.

Concept

The guided piercing tool was developed by adding electronic tracking and mechanical steering systems to two commercially available piercing tools: the pneumatically operated Hole-Hog® and the hydraulically powered Hydramole. Allied Steel and Tractor Products, Inc., manufacturer of the Hole-Hog tool, and Stanley Hydraulic Tools, manufacturer of the Hydramole, are both participating in the development of the new tool.

The tool integrates three subsystems. The mechanical steering system combines a slanted-face anvil on the front of the tool with control tail fins mounted on a rotatable housing on the rear. The slanted anvil generates a deflective side force as the tool bores forward through the soil, allowing the operators to turn the tool in the desired direction. A magnetic field attitude sensing system is used to track the subsurface position of the tool. A solenoidal coil onboard the tool produces a magnetic field which is detected by a sensor located at the entry or exit location. The tool face orientation system consists of two sensors for roll information and an array of sensors for pitch information. Data from both the tracking and orientation systems are transmitted,

Schematic of the guided piercing tool.

processed and graphically displayed on a small visual screen at the entry location for the tool operator's use.

Project Status

The mechanical steering and instrumentation subsystems were extensively tested in the laboratory and in field experiments at sites provided by Entex, Inc., of Houston, Texas. The tests confirmed that the slanted anvil and fin assembly can reliably change the direction of the piercing tool at a rate of two degrees per foot (equivalent to a 28-ft turning radius). The steering response guides the tool to a two-foot diameter target and steers around obstacles that may be

Potential savings for guided piercing tools as a function of distance and restoration cost.

encountered in the field. Reliability and range tests demonstrated that the electronic coil and the tool face sensors will survive the shock load generated during operation of the tool and that sufficient signal exists to track the tool to 120 ft. The systems do not require any major modifications to the present piercing tools and do not affect their normal operation or penetration rate.

Prospectus

Beginning in fall 1986, several pre-production models of the guided horizontal piercing tool will be field tested in a representative sample of soil types throughout the United States. These tests will be conducted in cooperation with several gas utilities to assess durability and reliability of the tool, as well as user acceptance. Based on the results of a successful field test, early market entry of a limited number of commercial units is expected in mid-1987 with full commercialization planned by Allied and Stanley for 1988.

Research was recently initiated to develop an extended-range guided boring tool for distances up to 2000 ft. This system will be used for horizontal boring in rocky and difficult soils, with penetration rates faster than available boring equipment. Prototype models will undergo field experiments in 1986-87.

For Further Information, Contact:

Steven R. Kramer
Manager, Distribution Operations

Renee M. Nault
Editor, Technical Communications

Gas Research Institute
8600 West Bryn Mawr Avenue
Chicago, Illinois 60631
312/399-8100

GRi

10.2 Two Post-Advance Stories

Both of these stories have public relations sources. They were used because the information is of value to this weekly newspaper's readers. The weekly emphasizes local news because it exists in the sixth-largest media market in the nation and competes for reader attention with four metropolitan newspapers and a number of suburban papers. Stories like this seldom appear in major metropolitan papers. Most PR people don't expect them to, although they send the releases anyway for information.

Groundbreaking held for Broadway Plaza

Groundbreaking ceremonies for The Broadway Plaza at Cityview, a Forum Group retirement community, were held Tuesday at the site, 5301 Bryant-Irvin Rd. A reception followed at Ridglea Country Club.

The Broadway Plaza, a $30 million, full-service retirement community, will consist of 88 clustered cottages, 136 apartments, a 120-bed health-care center, 40 personal-care units and leisure facilities in the Cityview development in Southwest Fort Worth. Already more than 50 percent reserved, The Broadway Plaza is scheduled for occupancy in late 1987.

Forum Group Inc., which currently owns or operates 11 retirement communities throughout the United States, purchased The Broadway Plaza in May 1986 from a local non-profit group.

Fort Worth News-Tribune, Sept. 19, 1986, p. 18B. Reprinted with permission.

Women voters open new headquarters

The League of Women Voters have opened their new location at 101 S. Jennings, Suite 210.

Twenty-five league volunteers and one part-time employee are available to answer questions about candidates, elections, polling places and the political process from 10 am to 2 pm weekdays through May 15. League publications are also available at the office.

The League is a non-partisan organization promoting political responsibility through informed and active participation in government.

Fort Worth News-Tribune, Sept. 19, 1986, p. 18B

Some PR stories are simple announcement stories—for example, those written to comply with Securities and Exchange Commission disclosure regulations for publicly held companies (see 10.3a). Other announcements are the results of research, like the one in 10.3b on breast cancer. Although the story carries an AP byline, the source for the information is the American Cancer Society.

For print media.   Given the abundance of PR material to choose from, reporters and news editors can and should be discriminating. Some material sent to the mass media doesn't belong there at all: The audience for the information is small; a specialized publication would be a more suitable target.

The criteria editors in the news media use for judging a release are based on their standards for news. Is the information significant? How many readers could benefit from it? Is the story timely? Is it reaching the readers early enough —so they can plan a visit to the museum before an exhibit closes, buy tickets to a ballet? Is the story local, or does it have some local impact? Do the people involved in the story mean anything to the readers?

10.3a Disclosure Release

SEC reporting calls for publicity like this Singer report.

Singer reports net rose 40% in 3rd quarter

By Patricia Bellew Gray
Staff Reporter of The Wall Street Journal

Singer Co. reported net income rose 40% in the third quarter, citing a gain from an accounting change.

For all of 1986, Singer, which spun off its struggling sewing machine and furniture operations in the second quarter, projected "satisfactory" gains in profit from continuing operations and slightly higher net.

For 1987, Singer, which is based in Stamford, Conn., said it expects that growth in its aerospace, motor and gas meter businesses will produce net "at least equal" to 1986 net, which includes several special items.

Third-quarter net was $17.4 million, or 77 cents a share, up from $12.4 million, or 62 cents a share, a year ago. Singer said the most recent quarter included a $5.2 million gain from a new pension accounting standard adopted at the beginning of the year. Excluding the year-earlier quarter's $2.2 million loss from discontinued operations, Singer said, third-quarter profit from continuing operations rose 19%.

The pension-related gain was included in profit from continuing operations. But if that gain also is excluded, earnings in the quarter declined 16%.

Third-quarter revenue rose 8% to $433.5 million from $401.5 million. The year-ago results were restated to reflect discontinued operations.

"The key factor in Singer's operating results for the third quarter was the substantially higher revenue and earnings recorded by the aerospace electronics operations, which now account for 80% of our business," Joseph B. Flavin, chairman and chief executive officer, said. "This primarily reflected the contribution of the Dalmo Victor and Allen (aerospace) divisions" acquired earlier this year.

Singer said growth in its traditional aerospace business "moderated," partly because customers delayed buying some equipment. However, the company said it expects shipments and sales to rebound in the fourth quarter. Singer said its backlog of orders for aerospace-electronics equipment is "significantly higher" than a year ago. It declined to give details.

Singer said profit from its motor-products division was flat and revenue fell, because of a change in Sears, Roebuck & Co.'s inventory distribution policy. Chicago-based Sears, a retail, financial services and real estate concern, is a major customer. Cost reductions helped buoy profit,

the company said. Singer's motor-products division, which accounts for about 13% of the company's business, makes power tools and floor-care equipment.

The gas-meter division's revenue and profit declined by an amount that wasn't disclosed from strong year-ago levels because sales to industrial customers dropped, the company said. The meter division accounts for about 6% of Singer's business.

Singer's net income for the nine-month period, which included a number of special transactions in the second quarter, declined to $50.9 million or $2.34 a share, from $54.4 million or $2.82 a share in the year-ago period. The special transactions, which were related to the spin-off of the furniture and sewing businesses, contributed $22.4 million to net income. Nine-month revenue increased to $1.2 billion, from $1.1 billion.

Singer said its projection of a fourth-quarter profit rise is based on expected "strong performance" by its aerospace and motor units. A spokesman declined to be more specific.

Breast cancer may strike 1 in 10 women

NEW YORK (AP)—One in 10 American women under age 40 will develop breast cancer someday and about one in 30 will die from it, according to new projections by the American Cancer Society.

The 1-in-10 figure is an increase from the 1-in-11 projected in 1980, a change reflecting longer life spans, better cancer detection and possibly a modest increase in breast cancer rates, experts said.

"It certainly points up the fact that this is still a very serious disease," said Dr. Virgil Loeb Jr., the society's national president. "There's no way we can be content with our present figure."

Breast cancer is the most prevalent cancer among women, and ranks second among cancers as a killer of women, the society says.

It will strike 130,000 women this year and kill 41,000, the society said in new projections. Lung cancer is expected to kill 44,000 women.

While females younger than 40 face the 10 percent chance of breast cancer later in their lives, older women who have not developed breast cancer face lesser lifetime risks, said Herbert Seidman, the cancer society's assistant vice president for epidemiology and statistics.

By age 50, the risk for the remaining lifetime falls to 8.7 percent, and by age 60, it is 7.2 percent, Seidman said. The decline results in part from the fact that although an older woman faces a larger risk of breast cancer in any given year, she has already passed through years of risk that a younger woman has yet to face, Seidman said.

The lifetime risk calculations follow federal statistics on breast cancer and on the overall risk of death at various ages, he said. The 1-in-10 risk was calculated after breast cancer rates for 1982 and 1983 became available, he said.

The rise in that risk comes from several sources, experts said.

"I think one of the major reasons is that women are living longer, and more women are living to develop breast cancer" rather than dying of something else first, said Lawrence Garfinkel, the society's vice president for epidemiology and statistics.

John Horm, statistician with the National Cancer Institute, said rates of diagnosed breast cancer have shown a modest rise of about 1 percent a year from 1975 to 1984.

But it's not clear how much of that is a real increase in the disease, and how much is simply better detection through screening programs, he said.

Garfinkel said the modest increases "may be a real change in incidence for reasons we don't know."

To fight breast cancer, the cancer society recommends monthly self-examination by women aged 20 and older, plus regular examinations by a physician.

For women without any symptoms, it also recommends a mammogram every year or two for women aged 40 to 49, and annually for women 50 and over. A single mammogram should be taken by women 35 to 39, the society says.

Another criterion is accuracy. If an editor or reporter hasn't had previous dealings with a PR source, he or she should make sure to verify details: times and dates, spelling of names. You'd assume that such details would be accurate, more so than if they had been gathered by the reporter as an outsider. Not so. Nobody's perfect; reporters should check details carefully before using a release. Most reporters are reluctant to use a release if they find some substantial inaccuracies on the initial check.

Editors always use caution in handling news releases. While some errors in PR releases are ones of carelessness and fairly easy for a knowledgeable reporter to discover, others are not so innocent and often not so easily recognized. To detect self-serving distortions in a news release, reporters have to keep reminding themselves that the source for the story is being paid by the institution.

Professional PR people will not deliberately lie to a member of the news media, because it destroys their own credibility and thus their usefulness to their employer. However, some releases fail to tell the whole story, especially in times of controversy. A reporter needs to read a release carefully to see where the holes are and then fill them in, by going to other sources for statements and explanations and going back to the source of the release for more details. As a reporter, you're charged with presenting to the public as objective and responsible an account as possible.

Time restrictions are sometimes placed on a release: "Hold for Release: Date, Time." Some reporters won't accept a restricted or embargoed release. Others will accept them from some PR contacts but occasionally get burned when competitors don't honor the restriction. PR people often abuse the restricted release, using it for their convenience in managing the news. The only legitimate use for it is when an announcement is pending, either because an event hasn't occurred or is not yet approved by someone or some groups, such as a board of directors. Then it's a courtesy for the reporters to already have the release in hand. Sometimes speeches that dignitaries or celebrities are to make are also released in advance with a hold. Different newsrooms have different rules for handling such stories, so it's best to ask. If you don't intend to honor a source's hold requirement, you're obligated to let him or her know. It may be a learning experience for the PR person. Some put "Hold for Release" on copy that could go anytime.

Responsibility is always to the consumers of information, both for the PR people and the reporters and editors. The reporter's primary responsibility is to be sure information given out is as accurate, fair and complete as possible. A PR source has the responsibility to be honest and cooperative, but often is constrained by top management or legal counsel from making some information available. Most PR people believe in being as forthright as possible to avoid having a story turned around on them. However, most expect that when only one side of a situation is given, the other side will be represented if a reporter is doing a professional job. Reporters handling news releases from

Reprinted by permission of Jefferson Communications, Inc., Reston, Va.

public relations people need to get to know both the institutions and the PR representatives to do the best job for their readers.

In contrast to the polished copy of public relations professionals, reporters frequently get the rough copy prepared by a publicity committee head. As a reporter, your responsibility is to examine the information submitted for the possibility of a story. Often you'll have to distill the few facts out of a lot of words and ask for names and phone numbers of people who might be able to furnish a story idea. Not only can you get some good stories this way, you can also develop some good sources to use on other stories.

Some publicity pieces don't go through the ordinary news channels. An example can be found in most newspapers' real estate sections. There the buyer of advertising signs a space contract that allows the organization certain editorial space—a picture only, a picture and story, or several stories and pictures over a certain time period (see 10.4). The information is identified as advertising so that readers don't mistake it for editorial content. In some cases, it is written by people working in the classified advertising department, but usually it has only been edited and checked by them. Most large advertisers employ PR and advertising agencies to produce such material.

Sometimes the travel section of a newspaper walks a fine line between publicity puff pieces and features about places to visit. (See Chapter 14 for an opinion piece on this ethical point.) Generally these pieces are written by travel writers, either staff or freelance, and while they do rely heavily on PR sources, they generally write their own material.

Broadcast news releases.   Most releases mailed to print newsrooms are sent to broadcast newsrooms as well. Broadcast reporters also receive tapes, audio and video.

Tapes no longer arrive via the mail, for the most part. In radio, "800" telephone systems are used instead. With a toll-free 800 number and an automatic answering machine, any organization, public or private, can issue taped messages. (These 800 numbers can be national in scope, regional or statewide.) A message is recorded on the machine, and an announcement is mailed to all radio stations in the target area informing them of the service. Reporters can call the number and receive an actuality or voicer each day.

In some cases, stations pay for the call, but colleges, universities, sports departments (professional and college), state, regional and national government offices, business and industry groups, labor unions, private companies, religious organizations, special-interest groups, hobbyists and even the Office of the President of the United States all provide "hotline" services to radio stations nationwide.

The voicers offered are well written and in many instances are delivered by former radio newspeople in order to ensure correct broadcast style and professional-sounding delivery. But in some cases, running these tapes unedited is like printing a news release unedited. With controversial issues, if the other side isn't sought out for comment, the station simply becomes a PR representative. Thus the criteria and action recommended for news releases apply equally to the use of these tapes and message services.

Satellite technology is making a service similar to these hotlines available

10.4 Advertising Copy That Looks Like Editorial Copy

This is pure publicity, not a news release, and it is in a section clearly labeled "Written and produced by the Classified Department." Space for the publicity and photos in sections like this are tied to advertising contracts. These stories about new houses may look like news stories at first glance, but when you read them, you'll see how differently these are written. You'll never find adjectives like "rich-looking, high-quality, beautifully designed" in a news story. PR writers know the difference between writing news for the news columns and publicity puffs for the paid advertising columns. The lead calls the area the "newest upscale alternative for homebuyers," and the sales representative is quoted. There's scarcely enough in the whole story for a real news lead, but one might be: "A new development community, Sherwood Village, is now open in Arlington, just off I-20." A transition statement might be: "Homes under $80,000 in seven styles are being sold." That's about all the news, unless you're in the market for a home. Then the publicity piece serves its purpose, because it tells you more about the styles, the builder, the location and when the sales office will be open.

Star-Telegram

SUNDAY'S NEW HOME GUIDE

September 21, 1986   *Written and produced by the Classified Department*   **G**

U.S. Home's Countryside homes have good curb appeal

Pulte sets grand opening prices on homes at Sherwood Village

Pulte's new Sherwood Village community in Arlington is the area's newest upscale alternative for homebuyers, said sales representative Tom Bepko.

Perhaps the most pleasant part of Sherwood Village as an alternative to existing subdivisions is its combination of low pricing and a stylish product, Bepko said.

Pulte's Design Series Homes in the community will be available for a limited time at pregrand opening prices from $79,990. All floorplans offer four elevations each from a total of seven architectural styles — including the popular Colonial and Georgian styles.

Luxury touches are standard at Sherwood Village, which offers such features as vaulted ceilings, hand-finished fireplaces with special wall treatments, wallpapered kitchens and baths, spacious master suites, wood window sills and more.

Sherwood Village also offers homeowners the aesthetic pleasure and convenience of a handsome community entry, to harmonize with Pulte's beautifully-designed homes.

Besides a distinguished appearance and full range of features and amenities, Sherwood Village gives homeowners valuable convenience to I-20 and a brief commute to Fort Worth and Dallas.

To visit Sherwood Village, drive on I-20 to the Matlock exit, go south three-quarters of a mile to Embercrest and turn left to the models. The sales office is open from 10 a.m. to 7 p.m. weekdays and from 10 a.m. to 8 p.m. weekends.

Homes at Pulte's Sherwood Village offer four elevations

U.S. Home offers convenience, drive-up appeal at Countryside

Priced from $53,450, U.S. Home's Countryside community combines convenient location and affordability with spacious designs, tremendous drive-up appeal and great schools, said Mark Ketcherside, a U.S. Home sales representative.

The Countryside homes are a popular choice among first-time buyers, both with and without children, he said. With affordable prices and the lowest interest rates in years, the payments are usually comparable to rent, and home-ownership gives home-buyers tax advantages, too.

U.S. Home is currently offering several financing plans at Countryside, including conventional, FHA and VA ($1 move-in). Today's low interest rates mean that the cost of home-ownership is not that prohibitive, Ketcherside added. The lower rates can also make qualifying for a loan easier than before.

Countryside is in southwest Fort Worth, a short distance from several major traffic arteries, shopping centers and medical facilities. General Dynamics, Carswell Air Force Base and downtown Fort Worth are only a few minutes away.

These spacious Countryside homes are available in three floor-plans and nine elevations, the largest of which is a three-bedroom, two-bath plan. Abundant windows bring the outside in and enhance the custom-like feeling created by the vaulted ceilings and tiled entryway.

Entertaining is easy in the gourmet, U shaped kitchen with late-model name-brand appliances, and extra cabinet and pantry space. The master bath features double vanities, walk-in closet and full tub with shower. Homebuyers may customize their home with choice of colors and styles in upgraded carpets and vinyl floor coverings.

Outside, Countryside homes are fully landscaped with trees, shrubs, flowers and fully sodded front yard. The homes are inspected regularly so homebuyers can be assured that Countryside homes carry the quality consistent in all U.S. Home's Ten 2-10 Year Homebuyers Warranty, which is backed by a full-time staff of warranty service technicians on hand to assist each homeowner.

Financing programs available through U.S. Home include excellent below-market 30-year fixed rate conventional plans plus variable-rate mortgages, and FHA and VA ($1 move-in) loans.

To reach Countryside, take McCart south from Loop 820 to Alta Mesa and turn left. Go two blocks to Brookhaven and turn right, which leads to the Countryside sales office. Countryside is open from 10 a.m. to 8 p.m. Monday through Saturday and 11 a.m. to 8 p.m. on Sunday. Three fully furnished models are available for viewing.

History Maker spotlights new designs at Hillcrest West addition in Mansfield

History Maker Homes has been famous for high-quality residential construction in the Tarrant County area for over 36 years. Its most recent Hillcrest West addition in Mansfield has met with outstanding success. Over 70 homes have been sold since opening just a few short months ago.

This weekend marks the first time History Maker's two newest floor-plans are being offered. Both one-and one-and-a-half-story homes are now available from only $48,950.

History Maker Homes' newest plan is a one-and-a-half story with two bedrooms and bath downstairs and another bedroom and bath upstairs. The 1026s model is a one-story home with three bedrooms, one and one-half baths and one-car garage. Both plans are brick homes located on full-sized lots.

Each plan has a comfortable living room with vaulted ceilings, modern recessed kitchen lighting, high-efficiency heating and air-conditioning systems as well as double insulated pane windows.

All of these quality carpeted homes offer long-lasting brick, rich-looking cultured-marble vanities, roomy walk-in closets and vaulted ceilings to add spaciousness.

Either the 1026s or 1202 plan is available for only a $450 down payment and $1,050 closing cost, making the total required investment only $1,500. The homebuyers first year's payments are only $373.

Many other one-story and one-and-a-half story professionally designed plans are available for the discriminating homebuyer from only $55,950.

To visit Jody Gilbert and the decorated models at 622 South Walnut Creek in Mansfield, take the Walnut Creek exit south off Highway 287 one mile to Broad Street, turn right at the light one block to Graves, then left on Graves two blocks, turn left on East Dallas Street by the First Baptist Church and follow the signs to the History Maker Homes information center.

---

to TV stations. TV newsrooms across the country are now being offered special news feeds via satellite. These feeds come from a variety of sources, which, in turn, receive their information, and taped stories, from PR people in many instances.

TV newsrooms still receive some videotapes in the mail from PR sources. But videotapes are expensive to produce and distribute. More commonly, PR departments send out slides (chromakey or regular). The printed releases continue to pour in, some with glossy pictures enclosed. While these are of no use technically, they do sometimes give a news director an idea of whether something is worth sending a camera crew to cover. Most radio and TV stations and cable systems put news releases in a futures file or incorporate them into newscasts or public affairs programs that give listings of upcoming events in the area. These listings are also a feature of some newscasts and are used on cable systems. They will probably be an essential part of the news and information service of videotex and teletext systems in the future.

An example of how television uses PR material can be found in 10.5.

PR news releases are not to be confused with public service announcements. A PSA is ad time or space donated by the medium to non-profit organizations (a status formally conferred by the Internal Revenue Service; see Chapter 13).

10.5 News Program Using PR Sources

The American Heart Association makes available to the news media experts in various areas of cardiovascular disease. This television program grew out of a series of contacts arranged by PR people. The AHA put the reporter in touch with the doctor, who was the contact for the patient, who had to give permission for the story to be told.

```
(THE KILLERS/PART 1)                    HEART STATS/CHAMBERS/2-1-82/5:00 &
                                        10:00PM
                                        (AUDIO UP FULL :18-:20)
VIDEO                                   MUSIC & HEART BEATS
VARIOUS PEOPLE & HEARTBEATS
                                        WE ARE A FAST PACED SOCIETY . . . RUSH
                                        HERE . . . RUSH THERE . . . QUICK SERVICE
                                        THIS . . . SPEEDY SERVICE THAT . . . AND
                                        ITS CLEARLY KILLING MILLIONS OF
                                        AMERICANS.
                                            THE NUMBER ONE KILLER TODAY IS
                                        HEART-DISEASE OR DISEASES RELATED
                                        TO THE BLOOD VESSELS THAT GO TO THE
                                        HEART.
                                            NATIONWIDE NEARLY ONE MILLION
                                        PEOPLE WILL DIE THIS YEAR FROM
                                        CARDIOVASCULAR DISEASE . . . KILLING
                                        5 OUT OF EVERY 10.
                                            CANCER BY COMPARISON KILLS ABOUT
                                        2 OUT OF 10. . .
                                            ACCIDENTS WILL TAKE ABOUT 1/10TH
                                        OF US . . .
                                            AND ALL OTHER CAUSES WILL
                                        ACCOUNT FOR THE REMAINDER OF
                                        THOSE WHO DIE IN 1982.
```

10.5 (continued)

AMONG THE CARDIOVASCULAR DEATHS
. . . OVER HALF WILL BE FROM 'HEART
ATTACK'. . .
    LIKE THE ONE TRAVIS BLAKESLEE HAD.
BUT HE LIKE MANY OTHERS DID NOT
THINK IT WOULD HAPPEN TO HIM . . .

SUPER: TRAVIS BLAKESLEE
HEART ATTACK VICTIM
RUNS :07 OPENS: "I'D BEEN ACTIVE . . .
          ENDS: . . . ANY TROUBLE AT
          ALL"

MEANWHILE, DOCTORS CITE ALL THE
THINGS WE DO WRONG IN OUR FAST
PACED SOCIETY AS THE LEADING RISK
FACTORS WHICH CAUSE HEART
PROBLEMS . . .

SUPER: DR. DAVID L. MORRIS
CARDIOLOGIST
RUNS :15 OPENS: "ELEVATED FATS . . .
ENDS: . . . AS WE SEE IT TODAY"

(AUDIO UP FULL :06-:08)
    RISK FACTORS INCREASE YOUR
CHANCES OF HEART-DISEASE, BUT SOME
ALMOST AUTOMATICALLY, BECAUSE OF
HEREDITY, HAVE A HIGH CHANCE OF
HIGH BLOOD PRESSURE OR
HYPERTENSION . . .
    OUT OF ALL ADULTS OVER 18 IN THE
U.S. 31% OF ALL BLACK MALES WILL
HAVE HIGH BLOOD PRESSURE . . .
31% OF BLACK FEMALES WILL ALSO
HAVE IT . . . 22% OF ALL WHITE MEN
HAVE HYPERTENSION . . . AND 21% OF
ALL WHITE FEMALES ARE AFFECTED.
    ADD THE HIGH BLOOD PRESSURE TO
TOO MUCH CIGARETTE SMOKING . . . AND
HIGH LEVELS OF FAT IN THE DIET . . .
AND YOU BECME A PRIME TARGET.
    IT CAN HAPPEN TO YOU . . . AND YOU
WILL BE OUT OF THE PICTURE . . . AS
FAST AS YOU CAN BLINK . . .
    IN OUR NEXT REPORT . . . A LOOK AT
A LUCKY SURVIVOR.
KEN CHAMBERS 36-EYEWITNESS NEWS

(THE KILLERS/PART 2)

HEART VICTIM/CHAMBERS/2-2-82/5:00 &
10:00PM

(continued)

10.5 (continued)

02 OF VIDEO BEFORE AUDIO

TRAVIS BLAKESLEE IS AN ATTORNEY FOR THE AUSTIN LAW FIRM OF MINTON & BURTON.
    HE'S 62.
    AND HE'S LUCKY THAT HE DIDN'T STOP CELEBRATING BIRTHDAYS AT THE AGE OF 50.
    12 YEARS AGO HE HAD A HEART ATTACK.
    EVEN THOUGH HE SMOKED HEAVILY, IT WAS STILL A SHOCK TO HIM TO COME DOWN WITH A HEART PROBLEM . . . AND AFTER HIS SURGERY THERE WAS EVEN MORE CAUTION . . .

SUPER: VOICE OF: TRAVIS BLAKESLEE
HEART ATTACK VICTIM
(0:22-:37)

OPENS: "AFTER YOU'VE HAD . . .
ENDS: . . . THINGS I COULD DO" RUNS :15

DOCTORS HAVE LOWERED THE NUMBER OF DEATHS FROM HEART DISEASE BY 31% . . . BUT THAT'S NOT ENOUGH . . . ALTHO DOCTORS ARE ENCOURAGED . . .

SUPER: COURTESY AMERICAN HEART
ASSOC.
(1:45-:57)

OPENS: "IT SOUNDS STRANGE . . .
ENDS: . . . PROCESS OF DOING THE
OPERATION"   RUNS :12

SUPER: VOICE OF BLAKESLEE
(1:58-1:14)

OPENS: "ANYBODY THAT HAS TO . . .
ENDS: . . . BUT TO DO IT"   RUNS :16

SUPER: VOICE OR GLADYS BLAKESLEE
WIFE OF HEART VICTIM
(1:15-:32)

OPENS: "AS FAR AS HEART ATTACK . . .
ENDS: . . . HIS NORMAL SELF" RUNS :17

SINCE HE WAS ONLY ABOUT THE 7TH OR 8TH PATIENT IN AUSTIN TO HAVE SUCH A DELICATE OPERATION AT THE TIME ... HE HAS SEEN A LOT OF CHANGES IN THE WAY THINGS HAVE IMPROVED IN THE LAST FEW YEARS . . .

SUPER: TRAVIS BLAKESLEE
HEART ATTACK VICTIM
(1:42-:51)

OPENS: "NOWADAYS . . . THEY KEPT ME . . .
    ENDS: . . . OUT IN ABOUT 10 DAYS"
                       RUNS :09

AND WHAT ADVICE DOES HE HAVE FOR OTHERS TO AVOID SUCH A PROBLEM???

10.5 (continued)	OPENS: ''I'M THOROUGHLY CONVINCED . . . ENDS: . . . AS WE GET OLDER'' RUNS :17 ((TOTAL 2:12))

(THE KILLERS/PART 3)	HEART DOCTORS/CHAMBERS/2-3-82/5:00 & 10:00PM AUDIO UP FULL :05-:07 MUSIC WHETHER TRYING TO KEEP FIT BY EXERCISE OR BY JUST WATCHING THE DIET . . . WEIGHT CONTROL IS IMPORTANT TO A HEALTHY HEART. YOU DON'T HAVE TO WIN A MARATHON, OR EVEN RUN IN ONE ... TO BE HEALTHY. BUT DOCTORS DO RECOGNIZE REGULAR EXERCISE AS ONE OF THE BEST WAYS TO KEEP THE BLOOD FLOWING THROUGH YOUR VESSELS AND PREVENT THE BUILDUP OF FATTY DEPOSITS WHICH WILL SLOWLY CUT OFF CIRCULATION TO THE HEART. IT'S THE NUMBER-ONE PROBLEM FOR AUSTIN HEART SURGEON DAVID L. MORRIS . . .
DELAYED SUPER: DR. DAVID L. MORRIS CARDIOLOGIST (:37-:45)	OPENS: ''IT'S A MAJOR FACTOR . . . ENDS: . . . IMMENSE PROBLEM.'' RUNS :14
SUPER: COURTESY AMER. HEART ASSOC. (:47-1:03)	OPENS: ''THE GREATEST ENEMY . . . ENDS: . . . AFTER A HEART OPERATION'' RUNS :29 THE CURRENT PRESIDENT OF THE AUSTIN/TRAVIS COUNTY CHAPTER OF THE AMERICAN HEART ASSOCIATION IS DR. AL LINDSEY . . . AND HE SAYS THE EMPHASIS FOR HEALTHY HEARTS IS STARTING MUCH YOUNGER, NOW . . .
SUPER: DR. AL LINDSEY PRES. AUSTIN/TRAVIS CO. HEART ASSOC. (1:27-1:39)	OPENS: ''OUR THOTS ARE THAT . . . RUNS :23 ENDS: . . . MESSAGE TO THE STUDENTS'' A YEARLY PHYSICAL MAY NOT BE NECESSARY IF YOU HAVE NO HISTORY **(continued)**

10.5 (continued)

	OF MEDICAL PROBLEMS . . . BUT STAY AWARE OF THE WARNING SIGNALS OF HEART ATTACK . . .
TAKE SUPER: PRESSURE OR FULLNESS PAIN IN THE CHEST (1:56)	. . . PRESSURE OR FULLNESS TYPE OF PAIN IN THE CHEST . . .
<u>ADD</u> SUPER: PAIN TO SHOULDERS, NECK OR ARMS (1:59)	. . . PAIN SPREADING TO THE SHOULDERS, NECK OR ARMS . . .
<u>ADD</u> SUPER: DIZZINESS, FAINTING OR SWEATING (2:02-:05)	. . . DIZZINESS, FAINTING OR SWEATING SPELLS
	AND DO WHAT YOU CAN TO CHANGE THE MAJOR RISK FACTORS THAT AFFECT YOUR HEART OF:
<u>MAJOR RISK FACTORS</u> TAKE SUPER: CIGARETTE SMOKING (2:07)	. . . CIGARETTE SMOKING
<u>ADD</u> SUPER: HIGH BLOOD PRESSURE (2:09)	. . . HIGH BLOOD PRESSURE . . .
<u>ADD</u> SUPER: HIGH CHOLESTEROL (2:10-:12)	AND HIGH CHOLESTEROL INTAKE.
	IT MAY NOT BE A CURE, BUT IT SURE WILL HELP . . .
	OPENS: "IT WILL LESSEN . . . ENDS: . . . OUR PROBLEM IMMENSELY"
	((TOTAL 2:15))

Used with permission of Channel 36, KTVV-TV; and the American Heart Association, Texas Affiliate, Inc.

Media kits Both print and broadcast outlets get their share of media kits. Some are sent through the mail, some are hand delivered, others are given out at news conferences or made available at special events. Media kits are the standard tool of most PR professionals (see 10.6). These vary in content with the situation. However, most kits contain a fact sheet, biographical sketches of the major personalities involved, a straight news story, news-column material, a news feature, a brochure and, in some cases, photographs. Most news media prefer to take their own photos, except when they'd be using a file photo anyway—for example, shots of people in costumes or celebrity mug shots.

A prominent part of a media kit is the fact sheet. There may even be two fact sheets: One has the basic information about the organization and the event or occasion for the media kit, the other can be historical, noting milestones in the event or the organization itself. These often serve as story ideas for reporters.

10.6a The Media Kit

The usefulness of this kit about a Texas health spa is explained by Cherri Oakley, president and owner of the PR firm that produced it: "This multi-function media kit serves all the various needs of the publications which might be interested in information on The Greenhouse. The attempt here was to try to offer a wide perspective from which an editor could zero in on his or her particular interest. Much of the kit has been quoted verbatim in publications, and the package has served beautifully to whet the appetites of many national, regional and local editors and producers in areas which range from gardening to makeup to low-calorie recipes and everything in between. The exercise and fitness area has been received tremendously."

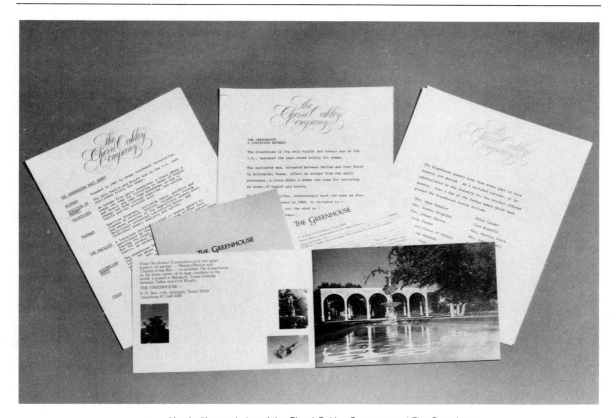

Used with permission of the Cherri Oakley Company and The Greenhouse

10.6b American Heart Association's High Blood Pressure Kit

This kit was prepared specifically for the 40th Annual Conference and Scientific Sessions of The American Heart Association Council on High Blood Pressure Research. It contains a fact sheet, background materials and five news releases based on scientific reports to be presented during the conference.

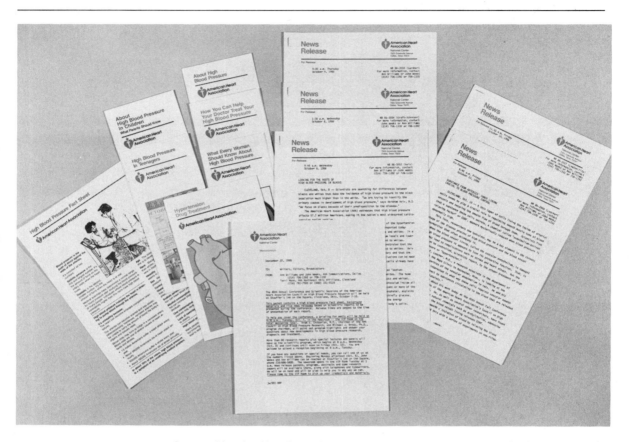

Courtesy of American Heart Association.   Photo: Richard Wheeler

Backgrounders and briefings

Reporters attending these sessions must wrestle with the question of how best to use the information provided. The news business is competitive, and some reporters will rush to use the material by finding a peg for it in the day's digest of news.

A background or briefing paper generally is in-depth information about an issue or event. Backgrounders are factual pieces, with sources listed so reporters can follow up by going to the original sources if these are outside the institution, or sometimes even inside in the case of government. The PR writer preparing one approaches it like a basic research paper, outline and all.

Some reporters keep files of handouts from backgrounders and briefings. (After one State Department "briefing," a reporter whose arms felt uncom-

10.6c Tobacco-Free Young America News Conference Kit

The news conference was jointly sponsored by The American Cancer Society, The American Heart Association and The American Lung Association. This kit contains materials from all three groups.

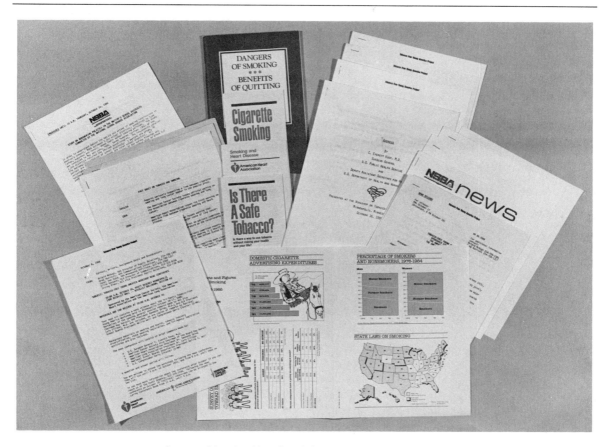

Courtesy of American Heart Association.   Photo: Richard Wheeler

monly tired when she got back to the newsroom weighed the material she had taken away—four pounds of documents!)

Background sessions offer little give-and-take. A principal news source makes a presentation and the handouts are distributed. This format originated with the government, but the private sector also uses it. For example, a real estate developer undertaking the restoration of a downtown section of a big city held a session with real estate writers of both mass and specialized media to draw the broad outlines of the plan before details could be filled in.

Briefings occur when an institution is involved in some continuing news event. It can be good news, such as a hospital representative discussing the rapid progress of a transplant patient, or unfavorable news, such as an industrial explosion, stalled strike negotiations or pickets being arrested at a nuclear plant. On such occasions a general "cover" release may be provided by the PR department, but not necessarily. News reporters should expect a great deal of resource material for stories and status reports from these meetings.

Briefings are sometimes considered mini–news conferences. Their intent is to provide some spot news on an ongoing situation that is attracting media attention. For example, if the U.S. launches a space probe, news briefings will be frequent until the general success of the mission is confirmed. For a disaster, like the explosion of the Challenger in 1986, the briefings will continue for months. In a sense, briefings not only present the breaking news but also help to set the agenda for the next day's coverage.

Special events

Despite Daniel Boorstin's observation that these are generally press agentry, or "pseudo-events" created to "make news," the fact is that because something does occur and people participate, it often becomes news.[3] Special events may be anything from a jump-rope-a-thon for the American Heart Association to a food lift for famine victims. PR people planning a special event have an objective—the event is designed to call attention to something. It may be manufactured news, but the message can nevertheless be important. The heart event focused attention not only on the role of exercise in a healthy lifestyle but also on the role of the association in education, and it raised funds for research. A food lift calls attention to the magnitude of the disaster, and in addition to helping the victims also helps get political support for some emergency funding.

Reporters must look at an event from the point of view both of those who are staging it and of the public, which may benefit in one way or another. For example, many cities host computer shows, boat shows, sports and vacation shows. Of course, the purpose of these events is to sell the products, and the producers also expect to make money from the show itself. Why report it? Why not let paid ads do the job? Like a state fair or rodeo or any other public entertainment, the interest in the event is the reason for news coverage. A reporter is neither compelled to play to the commercial objective nor to overlook it. Sometimes a special event even merits editorial page attention (see 10.7).

THE PR CONTACT: RESTRAINTS AND RELATIONSHIPS

PR people are often the spokespersons for their organization and are quoted as such by the news media. They are also suppliers of news tips and feature ideas.

All PR people are subject to the control of the person, agency or institution employing them. When that employer is government—local, state or federal—a natural adversary relationship springs up between the PR person and the reporter, because in a democratic society, the news media act as watchdogs.

In European countries such as England, France and Spain in the Middle Ages, society was rigidly divided into three "estates": the nobility, commoners

10.7 PR-Inspired Editorial

It's difficult to imagine how much more a public relations person could want than this piece about the Texas state fair, in which some PR source information is apparent.

State Fair
Sesquicentennial to hit full stride at fairgrounds

What a season this will be for the State Fair of Texas.

The sesquicentennial celebration, which has been under way in Texas for most of the year, will hit its stride Friday at the fairgrounds with the opening of this year's expanded State Fair. There could be no more appropriate place for the state to celebrate its 150th birthday than Fair Park.

This year is historically significant for the State Fair. It marks the 100th year of the fair's operation; and 1986 is the 50th birthday for Fair Park and the Cotton Bowl. Now, the National Park System has recommended that the Fair Park district be named as the first national historic landmark in the Dallas-Fort Worth area.

The fair will run a full month this year as part of the state's birthday festivities. And there will be evidence everywhere of the $18.3 million in improvements made to Fair Park. Among the most noticeable changes are the new main entranceway, the renovated Band Shell and the restored Automobile Building. All of these improvements, supported by voters on two city bond issues, will help make Fair Park a year-round tourist attraction.

The sesquicentennial celebration at the fairgrounds should remind visitors of the traditions and heritage that have built Texas. But Fair Park itself also should serve as a reminder of what Dallas has been able to accomplish.

Fifty years ago, this city was still in the grip of the Depression. Jobs were scarce, and money was even scarcer. And yet, the leaders of Dallas were able to bring about an unprecedented renovation of the fairgrounds in preparation for the Texas centennial celebration.

The art deco buildings that line the esplanade at Fair Park reflect the "can do" spirit that this city was able to retain in spite of the difficult financial times of the 1930s.

Today, Dallas is experiencing a downturn in the economy that again has challenged this city's positive outlook. Declining oil prices, increased office vacancies and a large number of business failures have caused some to wonder about this city's financial future.

The accomplishments at Fair Park a half century ago should serve notice that failure is in the minds of those who decide they cannot succeed. The leadership of Dallas today would do well to look back at the nearly insurmountable hurdles that stood in the way of this city during the year that the Texas centennial was held here. Only then can they fully appreciate how much Dallas has going for it as we kick off this sesquicentennial celebration.

Reprinted with permission of *The Dallas Morning News.*

---

and clergy. The press was separated into yet another category, the fourth estate. Now it is often referred to as "the other government," so far-reaching is its influence. Reporters must handle this social responsibility conscientiously, even, or perhaps especially, in an adversary relationship. William B. Blankenberg described it best:

> By "adversary relationship," I don't mean enmity—although that sometimes appears—but a posture of contention and antagonism whose tactics include sweetness as well as wrath, thrust and parry, guile and bluster. . . . *why* such an abrasive condition [exists] . . . lies in the differing responses of press and government to an undefinable thing called *news* that mixes two combustibles, timely disclosure and objective truth, one of which is chaotic and the other coercive.[4]

Government   PR professionals for government agencies are caught in the bind of trying to serve two masters. They have a responsibility to the public at large, because as government employees they are public servants, and to their immediate employer. Press secretaries are notorious for deceit in the "interest of national security." Most have been government appointees with no public relations background, selected for loyalty. President John F. Kennedy once told political columnist Scotty Reston that he wished Reston had broken the Bay of Pigs story (the aborted invasion of Cuba) and saved the United States from making a terrible mistake. In 1986, the government was scolded by the news media for a "disinformation," or propaganda, campaign (supposedly launched only abroad and not in the United States) designed to make Moammar Gadhafi think his country, Libya, was about to be attacked again by U.S. planes. The issue brought about the resignation of the State Department's chief spokesman, Bernard Kalb, who felt compromised by what he had been told versus the reality (see 11.8).

Neither policy nor law, however, is an excuse for lying to the news media. Reporters should probe all sources carefully to test for the truth, and they should test the facts against other sources for balance and consistency. If a source is frequently in error, either through carelessness or intentionally, it is time to work around that source.

Terminology.   Although the following terms are generally "understood" between reporters and PR sources, what any words really mean in a given situation should be spelled out. *Off the record* means that the information is for the writer's general understanding and not to be reported in any form. *Background only* means that information may be reported but not attributed to the source. *Not for direct quotation* means that information may be reported and the source named, but the writer must paraphrase, using neither quotation marks nor the official's exact words.

The problems a misunderstanding about terms can create are described by former Washington correspondent W.L. Rivers. Too often, Rivers says, officials who actually intend to offer information for "background only" will say, "This is off the record" or "Don't quote me directly." Some who want to speak "off the record" say, "This is for background only," thinking that the writers will not report the information but will use it only for their background understanding of issues. On Capitol Hill, some members of Congress who have been around some time occasionally use expressions like "This is neither *from* me nor *for* me." That is intended to mean the information may be reported but should not be attributed to the source or friends of the source.[5]

Further evidence that the backgrounder causes almost as much difficulty as the off-the-record pact is the following set of guidelines drafted by Bill Moyers when he was press secretary and counselor to President Lyndon B. Johnson.

1. "Backgrounders" should be designed to *explain* policy rather than *announce* policy. This rule would discourage the use of unattributed quotations.

2. "Backgrounders" in subjects other than national security and foreign affairs should be the exception rather than the rule.

3. The contents of a group "backgrounder" should not be disclosed for at least one hour after the conclusion of the session. This would permit time for cross-checking.

4. The rules should be clearly stated before the "backgrounder" begins by the principal or by the press spokesperson.

5. There should be only two levels of concealment. Either the reporter uses the information on his own—a practice that should be reserved for the most sensitive issues of national security—or it should be attributed as stated in the following principle.

6. The source should be identified by the specific agency. The loose anonymity of "high U.S. official," "top government officials," "friends of the President," or "visitors who've talked with the President" would be replaced by "a Defense Department spokesperson," or "a U.S. Army official," or "White House sources."

7. The reporters should refuse to deliberately increase the obfuscation through such tactics as withholding the information until the source has left town, or by attributing the information to plural sources when it comes in fact from one source.

8. When a public official in a "backgrounder" refuses to permit attribution of material that is patently self-serving but reporters nonetheless feel obliged to carry the story, they should carry a sentence attributing the information to a Pentagon (or State or White House) official "whose name is withheld at his insistence."[6]

Two newspaper reporters meeting with a group of PR professionals were asked, "What do you do with off-the-record remarks?" Both agreed that they did use the remarks, without attribution, but only after checking the facts thoroughly. So much for the "rules." These reporters had at least 10 years' professional experience but apparently never had been instructed that off-the-record agreements with sources mean just that: The comments are not to be used.

Some newspapers and broadcast stations will not let their reporters even listen to off-the-record remarks. One reason is that the information is probably available somewhere else, for attribution, but if the off-the-record source has been promised that the information won't be used, ethically it can't be. Another reason is that a reporter might promise to withhold the comments and then later in an honest slip of memory either use the material in a story or otherwise disclose it in framing a story or in talking to another source. Some sources count on such slips, because they are launching trial balloons to see what the climate of public opinion is.

Corporations and non-profit institutions

Dealing with corporations and non-profit institutions is in many cases like dealing with the government. Corporate and institutional operations also need "watchdogging" from the media, and therefore an adversary relationship often exists in this area as well.

But because private companies and institutions aren't publicly supported, they aren't under the same legal and political obligation to deal with the news media that government offices are. They do seek "good PR," though, and that means dealing with the news media at some time for some reason.

Beginning reporters need to realize that the private sector is as newsworthy as the public sector. Not all the stories reporters find in the private sector make the corporation or institution look good. If publicity harmful to a company or institution's image does appear in the news, an adversary relationship may result.

Reporters often encounter corporate PR people during times of crisis. At such times, these PR people can be as evasive as any government representative. The rules that apply to government sources apply to the private sector in these instances.

But not all relationships with government, corporate and non-profit institutions are adversarial. In many, perhaps most, instances, these relationships are quite friendly. In fact, PR people in both the public and private sectors can be of great assistance to the news media in a number of ways.

Sources of special assistance.   The PR person's role here is best illustrated in the story of the intern earlier in the chapter—getting all of the information to the newspaper on request so a deadline can be met. When you're on the news side and working on a story, you start with the PR person, whether it's a non-profit or business institution.

The PR director will get the background material, supply photographs or arrange for these to be taken to your specifications, and set up interviews you'll want. They'll get quotes for you or get you access.

PR people can help with broadcast reporters' and photographers' special needs. When covering speeches, for example, TV camera crews want front-row seats to get clear shots of the speaker. Radio reporters want podium mikes or mult boxes provided in order to tape a speech. PR people can ensure the broadcast reporter's cameras and mikes are on the reviewing stand during the parade, on the field during the big game and on the team plane on the way home, in the helicopter surveying the extent of the disaster, in the Oval Office when the president meets with the Soviet premier.

Getting to take some shots of the president and premier together, before the private talks begin, has come to be called a "photo opportunity." It is now a practice of many public officials, even at the local level.

PR-generated features.   Feature stories with a PR base that appear in the mass media usually are prepared by news staff writers. PR-written features generally appear in specialized media (see Chapter 11). PR representatives usually approach editors rather than reporters with feature ideas, although a PR person who has followed a reporter's work may call that reporter to propose an idea for a feature.

PR tip sheets often resemble freelancers' query letters in style. A tip sheet may call one editor's attention to only one feature idea, or a tip sheet may offer a number of ideas that may go to many different editors. A collection of ideas stated briefly might look like this:

(Organization's Letterhead, often especially designed with a name like "Editor's Tip Sheet" or "News Notes.")

(date)

TO: NEWS EDITOR
FROM: NANCY NEAL, University News Service

The following story ideas could be easily developed by your staff if you are interested. We have the basic information in our office, and for some of the suggestions we have black-and-white glossy 8½x11 photos. We will be glad to work with you in developing any of these story ideas.

1) Research on the reaction of stockmarkets to international events, especially crises—a combined project of political science, economics and mass communication professors. Model suggests some degree of predictability. Possible story for your business pages.

2) Geology Department working with Gas Research Institute on permeability problems. Potential restoration of some wells shut down due to low productivity. Possible story for your science page.

3) Visiting Professor in Philosophy says renewed demand for teaching ethics in professionally related disciplines is expanding research and scholarship. Professor Edwin Masters from Sincere University is lecturing this week in business, nursing, political science and mass communication classes. Story focus could vary for almost any page, including religion, but might be an interesting possibility for your lifestyle section.

When the approach is to only one editor or reporter, the tone is more personal.

(Standard Letterhead)

(date)

To: Carol Ortiz, Art Editor
From: Nancy Neal, University News Service

One of our alumnae has just offered to the university her mother's extensive collection of American glass. The collection of more than 2,000 individual pieces is currently being evaluated by appraisers, and the University is trying to decide where it could best be displayed.

Since our development office was just called about this last week, I thought you might be interested in an exclusive. We have made no announcement of the gift, and will not until the appraisers have completed their evaluation.

The collection has some rare pieces like a Steuben miniature that may have been made for a member of the glassmaker's family, and some exceptional pieces of the original milk glass patterns that are not rare, but are unusual.

We are photographing the collection now, and could provide you with black-and-white or color pictures. Of course, we would be glad to work with your photographer, if you prefer.

The alumna is willing to be interviewed and to talk about her mother, but she discounts their importance, saying, "One woman's obsession has created an interesting history of American glass."

Let us know if you would be interested in doing the story now. I think as we move toward determining the value of the gift and its display, we will be giving the story a general release.

Obviously such a story would be a feature, one to which an editor has been offered an exclusive, in writing.

Print media features are often contained in media kits. These may be very well done, but the newspaper that uses them "as is" runs the risk of seeing the same features in another paper. Most just follow up on the idea instead.

News features are a popular PR goal. For example, a PR person in charge of a sponsored golf tournament may offer a sports reporter a news feature about the 80-year-old greenskeeper who helped design the course so long ago that everyone has forgotten about it, or a profile on the person for whom the tournament is named.

The reporter wants to be sure that the same idea isn't going out to other reporters. After offering an idea, the PR person awaits a response of some kind from the reporter. If the response is silence or "no," the PR person is released from an "exclusive" offering and can suggest the idea to another reporter. Once a reporter expresses interest in that idea, he or she can rightfully expect "ownership" of it and full support from the PR person in developing it.

A PR person for a greeting-card store suggested to a local newspaper that their annual Valentine's Day story be a historical look at greeting cards and offered to do the research through the card companies whose wares the store carried. The idea for the feature was presented in early January; the PR person had already secured the cooperation of the card manufacturers' PR departments. The story was put together in late January and was ready, with excellent art, by Feb. 14.

The PR person who knows company employees well can be a continuing source of interesting subjects for personality profiles—the accounts-receivable clerk who trains falcons, the bank president who hang-glides. The name of the company doesn't have to be mentioned more than once or twice in the story. Some examples of PR-generated features are in 10.8.

Broadcast media features.   PR people generally direct features to TV rather than radio because television has more time in a newscast for features and it has the advantage of pictures.

10.8a PR-Generated Features

The first example is a feature in a national magazine that originated with a PR firm that handled the spa where Brooke Shields was staying. Cherri Oakley, president of the PR firm that prepared the material for *Vogue*, said: "The article was requested by and prepared for a national magazine and submitted along with color photography. The magazine subsequently chose to limit the story and use the photographs with expanded cutlines. Still, it was the printed word that got the client's message across and got national play for an event."

Brooke Shields at The Greenhouse
Exclusive to *Vogue* Magazine

By Yvonne Saliba

The sweet, youthful voice on the phone was asking for brochures and information on The Greenhouse, posh spa outside Dallas.

"I wasn't sure the lady believed me, but a few days later the stuff came in the mail," says Brooke Shields, who made the reservation herself for a week's stay at The Greenhouse for her and mother, Teri.

It was her vacation/getaway from a fast-paced life in the limelight, a chance, she said, to really look at herself and to spend precious time with her mother just talking about "things."

The starlet and her mother say they picked the Texas health and beauty spa because of the small guest list—38 maximum guests to a staff of 125—and because it's not co-educational. The Greenhouse, midway between Dallas and Fort Worth, was far enough away to allow the mother-daughter duo to do just what they had set out to do.

Besides, Brooke says friend John Travolta, who had recently been in the area getting some pilot training, had assured Brooke she'd like Texas. "I wanted to see what the *real* 'Urban Cowboys' looked like," she said with that patented Brooke Shields twinkle in her eye.

Once ensconced in the elaborate retreat, Brooke really got into The Greenhouse regimen of nurturing and pampering while at the same time teaching a woman how to change her body through exercise; alter her diet via strict, yet delicious, diets of only the freshest foods; and get in touch with all areas of herself.

Brooke really wasn't there to lose weight off that lithe size 7 Calvin body, but she took classes every day with all the other guests and confided to Greenhouse consultant Toni Beck that she's afraid of getting heavy in the hip area as she ages.

"She rides horseback every day," said Beck, "and I told Brooke that's probably the worst thing you can do for that below the buttocks area, because in riding you have to let go of those muscles back there." Beck, a dancer who formulated the original Greenhouse exercise program when it was founded in 1965, worked with Brooke all week to "stretch those hamstrings. Long, lean muscle-mass—that's what we want for her."

Beck says Brooke is very loose and moves very naturally. "She's just graceful, very graceful," said Beck, who works with all the women to show them how good exercise is not far removed from dance and a dancer's training. The exercise doyenne of Dallas, who also created the SMU School of Dance, observed that Brooke seemed happiest exercising to music—tunes like the themes from "Star Wars" and "Fame" seemed to especially relax her.

"Aside from riding, Brooke hasn't done anything physical. The dance-like routines seemed fun for her. She moves so well."

Asked if anyone had ever worked with her on exercise and toning her body during these important young years, Brooke said no. "I never had a routine to follow. Hopefully I will now," she said, adding she took Xerox copies of everything home with her, along with the five cassette tapes The Greenhouse offers to guests.

(continued)

10.8a (continued)

Shape-up Now

Spa secrets from a top model… fitness over fifty… shape-saving holiday diet

For athletes, now: a book to answer all your health/injury concerns about sports. Written by William Southmayd, M.D., and Marshall Hoffman, "Sports Health: The Complete Book of Athletic Injuries" (Quick Fox) discusses safest sports, minimizing risks, preparation, and covers injuries to every body part (fingers and hands are most injury-prone), with special sections devoted to nutrition and children's sports injuries. A worthwhile reference for every home library.

What happened when mother, Teri Shields, offered daughter, supermodel Brooke, "time off" doing anything she wanted? Brooke's idea: a week together at a spa. Final choice: The Greenhouse, Dallas. "It made me work harder to have Brooke there," says Teri. "I lost seven pounds; Brooke, on a maintenance diet only, toned hips and waist. We ate less *(far right)* but were never hungry; it was a total change—part-cooked salads, steamed-but-crunchy vegetables—from foods we usually eat and only 850 calories per day." Brooke's report: "It wasn't easy doing those exercises—it was nothing like gym—but it got me going." (Her favorites, *above* and *near right.*) Best part: "Time to talk and make plans." Says Teri, "We're applying the walking and exercise programs to our everyday life and two Greenhouse recipe books Brooke brought back have kept us on track." One: *Helen Corbitt's Greenhouse Cookbook* (Houghton Mifflin). More on spas, page 272.

"An older woman who has remained physically fit has no problem keeping up with exercise classes; but the older woman who hasn't will have a discouraging problem: her body will be out of condition. She cannot—should not—do the routines designed for physically fit women," says Sally Olins, who runs The Firm Company, a Los Angeles exercise studio. Her "Fitness After Fifty" classes ease a woman back—gradually; 213/478-6914.

First look at the "new" Helena Rubinstein Beauté in New York City, offering revitalizing skin treatments—from Swedish massage to facials (for the body, too, see *right*). To come: European skin-caring products. Look for them on-counter in February.

The same seemed true of the beauty program at The Greenhouse. Here was the hottest young star of the '80s, playing with the makeup and oohing and aahing over all the colors.

"I'm always being made up by a makeup artist. Then you can't really see what's being done. In the beauty school, I learned a lot."

The first day of her week's stay, in fact, the other guests wanted her to be the "volunteer" from the audience to be made up. "I said I would really rather sit there and do it myself.

You start with your eyes and learn to shade, and really just learn to put makeup on correctly by just playing with it."

Erica Miller, director of beauty, and the one who got the closest view of Brooke all week, described Brooke. "She's got beautiful facial structure, already built with all the shadows and highlights before makeup. No corrective shaping is needed at all. She has an almost mystical look with those thick lashes and brows. The complexion is flawless, although her skin may tend to dehydrate later."

While she doesn't like heavy makeup, The Greenhouse beauty staff got a big kick out of Brooke wanting to try every color in the Charles of the Ritz line, the makeup supplier from the spa's beginning.

"Easily, she is the most beautiful person I've ever made up. With so little makeup, it's so easy to create a goddess."

While Brooke and her mother don't really look alike, Erica Miller observed that there's that same twinkle, the same smile and the lips in both mother and daughter. The height, 5 feet 10½ inches, is from her father, Frank Shields, who is 6 feet 7 inches.

Mrs. Shields was on The Greenhouse weight loss program, while Brooke was on the maintenance diet. "I always thought you lose weight and that's it, but I lost inches— 1½ inches in my stomach and that's a lot," Brooke said. While she was at 1,200 calories a day, mother had 850.

"I ate desserts—mostly fruits—with my meals, but it was still nearly half of what I normally eat," said Brooke, who does not eat junk food but admits to a passion for chocolate.

"I never once thought how hungry I was; just before lunch maybe, and sometimes at the dinner table you'll look and it looks like a real small piece of steak and you look at it and think, I'm going to be hungry afterwards, but you're really not hungry at all. I was surprised because I eat a lot."

Mrs. Shields says she thinks the food service and presentation is the "biggest secret" to The Greenhouse success. "The diet—and I was used to candies and cakes and everything that's wrong for you—the diet is so great and it's nothing artificial, that you're not hungry, you don't have a craving. It's amazing."

Brooke did request a take-home treat, some of food service director Bertha Shields' yummy chocolate coconut cookies—something only a small percentage of The Greenhouse guests ever eat, since no sweets at all appear on the weight loss menu. Bertha Shields (no relation) directs the preparation of the delectable and beautifully presented foods. She is the protege of the late Helen Corbitt, who formulated the menus and ideas for the food in 1965 at the request of Stanley Marcus, who was her boss at Neiman-Marcus.

Corbitt, the force behind Neiman's Zodiac Room, came on board in the beginning because Marcus was the arbiter of taste in all facets of the original blueprint for the spa, owned by the Great Southwest Corporation, a conglomerate which had the good sense to bring in experts in all areas to format their idea. Neiman-Marcus still provides a weekly fashion show for guests.

Situated midway between Dallas and Fort Worth, The Greenhouse is an unobtrusive-looking but impeccably manicured haven away from the hustle bustle. The 38 guests, who pay $2,000 a week, are guaranteed a stay with the utmost security. The low-profile atmosphere—34 of the 36 rooms have no outside exit—and the 24-hour security system assures guests a privacy they can have nowhere else in the world outside their own home.

Even the highly visible Brooke had a good four days of life completely outside of the limelight from Sunday until she ventured out on Thursday (when most guests limp to N-M to shop) to Billy Bob's Texas, a Fort Worth country-western nightclub billed as the largest in the world, and for some shopping. She visited Sakowitz' new Dallas store and Neiman-Marcus in Dallas, as well as Morgan's, near the spa, where she and her mother bought lizard cowboy boots. And, from a flea market they happened by, the Shieldses bought some Royal Doulton china.

(continued)

10.8a (continued)

After a week of pampering and introspective study into herself, is there anything gleaned from The Greenhouse regimen that Brooke wants to work on?

"Well, I've been thinking a lot about my posture. And sometimes when I'm mad I look kind of like I'm snarling. I want to work on that," said Brooke. And to that, her mother added, "That's the only way I can ever tell when Brooke is mad. Her lip curls upward on one side." Otherwise, the consensus seems that she's perfect.

10.8b

A news feature on heart disease was the result of the American Heart Association's national meeting. Most of the material came from the media kit.

Healthier hearts beating in America

Heart facts

In its latest "Heart Facts," the annual publication of the statistical outlook for heart disease, the American Heart Association says:

☐ 110,000 more Americans had some kind of heart disease in 1984 than 1983. Some 63.4 million had one or more forms of heart or blood vessel disease in 1984.

☐ Heart attack, the major cause of death from heart disease, caused 540,400 deaths in 1984. That's nearly 7,000 less than in 1983.

☐ Nearly 5 million people alive today have a history of heart attack, chest pain or both.

☐ An estimated 202,000 coronary

bypass surgeries were performed in 1984, compared to 191,000 in 1983.

☐ Rheumatic heart disease increased slightly in 1984, causing 6,900 deaths, compared to 6,700 in 1983.

☐ Stroke killed 155,000 people in 1984; 156,400 in 1983.

By Ellen Hale
Gannett News Service

MONTEREY, Calif. — Some 3,000 fewer Americans died of heart disease in 1984, as deaths from cardiovascu-lar ailments continue their decline in this country.

Heart and circulatory diseases will kill almost 1 million Americans this year as the cost of the nation's major cause of death rises to $85.2 billion, the American Heart Association said Sunday.

Nearly 540,000 of the deaths will occur among 1.5 million heart attack victims, the non-profit group said in releasing its statistical outlook for the year, published in the booklet "1987 Heart Facts."

For the third year in a row, deaths from heart disease accounted for less than half—48.2 percent—of all deaths in the United States, claiming some 986,400 lives in 1984, the most recent year for which statistics are available. In 1983, nearly 50 percent of deaths—989,400—in this country were as a result of heart disease.

The decrease in deaths, accompanied by decreases in the rates of various kinds of heart disease, suggests the overall decline in the death rate from heart ailments that began in the 1960s has not yet abated. The rate has dropped 40 percent in 20 years.

Nonetheless, heart specialists are quick to point out, heart disease remains the No. 1 cause of death and disability in the United States, afflicting more than 63 million Americans. In 1983, heart deaths totaled more than twice the number of deaths from cancer.

And, despite the death-rate decline, the cost of heart disease in this country in 1987 will hit $85.2 billion, nearly $7 billion more than it did in 1986. That's $361 for every individual in the United States.

American Heart Association President Dr. Kenneth I. Shine credits research, improvements in treatment and changes in lifestyle. And he estimates the decline has saved the country as much as $60 billion a year in medical costs.

Current deaths could be cut in half by lifestyle changes alone, however, said Shine, who is also UCLA Medical School dean.

"Despite all the progress we've made, there are still very dramatic reductions in disease and death that can come about just from modifying lifestyle," he said.

Lower-fat diets, less smoking, more exercise and better control of blood pressure have helped to slash our coronary death rates, said Shine. "But about 50 percent of our current deaths are strongly linked to these known risk factors, and we could reduce our rates by that amount."

Moreover, the AHA recently has taken the stand that such lifestyle changes can and should be launched among children, as well, since the precursors of heart disease may begin in childhood.

The other half of deaths are due primarily to a genetic cause. "Even these genetic factors may be influencable at some time in the future as our research continues," Shine said.

Some of the most impressive progress has turned up in the nation's diet changes, added Dr. Virgil Brown of Mount Sinai Medical School, New York City, chairman of AHA's nutrition committee.

In the early 1960s, our diets were about 18 percent saturated fat. Now it's 13.5 percent. The AHA recommends only 10 percent of these fats—heaviest in liberally marbled meats, animal-derived oils and whole milk dairy products—because they clog arteries, spurring heart attacks.

"We've lowered saturated fats by almost one-third and are about halfway there (to the 10 percent goal) now," Brown said.

Slipping down to a 10 percent mark alone would cut cholesterol blood fats by an average of 10 milligrams, leading to a 10 percent to 15 percent overall reduction in coronary deaths, said Brown. "That's about 90 to 130,000 less deaths per year," he said.

But radio is not completely left out in this effort for publicity; almost any feature story that newspapers and television can do, radio can also do in its own way. The radio feature is often an interview story. The PR source usually has someone available to talk about the feature subject. Personalities are interviewed in the studio, and radio reporters do interviews, and voicers, from the scene of feature stories.

Radio sportscasters seem to do more features than do radio news reporters. Sports information departments constantly send out feature suggestions, and these features are heard almost every day on at least one radio station in town.

TV sports departments also do a large number of features. Special network sports programs, such as ABC's *Wide World of Sports*, consist almost entirely of features on some days, with stories on relatively obscure sporting events, interviews with sports personalities, sidebars, advance pieces on upcoming events and so on. Local TV sportscasts are also full of such feature material many nights.

MAIN POINTS

- PR writers prepare copy for mass and specialized media. It's their job to know exactly how a medium would get the story if a staff writer prepared it.

- Backgrounders, briefings, position papers, media kits, brochures, films and annual reports are all PR writing tasks.

- PR sources generate advance stories, coverage stories, follow-ups, and final, or "result," stories. Most advance stories need little editing for use. Reporters may prefer to do their own coverage and follow-up stories, using the PR copy as background.

- PR people can supply tips for reporters to do the story and will set up interviews, photos and provide background information.

- Sometimes PR people ask that copy be held for a particular release. Some media policies prohibit this.

- Reporters working with PR people as sources need to know source terminology like "background only" and "off the record."

- A reporter needs to know PR sources and learn which ones can be trusted.

- Experienced PR people are just as willing to help reporters develop a feature as cover a breaking news story.

- Reporters should always remember that the PR person must serve two masters—the client or employer and the news media.

EXERCISES

1. You have just seen the following news story and as public relations director for the Aircraft Owners and Pilots Association you have been asked to write a brief news release in response. List what you would do to prepare that release.

Air safety regulations tightened

By Marilyn Adams
USA TODAY

New rules aimed at averting midair collisions will soon take effect at 14 USA airports.

The Federal Aviation Administration Thursday ordered all aircraft flying near the big-city airports to have special altitude-reporting equipment by Dec. 1. Called a transponder, it shows a plane's exact location on air controller's radar.

Most affected: pilots of small, private planes. Minimum penalty for violation: 60 days' license suspension.

"The aviation community needs to know whether FAA—both their computers and controllers—can handle the additional workload from this," said Patricia Weil of the 260,000-member Aircraft Owners and Pilots Association. "We'd hoped for a . . . study."

The new FAA rule—coming four years earlier than scheduled—was hastened by the Aug. 31, 1986, midair crash of an airliner and small, private plane over Cerritos, Calif. The small plane could not report altitude; 82 died.

FAA is considering tighter controls at even more airports.

The new rule affects at least 2,400 planes—and possibly thousands more—flying in restricted airspace over Cleveland; Denver; Detroit; Honolulu; Houston; Minneapolis-St. Paul; New Orleans; Philadelphia; Pitts-

burgh; Seattle; St. Louis; San Diego; Kansas City, Mo.; and Las Vegas, Nev.

Of 215,000 private USA planes, only 84,000 have altitude-reporting equipment. Nationwide and commuter airlines and many business planes already are equipped. Cost: from several hundred to several thousand dollars per plane.

The equipment already is required in the most dangerous airspaces: Atlanta, Boston, Chicago, Dallas, Los Angeles, Miami, New York, San Francisco and Washington, D.C.

2. The air safety story has been given to you as a newspaper writer to rework. You are told to beef it up and find a local angle for the paper. What would you do?

3. Rewrite the same story for a radio news item. Would you use an actuality? Where would you get it?

4. Now prepare the same news story for the 6 p.m. television news. What pictures do you need? Sound? Indicate both in your script. Where would you go to get what you needed?

5. As a public relations writer, you are preparing a news release about the university's chorus going on a summer tour to Europe. What would you do differently in writing the story if you worked for the local newspaper? What would you offer a radio station with the release? A television station?

6. You are a public relations writer for the Gas Research Institute, and the marketing department has just brought you a copy of their newest technology profile that another PR writer has prepared (example 10.1). The writer is away on vacation and a news release needs to be written to go out with the profile. Try your hand at writing it, first for newspapers and then for a utility's house publication.

NOTES

1. Judy VanSlyke Turk, "Public Relations' Influence on the News," *Newspaper Research Journal* 7, no. 4 (Summer 1986): 15–27. Turk's findings were that about half of the information provided by public information officers for six state government agencies was used by newspapers, and the topics the public information officers identified as important to their agencies were the same topics given attention in media coverage. In her conclusions, Turk said: "Journalists said their decisions to use PIO sources were heavily influenced by craft norms of newsworthiness and by staff and space availability to 'massage' the information into news copy."

2. Public relations materials are sent to news media by wire service networks that cover the continental United States and by some international services. The largest is PR Newswire, which began operations in 1954. PR practitioners buy the distribution systems as needed for their news release coverage. Hookup for media is free.

3. Daniel Boorstin, *The Image: A Guide to Pseudo-Events in America* (New York: Harper & Row, 1962).

4. William B. Blankenburg, "The Adversaries and the News Ethic," *Public Relations Quarterly* 14, no. 4 (1970): 34.

5. William L. Rivers, *The Opinion Makers* (Boston: Beacon Press, 1965), p. 37.

6. Bill Moyers, "Press or Government: Who's Telling the Truth," *Television Quarterly* 7 (Summer 1968): 24–25.

SUGGESTIONS FOR ADDITIONAL READING

Bernays, Edward L. *Public Relations*. Rev. ed. Norman: University of Oklahoma Press, 1977.

Cutlip, Scott, Alan Center and Glenn Broom. *Effective Public Relations*. 6th ed., rev. Englewood Cliffs, N.J.: Prentice-Hall, 1985.

Newsom, Doug, and Bob Carrell. *Public Relations Writing, Form and Style*. Belmont, Calif.: Wadsworth, 1986.

Newsom, Doug, and Alan Scott. *This Is PR*. 3rd ed. Belmont, Calif.: Wadsworth, 1985.

Rivers, William L. *The Other Government: Power and the Washington Media*. New York: Universe Books, 1982.

Simon, Ray. *Publicity and Public Relations Worktext*. Columbus, Ohio: Grid, 1983. Also see Simon's *Public Relations, Concepts and Practice*, same publisher.

Features and Columns

Feature stories are "soft news"—the candy. A feature assignment is often considered a writer's reward for handling routine news well. The implication is that feature writing is easy. Actually, it makes more demands on writing ability than the straight news story, because it has no specific format. Neither does a column.

The difference between the feature story and a column is the personal tone of the column. Column writers indulge their own interests, and that's OK as long as they entertain. Column writing is probably the closest to creative writing in any medium, although opinion writers are really essayists.

The broadcast equivalent of a columnist is the personality who has a daily essay type of program or a how-to show on subjects like home repair or gardening. The major attraction of a columnist, print or broadcast, is his or her style —a reflection of personality. In features, the story is the star.

WHAT IS A FEATURE? Feature stories can be news. Features can be investigative. Features can be in-depth. Features can be for fun. The subject can be anything: *places*—a community, a farm, a business; *topics*—education, science, the economy, religion, philosophy; *events*—parades, programs, concerts; *people*—well known or unknown; *animals*—unusual or ordinary; *objects*—art or products.

A publisher of the *Denver Post*, Palmer Hoyt, asked his assistant to develop a definition of the feature to clarify categories in some newspaper competitions. The assistant, Alexis McKinney, wrote this definition:

A newspaper feature is an article that finds its impact outside or beyond the realm of the straight news story's basic and unvarnished who–what–where–when–why and how.

The justification, strength and very identity of the feature lie in its presentation of the imagination—not, however, departing from or stretching the truth, but in piercing the peculiar and particular truths that strike people's curiosity, sympathy, skepticism, humor, consternation or amazement.[1]

Common denominators   Most features draw on some element of human interest: drama, pathos, empathy, humor; something that involves the reader emotionally. Another distinguishing trait is that good feature stories are particularly well written, filled with solid information and detail, sparkling and imaginative. The reason for such qualities is simple: You can spend more time crafting the feature, because it usually isn't as timely as a hard-news story.

But that doesn't mean a feature story doesn't have news value. It's just a different kind of news value. For instance, instead of reporting the facts of a hotel fire in which 4 people died and 16 were injured, you might focus on one of the survivors and tell the story from his or her point of view. Or you could tell the story through the eyes of the firefighters who carried out the dead and administered first aid to the injured. You can create images and evoke emotions that you can't with the straight fire story.

Public relations writers find feature stories an important tool in getting their organizations outside recognition. Inside the organization, features are a useful device to convey information and build a sense of belonging. Features can capture the imagination, and their anecdotal nature makes them memorable.

Ideas for features   Anything that happens is potentially a feature—depending on how you, the writer, view it. Ideas are everywhere. One writer, Frank A. Dickson, demonstrated that in a book called *1,001 Article Ideas*. Actually, it contained 1,464 feature-story suggestions. That doesn't count the spin-offs that result naturally from a good feature idea. Dickson said of his suggestions: "Each idea . . . be it historical, current or futuristic—has been designed to enable you to give your readers—whoever they are—a personal interest and identification in the story."[2] Dickson intended his article ideas not only for newspaper and magazine writers but also photojournalists and broacasters. The public relations person can relate those ideas to the organization he or she represents and prepare stories to supply to the print and broadcast media.

Feature ideas characteristically call for a great deal of research in the subject area so you have a solid background for new information. In gathering the new information, you need to list everyone who could possibly contribute some insight. Then you narrow the list to the ones you have time to see, who have time to see you and who are within reach for an interview, even if only by phone. If you do your job right, you should be drowning in information by the time you're ready to write.

Types of features   Though the number of ideas for features is limitless, there is a finite set of categories for them. These categories aren't rigid; they're only labels to help you describe a story.

News feature.   Most common is the news feature, generally developed around a timely event. The news feature can be more personal than a straight news story. Considerably more human interest is brought to the story, through direct quotes, description and perhaps emotion (see 11.1). At the core, though, is

11.1a Human-Interest News Features

The lead plays it straight: The man's ambulance-driving experience helps him save a drowning victim. Then the unusual element is injected. Notice the last graph has the punch line, and makes use of the colloquial *whup* — here's a time to write it just like the person said it.

Owner breathes life back into pup

HOUSTON (AP) — Reid Millard used to work for an ambulance service — experience that came in handy this week when he succeeded in saving a drowning victim.

But this victim was a little different. It was Jake, Millard's 12-week-old chow.

"I didn't know what to do," Millard said. He discovered Jake at the bottom of the pool Monday. "I've given CPR (cardiopulmonary resuscitation) to some people before, but never to a dog. I worked on him for about 30 minutes, I guess, before I got him back to where he was halfway breathing right."

A veterinarian gave Jake a clean bill of health and sent him home to rest, saying it was a doggone miracle.

"I had let him out at about 7:20 Monday morning, and when I looked out at about 7:35, I didn't see him," Millard said.

"I looked in the pool, and he had gotten tangled up in a line (holding up a volleyball net). He fell in the pool and couldn't swim."

Millard, a 27-year-old real estate manager, said Jake seems to be taking it all in stride, and Millard is giving him preferential treatment for the time being.

"I told him I wouldn't whup him for the next month — 'do whatever you want' — so he's been chewing everything up," Millard said.

Reprinted with permission of The Associated Press.

Reid Millard cuddles his 12-week-old chow, Jake. Photo: Copyright © *Houston Chronicle.*

news. Often news features are written as sidebars to straight news stories. Color stories capture the flavor of an event, seasonals the spirit of the time of year. And problem pieces tackle social issues (see 11.2).

11.1b News Feature that Becomes an Anecdote to Tell and Share

As you read this, you can practically hear cheering—from anyone who has ever been mugged, and from all of the elderly who are tired of always being portrayed as victims. This story abounds with literary devices. First the scene is set. Next comes foreshadowing—what is it the robber learned? The narrative follows. Part of the narrative is told through an eyewitness. The last graph is the "good triumphs over evil" finale of so many fiction stories. But this one is true. It's the kind that gets told at the office and at parties.

87-year-old woman delivers thumping

Purse-snatcher picks on wrong victim

The New York Times

To the bicycle-riding purse-snatcher on the Upper East Side of Manhattan yesterday afternoon, 87-year-old Vera Tucker must have looked like an easy target.

But the robber quickly learned otherwise, when Tucker struck several blows for justice.

Tucker was walking home on East 66th Street near Fifth Avenue at about 5 p.m. when a man rode by on a bicycle, reached out, grabbed her purse and began to pedal away, the police said.

A surprised Tucker, dressed in an elegant floral print dress and a wide-brimmed hat, yelled at the robber to stop.

He did not.

Tucker gave chase, caught up to the bicycle and whacked away with her parasol until she knocked the man off his bike.

A doorman and a passer-by who heard the screaming and saw Tucker knocking the thief on the head then came to her aid.

The doorman, Charles Migliara, grabbed the bicycle, and the passer-by, Gregory Culley, tried to grab the man.

"I was on the side of my van and I heard these very loud shrieks," said Culley, who delivers food to city shelters for the Human Resources Administration.

"I saw this elderly woman whapping a man on the head. The umbrella had a good bend in it. I wouldn't like to have been him," Culley said.

Culley, who is 6 foot 5 inches, then wrestled the robber to the ground.

At that point a police officer, posted around the corner on duty in front of the Yugoslav Mission to the United Nations, arrived and arrested the man.

The man, identified as Jose Ramos, 38, was later charged with robbery, resisting arrest and criminal possession of stolen property.

11.2 News Feature about a Problem

This news feature from a Sunday newspaper magazine supplement obviously has a public relations source. In this case, the PR source worked with the writer to develop the story. A sidebar highlights special facts. The story itself is a fairly typical news feature, problem format.

How can we protect our elderly?

By Donald Robinson

Lead presents the status of the problem, what probably is a surprising fact, and a quote. —— Abuse of the elderly across the United States today has become almost commonplace, a recent investi-

Rep. Claude D. Pepper, who is proposing stronger legislation against abuse, visits elderly resident of nursing home.

Shephard Sherbell/Picture Group

gation by PARADE has found. Most of the abuse of the aged is by members of their own families. Rep. Claude D. Pepper (D., Fla.), who is himself 84 years old, calls the situation "a frightful national disgrace."

Ties the lead to the body by showing the prevalence of the problem in all parts of society. ——   Our inquiry found that more than a million men and women 65 and over are seriously mistreated—physically, psychologically and financially—every year. Such abuse, we learned, happens in all classes of society, in big cities and small, in suburbs and on farms.

Shows the source for the information in the story. ——   Some of the examples of abuse are hard to believe, yet all have been documented. They are based on a continuing six-year investigation by a subcommittee of the House Select Committee on Aging, which obtained statistics from police departments, hospitals and social-service organizations in all 50 states. In addition, I talked with more than 100 federal, state and local officials, law-enforce-

(continued)

11.2 (continued)

Some gripping examples, with a summary of the types of abuse.

ment officers, physicians, psychologists and social workers involved in the care of the elderly.

One out of every 25 old people is abused. Examples ranged from a 39-year-old Illinois woman who chained her 81-year-old father to a toilet and tortured him for several days, to an 8-year-old who beat his 81-year-old grandmother, urged on by his parents. Abuse can take the form of assault, neglect, deprivation, even rape. The average victim is 75 or older and, more often, a woman. Most victims must rely on others—generally, those who abuse them—for care, food and shelter.

Quote gives some idea of why such a prevalent problem has gone unnoticed, obviously answering a question readers might be asking themselves at about this point.

"Until now," says Representative Pepper, "no one has really recognized how widespread this terrible problem is. The truth is that no one wanted to recognize it. We ignored it because it was just too horrible to accept. We didn't want to believe that things like this could take place in a civilized nation."

Getting into the problem, the writer poses the question that readers also want an answer for.

How does it happen? The bond between parent and child might be seen as the fundamental link in society. How can it be rent so terribly?

Quote from an authority.

"We Americans have always abused our old people," says Dr. Suzanne K. Steinmetz, a professor of individual and family studies at the University of Delaware. Dr. Steinmetz, who warned the House committee six years ago about the growing menace, told me: "You can find case after case of elderly abuse in the court records of the 17th and 18th centuries. We have a tendency to physical violence. It has become second nature with many families. They are violent with old people as well as children.

"The situation is getting worse because people are living longer and are not economically productive anymore. Their families have to care for them and don't know how. Many lose control out of frustration."

Another authority.

Howard Segars, clinical director of Guardianship Services in Brookline, Mass., has made a study of the causes of abuse of the elderly. "Resentment at having to tend to a frail, bedridden, incontinent parent can push some people to the breaking point," he explains. "The situation can cause frustration, anger and resentment and can trigger some awful form of abuse. These people really want to do right by their parents, but they cannot cope with all the emotional and financial stress placed on them. Obviously, their early relationship with their parents can contribute to the tensions too." Segars stresses, however, that many people find fulfillment in caring for elderly parents.

Summary graph of information from a number of experts. —— Other experts say alcoholism, drug addiction, marital problems and long-term financial difficulties contribute most in leading people to abuse their parents. The son is the most likely abuser, accounting for about 21 percent of all cases, followed by the daughter and the victim's spouse who is providing care.

Information and examples gathered from the research. These "little stories" within a story help break the monotony of facts and spur reader interest. —— Significantly, people who were abused as children are most likely to mistreat their parents when they grow old.

Last July, Los Angeles newspapers reported that a middle-aged man and his sister, Michael and Nadine Pensis, had been arrested for holding their 90-year-old aunt a prisoner for four years in a metal shed behind their house. The neighbors ignored her cries for help because the sister said she was crazy.

Sexual abuse of old people also is all too common. A 74-year-old woman in New Jersey was beaten and raped by her son-in-law. The woman's daughter demanded that her mother keep silent about it. "I'm warning you," she said. "You won't have a home to sleep in if you say anything about this."

Risa Breckman, director of the Elder Abuse Project of the New York City Victim Services Agency, says that much rape of old people goes unreported. "Victims are reluctant to say, 'My child raped me,' and old men and women are not routinely checked for rape in hospitals," she explains. "There are two myths. One is

(continued)

11.2 (continued)

that rape has to do with sex. The other is that 65-year-old women no longer have any sexuality, so they can't get raped. Well, the truth is that women 65 years and older are often raped—and by members of their families."

Neglect is another form of abuse. An 84-year-old woman in Washington, D.C., terminally ill with cancer, was denied proper medical attention by her grandson because he didn't want to "dissipate" her income and property on hospital and doctors' bills.

The daughter and son-in-law of an elderly woman in New Jersey left her at home all day without food. One day, she fell and lay on the floor with a broken hip for eight hours. The daughter confessed that she wanted her mother to die. "It would make our life a lot easier," she declared.

Some old people are subjected to intense psychological abuse by their relatives. This can run from simple verbal assaults to a protracted and systematic effort to dehumanize, sometimes with the intention of driving an old person to insanity or suicide.

William Delahunt, district attorney of Norfolk County, Mass., tells of a woman in Quincy whose family ostracized her. "They ordered her out of the kitchen when the rest of the family ate," says Delahunt. "They instructed her to stay in her bedroom and not associate with the family. They told her she was not wanted. She ended up in tears on the steps of a church. A police officer eventually brought her to a city shelter."

Hundreds of cases of financial exploitation by relatives or caretakers also have been documented. An ailing Florida man was swindled out of a 40-acre orange grove by a nephew whom he trusted. The nephew fed him liquor with his medications, then threatened him physically until he signed. The old man had only his Social Security pension left. "I guess I signed too many papers," he said. "I still fear for my life."

Saddest of all are the cases of elderly people who have lived independently until illness or injury landed them in the hospital. Upon release, they learn to their dismay that their families have sold their homes out from under them. Some family members also have had relatives committed to mental institutions or placed in nursing homes as a means of obtaining their property.

In addition, thousands have been fleeced of their Social Security, disability and welfare benefits by crooked operators of boarding homes. "We see case after case where old people have to beg the boarding home operators for their own money," says Jack D'Ambrosio, New Jersey Ombudsman for the Institutionalized Elderly. "The operators use the money to control the old people. They punish them by depriving them of money if they don't perform jobs around the house that the operators insist they do—work that they should not have to do because Social Security is already paying for their maintenance."

Some boarding-home operators have been guilty of violence and neglect toward their aged residents as well. Last March, Chicago social workers had to saw through rusty steel bars to rescue eight gaunt, hungry old people from a boarding home strewn with human excrement and overrun by rats. Chicago newspapers reported that the old people were jammed into tiny rooms with coffee cans as urinals. The proprietor allegedly made the residents turn over their welfare checks to her. She was arrested.

This section tells why the abuse goes undetected.

Complicating the problem of abuse is the fact that elderly people seldom report incidents to authorities. More than 70 percent of all cases are reported by third parties. Old people apparently are ashamed to say that they've been abused by their own children, don't want to cause trouble for their children or simply are afraid.

Many state officials admit that the elderly are not adequately protected. On average, state governments devote merely 6.6 percent of their protective-services budgets to this group. A few states, however, provide the

(continued)

11.2 (continued)

elderly with better defenses against abuse.

For example, New Jersey's Office of Ombudsman for the Institutionalized Elderly, established in 1978, is the strongest of its kind in the nation. It has subpoena power and the right to enter any institution for the elderly 24 hours a day. New Jersey also recently enacted a law that requires doctors, nurses, social workers and other professionals to report any serious, unexplained bruise on an elderly person as well as any other sign of abuse. Failure to report can bring a $500 fine. South Carolina has a law that makes failure to report elderly abuse punishable by six months' imprisonment and/or a $1000 fine.

Delaware's Dr. Steinmetz says the one hope is for government agencies to provide counseling *and* financial help to families caring for aged parents.

Some local organizations are making a start. The Family Service Association of Santa Clara Valley in California is pioneering in the prevention of abuse by furnishing counseling to people who are under extreme stress while trying to care for an old person. The Veterans Administration hospital in nearby Palo Alto is helping by admitting aged veterans for week-long stays. This gives their families a respite from the endless, nerve-racking strain of caring for them.

Representative Pepper fears that the problem of elderly abuse will grow as the number of old people increases. By 1983, the number of people aged 65 and over had risen to more than 27 million. By the year 2000, it will be close to 35 million. "The more older people we have," warns Pepper, "the greater will be the incidence of elderly abuse—unless we take steps now to curb it."

Problem pieces need to offer hope and some solutions. This piece closes with both.

He proposes a six-point program:
1. Congress must enact legislation providing funds and directing every state to establish specific programs to protect its elderly.
2. Each state should enact an abuse-

reporting law with teeth in it and give an ombudsman power to protect the aged.

3. All states must insure that personnel at institutions for the elderly are qualified—that they don't have criminal records or histories of mental illness.

4. Prosecutors must move with all their resources against abusers of the elderly.

5. Judges must hand down stiff penalties to offenders, not slaps on the wrist.

6. Most important, Americans must stop denigrating the elderly. Children should be taught to respect old people for their insight, judgment and experience.

How to Spot a Victim

How do you recognize an elderly victim of abuse?

Dr. George Cornell, director of the emergency room at the New York Hospital-Cornell Medical Center in New York City, says: "There are many clues to look for. Bad bruises, black eyes and broken bones, for instance. And burns. It's astonishing how often abusers burn defenseless old people. If the old person does not have a convincing explanation for his injuries, you certainly may suspect elderly abuse."

Adds Dr. Cornell: "If an old person complains that he is constantly harassed by his family, cursed at, told that he's going crazy when he knows he is perfectly sane, you can be suspicious. He may well be the victim of deliberate psychological abuse."

What should you do about it?

"Call your local department of social services," suggests Dr. Edmund Dejowski, director of Project Focus, a federally financed program to improve protective services for endangered adults. "Tell them you'd like to report a case of elderly abuse. You may not even be required to give your name."

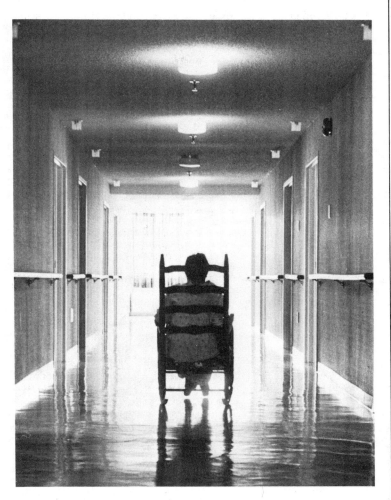

Financial exploitation is common: Family members often will place elderly relatives in nursing homes or mental institutions, then sell their homes. Photo: Peter Menzel/Stock, Boston.

Project Focus has information concerning services for adults who may need protection. Send a stamped, self-addressed envelope to: Project Focus, Dept. P, FAS, Room 9438, 60 Hudson St., New York, N.Y. 10013.

Where to Write

If you wish to contact the House Select Committee on Aging in connec-tion with the proposed legislation, write: Rep. Claude D. Pepper, Dept. P, Room 715, House Annex 1, House of Representatives, Washington, D.C. 20515.

Reprinted with permission of Donald Robinson and *Parade Magazine*.

Personality sketch or profile.   These pieces focus on accomplishments, attitudes and characteristics that make an individual stand out. Some writers make a distinction between the *personality sketch* and the *profile.* The sketch attempts to convey a sense of the total person, with emphasis on overall achievements, lifestyle and philosophy (see 11.3). The profile, usually a magazine piece, now depends a great deal on photographs to tell the story. Often it examines only one or two aspects of the person in depth, because profiles are generally based on news pegs. Public relations writers rely on the news peg to place profiles of their organization's leaders.

Magazines and lifestyle and entertainment sections of newspapers use personality pieces frequently (see 11.4). Some television programs, like *Entertain-*

11.3 Feature Obit: Personality Sketch

This unusual obit, similar to one mentioned in Chapter 5, is a personality sketch as well as an obituary.

Fort Worth man faced tough life, hard death

By Tom Anderson
Star-Telegram Writer

They called him the mayor of Vaughn Boulevard.

For much of his life, 46-year-old Philip Elwell faced the hardships of polio and epilepsy with a smile. He never considered anyone he met a stranger, friends said.

Elwell died Sunday night when fire swept through his room in the house he shared with a southeast Fort Worth family who had taken him in.

Fire investigators said Elwell apparently suffered an epileptic seizure shortly before midnight and dropped a cigarette in bed. Flames and smoke spread so quickly that members of the Jessie Watkins family, with whom Elwell lived at 800 Verbana St., were unable to save him.

Firefighters found his body against the bedroom door. His weight, plus the heavy smoke, kept the Watkins family from getting in, investigators said.

"They could hear Mr. Elwell, but they couldn't get to him," said fire department spokesman Butch Hall.

Arson investigator D.M. Eubanks agreed. "There was just so much

smoke in that room, they couldn't get to him."

Elwell's death was Fort Worth's 14th fire fatality of 1986, compared with 11 for all of 1985.

Life was never easy for Elwell.

"He struggled through life with a number of physical handicaps, but he never met a stranger," said his brother, Robert Elwell of Arlington.

When Philip Elwell was 19 months old, he developed polio, and when he was in his 20s he began suffering epileptic seizures, his brother said.

Philip Elwell was the 1946 March of Dimes poster child in Corpus Christi.

When the Elwell brothers' father died in 1953, the boys were sent to the Masonic Home in Fort Worth.

Despite the aftereffects of polio, which made walking difficult, Elwell spent much of his free time pacing the streets in front of the home talking to residents and passers-by.

Bill Remmert, former dean of the Masonic school, dubbed Elwell the "mayor of Vaughn Boulevard" because of his outgoing personality.

"He'd get to know anybody who was around," Robert Elwell said of his brother. "He enjoyed people."

"He would spend his time just talking and being with people. He would go up to anybody and talk about anything."

Even with his outgoing personality, physical limitations made life difficult for Elwell.

"Everywhere you turned there was a barrier," his brother said. Once he enrolled in barber college, but he found the strain too much and he couldn't hold the shears properly, Robert Elwell said.

Philip Elwell had been living with the Watkinses for nine months, said the Rev. David Donovan of Missionary Baptist Church.

"This was their way of showing him some companionship," Donovan said.

Funeral arrangements for Elwell had not been completed this morning.

Hickson on Marple

By Jeffrey Ferry

Meeting Joan Hickson makes you wish you had the energy of an eighty-year-old. She sits, back erect and hands firmly clasped in her lap, with eyes darting about taking in the feverish activity of the BBC crew rushing in and out of the drawing room of this sumptuous fin-de-siècle London woman's club preparing another take of *Miss Marple*, and answers all my questions sharply, concisely, and usually with another question.

Yes, she finds it "very gratifying" that *Miss Marple* is such a success, currently being shown in thirty-six countries and about to be screened for 300 million viewers in China. But her opinion doesn't matter, she insists. What do *I* think of it?

She prefers doing theater to television. Which do *I* prefer?

She loved playing Broadway but finds American stars a bit "grand." Don't I think? Perhaps she's misunderstood something?

Never mind that this lady has been in far more plays in more countries than she can remember, and that her first appearance on a London stage goes back, almost unbelievably, to 1927—she wants to know what her interviewer (scarcely a twist of ribonucleic acid in his grandfather's eye in 1927) thinks.

Her modesty is as genuine as her manners are ladylike. Both are products of the days when an English education meant a deeply instilled devotion to excellence, along with an equally deeply instilled sense of humor.

"Don't just write it all down," she says with a polite insistence that recalls the bygone days when actresses were slightly daring ladies and journalists were learned gentlemen. "Tell me what you think. I want to know."

She prefers the live stage to television or movies ("Playing to an audience, that's the real acting"), but her greatest pleasure, she says, comes from the enormous variety of roles she's played. "I've been very lucky. I've got to play different ladies in all sorts of ages and all sorts of nationalities."

The critics attribute very little of her success to luck. Her role of Delia in Alan Ayckbourn's *Bedroom Farce* won her a Tony in 1979 (a fact she forgets to mention), and praise from a British newspaper as "our most valuable comedienne."

Will she act again when the current series of *Miss Marple* is completed? "Definitely. Something quite different, I hope."

Doesn't she find it remarkable that someone of eighty should be working so hard?

"Not at all. We had somebody at the National [London's National Theatre] who came in to do a Chekhov. She walked to the theater every day, did the show, then walked home. She never missed a single performance. And how old you do think she was? Ninety-four.

"In 1946," she recalls as her nonplussed interviewer struggles to evade a horde of overenthusiastic prop-movers and stage managers, "I played an Agatha Christie on the London stage. It wasn't really a terribly big success.

(continued)

11.4 Entertainment Personality Sketch

Notice the interview treatment here. In Chapter 7 we advised you not to inject yourself or the interview situation into the story. Well, sometimes rules are made to be broken. Look at the insight you get into Joan Hickson because the author of this sketch shares with you what she said to him: "Don't just write it all down. . . . Tell me what you think. I want to know."

> "But," she continues, hands still primly clasped, completely unperturbed by the mounting chaos fast closing in on her, "Agatha Christie sent me a letter. She said that she'd like to have lunch with me one day, but at the moment she was rather domestic and wasn't really up to it. At the end of the letter she said she hoped that one day I'd play Miss Marple.
>
> "Now I think that's really rather extraordinary. What do you think?"
>
> Well, I find the whole thing rather extraordinary. Really.
>
> Reprinted from *DIAL magazine* with permission from Jeffrey Ferry.

ment Tonight, focus on entertainment personalities, or other celebrities, like *Lifestyles of the Rich and Famous*, or newsmakers, like the *Today* show or *Good Morning America*.

Informative.   These zero in on the little known, the odd or unusual aspects of a subject. Often these stories are about a place or process or both, like "Dressing for the Ascot" or "The Fine Points of Bullfighting." A news peg may be involved in publishing such stories, but ordinarily they are "time copy," which means "anytime." If you're putting out a publication, for the public or for an organization, it's a good idea to have these around to fill a sudden news hole. Such stories are popular, for they provide the audience with information to tuck away for future reference. Like the news feature, informative features are often packaged with a main news story.

Historical.   Holidays are often the occasion for these pieces. Each year copy is generated about Christmas, Thanksgiving, Yom Kippur and other special days. Likewise, national events such as Labor Day, Memorial Day, the celebration of statehood, the anniversary of the founding of a major business, school or organization also inspire historical features. In the case of the state, business, school or organization, these pieces generally are originated by the public relations writer. Whether the writer is a newswriter or a public relations writer, the prime concern in preparing this feature is to make the historical chronicle relevant to a contemporary public.

Personal experience.   Many personal-experience features recount the accomplishments of an individual or group. The disabled Vietnam veteran who rolls across the state in a wheelchair to raise funds for charity, the junior high school student who spells *prestidigitator* and wins the county spelling bee and the chance to go on to the state competition—these are examples of stories that capture audience interest.

Descriptive.   These stories center on places people can visit or events they can take part in or enjoy as spectators. Almost every community has tourist spots, historic buildings or sites, recreational areas, pageants, festivals, unusual restaurants.

Such stories are cyclic: They can be written and rewritten almost every year, for there's always a new audience looking for places to go and things to do, or for a vicarious experience if they can't go and do. The purpose of these features is to provide specific facts: about the weather, costs, special events and the like. They're usually found in the travel and entertainment sections of newspapers and magazines and in the feature segments of radio and TV programs. A substantial number of them are generated by public relations writers.

How-to.   These are popular because people now have more leisure time, want to save money, and want to experience the thrill of creative work. Flower arranging, furniture building, improving your golf or tennis game, buying at discount stores, using home computers, installing solar systems—all have appeal. You are limited in how-to articles only by your own limitations in understanding the subject, and authorities can usually be found to provide the technical expertise. (A number of public relations writers prepare how-to features as product publicity. These abound in the food section of most newspapers and in the crafts sections of family and children's magazines.)

The secret to a successful how-to feature is in its reward for the audience. A project or a suggestion that's too complicated, too expensive or too time-consuming is likely to lose the audience.

Enterprise.   For lack of a better generic label, stories that don't fit any specific category are called enterprise features. "This and that" stories can be written about the everyday occurrences in our lives. You look at a fairly common situation but ask "Why?" and a story results. As you cook breakfast you may wonder why some people call the utensil a skillet and others refer to it as a frying pan. You're on the way to a feature about regional slang. Ideas can develop from something you read or heard on radio or TV or picked up in classes or casual conversations. The list is as long as your curiosity.

Advertising features.   Some features that are really advertising look so much like editorial matter that readers don't consciously discriminate (see 11.5). You've probably seen an enticing travel feature that you discovered when you reached the end, two or three pages later, was a cruise ship's ad. Or you've read something that looked like a health feature, only to find out it was really a pharmaceutical company's ad.

When John Fischer was editor of *Harper's* magazine, he turned down such an ad because it looked like an article and didn't identify the supplier of the copy or tell the readers the space was purchased. Many readers don't care. Some are savvy enough to make the assumption that advertising is going to mean some treatment occasionally editorially anyway. In some publications, their suspicions are correct, as with stories on performance tests of new cars. Editors defend these by saying the story comes first. The advertising staff tells

weekend at macy's

A Parisian street on a rainy day, a pensive moment in a garden, the arrival of a train at the station—these are the everyday scenes painted by a small group of French artists just over a century ago. The seemingly innocent works those artists created and showed in eight exhibitions between 1874 and 1886 changed not only the history of art, but also the ways we see and understand the world around us. We call them the Impressionists. The M. H. de Young Museum is pleased to present "The New Painting: Impressionism 1874-1886," an extraordinary exhibition of 150 Impressionist paintings, opening today through July 6. The exhibition brings together a selection of paintings chosen by the Impressionists themselves and shown in the legendary original eight shows: "The New Painting" includes among its masterworks paintings by Cezanne, Degas, Gauguin, Pissarro, Renoir, Cassatt, Seurat and Monet. It also includes superb works by many of the lesser known artists who exhibited with the group. For the Impressionists, painting was no longer objective rendering in somber tones. These new artists sought realism in a startling way, by painting impressions of natural light in loose brush strokes and brilliant colors. Their choice of subject was no less unorthodox than their technique, for they portrayed ordinary people in ordinary circumstances and often painted them from unusual vantage points. Tickets for the exhibition are 6.00. Order tickets from the Museum at (415) 893-4444 or through BASS Ticket Center 762-BASS.

Meet Joanie Greggains of Macy's! Creator and star of "Morning Stretch," America's most popular and longest running TV exercise show, Joanie will be in the Bodywear Department, 1st floor, Macy's West, Saturday, April 26 at 1 p.m. Her latest workout videotapes will be available for purchase, 20.00. Have her autograph your tape! She is hosting the Third Annual City Sports magazine's Aerobics Expo, being held Sunday, April 27 at the Hyatt Regency. Pre-register for classes and workshops by calling (415) 762-BASS.

Macy's celebrates the newly expanded and renovated Dress department with a fashion show. See the best of spring and summer '86 Friday, April 25 at 12:30, 2nd floor Macy's San Francisco. You'll meet designer Karen Alexander and see her newest collection. You'll see dresses in impressionistic prints, body conscious shapes, designs influenced by exotic cultures, the elegant "Chanel" look and much more. Macy's Corte Madera is host to a fashion show of dresses, April 26, 2 p.m., 2nd floor.

THE GREAT SAN FRANCISCO BIKE ADVENTURE

Sign on for a day of cycling and celebration, June 8. Starting at 7:30 a.m. from the Presidio of San Francisco, you'll bike 20 of the most beautiful miles in the world of a friendly, enjoyable pace. Then meet for refreshment, prizes and entertainment at the Great Meadow of Fort Mason. You might win a 15-day bike tour of the wine country! Pick up an entry form at Macy's Customer Service areas at all Macy's. Be a volunteer ride marshal. Call (415) 393-3199. The Great San Francisco Bike Adventure is sponsored by Macy's California and KNBR-68 in association with California Bicyclist Magazine to benefit the Golden Gate Council of American Youth Hostels.

The African Children's Choir—30 boys and girls ages 5-12 from Uganda, East Africa—will perform Monday, April 21, 12:30-1:00, on the first floor stage of Macy's San Francisco West. The children, who are orphans, are here to bring attention to the plight of Ugandan children and to raise money for an orphanage. For more information, call 587-5028. Come hear this delightful concert Monday at Macy's.

Reprinted with permission of Macy's California.

11.5 Advertising Feature

Readers are not deceived by this ad's feature format, which has the look of a lifestyle section.

the car company when the story will run so they can buy advertising space to accompany the story.

Broadcast commercials have even adopted the mini-feature approach. These commercials tell a story, generally without words until the end. They show someone or people moving through different experiences, and the viewer is allowed to involve his or her imagination in creating the story line. This approach was Madison Avenue's response to "zapping," fast-forwarding through or cutting out the commercials with VCR controls.

WRITING THE FEATURE

A feature usually attempts to involve the reader emotionally in some way. As a feature writer, you will draw on the human-interest elements of pathos, drama, curiosity, humor. You strive for identification on the part of your audience. You want someone to say, "How would I feel if my grandmother were being abused?" or "What would I do if my dog almost drowned?" For that reason, humor is gentle; you laugh with, not at, the victims of the situation.

Creativity

Features dispel the notion held by so many beginning reporters that newswriting cramps creativity.

Don't confuse creativity with flamboyance, though. Creativity involves using all the writing and reporting skills you have to craft a story that probes under the surface, reveals the unknown, the unusual, the unique. Overwriting, hyperbole and imprecise language have no place in a feature story.

Think of a recent film or television program that you really enjoyed. Summarize the plot in your mind. Chances are that the plot summary is really rather simple, perhaps even dull. What made the film or TV program exciting and rewarding was a writer's creativity. The writer found an unusual approach to a simple story and then embellished it. You create a feature in much the same way, with an original angle, the discriminating use of facts and interesting language.

Structure

A feature is seldom written in the traditional inverted-pyramid pattern. It often is written in a chronological format, much as a story is told. The main point, always in the lead of a news story, may be withheld until the end as a climax when the feature is told in a narrative fashion like a joke or anecdote. In that case, the lead is a partial summary. You tell just enough about the story to attract interest and give just enough information so the story line can be followed easily.

You have to organize carefully. First decide what the theme is. Then carefully outline the subpoints so they will support the theme. The good feature requires as much organization as the straight news story, for the feature has to flow smoothly. News stories can be cut without severely damaging the sense, but generally all the parts of a feature story must be kept intact if it is to succeed. A good test is to cut paragraphs from the body of a feature. If the story doesn't suffer from the cut, then the graphs probably aren't necessary. In the well-planned story, every paragraph—every sentence—should add to the total effect.

Lead.   The lead must attract immediate attention and pull the reader into the story. Leads can vary in style and content. You can use description, narration (11.1), dialogue, questions, call to action (11.2), unusual statements (11.3), comparison–contrast. The question lead is just like the news story question lead, and the dialogue lead is often used in literary journalism. It begins much like a play, with two "characters" or "actors" in the story talking to each other.

Transitions.   No matter how good the lead is, you need a solid transition into the body of the feature. If you think of the lead as a lure to attract the audience, the transition sets the hook. It makes the reader want to continue. And it promises some kind of satisfaction or reward. The reward can be entertainment, information or self-awareness—but has to be something of value to the readers.

Body.   Sound knowledge of the subject, coupled with good writing skills, will let you take the reader through a variety of experiences. You should use the standard writing devices of crisp dialogue, documentable but vivid fact and detail, careful observation, suspense and, if appropriate, plot.

Conclusion.   The conclusion should give the reader a sense of satisfaction. You need to tie the conclusion to the lead so the story has unity. Often you can do this through a short, tight summary. Occasionally, you can conclude with an anecdote or a quote that sums up the substance of the story. With a narrative approach, you build toward a climax.

William L. Rivers, a prolific writer and journalism scholar, sums up the relationship between the beginning and the ending of a feature story thus:

Experienced writers can often spot the ending to an article among the interviews, notes, and other material they have gathered before even writing the lead. A good ending can even suggest a lead, or give the writer a sense of the direction in which the article is heading. There is a pitfall, however, in saving an item that appears to be a good ending—sometimes a good ending is really a good beginning in disguise. Writers must learn to tell the difference.[3]

Length   Feature stories can be of any length. Examine any newspaper or magazine, or listen to any radio or TV station and you'll note the range.

Editors and news directors want this variety. In the case of a newspaper, a hole in the page may require a short item. The same is true on radio or TV. A hole in the newscast can be plugged with a short feature—almost a filler.

Short feature fillers that have a light touch (sometimes called *brites*)—a bit of humor, something heartwarming—are particularly welcome in the newsroom. (Example 11.6 is a brite; regular readers of the *Wall Street Journal* know to look in the same place on the front page every day for a bit of humor.) Brites often have what is called an "O. Henry ending"—a surprise conclusion typical of that writer's short stories.

Today's computerized typesetting, with its pagination and automatic calculation of story length, has reduced the need to fill holes on a news page. Even so, the brief filler–feature is popular, for it gives the reader a break from the more serious straight news that dominates the page, and it helps add visual variety to the page.

Longer features are equally popular. In newspapers, they may be accompanied by photographs or artwork. As you work on a feature, think about possible illustrations or photographs to complement the story. For TV features, the visuals generally tell most of the story.

11.6 Brite

Personals: young bachelor seeks sensitive moose to share tiny isle

By Jacquie McNish
Staff Reporter of the Wall Street Journal

In the fall, a young moose's fancy turns to thoughts of love. And that's a problem on Bell Island.

This spot of land off the eastern coast of Canada has a population of 4,000 people and one moose. But some farmers and their cows suddenly think that's one moose too many. Thus the big question these days among Bell Islanders: Do we ship our moose out or ship another moose in?

Belle or Bill?

The current moose population, whose name is Bill, swam three miles out to Bell Island five years ago from the bigger island of Newfoundland.

In those days Bill was a cute little calf. "Everyone thought it was female, so we called it Belle," recalls Walter Tucker, mayor of Wabana, the island's only town. "Then it began to grow antlers."

Bill is now a 1,000-pound bull moose and, for the first time since he arrived, is observing the autumn moose-mating season. Early last month, two local farmers proposed that Bill be tranquilized and taken off the island because he was paying too much attention to their cows.

"They bunch up in little groups and roam the pasture when he gets close," says Henry Crane, a farmer who worries that cattle don't eat properly when Bill is around. The waist-high fence that surrounds the island's community cattle pasture affords little protection from a gamboling moose. Confides Mayor Tucker, "Seemingly, he tried to molest one cow."

But the mayor and others want to keep Bill on the island. The moose is Bell Island's biggest pet, and residents like to see him strolling down their streets and poking into their back yards. "He's a darling; we don't want to give him up," a spokeswoman for the town council says.

Like his cows, Mr. Crane is hard pressed to find anything cute about the enormous mammal. "How can you be fond of a big moose? They don't realize the danger that's involved."

Can You Spare a Moose?

Nevertheless, the council would rather have two moose than no moose at all, so it has asked officials in Newfoundland to airlift a lady moose to the island. The townspeople hope she will take Bill's mind off the cows. Newfoundland, with about 70,000 moose, is pondering the matter.

Mr. Crane argues the town council is ignoring the probable consequences of turning two moose loose on an island that's only nine miles long.

"We really don't know what we'll do if they start having babies," acknowledges Mr. Tucker.

Language Generally the language of features is simple, even when dealing with medical or scientific subject matter. Occasionally a story benefits from beginning with a literary or historical allusion. The writer has to be sure in choosing this approach that the allusion is familiar and appropriate, not strained or contrived. Literary techniques—metaphors and similes, narration and dialogue—can be used as well, but you must be sure that such techniques contribute and are not mere ornaments.

Symbols are used a great deal in feature writing. A person or an incident is chosen to represent a problem or a situation. For this reason, the present tense is used often in features. It creates a sense of ongoing activity. A story about a children's creative center starts this way:

> Six-year-old Scott Wattley sits in the middle of his classroom coloring pictures that he has just traced. "These are vegetables," he says, pointing to the carrot, cabbage and asparagus. "Legumbres—I can say them in Spanish, too."
> Across the room, Jade Burrowes, 5, is identifying pictures whose names contain the short "i" sound. "Bib, hit, fin, wig," she says, looking down the row of words she has spelled in plastic letters. "This is easy."[4]

These children represent all of the children, many from disadvantaged backgrounds, who are realizing high IQs from this creative learning environment.

BROADCAST FEATURES In broadcast news, the definition of a feature is almost always a story on the lighter side: "soft news." Studies have shown that audiences like features as an escape from the bad news of the day.

Features are more common in TV than in radio. Many TV reporters get feature assignments on a regular basis. In larger TV newsrooms, one reporter may be assigned full time to nothing but feature stories.

Broadcast writers look for the humorous, the cute, the offbeat or the heartwarming when selecting a story to do as a feature. In TV, they also look for ideas that will result in good pictures (see 11.7).

All stations keep "features files." However, the demands of covering the hard news often limit the number of local features each TV or radio station can do each day or week. Because of that fact, syndicated features have become popular. A large number of them are now available for both radio and TV; they run the gamut of topics and types. Here's a sampling of some of the topics of syndicated radio and TV features:

Health	Consumer buying	Home repair
Investments	Gardening	Advice for women
Employment	Car repair	Child rearing
Pet care		

Some of these features have public relations origins. Public relations people also generate their own video features. For example, Pacific Gas and Electric Company has a nine-person full-time video staff, and they call on three others in the organization's news services department who have TV experience. In

11.7 Television Feature

Television features have the same purpose as newspaper or magazine features—to capture audience attention and to provide them with something they may be unaware of, to inform them, or to provide them with a chuckle.

ANNCR. (CAT)

ROLL SONY TAPE SILENT VO
RUNS :47

AND NOW A TALE OF A MOOSE ON THE LOOSE . . . FOR AWHILE.
THESE ARE NOT THE WOODS OF NORTHERN NEW HAMPSHIRE OR MAINE . . . WHERE MOOSE ARE SUPPOSED TO BE. THIS IS A LITTLE WOODED AREA NEAR DOWNTOWN LOWELL, MASSACHUSETTS . . . WHERE MOOSE SHOULDN'T BE. IT'S UNNATURAL FOR MOOSE AND MAN TO MIX . . . EVEN LESS NATURAL FOR MOOSE AND MOTORISTS TO MINGLE.

SOT UP FOR :08

(SOUNDBITE :08)

IN: "CAR WHAT'D YOU:"
OUT: "PARKING LOT"
  SONY SIL/VO CONT.

OUT: ("PARKING LOT")

IT'S THOUGHT THE MOOSE MAY HAVE STRAYED DOWN TO MASSACHUSETTS IN SEARCH OF A MATE. TWO TRANQUILIZERS WERE FIRED, BUT THEY ONLY STUNNED THE MOOSE ON THE BANK OF A CANAL. AND THEN . . .

(CAT . . . PAUSE)

(PAUSE)

  SONY SIL/VO CONT.

HE WAS FISHED OUT, TIED UP, DRIED OFF AND SENT TO MORE SUITABLE SURROUNDINGS IN NEW HAMPSHIRE.

From WOWT-TV, Omaha, Nebraska. Used with permission.

---

a single year, PG&E produced about 100 video programs that were seen by most of the 30,000 employees and many of the 10 million people in their area. They duplicated and distributed 15,000 copies of their programs in 1985 alone.[5]

PR is often the source of the community calendar features that are the staple of local stations. "What to do this weekend" types of features on Thursdays or Fridays each week are also popular, especially in TV newscasts.

Broadcast sports departments do a lot of features, and sportscasters are always on the lookout for new and different sports feature ideas.

Features can be written and produced and then kept on the shelf until needed. Many larger broadcast newsrooms build up a backlog of these features, then insert them in newscasts as fillers or when they tie in to news stories of the day.

THE MARKETPLACE

By adding more detail, feature writers can place their stories in regional or national publications and stations. If you work for a newspaper or broadcast station, your feature has a good chance of being picked up by a news or feature service. Print and broadcast services are always looking for good feature copy, particularly stories that give readers a chuckle or make them feel good about something. A considerable amount of feature copy is used around holidays—Thanksgiving, Christmas and Hanukkah, Valentine's Day, Fourth of July. Exceptionally good features are often reprinted. Credit lines for local reporters appear in *Reader's Digest*, for instance.

If you are in public relations, you will want to get the feature placed where it will do the most good for your organization. If a national publication does take your story, though, you can't get paid for the piece. So some public relations people are willing to work closely with freelance writers in developing a piece rather than spending the time on it themselves: The freelancer can get paid. Since placing stories is part of the PR writer's job, accepting a fee would be unethical.

Public relations features appear regularly in publications that have a PR origin: magazines like American Express's *Departures* for its credit card holders; association publications of trade, professional and general-membership groups; employee publications. Some public relations magazines, such as Chamber of Commerce city magazines, are for employees, members and sold on newsstands for the public as well.

Some advertising copy also appears in a feature format. Some magazines will not accept this type of advertising copy. Other publications not only accept feature material that is ad copy, as *Reader's Digest* does, but will even help to generate and package it, as *Esquire* does. Many readership studies have shown that while editorial personnel make sharp distinctions between advertising and editorial content, their readers don't.

WHAT IS A COLUMN?

A column is the ultimate in journalistic freedom. It lets the writer indulge in creative expression and personal opinion that would not be appropriate in any other kind of story. Columnists can pass judgments, make recommendations, talk about themselves and otherwise violate most of the accepted tenets of newswriting. Columnists can and do use the language any way they want to. Sometimes, in fact, their unconventional style becomes a signature, an identifying characteristic. Few can write like Jimmy Breslin. Copy editors handle columnists gingerly.

In broadcasting the counterpart to the political column in the newspaper is often the commentary. Here, too, the rules can be broken, and often are.

Columns are often features; they can be editorials, too. They are not intended to be "news" in the traditional sense. Political columnists do write about timely topics, but they are generally read for their personal presentation rather than the factual content.

Columnists have such freedom that the variety of column content is beyond classifying except in very general ways. Column topics can range from the philosophical to the whimsical. Columns can be subject-oriented, such as those on hobbies or crafts. Or the column can be a reflection of the writer's personality, offering humor, opinion, anecdotes.

The column always carries the writer's byline; it also may carry the writer's photograph. Columns appear at regular intervals and usually in the same location in the publication so loyal readers will know where to find them.

And columnists do inspire fierce loyalty, especially sports columnists, many of whom command top dollar because of the sizable audience they can deliver. One disgruntled, maybe jealous, reporter complained that sports columnists for newspapers were now offering options on their talents each season and dealing through agents for six-figure contracts. In major metropolitan markets, that's only a slight exaggeration.

The other stars among local columnists are the entertainment and society columnists. They have name and face recognition and get their phone calls returned—even by the rich and famous.

Unlike features, which usually require considerable background and experience, columns can be written by the newest member of the staff. You need creativity, ambition and a conviction that what you have to say is interesting to others. You also have to persuade an editor to give you a try.

WRITING THE COLUMN

Do you have a special interest that intrigues you, motivates you and consumes at least some part of your leisure (and perhaps academic) time? Is it something you know more about than anyone around you? You could become a columnist.[6]

Getting started

Finding the topic is a starting point, but editors want evidence that you can write uniformly good copy over a period of time. They can't afford writers whose work begins to weaken after 15 or even 50 pieces. To build a reputation, and to test your endurance, you might begin writing a column for your school paper or a local weekly. If you're any good, other publications in the area may request permission to reprint some of your pieces. And if your work has appeal for a wide range of readers, you have a chance of being looked at by still other publications and even syndicates.

Style

The successful columnist is one who has developed a personal style. No formula exists for cultivating this, but here are some general principles:

- *Look at the ordinary from a different vantage point.* Give it a twist or turn it upside down.

- *Use humor.* Erma Bombeck and Art Buchwald both depend on interpreta-

Erma Bombeck, seen here with her dog Murray, is one of the most successful syndicated columnists in the U.S. A prolific writer, Bombeck has created a number of popular best-sellers, and many of her writings have inspired films and TV series.

tions of events to create humor. Russell Baker employs allegory. Other writers use amusing anecdotes and exaggerate for comic effect.

- *Express private thoughts.* Let the public know that you share their concerns, pleasures and fears.

- *Personalize your column.* Use specific names, places, events. Let readers identify with you as you wander through the community. Share ideas that you've picked up during workouts or tennis or social events.

- *Be creative.* Experiment with words and their meanings. Play with sentence and paragraph structure. Build images. Be descriptive.

- *Use dramatic elements.* Study good storytellers. Learn how to build suspense to a climax.

- *Borrow techniques from fiction.* Description and dialogue can re-create scenes and sharpen story lines.

- *Sharpen your vocabulary*. Search for precise words. Don't be content with coming close in the meaning of a word or sentence. Take the extra time with your writing to be exact.

- *Learn to listen to others*. Careful observation and keen perception result in evocative writing. Ask questions and probe others' interests.

- *Write for others*. Though the subjects you choose are your own, your responsibility is to please your audience.

Structure   Pointing out the different structures of columns may seem a useless exercise, since column writing is so individual. However, six basic formats recur:

Q&A.   The questions come from readers and the answers are supplied by the columnist, generally from his or her expertise, although some advice columnists often either cite or refer to other sources. The style can vary significantly.

Grab bag.   Some columns are a collection of events coming up, awards handed out, gossip and anything else too small for a headline. However, many newspapers are abandoning these for a thematic grab bag (see 11.8). A good example is the *Wall Street Journal's* Business Reports column on page 1.

Anecdote.   Columns built around a single anecdote resemble a mini-feature. Many of these also have the characteristics of personal essays.

11.8 Grab Bag Column

Kudos for Kalb

By Eleanor Randolph
Washington Post Staff Writer

The recipient of this year's top service award from the National Association of Government Communicators is no longer a government communicator.

Bernard Kalb, who resigned in protest Wednesday as chief spokesman for the State Department, was chosen almost two months ago to receive the award Nov. 7.

But does Kalb's abrupt departure, because of reports that the administration had undertaken a "disinformation" campaign, cause problems for the organization?

"Absolutely not," said Brenda Curtis-Heiken, immediate past president of the organization and a member of the Agriculture Department radio service.

"Now, he's like our hero," she said. "What he did in our minds makes him the ultimate communicator.

"We are the government information people who put out press releases and strive very hard to be fair and accurate and truthful," said Curtis-Heiken of the 1,000-member organization. "But, as you know and as he knows, it gets harder and harder every year."

Reprinted with permission of The Washington Post.

Feature.   A feature, usually a profile, is a common column format. The difference between this and a regular feature is the longer length of the regular feature (sometimes 2,500 words), and, sometimes, personal involvement of the columnist indicated by use of personal pronouns (see 11.9).

11.9 Feature Column

The press conference: an industry of 'events'

By Neil Henry
Washington Post Staff Writer

Narrative, to get you involved. Notice the number of literary devices—simile, description, dialogue. ___ Retired lieutenant general Daniel O. Graham looked like a bantamweight fighter on the podium in Room 562 of the Dirksen Senate Office Building, a feisty guy with one hand shoved deeply into a pocket of his blue suit and the other gesturing sharply toward the ceiling.

The television lights were burning. The cameras were rolling. Fifty or so reporters were scribbling notes. The subject: President Reagan's Strategic Defense Initiative (SDI), otherwise known as "Star Wars."

"We can be ready to deploy the system within 7½ years at a total cost of $30 billion," the white-haired figure gruffly declared. "Strategically, it's *far* better than the nuclear nudity we live in today."

Canons clicked. Pencils continued to scribble. Then someone in the crowd looked up and whispered, "Did he really say that?"

"Just like Strangelove," came a soft reply.

Finally you see that you are at a press conference. ___ "There's nothing quite like a press conference to bring out the best and worst of the human intellect, The "Press Conference"—it comes in so many guises in this city. It can be an event, an experience, a theater of ideas. It can be serious, tense or riveting. It can be downright silly.

Comparison and contrast. ___ If San Francisco is the city of cable cars and Chicago the city of broad shoulders, then Washington must surely be the city of press conferences.

Here you get an idea of what the writer means by calling Washington the city of press conferences.

There are dozens here each week. The topics range from the all-too-weighty to the utterly ridiculous.

A few days ago, on the same morning that Graham, Sen. Ernest F. Hollings (D-S.C.) and Rep. Jack Kemp (R-N.Y.) spoke about "pellet clouds," "time lines" and "Space-Born Early Trajectory Defenses," others were talking to journalists about "Encyclopedias, East and West," "the Supergirl Seatbelt Educational Program" and "Opposition to the Contra Aid Bill," to name just a few of the 20 listed in the UPI daybook.

Washington manufactures press conferences as commonly as other cities manufacture steel, lumber or cars. But no section of Washington manufactures quite as many as Capitol Hill. In fact, the term "press conference" is something of an anachronism for what transpires there almost every day. Often a press conference amounts to nothing more than another soap box for a politician who wishes to vent his or her views, even if that view is of the press itself.

The writer takes you to one to see the action for yourself. This conference is compared to the one in the lead. The technique of comparison shows you how much alike the events are. Ludicrous events from both are juxtaposed so that you are made to wonder how any news could possibly come from such events —the author's point, of course.

"This is a very important event," Rep. Patricia Schroeder (D-Colo.) said as she stood in a circle of bright light before a small gathering of sleepy reporters who were scattered like sea gulls on a pier in Room 2257 of the Rayburn House Office Building. "It's had very little coverage and I want to know why."

No one answered.

"One hundred and thirty-eight people were arrested at a nuclear test site in Nevada. It got only an inch of coverage in *Time*. I want to know why. Seems like a new disinformation campaign to me."

That out of the way, Schroeder introduced astronomer Carl Sagan and others arrested last month during an antinuclear demonstration organized by a group called Physicians for Social Responsibility.

His arrest was "an act of conscience," Sagan said in his singular

(continued)

11.9 (continued)

baritone, describing how he crossed a white line in the highway, was led to a bus by Nevada State police, handcuffed, "booked in the desert," then released on his recognizance.

There ensued a remarkable discussion that proved an almost mirror image of the SDI press conference. In both, opening statements lasted more than 45 minutes, while the time reserved for questions and answers was less than 10.

In both, history was used as fodder for political argument. The same historical figures—Kennedy, Hitler and Stalin—and the same recent tragedies—Challenger and Chernobyl—were bandied about, all for the participants' respective—and opposing—causes.

"In 1963 President Kennedy announced the nuclear test ban treaty," said Sagan, a crane-like man, as he bent forward to speak into a microphone. "Today we have an historic opportunity . . . to do what the people in 1963 did."

Kemp, at the SDI press conference, recalled how Kennedy announced his plans to put an American on the moon. "President Kennedy energized the American population," he said. "SDI should energize the public today."

H. Jack Geiger, a New York physician who was arrested with Sagan, likened the present to the 1930s. "We will not make the same mistake as physicians in Germany did when they joined the Nazi Party," he said.

On the other side of Capitol Hill, Kemp harkened back to Nazi Germany as well. "There is a clear parallel between the buildup of Soviet offensive capability and the unheeded buildup of the German military in the 1930s," he said. "We cannot afford not to learn the lessons of history."

Were the topic of both press conferences not so deadly serious—the 60,000 nuclear warheads in the world and what to do about them—a witness would almost think he was watching a vision of reality furnished by Hollywood, a movie so astonishingly bad it had to be a joke.

11.9 (continued)

At one point, Graham, who heads a technical research outfit called High Frontier, used a pointer to go over an array of colorful hand-drawn charts that showed various space-based defense systems. These were simplistic drawings of missiles and satellites, all pointing out how well-protected the United States could be with an SDI umbrella.

"Next!" he barked to the smiling young woman handling the charts. "Ah, now this is my favorite. I like this very much. Pellets. A cloud of pellets. We can use these pellets to intercept the missiles."

But it was Sagan who delivered perhaps the finest words of the day. He was listening to Lester Grinspoon, a Harvard University Medical School psychiatrist, answer a question concerning the difficulty of mobilizing the American public around the issue of nuclear war.

Grinspoon, a slender, gray-haired man, tried his best. Using terms such as "maladaptive behavior" and "affective cognition," he pointed out that one of man's greatest survival tools was "the strong ego defense of denial."

The best line is saved for the last graph, just so you won't forget how senseless the conferences can be made to appear.

Sagan, looking on from a nearby chair, took advantage of a pause to recall a line from a song by the rock group Dire Straits. "Denial," he said, "ain't just a river in Egypt."

Reprinted with permission of *The Washington Post.*

Instructive. The tone may vary from the direct approach to a more casual, informal style. The directions are always carefully written to eliminate ambiguity, and writers often give the material an "idiot run" to be sure there are no steps missing. The types of instructive columns range from game columns, like bridge, to hobby columns, like sewing, to home repair and gardening (see 11.10). Sperry also has a Q&A call-in broadcast column.

Informative. The informative column can provide very detailed information, like a how-to, but without the one-two-three approach (see 11.11). Advice, recommendations, suggestions are given with illustrations to make a point clear.

11.10 Instructive Column

In the shade of the old (red) oak tree

By Neil Sperry

Nothing you put into the landscape will be so permanent as shade trees.

The wise gardener considers the options, then elects only the types best suited. To streamline your selection process, let's categorize trees into the several use groups. Know that each of these trees will do well in our part of Texas, but also seek the advice of your nurseryman. He can interpret your specific environmental and aesthetic situations.

Large shade trees

These will be the dominant trees in your landscape. They'll reach heights of 40 to 60 feet with similar spreads. Use them to enframe your house and as backdrops.

Red oaks are native to most of Texas, although there are many different species lumped into this category. Shumard red oaks are most common in the central part. They offer great fall color, bold dark-green foliage during the growing season and superior durability.

Bur oaks are much less common. Their rough bark and large shaggy leaves give them a coarse and dominant appearance. They, too, are native over much of the state.

Live oaks are shorter and more spreading, but they're still fine structural trees for the landscape. They are evergreen and are well suited to the poorer Texas soils. Many are dug for the nursery trade from the rocky soils of North Central Texas.

Pecans are among our largest native trees. If you're planting one in your landscape, consider the improved varieties Choctaw, Desirable and Kiowa. Mohawk makes a particularly lovely shade tree, but bearing diminishes with age.

Chinese pistachios grow in much the same rate and habit as red oaks. They, too, provide fine fall color. Though not native, they're certainly well adapted.

Upright shade trees

If the shape of your landscape is narrow but you still want a shade tree, these are your best possibilities. Each will grow at least two times as tall as the width.

Cedar elms are fairly upright at the outset and later round out. They are the one elm well suited to our landscapes. They're native over the central part of Texas and are resistant to common elm problems.

Sweet gums are native to East Texas' sandy soils, but they'll grow in neutral or alkaline clays if they're properly managed. Apply iron and sulfur soil acidifier regularly in those conditions. Because of their distinctly upright habit, sweet gums are commonly used in medians, parkways and between buildings for vertical shade.

Bald cypress trees live for centuries. While they may eventually be broad and rounded, for decades they remain pyramidal, like deciduous Christmas trees. Their texture is light and airy, and their color is a bright medium green.

Bradford pear, which also happens to be the only recommendable fast-growing shade tree, is fairly upright. Young trees quickly grow to their mature heights of 20 to 25 feet, then fill out and broaden to mature widths of 12 to 15 feet. Spring flower color is bright white and lovely. Fall foliage is brilliant. Summer foliage is deep green. The trees bear no fruit.

Small trees

These are the best choices for today's small urban lot sizes. Use these trees near entries, around patios and in other locations where space is quite limited.

Crape myrtles are available in all sizes and shapes, with flower colors including reds, pinks, purples and white. The standard varieties grow to 15 to 20 feet tall. They bloom all summer, with good fall foliage color as well.

Yaupon holly is our most popular small accent tree. It's native to Central Texas, and is noted for its fine winter fruit color (on female plants only). It is adapted to sun or shade. Container-grown plants may be somewhat smaller, but will re-establish quickly.

Japanese maples are fine small trees for mostly shaded areas. Their foliage is finely cut and is available either in purple or green shades. Mature heights range from three feet (novelty pot-types) to 15 feet. Fall color of this tree is excellent.

(A specialist in Texas horticulture, Neil Sperry writes this weekly feature especially for Tarrant County readers. Sperry has the top-rated weekend lawn and garden program on KRLD-radio, writes a syndicated newspaper column, publishes in numerous trade and professional journals and has a syndicated radio show.)

11.11 Informative Column

Portrait of an artist as FBI target

By Jack Anderson and Dale Van Atta

This is the portrait of Georgia O'Keeffe, the eminent artist, as painted by the Federal Bureau of Investigation during the Red scare of the 1950s. O'Keeffe, who died earlier this year at 98, was not just a reclusive, intense woman who broke new ground in American art, according to her FBI file. She was an outsider, living near the Los Alamos nuclear laboratory, whose politics did not "sound entirely American."

Though born in Wisconsin, O'Keeffe spent much of her life in New Mexico, where she found the inspiration and subject matter for the masterpieces that made her a major figure in the history of American art. Her studio in Abiquiu was about 20 miles north of Los Alamos.

Our associate Stewart Harris obtained the file on a three-month FBI probe.

The bureau began checking out the reclusive artist after receiving a complaint about her on Oct. 29, 1953. The informer, whose name was deleted from our copy of the FBI document under Privacy Act rules, told the bureau that O'Keeffe was the only person in Abiquiu who voted for Henry Wallace, the former vice-president and Progressive Party candidate for president in 1948. He did not say how he knew the contents of her supposedly secret ballot.

The informer further reported that, in a discussion with O'Keeffe, he had called Wallace a "Bolshevik." O'Keeffe replied, the informant related, that she believed in Wallace's policies, including his desire for closer relations between the United States and the Soviet Union.

"Also," the FBI wrote, "the subject [O'Keeffe] had made remarks which were not [in accord] with his line of thinking, and remarks that would not be made by loyal Americans." She is "ultra-liberal," the informer said, and "her political philosophy doesn't sound entirely American."

At the height of McCarthyism, this was enough to set the FBI on O'Keeffe's trail. A Nov. 16, 1953, memo from the Albuquerque FBI office to headquarters explained the threat O'Keeffe posed to national security.

"Due to the closeness of Abiquiu to Los Alamos, it is recommended that a case be opened and that the subject be checked out.

The investigation was approved, and diligent detective work soon turned up further horrors regarding the artist. She "frequently entertains guests of foreign extraction in her home," the agents reported.

Of particular interest to the FBI was a man of either Chinese or Filipino extraction who stayed in her house while O'Keeffe was visiting the Ghost Ranch, a resort operated by her friends and neighbors, Earl Vance and Arthur Pack.

The FBI was frustrated in its research on him. "No further information was available in Abiquiu," the FBI reported.

The agents never interviewed O'Keeffe about her foreign guests or the Oriental house-sitter, and the file was closed on Feb. 5, 1954, "until such time as information is received that is of a substantial nature." The final report states: "It is to be noted that the New York files and the [Albuquerque] bureau files failed to reflect any information of derogatory nature regarding [O'Keeffe]."

Humor. The purpose of a humor column usually is just to entertain (see 11.12), but the humor sometimes masks an attempt to persuade.

Public relations. Most public relations publications carry a column from the head of the sponsoring group—the organization's president or the executive director of the association.

Ad columns. Many advertising columns are opinion columns, like those in Chapter 14, but some are entirely promotional in content, imitating (like ad features) editorial style (see 11.13).

Execs put a lid on 'Tupperware Song'

By Dave Barry

I have just about given up on the Tupperware people. I've been trying to get them interested in a song I wrote, called *The Tupperware Song*, which I am sure would be a large hit. I called them about it two or three times a week for several weeks.

"You wrote a song?" they would say.

"Yes," I would say.

"About Tupperware?" they would say.

"Yes," I would say. "It's kind of a blues song."

"We'll have somebody get back to you," they would say.

For quite a while there I thought I was getting the runaround, until finally a nice Tupperware executive named Dick called me up. He was very honest with me. "There's a fairly limited market for songs about Tupperware," he said.

"Dick," I said. "This is a killer song." Which is true. It gets a very positive reaction whenever I perform it. Of course, I perform it only in those social settings where people have loosened up to where they would react positively if you set their clothing on fire, but I still think this song would have widespread appeal.

I wrote it a while back, when friends of mine named Art and Dave had a big Tupperware party in their apartment. It was the social event of the month. Something like 50 people showed up. When the Tupperware Lady walked in, you could tell right away from her facial expression that this was not the kind of Tupperware crowd she was used to. She was used to a subdued, all-female crowd, whereas this was a loud co-educational crowd with some crowd members already dancing on the refrigerator.

The Tupperware Lady kept saying things like: "Are you sure this is supposed to be a Tupperware party?" and "This doesn't look like a Tupperware party." She wanted to go home.

But we talked her into staying, although she never really accepted the fact that Art and Dave were her Tupperware hostesses. She wanted to deal with a woman. All of her communications with Art and Dave had to go through a woman interpreter:

Tupperware lady (speaking to a woman): Where do you want me to set up?

Woman (speaking to Art, who is standing right there): Art, where do you want her to set up?

Art: How about right over here on the coffee table?

Woman (to the Tupperware Lady): Art says how about right over here on the coffee table?

Tupperware lady: Fine.

Once we got everybody settled down, sort of, the Tupperware Lady wanted us to engage in various fun Tupperware party activities such as "brain teasers" wherein if we could name all the bodily parts that had three letters, we would win a free grapefruit holder or something. We did this for a while, but it was slowing things down, so we told the Tupperware Lady we had this song we wanted to perform.

The band consisted of me and four other highly trained journalists. You know what *The Tupperware Song* sounds like if you ever heard the song *I'm a Man* by Muddy Waters, where he sings about the general theme that he is a man, and in between each line the band goes Da-DA-da-da-DUM, so you get an effect like this:

Muddy Waters: I'm a man.

Band: Da-DA-da-da-DUM

Muddy Waters: A natural man.

Band: Da-DA-da-da-DUM

Muddy Waters: A full-grown man.

And so on. This is the general approach taken in *The Tupperware Song*, except it is about Tupperware. It starts out this way:

Some folks use waxed paper
Some folks use the Reynolds Wrap
Some folks use the plastic Baggie
To try to cover up the gap
You can use most anything
To keep your goodies from the air
But nothing works as well
As that good old Tupperware
(CHORUS)
'Cause it's here
Whooaaa
Take a look at what we got
If you don't try some and buy some
Don't blame me when your turnips rot.

It has two more verses, covering other important Tupperware themes. Verse 2 stresses the importance of "burping" the air out of your container to make sure your lid seals securely, and Verse 3 points out that you can make money by holding a Tupperware party in your home.

As you can imagine, the crowd was completely blown away by this song. The Tupperware Lady herself was near tears. But the important thing was, people bought a LOT of Tupperware that night. People bought Tupperware they would never in a million years need. Single men who lived in apartments and never cooked anything, ever, that could not be heated in a toaster, were ordering Tupperware cake transporters. It was obvious to me right then and there that *The Tupperware Song* was a powerful marketing tool.

I explained all this to Dick, of the Tupperware company, and he said I could send him a cassette tape of the song. Which I did, but I haven't heard a thing. Not that I'm worried. I'm sure there are plenty of other large, wealthy corporations out there that would be interested in a blues song about Tupperware. In fact, I'm getting offers in the mail almost every day. Most of them are for supplementary hospitalization insurance, but that's obviously just a negotiating ploy.

(Dave Barry's column appears in Monday's Lifestyle section of the *Star-Telegram*.)

Reprinted with permission of *Fort Worth Star-Telegram*.

SYNDICATION: THE EPITOME OF SUCCESS

Some syndicated columnists become household names—at least among newspaper readers. The predecessors of today's big-time political columnists were journalists such as Raymond Clapper, Tom Stokes, Drew Pearson, Robert Allen, Marquis Childs, Dorothy Thompson and David Lawrence, who became widely known for their interpretative columns. They wrote about the volatile political life of the 1930s, when the United States was trying to recover from a depression and about to enter a world war.

Money was tight, and editors didn't have funds to send reporters to Washington. But readers wanted more interpretation of what was happening in the nation's capital. One writer could supply several editors on a regular basis— once a week, for example. Contracts were drawn between editors and writers stating that the writer would provide the newspaper with copy on a routine schedule at a reasonable rate. Editors were thus able to fill space with more detailed accounts of activities in Washington. Readers were pleased to be better informed about government, politics and public affairs. And the columnists were making more money and receiving wider recognition than they ever thought possible.[7]

Some of these columnists took to the airwaves. Among them were Walter Winchell, Hans Von Kaltenborn, William L. Shirer and Eric Sevareid—all trained as newspaper journalists. They became well-known radio personalities and, in some cases, television notables because of their interpretative efforts.[8]

The popularity of syndicated copy, coupled with its relatively low cost, resulted in the development of organizations that peddled columns throughout the country. Today, according to *Writer's Market*, 27 syndicates are soliciting material from writers, and *Editor & Publisher* lists 375 syndicates.[9]

The syndicate fee is usually based on the circulation of the subscribing publication or station. The author typically gets a commission of from 40 to 60 percent of the sales. However, some syndicates pay a flat salary; others may pay by the word. Syndicated columns generally run between 200 and 1,000 words. Some syndicates may specify longer or shorter articles, though, depending on the clientele they serve.[10]

Why consider syndication at all at this stage? Why not? You might just have a better product, a better idea. Who would have imagined that synopses of the daily soap operas would sell? Does your paper have a column on home computers yet? Your ideas and your interests are potential columns.

11.13 Ad Column

Dateline Dodgeville

The Lands' End letter to The Wall Street Journal

DODGEVILLE, WI, February 25—As we began planning our March catalog—traditionally an all-out, rousing welcome to a Spring that never comes too soon in this part of the country—someone had a brilliant idea.

"Let's go to the children of Dodgeville Elementary School and tell them to draw us a picture of Spring. Then we'll have illustrations for the whole issue."

So, through the good offices of Ms. Evie Odean, who serves as an itinerant art teacher for children in the grade schools of Southern Wisconsin, we did just that.

Among the 80 second graders who responded with an enthusiasm and a talent Jackson Pollock might have envied, was **Shawn Fiedler**, who gets us off to an uplifting start right there on the front cover. That's Shawn waving to us from the basket of a hot air balloon, as a smiling sun looks on. Inside, you'll find other efforts, including portraits of some rare birds and flowers we've never seen before, more's the pity.

FOR OUR PART, we've crammed the remaining space with 10 pages of sportshirts of every conceivable kind, and our biggest collection of swimwear, knits, shorts, jeans and other clothing items which have VALUE written all over them in letters THIS BIG!

If you haven't yet laid hands on this issue, call our toll-free number forthwith, or as soon as possible thereafter. That number: 1-800-356-4444.

*   *   *

IN THE SAME ISSUE, our first "Letters to Lands' End" page—a sampling of our mail we thought you might enjoy sharing. After all, we read <u>your</u> mail with great interest. And we learn from it as well. For instance, in this first mailbag, a lady pleads for us to restore a **100% cotton twill skirt** we had abandoned. But, thanks to that letter, that item will be back come Fall. So, feel free to write—whatever's on your mind.

*   *   *

Finally, in the course of preparing for the all-out offering of **Madras shirts** in the March issue, we picked up some geographic intelligence. The Indian federal state from which Madras shirting takes its name is no longer called Madras. (You know how it is. What once was Pekin, became Peking, and is now Beijing, and life goes on.)

Well, the state of Madras is now called Tamil Nadu, but we are not changing the name or the quality of the shirting we use. It's still the real thing, and our selections are all but irresistible, having survived a riffle through literally thousands of colors and patterns.

Look for them. Genuine Madras Shirts (from Tamil Nadu, if you like!) And great values at $21.50 to $26.00.

That's about it for now.

**As Always,
Your Friends at Lands' End**

Reprinted with permission of Land's End.

DATELINE DODGEVILLE
The Lands' End Letter to The Wall Street Journal

Dodgeville, WI, February 24—As we began planning our March catalog—traditionally an all-out, rousing welcome to a Spring that never comes too soon in this part of the country—someone had a brilliant idea.

"Let's go to the children of Dodgeville Elementary School and tell them to draw us a picture of Spring. Then we'll have illustrations for the whole issue."

So, through the good offices of Ms. Evie Odean, who serves as an itinerant art teacher for children in the grade schools of Southern Wisconsin, we did just that.

Among the 80 second graders who responded with an enthusiasm and a talent Jackson Pollock might have envied, was Shawn Fiedler, who gets us off to an uplifting start right there on the front cover. That's Shawn waving to us from the basket of a hot air balloon, as a smiling sun looks on. Inside, you'll find other efforts, including portraits of some rare birds and flowers we've never seen before, more's the pity.

FOR OUR PART, we've crammed the remaining space with 10 pages of sportshirts of every conceivable kind, and our biggest collection of swimwear, knits, shorts, jeans and other clothing items which have VALUE written all over them in letters THIS BIG!

If you haven't yet laid hands on this issue, call our toll-free number forthwith, or as soon as possible thereafter. That number: 1-800-356-4444.

* * *

IN THE SAME ISSUE, our first "Letters to Lands' End" page—a sampling of our mail we thought you might enjoy sharing. After all, we read your mail with great interest. And we learn from it as well. For instance, in this first mailbag, a lady pleads for us to restore a 100% cotton twill skirt we had abandoned. But, thanks to that letter, that item will be back come Fall. So, feel free to write—whatever's on your mind.

* * *

Finally, in the course of preparing for the all-out offering of Madras shirts in the March issue, we picked up some geographic intelligence. The Indian federal state from which Madras shirting takes its name is no longer called Madras. (You know how it is. What once was Pekin, became Peking, and is now Beijing, and life goes on.)

Well, the state of Madras is now called Tamil Nadu, but we are not changing the name or the quality of the shirting we use. It's still the real thing, and our selections are all but irresistible, having survived a riffle through literally thousands of colors and patterns.

Look for them. Genuine Madras Shirts (from Tamil Nadu, if you like!) And great values at $21.50 to $26.00.

That's about it for now.

As Always,
Your Friends at Lands' End

LANDS' END DIRECT MERCHANTS

In a world of the flimsy and flighty and fly by night, a label like this can be a wonderful thing.

Please send free catalog.
Lands' End Dept. AF-C5
Dodgeville, WI 53595

Name _____
Address _____
City _____
State _____ Zip _____

Or call Toll-free:
1-800-356-4444

MAIN POINTS
- While not necessarily timely, feature stories have news value. They give the audience insight and understanding of a person or situation that might not be incorporated into a straight news story.

- Ideas for features are everywhere. The shrewd reporter reads, listens and observes carefully, then makes a note of potential story ideas.

- Feature stories can be grouped into broad categories: the news feature, the personality sketch or profile, the informative, the historical, the personal experience, the descriptive, the how-to and the enterprise story. Public relations features in organization magazines may be any of these. Advertising features imitate the editorial style.

- All features need a central theme and some form of reward for the reader at the end.

- Feature structure is not the traditional inverted-pyramid pattern; it's sometimes more like that used in fiction, complete with suspense and climaxes.

- The language can deviate from the more objective style used in news stories. Dialogue, narrative techniques, vivid description and detail, comparison and contrast can be used to evoke the desired images and emotions.

- In broadcast news, the feature is almost always defined as a story on the lighter side.

- Broadcast news features can be locally produced or can be sent to stations from networks or syndicated news services.

- The marketplace for feature stories is unlimited. A feature story can be turned into newspaper, wire, radio and TV copy.

- Columns are highly personal statements that appear at regular intervals and generally in the same place.

- Columns have a loyal, constant readership, offer more variety of subject matter than is found in straight news and are more flexible in style and format than straight news or features.

- Some general principles of style for column writing are:

  1. Put an unusual twist on the ordinary.

  2. Inject humor into the writing.

  3. Explore private musings, concerns and ideas.

  4. Be personal. Talk to, not at, the reader.

  5. Be creative. Experiment with the use of words and language patterns.

  6. Draw on the qualities of drama and fiction writing.

  7. Use exact words.

  8. Always keep the reader in mind. The reader will pass final judgment on whether your column is worthwhile.

- Some typical formats for columns: the Q&A; the grab bag; anecdotal; the feature; the instructive; the informative. Public relations columns usually come from the organization's leadership, and some advertising columns look like editorial columns.

- Syndicates are a major source for columns that appear in the print media, though a local writer can also place columns with newspaper editors.

EXERCISES

1. Look through some newspapers and magazines and find straight news stories that you believe could be turned into feature stories. Decide the best approach to use: personality feature, historical feature and so on. Indicate how you could convert the news story into an interesting feature.

2. Based on your conversations of the day, your observations, your reading and your knowledge of the marketplace where you live, list 10 feature stories you think would appeal to the public.

3. Watch a television news program, either local or network. Count the number of feature items used and the time each takes. Also note the kinds of topics covered. Does the placement of the feature in the overall program affect the impact the feature has on the audience?

4. Read several different categories of columns in newspapers and magazines. Compare the style and format of writing to that of feature stories. How are they similar? Different? If you were to distinguish five separate characteristics for each, what would they be?

5. Assume that you have been invited to begin writing a weekly column for the student newspaper. Prepare one sample column and a list of topics for other columns.

6. The news director of the campus radio station wants a daily five-minute "behind the headlines" program. Write a promotional description ("promo") for your show. Write one sample program.

NOTES

1. William L. Rivers, *The Mass Media*, 2nd ed. (New York: Harper & Row, 1975), p. 285.

2. Frank Dickson, *1,001 Article Ideas* (Cincinnati: Writer's Digest Books, 1979), p. iv.

3. William L. Rivers and Shelley Smolkin, *Free-Lancer and Staff Writer* (Belmont, Calif.: Wadsworth, 1981), p. 78.

4. Cynthia Sanz, "Teaching the Children: Center's Exceptional Methods Get Students Off to Early Start," *Dallas Morning News*, Oct. 16, 1986, p. C1.

5. Grant N. Horne, "Anatomy of a Corporate Video Department," *Public Relations Quarterly* 31, no. 2 (Summer 1986): 26.

6. Peggy Teeters, in *How to Get Started in Writing* (Cincinnati: Writer's Digest Books, 1981), pp. 98–99, lists 50 marketable topics—for starters. There are more.

7. Kenneth Rystrom, *The Why, Who and How of the Editorial Page* (New York: Random House, 1983), pp. 272–73.

8. Warren K. Agee, Phillip H. Ault and Edwin Emery, *Introduction to Mass Communications* (New York: Harper & Tow, 1982), pp. 156-60.

9. "Syndicates," *Writer's Market* (Cincinnati: Writer's Digest Books, 1987), p. 947–52. *Editor & Publisher Yearbook* (New York: *Editor & Publisher*, 1986), Section V, p. 7.

10. Ibid.

SUGGESTIONS FOR ADDITIONAL READING

Burack, A.S. *The Writer's Handbook*. Boston: The Writer, 1980.

Caen, Herb. "Stitching Together Piffle and Profundities." In *Improving Newswriting*, pp. 47–50. Washington: American Society of Newspaper Editors Foundation, 1980.

Cohen, Richard. "On Being Oneself, Not Jim Breslin." In *Improving Newswriting*, pp. 40–43.

Harris, Julian, Kelly Leiter and Stanley Johnson. *The Complete Reporter*. New York: Macmillan, 1981.

Rees, Clair. *Profitable Part-Time/Full-Time Freelancing*. Cincinnati: Writer's Digest Books, 1980.

Safire, William. "Ten Commandments of Press Columns." In *Improving Newswriting*, pp. 44–46.

Schoenfeld, A. Clay, and Karen S. Diegmueller. *Effective Feature Writing*. New York: Holt, Rinehart and Winston, 1982.

Shaw, David. *Journalism Today: A Changing Press for a Changing America*. New York: Harper & Row, 1977.

Teeters, Peggy. *How to Get Started in Writing*. Cincinnati: Writer's Digest Books, 1980.

Zinsser, William. *On Writing Well*. Rev. ed. New York: Harper & Row, 1985.

Depth Reporting

A reporter enrolling in some journalism courses as postgraduate work asked about the difference between *interpretative* and *investigative* reporting. After listening thoughtfully to the explanation, he asked, "Then what is a *news analyst?*" He shook his head. "I wish I had learned that in journalism school. Now we're thinking more about what we're doing. I learned to just *do* it." The suggestion that what he is now doing for the newspaper is not any of the three he asked about but instead is *depth reporting* brought a surprised "Oh!"

ORIGINS AND DEFINITIONS

Neither the four reporting methods nor the names are new. The first copyright on *Interpretative Reporting* by Northwestern University professor emeritus of journalism Curtis MacDougall is 1938. (Its 1932 title was *Reporting for Beginners*.) *Investigative reporting* is likely to be mentioned in the same breath with the 1973 Watergate stories. But I.F. Stone began publishing his exposés of federal government in *I.F. Stone's BiWeekly* in 1953, and he was only following in the tradition of the muckrakers, who contributed exposés to *McClure's* magazine in the early 1900s. Much of their work resulted in social legislation still in effect today. Upton Sinclair's 1906 novel *The Jungle* about the Chicago meatpacking industry led to passage of the Pure Food and Drug Act. Ray Stannard Baker wrote about child labor conditions, and Ida Tarbell exposed the unfair labor practices of Standard Oil. The investigator of political corruption in government in that period was Lincoln Steffens.

Muckraking had a revival in the 1960s. Rachel Carson is given credit for starting the environmental movement with her 1962 book *Silent Spring*. And Ralph Nader, a leader of consumerism, wrote *Unsafe at Any Speed* in 1965, an indictment of the automobile industry. (Neither was a journalist by profession. Carson was a biologist and Nader a lawyer.)

The '60s also spawned what was called the "new journalism." It wasn't new. It was an attempt to give readers the experience of the event through the use of literary devices.[1] Journalists like Mark Twain and Ernest Hemingway who

334

had written fiction always had mixed techniques. R. Thomas Berner calls it literary newswriting:

> Literary newswriting is the marriage of depth reporting and literary techniques in newspaper writing. Among those techniques are narration and scene, summary and process, point of view, drama, chronological organization, rhythm, imagery, foreshadowing, metaphor, irony, dialogue, overall organization (beginning, middle and end)—all girded by good reporting.[2]

The depth report A step beyond straight news reporting, the depth report attempts to put a news event into perspective by relating it to other events or reports. When you work on a depth piece, you will research the *issue* the event represents. Neale Copple, dean of the University of Nebraska's journalism school, once defined depth reporting as "telling the reader all the essential facts in a way that brings the story into the reader's environment."[3]

Suppose you're motivated to do a depth piece after listening to a speaker discuss the difficulty college students will have finding jobs when they graduate. Is that true for your school's students? Is the job market better or worse for

I.F. Stone began publishing *I.F. Stone's Weekly* in 1953. Circulation was small, but his staff was even smaller —Stone, his wife and an occasional research assistant. His readers and his targets, however, were big —significant opinion makers. Stone targeted equally big subjects (like the red-hunting senator from Wisconsin, Joe McCarthy) until 1971, when he ceased publication because, he said, there was just no one to take over. He attributed his effectiveness to careful research, usually in public government documents like the budget and the congressional record.

Mark Godfrey/Archive Pictures

some majors? What can you add to the story to give it more meaning for students on your campus? You can find out what figures your school's placement office has on interviews and jobs. You can see what the deans of the various professional programs, like law and engineering, have to say about placement. You can build a story about opportunities for graduates at your school, and for graduates in particular fields, by going beyond what the speaker said. More than just localizing a story, you are putting an issue in focus. That is depth reporting.

The interpretative report

Although MacDougall calls interpretative and depth reporting the same thing, and W.L. Rivers calls the interpretative and the analysis the same, the most common definition of the interpretative report is a story that focuses on an issue that either is controversial, such as abortion, or isn't well understood, such as nuclear energy.

Interpretative reports delve into probable causes and possible motives of participants and attempt to explain the significance of various actions and events, to make comparisons with past or similar events and to project the outcome or resolution.[4] The emphasis is on the *why*. A common technique is to define the issue, give background on it to let past events explain the current development and then ask authorities to help project the future.[5]

With sufficient time, resources and experience, you might tie the employment of college graduates to the overall national employment picture and then to the employment opportunities of typical college career paths, including the always difficult to define "liberal arts" major. You could then project which areas of study might be the most in demand in the future. One ongoing debate in academe is whether to let the marketplace for talent affect planning, which includes advising and commitment of resources.

The news analysis

The dictionary definition of a news analyst is a commentator; the textbook definition of news analysis is synonymous with interpretative reporting. A news analysis is a report that also tries to put an issue, generally a controversial one, in perspective—the perspective of the writer. So a news analysis is commentary, but it's commentary intended to clarify and explain. This purpose makes it quite different from an editorial, an opinion piece intended to persuade.

Just as the print media label pieces "analysis," so do broadcasters alert listeners and viewers to the distinction between this type of story and a straight news story. On television, not only do an introduction and close inform the viewer, but the words "NEWS ANALYSIS" or "COMMENTARY" are supered at the bottom of the screen.

Investigative reporting

An investigative reporter does just what any other investigator does. He or she digs up something that was hidden, probably deliberately. (The *New York Times* once stated it would stop referring to some of its reporters as "investigative

Reprinted by permission of Jefferson Communications, Inc., Reston, Va.

reporters," because *all* reporters are supposed to investigate, then report.)

Investigative reporting is often dangerous to the reporters involved and to their employers. In 1975 an organization called Investigative Reports and Editors (IRE) was formed. The founders' idea was to band together to share sleuthing techniques; however, their most dramatic activity was their investigative reporting in Arizona following the death of a colleague, Don Bolles, in 1976. Bolles, an *Arizona Republic* reporter, was killed while looking into organized crime and political corruption in the state. IRE sent a task force in to complete Bolles' work to show "you can't kill a story by killing a reporter."[6]

Because of the time and resources invested in investigative reporting, some news media package their series for distribution. Television stations put theirs on videotape and newspapers generally print a tabloid. Some examples are the *Orlando Sentinel*'s weeklong series on malpractice by Rosemary Goudreau and Alex Beasley in 1986. A small number of doctors were involved in the malpractice suits and their victims were receiving large awards. The problem, the writers said, was the failure of the profession to monitor and report on its own members. Another example is the *Philadelphia Inquirer*'s tabloid reprint of a three-day series in 1983, "Death Ships: How the U.S. sends rustbuckets to sea, sailors to their graves." The 20-page tabloid presented information and pictures that Robert R. Frump and Timothy Dwyer had spent two and a half years gathering and assembling. Also in 1983, that same newspaper published a 68-page tabloid, "Above the Law: The questionable conduct of the Pennsylvania Supreme Court." This story took Daniel Biddle two years to write. The time, trouble and dedication investigations take is well documented in the various accounts of the *Washington Post*'s Watergate stories and in the story of the Pentagon Papers,[7] the *New York Times* 1971 series it called "The Secret History of the Vietnam War." Obviously, a news medium has to have a commitment and resources to get involved in investigative reporting.

The direction of investigative reporting should change, according to an extensive report in 1983 from the Women's Studies Program and Policy Center of George Washington University. It quotes Michael O'Neill, former editor of the *New York Daily News*:

". . . We need to put more emphasis on what I call preventive journalism — deliberately searching for the underlying social currents that threaten future danger so that public policy can be more intelligently mobilized. . . ."

He recognized the high cost of preparing reporters with specialized knowledge, skills and experience to do such work but thought the stakes for humanity so great that it must be done.

THE GROUNDWORK

The reason depth reporting is considered a step beyond basic newswriting is the combination of skills it requires. The skills have to be commanded by a resourceful thinker who is both persistent and optimistic.

Finding facts

As you learned in Chapter 3, you can get facts firsthand by asking questions, or secondhand by consulting libraries, public records and such. In depth reporting, the information you seek is likely to be on more specialized subjects, and easy answers are not as readily available. You may have to question specialists in a field you aren't familiar with — engineers, physicians, economists.

- *Be accurate* in getting all of the words spelled correctly, and the causes and effects sorted out.
- *Be meticulous* about taking notes you can read later — weeks, perhaps.
- *Keep asking* questions until you understand the subject enough to write about it. You can't afford to say "Oh, I see" when you don't.

The depth report's focus on *why* means you have to be patient and persistent. Accuracy, always critical, is more elusive when you're on unfamiliar ground. It helps to know where to go to check both yourself and your sources.

Developing sources

Almost anyone is a potential source, you'll discover. The person you met at a friend's house last week might be the authority on insurance regulation you need for a story. Collect business cards. Note on the cards where you met someone; sometimes jotting a key word from the conversation will help you remember the person better.

Discussing issues with acquaintances often leads to their saying something like, "Have you talked with Elizabeth Anderson? She's a real authority on property-damage claims." Remember the name and who mentioned it.

Be very careful when quoting authorities. Read the quote back to them to be sure you've got it right. Check the spelling of name and title. Ask about titles or academic credentials if you don't understand them, and it's wise to check even if you do. In quoting a source, you are presenting that person as an authority, and you won't be forgiven if you make him or her look foolish. Care will establish confidence; the source will be accessible to you in the future.

Understanding institutional systems

Our social, political, economic and even religious life is dominated by systems and the people who run them. You have to understand the systems before you can make sense of what's going on in them and how they interrelate.

Government. Federal, state and local governments are the framework for laws and processes—how things happen. You need to know what the different offices do, what they are authorized to do by legal authority. The court system can be mystifying unless you know how a case gets into a certain court and where it goes on appeal. Do you know where to find a copy of your city's charter? What about your university's own organizational tree? Do you know the academic appeals process at your university? What about your student government charter and constitution and that of the faculty senate? You can't make sense of information unless you understand the formal systems and channels of authority.

Business. Industrial and commercial businesses are set up differently, and within each of these two broad categories different systems exist. The utilities, for example, are different from the retail merchants in pricing, servicing and distribution. Within industry, you'll find whole product industries (like cars) differ from principally part manufacturers. Industries involved in defense contracts are organized differently from commercial-products industries. The reporter handling a story must understand the structure and mission of the business, because the story must be put in that frame. In gathering information, the reporter must exhibit this understanding in order to be treated seriously by sources. (A major complaint of business leaders interviewed by reporters is that reporters are ignorant of how businesses operate.)

Whether a business is publicly held or not makes a significant difference in the information readily available. Publicly held companies have to be accountable to their stockholders and must comply with federal regulations of the Securities and Exchange Commission. Becoming acquainted with the types of business, their organization, financing and supply systems will give you a starting point for developing stories beyond the basic facts.

Non-profit and not-for-profit organizations. Your university belongs to this category, and it also may be a part of a government structure if it isn't a private school. The function of non-profit organizations, to serve the public, makes them more like government than business in structure. However, some non-profits—some private schools, museums, hospitals—are organized and run more like corporations. But they don't operate to make a profit. They operate with a narrow margin and reinvest any profits in improving resources or redistribute them. Knowing the various patterns you're likely to find helps you give a story depth.

Economics is the base for most activities of institutions; how they get money to do what they are doing and to whom they are reportable is of great consequence. Sometimes what an institution is doing makes no sense at all unless you understand its funding. For example, a student newspaper once criticized the university for spending money on improving a dorm for athletes when other dorms also needed renovation. However, the paper's editors and reporters didn't realize that the athletes' dorm wasn't even in the university's regular budget, because all athletic activities generated their own money.

Informal structures.   All organizations have an informal structure as well as a formal one, and it often has a great deal to do with the way the organization is managed. Sometimes this is called management style or corporate culture. Often it's just referred to as the internal politics of an institution. In some places, the environment is an open one where employees have the privilege of participating in management by offering ideas and expressing opinions. In other places, the rule (unspoken, of course) is do as you're told and keep quiet. The more open the management, the more likely you are to get information through traditional sources. The less open a management is, the more you may have to rely on internal sources whose confidence must be kept, and you'll have to verify their information with other internal or, preferably, external sources. Banks and hospitals are generally not open management systems, but public universities as well as some private ones are.

Building files   You'll want to accumulate at least three types of files: issues, people/places, sources.

Issues.   You may find yourself following an issue and keeping clips on it because you're interested in it personally or because you once covered a story on the subject and thought you might later return to it in depth. You should also file your notes from previous stories by issue or topic so you can build from past information. You can't always count on a clipping file. Portions you need may have been deleted in editing. Or the story might not be there at all. Even well-kept media libraries have shortcomings.

People/places.   You don't need to keep files on the famous, because information on them is readily accessible in libraries. But your interview with an impressive freshman state legislator may come in handy when he or she is elected governor. Record observations and facts about cities, towns, countries visited. News often strikes the same place twice. The site of last year's world's fair may be the scene of this year's chemical spill.

Sources.   Maintain a card file of people you've used as sources and note the other areas where they might have some expertise—the surgeon who's also a jazz bassist or the banker who's an aerobatic pilot.

Clarifying explanations   Depth reporting calls on the ability to simplify the complex, discussed in Chapter 2. You can't do that effectively unless you understand the material yourself. Try to make abstract information concrete. Ask the poison authority who has given you a lecture in pathology: "You mean if I get that on my hands, my whole body will break out? In what—welts like hives, or red spots like measles?" Questions to keep in your simplification repertoire are: What will happen then? What will it do? What will this mean to the average citizen? What would that look like? Can you give me an example?

CONSTRUCTING THE DEPTH STORY

Writing the depth story is not nearly as much fun as gathering the information, confessed a reporter who also said he had difficulty turning loose a depth piece. His feeling that there's always something else to add is a common one. (The experience is not unlike doing a major research paper.) Ordering all of the material so that nothing important gets left out and the story makes sense to the reader is a formidable task. You get so close to a depth piece and the individuals involved, you need to make a conscious effort to set the scene, introduce the characters and summarize the plot for the reader before you detail the action.

Finding the start of the yarn

The notes for a depth piece will be voluminous if you've done your research well. The first step is to reread all of them and decide which ones you'll use. In rereading, you can devise a preliminary arrangement and decide what's the best starting point. One place to begin might be with an event or a situation that also allows you to introduce the principal participants (see 12.1). For a story about a controversial issue, you could begin by introducing the two sides and their advocates, or you could begin by describing the problem in a narrative format. Whatever form the introduction takes, it must clearly give the reader an idea of what the story is about and a sense of all it involves. This is particularly a problem if your research has resulted in a series, even if it's only two installments. It's difficult to recap and restate without losing the readers of the first segment, but you have a responsibility to the readers who are picking up the series after the first story. (See 12.2, a research depth series, and 12.3, an issue depth series.)

12.1 News Peg Depth Story

The discovery of the gene that acts to prevent one type of cancer in the eye is a major breakthrough in cancer research. The real significance goes beyond help in treating retinal cancer—it involves all malignancies that are considered hereditary. The story, then, is a complex one. Not only is this a good example of a depth piece, because it is a science story it is a good example of simplification.

Gene involved in eye cancer identified

Discovery is first of kind in research on human hereditary malignancies

Chicago Tribune

In a significant advance in the fight against genetic disease, medical researchers in Massachusetts announced Wednesday that they have identified the gene that acts to prevent formation of retinal cancer.

The achievement is expected to be important in helping to understand the processes by which cancers arise and why some people inherit a tendency to develop cancers while others do not. The findings are also expected to

(continued)

12.1 (continued)

clarify some of the mystery that surrounds the normal processes of cell growth and differentiation.

The researchers also may have found a genetic basis for osteosarcoma, the most frequent form of bone cancer, an ailment not previously considered hereditary.

Discovery of the retinoblastoma, or retinal cancer, gene by a team of scientists at Harvard University and the Massachusetts Institute of Technology will enable genetic screening and early diagnosis of the most common life-threatening eye tumor in young children.

"Retinoblastoma and at least a dozen cancers—maybe a majority—are caused by genes like this," said Thaddeus Dryja, a researcher with the Harvard-affiliated Massachusetts Eye and Ear Infirmary.

"For instance, the evidence is really strong in Wilms' tumor (a kidney cancer), one type of lung cancer and tumors of the spinal cord. We also know that colon and breast cancer tend to run in families."

Dryja said the finding, published in the latest issue of the British journal *Nature*, will bring closer understanding of the genesis of osteosarcoma, a deadly form of bone cancer that strikes youngsters at puberty.

Although bone cancer has not previously been considered a genetic disease, children who survive eye cancer are at high risk of osteosarcomas later in life.

"We cannot say that trouble with this gene is the only way you can get a retinoblastoma or bone cancer," said the co-leader of the research project, Dr. Stephen H. Friend of Children's Hospital and the Dana-Farber Cancer Institute, both in Boston. "But we can say for sure that this is an important cause of the majority of these tumors."

The discovery marks the first time that a gene governing a hereditary human cancer has been isolated.

Retinoblastoma strikes one child in 20,000, with about 200 new cases being reported each year in the United States. Treatment of this dangerous, fast-growing cancer usually involves the loss of one or both eyes, unless the tumor is detected while it is very small and can be cured by radiation.

Overall mortality is 20 percent in the United States, but is much higher in underdeveloped countries where the tumor is often undiagnosed until it has spread beyond the eye. Once the disease appears, all victims also are at risk not only for the bone cancer but also for other malignant tumors.

The gene has been isolated to a specific section—the long arm of chromosome 13 of the 46 human chromosomes—by Harvard's Dryja, and Friend and the celebrated cancer researcher Robert Weinberg at MIT's Whitehead Institute for Biomedical Research.

Osteosarcoma, the most frequent tumor of bone with about 250 cases being diagnosed each year, is a particularly vicious cancer that strikes down teen-agers—it has a peak age range from 10 to 25 years. Treatment involves amputation of the diseased limb, or bone transplantation, but often the cancer has spread throughout the body by the time it is diagnosed.

"Both these diseases may be caused by the same gene, or a cluster of genes that lie very close together on the 13th chromosome," Friend said. "We are fascinated by the possibility. Retinoblastomas occur mainly in infancy, while osteosarcomas strike in puberty. How could one gene, or a cluster, cause such different diseases that show up at such different times? This now becomes a major research question."

The discovery is extremely important to cancer research.

In recent years, scientists have determined that two types of genes play vital roles in causing many types of cancer. Both types are found in every human cell, and normally are essential for the growth and repair of cells. When these genes are damaged, or somehow changed, they can cause cancer.

The first type of gene is called a dominant oncogene. It can redirect the growth of healthy cells, making them spread wildly in the uncontrolled growth we call cancer.

A recessive oncogene is the other type. This gene routinely restricts the normal growth of cells, but if the gene is lost or somehow switched off, the cell may not receive the proper signal to stop growing. Cancer is the result.

The retinoblastoma gene is a recessive oncogene. "We believe that dozens of types of cancers—both solid tumors and leukemias—are triggered by recessive oncogenes," Friend said.

"Isolation of the retinoblastoma gene will allow us to study what the normal gene does in a retinal cell, and how lack of this gene results in a cancer. A similar process may be used to investigate other cancers governed by recessive oncogenes.

"Because this gene is missing in tumor cells, we want to put it back into such cells and see if we can reverse the cancer. That will be the next step in our work," Friend said.

Although retinal cancer may be passed on directly from parent to child, the disease often crops up spontaneously. Friend and Dryja say the discovery may soon result in an effective test for carriers of the defective gene. The technique also would allow the gene to be spotted prenatally.

"Moreover, we think the finding is likely to be of great benefit in the treatment of children who already have the disease," Friend said.

From the *Chicago Tribune*, printed in *The Dallas Morning News*. Reprinted with permission.

12.2 Research Depth Series

This week-long series resulted from the newspaper's own research into the lifestyles, opinions and attitudes of teenagers in the city. Each day one major story covered the issue, using statistics; a feature personalized the issue. The first of the series, "Messages to Adults," is drawn from an open-ended question in the research instrument. The methodology is explained in a box. Subsequent parts of the series were titled "Parents, Peers, Relationships," "Drugs and Alcohol," "Pressures, Values, Self-Worth" and "Education and Career." The series was presented in a graphically attractive package, with the series schedule and representative quotes from that day's topic set off in boxes.

ON DISCIPLINE...

"They (parents) may not be lenient because they care. Sometimes I get mad. But then I go in my room and sit down, and I realize that they're saying that because they care."

— *Willie Clayborne, 14, sophomore,*
W.W. Samuels High School, Dallas

Changes in attitudes as adolescents age

Almost never or never lie to their parents

10th-graders	29%
Recent high school grads	42%

Agree that teens get too much freedom

10th-graders	10%
Recent high school grads	23%

Believe their parents' rules are very fair

10th-graders	30%
Recent high school grads	43%

Almost never worry about being popular

10th-graders	43%
Recent high school grads	60%

Do you think your parents are too strict, not strict enough, or about right in their attitudes toward discipline?

Too strict	27%
Not strict enough	8%
About right	64%
No answer	2%

When do you expect to get married?

Before age 20	9%
Between 20-30	78%
Between 30-40	6%
Older than 40	1%
Never	6%

Do you want to have children?

Yes	79%
No	7%
Don't know	13%

THE TEEN SURVEY

☐ Sunday: An overview

☐ Monday: Relationships

■ **Tuesday: Drugs and alcohol**

☐ Wednesday: Self-worth

☐ Thursday: School

(continued)

12.2 (continued)

Today

Sunday, September 7, 1986   The Dallas Morning News   — Section F

Sunset High School football players (from left) Demarcus Odom, David Thompson and Charles Ignot take a break to watch the Bisonettes drill team practice.

THE TEEN SURVEY

MESSAGES TO ADULTS

Jimmy Lee of North Mesquite High School and Hyun Lim, a graduate of Berkner High School in Richardson, share the ups and downs of a day at Six Flags Over Texas.

ON UNDERSTANDING . . .

ON FREEDOM . . .

ON HYPOCRISY . . .

ON SEX . . .

ON COMMUNICATION . . .

Today

Monday, September 8, 1986   The Dallas Morning News   ... — Section C

THE TEEN SURVEY

A GIRL AT THE CROSSROADS: Angelica Cavazos is approaching the moment of decision, the time when she either follows family tradition or pursues her dream of college and a career. Her story is on Page 6C.

PARENTS, PEERS, RELATIONSHIPS

By Christine Wicker
Staff Writer of The News

ON LYING . . .

ON COMMUNICATION . . .

ON BIRTH CONTROL . . .

COMMUNICATION

HOW THE INFORMATION WAS GATHERED

Today

Tuesday, September 9, 1986   The Dallas Morning News   — ...... Section C

THE TEEN SURVEY

EIGHTEEN AND DRUG-FREE: David has reentered the mainstream of high school life and faces old situations with a new outlook. His story is on Page 4C.

DRUGS AND ALCOHOL

By Connie Prryant
Staff Writer of The News

ON ALCOHOL, DRUGS . . .

ON TRYING POT . . .

ON REASONS WHY . . .

HOW THE INFORMATION WAS GATHERED

ALCOHOL

Today

Wednesday, September 10, 1986   The Dallas Morning News   Section C

THE TEEN SURVEY

YOUNG MAN OF GOD: "My family and my church are probably the most important things in my life," says James Bush Jr., 19. His story is on Page 6C.

PRESSURES, VALUES, SELF-WORTH

By Steve Levin
Staff Writer of The News

ON WORRIES . . .

ON SUICIDE . . .

ON SELF-IMAGE . . .

SUICIDE

HOW THE INFORMATION WAS GATHERED

12.2 (continued)

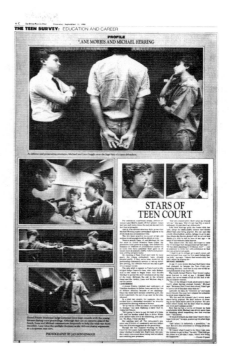

Reprinted by permission of *The Dallas Morning News*

12.3 Issue Depth Series

This student series was one of the winners in the Roy W. Howard Public National Writing Competition in Public Affairs Reporting in 1986. The first article in the series deals with student alcoholism, and the second points out the connection between the student and an alcoholic in the family. In presenting the information, the writer also offers a solution: Alcoholics Anonymous for the alcoholics and Al-Anon for their families.

Life in the fast lane drives drinkers to a dead end

By Faith Conroy
This is the first of a two-part series.

The party is over for Bonnie, a University of Montana staff member. There's no more drinking with friends or partying til dawn. She gave up being wild and wasted because she had to. Bonnie's an alcoholic.

When Bonnie was 16 years old, she discovered alcohol. She already knew that taking pills relieved emotional pain. But alcohol added a whole new dimension.

"I discovered that if I mixed alcohol with those drugs I got an incredible sense of relief. I reached oblivion. I didn't feel any pain and I had a good time. I could talk to people. I wasn't shy anymore. It was wonderful. I loved it."

(continued)

But she was afraid of it, she said. "I was very interested in school so I stayed away from it (alcohol) for the most part. I liked it too much."

"I was a very good student. I was straight A. But I felt like there was something missing in my life. I always felt kind of inadequate, even if I got straight A's."

Drinking relieved those feelings, she said. "In looking back, it was ridiculous because whenever I attempted something I usually succeeded at it."

It was difficult for Bonnie to see herself as an alcoholic, because most people think an alcoholic is someone on skid row—an unshaven derelict asleep on a park bench, hugging an empty wine bottle in a paper bag.

But the facts are that alcoholism affects 1 in 10 people in the country and many are intelligent, successful people. Other statistics indicate that half the children of alcoholic parents become alcoholic themselves and another 26 percent marry alcoholics.

Bonnie was one of those children. She came from an alcoholic family and her home life was chaotic, she said. "Emotional communication was missing. Feelings were never discussed."

Her father was an alcoholic and she didn't like him when he drank. He wasn't abusive, she said, but he was a little louder, a little rougher.

She remembers sitting in the car with her mother outside bars, while her father went inside to drink. "Sometimes we'd sit out in the car for two hours," she said.

But she didn't think her own life had become chaotic or out of control until she experienced her first blackout at a friend's party when she was 18. She said she woke up and didn't know where she was or why her friends were forcing her into a cold shower.

The sheriff was at her house when she got home because police had found her car at the bottom of a lake.

"After that experience I realized that I wasn't drinking like other people. When I drank, I drank solely to get drunk and I didn't stop drinking until I reached total oblivion.

"I remember my friends calling me an alcoholic. One friend said, 'Maybe you shouldn't drink so much.'" But Bonnie refused to believe she was an alcoholic.

"I was too smart to be an alcoholic. I drank because it was fun." She continued to drink until alcohol devastated her life.

"I think that it's hard for people to pull back from their partying situation and say, 'Yeah, I'm losing control and I'm hurting relationships with other people and with myself,'" she said.

John Garlinghouse, counselor at UM's Center for Student Development, said many students are unable to admit they have a drinking problem. "The biggest constant factor with the college community is rampant denial, which of course the afflicted person is never aware of.

"College people, by and large, are better at denying it because we're of average or better intelligence. A high IQ is a definite liability if you have a chemical problem.

"Its main effect is to allow you to bullshit yourself right into the grave," he said.

"Most people in school, if they're making their grades, they figure they're on top of their lives.

"This is a partying environment. It's not particularly unusual to find yourself partying more than you should. What is unusual is to realize that and fail to stop it.

He said if you have a bad experience while you're drunk and you say "'I'm not going to do that again' and then you do, I think that is when you really need to start saying, 'Hey, what is this?' you know? 'Where am I?'

"I think as a rule, more of us are at a greater risk of getting into abuse patterns here. I did it for years and years and loved most of it. It didn't get grim until later."

He said he believes some people are genetically predisposed to alcoholism but that heavy partying can also evolve into the disease. "It's a very insidious trip, this alcohol."

Jean Erickson, a recovered alcoholic and a chemical dependency counselor at Life Development Center, said that many alcoholics are over-achievers and lead productive lives—at least for a while.

"A lot of them finish school," she said. They work hard and produce well. "But somewhere inside we know the day is coming when we won't."

She said it is difficult for students to recognize alcoholism because drinking is a big part of the college experience and wild behavior is acceptable. But often, their behaviors are symptoms of alcoholism.

Young alcoholics are always living on the edge, she said. They like taking risks, driving fast, chugging beer, getting into fights, upsetting parents by coming home late and rebelling against society—one adrenalin rush after another.

"It starts when you're a little kid and it doesn't change," she said.

They don't pace themselves with schoolwork. Instead, they cram for exams. They drink faster and build up more tolerance for alcohol than other people. "They're the guy or gal that can drink anybody under the table," she said.

The amount of partying increases, "Where you used to go out on weekends and get blitzed, maybe now you're going out two or three nights a week."

Students have a great deal of stamina, she said. "A 20-year-old probably can go out five nights a week and still function in some manner. When you're 35 you can't do that anymore."

Many students don't wake up with hangovers, she said, but begin to feel bad later in the day as the alcohol leaves their systems.

Grades and class attendance decline and oversleeping increases. Often an alcoholic will change his or her major to one less demanding. "Everything they do in life will become less demanding so it doesn't interfere with their drinking," she said.

There's usually a preoccupation with drinking and always a reason to party. Friends evolve toward a crowd where alcohol is the primary focus. Friends and relationships mirror the drinking pattern or are short-lived. "The primary relationship in that person's life is with booze," Erickson said.

The more they lose control over their lives, the more they blame others.

(continued)

They have rotten professors, redundant classes or bad scheduling. "I don't think I've ever worked with a young person in 10 years that has come to the conclusion that they have a drinking problem," Erickson said. "They will have it forcibly pointed out to them.

"If I'm drinking and flunk out of school, it's because I didn't like school anyway or I wasn't ready for college. If I wreck a car, so did five other people I know.

"Young people have very little sense of morality. 'The alcohol may be tearing my family apart, my father may have died from it, but I'm not going to be like that,' as if they had a nickel's worth of control over it.

"It happens in spite of your plans," she said.

Erickson said many young alcoholics get into legal trouble, describing it as "delayed adolescent behavior."

"At the time alcohol abuse sets in, which for a lot of people is their first drink," emotional maturity stops, she said.

They consistently drink more than they intended, when they didn't plan to drink at all, and they do or say things that do not fit their perception of themselves.

They have a high investment in graduating, but they cut classes all the time. They have a high investment in their grade point average, but they get C's and D's on their tests.

Generally, alcoholics don't eat when they drink, Erickson said. "It takes the buzz off. 'What do you mean, go eat? I'm not going to ruin a perfectly good drunk with a hamburger,' but at 2 a.m., they'll eat so they don't get sick," she said.

But alcoholics don't see the discrepancies in their behavior, she said, because they will only party with people who like to get drunk. If you don't get drunk, "you're a dud. It won't be that I'm out of control, it'll be that you don't know how to have fun.

"And people make excuses for them. They say, 'Oh well, he's just drunk,'" she said.

Alcoholics assume they drink the same as everyone else. But they don't remember driving home, what they did the night before or how they got that incredible bruise.

"We're charming, we're witty, we're bright," Erickson said. "An alcoholic can fix the world, but they can't find their car keys to get to the White House to do it."

Eventually, alcoholics reach a stage in their drinking when they can no longer justify what they are doing. "If your use of alcohol interferes consistently in any area of your life, you have a problem with booze," she said.

They consistently break promises and lie to protect their habit, "without ever knowing we have the habit," Erickson said. Usually, it takes something drastic to trigger awareness.

Garlinghouse partied with the best of them when he went to UM, he said. "When I was in my 20s, I would've been hard pressed to be polite if anyone had told me that I had an abnormal drinking pattern.

"In fact, a few people had suggested it and I discounted them as reactionary fools," and continued partying without them, he said.

"A fool is a fool and I ain't got the time for fools" was his sentiment then, he said.

"With the exception of one quarter, I made almost solid incompletes. I call that an 'alcoholic transcript,'" he said.

"College was jive anyway," Garlinghouse recalled, "I stumbled around campus trying to find out how to withdraw with hangovers."

Garlinghouse said if 1 in 10 people is alcoholic, then there are nearly 900 student alcoholics at UM.

"That's a lot of undiagnosed people running around," he said. And it's not difficult to believe if you scan the Dornbiaser Field parking lot before, during and after a football game. Beer flows freely at tailgate parties and many of the parties never even enter the stadium.

"If indeed a student here is an alcoholic, he's a member of one of the largest groups on campus. And it's OK to have a problem. It doesn't make you lame and it doesn't make you immoral. Addiction is just real democratic. It can nail anybody."

Debbie, who begins classes at UM in January, said she was 10 years old when she began drinking with her dad.

"The consequences of drinking at that time weren't bad," she said. But because she suffered blackouts from drinking, she doesn't remember much of grade school or early high school.

What she does remember is how much she enjoyed drinking. "It got me out of reality and relieved a lot of pain," she said.

The pain came from her parents' divorce when she was 3 years old and from living with an alcoholic father.

She said she grew up in bars, and didn't do "average teenager things." Instead she took care of her dad and "drove them home from the bars after he passed out."

She got into drugs and spent most of her time loaded, she said. She was either thrown out of school for fighting or thrown in jail for drug dealing and robbery.

"No matter how hard I tried not to drink or use, or rip somebody off, even though I did want to stay in school really bad, I couldn't," she said.

"People started drawing away from me, even the people I drank with, because I was constantly obsessed with the idea of getting wasted all the time."

Eventually she attempted suicide, she said.

"I realized at that point I was going crazy on the inside and everything on the outside was crazy too." So three years ago, at age 16, Debbie was admitted to an alcoholism treatment center in Helena.

Anna Martin, UM's Blue Cross coordinator, said approximately 20 UM students use student health insurance to pay for alcohol or drug abuse treatment each year. UM's Blue Cross coverage pays up to $4,000 for hospital treatment and 50 percent of the expenses for out-patient care up to $1,000 per year.

Treatment costs about $7,000, Martin said, and students must be on UM's policy for a year before expenses for treatment will be paid.

(continued)

12.3 (continued)

But you don't have to wait until you bottom out, Garlinghouse said. There's free confidential help on campus "for anybody who is uneasy about their own or anyone else's chemical trip."

Some important questions students should ask themselves, he said, are: "Do normal people who are in control of their drinking do this? Does this happen to people who are on top of it? Boogie till you puke: Is that really the good life?"

If they answer yes, Debbie said, and continue to drink, "more power to them. I guess that's the way I look at it, really. I had to look at the consequences, not my fantasy world. I was convinced that everything in my life was OK and it wasn't. I had all the proof that I needed that it wasn't."

She said she knows that a lot of people won't get sober. "And that's real possible for me. I could go out and get drunk tomorrow. I really could. But I don't think I will and I hope not."

Alcoholics Anonymous meetings help, she said. Both Debbie, 19, and Bonnie, 35, regularly attend meetings to help them remain sober. Bonnie's last drink was six years ago. Debbie's been sober for two years.

"AA seems like such a drastic step to some people," Bonnie said. "I remember my family saying, 'You're going to AA? But alcoholics go there!'"

Bonnie said she didn't like AA at first because the members talked about God and spiritual matters. "I had that all confused with religion and Christianity and I didn't want anything to do with that. The spiritual aspect of AA is now the most important part of my life. It's not in the sense of religion. It's just in the sense of taking care of myself and improving the quality of my life."

"There's so much insanity in this life," Debbie said. "I just wanted more from my life and I sure wasn't getting it from drugs and alcohol anymore." Now with the help of the AA program, she said, "I'm working on my dishonesty, my denial. I'm learning to deal with reality instead of running from it."

Bonnie said, "AA absolutely ruined my drinking. You know that you will not drink normally, no matter what you do. It's awful. And it's wonderful, because the alternative is dying."

Alcoholism: a family affair

By Faith Conroy
This is the second of a two-part series.

Fran, a University of Montana senior, didn't know much about alcoholism when she started college. She didn't know that half of the children of alcoholics (COAs) become alcoholic themselves and that another 25 percent marry them.

However, statistics show that 1 in 8 Americans has at least one alcoholic parent. Several years ago, Fran realized she was one of the eight.

In high school, Fran was really "straitlaced." She said she was a good student and didn't party very much. Occasionally, she got drunk at cast parties after performing in the high school plays.

But the drunk she remembers the most was at a pool party while visiting her father for the summer. That was the summer she "was dumped" by her first boyfriend, she said. And it was the summer her stepmother asked her father for a divorce.

She remembers her father getting drunk, crying and asking her why everything was going crazy. She remembers getting drunk with him later that summer in defiance against the world.

Years later, when the pressure of college became intense, she remembered the relief she felt from drinking with her dad and she often partied herself into oblivion.

"One time I passed out while walking down a hall," she recalled. At that point, she was partying several nights a week. "Some people would party one night and then other people would party another night. I was partying with all of them." But she didn't think anything was unusual.

Unfortunately, Fran learned the facts after she became involved with an alcoholic, suffered several years of mental abuse and then turned to Al-Anon meetings for help.

Al-Anon is a branch of Alcoholics Anonymous and is designed for the relatives and friends of alcoholics.

Carl Bodek, a chemical dependency counselor in Missoula and a COA, said the biggest problem of alcoholics and COAs is denial.

"Denial, that's where it all starts," he said. It can be a refusal to see that behavior patterns exist, or it can be distorted thinking or distorted perceptions of the world and reality.

"It's really hard to wake up in the morning and say 'I hate my father. He's a drunk.' So we deny that.

"We grow up in a world that's not real. When you deny things, you're not even aware you're denying them. We look and act normal, but we're a mess," he said. "We don't really know what normal is."

He said if current statistics are accurate, "there are literally thousands" of COAs at the University of Montana. Bodek said UM Health Service's personnel know how to identify COAs and often refer these students to him.

"They go to the health service with a whole laundry list of problems," he said.

They're confused. They can't decide on a major. They're having an anxiety attack. Their grades aren't good. They're having problems with their families or with relationships.

In general, they're having problems adjusting to adulthood and they can't cope with stress. Many develop obsessive-compulsive personalities and become workoholics or overeaters.

Ben, a UM senior, doesn't worry about becoming alcoholic, he said. But he does feel a lot of pressure to do something with his life. His older brother and father are alcoholics.

"I probably put it on myself," Ben said, "but then see, I'm starting to be more like my dad. I'm a workoholic now."   **(continued)**

12.3 (continued)

Coral, a COA, said that many children of alcoholics don't learn how to communicate or how to label their feelings because feelings aren't discussed or shared at home.

"Things we were taught when we were young were not to talk, not to trust, and not to feel," Coral said. "So you spend most of your life doing those three things."

She said she performed like an actor on a stage to survive in the world. "You don't know why you feel the way you do. You go through the motions. You do everything everybody else does but you're dying inside," she said. "We just don't fit in."

Coral's friend Linda, another recovering COA, said she lived in fear as a child. There was a lot of alcohol abuse and a lot of violence in her family. "My mother was an addict and an alcoholic. She's dead. My father was an alcoholic. He died of alcoholism," she said.

Occasionally her mom would disappear for a few days, she said.

"She'd be gone for three days at a time. We wouldn't know where she was and we were so well conditioned we wouldn't tell anybody she was gone. When we got phone calls, we either didn't answer the phone, unless it was a signal ring, or we made up a story."

She said her mom had drug-induced multiple personalities. "I couldn't bring friends to my house," Linda said, for fear of what she would find at home.

"Our house," Linda choked, "was the most incredible, stinking mess you could believe.

"There were fleas everywhere," she said, crying. "I used to have bites all the way up to my knees. I begged for knee socks because I had so many bites on my legs."

"You wouldn't want to lift the lid of a pot in the kitchen because there was no telling how long it had been there. You could just vomit from the smell," Linda said.

And the fear doesn't go away, according to Coral. Often it grows out of proportion and is difficult to control. "It goes into a relationship, walking down the street, taking a new job, going back to school, taking a test.

"I don't know how in the hell I got through a BA in education," she said. "I put myself under that much stress."

But because COAs work hard and are tenacious, responsible people, they know how to get things done and are usually successful, Bodek said. They're overachievers and take on many projects at once. They have a compulsive need to be perfect.

But they don't recognize their successes, he said. Instead, they blame themselves for the world's ills and punish themselves accordingly.

"I always quit when I started to do well because I didn't believe I deserved to be prosperous," Bodek said.

COAs also try to control the feelings and behaviors of others and become anxious and defensive when they can't.

"We act OK out in the work force, socially and the whole thing," Coral said. "But when we get into intimate relationships, that is when our world falls apart. We've had no role models."

Bodek agreed with Coral. "We didn't learn what relationships were supposed to be. When we were kids, we were used to people storming out of houses, leaving if the wrong thing was said, somebody gets hit or drunk," he said.

As a result, COAs often fall in love with alcoholics—someone they can rescue. They don't recognize the destructiveness of the relationship because they ignore their own needs, Bodek said. Instead they cater to the needs of the alcoholic and lose their identity in the process.

"You give somebody else the option of controlling your self-esteem," Bodek said. It's a way to prove to the other person how much you love them.

"You think that they're normal and you're not," Coral said. "Your gut is telling you this is crazy behavior, but they have a way of manipulating things. All of a sudden you're feeling confused, crazy, guilty.

"They had done something to create a crisis in their life and all of a sudden it was my fault. After a while, because you isolate yourself, you do this head trip on yourself and you believe them.

"And then the guilt that you feel when you try to get out of that relationship is overwhelming," Coral said.

COAs are called "enablers" because they protect the alcoholic and prevent them from suffering the consequences of their behavior, hiding the problem from others.

COAs are also insecure and will do anything to hold onto a relationship to avoid the pain of abandonment. And even if they do leave, Linda said, "You feel so isolated and so alone, you will go back to the relationship more than likely."

That's because the outside world is "too scary," Coral added.

COAs often have more difficulty coping with healthy relationships because they only learned how to respond to alcoholic behavior. "We create a bunch of stress for ourselves," Coral said. "We sabotage things constantly. With irrational thought, we can sabotage a relationship."

"We're like sticks of dynamite with the fuses lit," Bodek said.

COAs are always on guard. They can't relax, let go and have fun. Many have difficulty with sexuality. In addition, they can't cope with conflict, people in authority or personal criticism.

However, COAs are overly critical of themselves and of others.

"It's like a movie critic," Linda said. "I mean, those people really get down. But we're twice as bad as that on ourselves and we're that bad with everybody else in our lives."

COAs take on the burdens of the world because of an overdeveloped sense of responsibility. Often, COAs are depressed because the grief they suppressed in childhood surfaces and is compounded in adulthood. Many suffer a higher rate of stress-related illnesses.

Coral said that many children of alcoholics also drink compulsively. "We have all the behaviors (of alcoholics)," she said. "It's easy to become overwhelmed and turn to drugs or turn to alcohol."

Linda agreed. "We're not supposed to feel. When we do start to feel, we have to cover it. It's too much for us."

Ben started drinking compulsively when he was 17. "If you're a student,

(continued)

it's a great way to release pressure. Maybe you don't set out with that in the forefront of your mind, but that's surely what you're doing.

"I was into drinking heavy in high school, and marijuana too," he said. "And then in college, after I turned 19, I was down at the bar five nights a week.

"I knew it was a problem. Waking up feeling like shit everyday. It's pretty obvious. I don't know why I did it. God, I'd just drink until I got sick.

"I've driven sometimes, hanging my head out the window just to stay awake, to try and focus," he said. And sometimes he'd have blackouts.

Everything in high school revolved around beer, he said, "and everybody partied. I mean, the only people who didn't party were the real straight stiffs.

"I think one of the reasons I used to drink was for the companionship," he said. "To be in, to be accepted. I couldn't make it as a jock so partying was just the next best thing."

And drinking was a way to act rebellious. "But you know, it got old real fast," he said.

He said he's "the total opposite" of his alcoholic brother and father. He said his dad drinks a beer in the morning for breakfast and gin in the afternoon. "He's in a permanent comatose state."

Ben said he doesn't remember when his brother started drinking, but it didn't seem to be a problem at first. "I'd see him come home and he'd be sloshed, but I did a lot too, so I didn't think anything of it."

"I think he's past hope. We've tried. My whole family's tried to talk to him and stuff. But you can't."

He said he's almost come to blows with his brother because of his drinking. He said his brother has driven a wedge between his parents, driven his father to drink and made his mother uptight. But "it's never really affected me," he said.

"If anything, it just makes me averse to ending up like that," he said. "I have a hard enough time finding time to do everything I want without having to worry about getting up in the morning.

"I think I went through my phase and I realized how lonely it can get going out to bars five nights a week, 'cause it really is," Ben said.

Karen, a recovering COA, always thought her childhood was normal. She had loving parents, a stable home life and lots of fun with her family and friends. There was drinking, but to her, the drinking was normal.

Lately, however, she has noticed that her dad gets out of control when he drinks. And so does she.

She said she's doing things she wouldn't normally do. "Like passing out in front of my kids." And she has trouble remembering what she did when she was drunk.

But she said she doesn't want to stop drinking. She likes the release and the freedom she feels. Besides, it's fun.

So instead she's trying to control her drinking by deciding ahead of time how much and what she will drink. But something tells her that isn't normal.

"If I didn't have a problem with it, then I shouldn't have to be that concerned about it," she said. "But I don't want to be an alcoholic."

Because COAs grow up in a tumultuous environment, they thrive on chaos. They're hooked on adrenalin and the feeling of power that accompanies it. "You can become addicted to your own rush," Bodek said. "You don't have to have alcohol.

"When there's nothing out there supplying that rush, you create it," by instigating fights or climbing mountains, he said.

"Adrenalin rushes are all right as long as they're not destructive," he added. COAs learn in recovery how to channel this energy in positive directions.

"Recovery isn't some magical thing," Bodek said. "It's a desire to deal with all this."

But counseling is only one means to recovery, he said. Not all COAs need it. Many benefit from COA meetings, church groups, self-help and close personal relationships. "There's no one way," he said.

COA meetings, which are structured much like Alcoholics Anonymous meetings, are held from 7:30 p.m. to 9 p.m. each Wednesday and from 7 p.m. to 8 p.m. each Sunday in the Warehouse Mall at 725 W. Alder in Missoula.

"I can't stress enough how much meetings have helped me," Linda said. "I can become an alcoholic or a drug addict but I don't want to be. I choose to be aware."

Fran, Karen, Linda and Ben are pseudonyms.

Reprinted with permission of the Roy W. Howard National Writing Competition in Public Affairs Reporting, and the Scripps Howard Foundation, Indiana University School of Journalism.

Tying it all together Your job in a depth piece goes beyond telling what happened — you must tell what it means. The inverted-pyramid form is only somewhat helpful in writing the depth piece. You will be introducing the elements in order of their importance, but many elements will be almost parallel in alignment. For example, with a controversy, you might present one side and follow immediately with a contrary point and continue alternating like that throughout the development. Or you might present the surface of the story and then develop each aspect in order.

In developing the story, you may find some holes that need to be plugged. You may have to go back to sources or seek new ones. When you do resume digging, there's always a chance you'll find something that will alter the story significantly. Time causes situations to change; other events may have occurred that you weren't aware of. You have to be willing to reorganize and rewrite, weaving in the new material. One reaction to the discovery of new material is annoyance at the disruption of a story plan, but there's also the thrill of finding yet another piece of the puzzle and putting it in place. Sometimes more than one person is working on the puzzle. This can be good or bad, depending on how well you learn to work with another writer. Sometimes the team is reporter–writer, with one doing most of the primary fact-finding and the other doing the secondary fact-finding and the writing. Sometimes both are involved in all aspects.

Constructing a depth piece generally involves working with these elements:

- Introduction to the issue or event and people involved.
- Current events; status of issue.
- Past events; background.
- Commentaries by and interviews with participants and observers.
- Research available from secondary sources (documents, public records and the like).
- Observations and conclusions or summaries—generally from authoritative sources.

The format may be almost any mixture of the above, but is likely to start with a current event that serves as a news peg. The event may be a speech or some action, such as the filing of a lawsuit or the proposing of an ordinance in a city council. The significance of the event or issue—what it means to the reader—should be established early. Who is involved and how they're involved must be made clear. After you've established what's going on, how important it is and who is involved, you can add the background material to help put the story in perspective. Other aspects of the story can be introduced by quotes from a variety of sources. To establish the credibility of the commentators, cite their authority and ties to the issue or event. You can document what they say by referring to reports or public records such as laws or court actions.

Winding up   You will want to end the story with some projection of what is likely to occur; several outcomes might be possible. Using quotes is one way to provide the reader with a summary and reduce the risk of your views' being injected into the piece.

To summarize: You'll need a lead that attracts attention and that ties to something in the news—a news peg. Make your main point quickly so the audience will know what the piece is about. Follow that by telling them why the issue is especially significant. Next, offer some explanations: sometimes background, sometimes processes, sometimes scientific basis for developments or discoveries. Then dissect the issues or the elements involved, and once you have taken the pieces apart, quote some authorities about the relative importance of each. Finally, put the pieces back together in a way that gives the reader the satisfaction of having learned something.

BROADCAST DEPTH REPORTING   Some argue that depth reporting doesn't occur in broadcast journalism, because the tight time formats of news programs barely allow the surface of stories to be scratched each day. *Does* depth reporting exist in broadcasting?

Each year thousands of broadcast news programs compete for awards for depth reporting (see 12.4 and 12.5). This would indicate that depth reporting is not a thing of the past in broadcasting. But perhaps the past was a better era for it than the present.

12.4 Broadcast Depth Reporting

Broadcast depth reporting takes several forms, Station WOWT-TV of Omaha, Neb., took an in-depth look at fire prevention and safety over a two-week period. This is a lead-in to the first of many reports on the subject.

ANNCR.

FIRE MARSHALL WALLY BARNETT SAYS FIRE DEATHS HAVE INCREASED THIS YEAR.

TWENTY PERSONS DIED FROM FIRE IN ALL OF LAST YEAR . . . AND 34 HAVE DIED BY THE END OF AUGUST THIS YEAR. HE RELEASED THE FIGURES AS FIRE PREVENTION WEEK BEGAN THIS WEEK.

GARY PFEFFER NOW BEGINS A TWO-WEEK LOOK AT FIRE SAFETY, WITH A REPORT ON MISUSE OF ELECTRICITY.

TAPE SONY SOT
TIME 2:18
END CUE ''ACTION NEWS SIX''

From WOWT-TV, Omaha, Nebraska. Used with permission.

12.5 Depth Report Script

This script illustrates the way almost all TV reports are packaged. The reporter leads off with a standup or voice-over open (see Chapter 5), and then inserts SOT or NAT SOT tape cuts throughout his V/O narration. These tape productions can become very complex and are often taught in advanced broadcast news courses.

TAPE SONY SOT
(STANDUP OPEN)

SCRIPT NARRATION   What you've just seen is what happens when a wire is overloaded or made to do a job that it was not designed to do. It's part of a demonstration given by the Lincoln fire department. Improper wiring and overloaded circuits are the oldest cause of electrical fire. Yet, surprisingly, these fires still occur.

SOT
SUPER (BILL DUNBAR
        OFD FIREFIGHTER)

NARRATION   One of the biggest fires Dunbar ever fought started with faulty wiring.

(continued)

12.5 (continued)

SOT
SUPER (DUNBAR)

NARRATION   Electricians and manufacturers of appliances say these kinds of accidents
can be avoided by making sure not too much is asked of any particular
appliance. Don't overload circuits, and don't try to go around safety
measures built into the wiring system. That's particularly important
around Christmas time.

SOT
SUPER (CAPT. DAVE KOZIOL
        OFD PUBLIC INFORMATION OFFICER)

NARRATION   With the cooperation of the Omaha fire department, we were able to set
some fires to demonstrate their quickness and intensity. If a Christmas tree
begins burning, firefighters say it's almost impossible to put it out. Their
only hope is to save the home after the tree starts burning in that house.

Cary Pfeffer . . . Action News Six.   From WOWT-TV, Omaha, Nebraska. Used with permission.

The early years of television, especially, saw some of the best TV depth
reporting ever. In the 1950s and 1960s, such historically acclaimed shows as
See It Now, *CBS Reports* and *NBC White Papers* were produced. Nothing really
compares to that era today, at least not on network television. High costs and
potential lawsuits have curtailed a lot of network depth reporting, especially
of an investigative nature. Network personnel are expensive, and the time
involved in putting together a depth piece is significant. And the audiences
for these shows are never large, although they may be elite, with a high percentage of opinion makers.

However, when the South African government banned coverage of areas
experiencing discontent or demonstrations in the mid-1980s, the TV reporters,
deprived of action, delved into issues. The government in Pretoria might have
been better off having them cover the action. One of the problems with television reporting is the spotty nature of the brief reports: a lot of gunfire, but
not much counting of the casualties. Reporters felt that the situation was such
that it had to be reported in some way; the result was real understanding on
the part of many in the network audiences of what apartheid was all about.

Local stations do depth reporting of many types, and in general the categories
of depth reporting for both local stations and networks are:

- The documentary, or "doc."
- The mini-documentary, or "mini-doc."
- Investigative reporting.
- Special reporting.
- The magazine program, such as CBS's *60 Minutes*, and interview shows.

Docs and mini-docs   The documentary format has certain identifiable characteristics: It is usually a half-hour or hour in length; it focuses on one subject, topic or issue; it often exposes social, political, economic or moral ills. At the end, the problem is summarized, and a call to action may even be included. Many documentaries simply let the audience draw their own conclusions from the facts, and pictures, shown.

The documentary creates a mood over the half-hour or hour. The writer often tells the audience in the introduction what he or she wants to accomplish in that time. For example, in *Hunger in America*, one of the most critically acclaimed documentaries ever, the audience is told to be prepared to see the faces and hear the voices of the hungry in this land of plenty and to think about why hunger exists in a country like America. This 1968 CBS documentary then takes you to visit families across the U.S. that are hungry and makes you see, hear and find out the problem for yourself.

Every broadcast newsperson in the country wants to do docs, but the percentage that ever gets the chance is small. The reason is that documentaries require the assignment of a reporter and camera crew full time, a luxury few stations can afford; documentaries cost money to write and produce; they traditionally draw low ratings, and thus lose money for the station, and they frequently stir up trouble.

The documentary begins with a reporter's idea, which is then developed and presented as a proposal to the news director. The proposal should include the topic to be addressed, why it's important, how you'll go about addressing it, how much time and money it will take to complete the documentary, and when it will be completed.

The news director must then decide whether the idea is worth doing, whether you can be freed from your regular reporting assignments to do it, whether a camera crew can be assigned to you, and whether extra money is available to cover all of these expenses.

Station management must be consulted as to whether time can be allocated in the schedule to air the documentary. And if the program will be on a controversial subject, management might also have to give its approval in this regard.

In the place of the doc has come the mini-doc, which usually appears in three or five parts, on separate days for several minutes each time, within newscasts (see 12.6). Attaching the term *doc* to these short stories may create the impression that they are close relatives of the Murrow-style documentary. In fact, they are more like news features.

You have to repeat, summarize or update the audience each day:

> Yesterday we told you about what Denver housing officials say they're doing to provide housing for the city's poor. Today we hear another side of this issue as TV-10's Preston Kendrick presents the second of his five-part series on "Denver's Homeless Citizens."

By the time the mood and stage are set, and reset, each day, often half the allotted time is over. And by the fifth day, or earlier, many in the audience will have lost the thread of the story, despite the summary. Thus the mini-doc format, which is more like a print series, is often less than attractive.

12.6 Mini-Docs

These mini-docs are two examples of a five-part series on heart disease and cardiovascular problems by Dennis Johnson, medical reporter for WFAA-TV, Channel 8, in Dallas. The reporter notes this series was designed to educate and inform people about the various aspects of cardiovascular disease. Note that in major market stations like those in Dallas, and in many stations in smaller markets, broadcast reporters are sent all over the state, country—and even the world—to get the story.

HEART DISEASE—JOHNSON—PART THREE

ANCHOR

> PEOPLE WITH HEART DISEASE ARE TREATED WITH DRUGS AND SURGERY. BUT THOSE MEASURES OFTEN MISS THE ROOT OF THE PROBLEM—THE PERSON'S LIFESTYLE.
>   AS CHANNEL EIGHT'S DENNIS JOHNSON REPORTS FROM HOUSTON TONIGHT . . . HEART PATIENTS MUST LEARN TO MAKE CHANGES IF THEIR RECOVERY IS TO BE SUCCESSFUL.

TAKE TAPE (SOVT)
TOTAL TIME 1:30
END Q "CHANNEL 8 NEWS IN HOUSTON"

JOHNSON ON TAPE—SOT AND V/O
SCRIPT NARRATIVE

JOHNSON V/O   Open heart surgery doesn't mean much to patients who return to the same lifestyle that put them on the operating table.

> (NATSOT) EXERCISE CLASS
> TIME :03 END Q "THREE AND FOUR AND FIVE . . . "

V/O   Exercise after surgery or heart attack is important therapy . . . but it does little if patients return to their old ways.

> (SOT) DR. J. ALAN HERD
> TIME :11 END Q "IN THE FUTURE."

V/O   Because he's already had heart surgery, Joe Pyle doesn't want that to happen to him. So he comes to the Institute of Preventive Medicine to shape his new lifestyle. First, under supervision, he is tested to find his safe tolerance level for exercise.

> (NATSOT) JOE ON TREADMILL
> TIME :02

V/O   Besides more physical activity, Joe's lifestyle reflects less stress, good diet and no smoking.

(NATSOT) JOE ON BICYCLE
TIME :02

(SOT) JOE PYLE
TIME :10 END Q "UNTIL I'M 46."

V/O   But strong hearts don't live on exercise alone.

(NATSOT) DIETICIAN AND FAMILY
TIME :05 END Q "JELLY ON IT."

V/O   To help patients and their families make that often difficult transition
to less fat in the diet, the Institute offers this nutrition class. The
students just don't sit there . . . they make the meals. Here it's a meal
using foods like low fat cheeses, potatoes, fruits and vegetables.

The old habits are the hardest to break, but the people at the Institute
say patients can discover it's worth the effort when the benefits are
looking and feeling better than before.

Dennis Johnson, Channel 8 News in Houston.

HEART DISEASE—JOHNSON—PART FIVE

ANCHOR   ACCORDING TO CENSUS FIGURES,
MEXICAN-AMERICANS COMPRISE THE
FASTEST GROWING MINORITY GROUP IN
THE UNITED STATES. RELATIVELY
LITTLE IS KNOWN ABOUT CERTAIN
HEALTH RISKS IN MEXICAN-AMERICANS.
BUT NOW THAT IS CHANGING . . . AS
CHANNEL EIGHT'S DENNIS JOHNSON
REPORTS FROM SAN ANTONIO.

TAKE TAPE (SOVT)
TIME 1:35
END Q "CHANNEL 8 NEWS IN SAN
ANTONIO."

JOHNSON ON TAPE—SOT AND V/O
SCRIPT NARRATIVE

JOHNSON V/O   Out of state visitors and Texans flock to San Antonio to see the
Alamo. They enjoy themselves along the riverwalk. They take in the
Hemisfair . . . and for the last three years the American Heart
Association has turned San Antonio into a giant laboratory.

(continued)

12.6 (continued)   The San Antonio Heart study is the first major attempt to determine risk factors in Mexican-Americans.

The early results show they are three times more likely to have diabetes than their Anglo counterparts. One of the complications of diabetes is heart disease.

In San Antonio, low, middle and upper income Mexican-American residents are first interviewed in their homes, and then tested in this mobile clinic.

> (NATSOT) NURSE AND MAN
> TIME :11 OUT Q "2 TACOS..OK."

> (NATSOT) BLOOD PRESSURE BEING TAKEN
> TIME :02

V/O   Lalo Galindo is one of 14-hundred people in this study. He's had blood tests and an electrocardiogram. Lalo has a very personal reason for being here.

> (SOT) LALO GALINDO
> TIME :05 END Q "TAKE THE TEST."

> (SOT) DR. MICHAEL STERN
> TIME :16 END Q "PARTICULAR NEIGHBORHOOD."

V/O   Researchers think obesity may explain the higher diabetes rates among Mexican-Americans. But they also suspect other factors as genetics, diet and exercise . . . so the testing goes on.

> (SOT) JOHNSON STANDUP CLOSE
> TIME :15 END Q "IN SAN ANTONIO."

Investigative and special reporting   The networks may present a special investigative report that is then localized by individual stations. The cumulative effect is often "hype." Television was accused of hyping drug abuse, especially the prevalence of "crack"—smokable cocaine—in 1986. ABC's reporter John Quinones did observe that "sometimes we have a tendency to feed on one another, and the story feeds on itself."[8]

Story ideas are copied. The source is often an award winner like WTVJ-TV, Miami. In one series of investigative reports, WTVJ followed health inspectors around to local restaurants, and then each night on the 6 and 11 o'clock newscasts viewers would see for themselves the dead mice and rats, live cockroaches, and the methods used to recycle and serve previously served but uneaten

BLOOM COUNTY   by Berke Breathed

Reprinted with permission of The Washington Post Writers' Group.

food at many Miami area restaurants. A visual medium like TV is especially suited for this type of investigative report. Other stations picked up on the idea, and it was popular with consumers.

Many TV newscasts feature an "Action Line" reporter, who investigates the complaints of disgruntled consumers and tries to resolve them.

Consumer reporters sometimes handle complaint reporting but are mainly involved in activities like comparison shopping. Syndicated consumer shows, such as *Consumer Reports*, are also available for stations to use within their newscasts.

Some stations have begun to do more in the way of depth business and economic reporting. Broadcast networks and Cable News Network are assigning reporters to specialize in the area.

News magazine and interview programs

The TV-magazine format, made popular by *60 Minutes*, calls for several stories of 10, 15 or 20 minutes in length to be aired in a half-hour or hour block, including as well some lighter feature segments, commentaries, reviews—known as the "back-of-the-book" section.

Many local stations wish they could do a local news-magazine show, but very few do. The same problems exist here as with documentaries. Magazine programs are expensive to produce, often raise controversy and must be scheduled at a regular time in the broadcast week or month?

The *PM Magazine* format, a mixture of national and local stories, became popular in the late 1970s. However, these types of shows were always considered entertainment, not news, and news departments rarely had anything to do with their production.

Instead, most local stations settle for the news interview show. At the network level, the best known of this type of show have been *Face the Nation, Meet the Press,* and *Issues and Answers*. Locally, similar programs air on nearly all radio and TV stations. They're often bland, poorly produced and rarely tackle local controversy. Many stations agree that the only reason these public affairs programs are aired is to appease the FCC; if the FCC didn't require them, they wouldn't exist. With the deregulation of radio, much news programming has been replaced with music and entertainment. Similar effects are predicted for the deregulation of TV.

MAIN POINTS

- Depth pieces are built around the *why* of a story, telling how something occurred and what it means.
- Depth writing requires research skills, the cultivation of sources and knowing how various institutional systems work.
- Constructing the depth piece involves introducing the issue or event and people involved, giving the current status of the issue, recounting past events and giving other background, offering the observations and comments of authorities (participants and observers), including information from documents and public records, suggesting what to expect—the outcomes and their significance.
- Some depth pieces are presented in a series, in print and in broadcasting.
- Depth pieces in broadcasting take on several forms: the documentary (doc), the mini-documentary (mini-doc), investigative reports, special reports, magazine and interview shows.

EXERCISES

1. Make a list of topics at your school that could be given a depth treatment. These can be matters that affect primarily students, such as the academic honesty policy, or ones that affect the university as a community, such as the school's endowment or university governance, or day-to-day subjects such as the bookstore purchasing and return policy, the cafeteria's meal planning and pricing, the medical service.

2. Do research for a depth report. Be comprehensive in your research, looking up available information and interviewing to search out additional facts and new aspects to research.

3. Write the depth story for your newspaper, a minimum of 20 inches.

4. Take that same depth story you wrote for the newspaper, or a different one, and develop a proposal for a broadcast depth report of about five minutes in length. Include the following in your proposal:

   - The issue or subject and why it's important.
   - Who you will interview on tape (audio or video) for the story and why.
   - An outline of how you see the report appearing on the air. Write an opening segment introducing the report, lead-ins to the tapes in the story, and a closing segment.
   - Cost of travel and equipment.
   - When you'll turn in this special report.

NOTES

1. The "new journalism" of Tom Wolfe (*The Electric Kool-Aid Acid Test, The Painted Word*) is really the new non-fiction, argue W.L. Rivers and Everette Dennis in *Other Voices: The New Journalism in America*. They see this dramatic narrative style with dialogue and scene setting as a distinct type, different from *alternative journalism*, practiced in magazines such as *Mother Jones* by reporters who feel the established media are ignoring some levels of society and some issues; different from *advocacy journalism*, which they see as more like the traditional newswriting of an earlier period, opinion interwoven with fact. They identify yet another splinter as *counter-culture journalism*, mostly a product of the 1960s but still alive in some publications. The original in this area, *Rolling Stone* (founded in 1967), is well established but has broadened its scope. Another new style they see as *precision journalism*, the origin of which is attributed to Philip Meyer while he was in the Washington bureau of the Knight newspapers. It involves applying social science methods to reporting, as in the *Dallas Morning News* series on teen-agers drawn from survey research represented in 12.4. They also define *alternative broadcasting* as an outgrowth of the videotape and video recorder as well as the proliferation of choice given by cable.

2. R. Thomas Berner, *Literary Newswriting*, Journalism Monographs, No. 99, October 1986, p. 22.

3. William L. Rivers, *The Mass Media: Reporting, Writing, Editing*, 2nd ed. (New York: Harper & Row, 1975), p. 221.

4. Curtis D. MacDougall, *Interpretative Reporting*, 7th ed., pp. 159–67.

5. William L. Rivers and Shelley Smolkin, *Free-Lancer and Staff Writer*, 3rd ed. (Belmont, Calif.: Wadsworth, 1981), pp. 62–63.

6. Ronald P. Lovell, *Reporting Public Affairs: Problems and Solutions* (Belmont, Calif.: Wadsworth, 1983), p. 119.

7. The Pentagon Papers were official documents about the Vietnam War that offered a view of the conflict different from the government position presented to the public.

8. "Though Crack & Cocaine Stories Dominated TV News Last Summer, 'No Evidence That Level of Drug Abuse Changed,' Only The Hype Did: NYU's News Study Group," news release from Howard Greene, Greene Inc., for *TV Guide*, Feb. 2, 1987.

9. The Fairness Doctrine said that broadcasters must seek out issues of controversy, importance, interest and concern in their local communities. This was a directive to broadcasters to act, and not sit and wait for someone to come to them with complaints. Once these issues were identified, the broadcast had to treat their presentations on the air with "fairness." The FCC checked to make sure stations were raising the issues, and then checked to see if they were reporting on them in a "fair manner." The majority of broadcast people, joined by many print journalists, claimed the Fairness Doctrine was not fair. The argument used was that newspapers are not required by the government to seek out any issues if they don't want to. Furthermore, if the newspaper *does* report an issue, it doesn't need to be fair at all but can show an editorial bias to one side or the other, and often does. The FCC dropped the Fairness Doctrine in 1987. Both houses of Congress passed legislation to "codify" the Fairness Doctrine, but President Reagan vetoed it as "antagonistic to the freedom of express." Congress is expected to try again.

SUGGESTIONS FOR ADDITIONAL READING

Dennis, Everette, and William L. Rivers. *Other Voices: The New Journalism in America*. San Francisco: Cartiche Press, 1974.

Downie, Leonard Jr. *The New Muckrakers*. Washington: New Republic Book Co., 1976, pp. 183–91.

Hage, George S., Everette Dennis, Arnold H. Ismach and Stephen Hartgen. *New Strategies for Public Affairs Reporting*. Englewood Cliffs, N.J.: Prentice-Hall, 1976.

MacDougall, Curtis D. *Interpretative Reporting*, 8th ed. New York: Macmillan, 1982. The only book in the field for a long time.

Meyer, Philip. *Precision Journalism*. 2nd ed. Bloomington: Indiana University Press, 1979. His book and work defined a whole new area of reporting.

Rivers, William L. *The Other Government: Power and the Washington Media*. New York: Universe Books, 1982. An excellent look at the news process with government as the source.

Rose, Louis J. *How to Investigate Your Friends and Enemies*. St. Louis: Albion Press, 1983. Secrets shared by a *St. Louis Post-Dispatch* reporter.

Schulte, Henry H. *Reporting Public Affairs*. New York: Macmillan, 1982. A news-paperman/teacher explains the mysteries.

Sheehan, Neil, Hedrick Smith, E.W. Kenworthy and Fox Butterfield. *The Pentagon Papers*. New York: Bantam, 1971. Also Chicago: Quadrangle Books, 1971.

Sussman, Barry. *The Great Cover-up: Nixon and the Scandal of Watergate*. New York: Signet, 1974.

Weinberg, Steve. *Trade Secrets of Washington Journalists*. Washington: Acropolis Books, 1981. Saves some steps for information-seekers in the capital.

Persuasive Writing

"All of us by nature fall in love with our own ideas, our own words. Excellence is born of intelligent criticism. And maturity is the product of the self-confidence that seeks, accepts, and benefits from criticism. To avoid it is a symptom of personal weakness or low ability or both."

"Technology and modern communications combine to get products accepted more quickly, copied more quickly, and replaced more quickly.

"The creative person doesn't have time for foreplay. Today is the day. The time is now."

William A. Marsteller, *Creative Management*, pages 13 and 34.

Writing Advertising Copy

Advertising copy has many of the qualities of good feature writing and opinion writing, including its use of literary devices, and it often has the qualities news demands, too: timeliness and high concentration of information.

Audiences tend not to discriminate between commercial and editorial messages. So advertising messages compete for attention not only with each other but with the editorial and entertainment content of a news medium as well.

Almost all advertising copy has something in common with broadcast copy: A few words have to accomplish a great deal. Another similarity is that the words must work well with other elements, such as pictures or sound; they must complement, not compete.

A commercial message has a specific purpose: to get someone to think something or do something. It must be compelling enough to get someone to read or listen to completion, so easy to understand that recognition of meaning is almost instantaneous, credible enough to be believed, memorable enough to be recalled, and persuasive enough to convince its audience to actually think or do what the message says.

RESEARCH The writer responsible for advertising copy has to do research in three areas— product, market and audience—or have it provided, so that he or she can do a credible writing job. What the writer is supposed to bring to the writing task is a thorough knowledge of the media: style and format requirements, deadlines, costs, as well as supplier requirements, deadlines and costs.

The product, the market and the audience Some copywriters like to have a sample of the product to try personally. In almost all cases, writers like to have a sample to look at as they write. If it is something large, like an airplane or a building, scale replicas help. Often all the copywriter really has are photographs and the R&D (research and development) report.

When the client is a service, like a rug cleaner or an interior decorator, the writer has to know all of the things the service will offer—in great detail. Many services are almost identical. The writer has to search for a competitive edge. Sometimes the writer will take advantage of the service, when that is physically possible. If the writer is miles away from where the service is being offered, as is often the case, he or she can arrange to call and interview some of the people who actually deal with the customers, either in taking the service calls or in making them. From these interviews, the writer can get an idea of the level of performance.

Seeing how complaints are handled, for either products or services, is also helpful, because it sometimes hints at the difference between the client and the competitors.

Looking for the competitive edge is important to remember, too, when writing about a person, like a political client, or an institution, like a museum. Generally, in these cases the emphasis is more on the quality of the client and less on a comparison.

The copywriter imagines the use of a product or service, anticipates the response to an institution, a person or even to an idea, such as a bond issue to raise money for public libraries. To do this properly, the copywriter has to know a great deal about the target audience for the product, service, institution, candidate or issue. Generally, this comes in the form of market research, which describes the audience demographically—age, sex, education, income and so on—and psychographically—lifestyles and interests. But the statistics have to be interpreted by the writer, who draws from some experiences with people of all types to make the statistics come to life and to envision a representative of that target audience to "talk to" through the ad's copy. The ad's creative strategy is designed to reach the particular segment of the audience the advertiser wants to affect. There is no "general" audience. There is a describable audience to reach, to inform, to persuade and maybe to entertain.

The way the writer talks to the audience is greatly influenced by the position of the product or service or institution in the marketplace. Is this an introductory campaign, a change-of-focus or -image campaign, or simply maintenance advertising to keep customers and market share? It may be an image campaign designed to make the audience aware or to give it a different view of the institution or to reinforce a favorable image. In any case, the writer has to understand the current market status and the purpose for the advertising being created.

Media and suppliers   The market research should show which media the target audiences use, but the writer should also know *how* those audiences relate to those media. In order to write for the media, the writer must understand that newspapers get generally less second-experience readership than magazines: A person looks at a newspaper and puts it aside, not to be looked at again, unless something comes to mind that needs to be referred to, like a sale ad. But a magazine may be read piecemeal and stays around as long as the person is still reading his or her way through it.

The person listening to radio probably is doing something else, maybe driving, and isn't likely to have pencil at hand to write a name or phone number, nor is that sort of information likely to be recalled. However, the setting for television, in the home or office, generally means pen or pencil is available, so an address or phone number can be shown on the screen, superimposed on the picture or alone, for audience response.

Writers are supposed to know which media are most credible, too, because that affects how copy is handled. You know that instinctively. You have to be much more persuasive explaining an absence to a teacher you've taken classes from before who knows you don't usually miss than one who doesn't know you at all.

In addition to knowing audience response to and use of media, the writer should be knowledgeable about the demands of the media. Each type of print media—newspapers, magazines, posters and so on—has specific format requirements. So do radio, television, videotex. The writer will be expected to have some knowledge of these format specifics and to know where to get the additional information. For example, *Editor & Publisher* lists the advertising specifics for every U.S. newspaper, daily and weekly.

Likewise, the writer is expected to understand the needs of suppliers. How should copy be marked to be sent to the typesetters? The writer is expected to know the production process—how corrections are made and what costs are involved.

THE WRITING ASSIGNMENT

What the writer must know to begin an advertising writing assignment falls into seven categories.

1. What is the *purpose* for the ad? What does the client want the audience to do: buy the product, come to the museum, vote for the candidate, gain additional insight into an institution—what it does and what it stands for.

2. What is the *persuasive strategy* to accomplish this purpose? What is being offered in terms of an appeal or incentive, a mild threat or unfavorable comparison? What is likely to work best for that audience, and in the medium being used to deliver the message? How can the purpose be accomplished through the planned strategy?

3. What is the best writing approach for the *audience*? What language is most appropriate? This may depend on educational background and age, and it may be related to experience with the product or similar ones. What you would say about binoculars in a *Time* magazine ad to someone buying a pair for the first time would differ from how you'd write for someone who might have a great deal of product experience, as the reader of *Audubon* might.

4. How well will the *medium* deliver the message you need? You know that if you are trying to talk about a complex subject like insurance but your

medium is television, you will have to go with images, not facts: the medium just won't accommodate a long, detailed message. You need to be sensitive to the visual element in print and television. The words and art must complement, enhance each other, not compete and distract.

5. How *accurate* is every single detail? How flexible can you be with the copy and still be accurate? Not only do you have responsibility to the audience, but there are legal concerns. How many ways can you state the terms of a warranty, or what a product will and won't do? You can't run the risk of false advertising.

6. Can you make special *creative* use of a medium? Can you design an ad that is so different that it becomes a trend setter? Examples are the fold-out ad in *Time* magazine's September 1986 edition, the scratch and smell ads, the silent action commercials that keep audiences from zapping. All of these are innovative uses of traditional media. What is your contribution?

7. What *overall effect* is the ad you prepare likely to have? How does it fit into the other part of the advertising campaign? You have to know what the rest of the advertising looks like—point of sale, billboard and so on.

Knowing all of this, where do you start writing your ad? You examine the elements of advertising copy appeals and determine your approach to satisfy each.

A focus for advertising copy

Five types of advertising copy appeals have been identified: attention, self-interest, desire, credibility and action. The first requirement is to capture the *attention* of your target audience. If you don't accomplish that, nothing else you do matters. In print, you capture their attention with the headline. For instance, "You Can Win One Million Dollars" is threadbare, but it still works. Headlines account for 80 percent of the attention-getting factor in any print ad. In radio, you have to count on the sound effects and music, and in television, you rely on motion, the action.

Second, you figure out how you can appeal to *self-interest*. People do things for their reasons, not yours. You have to find out what their reasons might be for doing what the ad is supposed to cause to happen. For example, the headline "Be Your Own Boss" will get attention, and the self-interest appeal is elaborated on immediately in body copy, which tells you how you can be self-employed and not only make more money (vested self-interest) but also be relieved of the stress of someone else controlling your life (quality-of-life self-interest).

You want the reader to become absorbed in the "how-to" of the ad. The first sentence of the body copy not only must fulfill the promise of the headline, it must entice the audience to receive the rest of the message and whet the *desire* for what is being advertised. The next sentence tells how the desire can be fulfilled, perhaps by sending away for the manual that tells how owning a franchise turns you into your own boss, and a rich one at that. This is the problem-solving portion of the message: You want to be your own boss, and you know that having control of life and working for yourself is in your own best interest. Now, this is how you do it.

Credibility is crucial to the message at this point. If in making the offer or the appeal you waffle or hedge, you will lose your audience. Sometimes delivering this part of the message without that risk is difficult, not because there's anything wrong with the product, but because of laws that govern how an offer or an appeal can be made. You have to be as direct as possible to be convincing. The audience's experience with these types of claims, offers or appeals is a consideration here, too. You may have to overcome some resistance. This part of the message needs to be successful, because your audience may not act right away. You want a residue of belief so a subsequent message might be more successful. In any case, you don't want your copy to be rejected for lack of credibility.

You want the audience to take the *action* that is the intent of the ad: buying the product, voting for the bond issue, making a donation. Action is how most advertising is measured for its effectiveness, even though most advertisers know that repetition of message, a cumulative effect, is what is really likely to get action. You have to approach each advertising copywriting assignment the way an editorial writer approaches an editorial—a one-shot effort to get someone to think or do something.

Creative thinking   Because words are so critical in advertising, writers need to develop creative thinking skills. Much native creativity is suppressed during our development in structured learning situations and has to be teased back to the surface. Creative thinking skills can be restored by learning to make unusual associations. To improve this skill, write a word, any word, then all of the other words it makes you think of. When you have a writing assignment, do this with some key words and you may find some unusual associations that will keep you out of the trite trap.

Another creative training device is learning to make the commonplace exotic. One advertising teacher always assigns students products like plumbing supplies, hardware, lumber, fresh produce like celery and broccoli instead of grapes and peaches. Such assignments are designed to stretch the imagination. One student captioned a pile of lumber "The stuff dreams are made of." A number of copy spin-offs resulted: "Dream house," for instance, was a home, a child's dollhouse, a doghouse, a children's tree house, a pool house. Associative ideas like this come from lifetime experiences, listening to and observing and learning from others and being exposed to music, literature, theater, painting and sculpture, since the fine arts are generally the source of the avant-garde.

Once the idea is there, the next choice is deciding what to show, what to tell and what to leave to the audience's imagination. This requires some creative thinking, too. You have to decide what is best represented by art and what by words. You have to determine what can be left unsaid and yet be understood. One ice cream ad had a child in a toy car holding an empty cone up for a dip. No ice cream was shown, just the name of the company. Obviously ice cream goes in a cone, and the implication is that all flavors are equally desirable. The caption said, "Fill 'er up." The television commercials with a visual narrative and few words, usually at the close, follow this same principle. The emphasis is on art or action as symbols. But you can't sell hospital insurance that way. Some items need an emphasis on the words. Sometimes the medium and not the product determines the emphasis. In radio, for example, words are the pictures.

The choice of symbols—words, music, art, action, characters—are a careful mix. Words can be almost neutral so as not to distract, or they can blend in delicately. They can strongly reinforce or they can dominate. The choice has to be carefully calculated.

Format   **Print.**   Print advertising generally implies ads in newspapers and magazines, although posters, billboards, flyers, inserts and any number of other types of print are also included in this category.

First you begin with a rough layout of the ad, measured precisely to size. Block in how much space the art is going to take, then block in the headline space. The size of the space and the size of type you think you will need to be effective will determine how many words you can use. Get the character count for the type style you want and see how much room you have. This is very much like headline writing for newspapers. Think of the space as an empty slot. You are going to insert something in the slot, but it has to fit. It can be a bit too small, but not too large. Computer terminals and laser printers have made desk-top publishing a reality. For advertising copy, you may also have a Kroy machine for type and an Artograph (an opaque projector) for design production.

Even with all of these machines, you will sometimes send material to type-setters. You need to know the correct format to use when someone else is following your directions in setting the type and handling the ad's design.

Write the headline on a separate sheet, because it will be set on a different machine from the body copy. The headline and copy sheets have to be fully identified with your name and your company's address or phone number in one corner, along with the client's ad topic represented by a slug line, so that once the headline is set, it can be reunited in the typesetting plant with the body copy. Mark the sheets with the type specs: the size and face you want and any other instructions, such as color and spacing, or leading (pronounced LED-ing). All instructions have to be circled, because the typesetter sets anything that isn't.

On the layout, the headline and body copy are represented with straight lines or bars. The copy block represents the amount of space you can fill with words. The count has to be accurate.

If one size and typeface are used throughout, you can put the body copy on one sheet. But chances are this won't be the case. You mark the layout

"Copy A" and put that designation on the copy that is to be set the same. You mark the layout "Copy B" and put on another sheet, also marked "Copy B," all of the type to be set in that size and face (see 13.1). Again, all copy must have your identification and the slug line, so it can be unified as a package once the type is set.

You will also want to mark a space for a logo on the layout. That does not need to go to the typesetter, only to the printer, but the logo may also

13.1 Print Ad Layout and Finished Product
An ad's layout is a set of instructions as well as an illustration of what the piece will look like.

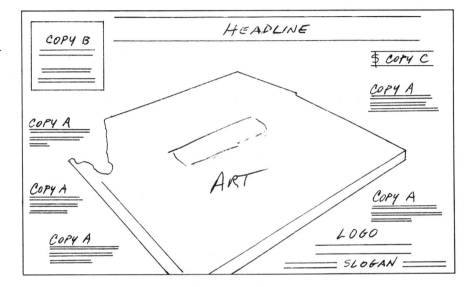

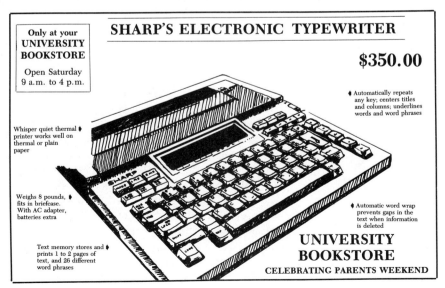

TOURNAMENT

November 11-13   4p.m. to 7p.m.

College Bowl:

Varsity
Sport
of the
Mind

*Team competition
of
organizations and individuals*

Deadline - Wednesday, October 22   *entry blanks*
Sponsored by Special Events Committee   *in Student Activities Office*

13.2 Public Service Ad

need some type associated with it, such as "registered trademark of XYZ Company." If so, the logo with a copy sheet attached does go to the type-setter so that line can be set. Again, this copy sheet has to carry full identification and instructions for typesetting.

Once it is set, the type will be sent with the layout to production, where it will be pasted up and prepared for the printing process. When the type comes back from the typesetter, it will be your job to check it to be sure the type was set *exactly* the way you wrote the copy, with every "i" dotted, literally, and every punctuation mark in the right place. For this reason, always keep a copy of what you have written, separate from the one that goes to the type-setter. If the type is set wrong and the typesetter made a mistake, corrections are free, but if you made the mistake, it costs your employer. You have to hold on to this copy because when the proof (the copy of the typeset material) comes back from the printer, you will be asked to check again to be sure that when someone was pasting up the type, a slip of the knife didn't cut off a comma or a digit of a zip code. You will have to check it yet one more time when the final proof comes. Then when you see the ad in the publication, you will need to check again. Some mistakes do find their way into print. You need to know where the error occurred. Again, if the mistakes are with the supplier, the correction, even reprinting, is free.

Radio.   In writing any broadcast copy, remember that you are writing for two audiences, not one. The announcer (or actor) is your first audience. If the person reading the copy has a difficult time with it, the delivery will be flawed. Try reading it yourself and listen to how it sounds. Some writers tape their copy as they read it and play it back. Others get someone else to read it cold to see if he or she stumbles. One advantage of doing both, reading it yourself and having someone else read it, is that you get a feel for the exact timing of the words. Although you know it's roughly four seconds per line, some words are easier to say than others. The emphasis that advertising copy needs means some parts need to be read more slowly than others. Furthermore, music and sound effects may deduct from the amount of time available for copy. You have to estimate this as accurately as possible. Some copywriters include music (any music) and some sounds in a recording to see whether they have too much or too little copy. Better too little than too much. If radio copy is too long going into the production studio, the producer will make cuts. These may not be the ones that you, the writer, would have made.

Radio commercials are written as scripts. Directors, producers, music and sound effects people, actors—all will be working from this script. You need to think constantly in terms of the medium's unique ability to use words to create images for listeners, which makes it a powerful means of persuasion. Radio is also a very flexible medium in production terms, so you can get on timely messages, ones that use a news peg, if you wish.

Radio scripts are fairly simple in composition. As with print copy, complete identification should be on the copy so you can be contacted if necessary, and for properly labeling the audiotape. This information goes in the upper left-hand corner with the dates the commercial is to be played.

> These read as START: JAN. 10, 1987
> STOP: FEB. 16, 1987
>
> SCHEDULE: (The time bought goes here.)

On the right goes the length of the commercial—for example, 30 seconds. The speaking parts are identified by all caps on the left side of the pages, and everything that is heard, words, music and sound effects, goes on the right. Thus the commercial script looks like any other radio script, except for the notations for music and sound effects (see 13.3).

Television.   The audio precautions you took with radio copy need to be taken with television copy, too: You want to be sure the people who have to read your words can do so easily and with meaning, and you want to be sure you have stayed within the time limits. With television, you really have less time for copy because movement is involved.

You want your words to complement the action, not compete with it. To do that effectively, you work from a storyboard, a series of panels that represent each scene in the commercial. Usually about nine panels make up a 30-second TV spot. The rule of thumb is about one frame per four or five seconds of video. The first and last frames are usually viewed a little longer, the first to establish and the last to close. This is not a hard and fast rule; it depends on the pace of the spot. Some award-winning commercials are so fast-paced that they have at least double that number. With too few shots, the pace will lag. Even in a 10-second spot, you need at least two visuals.

13.3a Radio Copy for British Caledonian Airways

This is what is called a "donut" in copywriting. These words, with music, are a recorded format into which other copy can be inserted. The insert can make the commercial 30 seconds or 60. The inserted copy that goes in the "hole" can be updated for marketing changes—price, schedule, specials. The copy in the hole is read by the station's announcer. This allows for lower production costs, because the music "frame" is already there. This particular copy takes advantage of radio's ability to have the listener imagine pictures. In some ways this is even more powerful than television.

HANNAH:	I am a 600 year old castle on the Isle of Skye.
	I am the kilts and bagpipes at a Highland gathering.
	I am the bright lights of Picadilly Circus.
	I am the footsteps of William Shakespeare along the River Avon.
	I am Robert Burns and Winston Churchill.
	I am the glowing colors of a proud Scottish tartan.
	I am Windsor Castle and the Tower of London.
	And I am only a non-stop flight away.
	I am British Caledonian Airways.
	I am an airline with over 40 world-wide destinations.
	I am Europe's largest independent airline.
	I am the best of Great Britain.
	I am British Caledonian Airways.
ANNC:	Fly the only daily non-stop from Houston to London. Fly British Caledonian Airways. We're the best of Great Britain. And we never forget you have a choice.
HANNAH:	I am Parliament and Big Ben.
	I am the Best of Great Britain.
	I am British Caledonian Airways.

Reprinted with permission of British Caledonian Airways.

As in TV newswriting, the page is divided into two sections. On the left go the video descriptions and instructions. The timing of each segment is either built into this or appears in a narrow column immediately adjacent. The right half of the page is devoted to the audio. At the top of the page is the identifying information: the name of the client, the writer, the length, the slug line or a production code, the start and stop dates, and instructions for the video and the audio. If anything special needs to be done in producing the commercial, instructions to the director and producer should be written in at the top of the page and marked off from the script. Most agencies, and all stations, have printed forms for TV scripts (see 13.4).

Style Ads follow six general styles, sometimes according to purpose.

1. *Humor*. Despite some adverse research findings about the effectiveness of humor, advertising messages are still being presented to get a smile, a chuckle

Motel 6 Radio Script

''Free Phones''

Hi. Tom Bodett. I'm sitting in room 201 of the Motel 6 in Yuba City, California, and I'm talking on the phone. Big deal, you say. Darn right it's a big deal. Because now, almost every Motel 6 has a telephone in every room—but that's not the half of it. We'll let you make free local calls on our new phones. But wait. There's more. Motel 6 now gives you free TV and movies. And kids stay free in their parents' room. It's wild. Plus you get all this for the lowest prices of any national chain, under 20 bucks* in most places, a lot less in some, a little more in others, but always a heck of a deal on a clean comfortable room. To make a reservation at Motel 6 call 505-891-6161. Then come make free local phone calls. Watch free TV and movies. You'll be thrilled. That's how it always is when something new comes along. You'll get the hang of it. I'm Tom Bodett for Motel 6. Keep both hands on the wheel and we'll leave the light on for you.

*Under 19 — Texas and Oklahoma

 Under 21 — California

Reprinted with permission of Motel 6 and The Richards Group.

13.3b Radio Commercial

The challenge here was to let people know about new benefits in a low-cost motel chain. Every hotel room has a phone, right? So the copywriter decided to do a spoof of the "new" benefit. Getting the client to laugh at himself or herself is a first-rate hard sell. A series of these commercials made a minor celebrity of the personality reading them.

or a good laugh (see 13.5). Some humorous appeals have a limited audience. Satire requires a fairly sophisticated audience, as does whimsy. But slapstick, if it's not overdrawn, seems to be accepted by most audiences. In international campaigns, the humor used has to be sensitive to the culture of the societies where it will be seen. For these reasons, many advertisers are cautious about using a humorous appeal.

2. *The hard sell.* The copy is direct, repetitive, often fast-paced and hard-hitting. Some of the late-night television commercials for furniture stores and used-car dealers belong to this category, as do much print catalog copy and newspaper sales copy.

3. *Information* advertising comes with higher-priced items, especially ones that are technical, like computers or luxury cars.

13.4 TV Ad Copy

HELP FIGHT POLLUTION CAMPAIGN

KEEP AMERICA BEAUTIFUL, INC.
"Clean Community"

Public Service Announcements available in
:60, :30, :10 lengths on 16mm film

ANNCR: (VO) Over the past
3 years --

America's becoming a
cleaner place to live in.

San Diego, for example,
has become 29% cleaner.

Weirton, West Virginia,
44% cleaner.

Indianapolis, 81% cleaner.

And all because of something
called the Clean Community
System.

The Clean Community
System actually changes the
way people think about
trash and pollution.

More important, it changes
the way people act.

The Clean Community
System makes a city so clean,

the citizens simply refuse
to let it get dirty again.

But though many
communities are part of
the system...

many more aren't.

What about your
community?

Write to learn if it's in the
system. And, if not, how to
change that.

With the Clean Community
System, our whole country
can be a cleaner place to live
in.

A Public Service Campaign of the Advertising Council

CNHF-0160
CNHF-0130
CNHF-0110

Volunteer Advertising Agency: Marsteller Inc.
Volunteer Campaign Coordinator: Marshall C. Lewis, Union Carbide Corporation

13.5 Humor in Advertising

4. *Testimonial* advertising is in between the hard sell and the informative: the person in the white lab coat telling you why one cold medicine is better for you than another (see 13.6).

5. *Endorsement* advertising is seen during political campaigns, but it's also occasionally used for products (see 13.7). This form has some strict regulations. The person "endorsing" really has to be voting for the issue or candidate or actually using the product. The laws were enacted to put an end to "endorsements" by celebrities of products that they had cases of in their garage but had never touched.

13.6 Testimonial Ad

This ad compares Advil, the newest pain reliever, with established competitors aspirin and Tylenol. The person testifying is a violinist, but she's not a celebrity. She's probably a professional model, which is why you see her face in the ad, but not her name. That's the difference between testimonial and endorsement advertising.

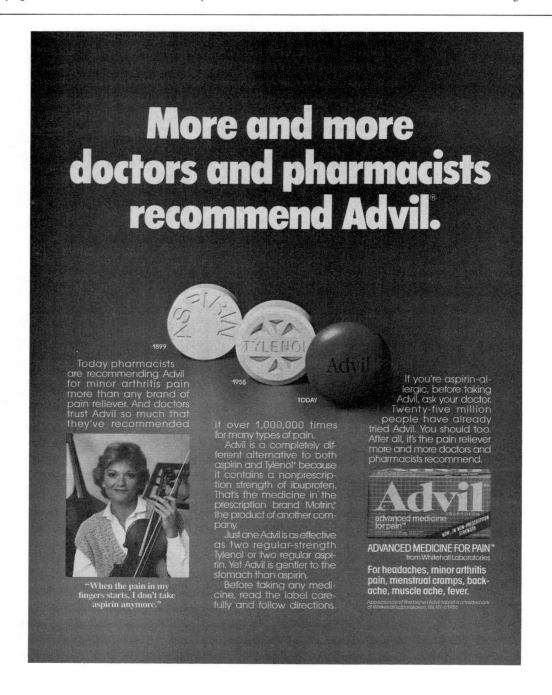

13.7 Endorsement Ad

This endorsement shows a musician recording on equipment related to the playback equipment being advertised. The copy indicates that he also uses that product as well.

To hear why George Benson records on Sony Digital equipment, play him back on a Sony Compact Disc Player.

When it comes to capturing the experience of live music, no audio equipment delivers the performance of digital audio.

That's why George Benson, creator of *Breezin'*, the best-selling jazz recording in history, has decided to invest in digital equipment.

And the name this leader in jazz/pop fusion chooses, interestingly enough, is the leader in digital audio: Sony.

Not only has Sony led the way in professional digital recording equipment, we also invented the digital system for playback—the compact disc player. Sony introduced the first home, car and portable CD players. And Sony sells more types of compact disc players than anyone else in the world.

But whichever Sony Compact Disc Player you choose, each allows you to hear the music the way the artist originally intended.

So why not do what George Benson does? Play back the top-selling compact discs the same way they were mastered. On Sony Digital equipment. You'll find that when it comes to bringing you close to the music, nothing else even comes close.

Presenting the Sony Discman,™ the world's smallest portable compact disc player.

Hardly larger than the disc itself, the fully programmable Discman* D-7DX comes complete with carrying case, headphones and a rechargeable battery. Everything you need for digital audio on the go.

SONY®
THE LEADER IN DIGITAL AUDIO™

© 1986 Sony Corporation of America. Sony is a registered trademark of Sony Corporation. The Leader in Digital Audio and Discman are trademarks of Sony Corporation of America.
*Headphones included with D-7DX only.

6. *Institutional* advertising is sometimes called image or idea advertising. **Image ads** are those that try to help an audience see the institution as it wants to be seen (see 13.8a). Or they might be trying to present an image of a company that sells a service rather than consumer products (see 13.8b). Institutional ads are quite different from the Mobil column ads, which are really *advertorials*, or editorials dealing with issues of interest to the company. In broadcasting, these advertorials are called *infomercials* (see 14.1). House ads are "self ads" for the institution in its own publication (see 13.9).

Public service announcements

PSA's for non-profit organizations can take the form of humor, hard sell, informative or image. Some PSA's come from the state or national headquarters of the organizations (see 13.10) and are elaborately produced. Most are locally produced for local non-profit organizations, so scripts are kept fairly simple.

13.8a Institutional Ads

The appealing child discovering something exciting about his world charms you into reading about the company's interest in and support of education and about their PBS series, which must run without commercials. This also represents a good use of art—fireflies flitting through the copy.

When curiosity flourishes, worlds can be changed.

Why? How? What if? Young people question. Taking joy in the search for solutions. Their worlds abound with endless possibilities. So, too, it is with scientists. Whose laboratories are as limitless as the universe. Whose ideas shape worlds. To interest young minds in the wonders of science, Phillips Petroleum has made possible a film series called "The Search for Solutions." Stimulating films aired on PBS and seen by over two million students per month. They capture the excitement of discovery. And the discoverer. To teach. To encourage. But most of all, to interest. Because childlike curiosity in the right hands can help turn darkness into light. **PHILLIPS 66**

Twenty years ago, George Hadfield discovered a broken, yet beautiful, 175-year-old grandfather clock. He also discovered that no one in all of England could repair it. So he learned how and found great pleasure in fixing it himself.

Now George Hadfield's pleasure is his business. And a visit to his unique clock shop in Shepshed, north of London, is, in many ways, a trip through time.

You can stroll the grounds among giant tower clock faces. And go inside his 18th-century farmhouse and fall in love with a meticulously restored grandfather clock.

But if you're planning to buy one, don't ask if it keeps good time. And don't forget your Visa card.

Because George won't sell anything unless it works as beautifully as it looks. *And he won't take American Express.*

VISA

It's everywhere you want to be.

Reprinted with permission of VISA U.S.A. Inc.

Many broadcast stations will handle the production of the spots as well as the presentation. Local agencies may provide the film or slides and a station announcer or local personality may volunteer to handle the audio. Radio PSA's are sometimes read live, but most of the time a television PSA is written so the audio can stand alone as a radio PSA. Station public service directors decide whether a spot will be used, and even then, the spot can be bumped if the time is sold.

13.9 House Ad

In its own publication, the *Wall Street Journal*, Dow Jones sells its on-line (computer) information service. The two sizes give the *Journal's* makeup editor a choice to fit an available hole.

GET YOUR FEET WET.

Sample and explore today's premier online financial news and information resource (which includes exclusive online access to *The Wall Street Journal*) without getting in over your head.

For just $49.95, a Dow Jones News/Retrieval® Membership Kit brings you 8 **free** hours of usage,* multiple passwords, a comprehensive User's Guide, subscription to *Dowline*™ Magazine and waiver of the $12 annual service fee for your first year.

To order, call toll free:

1-800-345-8500, Ext. 375.

Dow Jones News/Retrieval®

*Per account. New subscribers only. Free time must be used within 30 days of receipt of password. Some additional fees apply.
© 1986 Dow Jones and Company. All rights reserved.

1H689

GET YOUR FEET WET.

Sample Dow Jones News/Retrieval® — the nation's premier online business and financial resource—without getting in over your head.

For only $49.95, the News/Retrieval Membership Kit lets you and your colleagues plumb the depth of this valuable news and information service.

Eight free hours* of online time will get you started. There's a User's Guide to show you the way, step by step. And a year's subscription to *Dowline* (the magazine of News/Retrieval) gives you background on and suggested applications for our offerings.

Stay on top of the competitive situation in your industry. Check on the positions of your company and clients. Keep up with breaking news or call up past news from *The Wall Street Journal* (online exclusively with News/Retrieval) back to January 1, 1984. You can analyze a wealth of financial data, tap a pool of general knowledge, even plan a trip using almost any computer and modem, terminal or communicating word processor.

The Dow Jones News/Retrieval Membership Kit. It can help you embark on a wave of success. . .and not feel soaked.

To order or for more information, call **1-800-345-8500, Ext. 458.** (Alaska, Hawaii and foreign, call 1-215-789-7008, Ext. 458.) Or use the coupon.

YES! I WANT TO GET MY FEET WET!

☐ **Corporate offer-$49.95 Each** includes:	☐ **Personal offer-$29.95 Each** for
• 8 Free Hours* • Multiple Passwords	individual use, includes: • 5 Free Hours*
• User's Guide • 1 Year of *Dowline*	• Single Password • User's Guide
• $12 Annual service fee waived for 1 year	• 1 Year of *Dowline* • $12 Annual
☐ **Send more information**	service fee waived for 1 year

$_____ENCLOSED (Check/Money Order) ☐Bill me later Charge to ☐AmExp ☐ MC ☐ VISA
(If you pay by credit card, all subsequent usage charges will be billed to your credit card.)

Card No. _____ Exp. Date _____

Signature _____

Name _____ Title _____

Company _____

Address _____

City/State/Zip _____

Daytime Phone Number _____

**Mail to: DJN/R Membership Kit, P.O. Box 300, Princeton, NJ 08543-0300
ATTN: John McGovern**   HIWS0006E

*Per account. Limited to new subscribers only. Free time (8 hours per Corporate offer, 5 hours per Personal offer) must be used within 30 days after receipt of password(s). Certain databases have fees over and above usage charges which are excluded from free-time offer.

Dow Jones News/Retrieval®
Fuel for your ideas.

Copyright © 1986 Dow Jones & Company, Inc. All rights reserved. Dow Jones News/Retrieval is a registered service mark of Dow Jones & Company, Inc.   3H698

Print public service ads are used at the publications' discretion. They usually run in magazines, at the back of the book. That's because magazines are laid out from front to back, with jumps (continuations of stories). If an editor ends up with a hole and a public service ad that will fit, the ad gets exposure. Good public service ads try to compete with regular ads in compelling art and informative as well as persuasive copy (see 13.11). Notice that the Easter Seal's media ad kit hedges its bets with a one-inch ad. The editor may not have space

13.10 Radio PSA

Organizations sometimes get celebrities to do their PSA's in the expectation of increased use by stations and heightened attention as well as credibility. Most celebrities will respond to such appeals if they believe in the message and if they have some particular personal interest in the organization.

COPY FOR WWWW RADIO PSA (FOR USE
ON AND AFTER JULY 1, 1985):
30 SECONDS

BARBARA MANDRELL: HI, I'M BARBARA MANDRELL. MICHIGAN LAW NOW REQUIRES DRIVERS AND FRONT SEAT PASSENGERS TO WEAR THEIR SAFETY BELTS. IT'S A GOOD LAW AND IT WILL SAVE LIVES. I KNOW, BECAUSE A SAFETY BELT SAVED MY LIFE. BUT THE LAW IS <u>REALLY</u> ONLY AS GOOD AS THE PEOPLE WHO OBEY IT. HELP SAVE LIVES ON MICHIGAN STREETS AND HIGHWAYS BY OBSERVING THE SAFETY BELT USE LAW.

ANNCR: BUCKLE UP, MICHIGAN, IT'S <u>OUR</u> LAW. PRESENTED AS A PUBLIC SERVICE BY (RADIO STATION) AND THE MICHIGAN COALITION FOR SAFETY BELT USE.

Reprinted with permission of Casey Communications Management, Inc.

---

for the larger ad with photo and copy but could use a smaller "plug" to fill out a column.

CONSTRAINTS Although the law has defined organizations, profit and non-profit, as corporate citizens with First Amendment rights, occasionally newspapers will refuse an ad because they consider it in poor taste. The networks rigorously inspect nationally broadcast spots. Individual stations can also reject advertising copy and public service announcements. They are especially vigilant about non-profit organizations that try to get a station to carry a PSA while the organizations are buying print space.

Newspapers and magazines can refuse any advertising copy—even capriciously—because they are privately owned institutions. Broadcast stations, on the other hand, are governed by the FCC and have less autonomy. For example, if they are carrying one candidate's commercials, by FCC regulations they have to carry the other's. This has put some commercials using racist language on the air, much to the distaste of the station management and personnel.

13.11 Public Service Ads

The photo here is as important as the headline, but it's the headline that makes you look again at the picture. You have to look twice to notice that this "ordinary"-looking businessman has no hands. This carries the message that your money can make the difference in these people's lives—whether they are "handicapped" by their disability or able to live a full life. The smaller ad is also in the media slicks sent to the magazine to clip and use as space is available.

PUT ABILITY IN DISABILITY

People with disabilities come to Easter Seals looking for a chance, not charity. Share in their work and aspirations.

Support *Easter Seals*®

Magazine Ad No. 4 (2¼" x 5")
110-line screen

PUT ABILITY IN DISABILITY

Support *Easter Seals*®

Magazine Ad No. 5 (2¼" x 1½")
110-line screen

Reprinted with permission of National Easter Seal Society.

Regulatory agencies Advertising is regulated by the government through a number of agencies, including the Postal Service, the Food and Drug Administration and the Interstate Commerce Commission, but the primary regulatory body is the Federal Trade Commission. The FTC regulates the fairness of competition, unfair or deceptive trade practices and false advertising. The FTC's Bureau of Consumer Protection issues trade regulation rules that are legally binding.

The Bureau also has an advertising evaluation section that reviews advertising on its own from samples it pulls and also responds to consumer complaints. The FTC staff examines complaints to see whether a law has been violated. If it has, the FTC tries to get the advertiser to agree to stop, and if that fails, the FTC can start formal proceedings against the advertiser. The advertiser can sign a consent order agreeing to stop the offending practice, which halts the formal proceedings; if it disagrees it can contest the charges before a judge. The judge may dismiss all or some of the charges against the advertiser, issue another cease-and-desist order or order corrective advertising.

The advertiser can appeal such decisions to the U.S. Court of Appeals, and if it loses there may go on to the Supreme Court. While the case is being appealed, the advertiser can expect to win and continue the practice, thus running the risk of being charged with non-compliance and fined. When corrective advertising is ordered, the FTC specifies the language to be used. The commission can determine the amount of money or percentage of an advertising budget to be spent, the size of the ads and exactly which media to be used.

Self-regulation The Better Business Bureau is the way the industry tries to handle its own regulations. Two groups within the Better Business Bureau are designed to look into consumer and industry complaints. The National Advertising Division reviews the charges brought to it and does its own monitoring. If the NAB can't get the advertiser to change policies, the case is turned over to the National Advertising Review Board. If no resolution is reached at this point, the case can be referred to the Federal Trade Commission.

As another form of internal control, the National Association of Broadcasters used to have a code of ethics to which its members adhered. But the code has been abandoned with the deregulation of broadcasting.

However, the networks have impressive structures for reviewing and approving commercials. The NAB code initially served as much of the background for these policies. Advertisers clear storyboards or shooting scripts or both with all three networks at the same time. If a demonstration or testimonial is involved, documentation is usually provided when the script is submitted. Substantiation for all claims generally accompanies the copy, too. Copywriters need to know what sort of scrutiny their words will be under and by whom.

During the 1970s, Mobil couldn't get one of its infomercials about the oil and gas shortage by all of the networks, and the case of the 1980s is likely to be W.R. Grace & Co., which tried to buy airtime for a commercial about the federal deficit. The wording change that CBS insisted on was a line regarding "talk of an amendment." The network's point of view was that the commercial had crossed the line from issue to advocacy.[1]

MAIN POINTS
- Research means learning about the product or service to be advertised, the market environment for it and the audience.
- Research also means knowing all of the requirements of the media you'll be using in detail and those of the suppliers you'll be working with.
- Before you can write effectively, you have to know the purpose for the advertisement, the persuasive strategy, its possible impact on the audience, as well as how the audience uses the media, and the technical limitations and possibilities of the media being used, the accuracy of the information in the copy, the most creative approach to the use of the medium and the overall effect the message is likely to have.
- Focus is attracting attention, developing interest, creating desire, establishing credibility and getting the target audience to take action.
- Creative thinking involves making unusual associations, making the commonplace exotic, deciding what to show and what to tell, using words, sound and visuals effectively.
- Format can generally be divided into print, radio and television. Print copy has to be prepared to fit a dummy, or layout. The copy has to be marked carefully for the typesetters so it will be accurately reproduced. You have to check it through the different production stages. All broadcast copy has to be written for two audiences, those presenting it and the audiences receiving it. In radio, you can use words that create images in the minds of the listeners. For television, you have to be careful that the words don't compete with the action.
- The major types of commercial copy are humor, hard sell, informative, testimonial, endorsement and institutional. Institutional advertising can be idea advertising, as in advertorials and infomercials, or it can be image or identification advertising.
- Public service announcements (PSA's) from non-profit organizations are free ads run by broadcast stations and magazines.
- Constraints on advertising are laws, self-regulation and decisions about tastefulness.

EXERCISES
1. Write copy for an image ad about your school for magazines prospective students would read. Then write it for radio stations that have a programming format the same audience would listen to.
2. Write copy for an informative ad about your school for the local newspaper's education section.
3. Write a radio public service announcement for some event your school is sponsoring, such as a play or concert.
4. Write a hard-sell ad for your university's bookstore for the student newspaper.

NOTES
1. For a thorough discussion of all sides of the Grace case, see *Public Relations Journal* 42, no. 10: 30–33, 42–43.

SUGGESTIONS FOR ADDITIONAL READING

Burton, Philip Ward. *Advertising Copywriting.* 5th ed. Columbus, Ohio: Grid, 1983.

Heighton, Elizabeth J., and Don R. Cunningham. *Advertising in the Broadcast and Cable Media.* 2nd ed. Belmont, Calif.: Wadsworth, 1984.

Jamieson, Kathleen Hall, and Karlyn Kohrs Campbell. *The Interplay of Influence: Mass Media and Their Publics in News, Advertising, Politics.* Belmont, Calif.: Wadsworth, 1986.

Jewler, Jerome A. *Creative Strategy in Advertising.* 2nd ed. Belmont, Calif.: Wadsworth, 1985.

Meeske, Milan D., and R.C. Norris. *Copywriting for the Electronic Media: A Practical Guide.* Belmont, Calif.: Wadsworth, 1987.

Moriarty, Sandra E. *Creative Advertising: Theory and Practice.* Englewood Cliffs, N.J.: Prentice Hall, 1986.

O'Donnell, Lewis B., Carl Hausman and Philip Benoit. *Announcing: Broadcast Communicating Today.* Belmont, Calif.: Wadsworth, 1987.

Opinion Writing:
Reviews and Editorials

"Newspapers probably were a lot more interesting before anyone thought of 'social responsibility' and opinion was part of interpreting and reporting the news," a journalism department head said in a public forum on the responsibility of the press. Charles Arrendale, of the University of Texas at Arlington, left his audience in shocked silence. Most of them didn't realize that "social responsibility" and the elimination of opinion from news is historically recent. Joseph Pulitzer, whose name is attached to prestigious prizes in journalism, didn't invent "sensationalism," or the spirited injection into the news story of the reporter's view of the event, but he certainly practiced it with skill and enthusiasm in the 1890s.

The sanitation of news, the clinical separation of opinion from fact, was a U.S. journalistic reform that began with public reaction to the "yellow journalism" of the 1890s in the war between Pulitzer and William Randolph Hearst.[1] The trend took on the status of a theory during the two world wars, when "self-censorship" became an internal constraint and professional reform, to protect national security during the global conflicts. The idea was you didn't print everything you knew, because it might be useful to the enemy, and opinion was clearly labeled wherever it appeared.

In the lull between the two wars, the urgency for social reform created some opinionated writing by the muckrakers, most of it confined to magazines, notably *McClure's*.[2] Cynicism about protecting the government, right or wrong, grew during the Vietnam War, when muckraking reappeared, this time with a new name, "the underground press." The underground press was represented by periodicals of integrated fact and opinion.

Their impact on traditional journalism was manifested in a new type of writing, called the "new journalism." Most people give Tom Wolfe credit for originating the free-wheeling style that has become identified with the genre, but credit might really belong to his editor at *Esquire* who published a memo that Wolfe wrote because he didn't have time to write the magazine piece. The highly personal style, re-creating dialogue and setting the scene so that people felt involved in the story, moved swiftly from magazines, where opinion is still very much integrated into articles, to newspapers, but not without a great deal of controversy and criticism.

Serious newspapers clearly label all opinion pieces. So do broadcasters, because that is an FCC requirement. The airwaves belong to the people in the United States and are only used by licensed broadcasters with public permission. For that reason, anyone wishing to offer an opposing point of view may do so.

Newspapers also offer this opportunity for opposing-view formal essays, not just letters to the editor, with their op-ed pages, a name that came from the *New York Times*, which began running differing views on the page opposite the editorial page. The editorial page is traditionally regarded as the voice of the publisher. In fact, most newspapers, even those owned by chains, have editorial boards that meet representatives of different points of view (political candidates or others) and vote on a position. In the case of newspapers that belong to a chain, this form of decision making gives the newspaper the opportunity to reflect the community better than it would if the editorial positions were set at the national headquarters.

The op-ed pages furnish public relations writers with an opportunity for essays that will get exposure and reach opinion leaders. Editorials of public relations origin often appear in smaller papers that have limited resources for subscribing to syndicated editorial columnists. Sometimes the editorials are sent directly to the papers from the public relations source, but more often the PR-generated editorials are given to an editorial service to which the newspapers subscribe. Although these "canned" editorials are condemned by many, they seem to meet a need. PR writers also write editorials for their organization's publications. These opinions are often a source for news and taken as the official position of the organization on an issue.

Most beginning writers assume that opinion pieces are the easiest to write. Not so. Take the case of the student who couldn't resist ending all of her news stories with a statement expressing her personal opinion. After months of drilling from her instructors, she finally developed the habit of writing objective news stories. But when she enrolled in an opinion-writing course, she found, to her dismay, that she no longer felt comfortable framing an argument or expressing her own ideas.

She probably won't have to write editorials if she takes a job with a newspaper as a reporter. Reporters generally don't get the chance to write editorials. On many metropolitan dailies, the editorial-page staff has no reportorial assignments.

On many papers this is also true for those who review the arts. Reporting on the arts is quite different from critiquing them. The artists being judged insist on, and deserve, educated reviewers. The same case can be made for editorials and broadcast commentaries. A knowledge of government, economics and sociology is a prerequisite to an informed judgment of local, state and national affairs. Editorial writers also must understand persuasion theory and rhetoric if they are to be effective. They must also be good gatherers of facts. They must have all of the information a reporter has, all sides of an issue, before they can give legitimate support to an opinion.

Simply *having* an opinion is not enough to write a good opinion piece. Your demonstrated knowledge of the general topic, prior background, sensitivity to the specific subject at hand and expertise is what makes your opinion worth reading or listening to. A review by someone unfamiliar with the history of Elizabethan theater might refer to a Shakespeare-in-the-park performance as introducing Shakespeare to the people; an editorialist unaware of the congressional system of immunity and privilege might write about "libelous statements made on the floor of the Senate." Such gaffes damage the credibility not only of the writer but of the medium.

REVIEWING

Reviews are informed judgments about the content and quality of something presented to the public. The most common review subjects are books, films, theater, television programs, concerts, recorded music, art exhibits and restaurants.

The responsibility of a reviewer is to report and to evaluate. William Zinsser put it well when he said the reviewer is "the deputy for the average man or woman who wants to know: 'what is the new TV series about?' 'Is the movie too dirty for the kids?' 'Will the book really improve my sex life or tell me how to make a chocolate mousse?'" Zinsser advises the reviewer to "think what *you* would want to know if *you* had to spend the money for the movie, the baby-sitter and the long-promised dinner at a good restaurant."[3]

Reviews and criticism are not the same thing. Most reviews appear in mass media — print and broadcast, local and syndicated — and are really a form of interpretative reporting. Reviewers cover the industry of art. Critics write about art and artists. The mass media, especially newspapers, usually can't accommodate critics, whose detailed analyses are better suited to specialized magazines. Some metropolitan papers, however, do have critics, specialists in certain fields — art, dance, drama, television and so on.

Research for reviewing

It is easy to be critical, but that does't make you a critic.[4] You must know something about the subject. In addition to some prior training, you have to do research on the specific subject (see Chapter 3). If you're writing a book review, you should find out something about the author. What else has he or she written? Were previous works similar in content to the work being reviewed? Were they well received by other critics? The public? What kind of training, preparation or experience did the author have for writing the book? In other words, you must be familiar with the author and the author's other works to put the new work into perspective. The same is true of reviewing plays, concerts or other efforts. When the presentation is a collective effort, like a performance, a great deal of research must be done before you pass judgment. Many reviewers try to interview the artists involved to help them with their assessment.

Writing the review Because reviews have no prescribed format, framing them is sometimes a problem. Following this general pattern can help:

- *Write a brief paragraph or two about the nature of the subject.* If it's a play, indicate whether it's a comedy, tragedy, mystery, personality sketch or study. If it's a concert, let the audience know the music was classical, popular, jazz, rock, contemporary, experimental—and in what format: ensemble, orchestra, solo instrument, vocal. If it's a book, say whether it was an adventure, thriller, philosophical treatise—and in what style: first-person narrative, expository, historical.

- *Indicate your verdict early.* Because you're writing an opinion intended to influence the public, it's only fair that your personal point of view be clear at the outset. And don't feel obligated to always be favorable. If you don't believe the subject is worth the audience's time, let them know.

- *Support your opinion.* This is perhaps the most difficult step in writing the review, for it requires calling on your background and knowledge of the subject. Discuss the strengths and weaknesses of the work. Point out specifically what you liked and didn't like—and be explicit. At the same time, you might indicate what the audience reaction was, if it is a public performance.

In writing the review, avoid commonplace adjectives that have little meaning, such as *well-conceived* or *inspiring.* Avoid superlatives: "the best ever"; "never in history has anything like . . ."; "without doubt the most inept performance ever staged." A gross overstatement about the good or the bad is not likely to be accepted by your audience. A more effective approach is to note particular praiseworthy points and areas of inadequacy.

The final paragraphs can be a short, tight summary of your reaction. In some cases, the time, location and cost or ticket price are noted. Some publications and stations avoid such references, deeming them free advertising. If you're confident your review is thorough and reflects your honest evaluation of the worth of the book, concert or play, you can recommend a course of action to your audience: Read the book, attend the concert, see the play. But be certain your recommendation has been supported by your earlier statements.

Studying other reviewers As an opinion piece, a review will have your name on it. Someone might ask: How do you know that you're right? When is an opinion ever "right"? Probably when it is one you agree with. Author and critic Robert Lewis Shayon says that criticism should go beyond predictable observations, that it should offer some special insight that acts as a "cellfirer" to start others thinking.[5]

A level of social responsibility accompanies reviewing. *New York Post* theater critic Clive Barnes states it well:

The only responsibility a critic has toward an individual artist is that of being fair and informed. But when the critic looks at the institution, there is, I think, a special and different responsibility that might be called a social responsibility. . . . The institutions themselves do not need an easy review. Indeed, the more serious an institution is, probably the more stringent the review should be. But even a bad review—the worst review you can envisage—can be sympathetic. The critic needs to be free, maverick and honest. But he must not wilfully destroy the plaintive flowers of aspiration. He doesn't have to be easy, but he doesn't have to be cutting. It is easy to be funny at the expense of the unweaned.[6]

Read reviews of others critically and listen carefully to the film and music critics who appear on television. The same print reviews in 14.1–14.4 represent the thoughtful work of professional writers knowledgeable about their subject and skillful in sharing it.

14.1 Concert Review

This reviewer uses vivid descriptive words to let you experience the concert secondhand.

NSO: Beethoven, boldly

By Joseph McLellan
Washington Post Staff Writer

Last night's National Symphony concert ended in a burst of glory: the headlong finale of Beethoven's Seventh Symphony, where the orchestra, having danced itself to near-exhaustion, decides to finish up with a 100-yard dash.

Under the baton of guest conductor Gunther Herbig, the NSO was in a high-energy mode. The timpani crackled like artillery; the strings snapped out Beethoven's emphatic rhythms like booted feet stamping on a plank floor. But there was a refinement mingled with the peasant heartiness. The orchestra's many voices were beautifully blended and balanced and the ensemble sound was clear-cut and precise.

Above all, even in the most abandoned moments of Dionysiac frenzy, there was a reassuring sense of control. The orchestra was giving all it had, but it was not pushed beyond its limits.

Three hours earlier, a historic bit of music-making took place. Three of the orchestra's string players sat on the vast stage of the Concert Hall, performing Beethoven's String Trio in E-flat, Op. 3, in the first of the orchestra's "Prelude" concerts of chamber music. The audience was small— the Prelude concerts are still an unfamiliar idea—but the performance by violinist George Marsh, violist Denise Wilkinson and cellist Steven A. Honigberg was technically excellent and thematically significant.

The Op. 3 trio is not one of Beethoven's better known works, but it has a gentle grace and an 18th-century charm that make it immediately appealing. At first glance, it seems far removed from the muscular, exuberant symphony. Comparing them is like comparing a small pencil sketch with a gigantic, busy oil painting— but, in fact, such comparisons can be useful.

The trio gives a rather elementary preview of the art of dialogue in music that reaches great comic heights in the symphony (most notably in the scherzo). And the rhythmic variety and vitality of the symphony is curiously, gently foreshadowed in parts of the trio—for example, its second movement, which plays with a motif of three short notes followed by a long one: an early form of the rhythmic motto of the Fifth Symphony. Playing the two works in the same evening puts both of them into perspective. And, considering the very different kinds of performing forces they use, they are not normally heard on the same evening.

The opportunity to put oddly related works side by side like this is one of the good things about the new Prelude concerts. They also give the orchestra's musicians a chance to play chamber music under the orchestra's auspices, and they allow the orchestra to put a spotlight on some fine players whose work is usually, rightly blended into the ensemble. This season, there will also be Prelude concerts before the NSO concerts on Thursday, Oct. 16, and Thursday, Nov. 6, both at 7:15 p.m. In addition, NSO players are being featured, under the orchestra's auspices, in four chamber concerts at the Jewish Community Center in Rockville.

Orchestrally, last night's program also included Weber's "Oberon" Over-ture and Schubert's Fifth Symphony, both in excellent performances. Herbig was particularly effective in the Weber—a masterpiece of color and dynamic nuance that evoked this conductor's special qualities.

Reprinted with permission of The Washington Post.

14.2 TV Preview

This *Washington Post* piece is both intense and highly personal. Notice the very skillful use of quotes, generally a neglected technique in writing a review.

At home at the Phillips

By Paul Richard
Washington Post Staff Writer

Halfway through "The Phillips Collection," we hear Duncan Phillips speaking. His voice is strangely slender; antique static crackles 'round it. He was born 100 years ago, he's been dead for 20 years, yet here he is discussing his "frankly personal" collection. This mild, unpretentious show (to be broadcast tonight at 10:30 on Channel 26) is frankly personal as well.

It does not try to preach. It does not try to teach us the history of art. It is a program about people, about people who admired founder Duncan Phillips, and Marjorie, his widow, and the homey and beloved gallery they left us.

We meet Joseph Alsop first. The columnist and scholar is crusty and articulate. He says: "It is a miracle that the Phillips Collection ever happened at all because Duncan Phillips —who was as good and gentle, as nice and sweet a man as I ever knew —was entirely brought up in the American Genteel Tradition, and the American Genteel Tradition was certainly hostile to art of any very vigorous kind." Washington Post Co. Chairman Katharine Graham remembers seeing Phillips and his wife: "They were absolutely lovely . . . so refined and delicate." J. Carter Brown, the National Gallery's director, de-scribes walking through the Phillips at Duncan Phillips' side as a sort of "revelation."

Fine familiar paintings—by Renoir and Degas, Rothko and Cezanne—appear briefly on the screen. They are there to jog the memory; the camera does not linger. It is the voices that compel us. This 30-minute program is a sort of compound memoir and guided tour.

Marjorie, at ease, a silver tea service beside her, says Duncan's "happiest times with paintings were [seeing them] in a home where they seemed to belong."

The gallery, which opened in 1921 (eight years before the founding of New York's Museum of Modern Art), was homelike from the start. "It had big chairs one could sit in," recalls Richard Diebenkorn, the painter, "and—I can't believe this—but one could smoke. And one could look. And there was plenty to look at."

Laughlin Phillips, Duncan's son, now the gallery's director, speaks about the painters, all of them now dead, that he met as a child. Augustus Vincent Tack "had a monocle which he would keep in his eye until the punch line of his joke." When "John Marin painted his watercolors, he would use both hands. He had a large brush in one hand and a small brush in the other so they'd work sort of simultaneously." When Pierre Bonnard came to visit, he called for paints in order to redo one of his pictures. Marjorie, aghast, pretended hers were "in the country," so the work is unretouched.

Diebenkorn, most movingly, recalls a painting in the collection by Matisse. He says, "There's a figure on a couch . . . and a view across the Seine . . ." (We see the picture as he speaks.) "That painting has stuck in my head ever since I first laid eyes on it, and I've discovered pieces of that painting coming out in my own."

People still write Laughlin Phillips "saying that they've never forgotten the 10-minute walk-throughs" they had with Duncan Phillips "30 years ago." Both Marjorie and Duncan had a special sweetness. This program has it, too (it was produced and codirected by Edgar B. Howard). So does their museum.

Joe Alsop got the first word. He also gets the last. "It's not a giant collection. It's not a giant museum— thank God. But it is a marvelously beautiful and exceptionally valuable result of four—two pairs—of extraordinarily discerning eyes."

Reprinted with permission of The Washington Post.

14.3 Fashion Review

This piece was sent from Italy, where the *Washington Post's* fashion editor was previewing the spring collection.

Armani's feminine flair

By Nina Hyde
Washington Post Fashion Editor

MILAN—Scallop-hemmed skirts and petticoats, ruffles and lace, and then ribbons and bows all showed up here this week in the collection of Giorgio Armani, who first got women into tailored menswear more than a decade ago.

The rest of the fashion world followed, and then Armani turned women into boys with his androgynous style. That, too, started a worldwide trend.

So why the switch? "I know I created this tailoring. I've been copied for it. And now I'm bored with it."

Armani's new look, with full skirts and pants as loose and easy as pajamas, sweet blouses and jackets so softly constructed that lapels fall like ruffles, is in step with the entire shift to softer, more feminine clothes from Milan designers for next spring. But at Armani the ideas are more clearly expressed, from the crocheted caps to the high heel shoes.

His new femininity is not the only idea soon to spill from the runways here into the stores in Washington and elsewhere. Among the other themes surfacing this week for next spring are:

■ Short jackets, sometimes bolero in shape and often with a flare at the back. The other jacket style this season is quite long, often kimono-shaped and sometimes belted.

■ Empire silhouettes, achieved with a belt or seam under the bosom, other times emphasized with wide midriff cummerbunds or, quite the opposite, with bare midriffs.

■ Sheer fabrics, a natural in a season emphasizing femininity, used for

Giorgio Armani Spring/Summer 1987 Collection.

blouses, skirts and even long wide pants.

■ Full skirts and petticoats, often knee length, as a fresh alternative to the straight skirt, still very much around.

■ Ruffles and tiers, often on skirts teamed with tailored and soft jackets that make the look quite modern.

■ Brown is on all the designer palettes. Ecru, which is often paired with black, is the paler version. Gianni Versace and others hope to make navy the new black.

■ Pants that are wide and pajama-like, rather than man-tailored trousers.

■ Denim is a favorite for everything from citified suits to wedding dresses. And jeans, of course.

In a season when the emphasis is on feminine clothes, it is no surprise that high heels are back—Armani shows them with most of his pants—and that silk crêpe de Chine, which feels very soft, is more popular than crisp linen.

One designer who has always made sexy, feminine clothes goes in the opposite direction for next season. Versace has done more tailored clothes than ever, including pinstriped suits with calf-length pants. But he still can make some of the sexiest clothes imaginable, including dresses shirred over the hips and bare navy swimsuits shown with fringed piano shawls.

The few designers here who are holdouts for the maximum in minimum dressing are among the youngest and also the most talked-about. Romeo Gigli, who showed his first collection for Callaghan at the fairgrounds Thursday continued the same spare and almost Japanese spirit his collection showed earlier. He likes long skinny torsos and dresses with a hint of shirring for shaping at the hem, or skirts that burst out like bubbles.

Domenico Dolce and Stephano Gabbana are two under-30 designers whose clothes are also in the mood of those non-traditional designers from Japan. A favorite dress with many stores this season is a brown stretch jersey with steel snaps. The dress can hang loosely with the snaps just as decoration. But the snaps also function and can be used to vary the shape of the dress.

Ellin Saltzman, vice president and fashion director of Saks Fifth Avenue, wasn't surprised to see the softer, feminine styles show up on the runways here this week. "It's timely," she said. Missy LoMonaco, fashion director of Garfinckel's and Bonwit Teller, added, "Women are now secure enough in the workplace to wear soft and feminine clothes." However, LoMonaco thinks the ruffles and tiers are strictly for after working hours. And as for sheer, see-through styles, well, LoMonaco plans to be sure to show those with something opaque underneath.

Armani obviously worked to get his fabrics as lightweight and sheer as possible. His clothes have always been distinguished by exceptional fabrics, often subtly textured and patterned and always made just for him.

And he hasn't really forfeited his adeptness with tailoring. His jackets may be gently shaped and his blouses may have bows, but they are still beautifully tailored.

"This is Giorgio at his most exquisite best," said Bloomingdale's Kal Ruttenstein, who admired the way the designer applied his tailoring skills to the lightest wools and silks. "Even chiffon. Most people take chiffon and torture it—they drape it or twist it. He tailors it with ultimate subtlety."

Reprinted with permission of *The Washington Post*.

14.4 Theater Review

This theater review calls attention to something new about the medium of expression, which the reviewer calls a blend of journalism and theater. Then she supports her observation. Note, too, the specific detail about the audience, schoolchildren "too young for the show."

Tales of terror and tears
'Born in the R.S.A.': South African heroes

By Megan Rosenfeld
Washington Post Staff Writer

There is a nearly unbearable sadness about "Born in the R.S.A.", the fifth and final production in the "Woza Afrika!" series of South African plays imported by New Playwrights' Theatre. Some stone-hearted folks may not be moved by the stories, both horrifying and mundane, contained in this docudrama, but they will surely —one hopes—be few in number.

In creating this work, the gifted interracial cast and director Barney Simon have melded the techniques of journalism and theater. They interviewed scores of people in the period immediately after the South African government declared a state of emergency in mid-1985, then created characters based on these interviews and situations reflecting them.

They found several heroes, both black and white, people who in one way or another fight the apartheid system. But there is also the young single white mother (Terry Norton) who is—or wishes to be—apolitical, vaguely liberal but unwilling to throw in her lot with the activists, who make her uncomfortable. She describes her gradual withdrawal to her suburban apartment, spending her days "watching video and smoking grass" and waiting to pick her son up from nursery school.

One of the most intriguing characters is Glen (Neil McCarthy), the young mother's former husband. He is a university student gradually drawn into becoming a police informer. Initially Glen is sympathetic, ingratiating, a recognizable type uncertain about what he wants to do with his life. He is impatient with the Marxist babble he hears on campus, but attracted to the sort of people—especially a young art student—involved in the resistance. His is the evil of banality, the immorality of a person without strong principles, easily led into betraying his own lover. In the

(continued)

14.4 (continued)

end he muses about his future, professing, self-consciously, his indifference to being scorned by the friends he had betrayed. He says he's thinking about joining the forest service.

At one point Glen exclaims with passion: "We are the stars of the world. They watch us like voyeurs …" This touches a nerve in an American audience; there is something voyeuristic about smugly watching the injustice and turmoil in another country without having to do anything about it. We sometimes run the risk of becoming addicted to outrage experienced at a distance, to the rush of indignation that can obscure the individuals affected.

One particularly wrenching tale is that of Sindiswa, a young black woman played with extraordinary power by Gcina Mhlophe. Her 10-year-old son is arrested, and since there is no due process in South Africa, she has no way of finding him. Eventually policemen bring him home, only to take him away again and force him with violence to sign a false confession to having thrown stones at a bus. He is imprisoned and later released in the custody of the white activist lawyer who has taken on the spirit-crushing work of trying to help. A family friend, Zack (Timmy Kwebulana), speaks of his long bus journey from the township of Soweto to see the boy in the female lawyer's suburban house, describing the sedated child with a puffed-up face lying incongruously amid the flower-patterned sheets and curtains of his benefactor's bedroom.

It is in moments like these that the company most successfully combines the best features of journalism—the patient accumulation of telling detail —with the intensity of theater. At

Photo courtesy of Merle Debuskey

other times the staging is static, holding too closely to the pattern of spoken anthologies like "Under Milk Wood." But the conviction of the performers is unique and contagious, and their portraits rich. The cast deserves a special bow for never losing its concentration at yesterday's matinee, where a large part of the audience was made up of schoolchildren too young for the show.

There are times when the prospect of a play like this, which seems to offer only despair and horror, is more than one wishes to bear. It's like watching films of concentration camp victims; there comes a point when fleeing the horror seems the sanest re-course. But "Born in the R.S.A." does more than just manipulate the heart-strings. It is a worthy addition to the literature about man's inhumanity to man—a field that unfortunately appears to be growing daily.

Born in the R.S.A., *created by Barney Simon and the cast, directed by Simon. With Vanessa Cooke, Timmy Kwebulana, Neil McCarthy, Gcina Mhlophe, Terry Norton, Thoko Ntshinga, Fiona Ramsay. Originally produced at the Market Theatre in Johannesburg. At New Playwrights' Theatre through Oct. 12.*

Broadcast reviews   In larger as well as some medium-size radio and TV markets, at least one local station generally presents reviews of the arts. Film reviews, at least, are also available to local stations from syndicated services and the networks. The three major TV networks feature movie reviewers on their morning news programs, and they also send movie reviews via closed-circuit feeds to local affiliates, who may then run them in local newscasts.

On the local level, arts and film reviewer Arch Campbell of WRC-TV, Washington, D.C., notes:

[M]y movie reviews run 2 minutes and 15 seconds, including the time it takes to lead into me and show a clip. My theater reviews run 90 seconds—including lead-in. You must realize that although I feel the words are the most important part, the total effect is changed by the pictures—the theater slides and film clips used in the piece. Also, these scripts do not show emphasis or facial expressions, but they all contribute.

I try to use few words, not too many adjectives, short phrases, all leading to a definite point with a rating of one to four stars to emphasize the point. My theater reviews are often written in about 15 minutes, during the time between when I get back to the station and the time I'm due on the air.

Despite all of this, I restate my opinion that the words are the most important part. I also ad-lib off the scripts a lot, and these scripts serve as a guide to what I want to get across to the audience.[7]

Emphasis, vocal inflection and the general tone of the delivery are prominent in radio reviews. In broadcast reviews, the written word is important, as Campbell notes, but so is the overall picture the audience sees and hears when being told about art exhibits, films, music, dance, theater, concerts, restaurants and anything else broadcast reviewers can review (see 14.5).

14.5 Broadcast Reviews

One of the top film and theater critics in broadcasting is Arch Campbell of WRC-TV, Washington, D.C. The following pages contain a sample of a theater review and a movie review by Campbell. Note the use of pictures in the theater review and film clips in the movie review.

```
ARCH/MOVIES
ROMANCING THE STONE
30 MARCH '84/6PM/AC


ARCH/ESS MOVIES                          "ROMANCING THE STONE" IS A CRAZY,
REVEAL ROMANCING THE STONE               GIDDY ADVENTURE STORY—A "RAIDERS
                                         OF THE LOST ARK" PLAYED FOR EVEN
                                         MORE LAFFS. THE STORY—KATHLEEN
                                         TURNER—MISS BODY HEAT HERSELF—IS
                                         A TIMID ROMANCE NOVELIST—WHO SETS
                                         OFF TO COLOMBIA TO SAVE HER
                                         KIDNAPPED SISTER—SEEMS KATHLEEN
                                         HAS A TREASURE MAP EVERYBODY
                                         WANTS—SO ONCE A BEVY OF BAD GUYS
                                         GET ON HER TRAIL, MICHAEL DOUGLAS
                                         STEPS IN TO SAVE THE DAY—SORT OF—


EJ FULL (:56)                            TOTAL TIME: :56
```

14.5 (continued)

CHRYRON: SCENES FROM "ROMANCING THE STONE"	OUTCUE: ". . . THIS TURNED OUT TO BE ONE HELL OF A MORNING."
ARCH/HARDWALL	BESIDES THE JOKES—AND THE STUNTS—AND THE ALLIGATORS SNAPPING AT THE GOOD AND BAD GUYS—"ROMANCING THE STONE" HAS THE IRREPRESSIBLE DANNY DE VITO SLEAZING ABOUT AS A FOIL FOR OUR HERO AND HEROINE. MOST OF ALL—"ROMANCING THE STONE" HAS AN EXCITING CLIMAX—AND A SWEET ENDING. WHICH QUALIFIES AS MY PICK FOR BEST NEW MOVIE OF THE WEEK— "ROMANCING THE STONE"—3 STARS AND A P.G. RATING.
CHRYRON: ARCH CAMPBELL CHANNEL 4 NEWS	
ARCH/ESS MOVIES REVEAL STONE-3 STARS	

ARC VO EJ #2 FILMSTRIP WITH CHRYRON FULL ARCH'S BEST BETS	//HERE'S SOME OTHER PICK HITS—TERMS OF ENDEARMENT—THE DRESSER— BROADWAY DANNY ROSE—SPLASH—
	AND
ARCH VO EJ BK #3 CHRYRON: GREYSTOKE 3 STARS ARCH/HARDWALL	//GREYSTOKE—THE NEW TARZAN MOVIE—A FEW FLAWS BUT MOSTLY EXHILARATING—GREYSTOKE THE LITERARY TARZAN—THIS GUY'S AN ANIMAL.//
	THAT'S HOW THEY SHAPE UP THIS WEEKEND—I'M ARCH CAMPBELL—AND I HOPE YOU SEE SOMETHING GOOD AT THE MOVIES.

ARCH/1ST NIGHT DEATH OF A SALESMAN 27 FEB '84/11 PM/AC	
ARCH/ESS 1ST NIGHT	KENNEDY CENTER'S HANDSOME NEW PRODUCTION OF "DEATH OF A SALESMAN" IS AN UNFORGETTABLE NIGHT. FOR STARTERS, ARTHUR MILLER'S PLAY IS A TRUE AMERICAN CLASSIC—MAYBE THE GREATEST PLAY OF OUR CENTURY.

ARCH VO STILL #1	//HIS CHARACTER—WILLY LOMAN, THE BROKEN DOWN SALESMAN WHO FINDS HE CAN'T MAKE IT ON A SMILE AND A SHOE-SHINE ANYMORE—SPEAKS TO ALL OF US. AS WILLY LOMAN, DUSTIN HOFFMAN FINDS NEW DISTINCTION
CHRYRON: DEATH OF A SALESMAN KENNEDY CENTER	
ARCH/1ST NIGHT 2	//FOR HIS ALREADY PRAISEWORTHY CAREER, HOFFMAN MAKES YOU FORGET
ARCH VO STILL #2	THE MOVIE STAR—WITH THE AID OF MAKE-UP AND ABILITY, HE TRULY TURNS INTO AN OLD MAN WATCHING HIS DREAMS FADE. IT'S A MOVING, ELOQUENT PERFORMANCE.

ARCH VO STILL #3	//AIDED BY A WONDERFUL CAST—KATE REID AS HIS WIFE LINDA—JOHN MALKOVICH AS BIFF—STEPHEN LANG AS HAP—AND A SURPRISINGLY HAUNTING PERFORMANCE FROM DAVID HUDDLESTON—AS CHARLEY—THE NEIGHBOR WHO GETS THE
ARCH/1ST NIGHT-3	//INTANGIBLES WILLY WANTS WITHOUT EVEN TRYING.//
ARCH/ESS 1ST NIGHT REVEAL DEATH OF A SALESMAN	''DEATH OF A SALESMAN'' IS A CLASSIC PRODUCTION—WITH NEW MEANING FOR 1984 AUDIENCES—BRILLIANT, MOVING, ELOQUENT—ALL THE THINGS THAT MAKE THEATER MAGIC. I BELIEVE IT WILL BE REMEMBERED AS A HIGHLIGHT OF WASHINGTON THEATER. A FOUR STAR PLUS MASTERPIECE. SOLD OUT—SO IF YOU CAN TWIST AN ARM—OR EVEN JUST STAND IN THE BACK—DO IT. THIS IS THE ONE PLAY YOU SHOULD SEE THIS YEAR.
REVEAL 4 STARS PLUS	

Used with permission of WRC-TV, Washington, D.C.

EDITORIALS Like reviews, editorials reflect opinion. But the editorial is usually a reflection of management's attitude rather than the reporter's or the editor's personal view. Most editorials, unlike reviews, are unsigned. When people cite any editorial in conversation, they usually say something like, "Well, the *Post* said . . ." or "KRCK said . . .". The exception is the columnists who comment on political and social issues.

Reprinted by permission of Jefferson Communications, Inc., Reston, Va.

Framing an opinion   The editorial page is management's soapbox—the publisher's or the station manager's. Writers of editorials and broadcast commentaries do a great deal of fact-finding, checking to see what their own medium and others have said, conducting symposium interviews of people in the news, such as government officials and political candidates. As Curtis MacDougall observed: "Know what you're talking about or keep still."[8]

After the fact-finding, a decision has to be made about what to say, what position to take. Decision-making systems vary. Sometimes an editorial board hears all sides of a controversial issue and then votes. Of course, only one member of the board writes the piece. A writer usually isn't asked to write an editorial that takes a position different from his or her own beliefs (for a good reason: The piece is not as persuasive). When an editorial board takes a position that is likely to cause problems in the publisher's office, the publisher is generally advised. Few publishers today make much effort to "control" the editorial page. They have too many other things to do. The person responsible for seeing that the views the publication generally supports are presented to the public is the editorial-page editor.

This editor's views are generally in harmony with those of the publisher, and it's usually to the publisher that he or she reports. Occasionally, an editorial-page editor will report to the paper's editor-in-chief, who has overall responsibility for the news product. The editorial-page editor is the one who assigns and approves editorial ideas, reads the pieces and generally controls the content of the page, including the selection and editing of letters from the readers.

Purposes   Editorials either comment on a current issue or on something that is important but not timely. An editorial's purpose places it in one of three categories.

Commendation or condemnation.   Praising the school board, the fire department, the zoo is a way for the newspaper or broadcast station to act as the public's voice. And if someone's hand needs slapping, the editorial page can act for the community at large. In 14.6, the doctor speaks out about malpractice abuse in a professional journal.

Persuasion.   Editorials that condemn or complain are also intended to arouse public indignation and are close, therefore, to the persuasive category. Editorials that persuade try to get people to think or do something specific. They often pose problems and offer solutions. Persuasive editorials are written to support political candidates, with the obvious intent of getting readers to vote for them. Sometimes the persuasive editorial is one that judges the morality of some event, action or issue (see 14.7).

Keep in mind that a single editorial is not likely to result in immediate attitude shifts or action. Current research about editorial impact indicates that editorials over time about a subject of significance have long-range effect; the one-shot editorial does not, any more than the one-shot ad or commercial would.

Entertainment.   Some subjects, such as Groundhog Day, can inspire an editorial that is just meant to entertain. However, some lightly written pieces may have an underlying point (see 14.8).

Editorial topics   Ideas can come from anywhere—local, regional, state, national and international events, and the occasional offbeat occurrence.

The place to look for ideas is the news pages. Most editorial writers read five or more newspapers a day, most of the wire copy sent each day and all the national news magazines.

Meetings and speeches, sometimes not even covered by reporters, can spark an editorial idea. An editorial writer attending a civic luncheon as a guest saw a presentation on domestic violence and asked the speaker and the social agency for help in doing research to write an editorial on the impact of domestic violence on the community and what needed to be done.

Personal conversations and experiences are sources for editorial ideas. A writer who had his car insurance rate increased because of an accident in which he was an innocent party wrote an editorial stating that this practice makes the victims of accidents reluctant to file accident reports.

14.6 Condemnatory Editorial

This editorial is from a PR publication, *Contemporary OB/GYN*, published by Medical Economics Company.

March against malpractice?

John T. Queenan, M.D.

In any gathering of physicians, professional liability is a topic sure to generate strong feelings—and sometimes radical propsals. At a recent postgraduate meeting, one participant suggested it's time for doctors to stage a public demonstration to dramatize the medicolegal crisis that has enveloped us. He thought ACOG's [American College of Obstetricians and Gyne-

(continued)

cologists] annual meeting this month in Washington, D.C., would provide the perfect setting for a "March against Malpractice Abuse." The goal, of course, would be to use the media to let the public know how huge settlements and skyrocketing rates are driving up the cost of care and breaking down the physician-patient relationship.

I can't quarrel with this goal, but I believe that a national, public demonstration by doctors would probably backfire. Right now the public simply doesn't perceive the malpractice problem to be a crisis. Most people still regard doctors as comparatively well-off, or at least not under any real financial pressure.

Unfortunately, until the public recognizes the malpractice problem as a threat to society, enactment of corrective federal legislation is unlikely. As I've pointed out before, a national solution—perhaps in the form of no-fault compensation—is desirable, but not something we should count on in the immediate future. Therefore, we need to consider other measures.

Is there a better way to undertake public education? I believe there is, and that the key is concentrating on the local and state levels. People are much more likely to be sympathetic to their own doctors than to the profession in general. Effective local campaigning can lay the groundwork for action by the states, which have already provided much relief. . . . For example, a few weeks ago, many members of the Medical Society of the State of New York converged on the state capital to try to convince legislators to create laws to alleviate this crisis. In suggesting this approach, I'm encouraged by the fact that every state except West Virginia and the District of Columbia has passed some legislation to ameliorate the malpractice situation. Several states—in particular, Indiana and Maryland—have taken significant steps to make the medicolegal climate at least tolerable.

Here, then, is a realistic program of action:

■ Encourage state legislation mandating review panels for all potential malpractice cases.

■ Press for state laws placing caps on awards.

■ Support state legislation to eliminate punitive damages in malpractice cases. These are excess damages awarded when the plaintiff's lawyer is able to convince a jury that a doctor has engaged in "outrageous conduct." Though such conduct is extremely rare, unscrupulous lawyers use this charge as a weapon. Because malpractice insurance does not cover punitive damages, the physician is often forced into an unfair and costly settlement.

■ Encourage development of state expert witness panels. The panelists, respected physicians selected by state medical societies, would be available to both plaintiff and defendant at a modest fee. Their existence would discourage use of the "hired gun" by plaintiffs' attorneys and limit the credibility of such dubious witnesses.

■ Require health-care-plan subscribers to agree to binding arbitration in cases of alleged malpractice.

■ Suggest ways to eliminate the "deep-pocket" approach. That's the lawyer's tactic of suing physicians most likely to have the resources to pay damages—regardless of their responsibility in the case at hand.

Many feel that the chances for malpractice relief will grow as our health care system evolves from individual to corporate practice. As more doctors become employees, they say, the HMOs and for-profit hospitals that employ them will take the lead in campaigning for legislation, and will do so more effectively. While I don't dispute that in the future more physicians will practice as employees, I don't agree that we should sit back and wait for the corporations to bail us out. I believe organized action by individual physicians, focused at the state and local level, can have profound effects now. I suggest that state medical societies should make this a primary goal. Instead of a one big national demonstration, let's pledge ourselves to continuous efforts in our own communities and states. The march is on!

14.7 Persuasive Editorial

This editorial is a persuasive piece, although it also has a tone of condemnation. The stance of the *Wall Street Journal* in criticizing the government's controlling the new drug is consistent with its pro-business stance.

AIDS research: who benefits?

After federal officials announced recently that an experimental drug had successfully delayed death and relieved the suffering of AIDS patients, the National Institutes of Health had to set up a telephone hot line to handle calls from sick patients wanting to know how to get it. Calls came in at the rate of 1,000 a day. The Food and Drug Administration hasn't approved the drug for sale yet, but the government's fast-track processing for AIDS drugs may make it available through a doctor's prescription by early next year. In the meantime, the FDA has given Burroughs-Wellcome Co., the developer of azidothymidine (AZT), permission to distribute the drug to certain AIDS patients, so long as it does so for free.

We assume that all those AIDS patients phoning in fully understand that the drug's success is preliminary, that it has toxic side effects, and that other side effects may show up later. Knowing all this, they, like people with so many other life-destroying diseases, want to brave the risks and take the drug. Many, however, are told they can't have the drug. The alliance of researchers and regulators says only it will decide who may benefit now from AZT and who may not.

The drug is being offered only to patients who have had a specific kind of AIDS-related pneumonia. About 7,000 people may qualify. The people mainly left out by the FDA's rules have what is known as AIDS-related complex, or ARC, a set of debilitating symptoms similar to AIDS. They number in the tens of thousands.

The decision to forbid ARC patients access to the drug is difficult for them because their malady was included in the clinical trial that precipitated the extraordinary decision to take the control group off placebos and put them on AZT. The test included 282 people with either fully developed AIDS or AIDS-related complex. In the group of 137 patients treated with a placebo (meaning no treatment), 16 died. But of the 145 patients treated with AZT, only one died. With such dramatic results in hand, the company said it couldn't ethically withhold AZT from the pla-cebo patients. It shut down the trial and began distributing the drug free to a restricted class of patients. The formal reason for denying ARC patients access is that the drug's benefits for them were less clearly defined.

Does this make sense? How can the government ethically withhold AZT from one class of AIDS patients while handing it out to another?

The AZT story is an unusually visible example of the arbitrary authority of the research-regulatory alliance in the U.S. Its authority to decide who shall benefit from science and when is too great and deserves challenge. With AZT, another class of gravely ill individuals have found themselves in the unfortunate Catch-22 dilemma of the current drug-approval process. These patients learn of extremely promising therapeutic results with drugs used in research protocols but quickly discover they can't buy the drug or assume its risks until months or even years of additional research make it ready for formal approval by the FDA.   **(continued)**

14.7 (continued)

However, AZT raises a particularly volatile issue: What is going to happen when the research-regulatory alliance can't deny that an experimental AIDS drug significantly benefits ARC patients? The costs of distributing that drug "free" will be enormous. The per-patient cost of these free distributions of experimental drugs are substantial and can become prohibitive for a company without the resources of Burroughs-Wellcome.

Current federal regulations effectively prevent companies from recovering distribution costs from patients in large part because of a distaste for "commercializing" a drug prior to its approval for sale. In the event of an ARC breakthrough before the FDA is prepared to release the drug into the tainted world of profit, it's likely that the government would "buy" the unapproved drug from the developer to subsidize distribution.

The government's regulatory apparatus, with its emphasis on "free" or "compassionate" distributions of experimental drugs to restricted patient populations reflects a flawed understanding of the role of capital in bringing benefit to sick people. The deep base of public support for new medical therapies, however, has led to a rediscovery of the fact that research-based companies, large or small, use their income stream to underwrite additional research, whether for AIDS or for other purposes.

The questions before us here are whether the research-regulatory alliance should have such total, unchallenged authority to interpose itself between patients and medicine that promises respite from suffering. And is there a net gain or a net loss to the public's welfare when this alliance holds arbitrary authority to decide at which point a patient's willingness to spend his own money to relieve his suffering is ethical and when it is unethical?

14.8a Entertaining Editorials

These essays are good examples of condemnation written with a light touch.

Ten things I hate about public relations

By Joseph M. Queenan

1. *The remorseless use of the word "unique."* In a five-day study of the mail received at American Business, we found that the word "unique" turned up in 20.2% of our total mail, and in 42.7% of p.r. materials. Included in this galaxy of uniqueness were unique training programs, board games, publications, planning systems, staffs, end-user and reseller marketing opportunities, weekends, aspects, formats, looks, properties, audio cassettes, seminars, on-site training programs, microfiltration systems, travel options, and a software program unique to the Turkish banking system.

Backgrounds, dishwater filters, pizzeria openings, wall safes and two-day seminars were all unique, as were support systems, pulse-jet dehydration units, and four-day seminars. Rare was the telecommunications firm whose products, marketing ploys or executives were not unique. One release mentioned a "unique set of fingerprints," another the "very unique" feet of different runners.

Even if a press release contained several uses of the word "unique," we counted it only once. Otherwise, our stats would have been ever more bloated by the uniquely practical guide to the unique genre of business planning, and the unique pasta keeper, from the people who brought you the unique microwave turntable with the unique dual-action motion. Likewise when our art department was invited to "add impact and drama to a wide variety of unique graphic presentations" by using a "unique proprietary embossing technique." No thanks, we already have one.

2. *Stories about entrepreneurs who started their businesses in their parents' basements, garages, or with their bar mitzvah or Holy Communion money.* No they didn't.

3. *"Requested material."* Every time I open an envelope marked "Requested Material" and read that "Jake Wogan, VP, Sales, has been promoted to VP, Marketing, at Rectolinear Biscuit," I wonder if somebody who doesn't like me isn't sneaking into my office while I'm out, and calling p.r. firms all over the U.S., begging for their least interesting story ideas.

4. *Messengered materials.* Account

execs who express-mail or messenger materials to editors mistakenly believe that it improves the odds of acceptance. Personally, I'd welcome a service that slows down delivery of press releases, delivering them at the speed they deserve: say, in two to 36 weeks. A friend notes that such a service already exists: the U.S. Postal Service.

5. *Having press releases read to me over the phone.* The tip-off is hearing words like "burgeoning," "vertical integration" and "matrixing." Nothing ever burgeons, matrixes or gets vertically integrated in normal conversation.

6. *Stories my readers "will want to know about."* Not long ago, I got a release explaining that the candle industry was not growing, was not expected to grow, and could very well disappear by the year 2000—all of which my readers would want to know. "Sure enjoyed that story about how the candle industry isn't expected to grow this year, next year, or any year," I can imagine readers writing. "Cleared up a big argument we were having out here in Heathen's Fork, Neb."

7. *Stories about business support for the arts.* Whenever I'm told that a major corporation has awarded an artist $6 million to put up an oversized baggage check in downtown Baltimore, I check the paper to see how many of the firm's employees were maimed by chemical gas that weekend.

8. *The athlete as corporate spokesman.* Athletes plug sneakers they don't wear, charities they don't contribute to, and concepts they don't understand. Once the goodness of their quickness and their debt to Mom have been removed from the agenda, jocks are on pretty thin ice. Let's face it: Nobody ever became an athlete because Yale was closed that weekend.

9. *Stories about the "maverick"* *CEO.* I know, I know, your client is a poet, a Master of Go, a hot-tub repairman, a used-skateboard dealer, a psychic healer, a jacket designer for the Khmer Rouge, the reincarnation of Immanuel Kant's third cousin, a bisexual snowman impersonator, and the first one-legged jitney hijacker ever ejected from Mensa. But the fact that Daddy owns the $567 billion software company must have had something to do with Junior's getting the CEO post.

10. *Being told that it was a pleasure speaking with me the other day.* Not if I can help it it wasn't.

Mr. Queenan is editor of American Business, a publication mailed to small investors.

14.8b

Journalese: a ground-breaking study
By John Lee

Unbeknown to an unsuspecting public, Boy George's drug troubles touched off a severe crisis in the journalese-speaking community. How should reporters and pundits, all fluent in journalese as well as English, refer to the suddenly woozy singer? Naturally enough, conventions of the language demanded a hyphenated modifier. "Much-troubled" might have been acceptable, but that adjective is reserved, as are "oil-rich" and "war-torn," for stories about the Middle East. One tabloid, apparently eager to dismiss the celebrity as a wanton hussy, called him "gender-confused pop star Boy George." This was a clear violation of journalese's "most-cherished tenet": while doing in the rich and famous, never appear to be huffy. One magazine settled for "cross-dressing crooner," and many newspapers temporarily abandoned the hyphenated tradition to label George "flamboyant," a familiar journalese word meaning "kinky" or "one who does not have all of his or her paddles in the water."

Few readers realize how much effort is devoted to meshing the disparate tongues of journalese and English. In journalese, for example, the word *chilling* is an omnibus adjective modifying "scenario" in nuclear-weapons stories, "evidence" and "reminder" in crime stories and "effect" in any story on threats to the First Amendment. In English it is merely something one does with white wine. Reforms and changes can only be "sweeping" and investigations "widening," especially on days when the investigators have no actual news to report. "Mounting" is always followed by pressures or deficits. All arrays are "bewildering," whereas all contrasts are either "striking" or, if the story is weak, "startling."

Many sociologists have speculated (widely, of course) about the love affair between journalese-users and hyphenated modifiers. The gist of all this

(continued)

14.8b (continued)

cerebration seems to be that readers cannot stand the shock of an unmodified noun, at least on first reference. Thus we have Libyan-sponsored terrorism, Ping-Pong diplomacy, debt-laden Brazil and the two most popular hyphenated modifiers of the 1980s, "financially troubled" and "financially plagued," which can fairly be used to describe most Latin American nations, many banks and the United States Football League. The Syrian-backed P.L.O., an earlier hyphenated champion, had to be retired when the Syrian backers began shooting at the P.L.O. backs. Any dictator who leaves his homeland hastily, with or without his bullion and wife's shoe collection, is not fleeing in disgrace, merely heading into self-imposed exile.

Some multiple modifiers in journalese have no known meaning, much like "clinically tested" in headache-remedy advertising. Many seem to have been invented solely for their soothing rhythm: "Wide-ranging discussions" refers to any talks at all, and "award-winning journalist" to any reporter employed three or more years who still has a pulse. A totally disappointing report, containing nothing but yawn-inducing truisms, can always be described as a "ground-breaking study." The most exciting news on the hyphen front is that adventurous journalese users, like late-medieval theologians, are experimenting with new forms, to wit, multihyphen adjectives. So far, "actor-turned-politician," which can be found just to the left of Clint Eastwood's name in any story about Carmel, Calif., is the most beloved two-hyphen entry, while "state-of-the-art" is such a successful three-hyphen innovation that it may be used several times a week without risking reproof from an editor.

Though of lower wattage, nonhy-phenated modifiers also count for something in journalese. Since "buxom blonde" and "leggy redhead" are no longer in fashion, journalese has evolved alternate descriptions of females, like a "handsome woman" (virtually any female over 50) or an "attractive woman" (any woman at all). Negative journalese, a strong branch of the language, combines a complimentary word with an apparently innocent but actually murderous modifier. "She is still pretty," for instance, means, "She is long in the tooth" or "Good grief! Is she still around?" Other useful adjectives include "crusty" (obnoxious), "unpredictable" (bonkers), "experienced" (ancient) and "small but well-financed" (don't invest in this turkey).

A subcategory of journalese involves the language used to indicate a powerful or celebrated person who is about to self-destruct or walk the plank. Anyone referred to as an "American institution," for example, is in trouble. In politics, two or more stories in the same week referring to a power person as clever or, worse, brilliant indicate that the end is near. Soon Mr. Brilliant will be labeled a "loose cannon" and transmute himself into an adviser, the Washington version of self-imposed exile. In business journalism, the phrase "one of the most respected managers in his field" informs knowing readers that envy is unnecessary — the respected manager is on the way out. Before long there will be hints that his managerial ferocity is insufficient, and perhaps a profile mentioning that he drinks decaffeinated coffee, collects porcelain miniatures or loves San Francisco. This means that in a week he will be "leaving to pursue outside interests." In sports, it is understood that all such rapid declines are drug-related, and sportswriters, the original masters of journalese, are

constantly casting about for nonlibelous ways of suggesting that Johnny Jumpshot is deeply in love with controlled substances. The current code words are "listless" and "lacking motivation or concentration." If the reporter writes that the athlete "occasionally misses the team bus," the astute reader understands that Jumpshot is a walking pharmacy who no longer knows where or who he is, though his body still turns up for games.

One of the many challenges in journalism is turning out serious articles about celebrities who say they served in Joan of Arc's army or strolled through Iran with Jesus Christ. "Free spirit," "flamboyant" and "controversial" are not really up to the task. In a profile of a well-known woman who insists that she has lived several times before, one journalese speaker came up with this deft line: "More than most people on this earth, she has found spiritual answers." In crime journalese, the top thug in any urban area is always referred to as a "reputed Mafia chieftain" and generally depicted as an untutored but charismatic leader of a successful business operation. The chieftain's apprentice thugs are his "associates." This sort of coverage reflects the automatic respect and dignity accorded crime figures who know where reporters live and recognize the understandable desire of journalists everywhere to keep their kneecaps in good working order.

As all users know, journalese is a formidable bulwark against libel, candor and fresh utterance. Any threat to its state-of-the-art ground-breaking terminology would have a chilling effect on everybody, especially us award-winning journalists.

Writing the editorial Because an editorial presumably reflects the beliefs of management, the editorial *we* is used. The assumption is that the audience recognizes the anonymous first-person plural as representing the medium, not the individual who wrote the copy.

Form. Editorial organization is different from that of the straight news story. Because an editorial takes a point of view, it cannot be edited and trimmed in the same manner as news. The editorial has three essential units: the lead, the body and the clincher.

- *Lead*. The first sentence or two should be explicit. You need to state the topic and why it's important to the audience. The lead should be short, crisp and to the point.

- *Body*. Here you present your pertinent facts, persuasive language and logical arguments. One way you can develop the body is to point out alternatives, options or solutions, particularly if you intend to call for action or for a shift in attitudes. Above all, use hard facts to support your ideas. Give examples and illustrations, draw comparisons, cite authority. Avoid glittering generalities and clichés. Be specific, concrete. A popular technique is to start with the least desirable of options or alternatives and end with the one you believe is most acceptable and reasonable.

- *Clincher*. The clincher is where you provide what you believe is an inevitable conclusion. The clincher should be carefully composed, but it cannot be totally didactic. If you've done a good job of presenting the facts and of building an argument, the conclusion can be one logically drawn by the audience. All you have done in the clincher, in fact, is to put into a coherent sentence what you hope the audience already has deduced.

Style. After you have written the editorial, you need to review it for logic, consistency of thought and style. Be certain there are no ambiguities, no possibility for misinterpretation. Check sentence and paragraph length carefully. Apply a readability index, if necessary. A basic tenet in persuasive writing is the more complex the subject, the simpler the sentences should be.

Newspaper editorials. Even more important than sentence and paragraph length is the total length of the editorial. Readership studies of newspapers indicate that the average reader just skims the editorial page unless a topic is compelling. The wise editorial writer knows that a long, gray column of copy will turn the reader off. Short, tight editorials are the best.

Broadcast editorials. Almost every newspaper carries editorials, whereas only about 1 in 10 broadcast stations do. Part of the reason for this low percentage is regulation. Broadcasters maintain that the Fairness Doctrine and other regulations inhibit broadcasters from stating their opinions on the air.

Hundreds of stations, both radio and TV, do carry editorials, though they aren't always of the hard-hitting variety. A former, and outspoken, chairman of the FCC, Newton Minow, once said that practically the only things broadcasters editorialize about are "canoe safety and milk for children."

Editorials are the responsibility of station management, in most cases. Station managers often form editorial committees to advise on topics and content; the news director and other news staff usually serve on these committees, assist in the research and do any reporting that needs to be done. Unlike features or commentaries, though, in the end editorials are the product of station management; station managers usually read them on the air themselves.

However, today's TV editorials are often much more than a general manager sitting in front of a camera reading copy. The award-winning editorials in 14.9 demonstrate how copy is written for broadcast, but this copy is often just one part of a total package for airing that may include interviews with people, scenes from the place discussed, or even reporters on the scene. One unusual treatment is Charles Osgood's commentary in rhyme for CBS News.

Some stations also handle letters to the station on the air, much in the same way newspapers do—selecting and editing letters that represent different points of view. These are often shown in chromakey as the station manager is reading them. A good example is the way *60 Minutes* handles its letters.

Broadcast commentaries.   The distinctions between a broadcast editorial, commentary, news analysis (depth piece) and a feature are sometimes subtle. The feature, as you have seen, is defined by broadcast newspeople as being on the lighter, or softer, side of the news. Editorials are the position statements of management. They can also be light, or they can be hard-hitting, but the news department is usually not in full control of their content. Broadcast commentaries fall somewhere in between features and editorials. These commentaries are about the closest thing broadcasting has to newspapers' political columns.

Paul Harvey is perhaps the best known broadcast commentator today. His staccato, sometimes caustic style has won him many followers. Probably just as many listen to him each day because they *don't* like him. Harvey labels his daily program "news and commentary." His method of news selection involves looking for the offbeat as well as covering some of the top stories of the day. His commentaries are often slipped into his news stories; for most broadcast newswriters and announcers, that's a violation of good journalistic practice. But Harvey does say his program is news *and* commentary—he just doesn't announce where one leaves off and the other begins.

Harvey is syndicated, as are other national commentators. The various radio and TV networks also supply commentaries. Commentaries are sometimes included in network newscasts.

In some instances, the commentary is a news analysis. The commentator attempts to provide a closer look at a major news story. However, a broadcast commentary can also be a philosophical piece, as print columns often are,

The informal, narrative style of CBS news commentator Edward R. Murrow told radio and television audiences about war, famous people and significant events. His compelling style made listeners feel a part of the occasion. For a story of his career, read *Prime Time* by Alexander Kendrick.

The Bettmann Archive

as well as a personal essay on a political or social issue in the news. The commentator supplies the personality the audience can identify with.

Except on election nights, commentaries on local radio and TV stations are not that common. Local stations generally subscribe to a national syndicated commentator. These national commentators have some of the attributes of newspaper columnists. Their broadcasts are aired at the same time each day so listeners and viewers can tune in; they write in any manner they choose, or so it seems, on a wide variety of issues.

The Fairness Doctrine required that broadcast commentary be labeled as such. In TV the word "COMMENTARY" still is often supered on the screen, and in radio the lead-in to the tape of the commentator often states that what you are about to hear is commentary and does not necessarily reflect the views of the station. Commentators may be totally objective in their presentations, but stations are usually careful to make sure the audience can tell the commentary from the news.

14.9 TV Editorials

Both of these TV editorials are responses to incidents in the community. Both are strong pleas for action, and both offer listeners a course of action. Editorials that just arouse without offering some way to respond only frustrate listeners.

Editorial

WCVBTV **BOSTON, CHANNEL 5**
Editorial Department
5 TV Place, Needham Br. Boston, MA 02192
(617) 449-0400

Title: Following up on Incidents of Violence   Reference No.

Presented By: S. James Coppersmith, Vice President & General Manager   23-85

Broadcast:

February 18: 6:57 AM; 12:28 PM; 6:55 PM; 3:40 AM
February 23: 6:58 PM; 3:50 AM

A recent shooting in Boston drew national attention and outrage. A young Dorchester woman was shot by a teenager who tried to rob her after she left a bus on Blue Hill Avenue. The next day, by chance, the victim's mother sat on the subway near a teenager allegedly bragging about having committed that very crime. The mother followed the youth downtown and called police, who made the arrest. The following day, the 14 year-old suspect was free on $500 cash bail. Judge Darrell Outlaw said he had no choice, and then added, an attempted murder charge is "not that big a deal" in his court.

"Not that big a deal?" We don't blame the judge for his candor about the frequency of violent crime in his jurisdiction. But what does it say about our society?

Guns are too easily available. Crime is too casually committed. And the slow-moving court system is too burdened to be a real remedy. When 14 year olds brag about shooting people, you know our community is in deep trouble.

And we must respond as a community. Citizens and legislators should press for a ban on handguns. Our court system should be revamped to deal effectively with violent offenders. All of us should channel our outrage over one bizarre incident into sustained lobbying for safer streets and a more civilized society.

WCVB-TV. Boston, MA. Used with permission.

Editorial

WCVBTV **BOSTON, CHANNEL 5**
Editorial Department
5 TV Place, Needham Br. Boston, MA 02192
(617) 449-0400

Title: Fighting Poverty in Massachusetts

Presented By: Marjorie Arons-Barron, Director of Editorials   65-85

Broadcast:

                May 15: 6:57 AM; 12:28 PM; 6:55 PM; 3:40 AM
                May 19: 6:28 PM; 10:58 PM; 3:20 AM

When was the last time you ran out of money and couldn't afford to put food on the table? It happens almost every month to many welfare families because Massachusetts is stingy with benefits. We pay about 40 percent less than the Reagan administration allows for welfare recipients. Federal officials say it takes a family of four about $10,000 to live at the poverty level, but Massachusetts pays that family a little under $6,000. We can no longer ignore what those numbers mean to the average welfare mother.

> "The kids are constantly saying "I'm hungry." Basically, right now, if my kids eat twice a day, we're lucky - because I can't afford to cook three times a day."
>
> Ellen Hogan, Dorchester, MA

This is a time of prosperity in Massachusetts; we can't keep our poor living on the edge of hunger. For years we've been skimping on assistance, some years giving meager increases, some years none. So while the cost of living has risen 180 percent since 1970, welfare benefits have gone up just 50 percent.

That painful gap must close, and Governor Dukakis' proposed five percent hike won't do it. Proposed legislation would bring Massachusetts' welfare payments up to the federal poverty line. $500 million cost may not be possible all at once, even with Washington paying half. So legislators should approve nothing less than a ten percent increase for next year and pledge to meet the federal guideline soon thereafter. Because with more than half of welfare recipients children just ten years old or younger, it's the state which has them going to bed hungry. And that's not right.

Reprinted by permission of Jefferson Communications, Inc., Reston, Va.

A formula of sorts exists for a good broadcast editorial:

1. Define the issue to be addressed.

2. Provide some background information on the issue.

3. Call for some action on the issue, or provide a recommendation.

4. Expand on Step 3 by stating why your recommendation should be followed, who must do it, when and where it should begin, and how the action called for can be accomplished.

The impact of editorials

If nothing else, the experience of writing editorials will teach you that everyone has an opinion about something. Try as you might to compose a well-reasoned, coherent and convincing editorial, you will undoubtedly draw some responses you didn't anticipate: letters to the editor or crank calls or hate mail. But isn't that the point of an editorial—to make the public think about a subject and elicit some response?

The role of the editorial in influencing public opinion has been studied by professionals and academics alike. As more is learned about how the public reacts to editorials, editorial writers (and those who suggest editorial topics) are changing their approach. Editors once thought that their editorials would cause significant change. That isn't true today. Research studies—and they are many—indicate that compared to the news, sports and feature pages, editorials have relatively low readership.

Other media, not just other parts of the paper, compete for the public's attention. The old lament from politicians and other public figures that a single editorial could ruin them is not heard so often today as it was during the muckraking era of the 1880s and '90s.

Publishers are well aware of the diminishing effect of editorials on public opinion. The National Conference of Editorial Writers frequently explores this topic during its annual sessions. Kenneth Rystrom refers to it:

A number of vivid ways have been used to warn editorial writers against expecting too much from editorial campaigns. Bernard Kilgore, publisher of the *Wall Street Journal*, said he thought it was all right for newspapers to regard themselves as thunderers and for editorial writers to picture themselves "with a bolt of lightning in each hand about to smash down on something." But he urged writers to be "very careful about demolishing a subject with one swoop, because good subjects for the editorial page are hard to come by." His point was that most editorial topics require analysis and study over a period of time, not a single definitive pronouncement. Donald Tyerman, former editor of the *Economist* of London, reminded editorial writers at an NCEW meeting that they are neither Moses nor God. He warned against the Tablets of Stone theory—"that you can hand down the truth or, indeed, that you have it to hand down." Nor did he believe that editorial writers can effect a conversion, such as occurred to Saul of Tarsus on the road to Damascus.[9]

All of this is not to denigrate the importance of the editorial page. For despite its low readership and sometimes inane or turgid content, the editorial page remains a bastion of expression of opinions and ideas.

While editorials don't exert immediate impact on a majority of the public, they are influential in what has been termed "agenda-setting," establishing for the public the importance of topics. Agenda-setting helps give the public a syllabus, a list of things to think about. The more a subject is brought before the public, the more significance it takes on.

Ethics for editorial writers includes not only presenting facts accurately but refraining from propaganda. The opinion presented should be the best judgment you, as a writer, can make from a thorough investigation. To produce a piece without adequate information is to jeopardize the credibility of the medium's news as well.

ADVERTORIALS Advertisers often buy space to address concerns of theirs. Sometimes the concern is one that editorial writers have acknowledged, sometimes it isn't.

The advertorial by Pfizer pharmaceuticals in 14.10 addresses the need for biomedical research funding in two ways. Pfizer is saying research is an expensive process that private companies can't handle alone. Private companies need research grants from government and from voluntary health agencies. As a reader, you are urged to take two specific actions: (1) Write your legislators to be sure government funding for biomedical research doesn't become a victim of budget cuts. (2) Give money to voluntary health agencies, like the American Heart Association, American Cancer Society and others who offer grants to individuals and to colleges and universities to do biomedical research.

Another type of advertorial urges legislative action as well. Mobil's editorial column (14.10b) makes it a partner with consumers to attack the government's Superfund to clean up toxic wastes and the proposed legislation to prevent acid rain. It calls attention to independent research from the gas industry, without acknowledging it, that shows how the acid rain proposals will increase the costs of electricity, and by causing electric utilities to use more gas also increase

14.10 Advertorials

Medical Research– building a healthier future

If you've ever been treated for high blood pressure… heart disease…diabetes…or almost any health problem, medical progress based on research has already touched your life.

Because of medical research, polio no longer strikes in epidemic proportions every summer. Today about three-quarters of patients diagnosed as having Hodgkin's disease will survive five years or longer—as opposed to less than half twenty years ago. Current treatment options for people with heart disease and high blood pressure include medication that helps the body's natural regulators to control blood pressure and volume, enabling the heart to function with less strain.

Scientists are now working on new ways of treating such devastating afflictions as heart disease, cancer and Alzheimer's disease. They are testing new enzyme inhibitors that may control or reverse the late complications of diabetes. Forthcoming breakthroughs in understanding biological processes and treating disease may change the quality and perhaps the length of your life.

Medical research leading to such results takes years of patient, often frustrating experimentation by many different teams throughout the public and private sectors of our scientific community. The tasks involved are not simple.

Advances in research stem from a partnership that includes federal agencies such as the National Institutes of Health (NIH) and the Alcohol, Drug Abuse and Mental Health Administration (ADAMHA), universities and teaching hospitals across America, and private industry laboratories. Each partner often works independently to acquire knowledge and test new concepts. They must build on the knowledge developed in all laboratories, and they often coordinate efforts in their search for answers.

Whether an idea originates in a university laboratory or starts with basic product research carried on in the private sector, important findings percolate through the entire scientific community, where each new finding serves as a building block to establish a deeper understanding of what we are and how we function.

Medical research is an expensive process. It needs steady funding for equipment and personnel—even when progress is slow. Government and industry often work with university-based scientists and the medical profession not only in the acquisition of new knowledge and the development of new treatments, but also in funding these advances.

Now more than ever, we all must do our part to help keep the flow of discoveries active and ongoing. If funding for medical research is reduced, major advances in knowledge about some of the most dreaded diseases facing us today could be delayed for years to come.

What can you do?

- *Speak up.* Let your legislators know that you want funding of biomedical research by NIH and other government agencies to be kept at the highest possible levels.
- *Contribute* to voluntary health organizations supporting disease research.

Research-based pharmaceutical companies such as Pfizer are also increasing their financial investment in research. For instance, in 1984 alone, pharmaceutical companies in the United States spent over 4 *billion* dollars on research and product development.

At the same time, we at Pfizer realize the importance of committing more than money to research. As a partner in healthcare, we are continually working to discover new ideas, test new concepts, and turn new understanding to practical and beneficial uses. Now we are working harder than ever to make sure that this nation's medical research effort receives the attention—and funding—it deserves.

For more information on the future of medical research in America, write to Health Research U.S.A., P.O. Box 3852 FR, Grand Central Station, New York, NY 10163.

Pfizer PHARMACEUTICALS • A PARTNER IN HEALTHCARE

14.10 (continued)

Taxes that miss the target

With all that has been written recently on tax theory and tax "reform," we find it incredible that nobody, to our knowledge, has decried an alarming trend in the way America's lawmakers choose to solve certain problems. The problems, such as toxic waste disposal and acid rain, affect society as a whole. But Congress is debating solutions based on special-purpose taxes aimed at specific industries.

Basically, here's why we feel special-purpose taxes are wrong:

• They are directed at those who are perceived as being able to pay, whether or not these handy targets caused the problem, and whether or not they can actually afford to pay.

• They depart from the concept that funds from the general treasury, raised from all the taxpayers, should be used to provide benefits for all. We're not saying that identifiable polluters, for example, shouldn't pay to clean up their messes. But when those responsible can't be found, and everybody benefits from the cleanup, we believe everybody should share in the costs.

• Such special-purpose taxes create special-purpose funds, and as a result, expenditures are often driven not by the size of the problem, but by the amount of money available.

• Special-purpose funds give rise to priority-setting and decision-making by a bureaucracy with its own direction and momentum—and without the proper annual review and supervision provided by the budget and appropriations processes.

• Finally, special-purpose taxes distort the free market. By targeting certain industries, they, in effect, subsidize others.

Some examples:

Superfund was created in 1980 to clean up orphan toxic waste sites—sites where the dumpers cannot be identified. Started as a $1.6 billion program, Superfund has been financed almost totally by a tax on the oil and chemical industries—although other industries contributed much of the toxic wastes. Senate and House conferees recently agreed on a new Superfund program to cost $9 billion over the next five years—in spite of protestations by the Environmental Protection Agency that it could efficiently spend only about $5.3 billion.

To pay for the program, the tax on the oil industry was raised by more than 13 times to $2.75 billion over the next five years. One industry—oil—was singled out to pay for almost a third of the program. No other industry was asked to pay anything close to this amount. Part of the levy is a new tax on domestic and imported crude oil, which will raise the energy costs of American factories and farms, thus making them less competitive in world markets. American consumers will pay more and American exporters will be further disadvantaged in international trade.

Another example: The House is currently considering a measure to curb acid rain by imposing new limits on emissions from electrical power plants and other industrial facilities and by additional curbs on auto emissions. But the framers of the bill are worried about the impact of the legislation on residential users of electricity, because utility rates would have to rise by some undetermined amount as power plants either add costly hardware to their stacks or change to costlier fuels.

The proposed solution? A special-purpose tax on those utilities that burn coal or oil, collected by the federal government and dispensed in a manner to ensure that residential customers suffer no more than a 10 percent rate hike.

The implications are staggering. For one thing, major industrial users of electricity would see their costs go up—another favor for foreign producers. Consider, too, the bureaucracy of a federal agency—the EPA—sitting in Washington attempting to determine local conditions in 50 states, pondering at least 50 sets of utility rates and the basis for setting each of them. Where would this leave the 50 public utilities commissions already charged with this chore?

Sometimes, a special tax may have no special purpose beyond political expediency. The so-called "windfall profits" tax, imposed on oil in 1980, was never really a tax on profit; it was a tax on production. Uncollected now because oil prices are below its trigger price, the tax is still on the books, waiting for oil prices to recover. Meanwhile, it cost the industry almost $74 billion in less than five years—money that went into the general treasury in spite of an early "commitment" to finance energy conservation and synfuels development.

In our view, Congress still has plenty of work to do in the area of genuine tax reform. And it might start by eliminating special-purpose taxes, and returning to the principle that the general treasury should finance the general good.

the cost of natural gas. The emotional element in this persuasion is an attack on government bureaucracy and the suggestion that the federal government is making decisions the states could make better for themselves. The other suggestion is, of course, that your tax dollars are paying for this bureaucracy. Environmentalists are not likely to agree with this column, and they'll probably write the publication that ran the ad. But, of course, it's not the view of the publication. It's Mobil's point of view.

MAIN POINTS

- The mass media express opinions and judgments in reviews and editorials.

- Reviews can range in subject from opera to restaurants, but they have these characteristics in common: They should inform with fact, give some idea of content and express an opinion about quality.

- Reviewers must have background in the subjects they critique. Expressing an opinion without supportive detail is unfair to the audience and to the artist.

- Although print reviews are the most common, the electronic media, especially television, are giving the audience more critiques than in the past.

- Editorials represent an institutional point of view. The editorial stance is determined by management rather than the individual writer.

- Opinion columnists and broadcast commentators express their own opinions in any style they choose.

- Editorials have particular purposes. Among these are commending, condemning, persuading and entertaining.

- The editorial has three essential units: a lead, which specifies what the topic is; a body, which presents options, alternatives or possible conclusions; and a clincher, which makes clear the course of action recommended. In all cases, the recommendations should be supported by examples and illustrations that are logical and coherent.

- Careful attention must be given to clarity and brevity. Long editorials turn the audience away.

- Research studies indicate that individual editorials have little direct effect on audience opinion. Rather, the long-range effect of editorials seems to be that of agenda-setting— letting the public know what issues are important.

- Advertorials are editorials that an advertiser has paid to have published. They often read like editorials and may address some of the same issues.

EXERCISES

1. Attend a play or concert. Using the principles outlined in this chapter, write a 250-word newspaper review. Then get a copy of the local newspaper to compare your review with a professional's. Analyze the differences, strengths and weaknesses of your copy compared to the other.

2. Select an artistic production you know something about—an art show, a sculpture exhibit, a film. Write a review that will (a) interest readers in attending the same event and (b) reveal your knowledge of the subject. Rewrite this for broadcast.

3. Find a magazine editorial you disagree with. Tell why. Be specific in evaluating the reasons the editorial didn't succeed in causing you to shift an opinion.

4. Read the editorials in the school newspaper. Select one. Analyze the style and content. Did the editorial tell you something you didn't already know? Did it persuade you to think or do something, if that was its purpose? Rewrite the editorial to improve it.

5. Write an editorial in radio news style. Write the same editorial in TV style, incorporating visuals into the script.

6. Take an issue and write an editorial from your own perspective, then think of a company that would be likely to take either the same or a different point of view and write an advertorial for that company. (It will be easier if you choose one that is the same as your point of view. You can write the other side, just as you can learn in debate classes to debate the other side. But it's difficult to be as persuasive.)

NOTES

1. The two titans of journalism, Pulitzer and Hearst, battled in New York in 1896–97 with their respective Sunday papers, the *World* and the *Journal*. Hearst eventually won the hiring competition for talent between the two. He developed a Sunday comic section to compete with the *World*'s eight-page color section. One of the talents he had lured away was Richard F. Outcault, whose cartoon character "The Yellow Kid" had left the comic pages and begun to be associated with public issues. The *World* responded with another "yellow kid" to replace the one lost to Hearst. The character, dressed in a loose garment like a stretched T-shirt, with vacant eyes and a toothless grin, came to symbolize the sensationalism of the era created by the competition for readers between the two papers; hence the term "yellow journalism."

2. The muckrakers were given their name by President Theodore Roosevelt in a 1906 speech, in which he borrowed from John Bunyan's *Pilgrim's Progress*: "the Man with the Muckrake . . . who could look no way but downward." The name came to be associated with those who turned up unpleasant social and political facts and urged reform, probably in reaction against the "yellow journalism" of the 1890s.

3. William Zinsser, *On Writing Well*, 2nd ed. (New York: Harper & Row, 1980), p. 147.

4. Ibid.

5. Robert Lewis Shayon, *Open to Criticism* (Boston: Beacon Press, 1971), pp. 3–8.

6. Clive Barnes, "The 'Terrible Power' of Critics over Institutions," *New York Times*, July 25, 1976, pp. 10, 15.

7. Used with permission of WRC-TV News.

8. Curtis MacDougall, *Principles of Editorial Writing* (Dubuque, Iowa: Wm. C. Brown, 1973), p. 289.

9. Kenneth Rystrom, *The Why, Who and How of the Editorial Page* (New York: Random House, 1983), pp. 44–45. Used with permission.

SUGGESTIONS FOR ADDITIONAL READING

Anderson, Jack, and James Boyd. *Confessions of a Muckraker*. New York: Random House, 1979.

Babb, Laura Longley. *The Editorial Page*. Boston: Houghton Mifflin, 1977.

Hulteng, John L. *The Opinion Function: Editorial and Interpretive Writing for the News Media*. Hayden Lake, Idaho: Ridge House Press, 1973.

MacDougall, Curtis D. *Principles of Editorial Writing*. Dubuque, Iowa: Wm. C. Brown, 1973.

Osgood, Charles. *Nothing Could Be Finer Than a Crisis That Is Minor in the Morning*. New York: Holt, Rinehart & Winston, 1979.

Rystrom, Kenneth. *The Why, Who and How of the Editorial Page*. New York: Random House, 1983.

Stonecipher, Harry W. *Editorial and Persuasive Writing: Opinion Functions of the News Media*. New York: Hastings House, 1979.

Glossary

ABC Audit Bureau of Circulations, an organization giving accurate circulation data on U.S. print media.

Account executive (AE) Agency representative who is liaison between client and agency.

Actuality A radio report from the scene. Actualities can be live, on-tape or phone reports.

Ad-lib Unscripted reports or comments.

Advance News story about an event to occur in the future.

Advertising insertion order An authorization to reserve space in a print medium for an ad.

Aerial shot Photo taken from helicopter or plane. (Has different meaning for movie film production and printing — refers to a particular effect.)

Affidavit Proof that commercials were aired at specific time periods, a sworn statement. Affidavit is a legal term.

Affiliate A station that is part of a network, but not owned and operated by the network.

Agate Typographic term for 5½-point type, standard unit of measurement for advertising lineage; fourteen agate lines to the inch.

Air brushing Artistic improvement of photographs used in ads to remove undesirable elements.

Air check Tape made of radio or TV program or a commercial when it is aired.

Air time Time when a radio or TV program starts.

Alignment (1) Straightness or crookedness of letters in a line of type. Also refers to positioning of the elements in an ad for desirable effect. (2) Setup of head on audio or videotape machine.

AM May mean either a morning newspaper or standard radio broadcasting (amplitude modulation) of 535 to 1605 kilohertz.

Angle Particular emphasis of a media presentation; sometimes called a slant.

Animation Process of filming a number of slightly different cartoon drawings to create the illusion of movement.

Answer print In 35mm film, the first print off a negative or, in 16mm, off a reversal after work print is completed; used to check quality.

AOR Designation for a type of radio station format, album-oriented rock music.

AP Associated Press, a cooperative membership news-gathering service dating from 1848; serves both print and broadcast media with stories and pictures. AP is international in scope and has its own correspondents, in addition to receiving material from member media.

Arbitron Ratings Company Sales research organization for broadcasting. (Also known as ARB).

Art General term for all illustrations in any medium.

Art director Creator of the graphics section of ad or commercial.

Art-type Adhesive-backed, paste-on type used for special effects.

Ascender The element of a lowercase letter extending above the body of the letter such as in *b, d, h*.

Assignment(s) desk The desk in a broadcast newsroom where assignment(s) editors keep files on all upcoming events and assign reporters stories for coverage.

Audience Group or groups receptive to a particular medium.

Audio Sound.

Author's alterations (AAs) Typesetter's term for changes made on proofs by the author after type has been set.

Availabilities Unsold time slots for commercials.

B&W Black and white (monochrome) photograph (as opposed to color photo).

Back of the book In magazines, the materials appearing after the main editorial section.

Backroom or backshop Mechanical section of a newspaper plant.

Backtiming (1) In broadcasting, a method of determining the time at which various program segments must begin to bring a program out on time. (2) In PR campaign, a scheduling to determine completion dates for various component parts to climax.

Backup (1) In newspaper assignments, a second reporter or photographer used as a backup in case the first does not or cannot complete the job. (2) In printing, when one side of a sheet has been printed and the reverse side is being printed.

Bad break In typesetting, an incorrect word division at end of line of type.

Bank (1) Composing-room table for galleys. (2) A strip of lights.

Banner Also called a streamer, a long line of type.

Banner head Headlines set in large type and usually stretching across a page.

Beat A reporter's regular run, such as "city hall beat."

Beeper (1) Recorded telephone conversation or interview. (2) Device frequently attached to the telephone that beeps every fourteen seconds as required by FCC to indicate that a recording is being made.

Ben day Process carrying its originator's name which makes possible a variety of shadings in line plates through photoengraving rather than the more expensive halftone.

Bicycling Transporting of film or audio or video recording from one station to another instead of making a duplicate.

Black leader or opaque leader (1) Black film used in editing. (2) Film used in 16mm "A" or "B" or checkerboard editing. The

black film, without images, makes putting sequences together easier.

Blanking out Printing in two or more colors means forms must be broken or separated and spacing material placed where lines or illustrations have been lifted to print in different colors. Also called breaking for color.

Bleed Printing (photo, art or type) that goes to the edge of the page. Has higher impact, but costs more.

Bloop To erase sound track by degaussing (wiping out) if magnetic, or by opaquing (blocking out) if optical.

Blow up Photographically enlarging the visual size of any item.

Blurb Short promotional description of story or article.

Board Audio control board that sends programming to the transmitter for broadcast or to the tape machine for recording.

Body type Type used for text matter, as distinguished from display (headlines or headings) type.

Boldface type (bf) Blacker, heavier type than the rest of the type face, so it stands out from surrounding copy.

Booklet Compilation of six-plus pages, printed with paper cover and bound.

Boomerang effect When person affected by public opinion reacts in opposite from expected way.

Border Frame around piece of type matter.

Box or boxed Type enclosed with printed borders.

Break (1) Story available for publication. (2) Stopping

point—may designate commercial break.

Break up To kill or break up a type form so it cannot be used to print from again.

Breaking story Fast-breaking story usually written in sections.

Bridge (1) Phrase or sentence connecting two stories. (2) In broadcasting, transitional program music.

Brite (or bright) Light, humorous news story.

Broadcast wire Wire copy stories written in broadcast style.

Broadside Message printed on one side of a single sheet no smaller than 18 x 25 inches. Designed for quick reading and prompt response.

Brochure Printed piece of usually six or more pages. More elaborate than a booklet, but without a backbone. Differs from a pamphlet by its use of illustrations and color.

Bulletin (1) Important news brief. (2) Wire service message to kill or release a story.

Burnish/burnishing Spreading dots in a halftone to deepen certain areas; also rubbing down to make paste-ups stick.

Business publications Periodicals published by and/or directed toward business.

Busy Too cluttered, as in a print illustration, still photograph or TV scene.

By-line Reporter's name preceding a newspaper or broadcast story.

Cable TV A system in which homes receive TV (and radio) signals via a coaxial cable rather than from an over-the-air broadcast signal.

Cameo lighting Foreground figures are lighted with highly directional light, with the background remaining dark.

Camera chain TV camera and associated equipment, including power supply and sync generator.

Camera copy Copy ready for reproduction. Also called repros.

Camera negative Original negative film shot by film camera.

Campaign Organized effort to affect opinion of a group or groups on particular issue.

Caps Capital letters.

Caption or cutline Editorial material or legend accompanying illustration.

Card image Computer language for image of punched card as represented by some other medium, such as a tape or disc.

Casting off Estimating space required for copy set in given type size.

Cell or photocell Optical reader.

Center spread Two facing center pages of publication; printed on single, continuous sheet.

Channel (1) In broadcasting, a radio spectrum frequency assigned to a radio or TV station or stations. (2) In computer science, path for electrical communication or transfer of information; imaginary line parallel to edge of tape along which lines are punched.

Character Any single unit of type—letter, number, punctuation mark.

Character generation Projection on the face of a CRT of typographic images, usually in high-speed computerized photocomposition system. The series of letters and numbers appears directly on the television screen or is keyed into a background picture.

Cheesecake Photographs depending for their appeal upon display of sex appeal.

Chromakey A process placing an electronic image on the screen behind the newscaster. The image can be a live shot, a still, videotape or film.

Circular Flyer, mailing piece, free distribution item; usually one sheet and inexpensive.

Circulation (1) In broadcasting, refers to number of regular listeners or viewers or area in which they regularly attend to a station. (2) In print media, refers to subscribers, but may include street or newsstand sales.

Class publications Periodicals designed for well-defined audiences, with focus limited to certain subjects.

CLC Capital and lowercase letters, to designate typesetting.

Client Organization an advertising agency or PR agency represents.

Clip (1) Newspaper clipping. (2) In broadcasting, a short piece of film or tape.

Clipping returns Clippings, mentioning a specific subject, from newspapers, magazines, trade journals, specialized publications and internal publications.

Commercial services supply clippings from numerous publications for monthly charge and per-clipping charge, or flat rate per clipping.

Clipsheet Stories and illustrations printed on one page and sent to publications. Offers a number of releases in one mailing; works best with small publications that cannot afford syndicated matter.

Close The end segment of a newscast.

Coated paper Paper with enameled coating to give smooth, hard finish suitable for best halftone reproduction.

Coincidental interview Method of public opinion surveying in which a phone interview is conducted to gain information.

Cold comp Type composition by various cold methods— from typewriter to high-speed computerized photocomposition systems.

Cold light Fluorescent.

Cold reading Broadcasting copy read by announcer without prior rehearsal.

Colophon (1) Credit line at end of book for designer and printer; tells what type faces and paper stock used. (2) Publisher's logo.

Color (1) Mood piece to go with a straight news story. (2) Lively writing. (3) Exaggerate, falsify. (4) Colored ink or art.

Color separations Negatives made of full (four)-color art. A step that most publications still find necessary, although an electronic process exists that will transmit a color images without film to print.

Column rule Vertical line separating columns of type.

Combination plate Halftone and line plate combined in one engraving.

Commercial protection Specific time between competitive commercials granted by a station.

Community Immediate area affected by company policy and production.

Composition (1) Typesetting and make-up. (2) Arrangement of words into stylistic format.

Compositive or composite (1) In broadcasting, sound track with desired mix of sounds. (2) In photography, mixing of elements from different negatives to create false image.

Comprehensive layout A more elaborate version of the rough, as close as possible to the finished ad. Used to get client approval and to guide production people.

Computer network Two or more computers interconnected.

Computer program Set of instructions that, converted to machine format, causes computer to carry out specified operations to solve a problem.

Condensed Type that is narrower than regular face.

Conservation Support of an existing opinion held by a public to keep it from changing.

Console Part of computer through which operator or repairman communicates with machine and vice versa. Normally has display device such as typewriter.

Continuity Radio and television copy.

Continuity strip Ad in comic strip format.

Control group Group comprised of members chosen for particular characteristics or opinions.

Conversion To influence opinion away from one side of an issue to another.

Coppering Revising old news to give it feeling of currency.

Copy Verbal part of ad or commercial.

Copy desk News desk at newspaper or magazine, where copy is edited and headlines written.

Copyreader Newsroom employee who reads and corrects (edits) copy and writes headlines.

Copywriter Person who creates the verbal portion of an ad or commercial.

Core (1) Memory of computer. (2) Small hub on which film is wound for storage or shipping.

Correspondent Out-of-town reporter.

Cover (1) To reporter, getting all available facts about an event. (2) Outer pages of a magazine—specifically, outside front (first cover), inside front (second cover), inside back (third cover) and outside back (fourth cover).

Cover stock (1) Sturdy paper for magazine covers. (2) Also used for pamphlets, booklets, tent cards, posters and other printed matter where weight and durability are important.

CPI (1) In typesetting, characters per inch. (2) In computer science, density of magnetic tape or drum.

CPM Cost per thousand ("M" means "thousand")—the ratio of the cost of a given TV segment to audience reached in thousands.

CPS Characters per second; relates to paper tapes, typewriter speeds or computer printer speeds.

Creative director Person who coordinates art and copy for ad or commercial.

Credits List of people who participated in a TV or film production.

Cropping Changing the shape or size of an illustration to make it fit a designated space or to cut out distracting or undesirable elements.

CRT Cathode ray tube; computer terminal screen or television screen with keyboard for writing.

Crystallization Creating an awareness of previously vague or subconscious attitudes held by a public.

CTC or CTK Copy to come.

CTG Copy to go.

Cue (1) In TV, film or radio, signal to initiate action. (2) Mark in a TV script for technical and production staffs. (3) To find the proper place of a transcription.

Cumulative audience (cume) Audience reached by a broadcast station in two or more time periods or more than one station in a specific time period (such as a week).

Cut (1) To delete part of some copy or to end a program suddenly. (2) Track or groove in a transcription. (3) Engraving, metal plate bearing an illustration, either lined or screened, to be used in letterpress printing (with a raised printing surface made from a matrix). (4) Instantaneous transition from one video source to another. *See also* Engraving

Cutline Caption or legend accompanying illustration.

Data base/data bank A collection of data used by an organization, capable of being processed and retrieved.

Dateline Line preceding story giving date and place of origin; usually only one location is printed.

Deadline The time a completed assignment is due and *must* be delivered.

Dealer imprint Name and address of dealer printed on leaflet, pamphlet, poster or similar matter, usually in space set aside for this purpose.

Deck head Headline having two or more groups of type.

Deckled edge Ragged edge of a sheet of paper.

Demographics Statistics that describe an audience by specifics such as age, sex, education, occupation.

Department Regular section on a particular subject in a newspaper or magazine.

Descender Bottom part of a lowercase letter which extends below the body of the letter, as in *p, q, y.*

Dirty copy Written material with considerable errors or corrections.

Disc Record or transcription.

Display type Type or hand lettering for headlines; usually larger than fourteen points.

Documentaries Informational film presentation with specific message.

Dolly To move the camera toward (dolly in) or away from (dolly out or back) the object.

Dope News information or background material.

Double-page spread Two facing pages; may be editorial material or advertising, with or without illustrations.

Double truck Center spread, or two full facing pages.

Download The news release will be in the organization's computer; a newspaper or other medium can call the computer by phone and have the information fed directly into the medium's computer for typesetting.

Dress (1) The appearance of a magazine. (2) In broadcasting, a final dress rehearsal, or what people will wear on camera. (3) Set dressing, properties.

Drive out In typesetting, to space words widely to fill the line.

Drop folio In books and publications, page number at bottom of page.

Drop-in ads Small advertising messages added to or dropped in regular advertisements of a different character; for example, a one-column-inch community fund drive ad in a department store's regular half-page ad.

Dry A slow or dry news day when not much is going on.

Dry brush drawing A drawing, usually on coarse board, made with a thick ink or paint.

Dry run A rehearsal, usually for TV, before the taping or airing, if live.

Dummy Suggested layout for a publication showing positions of all elements. A

hand dummy is rough and general. A paste-up dummy is proofs carefully pasted in position.

Duotones Two-color art. Two halftone plates are made from a one-color illustration and etched to produce a two-tone effect.

Dupe Duplicate proof.

Ears Boxes or type appearing at the upper left- and right-hand corners of publications alongside the flag (newspaper nameplate).

Edge key A keyed (electronically cut-in) title whose letters have distinctive edges, such as dark outlines or a drop shadow.

Edit To modify, correct, rearrange or otherwise change data in the computer.

Editing Emphasizing important matter or deleting the less significant.

Edition All identical copies, printed in one run of the press.

Editorial matter Entertainment or educational part of a broadcast program or publication, exclusive of commercial messages.

Editorialize Injection of opinion into a news story.

EDP Electronic data processing.

Electronic newspaper Teletext or videotex system in which the individual becomes his or her own gatekeeper, selecting a tailored mix of news and other information.

Em The square of any given type body. Usually refers to the pica em, which is twelve points square. Common method of measuring type composition: number of ems in a line is multiplied by the number of lines.

Embossing An impression made by pressing a piece of paper between two metal dies so that it stands above the surface of the sheet.

En Half an em, unit of measure in typesetting. Equal to width of a capital "N" in the particular size of type face being used.

Engraving ("cut") Zinc or copper plate that has been etched, generally with acid, to get a raised surface that, when inked, will print on paper. Engravings are reproductions of either line illustrations or halftones (screened); also called photoengravings, because they are made by being brought into contact with film negatives of illustrations. In today's commercial usage, *engraving* refers almost solely to letter-press printing, although in the past it referred to the intaglio processes.

Etching proofs Sharp, clean proofs from which zinc etchings can be made.

Exclusive Correspondent's report or story limited to a single station, network or periodical.

Extended or expanded Extra wide face of type.

External publication Publication issued by an organization to people outside its own employee or membership groups, such as customers, the local community, the financial world, and so on.

Extra condensed Type compressed, very thin.

Face The printing surface of type. Also used to identify one style of type from another, such as plain face, heavy face.

Fact sheet Page of significant information prepared by PR people to help news media in covering a special event.

Family Complete series of one type face, with all variations (bold, italic, small caps, and so on).

Fax Slang for facsimile. Exact reproduction of printed matter (words and photos).

FCC Federal Communications Commission, the government regulatory body for broadcasting.

Feature (1) To play up or emphasize. (2) A story, not necessarily news; usually more of human interest.

Feed Electronic signal. Generally a source like a network from which a station can record, or what one station sends to another station or stations.

File Send story by wire, Telex or other form of transmission. In computer language, information on a related record, treated as a unit.

Fill (1) In broadcasting, additional program material kept ready in case a program runs short. (2) To fill out for timing or space.

Fill copy Pad copy. Material not significant used to fill out.

Fill light Additional direction light, usually opposite the key light, to illuminate shadow areas.

Filler A short, minor story to fill space where needed in making up the page of a publication. Copy set in type for use in emergencies.

Fixed position Spot delivered at a guaranteed time.

Flag (1) Front page title or nameplate of a newspaper. (2) Device to block light in film lighting.

FM Frequency modulation. Radio broadcasting (88 to 108 megahertz) with several advantages over standard (AM) broadcasting, such as elimination of static, no fading, generally more consistent quality reception.

Fold Where the front page of a newspaper is folded in half.

Folder A printed piece of four pages, or a four-page, heavy-paper container for other printed materials.

Folio Page number.

Follow copy Instruction to typesetter to set type exactly like copy in every detail.

Follow-up A story presenting new developments of one previously printed; also known as a second-day story.

Font An assortment of type face in one size and style.

Form Pages of type and illustrations locked in a rectangular iron frame called a chase.

Format (1) The size, shape and appearance of a magazine or any publication. (2) The skeletal structure or outline of a program, or even the kind of programming a station does.

Foundry proofs (1) Etching proofs. (2) Heavy borders of black foundry rules.

Four-color process Reproduction of full-colored illustrations by the combination of plates for yellow, blue, red and black ink. All colored illustrations are separated photographically into these four primary colors. Four-color process is available to the letterpress, offset and gravure process.

Frame (1) A single picture on a storyboard. (2) A single picture in film footage. (3) $\frac{1}{30}$ second TV; $\frac{1}{24}$ second in film. (4) A command to a camera operator to compose the picture.

Free lance An unaffiliated writer or artist, available for hire on a per-story basis or retainer.

Freeze frame Arrested motion, which is perceived as a still shot.

Frequency discount Lower rate available to volume advertisers.

Front of the book Main editorial section of a magazine.

F-stop The calibration on the lens indicating the ratio of the aperture diameter or diaphragm opening to the focal length of the lens. (Apertures control the amount of light transmitted through the lens). The larger the f-stop number, the smaller the aperture or diaphragm opening; the smaller the f-stop number, the larger the aperture or diaphragm opening.

Fully scripted A TV script indicating all words to be spoken and all major video information.

Futures file Also called future(s) file, advance folder, datebook. A file of upcoming events divided into thirty-one days and twelve months.

Gain Amplification of sound.

Galley Shallow metal tray for holding type after lines have been set.

Galley proofs Proofs reproduced from the type as it stands in galley trays before being placed in page forms; or, with cold type, as photocopied from the master print or repro.

Gel or cell Sheet of transparent colored plastic used to change the color of a still photo, key light or graphic, or clear material used in film animation. (Inserted in front of key lights, on top of art.)

Ghost writer Writer whose work appears under the by-line of another.

Glossy print A smooth, shiny surfaced photograph; most suitable form for black and white reproduction in print media. Also called glossy.

Grain (1) Direction in which paper fibers lie and the way paper folds best. Folded against the grain it is likely to crack or fold irregularly. (2) Unwanted silver globs in a photograph.

Graphics (1) All visual displays in broadcasting. (2) Art and display lettering as well as design in print media.

Gravure A form of intaglio printing.

Guideline Slugline. Title given news stories as guide for editors and printers.

Gutter The space between left- and right-hand pages of a printed publication.

Halftone A screened reproduction (composed of a series of light and heavy dots) of a photograph, painting or drawing.

Hand composition Type set by hand.

Handout Publicity release.

Hard news Reports of current events that are of importance because of timeliness, proximity and impact. Feature stories are not considered hard news.

Hardware Physical equipment of the computer.

Head Headline. Name, title of a story.

Headline (broadcast) A short sentence, or phrase, at the beginning of the newscast summarizing a story within the newscast.

Headnote Short text accompanying the head and carrying information on the story, the author or both.

Highlight halftone A halftone in which whites are intensified by dropping out dots, usually by hand tooling.

Hold Not to be published without release or clearance.

Hold for release (HFR) News not to be printed until a specified time or under specified circumstances.

Holdover audience Listeners or viewers inherited from a preceding program.

Home Box Office A company that supplies pay TV programs to cable systems.

Home information system (H.I.S.) A computer-based, electronic information system that links the home to a variety of data bases; individual consumer controls information mix delivered.

Hometown stories Stories for the local newspapers of individuals participating in an event or activity, usually written so the name and perhaps address can be filled into a general story.

Horsing Reading a proof without the copy.

House magazine   House organ, company magazine. Internal house publications are for employees. External house publications may go only to company-related persons (customers, stockholders and dealers) or to the public.

HTK   Head to come. Information telling the typesetter that the headline is not with the copy but will be provided later.

Human interest   Feature material appealing to the emotions—drama, humor, pathos.

ID   Identification. In broadcasting, includes call letters and location in a ten-second announcement that identifies the station, usually in a promotional way.

Impose   To arrange pages in a chase so they will be in sequence when the printed pages are folded.

Independent station   A broadcast station not affiliated with a network.

Indicia   Mailing information data required by the Postal Service.

Initial letter   First letter in a block of copy, usually two or three copy lines deep; used for emphasis; frequently in another color.

Inline   Letter with a white line cut in it.

Insert   (1) New material inserted in the body of a story already written. (2) Printed matter prepared for enclosure with letters. (3) In film, a matted portion of a picture or an additional shot added to a scene.

Institutional ads, commercials and programs   All planned for long-term effects rather than immediate response.

Integrated commercial   May be either a cast delivered commercial incorporated into a show or a multiple-brand announcement for a number of products by the same manufacturers.

Internal communications   Communications within a company or organization to personnel or membership.

Internal publication   A publication directed to personnel or membership of a company or organization.

Interviewee   Person being interviewed.

Interviewer   (1) A person who seeks information by asking questions either formally or informally. (2) One who asks respondents the questions specified on a questionnaire in an opinion or market survey.

Intro   Introduction to taped pieces. *See also* Lead-ins

Investigative reporting   Searching below the surface for facts generally concealed.

Island   An ad surrounded by editorial material.

Italic   Type in which letters and characters slant.

Item   News story, usually short.

Jingle   Musical signature or logo used as broadcast identification and as vehicle for message.

Job press   Press taking small sheet size, normally under 25x38 inches.

Jump head   The title or headline over the continued portion of a story on another page.

Jump lines   Short text matter explaining the destination of continued text.

Jump the gutter   Titles or illustrations that continue from a left- to a right-hand page over the center of the publication.

Justification   Arranging type and spacing in a line so the type completely fills the line and makes it the same length as adjoining lines.

Key   An electronic effect. Keying means the cutting in of an image into a background image.

Kicker   A short, humorous or lighter story at the end of the newscast. Also called a tag story or a brite.

Kill   (1) To strike out or discard part or all of a story. (2) In TV, to stop production.

Layout   Dummy.

LC   Lowercase (uncapitalized) letters.

Lead ("led")   Spacing metal, usually lead alloy, placed horizontally between lines of type to give more space between lines. Leads can be 1, 2 or 3 points thick. Ten-point type lines separated by 2-point leads are said to be "10 point leaded 2 points."

Lead ("leed")   (1) Introductory sentence or paragraph of a news story. (2) A tip that may develop into a story. (3) Also the news story of greatest interest, usually placed at the beginning of a newscast and generally in the upper right-hand corner of a newspaper, although some papers favor the upper left-hand position.

Leaders (1) In print, dots used to direct the eye from one part of the copy to another. (2) In broadcasting, timed visuals used at the beginning of sequences for cues.

Lead-ins A lead-in, or intro, is the copy written to introduce the audio or videotape segment that follows.

Leaflet Printed piece of about four pages, usually from a single sheet, folded.

Leg Part of any network; usually a principal branch off the main trunk.

Leg man Reporter who calls in information to a rewrite person.

Legend Cutline or caption

Letterpress Printing process in which raised type and plates are inked and then applied to paper through direct pressure.

Letterspacing Putting narrow spaces between letters.

Level (1) In audio, it means volume. (2) In video, it means number of volts.

Light level Measured in footcandles, or in lumens.

Light pen A penlike tube containing a photocell, which, when directed at a cathode-ray tube display, reacts to light from the display. The response goes to the computer and text in the data store can be deleted or inserted.

Lineprinter Drum, chain or cathode-ray tube printer that is usually capable of printing a complete line of characters in one cycle of operation. The whole line is composed in the computer.

Lineup The arrangement of stories in a newscast in the order in which they will be aired. Also called a rundown.

Linotype Typesetting machine that casts line instead of single characters.

Lithographic printing Chemically transferring an inked image from a smooth surface to paper, as in offset lithography, offset printing, photo-offset.

Lithography Printing from a flat surface.

Live On-the-air. A live story is not taped beforehand.

Localize To stress the local angle.

Log Second-by-second daily account of what was broadcast.

Logo Logotype, the commercial signature of an organization.

Loop (1) In audio, a technical way to keep up special sound effects or a background noise like rain, by constant transmission from one spot of tape. (2) In video, loops used with videotape may replace kinescope pictures and sound recordings for national dissemination of TV programs. Loop feeds make it possible for the affiliated local station's programs and news reports to be picked up by the network. Film loops permit continuous repetition of picture.

Magazine format In broadcast, a news program airing just a few longer stories each time, instead of many shorter stories.

Make ready Preparing a form on the press for printing.

Make-up (1) Getting type and engravings in printing form correctly. (2) Placement of information and pictures on a publication's page. (3) Planning a group of pages. (4) In film, putting several films on one big reel.

Markup Proof with changes indicated.

Mass publications Periodicals with a wide appeal and large, general circulation.

Master Original of a film or videotape.

Master positive Positive film made from edited camera negative and composite sound track with optical effects.

Masthead Name of publication and staff which appears in each issue of magazine or paper, usually on the editorial page in a box also giving information about the paper such as company officers, subscription rates and address.

Matrix or mats A papier-mâché impression of a printing plate that may be used as a mold for a lead casting to reproduce the copy or art. Used for publicity primarily because of economy of mailing and used by small publications without engraving facilities.

Matte (1) Imposition of a scene or title over another scene, excluding background. Not a blend or a super. (2) Name for a box placed in front of lens to shade and hold filters and effects. (3) Dull finish needed for still photos used by TV so lights will not be reflected.

Media buyer Ad agency employee who recommends media schedules for clients and places the approved orders.

Media mix Also, media schedule. A detailed account

of all the media bought by an advertiser during a specific budget period. It includes ad slug lines, size, frequency, cost, publication or airing dates, and names and addresses of media.

Media rep Media representative. Salesperson from the medium that tries to sell that medium to an advertiser.

Memory Storage.

MICR Magnetic Ink Character Recognition. Automatic reading by machine of graphic characters printed in magnetic ink.

Milline Unit of space and circulation used in advertising to measure the cost of reaching an audience. Milline rate means cost per million for a one-column line of agate type.

Minicam A highly portable TV camera and videotape unit that can be easily carried and operated by one person.

Mock-up Scale model used for study, testing or instruction.

Model release Document signed by a model allowing use of photographs or art in which he or she appears.

Monitor A television receiver. A monitor is the TV set in the home, and the TV set specially designed for use with computers.

More Written at the bottom of a page of copy indicating a story is not complete, that there is more to come.

Morgue Newspaper library for clippings, photos and reference material.

Multigraphing Trademarked process for making numerous copies of typewritten or hand-drawn material. More closely resembles hand typing than does mimeographing.

Must Written on copy or art to designate that it must appear.

Nameplate The name of the publication appearing on page one of a newspaper.

National rate Rate offered to advertisers in more than one market.

Natural sound Also called background sound or wild sound. Natural sound can be defined as the noise around us at any news event. It is not sound recorded for any specific purpose, or to fit any particular copy in a story.

Neilsen The A. C. Neilsen Company is the biggest name in broadcast rating. Reputations and shows literally live or die on their Neilsen ratings.

Network Any link, by any technology, of two or more stations so they can each separately broadcast the same program.

New lead Replacement for a lead already prepared, usually offering new developments or information.

News wheel News show in which content is repeated with some updating.

Newsprint A rough, relatively inexpensive paper, usually made from wood pulp, used for many newspapers and also for other inexpensive printed material.

NPR National Public Radio.

O & O Refers to broadcast stations owned and operated by the networks.

Obituary News biography of a dead person.

O/C On camera. A cue used to indicate the announcer should appear on camera without any visuals to accompany the shot.

OCR Optical Character Recognition. Electronically reading printed or handwritten documents.

Offset Lithographic process.

On the nose (1) On time. (2) Correct.

Online To be in direct communication with the computer CPU.

Open, opening The beginning portion of the newscast.

Open spacing Widely leaded spacing.

Open-end Recorded commercial with time at close for tag.

Optical center A point equidistant from the left and right sides of a sheet of paper and five-eighths of the way from the bottom. In the optics so important to film is the optical center point of a lens, a point that may have no relationship to equal distances from perimeters.

Optical reader Electronic reader of copy.

Optical scanner Visual scanner. Scans printed or written data and generates their digital representation.

Out cue The last several words of the tape cut used on the air.

Outline The gist of a written article or program.

Overline Kicker.

Overrun Legitimate printing trade practice that permits delivery and charge for up to ten percent more than the quantity of printed matter ordered.

Overset   More type set than there is space to use.

Pace   Overall speed of show or performance.

Pad   Fill.

Page proof   Proof of type and engravings as they will appear.

Pamphlet   A printed piece of more than four pages with a soft cover. Differs from brochure in its size and simplicity, lack of illustrations.

Panel   (1) An area of type sometimes boxed but always different in size, weight or design from the text and partially or entirely surrounded by text. (2) In communication research, a group brought together to discuss one subject or related subjects.

Participation spot   Shared time in a program for spot commercials or announcements.

PBS   Public Broadcasting System.

Perforator   Keyboard unit used to produce punched paper tape.

Personal   A brief news item about one or more persons.

Photo composition   A photographic method of setting type to produce proofs on paper.

Photoprint   Reproduction of art or a printed or written piece by any one of many different photographic copying processes.

Photostat   A trademarked device for making photographic copies of art or text.

Pic   A still picture. *Pix* is plural.

Pica   Standard printing measure of twelve points. There are six picas to the inch.

Pied type   Type that is all mixed up.

PIQ   Program Idea Quotient. Annual study by Home Testing Institute to get reactions to new program ideas. Ratings are on a six-point scale from "favorite" to "wouldn't watch."

Plate   Refers to all types of printing surfaces, as well as the engravings and electrotypes.

Play up   To emphasize, give prominence.

Plug   A free and favorable mention.

PM   Afternoon paper.

Point   Printers' standard unit of measure equal to 0.01384 inch. Roughly seventy-two points equal one inch. Sizes of type and amount of leading are specified in points.

Poll   Survey of the attitudes and beliefs of a selected group of people.

Pool   Coverage of news events when news organizations agree to share facilities, equipment and staff for the coverage.

Position   Where elements in any publication appear; usually indicates relative significance.

Poster type   Large, garish letters.

Power structure   The socially, politically and economically advantaged.

PR wires   Commercial wire services received by print and electronic media.

Precinct principle   Organization of a campaign through delegation of local responsibilities to chosen leaders in each community.

These may be opinion leaders and not necessarily political leaders.

Pretesting   Testing a research plan, any of its elements or any elements in a campaign before launching the entire program.

Printer's error (PE)   Typographical errors made by typesetter.

Privilege   Constitutional privilege granted the press to print with immunity news that might otherwise be libelous— for example, remarks made in open court.

Process plates and progressive proofs   Each of the color plates in a set printed singly. These may be laid over each other for effect. In progressive prints, in addition to the single prints of each color, the colors are shown in proper color combination and rotation to suggest the final printed result.

Producer   The producer is the person in charge of all content for each broadcast news show.

Production manager   Person who puts advertising into a format usable by each medium in which time or space has been bought.

Program   Set of instructions that makes the computer perform the desired operations.

Promo   Broadcast promotional statement, film, videotape/ recording, slide or combination.

Promotion   Creating interest in a person, product, institution or cause through special activities.

Proof   Trial impression of type and engraved matter

taken on paper to make corrections.

Propaganda devices Specific devices—Spoken, written, pictorial or even musical—to influence human action or reaction.

Psychographics Statistics that describe the emotional or behavioral characteristics of an audience, such as attitudes or opinions, lifestyles, and so on.

Public, publics Any group of people tied together by some common bond of interest or concern.

Public relations All activities and attitudes intended to judge, adjust to, influence and direct the opinions of any group or groups of persons in the interest of any individual, group or institution.

Public Service Announcement (PSA) Announcement for some non-profit activity in a time slot donated by the broadcast station.

Public television and radio Noncommercial broadcasting. Stations are financed by federal grants, private donations and public subscriptions.

Publicity Information about a client (person, company or institution), about a product, or about services which appears as news in any medium, print or electronic.

Puffery Unsubstantiated and exaggerated claims with no factual basis that appear in either advertising or publicity.

Pulp Refers to magazines printed on rough, wood-pulp paper in contrast to slicks, magazines printed on coated or calendered stock.

Punch To give vigor to the writing or editing process.

Query Letter addressed to an editor that summarizes an article idea and asks if the piece might be considered for publication.

Questionnaire The body of questions asked of subjects in a research effort.

Quote Quotations, estimate of costs.

RADAR Radio's All Dimension Audience Research, a survey conducted by Statistical Research Inc. for NBC, CBS, ABC and Mutual networks.

Radio-TV wire (1) Broadcast wire. (2) The news service's wire copy written in broadcast style.

RAM Random Access Memory. A storage device in which the time needed to find data is not affected significantly by where the data are physically located.

Rating service Company that surveys broadcast audience for total homes or individuals listening, or gives percentages of total listening for specific stations and also for specific shows.

Reach Number of people or households a station, commercial or program is heard by in a given time period. Used with frequency to measure station's audience for evaluation of worth, generally for advertising dollar.

Recap Recapitulation of news.

Reduce Decreasing the size of anything visual when reproducing it.

Register (1) The correct position in which a form is to print so that the pages when printed back to back will be in the proper places. (2) In color printing, the precise position for superimposition of each color for the colors to blend properly.

Rejection slip Letter or printed form from a publication's editor accompanying a manuscript returned to its author.

Relief printing Letterpress. Letters on the block or plate are raised above the general level so that when an inked roller is passed over the surface the ink can touch only the raised portions.

Remote A broadcast live videotape recording originating outside the regular studios.

Reprint A second or new impression of a printed work, either text or art.

Respondent Those to whom questions are directed in a survey.

Retail rate Local rate or lower for advertising.

Retouch To improve photographs before reproduction by artwork.

Reversal print A copy made on reversal print stock.

Reverse To print text or art in white on a dark background, or, in making a cut from a picture, to turn over or flop the negative so that everything goes in the opposite direction.

Review Critique or commentary on any aspect of human events—politics, society or the arts.

Rewrite person Newspaper staff member who rewrites

stories and takes phoned-in reports but does not leave the office to cover news.

Rim On newspapers, outer edge of a copy desk where copy readers work under the direction of a slot person or copy chief.

Rip 'n read A derogatory term used to indicate that the broadcast news department does not rewrite the copy, but simply rips it off the wire and reads it over the air.

Roots of attitudes Attitudes are grounded in our institutions, observations, responses of others to us, socialization, education and media.

ROP Run of paper. Means ad may be placed on any page of the publication.

ROS Run of station or run of schedule. Costs less; usually preemptible.

Rotary press Press that prints from curved stereotypes bolted to a cylinder.

Rotogravure Printing by means of a sensitized copper cylinder on which is etched the image to be reproduced.

Roughs Sketches in black and white that show a client what an ad generally will look like.

Roundup Comprehensive story written with information gathered from several sources.

Routing Cutting out a part of plate or engraving to keep it from printing.

Rule Thin strip of type-high metal that prints as a slender line.

Run-in To combine one or more sentences to avoid making an additional paragraph.

Running foot Identification information printed in the bottom margin in some magazines.

Running head Identification information printed in the top margins.

Saddle stitching Binding pages by stitching with wire through fold.

Sample The portion of the total population queried in a survey, intended to be representative of the total population.

Sans serif Type face without serifs.

Scaling Measuring and marking illustrations for engraving to be sure illustration appears in appropriate, designated size and in proper proportion.

Scanner Optical scanner.

Scanning The movement of the electron beam from left to right and from top to bottom on a screen.

Scanning area Picture area that is scanned by a television camera's pickup tube; more generally, the picture area actually reproduced by the camera and relayed to the studio monitors.

Scoop To report a story first, or, as a noun, a story reported before the competition. Also called a beat.

Script Written copy in television. Scripts contain all of the copy the announcer will read, plus all technical cues.

Set close To thin space and omit leads.

Set open To open spaces with leads as slugs.

Set solid To set without extra space between horizontal type lines.

Setwise Differentiates width of a type from its body size.

Shelter books Magazines that focus on housing or related subjects.

Short rate Charge back to advertiser for not fulfilling contract.

Show Program.

Side stiching Method of stitching thick booklets by pressing wire staples from the front side of the booklet and clinching in back, making it impossible to open the pages flat.

Silhouette or outline halftone Halftone with all background removed.

Silk screen Stencil process using fine cloths painted so that the surface is impenetrable except where color is supposed to come through.

Silver print or Van Dyck Proof of negative for offset plate taken on sensitized paper and used as a final proof before plates are made.

Sizing Scaling.

Skip frame Printing of alternate frames to speed up action on film.

Slant Angle. (1) Particular emphasis of a media presentation. (2) To emphasize an aspect of a policy story.

Slanting (1) Emphasizing a particular point or points of interest in the news. (2) Disguised editorializing.

Slick A publication, usually magazine, published on coated, smooth paper.

Slicks Glossy prints used instead of mats in sending releases or art to offset publications.

Slides Individual film frames, usually positive but can be negative transparencies, projected either in the room where an oral presentation is being given or from a TV control room.

Slip sheet Paper placed between sheets of paper to prevent smudging.

Slot On newspapers, the inside of a copy desk where the copy chief or copy editor sits.

Slug Lead thicker than four points used between lines of type.

Slug lines Notation placed at the upper left of a story to identify the story during typesetting and make-up of a publication.

Slushpile Collection of unsolicited manuscripts received by magazines.

SOF Sound on film.

Soft news Feature news or news that does not depend on timeliness.

Software The programs and routines associated with the operation of a computer; as opposed to hardware.

SOT Sound on videotape.

Sound bite The sound of the newsmaker, news source or natural sound on tape.

Sound under In sound under, the audio level on a tape cut is kept low so as not to drown out the voice of the announcer reading voice-over.

Soundup The audio level on a tape is turned up to normal

Sources of motivation Motivations are founded in socially based or personal need and avoidance or elimination of stress often caused by the power of others.

Splice The spot where two shots are actually joined, or the act of joining two shots.

Generally used only when the material (such as film or audiotape) is physically cut and glued (spliced) together again.

Split run The regional division of a national magazine before printing to accommodate advertisers desiring a specific regional market and often with regional editorial emphasis.

Sponsor (1) The underwriter of broadcast programming whose messages are presented with the program. Most advertisers buy spot time and are not sponsors. (2) Underwriter of an event or activity who gets publicity for participation.

Spot announcement or spot Broadcast commercial that lasts usually less than one minute.

Spread (1) Long story, generally illustrated. (2) Ad group of related photographs. (3) Copy that covers two facing pages in a publication, generally without gutter separation and usually printed from a single plate.

SPSS Social Science Statistical package used in research.

Standard Rate and Data Service SRDS. Monthly publications for all media, commercial and non-commercial, such as house publications, that accept advertising, their rates and specifications— physical requirements of what is sent. Also gives information on audiences and purpose of publication.

Standing head A regularly used title.

Standing matter Type kept set from one printing to

another, such as staff names on a newspaper.

Standup Also called a standupper. A TV report where the camera is focused on the reporter at the scene.

Station break On-the-hour legal identification required of broadcasters by the FCC.

Stereotype Plate cast by pouring molten metal into a matrix or flong. Inexpensive form of duplicating plates generally used by newspapers.

Stet Proofreader's designation to say that the copy should stand as originally written, that the change marked was an error.

Still A photograph, but can also be a drawing or a map.

Stop-motion A slow motion effect in which one frame jumps to the next, showing the object in a different position.

Storyboards Sketches in a series of frames with copy underneath to show what commercial will look like. Used for TV commercials; the equivalent of the print rough.

Straight matter Plain typesetting set in conventional paragraph form, as opposed to some kind of display.

Straight news Hard news. A plain recital of news facts written in standard style and form.

Stuffer Printed piece intended for insertion into bills and receipts, pay envelopes, packages delivered to customers or any other medium of delivery.

Subhead Small head inserted in the body of a news story to break up long blocks of type.

Summary lead Beginning paragraphs in a news story usually including the H and five Ws (who, what, when, where, why and how).

Super In TV, electronic characters are combined with another scene, as a studio shot, tape or film.

Super card A studio card with white lettering on a dark background, used for superimposition of a title, or for keying of a title over a background scene. For chromakeying, the white letters are on a chromakey blue background.

Subprint In printing, superimposing type or lettering on an illustration so the type remains solid, unbroken by a screen.

Survey An analysis of a market or opinions held by a specified group.

Suspended interest News story with climax at the close.

Tabloid Newspaper format, usually five columns wide, with each page slightly more than half the size of a standard paper. *Tabloid format* often is the use of just a picture and headlines on page one.

Tag or tagline Final line or two in a story. The final portion of a newscast.

Tailpiece A small drawing at the end of a story.

Take (1) In print, a portion of copy in a running story. (2) In broadcasting, a complete scene. (3) Also means to cut.

Talent Any major personality or models for ads or publicity photos. In TV, anyone in front of the camera.

Teaser (1) In print or broadcast, ads or statements that pique

interest or stimulate curiosity without giving away facts; used to build anticipation. (2) Technique in which the beginning of a film has scenes and sounds related to the theme of the program rather than a title.

Tele line Equipment room where film and slide projectors are located.

Telecommunications Long-distance transmission of signals by any means.

Teleprocessing Information handling in which a data-processing system uses communication facilities.

Teletext A one-way electronic information system; noninteractive.

Teletypesetter (TTS) Trademark applied to a machine that transmits to a linotype and causes news to be set into type automatically.

Terminal Point in a communication system or network where data can either enter or leave.

Test group Selection of a group used to measure reactions to or use of a product or an idea.

Testing Sampling of opinions, attitudes or beliefs of a scientifically selected group on any particular set of questions.

Text Written material, generally used in referring to editorial, rather than commercial, matter; excludes titles, heads, notes, references, and so on.

TF Till Forbid. Means to run until advertiser terminates or contract expires.

Thirty (30) In newspaper, means "that's all." Reporter writing story places at the

last of the written material to signify end.

Thumbnails A series of small roughs.

Tie-back Previously printed information included in a story to give background or frame of reference and to refresh the reader's memory.

Tie-in Promotional term used to describe the joint or combined activities of two or more organizations on a single project, or to describe a promotional activity designed to coincide with an already scheduled event.

Timesharing Use of computer hardware by several people simultaneously.

Tint block Solid color area on a printed piece, usually screened.

Tip Information offered that could lead to a story.

Tipping-in Hand insertion or attachment of extra pages in a publication, usually of a different stock than other items.

Trade publications Periodicals carrying information of interest to a particular trade or industry.

Traffic Department in ad agencies that handles production schedules; in broadcasting handles everything that goes on the air.

Traffic manager Person who handles the flow of work through an agency so deadlines are met.

Trim (1) In newspapers, means shorten copy. (2) In printing, the final process that cuts all pages to the same size.

Turnover In advertising, refers to ratio of *net unduplicated* cumulative audience over several time periods to average audience per time period.

TWX "TWIX," a teletype machine.

Type face Particular type design; sometimes carries the name of the designer or a descriptive name.

Type family Name given to two or more type series that are variations of the same basic design.

Type page Printed area on a page bordered by margins.

Type series Collective name for all sizes of one design of type faces.

Typo Typographical error.

UC and LC Upper and lower case; capitals and small letters.

UHF Ultra High Frequency; TV channels broadcasting at frequencies higher than channel 13.

Underrun Printing practices permit an allowance ten percent less than the total printing order as completion of an order when excessive spoilage in printing or in binding causes a slight shortage.

Update To alter a story to include the most recent developments.

Upper case Capital letters.

Varitype Typewriter with alternate type fonts.

VDT Visual or video display terminal. Electronic device for use in typesetting or word processing, with a television-type screen to display the data.

Vertical saturation Scheduling commercials heavily on one or two days before a major event.

VHF Very High Frequency. TV channels broadcasting at channels 2 through 13.

Video All television is video. Anything seen on the television screen and anything photographed on videotape.

Videotex Electronic data transmission system; interactive; establishes two-way link from individual's television set or home computer to a data base.

Vignette Story or sketch, often a slice of life drama.

Vignetted halftones A halftone with edges that soften gradually until completely faded out.

Visual scanner Optical scanner.

Voice-over The announcer reading copy with tape running on the screen at the same time. The audience sees the tape and hears the announcer's voice reading the copy.

Voicer The voice of the reporter on tape.

VTR Videotape recording.

Wash drawing Water color or diluted India ink brush drawing requiring halftone reproduction.

Watermark Identification mark left in texture of quality paper stock. Revealed when paper is held up to the light.

When room Designation on copy or art that means usable any time.

White space Used in ads to improve design; place where there's no art or type.

Wide open Publication or news script with ample room for additional material.

Widow Short line (one word to two) at the end of a paragraph of type. To be avoided, especially in the first line of a column and in captions.

Wood cuts Wooden printing blocks with impression carved by hand. Now an art form, was forerunner to zinc engravings.

Woodshedding In broadcasting, reading and rehearsing news script.

Working drawings Final drawings, usually black and white, prepared for use by engraver. Shows how final art will appear.

Wrap-up Summary or closing.

Wrong font Letter from one font of type mixed with others of a different font.

Yak Narration.

Zinc etching Line engraving etched in zinc.

Index